The Russian Way of War

MODERN WAR STUDIES

Theodore A. Wilson
General Editor

Raymond A. Callahan
J. Garry Clifford
Jacob W. Kipp
Jay Luvaas
Allan R. Millett
Carol Reardon
Dennis Showalter
Series Editors

The Russian Way of War
Operational Art, 1904–1940

Richard W. Harrison

 University Press of Kansas

355.40947
H32r

 © 2001 by the University Press of Kansas
All rights reserved

Published by the University Press of Kansas (Lawrence, Kansas 66049), which was organized by the Kansas Board of Regents and is operated and funded by Emporia State University, Fort Hays State University, Kansas State University, Pittsburg State University, the University of Kansas, and Wichita State University.

Library of Congress Cataloging-in-Publication Data

Harrison, Richard W., 1952–
    The Russian way of war : operational art, 1904–1940 / Richard W. Harrison.
      p. cm. — (Modern war studies)
    Includes bibliographical references and index.
    ISBN 0-7006-1074-X (cloth : alk. paper)
    1. Operational art (Military science)—History—20th century. 2. Military art and science—Russia—History—20th century. 3. Military art and science—Soviet Union—History. 4. Russia—History, Military—20th century. 5. Soviet Union—History, Military. I. Title.
    U163 .H38 2001
    355.4'0947'0904—dc21   00-047775

British Library Cataloguing in Publication Data is available.

Printed in the United States of America
10 9 8 7 6 5 4 3 2 1

The paper used in this publication meets the minimum requirements of the American National Standard for Permanence of Paper for Printed Library Materials Z39.48-1984.

To my daughter, Anna

Contents

List of Tables and Maps   ix

Acknowledgments   xi

Introduction   1

1. Twilight of Empire, 1904–1917   5
2. Wars Within and Without, 1918–1920   73
3. The Birth of a Theory, 1921–1929   119
4. Maturation, 1930–1936   169
5. The Road to War, 1937–1940   218

Conclusion   270

Notes   275

Bibliography   305

Index   339

Tables and Maps

TABLES

1. Red Army Consecutive Offensive Operations, 1918–1920   156
2. Soviet Industrial Production, 1928–37   171
3. Soviet Weapons Production, 1930–37   173
4. The Red Army's Weapons Park, 1928–35   173

MAPS

1. The Sha-ho Operation, 4–17 October 1904   14
2. The Mukden Operation, 19 February–10 March 1905   18
3. The Western Theater of War, August–September 1914   46
4. The Lutsk Operation, Summer 1916   64
5. The Eastern Front, April–June 1919   89
6. The Southern Front, October–November 1919   96
7. The Northern Tauride, October–November 1920   101
8. The War with Poland, June–August 1920   109
9. Consecutive Operations   161
10. The Army Deep Operation   206
11. The Front Deep Operation   212
12. Khalkhin-Gol, August 1939   238

Acknowledgments

I have been fortunate throughout in being assisted by a number of organizations and individuals who have given freely of their time and funds in helping this project reach fruition. Among these, I should like to single out for special thanks the Madison Center for Educational Affairs, the United States Army Center of Military History, and the Kennan Institute for Advanced Russian Studies, all of Washington, D.C., and the University of London's Central Research Fund for their generous financial support. Special thanks are also in order to Professor B. J. Bond of King's College London, whose patience and guidance proved invaluable throughout the course of my dissertation work.

Introduction

For more than a hundred years, Russian and Soviet military thinkers have grappled with the intricacies of conducting war at the operational level and have produced a number of outstanding works on the subject. The Soviets were among the most prolific publishers of military-historical and military-theoretical literature, and questions of operational art figured prominently. The Russian-Soviet conduct of past conflicts, despite major flaws in execution, also has much to teach us about the operational level of warfare. Unfortunately, due to a tradition of official secrecy and ideological hostility, much of this material has been denied Western readers until recently. This book is a start at remedying the years of neglect.

The American military's own appreciation of operational art has also evolved considerably from the time when it airily dismissed the Soviet concept as "not a fundamental or significant contribution to military science."[1] And while official efforts over the years toward improving our understanding of operational art have generally been positive, progress has not always been even. This was certainly the case with the army's operational manual *FM 100-5: Operations,* which appeared in 1982. Unfortunately, the manual was a defensive-minded failure, betraying a marked preference for the purely organizational aspects of war, much to the detriment of the reader's understanding of basic operational principles. A particularly serious flaw was its failure to examine the conduct of war at the army–army group level, which is the true realm of operational art. Subsequent editions have been successful in correcting many of these shortcomings, with the 1993 version taking into account the valuable operational lessons of Operation Desert Storm. It is to be hoped that the appearance of these and other works related to the subject heralds the beginning of a fruitful period in the West's military-theoretical research.[2]

However, it would be a serious mistake if, in our rush to master this discipline, we failed to take into account the rich heritage of operational thought and practice accumulated by the Soviet army and its imperial predecessor. Unfortunately, the disappearance of the Soviet Union now threatens to relegate the study of Russian-Soviet operational art to the backwaters of purely historical research, with little or no perceived application to current problems. But the present instability in Russia does not preclude the country's revival as a military power whose interests will not always coincide with ours. A resurgent Russian military would likely embody many of the practical and theoretical traditions of its predecessors. Moreover, the Soviets extensively propagated their operational ideas to officers from a number of Third World countries who studied in the USSR's military academies. These officers, who are now moving into or occupying senior positions at home, are presumably willing to put the precepts they learned into action in a future conflict with Western forces.

The subject of this work, operational art, is the theory and practice of waging war at the operational level. Unfortunately, this theory remains almost completely unknown in the West, even among the professional military. Moreover, those who have been aware of the theory's existence have often dismissed it outright, failed to understand it altogether, or concerned themselves only with its individual aspects. For the sake of clarity and consistency, this study will be guided throughout by the definition given in a 1958 Soviet work, which describes operational art *(operativnoe iskusstvo)* as

> a component part of military art, concerned with the elaboration of the theory and practice of preparing and conducting front and army operations of the different services of the armed forces. Operational art is the connecting link between strategy and tactics. Proceeding from the demands of strategy, operational art determines the methods of preparing and conducting operations for the achievement of strategic goals and serves as the point of departure for tactics, which organizes the preparation and conduct of the combined arms battle in accordance with the operation's goals and tasks.[3]

The goal of this book is to trace the practical and theoretical development of operational art from its infant beginnings in 1904 to the eve of the German invasion of the Soviet Union in 1941, an event that put the Red Army and its theory of operational art to the ultimate test. Such a broad scope of investigation will enable the reader to examine at length the imperial army's early attempts to understand the new operational level of war, as well as similar efforts by the follow-on Red Army.

In the course of this study, a number of issues central to the theory's evolution during this period will be examined. Among these is to what degree the Soviet theory of operational art up to 1941 owes its existence to the practical and intellectual inheritance of the prerevolutionary Russian army. Many of the theorists whose writings contributed to the development of operational art served in the imperial army and willingly or unwillingly joined the Red forces during the Russian civil war and continued to serve the Soviet regime in the postwar years as well. As the living embodiment of the imperial military tradition, their role is critical to any attempt to determine the degree of theoretical continuity, or lack thereof, between the two regimes. Particular attention will thus be paid to their theoretical and practical work in both the pre-1917 and postrevolutionary periods and how their ideas were received by the political-military authorities.

Among other factors to be considered are those that inevitably distinguish the Red Army from its imperial predecessor. Thus it will also be necessary to examine to what extent the Red Army's operational thought may be ascribed to circumstances peculiar to the Soviet regime. Such factors include the Bolsheviks' imposition of a radical political ideology upon the army, in contrast to the relatively apolitical outlook of the Russian officer corps before the revolution. Another is the forced industrialization of the Soviet economy, beginning in 1929, which also had no counterpart in the prerevolutionary years. In short, the utterly new political-economic situation that obtained following the Bolshevik coup influenced the Red Army's technical and theoretical development in ways not dreamed of by the old regime's officers and was in many ways fundamentally at odds with the military legacy of imperial Russia.

A number of other factors will also be examined. Chief among these are organizational-administrative questions, such as the persistence of the front (army group) instance of command, and the enduring system of Stavka (supreme command)–front–army subordination in wartime, which existed in both the imperial and Red armies. On the other hand, organizational incongruities, such as the post-1929 creation of large air and mechanized formations, which had no counterpart in the prerevolutionary era, will also be evaluated.

However, no military theory is a mere abstraction, but rather exists as a tool to achieve particular ends deemed important by a nation and/or its ruling elite. This theory, in turn, is the product of any number of historical, economic, political, cultural, geographic, and other factors extant in the society. This question immediately raises the problem of "military culture" as the expression of a particular state's approach to the problem of conducting war. Military cultures arise as the result of the interaction of the preceding factors, which determine the state's approach to armed conflict. The interaction of these factors gives rise to a military culture, which while it may share common technological aspects with other armies, is nevertheless unique.

For example, the evolution of Russian military culture, like that of its Western counterparts, represents a unique mixture of objective and subjective factors that played a role in the country's development. Among the former are Russia's position on the eastern edge of the vast European plain, which offers few natural obstacles to an invader. The country's location far from the major oceans has also lent a decidedly continental "tilt" to Russia's military development, as opposed to the maritime traditions of Great Britain and the United States. Among the more important subjective factors are the country's large population, as well as its economic backwardness vis-à-vis its Western neighbors for most of its history.

Russian military culture traces its beginnings to the wars for the creation of the modern Russian state, beginning in the fourteenth century. These wars took the form of a national struggle against a foreign oppressor, the Tatars, as well as an internal one, as the numerous Russian principalities vied for primacy among themselves. In this sense, the Grand Duchy of Moscow played much the same role as Prussia in Germany during the eighteenth and nineteenth centuries. This long and bloody struggle contributed to the development of a siege mentality among the ruling elite and the growth of an autocratic centralizing power. These factors, together with the deepening institution of serfdom, created a society in which democratic principles failed to take root.

Things changed outwardly with Peter the Great's opening to the West at the beginning of the eighteenth century. As a result of the emperor's reforms, the state and army acquired the outward trappings of a Western country, although fundamental changes were slow to take hold. In essence, the system remained a feudal one, headed by an autocrat and supported by an increasingly Westernized gentry, while the great majority of the population continued in its centuries-old way of life as virtual slaves. This social schism led to a culture that viewed heavy casualties among the peasant rank and file with an equanimity bordering on the criminal.

For many years this did not seem to matter, as Russian armies performed with credit in the major European wars of the eighteenth and early nineteenth centuries, during which Russia defeated successive Swedish, Turkish, and French enemies. However, the gathering pace of the Industrial Revolution in western Europe soon threatened to leave Russia behind. This backwardness was made abundantly clear as the result of Russia's defeat in the Crimean War of 1853–56. Attempts were made to address these problems during the period prior to 1914, but despite some impressive achievements in some areas, Russia continued to lag dangerously behind its probable opponents.

These manifold weaknesses led to the disasters of the Russo-Japanese War and World War I. In the latter conflict Russia was easily the weakest of the major belligerents, and its enormous military machine performed poorly against the smaller but better-armed and better-trained German army. Here, Russia's traditional advantages in mass and space proved useless against modern weapons, and throughout the conflict the country's military effectiveness was extremely low. The enormous losses of 1914–17, combined with the country's other social ills, finally led to revolution and the emergence of a new society.

The Bolshevik regime, which came to power in 1917, sought to create an entirely new army, one that reflected the Bolsheviks' sense of revolutionary impatience and brutality. The resulting Soviet military culture was an eccentric mix of old and new, which reflected the peculiar conditions of the country's development. The Red Army, like its imperial predecessor, continued to rely on the country's enormous manpower reserves to overwhelm the enemy, while the USSR's post-1929 industrialization drive brought the armed forces up to the technical standards of its Western counterparts. These factors found their expression in the development of the theory of operational art, a uniquely Russian-Soviet response to the problems of waging modern war.

1
Twilight of Empire, 1904–1917

The Russo-Japanese War was a humiliating military and moral defeat for the Russian Empire and its army. A series of bloody battles during 1904–5 led only to defeat and stalemate on land and the destruction of the Russians' Baltic Fleet in the Tsushima Strait in May 1905. The government, with support for the war almost gone, was forced to accede to a humiliating peace with Japan, in which Russia surrendered the southern half of Sakhalin and Port Arthur.

That Russia agreed to these terms had less to do with the military situation in Manchuria than with the shaky position of the czarist regime, which was beset by the pent-up demands of the country's industrial workers and liberal intelligentsia. The regime's clumsy attempts to deal with the mounting crisis only made matters worse, and by the autumn of 1905 the country was awash in a sea of industrial strikes, which threatened the autocracy's very existence. Emperor Nicholas II, faced with the collapse of his personal rule, finally bowed to pressure and granted the opposition's demands by agreeing to a package of broad constitutional reforms on October 17, 1905. The reforms, while limited and not always adhered to by the government, did guarantee basic civil liberties, for the first time in Russian history. Equally important, the emperor's proclamation called for the creation of a representative assembly, the Duma. Unfortunately, the several assemblies elected between 1906 and 1912 never evolved into a true parliament, and Russia's brief experiment in democracy would not survive the upheavals of 1917.

Nicholas's October Manifesto marked the high point of the revolutionary tide, and the reaction that followed was both violent and swift. A worker's uprising in Moscow in December 1905 was put down with particular brutality, although political terrorism directed against the regime and its supporters continued for several years afterward. The government gradually regained control of the situation from 1906, although its authority had been undermined forever.

The driving force behind the repression, and much of the reform that accompanied it, was P. A. Stolypin, who served as prime minister from 1906 until his assassination in 1911. Under Stolypin Russia returned to something approaching normalcy, particularly in the economic sphere, following years of stagnation. Recovery, in fact, was so swift that by 1913 Russian industry was producing 29.1 million tons of coal, 9.2 million tons of oil, 4.2 million tons of iron, and 4.2 million tons of steel. Overall industrial growth between 1908 and 1913 was 50.8 percent, although economic development remained uneven, and as late as 1913 Russia ranked only fifth in the world in total industrial production.[1] Similar changes were taking place in the agricultural sector, where the prime minister sought to create a class of private farmers as a bulwark for the regime in the countryside. However, this positive step was also taken too late and was soon swept aside by the coming storm.

The confrontation between Russia, Germany, and Austria-Hungary, which came to a head in 1914, had its roots in these nations' conflicting dynastic ambitions during the previous quarter century. As recently as 1887 they had been joined in the Three Emperors' League, which collapsed because of growing rivalry between Russia and Austria-Hungary in the Balkans. Germany subsequently allowed its own Reinsurance Treaty with Russia to lapse in 1891. Emperor Aleksandr III, fearing diplomatic isolation, thereupon concluded an alliance with France in 1892, which obliged both parties to come to the other's aid in the event of an attack on either by Germany. Russia's position was further strengthened by the signing of a diplomatic accord with Great Britain in 1907, which brought the two countries closer together by resolving their long-standing differences in southwestern and central Asia. This agreement completed the division of Europe into antagonistic camps: the Triple Entente of Britain, France, and Russia, and the Triple Alliance of Germany, Austria-Hungary, and Italy.

This was the lineup that prevailed on the outbreak of war in 1914, with the exception of Italy, which first declared its neutrality and then joined the Allies in 1915. The Allied coalition was strengthened by the addition of Belgium, Serbia, and other countries, as well as the United States in 1917. Germany and Austria-Hungary, known as the Central Powers, were later joined by Turkey and Bulgaria.

Russia was the weakest of the major Allied powers, both militarily and economically, and by the winter of 1916–17 the country was reeling from the effects of an economic crisis caused by the enormous exertions of the war. In all, Russia mobilized some 15.5 million men following the outbreak of the conflict, which strained its underdeveloped economic infrastructure to the breaking point. The steady round of defeats and the horrible losses also took their toll on public support for the war effort, particularly among the lower classes. Of the approximately 17 million men who served, nearly 8 million became casualties, of which 1.3 million were killed, 4.2 million wounded (of which 350,000 subsequently died), while over 2.4 million were taken prisoner.[2] These factors, combined with widespread public disgust with court intrigues and the regime's incompetent handling of the war, finally led to the overthrow of the 300-year-old Romanov dynasty in March 1917 and the proclamation of a democratic republic.

The Provisional Government that emerged was determined to continue the war, and at first it enjoyed a good deal of popular support. However, the failure of the new regime's highly touted offensive in the summer of 1917 showed how illusory the pro-war consensus was, particularly in the enlisted ranks. Behind the front, the government's position was fatally undermined by the worsening economic situation. A ruinous inflationary spiral, coupled with the gradual breakdown of the country's transportation system and food distribution network, meant that by autumn large sectors of the country's urban population were close to starvation. The Provisional Government, its authority increasingly diminished by its inability to enact reforms, and beset by coup attempts from both right and left, limped into the autumn, although its days were clearly numbered. In this situation, the Bolshevik coup of November 7, 1917, was almost anticlimactic.

THE RUSSO-JAPANESE WAR, 1904-5

Modern operational art is directly linked to the rise of the operation as an independent sphere of military activity during the nineteenth century and its continued evolution into the twentieth. However, to understand the present state of affairs, it is necessary to go back to a time when there were neither operations nor operational art.

Strategy and tactics have existed since the beginning of organized conflict itself. Strategy determined the overall plan for prosecuting the war and delivered the armies and fleets to the battlefield, while tactics executed the plan by actually engaging the enemy. In the past, some of these tactical actions have led to the defeat of one side's forces in a single climactic battle. At other times, the tactical-strategic link has been less immediate, and it often took years of seasonal campaigning, or longer, to bring about a final result. For much the greater part of military history, this two-tier arrangement sufficed. However, as in so many other areas, the Industrial Revolution ushered in enormous changes in the way men made war—changes that rendered the old formula increasingly obsolete.

The most startling of these innovations was the vastly increased ability of the developed countries' economies to feed the material demands of war. The large-scale introduction of the factory system ensured that late-nineteenth-century armies could be supplied with heretofore undreamed-of amounts and varieties of military equipment. The growing power and flexibility of this system made it possible not only to remake a nation's arsenal within a few years but also to increase output dramatically to meet the voracious demands of the large national armies that were beginning to appear. The crucial importance of these factors became apparent as early as the American Civil War of 1861–65, in which the North's substantially larger military-industrial base finally overwhelmed the Confederacy's primitive war economy, despite the advantage in traditional military virtues that the latter enjoyed. As any study of that conflict reveals, individual valor, while still important, had begun to yield pride of place to the cold, quantitative indices of national military production.

The Industrial Revolution also brought about important changes in the existing tools of war, while producing a number of radical innovations as well. The most far-reaching of these were the enormous qualitative improvements in firearms and artillery. The large-scale introduction of rifled firearms after 1850 increased both their range and their accuracy to deadly effect. This was followed by the introduction of breech-loading weapons, magazine rifles, and smokeless gunpowder, all of which dramatically increased the individual soldier's rate and effectiveness of fire, particularly on the defensive. Similar developments were also taking place in the artillery arm, where advances in fire control and range finding soon made the indirect laying of fire possible against enemy artillery and infantry positions. By the turn of the century, artillery ranges were being computed in the thousands of yards, considerably increasing the "killing zone" through which an attacker would have to advance. These changes were highly advantageous to a defender who, fighting from trenches and fortified positions, could now engage an attacker from a greater distance and with more fire and a higher degree of accuracy than had ever been known before. Under these conditions an attacker was likely to be repulsed with horrendous losses, as happened to Union troops at Cold Harbor in 1864 and the Germans at St.-Privat in 1870.

The growing primacy of the defensive gradually forced the attacker to adapt his methods to the new reality. As advancing in close column formation became increasingly suicidal, the less compact extended order came into being, as the attacker sought to moderate the murderous effects of the new technology. As the likelihood of a successful frontal attack decreased, commanders resorted more and more to trying to outflank the defender in order to turn his position. The efficacy of this maneuver was dramatically illustrated during the Franco-Prussian War during the fighting at Metz and Sedan, where two French armies were surrounded and forced to capitulate. The victorious German army came to make the turning movement the centerpiece of its military art after 1870, and by 1914 the scope of this maneuver had grown from the tactical to the strategic sphere, as embodied in the famous Schlieffen Plan, which foresaw the strategic envelopment of the French army in a single great turning movement.

Technological breakthroughs in the means of communication during this period also played a major part in revolutionizing the art of war among the industrialized states. The most prominent of these were the invention of the telegraph, telephone, and wireless telegraph—innovations that greatly increased the control a commander could exercise over the battle, even from a great distance. Now he could more effectively maneuver his scattered forces from a single location, as von Moltke had done in 1870–71. A single commander could now control the actions not only of several corps but of a number of armies as well, thus setting the stage for the appearance of the front, or army group, level of command. This impetus to centralized control also added greatly to the power and authority of the emerging general staff system.

The invention of the railroad was yet another factor that profoundly affected the conduct of war. With the spread of a rail net over much of western Europe and the United States after 1850, military planners were quick to discover that men and supplies could be swiftly transported over great distances in a fraction of the time required to cover the same ground on foot or by horse. As with the telegraph, the railroad's influence was first felt at the strategic level in the American Civil War, where large-scale movements from one theater of war to another were common. The Prussians owed much of their success in the several wars of German unification (1864–71) to their mastery of the railroad and its possibilities for strategic deployment. The war plans of the major European powers after 1870 came to be built increasingly around precise mobilization tables based on the carrying capacity of the railroads.

Along with these myriad economic-technological changes came equally significant social ones, by far the most important of which was the appearance of the mass national army. Until the end of the eighteenth century, most European armies were staffed by professional soldiers. These armies were relatively small, expensive to recruit and maintain, and even more expensive to lose. The caution and indecisiveness often displayed in European conflicts from 1648 to 1789 may be traced in part to the fear of losing such a large investment in a risky battle.

The French Revolution brutally swept aside this pleasant system. The modern national army was born in 1793 with the proclamation of the *levée en masse,* as France mobilized its adult male population to defend the republic against the invading armies of monarchist Europe. Although these drafts were often unwieldy on the battlefield and lacked the discipline of the old armies, Napoleon's military genius forged this explosion of nationalist enthusiasm into a formidable military weapon. Alone among the members of the anti-Napoleon coalition, Prussia adopted universal military service in 1813 and maintained it up to and beyond the unification of Germany in 1871. The success of this policy was so complete as to compel most of the major European powers to adopt some form of conscription soon after: Austria-Hungary in 1868, France in 1872, and Russia in 1874. By the turn of the century, such measures ensured not only that most industrialized nations could field a large army immediately upon the outbreak of war but also that the call-up of trained reservists and new recruits could raise the strength of the armies to several million men within a few weeks. What is more, these armies were now equipped and supported by the fabulously productive energies unleashed by the Industrial Revolution. And while modern armies demanded infinitely more in terms of matériel supply, the industrial capacity of post-1870 western Europe allowed the belligerents a great deal of latitude in the allocation of human and productive resources.

It is therefore one of the ironies of history that despite the tremendous growth in the destructive power of modern armies, by the end of the nineteenth century the leading industrialized nations had actually become more resistant to a single "knockout" blow by the enemy. The vastly increased human and productive resources at the disposal of the modern state had the cumulative effect of increasing its defensive "depth" and making it nearly impervious to the kind of climactic warfare practiced by Napoleon. Now a major state could suffer even a number of heavy reverses and, by drawing upon its vast internal resources, put together new armies to continue the struggle, as France succeeded in doing for a time following the disasters of Metz and Sedan. After 1870 the fact of the modern state's war potential was implicitly recognized in the growing emphasis on the factor of time and the necessity for rapid mobilization and attack in order to preempt the enemy's preparations.

In view of the augmented "staying power" of the modern state and its military consequences, the European art of war was in serious need of revision by 1900. Prior to this time the strategic art of maneuvering one's forces to the decisive point for the grand battle of annihilation was deemed the pinnacle of generalship in the manner of Napoleon and was the object toward which all commanders strove. Von Clausewitz, Napoleon's great interpreter, stated this succinctly in his *On War:* "The major battle is therefore to be regarded as concentrated war, as the center of gravity of the entire conflict or campaign."[3] And while the commanders persisted in their search for the Napoleonic ideal, the passage of time rendered this approach increasingly at odds with reality.

Now the generals were discovering that heightened enemy resilience had made an Austerlitz or Marengo all but impossible. Following a defeat, the enemy could slip away to regroup and replenish his forces, while the victor could rarely pursue effectively, given the effects of his own losses and the heightened defensive powers of modern weapons. Instead of a single battle deciding the war, one battle now served merely to set the stage for the next, which might follow quickly on the heels of the previous one. This tendency for formerly separate battles to fuse together in time became apparent as early as the Wilderness fighting in Virginia in 1864. As one participant in these battles later remarked: "Usually in military operations, the opposing armies come together, fight a battle and separate again, the strain lasting only a few days. . . . But with these two armies it was different. From the 5th of May, 1864, to the 9th of April, 1865, they were in constant contact with rare intervals of brief comparative repose."[4]

This phenomenon was repeated in the fighting around Metz during the early stages of the Franco-Prussian War. Here, in the space of five days (August 14–18, 1870), the German armies fought battles at Colombey and Nouilly, Vionville and Mars-la-Tour, Gravelotte and St.-Privat. At times, when the fighting was most intense, spreading out over several days, it became increasingly difficult to distinguish when one battle ended and another began. Often two or more major battles would rage simultaneously, as the single battlefield of old was gradually absorbed into the continuous melee of modern war.

Just as the formerly separate battles were merging in time, so were they also joining together in terms of space. This was due in part to the growing size of modern armies, which now had to spread out over greater distances in order to deploy effectively and turn the enemy's flank, as well as to ward off similar attempts on the enemy's part. The battle was also growing in depth, as the increasing range of modern weapons ensured that the fighting would begin at ever-greater distances from the actual front line, as even the formerly inviolate rear areas became part of the battle zone. The spatial growth of the modern battlefield can be shown by comparing two important nineteenth-century battles. In 1812 the French and Russian armies met at Borodino along a front of six to eight kilometers, while in 1870 the Germans and the French fought the simultaneous battles of Gravelotte–St.-Privat along a continuous front of some 20 kilometers in width.[5]

Even given the presence of modern communications technology, the enormous spatial growth of modern war after 1870 made it increasingly difficult for a single commander in chief to control all his armies. A Russian commander, for example, would be responsible for armies that would likely deploy along a front hundreds of kilometers in breadth. The Russian high command sought to alleviate this problem by creating the front, or group of armies, to serve as an intermediate command link between the commander in chief and the individual army commanders. This organizational response to the peculiarities of war in the East first appeared in the 1900 Russian war plan, which called for the creation of two fronts, directed at Germany and Austria-Hungary, respectively.

The single battle thus lost its former significance and spatial "separateness" and became increasingly subsumed under what came to be known as the "operation" *(operatsiya),* which later Soviet theoreticians have defined as the "totality of various combat actions, conducted according to a single plan by operational major field forces, of one or several services of the armed forces, for achieving the assigned strategic or operational goal."[6] While ranking above the purely tactical battle in terms of goals and forces engaged, the operation remains subordinate to strategy, due to its inability to bring about a strategic decision through its own resources, which are only a portion of the state's entire armed forces. It is this very intermediacy that defines the modern operation and sets the stage for the elaboration of a theory of operational art.

Thus, as opposed to the colorful spectacle of the past, war by 1904 had acquired a distinctly modern countenance. The necessary economic, technological, and social requirements were now in place and had developed to such an extent that the next major war would show just how far the operation had come.

This opportunity soon presented itself in northeast Asia, where the conflicting colonial ambitions of Russia and Japan finally came to a head in February 1904 with the surprise Japanese attack on the Russian Pacific Squadron, anchored at Port Arthur, in southern Manchuria. And although Admiral Togo's ships failed to destroy the squadron as planned, they did succeed in bottling up the Russian vessels within the harbor, which was a prerequisite for the next, continental phase of Tokyo's strategy. Unhindered at sea, the Japanese proceeded to carry out a series of amphibious landings along the Korean peninsula and southern Manchuria over the next few months. By May they had driven the small Russian covering force back across the Yalu River and cut off the garrison at Port Arthur from the main Russian forces based on Mukden.

Japanese strategy in the war was driven by the need to score a quick, decisive victory over the small Russian contingent in Manchuria before it could be reinforced from Europe. The Japanese armed forces, despite their impressive growth over the preceding thirty years, were still highly dependent on foreign military imports, particularly naval, and the country's economic situation was such that it could ill afford to wage a lengthy war with its potentially far stronger adversary. The Japanese instead relied on surprise, speed, and Russia's well-known internal weaknesses to bring them a quick and cheap victory. The Russian problem was just the opposite. At the beginning of the war, the Russians had only about 98,000 troops in the Far East, left over from their 1900 occupation of Manchuria during the Boxer Rebellion.[7] This force depended almost entirely for reinforcements and supply on a single unfinished rail line stretching thousands of kilometers back to European Russia. Russian strategy, thus hampered by nearly insuperable logistical difficulties, was necessarily defensive during the war's early months and sought to avoid large encounters with the stronger Japanese forces until sufficient reinforcements arrived to enable the Russians to take the offensive. While this strategy was undoubtedly correct for the first six months, the Russian effort was hobbled throughout by the senior generals' inability or unwillingness to adopt a more aggressive attitude, even after they had achieved a numerical superiority over the enemy. This stood in poor contrast to the Japanese approach, which invariably sought to carry the battle to the Russians, even in the face of superior numbers.

However, despite aggressive Japanese efforts to score a quick victory, the land war dragged on inconclusively throughout the spring and summer of 1904. Following the investment of Port Arthur, the Japanese, under the overall command of Marshal I. Oyama, moved north to meet Gen. A. N. Kuropatkin's Manchurian Army, which guarded the approaches to Mukden. The first major clash occurred at Lyao-Yang (August 24–September 3), during which the Japanese managed to dislodge the Russians from their positions through a skillful combination of frontal assault and flank attacks. The battle accomplished little except to cause casualties estimated at 15,890 Russians and 17,539 Japanese.[8] It was otherwise indecisive, except for the negative impression it left in the minds of the Russian command, as well as the common soldier. The Japanese, however, did not follow up very smartly upon their victory, and the Russians were able to withdraw unmolested to the north. During the next four weeks the two armies eyed each other warily across a 40-kilometer no-man's-land and gathered their forces for the next battle. Thus the stage was set for the battle along the Sha-ho River.

Kuropatkin, under pressure from St. Petersburg to relieve Port Arthur, resolved to attack the Japanese before they could recover fully from the Lyao-Yang fighting. The moment was certainly favorable, as the Russians had recently been reinforced and now numbered some 210,000 men and 758 guns against a Japanese force of only 170,000 and 648 guns, along a 60-kilometer front.[9] The Russian commander, to facilitate control of this large force, divided his army into several detachments, each of which was the equivalent of a small army. This made Kuropatkin, in effect, the first Russian front commander in everything but name.

Kuropatkin's plan called for Gen. Lt. G. K. Shtakel'berg's "Eastern Detachment" (1st, 2d, and 3d Siberian Corps and a cavalry detachment) to move south across the Sha-ho River (see map 1) in order to turn the weakly held Japanese right flank manned by General Kuroki's First Army and force it back on Lyao-Yang. At the opposite end of the Russian front, Gen. Lt. A. A. Bil'derling's "Western Detachment" (10th and 17th Corps and a cavalry detachment) would attack due south to pin down the Japanese and prevent them from switching troops against the main effort. A general reserve under Gen. Lt. N. P. Zarubaev (1st Corps and 4th Siberian Corps) occupied the interval between the detachments, echeloned slightly to the rear, while the 6th Siberian Corps constituted yet another reserve behind the Western Detachment.

The Russian plan contained a number of faults, the most serious of which was the even distribution of force along the front, which effectively precluded a decisive attack on any one sector. Kuropatkin exacerbated these faulty initial dispositions by tying the pace of the general advance to that of the left flank, thus making the entire attack hostage to the ostensible main effort, which was so understrength as to be doomed from the start. For example, the Eastern Detachment's main attack involved only a quarter of the entire Russian force, while half of the troops and more than half of the artillery remained idle in the reserve.[10] This egregious dispersal of force dovetailed exactly with the plan's lack of a clear, decisive objective and foresaw nothing more ambitious than the gaining of ground on the Japanese right, a move that neither threatened the enemy nor held out any promise of relief to Port Arthur. Also, whereas an attack on the Japanese left would have taken the Russians across relatively level ground, by attacking the enemy right the Eastern Detachment would be forced to advance over mountainous terrain in which large-scale movement would be limited to a few narrow and easily defended passes. In retrospect, it is obvious that a determined and well-supported attack against the Japanese left would have been far more effective, forcing the Japanese to fight where they stood or fall back.

Such cautious dispositions were not accidental, and they reflect Kuropatkin's entire philosophy of war. The latter was best summed up by the Russian commander's observations on the eve of the Battle of Lyao-Yang, when he wrote: "In my opinion, the best means of attaining success is to leave more than half of all forces in the reserve, so as to be able to meet any attack, no matter where it

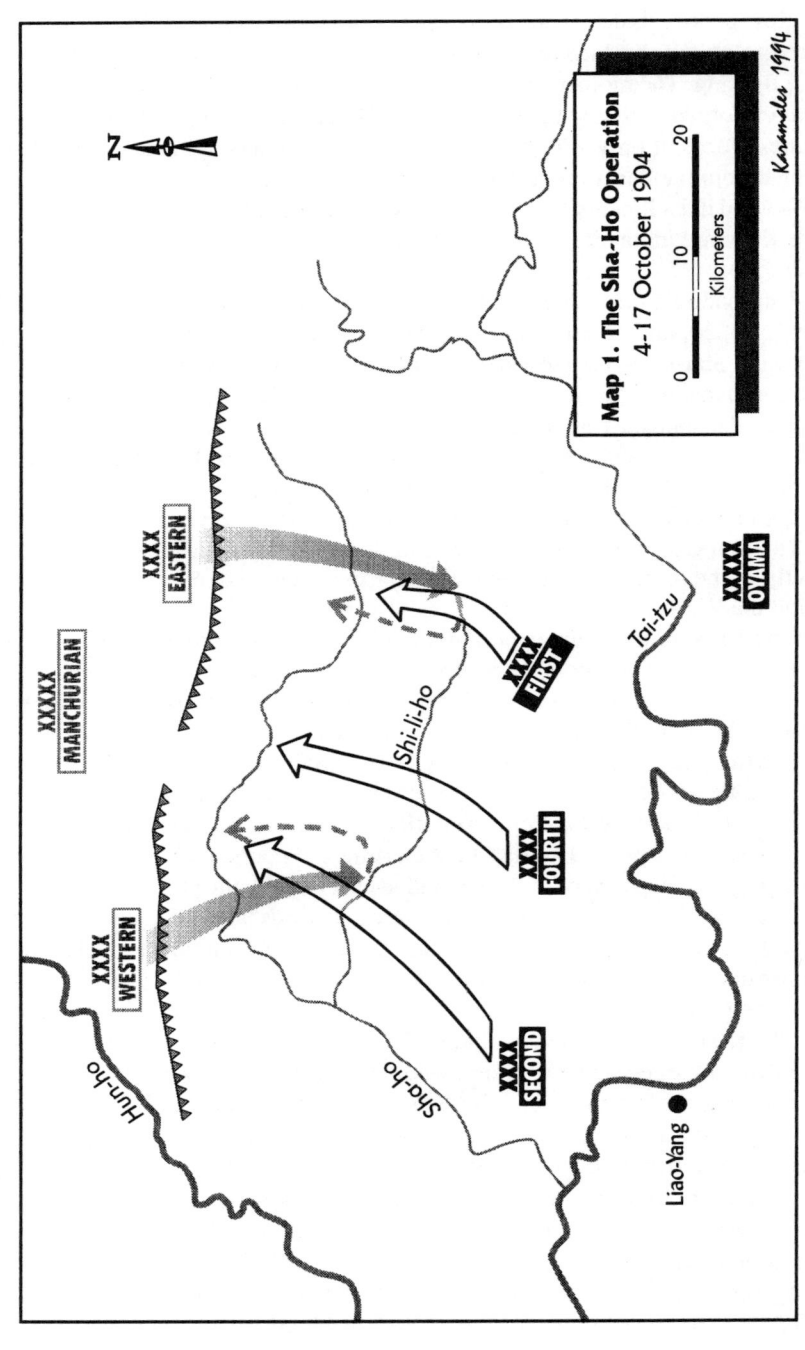

comes from."[11] Small wonder that one observer, writing after the war, called Kuropatkin and the generals around him "representatives of the Russian army's decadent era."[12]

The Russian offensive began on October 4 on the left flank, followed a day later by the Western Detachment on the right. Given the distance separating the opposing armies, the Russians encountered little initial resistance, although they advanced none the less slowly for that. The Russians reached the Sha-ho on October 6 and immediately and inexplicably dug in upon encountering a brigade-sized Japanese screening force, although the enemy's main body was still some distance away. In this manner the Russians, in the words of a British military observer assigned to the Japanese army, "parted for ever with that moral ascendancy which is the greatest of all the assets of an attack."[13] Shtakel'berg did not venture to attack when a serious assault would have easily routed the defenders. The Russian general even gave his troops a day's rest on the seventh and was no more aggressive the next day, which enabled the Japanese to withdraw southwest to a stronger and less-exposed position. The Russians followed slowly and finally closed to the Japanese line along the upper Tai-tzu River, but the element of surprise that their unexpected offensive had afforded them was now lost. The Western Detachment, its movements dictated by the progress of the "main attack," advanced in an equally dilatory manner, and everywhere the Russians' progress slowed to a crawl. And although the Russians would continue to attack fitfully, the overall initiative at this point passed to the Japanese.

Kuroki reacted swiftly to Shtakel'berg's threat and dispatched a division to his threatened right to shore up his position along the mountain passes. However, the Japanese were not content to merely blunt the Russian attack, and instead of allowing his actions to be dictated by the enemy, Oyama made the prompt and soldierly decision on October 9 to carry the battle to the Russians. The Japanese commander's plan called for General Oku's Second and General Nodzu's Fourth Armies, and Kuroki's left wing, to close to the Russian positions along the Shi-li-ho and pin the enemy along this line, while at the same time trying to turn the Russian right on the western bank of the Sha-ho. In fact, the first frontal collisions had taken place that very day south of the Shi-li-ho River.

The Japanese attacks continued throughout the morning and afternoon of October 10, and the Russians slowly began to give ground, although they retired in good order. Kuropatkin made no attempt to alleviate the pressure on his right by reinforcing the Western Detachment or by prodding the Eastern Detachment into action. The latter group limited itself to ineffectual cavalry probing and a number of attempts to dislodge the Japanese from the mountain passes. However, these attempts were unsuccessful, and Shtakel'berg began to withdraw his forces to the north and construct defensive positions, in spite of his three-to-one superiority over the enemy in men and guns.[14] Thus ended the heralded Russian offensive, which had been brought down by a combination of bad planning and the lethargy and timidity of the command echelon.

The Japanese offensive was resumed with vigor on the morning of October 11. Oyama had decided to give up his attempt to turn the Russian flank, due to a shortage of forces, and the Japanese shifted their attacks to the center of the line, where repeated assaults gradually wore down the defenders. The pressure here and farther east finally compelled the Russians to pull back their forces in the center toward the Sha-ho, a move that exposed the flank of the Western Detachment, forcing it to fall back as well. Unfortunately for the Russians, Kuropatkin's notion of command and his disjointed view of the battlefield meant that there was no attempt to relieve the pressure on this wing in spite of the Russians' overall numerical superiority. Thus even as the Japanese were threatening to break through the Russian center, a large percentage of Kuropatkin's forces remained unengaged. The fighting began to die down over the next few days, as the Japanese, by now exhausted, were content to let the Russians withdraw. Only in the center were the attacks launched with any energy, causing the Russians here to fall back behind the Sha-ho, where they had already begun fortifying the northern bank. Kuropatkin attempted a halfhearted counterattack west of the river on the fourteenth with the 6th Siberian Corps, which up until now had been idle. However, this attempt quickly faltered as a result of the Russians' usual inability to coordinate their efforts, and the fighting gradually began to peter out due to mutual exhaustion. There followed a final, brief burst of fighting along the Russian bridgehead south of the Sha-ho, which the defenders managed to hold in the face of furious Japanese infantry assaults. Both armies then settled down into a prolonged period of positional warfare known as the "Sha-ho sitting," which lasted, with minor breaks, for four months. Thus the operation's end found the Russians back at their starting point, although considerably the worse for wear in terms of casualties, and especially in morale. According to one source, the Russians lost 46,330 men, compared with Japanese casualties of 15,879, although the latter figure is probably too low by a good deal.[15]

The fighting along the Sha-ho River may rightly be described as the first modern operation. This view is justified by the appearance of a number of factors, called "operational indices"—a term to which I will have occasion to return often in the course of the narrative. These are the various quantitative indicators such as the number of forces engaged, the length of the front, the depth to which operations are conducted, and the duration of the particular operation. In this case, forces totaling almost 400,000 men were engaged in nearly continuous fighting for two weeks, along a more or less solid front some 90 kilometers in breadth and 20 in depth. It is precisely the accumulation of such indices that qualitatively distinguishes the Sha-ho fighting from anything that had gone before.

This is not to say that these indices have developed in any way harmoniously, as the experience of past wars showed. Previous battles (Leipzig, Waterloo) had involved large numbers of troops, and the 1864 Virginia campaign had witnessed extended fighting. However, while these battles may have come close in terms of numbers and duration, none compare with the Sha-ho fighting regarding the length of front occupied by the armies or the depth to which operations were conducted. The unprecedented appearance of all these indices in a single operation caused a later Soviet-era pioneer in the field to remark on the "amazing imprint of modernity" that "lies upon the operation along the Sha-ho River."[16]

By February 1905 both sides had sufficiently recovered from the October fighting to contemplate renewed offensive activity. The Japanese, numbering 270,000 men and 1,062 guns, were spread along a 110-kilometer front. The Russians, who lived in deadly fear of the enemy's turning movements, were even more extended, occupying a 150-kilometer front with 330,000 men and 1,266 guns, which effectively negated their numerical superiority.[17] The Russian position was further echeloned to a depth of 85 kilometers and consisted of three defensive positions, of which only the first was occupied. Kuropatkin, despite his failure of the previous autumn, remained in overall command of a force now divided into three armies, once again constituting a front command in all but name. At the same time, he was also commander in chief of all Russian forces in the Far East, which included both land and naval units. This was an organizational expedient to which the Soviets would resort in 1945 with considerably more success.

The czar had been pressing Kuropatkin to launch a decisive offensive against the Japanese, so as to extricate Russia from a war that was becoming increasingly unpopular at home. The latter dutifully responded with a plan that, even by the standards of late-imperial thinking, was striking in its lack of imagination. Its most glaring fault was that Kuropatkin once again utterly failed to pursue a decisive goal, either by means of battle or by maneuvering against the Japanese communications in anything approaching a forceful manner. Instead, Kuropatkin planned to make his main attack with Gen. A. V. Kaulbars's Second Army (8th and 10th Corps, plus a composite rifle corps) (see map 2) between the Hun-ho and the Sha-ho, with the vague notion of threatening the enemy's left flank and forcing him back on Lyao-Yang. If this effort were successful, General Lieutenant Bil'derling's Third Army (5th and 6th Siberian Corps and 17th Corps) and Gen. N. P. Linevich's First Army (2d, 3d, and 4th Siberian Corps) would support the attack by moving south against the Japanese center and right.

Kuropatkin's latest plan was again flawed in its very conception by its failure to employ the Russians' numerical superiority to any end other than the geographic objective of reaching the Tai-tzu River, in what was little more than a massive frontal attack. If Kuropatkin at least planned this time to attack across the more favorable terrain west of the Sha-ho, he still had not learned the wisdom of concentrating his forces for a decisive blow. Only a fraction of his force was assigned to take part in the main offensive, with the rest slated for supporting roles, while two corps languished in the army's more than ample reserve. Kuropatkin further reduced his chances by clinging to his practice of tying the supporting units' advance to the success, or lack thereof, of the main effort, thereby rendering the entire offensive dependent on the enemy's defensive prowess along a particular sector. In practice this meant relegating the greater part of his army to the role of

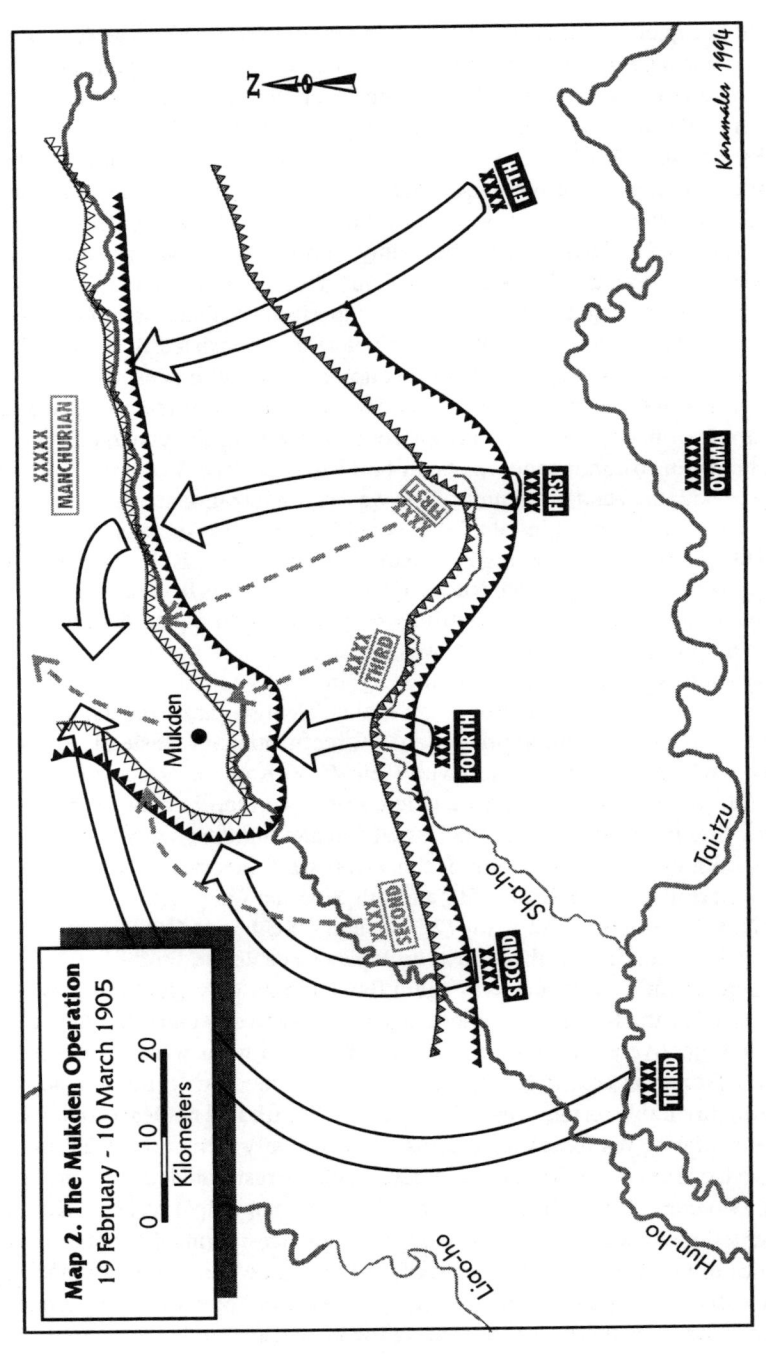

passive bystander. Finally, given his heavy investment in the previously named defensive positions, there is every reason to doubt Kuropatkin's commitment to any offensive action. Whatever the truth, he saw no reason to hurry his preparations, and he scheduled the offensive to begin on February 25.

The Japanese were also making offensive plans but of an entirely different kind from the halfhearted Russian efforts. Marshal Oyama's plan called for nothing less than the destruction of the entire Russian force in a single operation. He particularly sought to take advantage of the Russians' extended deployment, in which most of their forces were spread out in a single line, which made mutual support difficult and encouraged turning movements by an attacker. According to Oyama's plan, General Kawamura's Fifth Army was to attack the Russian outposts in the mountainous area north of the Tai-tzu and move northwest in conjunction with Kuroki's army to hit the Russian First Army's left flank. This attack, aside from having the objective of turning the Russian left, was also given the task of drawing away Russian reserves from the Japanese left wing, where Oyama planned to deliver his main attack. Here, General Nogi's Third Army, recently arrived from the successful siege of Port Arthur, was to swing around the Russians to turn their flank west of the Hun-ho and to cut Kuropatkin's communications north of Mukden and link up with Kawamura to encircle the defenders. The attack would be supported by the Japanese Second and Fourth Armies, which would launch simultaneous frontal attacks against the Russian positions along and to the west of the Sha-ho to prevent Kuropatkin from switching forces to either flank.

The contrast between the two plans could hardly be more striking. Whereas Kuropatkin, with an overall superiority in men and matériel, frittered away this advantage by allocating his forces evenly along the front, Oyama consolidated his smaller force into two strike groups and a ready reserve. Moreover, Oyama would be attacking with all his forces simultaneously, in pursuit of a single, clearly defined goal, while the Russian effort was fitful and uncoordinated, aiming at amorphous geographic goals instead of the enemy army. If there was a flaw in the Japanese plan, it was that it was probably too ambitious for the forces at Oyama's disposal. One can easily detect in the Japanese commander's design his personal experience at Sedan in 1870 and the strong influence of German military ideas in Japan at this time.[18]

The Japanese were first off the mark with a night attack by units of Kawamura's army against the Russian left on February 18. The attack made little progress at first due to stout resistance and the hilly terrain, which restricted the attackers' room for maneuver. Gradually, however, the Russians fell back in the face of Japanese turning movements on either side of their position. Kuroki's right wing applied additional pressure, beginning on February 24, by moving against Linevich along the upper Sha-ho. But the Russians retreated skillfully, and although the Japanese persisted in their efforts to turn their flank, they made little headway. However, they were more than successful in achieving their other goal of drawing the defenders' attention from the decisive front. In fact, the Japanese attacks so alarmed Kuropatkin that he ordered Second Army's reserve and his own general reserve of two infantry corps eastward to counter the threat. Kaulbars thereupon decided to cancel Second Army's "main effort," a move to which Kuropatkin readily acceded. The ruse had worked perfectly; the Russian command not only was fooled into weakening its forces in the area of the forthcoming main attack but also had completely surrendered the initiative to the enemy.

On February 27 Nogi began his move around the Russian right. His 3½ divisions quickly wheeled to the northwest, screened by a cavalry brigade on the Ta-lyao River's west bank. That same day Second Army began its attack to divert the Russians' attention from the envelopment being prepared against them. The Japanese turning movement caught the Russians completely by surprise, even though they had long been aware of Nogi's presence. In fact, so ineffective was the Russian cavalry west of the Hun-ho that Kaulbars was not even made aware of the enemy's move until the next day, by which time the Japanese were well around the Russian flank.

Kuropatkin's response to this developing threat was to dispatch a brigade to cover his communications north of Mukden, the first in a series of half measures that came to exemplify his conduct of the operation. At this point the commander in chief still saw the main danger on his left wing, where the Japanese had resumed their attacks on March 1. Had an energetic counterattack been made at this point, where the Russians enjoyed a better than two-to-one superiority, the Japanese might well have been thrown back against the Tai-tzu and Nogi's attack disrupted altogether.[19] However, such decisive actions were foreign to Kuropatkin's nature, and he proceeded to compound his previous error by ordering one of his infantry corps back to Mukden, where it would be of no immediate use to either wing. Kuropatkin's perverse refusal to seize his opportunities and his desire to be secure everywhere ended the best hope the Russians had of defeating the Japanese offensive.

In contrast to the confused Russian response, Nogi pressed on with his turning movement, meeting as yet only sporadic opposition. Kaulbars remained only dimly aware of the threat to his right, although the situation was growing more serious by the hour. As of March 1, Second Army still had just 22,000 men on the Hun-ho's north bank to oppose Nogi's entire army, the forward units of which were already northwest of Mukden.[20] Second and Fourth Japanese Armies, meanwhile, persisted in their unsuccessful efforts farther to the east. Kuropatkin's response to this concerted effort was to hurriedly reinforce and extend his right flank by creating small scratch units of strictly tactical significance in order to keep pace with Nogi's left wing and deflect it from the rail artery at Mukden. As the battle developed, this "system" of reinforcing the Russian right wing gradually bled Third and First Armies of men and equipment, while Second Army never received the decisive infusion of strength that would have enabled it to turn on the Japanese in a decisive fashion.

The Russians recovered somewhat during the first few days of March and began striking back in several places along their lengthening right flank. However, these attacks were poorly coordinated and usually not pressed very hard. The Japanese were only slightly inconvenienced by these moves and continued to press the enemy all along the front. Oyama continued to reinforce Nogi from his general reserve, and the latter castled his divisions northward as the line gradually snaked beyond Mukden. Elsewhere, Second Army maintained pressure on the Russians still south of the Hun-ho, while First and Fifth Armies continued to harry Linevich, despite being outnumbered 100,000 to 130,000.[21] However, as before, the Japanese could make little headway here, although their attacks continued to pin down disproportionate numbers of enemy troops.

Both sides traded attacks throughout March 5, 6, and 7, although the Japanese generally got the better of the fighting. The Russians kept searching for the Japanese left flank but failed to find it; as a consequence, most of their attacks became costly frontal assaults that did little to deter the Japanese from their objective. Nogi was now closing in on the railway north of Mukden, and Japanese cavalry was even able to raid the outposts defending this artery and destroy sections of the line. Kuropatkin, by scraping together his last reserves, was able to organize a blocking group west of the railroad. However, although this latest scratch group was temporarily able to stave off the threat to the Russian communications, it was far from being a force capable of pushing back the Japanese.

The bankruptcy of Kuropatkin's policy was now revealed. By failing to use First and Third Armies for anything more than a general reserve for his right wing, the Russian commander surrendered the initiative along his center and left to the enemy. The Japanese, in turn, ceaselessly pressed the Russians south of the Hun-ho, threatening a breakthrough there and preventing Kuropatkin from shifting more forces to his right. By the end of the first week in March, Kuropatkin could no longer maintain this balancing act, while the Japanese, with fewer troops, continued to attack everywhere.

The Russian commander was thus faced with the necessity of shortening his front south of the Hun-ho by pulling back First and Third Armies behind the river to build up a sufficient blocking force west of Mukden. An order to this effect went out on March 7, and the two armies began to pull back later that evening. The Japanese followed none too aggressively, and by the morning of the eighth the Russians were ensconced in their new positions along the north bank of the Hun-ho. On that day General Oku's Second Army moved its last division north of the river, so that the full weight of two Japanese armies was now brought to bear against the beleaguered Russian right. With the closing of the Fourth, First, and Fifth Armies to the Hun-ho, the Russian front came to form a very narrow and dangerous corridor, with its apex southwest of Mukden and the Japanese nibbling at its flanks. The Russian position was plainly untenable, although when disaster did strike it came from a wholly unexpected quarter.

As a result of poor staff work and the confusion caused by the hurried retreat, the troops who fell back behind the Hun-ho sometimes occupied their unfinished positions in a haphazard fashion. Kuroki's forces struck one of these weak points during a blinding sandstorm, and the Japanese flowed into the breach and into the Russian rear, hardly hindered by the demoralized defenders, who, in the absence of centralized control, offered little in the way of resistance. By nightfall Kuroki's army had wheeled to the northwest and was within a few hours of the Mandarin Road north of Mukden. The Russian army now faced the very real threat of encirclement.

Fortunately for the Russians, by this time Kuropatkin had already admitted defeat and had decided to pull the entire army back to Tieh-ling before he was even aware of the magnitude of the Japanese breakthrough. The Russians began their retreat on the evening of March 9 through an 11-kilometer corridor along the railroad leading out of Mukden. The most difficult task fell to the lot of Third Army, which had the greatest distance to travel, over roads clogged with men and supply wagons, and periodically shelled from both flanks. In these desperate hours a number of Russian units performed heroically and managed to keep the Japanese at bay just long enough for the main body to get away. By the evening of the tenth the greater part of the Third Army had escaped, followed closely by Second Army. First Army, which was effectively cut off from its neighbors, took a more easterly route and also managed to elude its pursuers. On the morning of March 11, units of the Japanese Third and First Armies finally linked up north of Mukden, although the greater part of the Russian army had gotten away.

The Russians did not linger long at their Tieh-ling positions but continued their retreat northward, only halfheartedly pursued by the Japanese, who in any case were in no condition to engage the enemy after two weeks of continuous fighting. By March 30 the Russians had reached their final defensive position at Ssu-ping-chieh. Linevich replaced Kuropatkin, and the Russian army was reinforced to a strength of 446,500 men to 337,500 Japanese, but the dispirited Russians undertook no more offensive operations.[22] The Japanese, for their part, had reached the limits of their resources and were content merely to observe their foes and allow the revolutionary situation in Russia to take its course. The latter's final defeat came at the naval disaster at Tsushima (May 27–28, 1905), where the Russians lost twenty-seven ships, and peace negotiations began soon afterward.[23] The Treaty of Portsmouth ended the war on September 5, 1905.

The Mukden operation was the war's largest land battle and the greatest single clash of arms before 1914. In it the Russians lost some 89,000 men, of whom 30,000 were prisoners, against Japanese losses of approximately 70,000.[24] In operational terms the fighting here represents a significant growth of those operational indices already mentioned, particularly as regards the increase in the size of the armies engaged (600,000 men) and the spatial growth of the battlefield, which now exceeded 100 kilometers. There is every reason to believe that had the two sides elected to fight along the Ssu-ping-chieh position, these figures would have grown even further, particularly as regards the creation of a continuous front. The operation had come a long way since its infant beginnings during the previous century, and in Manchuria the ghastly contours of 1914–18 were already visible.

The fighting in Manchuria, which one historian aptly termed an "epic of incompetence," revealed a number of weaknesses in the Russians' conduct of operations, particularly at the army and front level, where the high command utterly failed to master the complexities of controlling large formations.[25] It was one of Kuropatkin's many shortcomings as a commander that he was incapable of seeing beyond the immediate tactical level, when his army of over 300,000 demanded something quite different. Instead, Kuropatkin behaved like a division commander and threw away his chances for victory because of his preoccupation with the minutiae of battle, which during the Mukden operation reached down to the battalion level.

The Manchurian fighting also showed the importance, in the new operational setting, of the turning maneuver and outflanking the enemy, and, conversely, the fruitlessness of the frontal attack for any purpose other than a diversion. This was particularly important in this pre–World War I era, when there still existed open flanks. Kuropatkin's attempts, however, were halfhearted, understrength, and therefore stillborn. It was the Japanese, on the other hand, who continually employed this maneuver, using entire armies, and it ultimately brought them victory.

However, in a larger sense the Russians lost the war because of the almost-otherworldly pusillanimity of the command echelon, which, when faced with the choice of attacking or defending, almost always chose the latter. Kuropatkin's offensive efforts were invariably slow in their preparation, begun with insufficient forces, poorly coordinated, and all too quickly canceled at the first sign of resistance. The utter lack of offensive spirit at the top seriously damaged the troops' morale and greatly undermined the Manchurian Army as a fighting force. In Manchuria the Russian command suffered much less from a failure to master any principles of operational art than from a shortage of the traditional military virtues. In Kuropatkin's actions are evidence of an unmistakable systemic decline in the Russian army.

ACADEMIC CONCERNS

"We did not know modern war" was one observer's verdict on the Russian army's failure in the Far East.[26] Indeed, of the major European powers, the Russians had probably been the least successful in adapting to the late-nineteenth-century revolution in military affairs. However, a defeat may also have the positive effect of forcing a nation's political-military establishment to reexamine its fundamental beliefs to avoid a repetition of the mistakes that led to disaster. This was partly the case with Russia, whose humiliation in the war with Japan not only had led to

domestic unrest and far-reaching political changes but also resulted in a measure of reform within the chastened army. The intense soul-searching occasioned by the army's poor showing against the despised Japanese prompted several gifted thinkers to ponder the implications of recent military developments and attempt to draw lessons for the future. These studies, carried out in the decade preceding the outbreak of war in 1914, resulted in a number of interesting and influential conclusions regarding the nature of modern war and, in particular, the nascent field of operations.

Needless to say, the term "operational art" was not in use at this time and would only gain widespread currency under the successor Red Army some twenty years hence.[27] Nor would it be correct to assume that the rich vein of operational thought that emerged between 1905 and 1914 is entirely original to these years. In fact, many of the ideas that agitated Russian military thinkers during this time had their genesis in the decades preceding the turn of the century. In this regard, the most outstanding thinker during the pre-1904 period was the military theorist Genrikh Antonovich Leer (1829–1904), the author of several detailed works on strategy and other subjects. From 1889 until 1898 he was also the chief of the General Staff Academy, from which advantageous position he was able to shape the thinking of many of the country's best officers. In Leer we find one of the earliest Russian attempts at the systematic study of operations and an effort to incorporate this phenomenon into the existing fields of strategy and tactics.

Appropriately enough, his main work on the subject was entitled *Strategy (The Tactics of the Theater of Military Activities)*, which first appeared in 1869 and was reissued regularly over the next thirty years. As the title suggests, there was as yet no place for an independent field of operations in Leer's system; nor did the author put forth a working definition of the operation, although considerations of this sort occupy a prominent place in the book. Rather, the operation was subsumed under the rubric of strategy, which Leer divided into two parts, the ideal and the practical. The first, or strategy in the "broad sense," deals with what he called the "philosophy of military affairs" and constitutes a holistic understanding of the phenomenon of war. The second, or strategy in the "narrow sense," is more concrete and corresponds closely to the spatial parameters of modern operational art. Leer called this sphere the "tactics of the theater of military activities," which he identified with the "higher tactics" of Napoleon. This, in turn, was distinguished from what Leer called the "tactics of the battlefield," which is geographically much more limited in scope and restricted to the immediate task of engaging the enemy.[28]

Of equal importance with the delineation of these separate spheres of activity was their hierarchical relationship to one another. Thus while the operation blends into Leer's notion of applied strategy by virtue of the former's physical identification with the theater of military activities (the tactics of the theater of military activities), it is by inference superior to the "tactics of the battlefield" and is in fact made up of "a series of local actions, maneuvers and local battles."[29] In practice, strategy devises the operational plan and deploys, supplies, maneuvers, and provides for the security of the army in the given theater of military activities, while the issue is ultimately decided by a series of purely tactical actions, that is, battles.[30]

In spite of what is by current standards a confusing terminological overlap, it is clear that Leer had recognized the operation as a separate entity, in much the same way as battles and campaigns were seen as subdivisions of the larger phenomenon of war. As a separate theory, however, the sphere of operations was as yet far from achieving full independence from the more established fields of strategy and tactics. Rather, they—in particular, strategy—tended to encroach upon operations and to lend their terminology to the latter almost to the point of masking its salient features. Nevertheless, the distinctions that Leer did make indicate that the art of conducting operations was beginning to separate itself from its elder brothers. The seeds of future operational autonomy had been planted, although it would be left to another army to complete the process.

Of particular significance for the future development of operational art were Leer's thoughts on the nature of the theater of military activities *(teatr voennykh deistvii)* and the organization of the masses of men and matériel that would occupy it. The author, in the 1898 edition of *Strategy,* defined for the first time the theater of military activities as "the space in which one or two armies operate, having one and the same objective." The theater of war *(teatr voiny),* on the other hand, is "the entire space in which the war is waged" and may consist of several theaters of military activities.[31] More than ten years earlier, Leer had speculated that a theater of military activities might be occupied by as many as five armies, numbering up to a million men. Depending on a variety of geographic and political factors, these units might be further organized into what Leer called "groups of separate armies" *(gruppy chastnykh armii),* each of which would be responsible for a separate theater of military activities.[32]

This huge and unwieldy mass would inevitably present enormous control problems that could no longer be resolved using previous methods of direct field command, even given the remarkable advances in communications during the previous half century. Leer's solution was the post of commander in chief *(glavnokomanduyushchii),* each of which would be responsible for a group of armies.[33] However, the name belies the weak powers actually accorded the position, as Leer preferred a distinctly "hands-off" approach to command at this level more reminiscent of the elder von Moltke's practice in 1870. According to Leer, the commander in chief would be strictly limited in his ability to interfere in the activities of his individual army commanders and would be restricted to informing the latter of the operation's "general idea" and the overall situation in the theater of military activities.[34]

The appearance of the front at this stage, at least in theory, was conditioned by a number of factors, both objective (geographic) and subjective (political). The first involved a recognition by Leer and others of the command and control difficulties inherent in operations in the vast expanses of eastern Europe, even given recent advances in communications. The more subjective element had to do with the likelihood of war with both Germany and Austria-Hungary along most of this front. Given this alignment, one front would inevitably be pulled due west toward Berlin, while the other would incline toward the southwest, in the direction of Vienna and Budapest.

Leer's ruminations on the need to combine the heretofore independent armies into larger groups of armies, operating toward a common goal in a single theater of military activities, was, in retrospect, a seminal event in the development of Russian operational thought. Here, in a rudimentary form, was the theoretical justification for organizing what would later become known as the front, an operational-strategic command instance lying midway between the supreme command and the individual field armies. Leer's recommendations became a reality in 1900, with the division of the western theater of war into two theaters of military activities, each manned by a single front. These fronts were directed, respectively, against Germany and Austria-Hungary. The imperial army, in the years remaining to it, would further develop Leer's ideas on this score, and the notion of the front would quickly become one of the major tenets of the Red Army's operational heritage after 1917.

While Leer's work was certainly incomplete by current standards, his efforts were nevertheless advanced for his time and would continue to serve as a valuable reference point for succeeding theorists. Long regarded as the army's leading theoretician, Leer was particularly influential at the General Staff Academy, even after his departure in 1898. To judge from later sources, a number of Leer's ideas had already been introduced into the students' course of study at the end of the century, notably the author's notions of the theater of military activities and the necessity for creating groups of armies.[35] One student, who passed through the academy at the end of the century, later recalled that one of his final examination assignments was to elaborate a "strategic operation" in a theater of military activities.[36] And while it is doubtful that the forces engaged matched the numbers of men and equipment presumed under the later Soviet definition of this term, the spatial scope implied is certainly very close.

Among the later theorists were the academy graduates A. V. Gerua and E. E. Messner, who are credited with coining the term "operatics" *(operatika)*. One observer of the period's theoretical controversies later wrote that, according to this scheme, strategy is the waging of war in its entirety, while operatics is the conduct of the battle at the army level, and tactics is the waging of combat from the corps level down.[37] This early division of military art into strategy, operatics, and tactics is of decisive importance to the development of later operational thought, helping to further the liberation of operational art from the two older disciplines. This theoretical (the hierarchical arrangement of the three fields) and organizational (the size of the units engaged) division is one of the earliest pieces of evidence pointing to a link between prerevolutionary and Soviet operational thought. From this formula it was but a short step to the later Soviet division of military art into strategy, operational art, and tactics.

This is not to suggest that there existed anything like unanimity on this and other matters in the army in the wake of the Manchurian debacle. On the contrary, the Russian army during the interwar period was continually riven by a number of theoretical, practical, and personal controversies. One chronicler of the time saw the army as being divided into three antagonistic camps. The first group, according to this view, consisted of those senior officers who completely failed to understand the lessons of the recent war and the need for reform within the army. The leading members of this clique included War Minister V. A. Sukhomlinov and Chief of Staff Ya. G. Zhilinskii (1911–14), among others.[38] As a group, these men represented most clearly the official views of the court and the military bureaucracy. And while they were not wholly indifferent to the idea of reform, their innate conservatism and lack of resolve in implementing even the most inoffensive changes certainly retarded the army's development into a modern force.

By far the most interesting of these groups was the so-called Young Turks, whose writings and educational efforts did so much to revitalize Russian military thinking during these years. Intellectually, this group stood head and shoulders above its stultified opponents in the war ministry, although its academic virtues did not save it from defeat by the obscurantists' bureaucratic intrigues. These intelligent proponents of reform included D. G. Shcherbachev, chief of the General Staff Academy from 1907 to 1912, and the military intellectuals N. N. Golovin and A. A. Svechin.[39] The latter would eventually become one of the Red Army's leading and most controversial military theorists in the 1920s.

Finally, a third and much less influential camp consisted of those who tended toward a romanticized view of Russian military history. Headed by A. Z. Myshlaevskii and A. K. Baiov, this group made few practical recommendations, and its existence was due more to a deep-seated reaction against Western influences and a vague search for a native military method.[40] In spite of its weak theoretical base, this faction's strongly nationalistic appeal made it potentially the most powerful of the contending groups. Ironically, the nationalist school would come to enjoy its greatest success under the ostensibly "internationalist" Soviet regime, which assiduously promoted the idea, particularly after World War II, of a distinctly Russian-Soviet military tradition.

Much of the intellectual ferment during the interwar decade took place in the General Staff Academy, which served briefly as the reformers' base for disseminating their ideas within the army through successive classes of young, would-be staff officers. The reformers managed to get the upper hand during the period of recrimination that followed the Russo-Japanese War, when the army establishment and its methods stood in temporary disgrace. The academy itself was certainly in need of reformation and had been heavily criticized for failing to prepare its students to meet the demands of modern warfare. Indeed, the quality and relevance of the instruction in many areas left much to be desired, even under the reformist administration. For example, a preoccupation with abstractions at the expense of practical knowledge was a chronic problem in the academy's program for several years.[41] B. M. Shaposhnikov, who would later enjoy a brilliant career in the Red Army, complained of his student years that despite the outward signs of reform, the academy still "prepared more of a theoretician than a practitioner for service on troop staffs."[42] I. I. Vatsetis was another former student who was to rise high in the Red Army's ranks. While he was willing to give the academy its due, he nevertheless criticized it for what he called the reigning "intellectual anarchy."[43]

Whatever its shortcomings, the interwar academy did attempt to impart to its students some idea of modern war, and it offered what one former officer called a "well-founded knowledge" in tactics, operatics, and strategy.[44] However, the academy's approach to the field of operations was often hobbled by the same terminological muddle that had characterized Leer's writings on the subject and would continue to plague his successors. For example, the academy's leading authority on operations, Col. A. A. Neznamov, was during these years a professor of strategy, ample proof of the operation's continuing absorption by the latter discipline. This duality was reflected in the colonel's lectures, in which his teaching of operations was described as "something similar to operational art, not exactly grand tactics as defined by Napoleon, and not exactly the strategy of the theater of military activities according to Leer."[45] Likewise, another instructor referred to his teaching duties in the realm of operations as lecturing on the "higher tactics" of large combined-armed arms formations.[46]

Despite these continuing problems, there can be little doubt that the reformists' academic efforts during these years did much to raise the quality of the interwar graduates' understanding of operations. However, such victories proved fleeting, as the reactionary clique within the army regained its strength and confidence. The struggle between the competing factions ended in 1913 with the complete victory of the Sukhomlinov faction and the dismissal of many of the Young Turks to other posts and a restructuring of the academic program along more traditional lines. The housecleaning even went so far as to include the replacement of the academy's head with the chief of gendarmes![47]

Much of the significant writing on operations during this period, both inside the academy and without, dealt with a range of questions that were central to developing a coherent theory of operations. Some of these had already been raised in basic form by Leer and would continue to animate military thinkers through what remained of the imperial era and well into the Soviet regime. These issues can be reduced to four basic questions. The first concerned the place operations were to occupy in relation to the fields of strategy and tactics. This was more than just a problem of semantics, and its resolution would have consequences for the theoretical independence of operations and creating the basis for elaborating a broader theory of operational art. The second question concerned the operation itself and dealt with the different categories of operations, as well as their preparation and conduct. The third dealt with the notion of the front/group of armies in the theater of military activities—its mission, composition, and system of command. Finally, the fourth question concerned the early theoretical speculation into what in the 1920s came to be called "consecutive operations," or the conduct of successive offensive operations to final victory.

Easily the most outstanding figure to explore these and other problems during this period was the aforementioned Aleksandr Aleksandrovich Neznamov, whose highly productive academic career spanned both the czarist and communist regimes. Neznamov was born into a peasant family in 1872 and finished military-engineering school in 1893. In 1900 he graduated from the General Staff Academy, where he doubtlessly imbibed many of the reigning ideas on the place and conduct of operations according to Leer. Following service in the Manchurian theater, Neznamov returned to the academy as an instructor and was appointed professor of strategy three years later. At the same time he served as a member of the army's commission to write a new field manual. Neznamov held a variety of command and staff posts during the Great War and was promoted to the rank of general-major in 1915. He joined the Red Army in early 1918 and taught briefly at its new General Staff Academy before moving to the Military-Engineering Academy, where he worked as a professor until 1925. Neznamov continued to write under the Soviet regime and served on a number of administrative and historical commissions until his death in 1928.[48]

Neznamov's interwar writings reveal him to be the sort of clearheaded analyst that the army so desperately needed. As opposed to Leer's lengthy discourses on the immutable principles of war, Neznamov believed in the primacy of technical and economic factors in determining the development of military art. This shift away from the fuzzy and idealistic conceptions of the past helped pave the way for a more realistic study of modern war within the army.

Neznamov's views on the subject of operations were most cogently expressed in his 1911 work, *Modern War: The Activities of a Field Army,* which was reissued a number of times under the Soviet regime. Even a cursory reading of the book reveals the extent of the author's debt to Leer, although he was able to improve upon the latter's ideas in a number of areas. Most important, Neznamov was able to advance somewhat the terminological independence of the operation from strategy and tactics. This was most clearly expressed in the following passage: "Just as the entire war is broken up into an entire series of operations, so each operation is broken up into an entire series of local *immediate objectives,* . . . and they are all together united by the operation's common goal, just exactly as all the operations are linked among themselves by . . . the *war's fundamental guiding idea according to objective and direction.*"[49]

Neznamov's formula reaffirmed the primacy of strategy over operations and further delineated their relationship in an emerging three-way division of labor. Thus strategy determines the overall military goal and attempts to achieve this through the grouping of various operations. The connection between the two is obvious even before the outbreak of war, during which time strategy determines the relative importance of the various theaters of war and the forces assigned to each. In practical terms this involves drawing up a plan for the strategic deployment of the country's armed forces. This plan, in turn, determines the armies' placement and objectives at the beginning of the war and constitutes, in effect, the first operational plan.[50] As the war progresses, strategy will continue to regulate operations by orienting the fronts' axes of advance and allocating reinforcements, and by otherwise reacting to changes in the overall situation.

At the operational-tactical nexus the operation is clearly dominant over the innumerable tactical actions that constitute it. In practice, the operational plan establishes the number, type (offensive or defensive), and objective of these tactical actions, according to the forces allocated to them, in order to achieve the more long-range goals previously established by the strategic instance.

Neznamov fleshed out his notion of the operation with a battlefield definition, which served as a useful counterpoint to the more theoretical exegesis just cited. According to this view, a future war was likely to unfold in a series of forward movements by the attacker and corresponding withdrawals by the defender. These periods of activity would, in turn, be punctuated by periods of relative inactivity, during which both sides would seek to improve their position by bringing up reinforcements and otherwise refitting in preparation for the next round of fighting. It was to these self-contained periods of preparation and fighting that Neznamov gave the name operations, thereby continuing Leer's practice of subsuming the various preliminary measures under that rubric.[51]

Taken together, these examples offer a definition of the place occupied by operations in military affairs that later Soviet theorists would find it difficult to improve upon. One sees, in fact, in these passages the outline of what would eventually become the standard definition of operational art from the mid-1920s. And while Neznamov did not set himself the task of creating a new discipline, his work in further separating the sphere of operations from that of strategy and tactics certainly helped to further the movement toward the operation's ultimate theoretical independence.

Neznamov was less successful, however, in his discussion of phenomena at or near the operational level of war. This confusion chiefly revolved around his use of the term *srazhenie* (engagement, or battle) and a number of concepts derived from it. Neznamov, taking his cue from von Clausewitz, defined the engagement as "that toward which every operation tends" and which serves as the operation's "logical end."[52] Of somewhat greater substance were the "army engagement" *(armeiskoe srazhenie)* and the "general engagement" *(general'noe srazhenie)*. The former was a "series of more or less simultaneously occurring, independent battles of columns, which are connected with each other only by a single and general goal," while the general engagement involves the collision of a large part of the belligerents' armed forces in a single climactic battle, as was common during the wars of antiquity and Napoleon.[53] By way of historical example, one may consider the Battle of Mons of 1914 and the destruction of General Samsonov's army in East Prussia as modern examples of the army engagement, while the Battles of Galicia and the Marne correspond more closely to the author's notion of the general engagement.

However, these terms confuse as much as they elucidate, particularly regarding the place of the operation vis-à-vis either type of engagement. As defined by Neznamov, it is difficult to determine whether the different kinds of engagements are an integral and culminating part of the operation or something separate for which the preceding operation functions merely as the maneuver prelude to the actual fighting. Neznamov, by seeming to separate the engagement from the operation, inadvertently struck at the heart of the modern understanding of the latter, which holds that it is the engagement that has been absorbed by the operation. In this respect, Neznamov reveals himself as a typical representative of the nineteenth-century Napoleonic-Clausewitzian school, which holds that the engagement/battle is the supreme act of war, to which everything else is subordinate.

Neznamov was more fortunate in his examination of the various kinds of operations, which he divided into three types: offensive, defensive, and the meeting operation. As opposed to previous efforts, the author's functional delineation of the operation was more in tune with modern demands and would persist well into the Soviet period. Of the three, Neznamov considered the offensive operation the most important and devoted by far the most space to its study. In this regard he was not unlike many of his colleagues in the West before 1914, who looked forward to an offensive war of maneuver, despite the ominous hints of 1904–5. In the case of Russia, this more pugnacious approach also represented a healthy reaction to the army's chronic passivity during the Russo-Japanese War, in which the numerically inferior Japanese won repeated victories by seizing the initiative from the languid Russian command.

As to the various offensive forms available to the commander, Neznamov spoke approvingly of what he called the "strategic breakthrough" *(strategicheskii proryv)*, followed by a subsequent attack against one of the separated wings of the enemy front. Such an option, he claimed, had become more attractive of late because of the extreme elongation of the armies' fronts, which would impede any defensive countermeasures.[54] This is a surprising assertion, in light of Neznamov's experience in Manchuria, which saw not a single instance of a breakthrough of operational importance. Moreover, the approaching world war would clearly show that the prospects for such a breakthrough had been reduced dramatically, even under the more favorable conditions of the eastern front.

Neznamov's real preference was for the envelopment maneuver against the enemy's communications, carried out by a single army acting semi-independently in the theater of military activities. The main exponents of this method were the chief of the German General Staff, von Schlieffen, and his predecessor, the elder von Moltke, whose encircling operations at Metz and Sedan continued to mesmerize European military thinkers forty years after the event.[55] Neznamov, however, had certain reservations and was quick to point out that the fortuitous circumstances of the Franco-Prussian War were unlikely to be repeated, given the increasing tendency of the battlefield to coalesce into a single front, with the corresponding loss of room for maneuver. To this list of factors he added modern communications and intelligence means, which had rendered the old-style turning movement *(obkhod)* all but impossible, although he did not entirely rule out its use in the operations of a group of armies.[56]

As an alternative, Neznamov proposed the less ambitious flanking maneuver *(okhvat)*, which he felt to be the most acceptable expedient under modern conditions. However, the inherent limitations of this maneuver were that the smaller forces involved and the movement's shallow scope were of tactical significance only and could not lead to a decisive operational result. According to this scheme, the main flank attack would be accompanied by a secondary attack elsewhere along the defender's front. This not only would divert the defender's attention from the main blow but also would draw the latter's reserve into the battle against the secondary attack, leaving it vulnerable to a flanking movement by the main effort.[57] This was a prescription for a maneuver as old as military art itself, one that would be greatly expanded upon, both in theory and in practice, under the Soviet regime.

The "waiting operation" *(vyzhidatel'naya operatsiya)* was Neznamov's term for what otherwise was a defensive operation. However, as the name implies, the defender's mission was not limited to merely repelling the enemy's attacks but also included actively preparing for future offensive operations. Here, perhaps more than in any other area, was felt the searing experience of the Russo-Japanese War and the widely held belief that the war had been lost in large part due to the commanders' lack of offensive spirit. One can even detect traces of the prewar French cult of the offensive, which was all too willing to turn any defensive posture into the basis for an attack. Thus even when attacked by superior forces, the defender is to begin preparing a decisive counterattack, preferably against the enemy's flanks. This would involve stripping as many men as possible from the passive sectors in order to form a reserve capable of taking the attacker in flank and disrupting or halting his attack, preparatory to a counteroffensive.[58]

Neznamov's preference for viewing the defensive as a forced measure, dictated by temporarily adverse conditions, was an approach that enjoyed great support among a later generation of Soviet theorists, as did his desire to promptly transform almost any defensive action into a counteroffensive. A serious shortcoming in his analysis, however, was his narrow focus on the army defensive operation, which necessarily confined his prescriptions to the operational-tactical sphere. Unfortunately for posterity, Neznamov chose not to address the idea of waging defensive operations at the front level or theater of military activities. This omission would be repeated, with tragic consequences, by later Soviet theorists prior to 1941.

Neznamov's final category was the "meeting operation" *(vstrechnaya operatsiya)*, which occurs when both sides are in motion. This was a comparatively recent phenomenon, brought about by the enormous growth of late-nineteenth-century armies and their resulting tendency to form a continuous front. This was even more likely to be the case when both sides pursue an offensive strategy, as actually occurred in 1914. Neznamov thought it likely that, given the limited space available for maneuver at the beginning of a European war, the first operations would inevitably unfold as frontal collisions, only after which would the future course of action become clear.[59] It is unfortunate, given the likelihood of the next war beginning as a series of meeting operations, that Neznamov did not devote more attention to this phenomenon.

Neznamov, like other theorists of his time, felt the need to address the problem of operational-strategic troop control; and in this area, as in others, his views are an interesting blend of foreign and domestic influences. For example, Neznamov's preferred army numbered approximately 200,000 men.[60] However, a future European war might well involve the mobilization of millions of men and their deployment into many such armies, thus vastly increasing the problem of command and control from the center. Because the coordination of this unwieldy mass would be beyond the powers of even the most brilliant commander in chief, Neznamov proposed combining up to four of these armies into groups of armies for greater ease of control.[61]

A number of other reasons also prompted Neznamov to advocate the creation of groups of armies. He thus approvingly quotes the German von Schlichting's criteria for forming groups of armies, of which the most important is that the armies in question pursue the same goal and attack along the same strategic axis.[62] This condition, as we have seen, corresponds closely to Leer's definition of the theater of military activities, which was later given flesh in the Russian 1900 war plan, which posited the formation of two fronts: one moving due west against Germany and the other moving west and southwest against Austria-Hungary.

A "group commander" *(komanduyushchii gruppoi)* would command each of these bodies and would answer directly to the commander in chief at the center. However, as had Leer, Neznamov preferred a weak group commander and proposed to severely restrict his powers over the armies in the field. He believed that the commander in chief should orient the group commander only as to the larger goals being pursued, while the latter "will regulate only the *movement of the armies,*" thus leaving the individual army commanders a great deal of latitude.[63] Neznamov's penchant for decentralized control in this instance may have been a reaction to Kuropatkin's petty interference at Mukden, or admiration for the elder von Moltke's practice of giving his army commanders broad operational freedom. But however laudable these ideas may have been in theory, Neznamov's recommendations tended to undermine the authority of the group commander and reduce him to a mere transmitter of instructions from the center to the field armies, thus rendering the entire group/front command level superfluous. This also placed a premium on selecting army commanders who not only would display initiative but also would be able and willing to work together—a rare combination in any army.

Neznamov was probably at his most prescient when analyzing the inconclusive nature of modern operations. The increased viability of modern armies from the mid–nineteenth century had made their destruction in a single general engagement increasingly unlikely, although Neznamov continued to hail the latter as the "ideal" of military art.[64] This lesson had been driven home repeatedly during the Russo-Japanese War, in which the hapless Russians had abandoned the field at Lyao-Yang, been fought to a standstill along the Sha-ho, and barely escaped disaster at Mukden. However, in spite of these victories, the Japanese army had never achieved anything approaching a decisive success, and the land war eventually ended in a positional stalemate.

In these and other cases the losing side had avoided a decisive defeat by breaking contact with the enemy and slipping away to regroup and fight again. Furthermore, the fighting in Manchuria revealed that the victor, instead of immediately following up on his success and finishing off his weakened opponent, is often equally hurt and exhausted. He must first make good his losses before resuming the advance, lest he be defeated in turn by the defender, who has been able to replenish his forces more easily by falling back on his sources of matériel supply, while the farther the attacker advances, the more matériel he expends and the farther he moves from his own base. Thus the victor is forced to halt his pursuit, lest he risk a counterattack and possible defeat at the hands of a revived foe. This matériel regrouping would necessarily entail a pause in the fighting until the army or front was brought back up to strength and able to resume the advance. This novel situation caused Neznamov to note that modern wars have come to unfold "in the form of separate leaps of the attacker forward and the defender back," punctuated by periods of relative quiet as the opponents prepare for the next phase of fighting.[65] In this characterization of modern operations was an insight into a pattern of war that would become all too familiar within a few short years.

Here, in an admittedly rudimentary and incomplete form, was the germ of what, under the Soviets, came to be known as the theory of "consecutive operations," which sought to achieve a final strategic result through the uninterrupted conduct of successive offensive operations. This area was to become one of the Red Army's most interesting and productive fields of theoretical endeavor during the 1920s, when, armed with the rich operational experience of World War I and the Russian civil war, a number of outstanding thinkers would build upon Neznamov's original notions to fashion a unique theory of conducting operations.

For all his foresight, however, Neznamov was not without his faults as a military thinker. Perhaps the most glaring of these from the modern point of view was his stubborn belief in the continuing utility of the Napoleonic decisive engagement, when the experience of 1870 and 1904–5 clearly indicated that the general engagement had been absorbed by the operation and was now, at best, merely the battlefield culmination of the latter's efforts. Neznamov's sometimes confusing and contradictory approach to the place of operations in military art also dogged his thinking and prevented him from making a truly imaginative leap forward. However, his shortcomings were those of his time, and they should not blind us to his importance as a transitional figure who, while serving both the czarist and Soviet regimes, made a profound contribution to the development of his country's military theory. As his student, Shaposhnikov, later recalled, "It is doubtful that anyone ... so revealed the character of modern operations like Neznamov."[66]

Among the other writers on operations during these years were two officers whose subsequent careers mirror the tragedy of the Russian officer corps after 1917. The more noteworthy of these was Gen. Nikolai Petrovich Mikhnevich, who was born in 1849. Following service in the Russo-Turkish War, Mikhnevich graduated from the General Staff Academy in 1882, and from 1892 he taught there as a professor of Russian military art. He also served briefly (1904–7) as the academy's chief as it was beginning to recover from the shock of the Manchurian defeat. Mikhnevich wrote widely on questions of military strategy, areas of which would later be considered the proper sphere of operations. His most famous works in this area were *Strategy* (1911) and *Fundamentals of Strategy* (1913), in which he examined the changing nature of modern war and the place of operations in it. Mikhnevich, upon leaving the academy, served as a division and corps commander and from 1911 to 1917 was chief of the army's Main Staff. He joined the Red Army in 1918, but because of his advanced age he took no part in the fighting. However, Mikhnevich did resume his teaching duties under the new regime and served as an instructor in the Artillery Academy until two years before his death in 1927.

The other was Col. Andrei Grigor'evich Elchaninov, who was born in 1868. Elchaninov entered the army in 1888 and graduated from the General Staff Academy six years later; from 1908 he was a professor of strategy at the same institution. His enthusiastic lectures on the exploits of the great Russian commanders and his belief in the applicability of their principles to modern conditions mark him as an adherent of the "nativist" school of military art. These and other views were most forcefully presented in his *Waging of Modern War and Battle* (1909) and *Strategy* (1912). Elchaninov died in 1918 in southern Russia, where the anti-Bolshevik armies were beginning to coalesce.

Mikhnevich's views about the place of operations in military art reflect the consensus on the subject that had emerged in the army. This he expressed in the following formula: "Each war consists of one or several *campaigns;* each campaign—of one or several *operations,* representing a certain complete period from the army's *strategic* deployment at the operation's starting point, to the resolution of the latter through a victorious combat on the battlefield."[67]

As this passage indicates, the operation, in Mikhnevich's mind, continued to occupy a sort of theoretical no-man's-land between strategy and tactics. As did Neznamov, the author evidently believed that the end result of a number of operations and/or campaigns would be the general engagement—the culmination of all previous operational activity. Again, this formula left precious little to the operation except to maneuver the armies in preparation for the climactic battle, which remained theoretically and spatially separate from the preceding operations. On the other hand, Mikhnevich did correctly subordinate the operation to the campaign, which is nothing more than a seasonal or geographic subset of strategy.

Mikhnevich divided operations into two types, according to goal, a delineation that was at once more precise than Leer's abstractions and less concrete than Neznamov's functional approach. Thus the "main operation" *(glavnaya operatsiya)* has a decisive effect on the course of the war, while the "secondary operation" *(vtorostepennaya operatsiya)*, as its name implies, is of local significance only.[68] Presumably either of these may be of an offensive or defensive nature, although the reigning offensive mentality within the army almost assured that the former would predominate. And although Mikhnevich did not elaborate on this point, it could be inferred that the main operation would be conducted in the chief theaters of military activities, while the secondary operations would be confined to less important theaters or would be launched in support of major efforts in the more important theaters.

Mikhnevich also divided operations into two types, according to scale: simple and complex. The first would likely involve a spatially restricted operation by limited forces, pursuing a single objective. The complex operation, on the other hand, would involve larger forces operating over a wider area, pursuing multiple objectives simultaneously.[69] This, in crude form, was the theoretical basis for distinguishing between simple (army) and complex (front) operations. Unfortunately, Mikhnevich failed to develop this interesting notion further, but the ideas and terminology he employed would resurface as the basis for Soviet work in the 1920s in the area of army and front operations.

Regarding the latter, Mikhnevich recommended organizing the nation's forces into groups of armies, each one numbering as many as 1 to 1.5 million men. These groups of armies might have a permanent or temporary organization and would control those armies acting along a single "operational line" *(operatsionnaya liniya)*.[70] The latter corresponded closely to Leer's and Neznamov's notions of organizing similar groups on the basis of their ultimate objectives within the theater of military activities. Like the others, Mikhnevich favored a loose form of control from the center, in which the commander in chief would regulate the groups' and armies' actions in only the most general fashion, thus according the group commanders and their subordinate army commanders great freedom of action.[71] Unfortunately, the ticklish problem of relations between the latter two command levels was not examined at all.

The spatial growth of the formerly restricted battlefield into the theater of military activities and the corresponding need for new forms of troop control attracted Elchaninov's attention as well. Elchaninov, as did others, supported the creation of the front level of command, which would serve as an intermediary between the commander in chief and the armies in the field. The author also belonged to that group of thinkers who sought to restrict the front commander's powers to indicating his subordinate armies' "overall objective of activities," with the individual army commanders free to pursue their goals within these guidelines.[72]

Finally, of particular interest for the future are Elchaninov's thoughts on the periodization of a war into a number of operational episodes. Thus instead of a conflict crowned by a decisive general engagement, wars would henceforth take the form of what he called an *"unbroken series of local decisions,"* or local operations. These would unfold in a succession of operational efforts, which would yield a final result only after a prolonged effort.[73] Here again, in rudimentary form, was the outline of what became known in the 1920s as the theory of consecutive operations.

The most common theme among the more progressive theorists during these years was the broad agreement on the necessity of establishing the front/group of armies command instance in order to control the various armies in a given theater of military activities. Leer's early thoughts on the subject eventually found more concrete expression in the Russian army's 1900 war plan, which called for the creation of two separate fronts to coordinate operations against Germany and Austria-Hungary. And although this plan was revised periodically during the following years, the notion of two fronts operating along diverging axes in the western theater of war remained unchanged. The imperial army's most comprehensive official statement on operations was contained in *Regulations on the Field Control of Troops in Wartime,* which were issued on the eve of war in 1914. The *Regulations,* while primarily an administrative document, were nevertheless a useful attempt to delineate the responsibilities of the various commanders at the operational-strategic level.

The most important link in the chain was the emperor himself, who, as head of state, exercised ultimate control over the armed forces. In the event of war, the emperor had the option of assuming the position of supreme commander in chief *(verkhovnyi glavnokomanduyushchii)* or appointing someone else. In the latter case, the supreme commander in chief would report directly to the emperor and was to enjoy broad military powers, even to the point of being authorized to conclude an armistice with the enemy. He would be assisted in his work by a chief of staff, who would keep his superior informed of events at the front and present his views on the future course of military operations.[74]

Immediately below this level stood one or more front commanders in chief. The *Regulations* stated that the prime requirement for creating a front is that several armies must be acting in concert in pursuit of a single strategic goal in a specific territory, or theater of military activities.[75] This was simply a rehash of what had been stated by a number of theorists, from Leer onward. These criteria served as the basis for forming the first wartime fronts in 1914, as well as others during the course of the war. They were later adopted by the successor Red Army and served, with little change, as the justification for the creation of similar bodies during the civil war and World War II.

More at variance with past theory, however, were the *Regulations'* views on the extent of the front commander's authority. Leer, Neznamov, and Elchaninov had tended to exalt the role of the individual army commanders at the expense of the front commander in chief, whereby the latter became little more than a figurehead, charged with relaying orders from the commander in chief to the army commanders. The *Regulations* stood this formula on its head, declaring that "the commander in chief of the front's armies is the chief of the armies, fortresses and fleet designated for joint activities with the armies of a given front."[76] This article represented a significant expansion, at least in theory, of the front commander in chief's powers; it has much in common with Kuropatkin's wide-ranging authority in Manchuria during the Russo-Japanese War.

As before, the front commander was subordinated to the commander in chief and charged with carrying out the latter's instructions by directing his subordinate armies toward the objective. However, the *Regulations,* in contrast to many of the views expressed earlier, unequivocally stated that the army commanders would be "subordinate in all respects to the front commander in chief" and are given only the latitude necessary to carry out the latter's instructions.[77] This "tilt" in favor of a strong front commander would yield the imperial army only variable success in the few years remaining to it. The follow-on Red Army, with its systemic tendency toward a high degree of centralization, would later develop this idea even further.

However, the *Regulations'* wartime application was far from satisfactory. One general, who served as both an army and a front commander, dismissed the document as "good for nothing."[78] Another, less harsh criticism was delivered by a professional staff officer who criticized the high command for issuing the *Regulations* only after the war broke out.[79]

The evolution of Russian views on the operation during this period presents a complex and often contradictory picture, with many progressive steps often matched by retrograde ones. To cite only the most egregious example, despite commendable progress in this area, the consolidation of the art of operations into a self-contained discipline was still hampered by the reigning confusion over the relationship of the operation to strategy and tactics. Likewise, the otherwise progressive invention of the front/group of armies was still hobbled by the refusal of several theorists to endow the front commander with powers worthy of the name. However, progress had been made toward a functional delineation of operations into offensive, defensive, and meeting types. Finally, the era's tentative investigation into the nature of successive operations held great promise for the future.

However, as might be expected, the picture is murkier as regards the more immediate and practical results of the Russian army's theoretical endeavors. It is difficult to trace concrete steps back to a particular theory, and important decisions are usually made for a variety of reasons, without conscious reference to theoretical writings. A prime example of this is the creation of the front level of command in 1900, an organizational step that arose as much out of administrative, geographic, and political necessity as out of any theoretical justification offered by Leer and those who followed him.

Moreover, Russian history is replete with efforts at reform that have begun in a period of hope, only to be defeated by the conservative nature of the regime. At best, these endeavors have survived in a truncated form to serve as the inspiration for the next cycle of flux. This was the military reformers' fate during the period 1905–14, and they left behind a rich operational legacy that would serve as the basis for much of what was to come. The task of completing this work, however, would fall to a more vigorous regime, which by suffusing many of these ideas with its own peculiar energy would take the next important steps in the development of operational art.

OPERATIONS IN THE FIRST WORLD WAR, 1914–17

During World War I the modern operation truly came into its own. Compared with the modest scope of earlier operations, those of the 1914–18 period were gigantic struggles, waged along extended fronts stretching hundreds of kilometers in breadth. And, whereas previous operations in the Russo-Japanese War had been relatively short-lived and had involved, at most, a few armies, the Great War's operations often lasted weeks, or even months, and embraced entire groups of armies. Unfortunately, however impressive the increased scope of operations during the war, it was not matched by a similar growth in the skill with which they were conducted. As the war passed from its initial maneuver phase to a positional stalemate, military art at the operational level became increasingly devalued in favor of a purely tactical approach to the trench deadlock. The combatants' failure to find an operational solution to this unique situation led to the slaughter of Verdun and the Somme and to even greater carnage on the eastern front. In Russia the price of failure was too great and brought in its wake military collapse and social revolution.

Before studying the Russian army's wartime operations, however, it is necessary to briefly examine the state of the armed forces as a whole prior to the war. The defeat in Manchuria had been a serious blow to Russia's military capability and prestige, and it would require some time to restore either of them. The army's wartime quartermaster general later described the years from 1905 to 1910 as a "period of complete military helplessness."[80] The country's weakness was manifestly demonstrated during the 1908 Bosnian crisis, when Russia was unable to protect its ally Serbia and prevent Austria-Hungary from annexing the province.

That the armed forces recovered at all was mostly due to the government's strenuous efforts at rearmament, fueled by the certainty of a general European war. This was particularly true of the navy, which was extensively rebuilt following the twin disasters of Port Arthur and Tsushima. The emperor was especially eager to reconstitute his fleet, and the years before World War I saw a sharp increase in shipbuilding, involving orders for domestic and foreign shipyards. However, the long construction schedules involved meant that many vessels remained unfinished when war broke out. For example, all seven dreadnought-class battleships were still under construction in July 1914, as were all four battle cruisers, ten light cruisers, forty-five destroyers, and nineteen submarines.[81] The wisdom of such disproportionate spending on the fleet cannot be justified, however, either by the country's geographic position or by the nature of the military threat it faced. The government's actions in this regard are particularly incomprehensible in light of its ongoing rapprochement with Great Britain, the world's strongest sea power.

This was because Russia's fate in a European conflict would ultimately be decided on land, and during these years a number of steps were taken to turn the backward army into a modern force, among which were improvements in the army's mobilization and reserve system, as well as attempts to reduce its reliance on outmoded fortresses along the western frontier. The cornerstone of these efforts was the so-called Great Program, which was inaugurated in 1913. The Russian army, according to this ambitious plan, was to increase in size by 1917 from 1,230,000 men to 1,710,000, of which 274,000 would go toward building up new infantry formations, while the cavalry arm would grow by 38,000.[82] The artillery was to be improved by increasing the number of guns to 8,358, of which 1,176 would be howitzers and 468 heavy guns.[83] However, this project, like its 1940–41 counterpart, was also adopted too late and was only beginning to be implemented when war broke out in 1914.

For all these improvements, the army still lagged dangerously behind its probable enemies. For example, by the beginning of the war the Russians possessed only 6,720 artillery pieces, compared with 6,004 in Germany and 3,090 in Austria-Hungary.[84] The Russians were particularly deficient in heavy guns, which was to prove disastrous in the war's first months. In 1914 a Russian corps of two divisions contained only 108 guns, of which the largest were 12 122-mm howitzers, while a similar-sized German corps had 160 guns, of which 16 were of the heavy 155-mm variety.[85]

Moreover, these quantitative disadvantages were exacerbated by a number of qualitative shortcomings. Among these was a high command that had never fully recovered from its defeat in the Far East and remained psychologically crippled and unsure of itself.[86] Continuity in strategic planning was severely impaired by the fact that six men occupied the post of chief of the General Staff from 1905 to 1914. Moreover, an obtuse military bureaucracy made it nearly impossible to push through even the most inoffensive reforms. Turnover was also high among midlevel and junior officers, whose pay and social status were well below those of their counterparts in other countries.

The army's weakest link was undoubtedly its rank and file, which was drawn overwhelmingly from the country's vast peasant population. These recruits, who were shockingly backward and, for the most part, illiterate, were ill suited to man a modern army in which personal initiative and a degree of technical proficiency were at a premium. Moreover, their ignorance of the outside world and even their own country made it difficult to turn them into motivated soldiers capable of withstanding a protracted struggle.

Despite these drawbacks, Russia nonetheless enjoyed a number of seemingly insuperable advantages over its likely enemies. The army had a peacetime strength of 1,284,155 in mid-1914, which made it easily the largest in Europe, outnumbering both Germany and Austria-Hungary, which maintained peacetime establishments of 768,000 and 478,000 men, respectively. Moreover, Russia's population of 136.2 million dwarfed that of its future opponents, and its manpower pool of more than 17 million men threatened to make the vaunted Russian "steamroller" a reality.[87] In fact, it was probably the realization of Russia's nearly limitless military potential that finally decided Germany on war in 1914.

One of the most notable features of World War I was the multiplicity of war plans drawn up by the belligerents; these plans were endlessly revised and honed to a peak of theoretical perfection by the various general staffs in the years preceding 1914. Some of these, such as Germany's Schlieffen Plan, are so well known as to have become household words in the field of military history. The other powers, both great and small, had their schemes that strictly governed the mobilization, concentration, and deployment of their armed forces. The same was true of Russia, whose numerous war plans bore the imprint of multiple political, geographic, economic, and other considerations. As many prewar writers had pointed out, these initial dispositions inevitably have a decisive influence on an army's first operations. Thus the importance of this question merits an extended examination of the factors that influenced Russian strategic thinking before the war.

The great constant in Russian strategy was the growing enmity with Germany and Austria-Hungary and the likelihood that, in the event of war, Russia would have to face both powers simultaneously. The collision was made nearly inevitable by Russia's defensive alliance with France, which obligated it to come to the latter's aid if attacked by Germany. In the Balkans, Russia's support for Serbia made conflict with Austria-Hungary likely, which in turn meant war with Germany, which was bound to the Dual Monarchy by an anti-Russian defensive pact.

These and other concerns were aired in a detailed appreciation of the country's strategic situation, drawn up by the Main Directorate of the General Staff in early 1914. According to this document, Russia's likely opponents in a future war would be Germany and Austria-Hungary, with Romania and Sweden also listed as possible threats. Attacks by Turkey, China, and Japan were not excluded, although these would be of a secondary nature, far removed from the main theater of war. Russian strategy assumed that in the event of war, Austria-Hungary would throw its main forces against Russia, leaving only a token force in the south to guard against the Serbs. The wild card in Russian planning was the question of whether Germany would deploy its main forces against France in the west, with only a small covering force in the east, or whether the Germans would put up only minimal forces in the west, while launching their main effort against Russia, in conjunction with the Austro-Hungarians.[88]

In either event, it was expected that military operations in the east would unfold along the flanks of the large Russian salient in Poland. This area, centered on Warsaw, presented the Russian command with obvious strategic opportunities, as well as equally obvious dangers. On the one hand, the territory to the west of the Vistula River afforded the Russians the most direct route to Berlin through Posen (Poznan), as well as the opportunity to cut off any German forces defending East Prussia. On the other, a Russian advance due west ran the risk of being taken in the flank by these same forces. To the south, the situation was both less promising and less threatening. Here a Russian attack into Galicia, even if successful, would soon encounter the formidable barrier of the Carpathian Mountains, which hindered a further advance into the enemy's heartland. Conversely, the Austro-Hungarian army, small and debilitated by nationalist tensions, was a less serious threat than its German ally.

The Russian high command expected that in the event of war with Germany and Austria-Hungary, the latter would bear, at least initially, the main burden of the fighting in the east. This assumption was based on a number of factors, the most important of which was the Russians' detailed knowledge of the Austro-Hungarian mobilization plan, which had been obtained through intelligence sources. Accordingly, the Russians calculated that the Dual Monarchy would deploy in southern Poland 43 to 47 infantry, 11 cavalry, and 2 independent Landwehr divisions, with the remainder assigned to the Serbian frontier. The bulk of the Austro-Hungarian force in Galicia—24½ infantry and 5 cavalry divisions—would be grouped into two armies (First and Fourth) and make the main attack to the northeast, in the general direction of Siedlce and Brest-Litovsk (Brest). To the southeast another two armies (Second and Third) would deploy, numbering 22 infantry and 5 cavalry divisions. This force would cover the main advance by attacking due east toward Rovno and Zhmerinka, possibly assisted by the Romanians.[89]

The Russians' knowledge of German intentions was much less certain. In the unlikely event that Germany chose to make its main effort against Russia, the document's authors estimated that it could eventually deploy up to 63 infantry and 8 cavalry divisions in the east, which, together with the expected Austro-Hungarian forces in southern Poland, would create a clear superiority of force over the Russians. However, the more plausible scenario foresaw the Germans making their main attack in the west against France, while leaving only a minimum covering force in the east. In the latter case, it was calculated that this force might total as many as 25 infantry and 3 cavalry divisions. However, this figure seriously overestimated German intentions in the area. In either case, the Russian command expected the Germans to attack southwest out of their East Prussian salient in the general direction of Belostok, so as to link up with the Austro-

Hungarian armies advancing from the south. This move, if successful, could trap sizable Russian forces west of the Bug River.[90]

The Russian war plan prior to 1914 underwent a number of evolutions in response to shifting perceptions of the threat. However, even as Russian strategic planning increasingly inclined toward a simultaneous conflict with both Germany and Austria-Hungary, the problem of against whom to deploy the country's main forces remained unchanged.

One approach, as embodied in the 1910 war plan, sought to direct the bulk of Russia's armies against Germany. The plan foresaw the deployment of four armies (First, Second, Fourth, and Fifth) against East Prussia, leaving only the Third Army to hold the Austro-Hungarians in Galicia. Another two armies, the Sixth and Seventh, guarded the approaches to St. Petersburg and the Romanian border, respectively.[91] However, the plan quickly ran into strong criticism because of its extremely conservative proposal to deploy the armies slated for the German front east of the Bug River, which meant giving up most of Poland without a fight. Also, the single army left to watch the Austro-Hungarians was deemed too weak to prevent the latter from attacking across the base of the Polish salient and taking the main Russian advance in the rear.

In response to this criticism, a new plan was drawn up in 1912, which dramatically altered the 1910 plan according to two possible scenarios. The first, or Plan A, foresaw the Germans making their main effort against France. In this case, three Russian armies (Third, Fourth, and Fifth) would move against Austria-Hungary, while two more (First and Second) attacked into East Prussia. The second, or Plan G, would come into effect should Germany launch its main attack against Russia. In this case, First, Second, and Fourth Armies would deploy against East Prussia, leaving only the Third and Fifth Armies to meet an Austro-Hungarian attack. As before, two entire armies (Sixth and Seventh) remained idle against the specter of a Swedish and Romanian attack.[92]

However, while this plan was certainly an improvement over its timorous 1910 counterpart, it nevertheless bears all the earmarks of a bad compromise. The most egregious of these was the Russians' irrational dispersal of forces along the front. For example, Plan A allotted only 52 percent of the Russian forces against Austria-Hungary, while leaving a full 33 percent against the Germans and another 15 percent to watch the Swedes and Romanians.[93] This was a serious and perhaps fatal error, and it guaranteed that Russia would lack the forces to decisively defeat either enemy immediately upon the outbreak of war. In retrospect, it would have been wiser to have thrown overwhelming (two-thirds) forces against the weaker Austro-Hungarians, particularly because it was almost certain that the bulk of the German forces would be engaged in France during the war's first weeks and thus would not be a significant factor in the east. The Russians, by destroying or fatally weakening the Dual Monarchy's armies from the outset, might well have compelled the Austro-Hungarians to make peace. Failing that, the necessity of propping up their ally would certainly have forced the Germans to divert considerably more forces to the east earlier on than would actually become the case. As it was, this division of effort led to predictably mixed results: to Tannenberg, where the Germans destroyed most of a Russian army, and to Galicia, where the Russians soundly defeated the Austro-Hungarians after serious fighting but lacked the strength to exploit their victory.

Moreover, this plan, like preceding ones, was hobbled by the slowness of the Russian mobilization system, which was a product of the country's vast distances and underdeveloped economy. For example, in 1910 Germany had 10.6 kilometers of railroad for every 100 square kilometers of territory, while European Russia contained only 1 kilometer for the same area.[94] And whereas both Germany and Austria-Hungary had built excellent rail lines close to their respective frontiers to facilitate rapid maneuver, the Russians, in a fit of defensive thinking, had deliberately neglected their Polish rail net in order to delay an enemy attack. As a result, while the two Germanic powers could mobilize the bulk of their forces in about two weeks, the Russian armies deployed against Germany according to Plan A would reach only 63 percent of their infantry and 77 percent of their cavalry strength by the fifteenth day. Against the Austro-Hungarians, the rates were even worse—49 and 46 percent, respectively. In fact, the Russian armies would not be fully concentrated until the fortieth to forty-fifth day of mobilization.[95] However, this simple fact did not prevent the then Russian chief of staff, Zhilinskii, from foolishly promising his French counterpart in 1913 that Russia would put 800,000 men into the field by the fifteenth day of mobilization. This rash vow was beyond the country's capabilities and would have serious consequences for the war's opening battles.

When war broke out in August 1914, the czar's uncle, Grand Duke Nikolai Nikolaevich, was appointed supreme commander in chief *(verkhovnyi glavnokomanduyushchii)* of the Russian forces. One observer, not known for his flattering evaluations of the war's chief protagonists, nevertheless praised the grand duke as an excellent soldier who enjoyed the army's complete confidence.[96] The army was less fortunate in the selection of Gen. Lt. N. N. Yanushkevich as the grand duke's chief of staff. He had previously held the post in peacetime and had also been a professor at the General Staff Academy. However, Yanushkevich lacked authority among his peers, and it was rumored that he owed his advancement to the personal favor of the czar and the war minister, Sukhomlinov.[97]

The organizational deployment of Russia's forces also unfolded according to plan. The western theater of war was divided into two theaters of military activities, each represented by a front. The Northwestern Front had the strategic assignment of driving the Germans out of East Prussia and advancing on Berlin; the Southwestern Front was given the strategic task of destroying the Austro-Hungarian forces in Galicia before crossing the Carpathians and moving on Budapest and Vienna. As the war progressed, the Russian supreme command, or Stavka, in turn created the Northern (1915), Romanian (1916), and Caucasus

(1917) Fronts. The French and Germans also went on to create analogous army groups.

The creation of these two fronts, each tasked with taking out a member of the enemy coalition, qualifies the war's opening front operations as strategic in character. This differs somewhat from the Soviet definition, which describes a strategic operation as one conducted by a group of fronts.[98] This definition, however, relies exclusively on organizational factors (the number of fronts engaged) and fails to take into account the magnitude of the goals pursued. These operations will be examined to determine the strengths and weaknesses of Russian operational art at the beginning of the war.

The Northwestern Front was commanded by General Zhilinskii, in his capacity as commander of the vital Warsaw Military District. This was the same Zhilinskii who, as chief of staff in 1913, had committed the Russian army to a ruinous mobilization schedule. He was infamous among the general staff's officers as the "living corpse," for his brutal treatment of subordinates, and was dismissed by another officer as being completely unsuited for the position of front commander in chief.[99] However, if Zhilinskii was incompetent, his army commanders failed to rise above the level of mediocrity. These included Gen. P. K. von Rennenkampf, the prewar chief of the Vilna (Vil'nius) Military District, who was appointed to head the First Army. The Second Army was commanded by Gen. A. V. Samsonov, who arrived at his posting from Central Asia, where he headed the Turkestan Military District. Unfortunately, Samsonov had not commanded anything larger than a division since the Russo-Japanese War and had spent the intervening years in administrative posts.

To offset these command liabilities, the Russians would be attacking with an overall superiority of force. The First (20th, 3d, and 4th Corps, five cavalry divisions, an infantry brigade, and an independent cavalry brigade) and Second (2d, 6th, 13th, 15th, and 23d Army Corps, 1st Guards Corps, and three cavalry divisions) Armies numbered roughly 250,000 men, deployed along an arc from Kovno (Kaunas) to Warsaw. Opposing them was the German Eighth Army, composed of 1st, 17th, and 20th Army Corps, 1st Reserve Corps, a cavalry division, plus two independent divisions, four independent brigades, and garrison troops, or about 200,000 men.[100] However, the Russians enjoyed only a slight superiority of 1,444 guns to 1,044; of these, the Germans had 39 heavy guns to the Russians' 12.[101]

Moreover, the Russians would be advancing into an area seemingly configured by nature for defense (see map 3). The most salient obstacle was the chain of the Masurian Lakes, which stretched 70 kilometers from Angerburg to Johannisburg. The few passages between the lakes, such as at Lotzen, could easily be blocked by relatively small forces. This had the effect of dividing any westward advance into East Prussia into nonsupporting halves. The Germans, by taking advantage of their interior lines and excellent east-west rail network, were in a position to rapidly switch their army from one front to another and defeat an invader in detail.

46   THE RUSSIAN WAY OF WAR

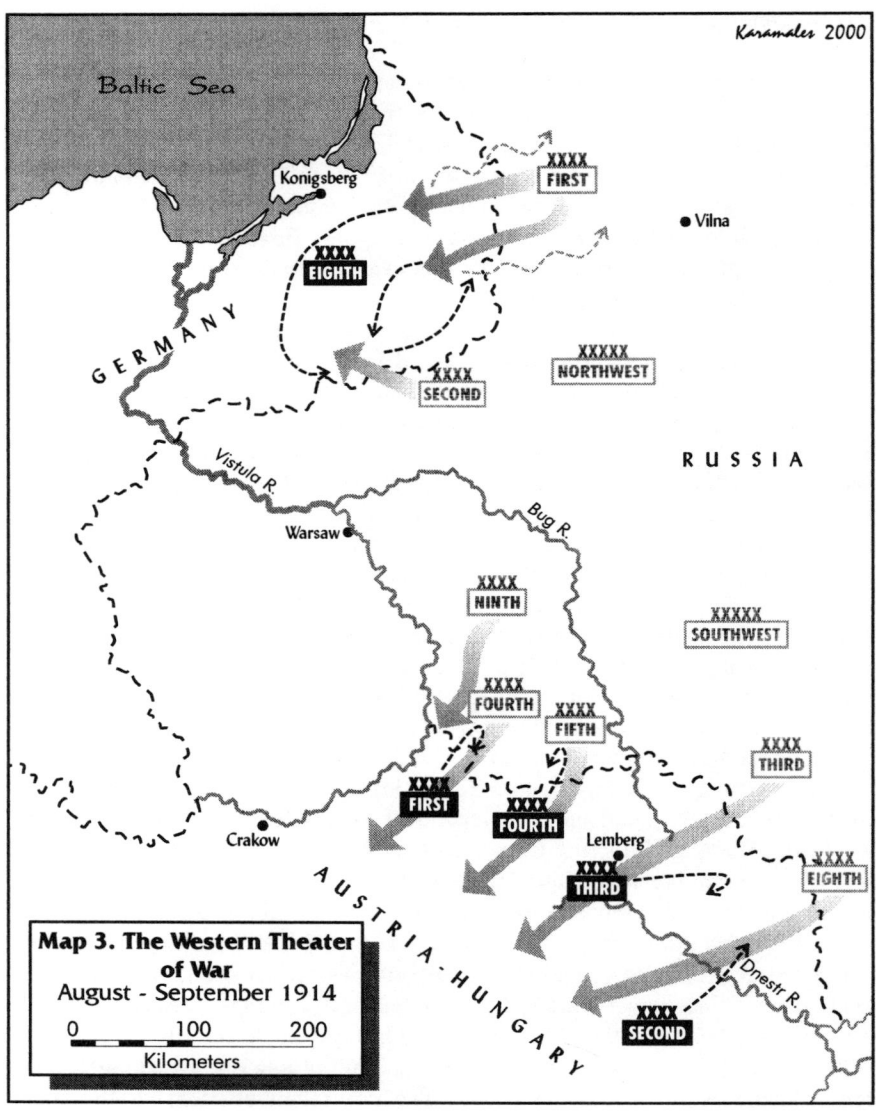

Map 3. The Western Theater of War
August – September 1914

Nonetheless, Zhilinskii elected to press forward. He revealed his plans to his army commanders in two August 13 directives. First Army was to advance due west from the Neman River into the gap between Insterburg and Angerburg and then drive west to isolate the garrison at Königsberg. Second Army would move almost due north from the Narew River in the general direction of Rastenburg.[102] At no point did Zhilinskii even raise the prospect of a double envelopment by the two armies. On the contrary, his order essentially called for merely pushing the Germans out of East Prussia, despite all the geographic prerequisites for a major encirclement battle.

Zhilinskii's conservative approach immediately brought him into conflict with Samsonov, who harbored ambitious designs of his own. On August 16 he sharply shifted the axis of his army's advance to the northwest. According to this scheme, the main blow would be launched west of the Masurian Lakes, so as to cut the Germans' path of retreat across the Vistula. Theoretically, this was certainly the proper step, as a prompt advance along this axis would either compel the Germans to fall back upon the Vistula or risk encirclement by the Russians. However, given the front commander's previous dispositions, this unauthorized change of direction would soon lead to disaster.

The East Prussian operation (August 17–September 15) began when Rennenkampf's infantry crossed the frontier. Facing him was the greater part of the Eighth Army, under General von Prittwitz, which was deployed expectantly along the Angerapp River. However, the commander of 1st Corps impetuously moved forward and attacked the Russians around Stalluponen the same day. The corps' unsupported attack failed to yield a result, however, and the Germans pulled back to Gumbinnen.

The fighting resumed here on August 20, this time with all three German corps in the area attacking. However, the assaults were poorly coordinated, and while the German forces on either flank made respectable progress, the attack in the center broke down and was repulsed with heavy losses. Nevertheless, Gumbinnen must be counted a German victory, and the Eighth Army command looked forward confidently to renewing the attack the next day.

However, that same evening von Prittwitz received word from the commander of 20th Corps, which was deployed around Allenstein, that Samsonov's army had crossed the border near Willenberg. The Russian army's appearance this far west so unhinged von Prittwitz that he immediately ordered his army to fall back behind the Vistula! Cooler heads soon prevailed, and von Prittwitz revoked his order in favor of a more aggressive design. Now 20th Corps was to move forward on Hohenstein, while 1st Corps was to entrain immediately to the southwest and Samsonov's left flank. The two remaining corps would stay in place, for the time being, to watch Rennenkampf.

However, von Prittwitz's loss of nerve spelled the end of his career as an army commander. He was immediately relieved and replaced by Paul von Hindenburg, who was called out of retirement. Erich Ludendorff, the hero of Liege, was brought from the west as his chief of staff. This was the beginning of a partnership that would wreak havoc among the Russian armies for the next two years and would eventually elevate the team to the pinnacle of the German Empire's political-military command.

In reality, Samsonov's movements were not as threatening as the Germans feared. Zhilinskii's insistence on a rapid advance put Second Army on the move before it could put its rear services in order. Several divisions, for example, lacked organic transport, and 23d Corps' situation was so bad that it had to be maintained through other units' rear services. Communications were in a state of chaos, and everywhere there was a lack of trained personnel and equipment. The virtual collapse of the army's supply services meant that some units did not eat for days at a time. These conditions were especially hard on the army's many reservists, who had only recently arrived from their civilian occupations. However, Zhilinskii's inflexible schedule gave Second Army no time to make the necessary adjustments.

The first serious clash between Second Army and the German covering force took place on August 23, when the Russian 15th Corps collided with 20th Corps' left flank in the Orlau-Frankenau area. The Russians suffered heavy casualties and had to call on 13th Corps for assistance. This move had the effect of pulling the latter sharply to the west and opened a sizable gap between it and 6th Corps, which was guarding the army's right flank in the Ortelsburg area.

Samsonov did not learn of the fighting until the next day, due to the poor communications between the corps and his headquarters. The minor German withdrawal that followed nevertheless seems to have made a strong impression on Samsonov, who took it as proof of a major German retreat. The "pursuit" that followed, however, only widened the gap between 6th Corps and the rest of the army, which continued its slow advance to the northwest. This movement, moreover, directly contradicted Zhilinskii's instructions of August 23, which specified a more northerly advance in the Allenstein-Sensburg direction for the purpose of cutting off the Germans' supposed withdrawal to the Vistula.[103]

Because of the chaos reigning in Second Army, Samsonov's instructions were sent out over the wireless in uncoded form and were immediately intercepted by the Germans; they proved to be the first of many such invaluable messages. This amazing piece of negligence was of considerable help to the Germans in drawing up their plans for a counteroffensive.[104]

German efforts were also considerably aided by Rennenkampf's dilatory movements following the Battle of Gumbinnen. First Army did not undertake to resume its advance until August 23. This enabled the German 17th and 1st Reserve Corps to break contact and move south to complete the combination against Samsonov, leaving only a thin cavalry screen to dispute Rennenkampf's advance. The First Army commander seems to have been more concerned with investing Königsberg than cooperating with Samsonov. Zhilinskii certainly made no effort to hurry Rennenkampf and was content to allow the First Army commanders to pursue his own goals.

However, if the Russians' moves were slow and unfocused, the Germans were acting with murderous intent, and their counterattack began on August 26. However, because of the 1st Corps commander's reluctance to attack before he was ready, little progress was made against the Russian left flank. Another German assault in the center briefly threw back 15th Corps, although the Russians did manage to capture Hohenstein. By far the heaviest fighting occurred on the Russian right, in the Bischofsburg area. Here two German corps (1st Reserve and 17th) hit the unsuspecting 6th Corps, after having marched for up to 50 kilometers the previous day. In spite of their undoubted exhaustion, the Germans steadily pushed the Russians back, and by nightfall the latter were streaming in disorder toward Ortelsburg. The corps commander failed to notify Samsonov of the collapse until that evening, and Samsonov did not get even this belated message in time.

The German offensive continued with increased vigor on August 27. This time the attack on the Russian left was pressed to the utmost, and the hungry troops of 1st Corps quickly broke under the massive German bombardment. The Germans quickly poured into the gaps in the Russian line and by noon had retaken Usdau. The bulk of 1st Corps fell back on Soldau, leaving only a small force to oppose a German advance on Neidenburg, in Second Army's rear. Here, once again, Samsonov was let down by a subordinate's criminal incompetence. The commander of 1st Corps failed to inform Samsonov of his defeat, and the army commander learned of the disaster only the next day.

In the center, 15th Corps continued to press its attack against the German 20th Corps, although the Russians could make little headway here. On the right, 6th Corps continued its southward retreat, now pursued by a single German corps. Indeed, so confident were the Germans of success on this flank that 1st Reserve Corps was rerouted to Allenstein, which the Russians had captured that afternoon. However, despite these successes, the German position in this area was becoming more precarious with each passing hour, with the belated approach of First Army's forward units. Rennenkampf's infantry had reached Rastenburg, while his cavalry was probing as far west as Heilsburg. In the hands of a more energetic commander this movement might well have ended in a German disaster.

As it was, Samsonov's own situation had become critical by August 28. Both of his flanks had been shattered, although he did not yet know about the rout of 6th Corps on his right. With the Germans pressing from both sides, 13th, 15th, and 23d Corps were now dangerously forward and exposed. Samsonov exacerbated his unfavorable position by needlessly pressing 13th and 15th Corps to continue their attack, thus moving them farther into the trap. Samsonov then compounded his error by abandoning his headquarters and riding forward to take charge of the attack in the center. This desperate move effectively put him out of contact with higher and lower headquarters at the most critical time and effectively sealed the fate of his army.

At front headquarters in Belostok, Zhilinskii had finally realized the danger of Samsonov's situation and had begun to act with unaccustomed energy. He now ordered Rennenkampf to "render assistance" to Second Army by moving his left flank to Bischofsburg.[105] This was hardly the stuff of urgency, however, and in any event, Zhilinskii's orders were issued too late to be of any use.

Meanwhile, the Germans continued to press their attack. The Russians were easily ejected from Soldau on August 28, while the main body of the German 1st Corps took Neidenburg. The Germans continued eastward to Willenberg, which enabled them to establish a thin blocking force astride Second Army's communications. And although the two German wings never did link up to form a solid encirclement, what they did achieve was sufficient to trap the greater part of Samsonov's army.

Samsonov had also come to realize the hopelessness of the situation and belatedly ordered the surrounded corps to withdraw on the evening of August 28. Inside the pocket there was complete chaos, as the trapped units struggled desperately to extricate themselves. Units quickly became lost or entangled during the exhausting marches that followed, and any semblance of centralized control quickly broke down. Efforts to relieve the isolated troops from without were equally ineffectual. Both 1st and 6th Corps made halfhearted attempts to relieve their comrades, but these efforts quickly came to naught and were, in any event, soon canceled by front headquarters.

At least Second Army's death agony was mercifully short. The hungry and demoralized Russians began surrendering as early as August 30, and by the end of the next day most of the rest had given up as well. In all, five Russian divisions were destroyed, and a German source put the haul of prisoners at 92,000 men.[106] What remained of Second Army fell back to the Narew River, where, under a new commander, Gen. S. M. Sheideman (Samsonov had committed suicide in the pocket on August 30), it sought to put itself in order. In fact, so great was the damage to the army's morale and personnel strength that it remained an impotent spectator during the operation's next stage.

The Germans now prepared to turn their forces on Rennenkampf, who continued to occupy a significant portion of East Prussia. The decision was certainly a disappointment to the Germans' Austro-Hungarian allies, who were being hard pressed by the bulk of the Russian army in Galicia. However, the Germans could hardly be expected to launch a major offensive into Poland with an entire Russian army in their rear, in spite of the promise of great strategic gain that the plan held, and so this grand project remained unrealized.

Even so, the possibility of a German thrust aimed at Warsaw continued to haunt the Russian command. These fears, in turn, formed the basis of Zhilinskii's September 4 instructions to Rennenkampf. The front commander "authorized" First Army to advance in the direction of Bischofstein and Rastenburg to forestall what he felt was a likely enemy attack across the Narew toward Warsaw.[107] This less than fiery exhortation indicates that Zhilinskii's offensive ardor had cooled considerably from the time when he had so precipitously hurried his armies into the disastrous campaign.

The Germans suffered from no such qualms and spent the days following the elimination of Samsonov's army reorganizing their forces for the upcoming offensive. The German plan called for a vigorous assault against the Russian left in the Lotzen-Johannisburg area. While the greater part of the Eighth Army attacked Rennenkampf's center north of the Masurian Lakes, the strike force was to turn the Russian flank and drive to the northeast, cutting off First Army's retreat across the middle Neman and pinning it against the river. So confident were Hindenburg and Ludendorff of victory that they left only a small covering force in the Mlawa-Myszniec area to watch the remnants of Second Army.

The German attack jumped off on September 5. The first two days were uneventful, as the Eighth Army's units made forced marches to close the gap with Rennenkampf, who had already pulled back to the line Allenburg-Johannisburg. The first major fighting occurred on the seventh, when the Germans captured Bialla in the south. This was followed a day later by the fall of Arys, although further progress was halted briefly by the arrival of Russian reserves in the Lotzen area. The fighting resumed along the entire front on September 9, as the main German body struck the Russians north of Angerburg. By now Rennenkampf realized the seriousness of his situation and ordered his army to fall back that night. His position was only worsened by Zhilinskii's inexplicable directive issued that same day, ordering two of the newly formed Tenth Army's corps to withdraw from the Grajewo area, where their presence alone posed a threat to the flank of Eighth Army's turning movement.[108]

The Russian retreat began in earnest the next day, accompanied by vigorous German attempts from the Goldap area to cut them off. However, Rennenkampf's order had been given in the nick of time, and his units, by dint of hard marching, barely managed to evade the trap. Still the cost of defeat had been heavy, and First Army is estimated to have lost 100,000 men since the start of the invasion.[109] The only bright spot in this string of disasters was the removal of the incompetent Zhilinskii as commander in chief of the Northwestern Front on September 16.

Zhilinskii is certainly the chief culprit in this sorry episode. His baleful influence was felt throughout, from his irresponsible prewar pledge to force the pace of Russian mobilization to his biased treatment of the two generals. His kid-glove treatment of Rennenkampf no doubt encouraged the latter to continue his unhurried advance, when a more energetic pace would have certainly saved Samsonov. On the other hand, Zhilinskii bullied Samsonov throughout the operation and pushed him to take risks that he otherwise might have avoided. However, Samsonov's own failings were no less serious and, in the end, decisive. His outright insubordination did much to create a climate of mistrust between himself and Zhilinskii, at a time when cooperation was essential. And while it is true that the front commander's plan was too conservative to yield a decisive result, had Samsonov followed Zhilinskii's instructions regarding the direction of his advance, he undoubtedly would have saved his army.

The East Prussian operation was a moral defeat for the Russian army of the first order, and it seriously undermined the troops' faith in themselves and their commanders. It was also the beginning of a depressing pattern in which the Russians could generally defeat the Austro-Hungarian armies but were consistently bested by the better-trained and better-led Germans.

Simultaneous with the events in East Prussia, an even larger drama was being played out between the Russian and Austro-Hungarian armies in southern

Poland (see map 3). Russian forces in the area were organized into the Southwestern Front, which was commanded by Gen. N. I. Ivanov, the prewar chief of the Kiev Military District. Ivanov has been unflatteringly described by a subordinate as "narrow, indecisive and incoherent." The subordinate felt that the commander in chief, a veteran of the Russo-Japanese War, had been irretrievably scarred by that conflict and had become cautious and unsure of himself.[110] The same observer rated the front's chief of staff, Gen. M. V. Alekseev, as "quite intelligent" and an "excellent strategist," while nevertheless reproaching him for being "indecisive and lacking character."[111]

Ivanov's command included the Fourth Army, commanded by Gen. A. E. Zal'ts, chief of the Kazan' Military District, and Fifth Army, headed by Gen. V. K. Pleve, commander of the Moscow Military District. Third Army was headed by Gen. N. V. Ruzskii, Ivanov's deputy, and the newly created Eighth Army was placed under Gen. A. A. Brusilov, who had previously commanded the Kiev Military District's 12th Corps. These armies deployed in a broad arc stretching over 400 kilometers from Lublin to Proskurov, while the small Dnester Detachment anchored the Russian left in the Kamenets-Podol'skii area.

The Austro-Hungarian First, Fourth, and Third Armies were spread out to meet them along a slightly shorter front from the mouth of the San River in the west to Chernovtsy in the east. This force was under the nominal command of Archduke Ferdinand, although actual control was wielded by Gen. Conrad von Hotzendorf, chief of the General Staff. The Kummer Group and parts of the German Woyrsch Detachment guarded the Austro-Hungarian left flank west of the Vistula, while the Kovess Group watched the Russians along the Dnestr. At the beginning of the Galician fighting the Austro-Hungarians outnumbered their adversaries by a margin of 787,000 to 691,000, due to the Russian army's slower pace of mobilization, although new units continued to arrive on both sides throughout the battle.[112] The Russians did, however, enjoy a slight superiority in artillery of 2,099 guns to 1,782.[113] Moreover, the Russians' morale was certainly higher than in the heterogeneous forces of the Dual Monarchy.

Both sides' initial plans called for an opening offensive and were suffused with a desire for a quick victory, characteristic of the major belligerents' prewar beliefs. Each sought to re-create a new Sedan on an even larger scale by turning one or both of the enemy's flanks and destroying his forces in a gigantic battle of annihilation. The Russians planned a concentric advance by all four armies against the Austro-Hungarian armies in southern Poland in order to cut off their retreat across the Carpathian Mountains into Hungary. According to this scheme, Fourth and Fifth Armies would advance due south on Przemysl and Lemberg (L'vov), while Third and Eighth Armies would move on Lemberg and Galich from the east. The Russian forces were divided almost equally between the Fourth and Fifth Armies (337,000 men and 942 guns) in the west and the Third and Eighth Armies (354,000 men and 1,157 guns) to the east.[114]

The Austro-Hungarian plan was conditioned by the need to tie down Russian forces in the east until their German allies could finish their campaign in France. Thus Conrad planned to launch his main attack with the forces of Dankl's First Army and Auffenberg's Fourth Army (430,000 men and 954 guns) due north between the Vistula and western Bug Rivers, in the general direction of Lublin. Brudermann's Third Army and the Kovess Group (297,000 men and 684 guns) would guard the advance's flanks around Lemberg.[115] Conrad, after defeating the Russians, evidently hoped to continue the advance north to what he believed would be a converging German attack out of East Prussia, thereby capturing Warsaw and cutting off the Russian forces in the Polish salient west of Brest-Litovsk.

However, both plans were founded on a number of serious miscalculations, which would come to have a decisive influence on the course of the battle. The most serious of these was Conrad's mistake in assuming a major German thrust across the Narew, without which the Austro-Hungarian plan made no sense at all. This astounding lack of even the most elementary strategic coordination between the two powers was shortly to bring the Austrian armies to the brink of disaster. Another serious error was the conviction that the Russians would not deploy sizable forces east of Lemberg, and that the Third Army and the Kovess Group alone were strong enough to meet any threat from that direction. This was compounded by Conrad's foolish dispatch of the Second Army to the Serbian front instead of deploying it to the right of the Third Army, as had originally been planned. This army was only beginning to arrive in Galicia when the fighting began.[116]

The Russians erred by assuming that the Austro-Hungarians would deploy their forces along the border in a way that would facilitate their planned double envelopment.[117] As it transpired, Conrad's decision to concentrate his forces farther south and west of the frontier seriously reduced the Russians' chances of a successful turning movement and ensured that the opening battles would play out as frontal collisions. Ivanov further weakened his attack by dividing his forces evenly between the front's two wings. This reduced the chances that either could achieve a decision and harked back to Kuropatkin's timid methods of 1904–5. The fact that the Russians were able to create a healthy superiority east and southeast of Lemberg owed more to Conrad's faulty dispositions than to any insights on Ivanov's part.

The Battle of Galicia (August 18–September 21, 1914) is conventionally divided into the Lublin-Chelm (August 21–September 3) operation by the Russian Fourth and Fifth Armies, later joined by the Ninth Army, and the Galich-L'vov (August 18–September 3) operation by the Third and Eighth Armies. Both of these operations had their seesaw offensive and defensive components, followed by a general offensive by all the armies and a subsequent pursuit.

Fighting broke out first on the northern wing, where the Austro-Hungarian First Army crossed the frontier on August 20. North of the San River it collided head-on with Zal'ts's Fourth Army (14th and 16th Corps, a Grenadier Corps, and two cavalry divisions), moving south from Lublin. On the twenty-third the Austro-Hungarian left wing struck one of the Russian corps south of Krasnik and drove it back. Austro-Hungarian efforts to turn the Russian right flank along the Vistula continued the next day, as the latter gave ground slowly before superior forces. The Russians struck back in the center, but the fighting here yielded no clear-cut result; nor did it relieve the enemy pressure on the right. Zal'ts, worried about the threat to his communications with Lublin, ordered his army to fall back late on the twenty-fourth to a position south of the city. For his poor handling of the fighting, the elderly Zal'ts was removed from command on the twenty-fifth and replaced by A. E. Evert.

Ivanov, concerned about the heavy enemy pressure on Fourth Army, ordered Pleve's Fifth Army (25th, 19th, 5th, and 17th Corps, plus three cavalry divisions) on August 25 to come to the assistance of its hard-pressed neighbor by changing its axis of advance from due south to southwest, in the direction of the lower San, with the object of striking the Austro-Hungarians in the flank. This change of direction through Zamosc and Rava-Russkaya, however much it may have been warranted by Fourth Army's situation, did not take into account the Austro-Hungarian Fourth Army, which was moving northeast from Przemysl. Fifth Army, which was also charged with maintaining contact with the Third Army on its left, would be stretched dangerously thin.

The two armies collided the next day in a series of battles between the Wieprz and Bug Rivers. The Austro-Hungarians quickly attacked and defeated Fifth Army's right flank, forcing it to fall back on Krasnystaw south of Chelm, while the Russian center was likewise bested north of Tomaszow. The fighting continued in the area for the better part of a week, with both sides suffering heavy casualties, but with the Austro-Hungarian superiority in numbers gradually beginning to tell. Fifth Army's units were slowly pushed north and east toward Krasnystaw and Hrubieszow. However, the army's divergent paths of retreat left its central and left-wing corps semi-isolated and in danger of encirclement, and opened the way for a determined Austro-Hungarian advance on Chelm. To the west, enemy pressure continued against the Russian Fourth Army, although the danger of an Austro-Hungarian breakthrough toward Lublin was receding, thanks to a combination of heavy enemy casualties and the timely arrival of Russian reinforcements to the army's beleaguered right wing. The serious threat to Pleve's flanks continued, however, and he was finally forced to order a withdrawal on August 30. The Russians here conducted a skillful fighting retreat, and the exhausted Fourth Army was unable to pursue them with any success. By September 3 the Russians had safely retired to positions stretching from the Vistula, west of Lublin, southeast to the area of Vladimir-Volynskii. Losses were heavy on both sides. Pleve's army alone suffered 30,000 casualties, while the Austro-Hungarian Fourth Army lost up to 40,000 men.[118]

To the east matters developed more slowly, although the fighting was no less fierce. Here the battle began with the movement of Gen. Brusilov's Eighth Army

(7th, 12th, 8th, and 24th Corps, although the latter had not yet arrived) from Proskurov to the frontier on August 18, followed the next day by Ruzskii's Third Army (21st, 11th, 9th, and 10th Corps, and three cavalry divisions) out of Dubno. At first the two armies encountered no serious resistance, and the Austro-Hungarians seemed content to remain behind their Lemberg positions. In spite of the Russians' preponderance of strength, their advance here was not as swift as it might have been, particularly in light of the developing threat to the front's northern wing. In fact, as early as August 25 the front command had ordered Third Army to swing its main forces north of Lemberg in order to maintain contact with Fifth Army's left wing as it executed its wheel to the southwest. However, Ruzskii disregarded these instructions and continued his advance toward Lemberg, creating a large gap between the front's two wings.

The first heavy fighting occurred along the Zolotaya Lipa River, southeast of Lemberg, where the Austro-Hungarians attacked Ruzskii's forces, despite being heavily outnumbered. During the first two days (August 26–27) the Russians fought off repeated enemy attacks along a 60-kilometer front, inflicting heavy casualties. On the twenty-eighth the Russians themselves attacked and drove the Austro-Hungarians out of their positions back to the Gnilaya Lipa. The fighting resumed the next day as the Austro-Hungarian Third Army and newly arrived Second Army under Bohm-Ermolli launched another series of attacks, which were met by equally determined Russian ripostes. In a three-day battle (August 29–31) the Russians broke through the enemy position southeast of Lemberg. Another enemy attack was beaten off north of Galich by Brusilov's army, which then began its own advance on Lemberg from the southeast. With their last defensive line broken, the Austro-Hungarians abandoned the city and retreated to a position along the Vereshchitsa River. On September 3 the Russians entered Lemberg.

Although the Russian armies in the east had won a significant opening victory, it had been purchased at the expense of Fifth Army, which by now was falling back on Chelm. Third Army's fixation on Lemberg had continually drawn it due west, away from the critical situation on Fifth Army's front. The Austro-Hungarian Fourth Army, in fact, had been seriously alarmed by Ruzskii's belated dispatch of a single corps toward Rava-Russkaya and had slowed its pursuit of the Fifth Army accordingly. Only now, however, under intense pressure from both Ivanov and the Stavka, did Third Army turn to the northwest.

The results of the two operations were decidedly mixed, although the overall state of the Southwestern Front's two wings gave grounds for optimism. In the north, Fourth and Fifth Armies had been roughly handled but not beaten. In fact, the Russian forces here were growing stronger each day, with the arrival of fresh units, of which the creation of P. A. Lechitskii's new Ninth Army (14th and 18th Corps, a cavalry division, and a rifle brigade) on September 3 was the most tangible result. The state of the eastern armies was even more favorable following the capture of Lemberg. Here the Russians had an excellent opportunity to finish off the Austro-Hungarians and roll up their entire right wing, with results that would inevitably affect the situation to the northwest. The foundations of a Russian victory were already present, if Ivanov could only get his armies to act in concert.

The situation called for a reappraisal of both sides' plans. Of the two, the Austro-Hungarian solution was the most radical, corresponding to its weaker position. With the hope of a German attack from East Prussia all but gone, and the growing threat to Fourth Army's rear, Conrad realized that a further advance on Lublin and Chelm was pointless, especially in light of growing Russian strength in the area. The chief of staff thus ordered his First Army to take up defensive positions against Ninth and Fourth Armies. To the south, Third and Second Armies were to regroup for an attack against Eighth Army. Most audaciously, Conrad then left part of Fourth Army to watch the supposedly beaten Russians in the Zamosc-Hrubieszow area, while the greater part of the army was to turn 180 degrees due south to close the gap in the Austro-Hungarian line and strike the Russian Third Army in the flank. The plan was daring, even foolhardy, given the odds, but it was the only alternative to a major Austro-Hungarian withdrawal from what was becoming an increasingly untenable situation.

The Russian plan, on the whole, remained faithful to Ivanov's original idea of a concentric offensive by all his armies. Ninth and Fourth Armies would resume the attack southwest toward the lower San, while Fifth Army was to put itself in order and move south on Tomaszow. Third Army would advance with the greater part of its forces north of Lemberg in the direction of Jaroslaw, and Eighth Army was to support this move from the south by pushing the enemy out of his Gorodok position and back on Sambor. Ivanov's plan was cautious and unimaginative, but it had the virtue of simplicity, compared with Conrad's scheme, and for that reason alone was probably superior. The plan may also have reflected the Russian commander's lingering fear of a German attack in the rear of his front, particularly following the spectacular defeat of General Samsonov's Second Army at Tannenberg, which effectively uncovered the route to Warsaw from the northwest. However, for reasons of their own, the Germans elected to move against the remaining Russian First Army and left their Austro-Hungarian allies to their own devices.

The Russians began their counteroffensive with a healthy overall superiority, particularly in the west, where Ninth, Fourth, and Fifth Armies now heavily outnumbered the Austro-Hungarian First Army and the remains of Fourth Army by some 26½ infantry and 9½ cavalry divisions to 15½ infantry and 4 cavalry divisions. In the east the forces were now more equal, with the Russian Third and Eighth Armies mustering 21½ infantry and 8 cavalry divisions against the Austro-Hungarian Second and Third Armies, plus the greater part (three corps and 2 cavalry divisions) of Fourth Army, numbering 27 infantry and 6 cavalry divisions. However, even here the Russians enjoyed an artillery superiority of 1,302 guns to 1,054.[119]

The Russian counteroffensive began in the north on September 4 with a concerted attack by all three armies. These forces advanced cautiously against the outnumbered Austro-Hungarian defenders, who nonetheless launched a number of local counterattacks. However, the Russian superiority slowly began to tell, and the Russians took Zamosc on the sixth, as the outnumbered Austro-Hungarian left wing started to bend back under the pressure. To the east, the bulk of the rejuvenated Fifth Army bore down on the weak enemy screen in the Komarow area and was approaching the rear of Fourth Army's main forces, which had pivoted south in accordance with Conrad's instructions and now occupied positions in the Rava-Russkaya area. On the ninth, Fifth Army took Tomaszow, thereby increasing the pressure on Fourth Army's exposed left flank. To the west, Ninth and Fourth Armies continued their methodical advance against First Army.

West of Lemberg, Third and Eighth Armies had reached the Gorodok position along the Vereshchitsa River in most places by September 5. Once again, the fighting took the form of an extended meeting engagement along most of the front, while both sides tried to outflank the other north of Rava-Russkaya. However, the approach of Fifth Army's units from the north caused the Austro-Hungarians to break off these attempts and pull back their line, first to the west, then farther to the southwest, where it came under increasing pressure from the reunited Russian forces. Farther south, Third and Eighth Armies had to withstand repeated attacks over several days (September 6–11) along the entire front south to the Dnestr by the greater part of three enemy armies. At times it seemed as though the Austro-Hungarians would break through to Lemberg, but the Russians managed to hold on, and on September 12 the exhausted attackers broke off the action.

Far to the northwest, meanwhile, First Army continued to fall back against Russian attempts to turn its flanks. By September 10 it had withdrawn south of Krasnik under growing pressure. The impending collapse of the Austro-Hungarian left wing was fraught with danger for the main armies fighting to the east and southeast, which now risked having their escape routes to the west cut off. Here, Fourth Army was in particular danger of being outflanked by Russian attacks north and east of Rava-Russkaya. The town fell on the eleventh, and the situation became critical for the three eastern Austro-Hungarian armies, and it seemed as though the Russians would soon break into their rear. At this point, Conrad at last realized that he was beaten, and that same day he issued an order for a general withdrawal to the west.

The Austro-Hungarian retreat soon got out of hand as the armies streamed back to the west and southwest. By September 15 the Russians had reached the line of the lower San and were approaching Sambor on the upper Dnestr. The Russians pursued as best they could, but the terrible state of the primitive roads, exacerbated by heavy rains, and their own supply shortages enabled the enemy to escape. The front line finally stabilized east of the Dunajec and the foothills of the Carpathian Mountains. And although the Russians were unable to cut off any large enemy units during the retreat, they did succeed in blockading two Austro-Hungarian corps in the fortress of Przemysl.

Although the Russians had failed to achieve their goal of destroying the Austro-Hungarian armies, the Battle of Galicia was nevertheless a great victory and a much-needed antidote for the disaster in East Prussia. According to Soviet figures, the Austro-Hungarians lost 326,000 men in the fighting, of which more than 100,000 were prisoners, as well as 400 guns. Russian losses are put at 230,000, of which 40,000 were prisoners, plus 94 guns.[120] Losses on both sides were extremely heavy, with the Austro-Hungarians suffering, on the average, 7,500 casualties per division during the battle, and the Russians 4,500. As a result of the fighting, the overall strength of the Austro-Hungarian armies in Galicia fell by 45 percent, with Third Army losing 109,000 men, Fourth and Fifth Armies 90,000 each, and the Second Army about 37,000 men.[121] The Dual Monarchy had suffered a major defeat, from which it would never recover, and henceforth would need substantial German assistance in order to survive.

However, the battle had been more of a near thing than these figures would suggest, and the outcome was ultimately due more to the Austro-Hungarians' mistakes than to any skill shown by the Russian command. Chief among these errors was Conrad's dispatch of his Second Army to Serbia and then to Galicia, where it arrived too late to affect the battle's opening phase. This weakening of the Austro-Hungarian right flank was exacerbated by the Third Army commander's stubborn insistence on launching expensive frontal attacks against superior Russian forces.

Apart from their immediate battlefield results, the two operations examined here are significant for what they reveal about the further development of the operation, according to a number of indices. In purely quantitative terms, the operation had grown immensely in scope in the ten years since the Russo-Japanese War. For example, more than 400,000 men took part on both sides in the East Prussian operation, which lasted thirty days. Here the operation was conducted in depth to 100 kilometers and in width to 200 kilometers, although the two Russian armies were never in full contact. An even greater leap occurred during the Battle of Galicia, which saw nearly 2 million men committed to the operations and the related fighting that followed. This fighting lasted thirty-five days along a more or less continuous front, which at its greatest length stretched some 400 kilometers and ebbed and flowed in places to a depth of 200 to 250 kilometers.

The two operations also help to clear up some of the theoretical confusion left over from the interwar period. It will be recalled that Neznamov, writing in 1911, felt that the battle/engagement was a thing separated from the operation, and in fact was its culmination point. However, the war's opening operations showed otherwise. In East Prussia we have the case of the Gumbinnen-Goldap meeting engagement occurring at the very beginning of the operation as a mere episode. In Galicia the distinction is even clearer, and such actions as the Battle of Krasnik and the Battle of Tomaszow, and the meeting engagements on the Zolotaya Lipa and Gnilaya Lipa Rivers, are clearly component parts of a larger operation. And while Neznamov was certainly more correct in his description of the "general engagement," strictly in terms of the forces involved, he nevertheless once again erred in separating this phenomenon from the operation.

The two examples also have much to say about the Russian army's use of operational maneuver, or the lack of it. In the case of East Prussia, geography itself demanded a decisive turning movement against the German Eighth Army to cut off its retreat to the Vistula. However, front commander Zhilinskii remained obtusely unaware of the possibilities until it was too late. For the most part he was content to push the Germans out of East Prussia by means of a frontal assault. Only Samsonov, of the Russian principals, seems to have been aware of the operational possibilities from the outset. His fatal mistake lay in attempting to carry out what was a front operation with the resources of a single army, and against the wishes of his front commander.

In Galicia the possibilities for a turning movement were much more limited, due to both the configuration of the enemy frontier and the number of enemy forces involved. Ivanov, to his credit, persisted in attempting to turn the enemy's flank, even as the prospects for a successful maneuver receded. If one takes as a given that in a nonpositional war, in which both sides' flanks are still open, it is better to attempt a turning movement than attack the enemy head-on, then Ivanov is to be commended for his persistence.

These early operations also represent the first clear-cut example of Russian operational command and control at the front level. Kuropatkin commanded a front in all but name at Mukden, but his insistence on acting like a division commander negated the operational significance of this development. Unfortunately, General Zhilinskii's incompetent handling of the Northwestern Front's armies during the East Prussian operation indicated that he had no clear conception of his role as commander in chief in a theater of military activities, and Ivanov's front-level conduct of the Battle of Galicia showed that he understood his role little better.

Both commanders were at fault in their "hands-off" approach to their respective operations and the activities of their subordinate army commanders. Zhilinskii's coarse treatment of Samsonov contrasts sharply with his delicate approach toward Rennenkampf and may have had something to do with the latter's alleged ties to the czarist court.[122] In Galicia, General Ruzskii's conduct in blatantly ignoring the front commander's orders in order to have the glory of capturing Lemberg is a particularly egregious example of the freedom some army commanders evidently felt they enjoyed. The impunity with which he acted may stem as much from the prewar Russian belief in giving the individual army commanders the maximum freedom of action as it did from the front commander's own lack of will in imposing his vision of the operation on his subordinates. However, the 1914 *Regulations* called for a strong front commander. Whatever the reason, Ruzskii's subsequent appointment to head the Northwestern Front in place of the incompetent Zhilinskii showed that an insubordinate army commander had little to fear by disobeying orders and did nothing to enhance the front commander's authority vis-à-vis his subordinates.

The Russian front system was also criticized from another angle for allegedly giving the individual front commanders too much freedom vis-à-vis the supreme commander in chief and his chief of staff. This charge was made by Gen. Yu. N. Danilov, who at the time served as the army's quartermaster general. He claimed that the broad territorial scope of the front commander's responsibilities necessarily diminished the role of the Stavka and its chief. This meant, he continued, that the front commanders all too often felt free to place the interests of their commands over the common good, to the detriment of the overall strategic situation. To remedy this, Danilov recommended breaking up the fronts into smaller units, presumably armies, which would lack the fronts' semiautonomy. Such a move, he maintained, would ease command and control problems by concentrating more power in the hands of the supreme commander in chief and his apparatus. Indeed, his animus against the front structure was such that at one point he claimed that the entire system was nothing more than an organizational expedient designed to ease the command burden on Nicholas II. However, Danilov does not elaborate on how the coordination and control of the resulting multiplicity of independent armies by the Stavka would have been any less difficult for the emperor, who had no formal military training. In this respect, Danilov's criticisms, whatever validity they may have, should nevertheless be understood as the views of a man who served in the army's central command apparatus and who sought, not surprisingly, to increase the latter's authority over the armies at the expense of the front instance of command.[123]

The Russian victory in Galicia posed a serious threat to Cracow and Germany's upper Silesian industrial area, bringing about a shift in both sides' efforts to the left bank of the Vistula. The Germans concentrated by rail the newly formed Ninth Army in the Czestochowa area, where, in conjunction with the Austro-Hungarian First Army, they were to threaten the flanks of the Russian forces in Galicia. The Russians, meanwhile, were planning their own offensive into Silesia from the same general area. This involved the transfer, primarily on foot, of Fifth, Fourth, and Ninth Armies from the Southwestern Front and the newly reconstituted Second Army from the Northwestern Front, between Warsaw and the upper Vistula.

The Austro-German attack began on September 28. At first the advance made good progress, sweeping aside the small Russian covering force west of the Vistula. Farther south, an Austro-Hungarian supporting attack against the Southwestern Front's weakened left wing (Third and Eighth Armies) succeeded in pushing the Russians back and temporarily relieving Przemysl, although the attackers failed in a forcing of the San. Meanwhile, the main Austro-German attack continued, although Russian resistance was stiffening with the arrival of forces from the south. By October 12 the Austro-Germans had reached the Vistula from Sandomierz north and were within a few kilometers of Warsaw. However, Russian counterattacks all along the line from the middle of October halted any further advance. By the end of October, growing Russian superiority and the parlous state of the Austro-

Hungarian First Army contrived to force the Austro-German armies back to their starting positions.

With the initiative temporarily in Russian hands, the way now seemed open for a full-scale invasion of the Silesian industrial basin. The Stavka planned to launch an offensive along a broad front between Posen and Katowice with four armies (Fourth, Fifth, Second, and Ninth). However, before the Russians could move, the Germans once again preempted them with an offensive of their own. Again the Ninth Army, which had been moved north to the Thorn area, spearheaded the attack, which was designed to drive a wedge between the Russian First and Second Armies and encircle the latter in the vicinity of Lodz. Although the German attack on November 11 made good initial progress, the Russians struck back with unaccustomed speed and soon had the Germans' lead corps boxed in. However, Renenkampf's incompetent handling of his army allowed the Germans to escape from the trap. Although the battle was a tactical draw, it had stopped the Russian invasion of Silesia. Thereafter, the front in the east stabilized for the winter.

By 1915 the problems of waging war under modern conditions had fully matured into a positional stalemate on both the eastern and western fronts. This novel situation was in direct contradiction to much of prewar Russian and foreign theory, which held that a decision would most likely be achieved on the enemy's flanks. By 1915 the possibilities for such a maneuver were nil, as the extremes of both fronts were now anchored on the sea or in neutral territory. This meant that any offensive would necessarily be a frontal attack against a fortified position, behind which the defender enjoyed most of the advantages. The difficulties of such an undertaking were amply illustrated during the inconclusive fighting of January–April 1915, when both sides launched offensives through the Carpathian Mountains. Here the Austro-Hungarians sought to relieve the garrison once again isolated at Przemysl, while the Russians attempted to break through to the Hungarian plain. Both armies suffered staggering losses during this fruitless campaign, which netted the Russians only a few kilometers of snowbound mountains. The Russians' efforts were particularly hampered by their increasing shortage of artillery shells, due to myriad production and supply difficulties. The only positive result of the fighting for the beleaguered Russians was the fall of the Przemysl fortress on March 22, with a loss to the Austro-Hungarians of some 120,000 men and over 900 guns.[124]

The conditions of trench warfare were by no means uniform, however, and on the eastern front a greater degree of fluidity always existed, due to the vast distances involved and the uneven quality of the opposing troops, which stood in contrast to the western front, where the British, French, and Germans were more or less evenly matched. These factors made breakthroughs in the trench line and the restoration of limited maneuver somewhat easier than in the west. This was demonstrated most clearly at Gorlice in May 1915, when a powerful Austro-German assault broke through the Russians' position and proceeded to roll up their entire front in Galicia. The Germans launched another blow from East Prussia to cut off the Polish salient, but the Russians managed to withdraw from the trap in time. The retreat continued throughout the summer, as the Russians yielded up Poland and Lithuania in a campaign that eventually cost them more than 2 million casualties, plus 1.3 million prisoners.[125] Losses were particularly heavy among the prewar cadre, which had to be replaced by inexperienced conscripts. This retreat marked the beginning of the army's descent into the chaos of 1917. Thereafter the front stabilized once again as the Central Powers turned their backs on Russia to seek a decision in the west.

By the spring of 1916 the Russian armies had recovered sufficiently from the previous year's disasters to once again consider offensive operations against the Central Powers along a front stretching more than 1,200 kilometers from Riga in the north, southward through Dvinsk (Davgavpils), Baranovichi, Pinsk, Rovno, and Ternopol', and ending at the Romanian border. The Russian forces were now organized into three fronts: Northern, Western, and Southwestern, numbering some 1,732,000 men and facing a combined Austro-German force of 1,061,000.[126] However, the Russian advantage should have been much greater, especially because the army numbered some 6,206,000 men by the beginning of the year.[127] However, the great mass of these troops remained far from the front in overly large garrisons or rear-area training units. Moreover, the overall quality of these troops was extremely low, and it is doubtful if any real use could have been made of them, even had there existed sufficient amounts of artillery, shells, and even rifles. The wasteful offensives of the war's first months had quickly killed off a large portion of the army's prewar cadre, particularly among the officer class. Brusilov, as early as the autumn of 1914, had noted that the army was no longer what it had been and had come "more and more to resemble a poorly trained militia force."[128]

The Russian high command met in April 1916 at Stavka headquarters in Mogilev to map out the details of the summer campaign. This group included Czar Nicholas II, who had replaced the Grand Duke as supreme commander in chief the previous autumn; the chief of staff, General Alekseev; and the three front commanders. The conferees decided to make the summer's main attack by General Evert's Western Front toward Vilna, just south of the site of the disastrous March offensive at Lake Naroch. General Kuropatkin's Northern Front would assist this effort with an attack toward Vilna from the Dvinsk area. General Brusilov, the newly appointed commander of the Southwestern Front, was to begin the offensive cycle by attacking toward Lutsk in order to draw enemy reserves away from the main blow. That the Southwestern Front would attack at all was due chiefly to Brusilov's insistence on an offensive role for his forces, as opposed to the other front commanders, who openly despaired of success.[129] The attitude of those commanders entrusted with the main offensive role is especially perverse, given the Russians' healthy superiority in men along the front north of the Pripyat Marshes.

Returning from the conference, Brusilov assembled his army commanders to dictate his plans for the upcoming offensive. As had been decided at Mogilev, the Southwestern Front's main effort would be made from the Rovno area toward Lutsk. However, Brusilov, instead of following the usual practice of massing all his forces here for a single narrow breakthrough, selected a radically different approach. The front commander demanded that each of his four armies prepare an attack zone along its front, as well as in a number of corps sectors. This meant, in effect, that the Southwestern Front would be attacking along almost the entire length of the 450-kilometer front in order to deprive the enemy "of the possibility of gathering all his forces in one place," so that he would not be able to determine "where the main blow will be launched against him."[130]

Such a radical dispersal of force was particularly daring in light of the slight overall advantage in men and matériel that the Southwestern Front possessed. On the eve of the attack the Russian forces outnumbered the Austro-Hungarians in infantry 573,000 to 451,000, and even more in cavalry, 60,000 to 31,000. However, the Russians' chronic inferiority in artillery continued to plague them. While Brusilov's forces disposed of 1,593 light artillery pieces to the defenders' 1,299, they nevertheless remained inferior in the all-important category of heavy guns, 335 to 583.[131] However, if the Russians would be attacking with what was a bare superiority of force, they nonetheless possessed a number of distinct advantages over the enemy. The most salient of these was their clear moral superiority over the dispirited Austro-Hungarian armies, many of whose Slavic contingents were less than eager to support the Dual Monarchy against their Russian cousins. The Austro-Hungarian chief of staff further compounded the weakness of his forces by siphoning off many of his best troops and artillery to carry out his Asiago offensive against the Italians in May. Thus Brusilov would be attacking the enemy coalition at its weakest point along the greater part of his front, with the tougher Germans holding only the area north of Lutsk.

Brusilov chose to make the front's main effort in the north (see map 4) with Gen. A. M. Kaledin's Eighth Army (225,000 infantry and cavalry, 706 guns) against Archduke Ferdinand's Fourth Army and Puhallo's smaller First Army.[132] Kaledin was to make his main attack from the Rovno area with four corps (39th, 40th, 8th, and 32d) northwest toward Lutsk and Kovel'. A mixed cavalry-infantry force on the army's right flank would assist the main effort by raiding to the southwest toward Kovel'. Brusilov also planned a major supporting attack along his front's extreme southern flank. Here General Lechitskii's Ninth Army was to move across the Dnestr into Bukovina against Pfanzer-Baltin's Seventh Army. It was hoped, despite the secondary nature of this sector, that a success here would induce the wavering Romanians to enter the war on the Allied side.[133] The front's weak central armies were assigned purely secondary objectives against Bohm-Ermolli's Second Army and the Southern Army under the German Bothmer. Gen. V. V. Sakharov's Eleventh Army was to attack due west toward Lemberg, while General Shcherbachev's Seventh Army would move along the Dnestr in the direction of Galich.

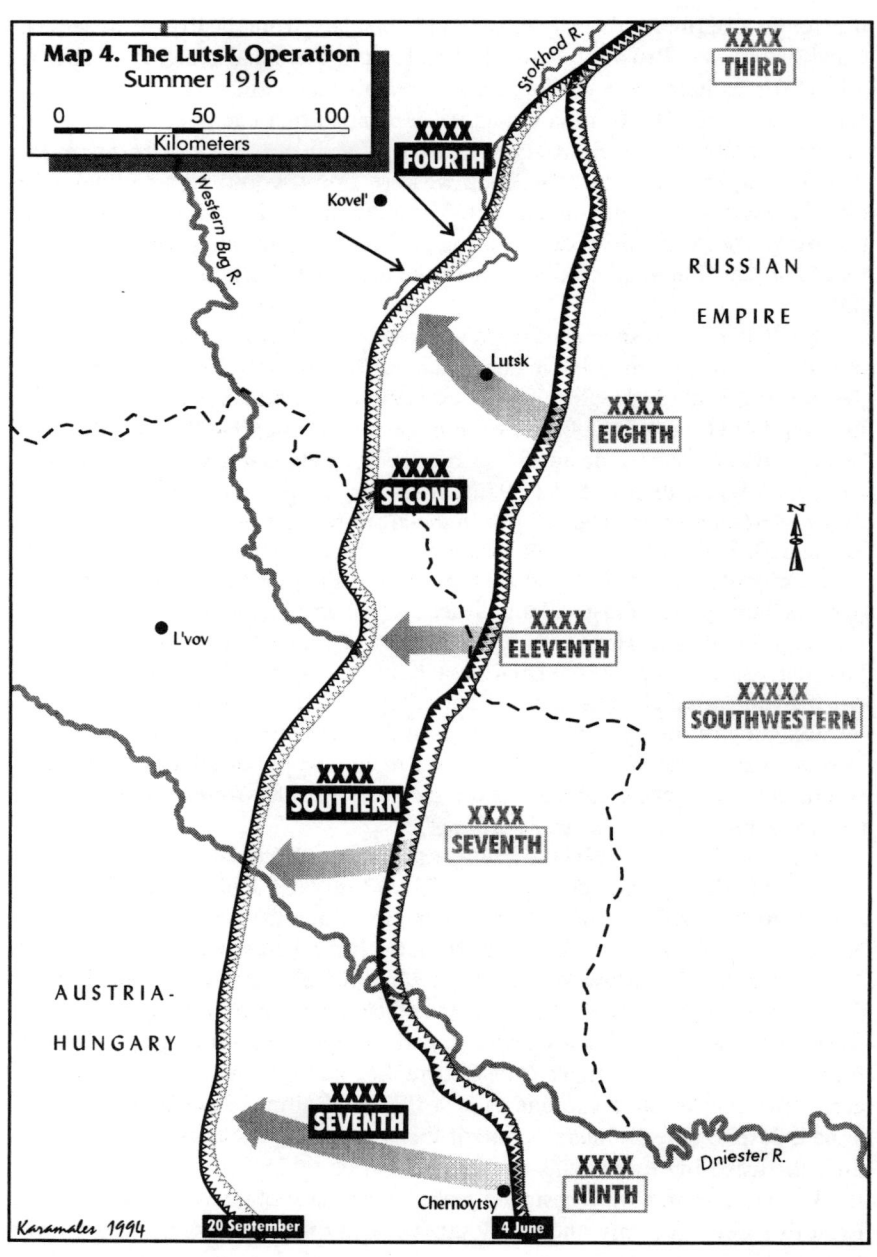

However, if Brusilov's operational plan called for dispersing his front's attacks widely along the line so as to disguise his true intentions, his army commanders' concerns were dictated by the necessity of concentrating sufficient forces to ensure a breakthrough of the enemy's defenses. Each Austro-Hungarian division occupied, on the average, a frontage of between 10 and 13 kilometers, while most of the Southwestern Front's divisions occupied sectors ranging from 9 to 10 kilometers in breadth. The Russians sought to increase their chances by organizing their breakthrough attacks along very narrow sectors of the front. The Eighth Army would launch its main attack with 4 corps along a 16-kilometer front; the Eleventh with 1 corps along an 11-kilometer front; the Seventh with 1½ corps along a 7-kilometer front; and the Ninth with 2 corps along an 11-kilometer front.[134] This formula, which involved a concentrated tactical effort along a narrow front against the background of a larger and more dispersed operational one, would later serve as a point of departure for Soviet theoreticians wrestling with the problem of organizing an operational breakthrough.

Brusilov's formula was certainly novel for its time. Heretofore, the Russians had essentially copied Western methods of organizing a breakthrough, which involved the massing of overwhelming numbers of artillery and infantry along extremely narrow sectors of the front, in order to punch a hole through the enemy's defense. Such preparations were typical of offensive operations for most of the war, particularly on the western front, in spite of the many and obvious drawbacks. Not only was this procedure tremendously expensive in terms of shells and manpower; the factor of surprise was also completely negated because such large-scale offensive preparations could rarely be hidden from an opponent possessing modern reconnaissance means, particularly aircraft. Any remaining doubts regarding the actual sector of the attack were soon removed by a lengthy artillery bombardment, during which time the defender could always bring up reserves to meet the impending offensive. Brusilov's solution not only was the proper one, given his limited resources, but also was more in tune with the peculiar conditions of the eastern front.

The Russian attack commenced in the early hours of June 4 with an artillery bombardment along the entire front, which lasted from six to forty-six hours, depending on the location. The infantry attack was quite successful, except in the north, where the combined infantry-cavalry raid quickly broke down in the swampy terrain. Repeated attacks in this area brought no more than minor gains at great expense. To the south the Eighth Army's main effort made good progress and completely uprooted the defenders from their heavily fortified positions. The breakthrough here was complete, and by June 7 the Russians had taken Lutsk and advanced 25 to 35 kilometers along a 70- to 80-kilometer front. Even more profound was the almost total collapse of the Austro-Hungarian Fourth Army, which had quickly "melted away into miserable remnants," according to one disgusted German observer.[135] Indeed, such was the magnitude of the disaster that Russian sources report capturing over 72,000 prisoners and ninety-four guns in this sector alone in the first five days.[136]

Unfortunately for the Russians, Brusilov lacked the means to properly exploit his success. Eighth Army's units were already fully committed to the battle, and what should have been the army's mobile reserve (4th Cavalry Corps) was being frittered away in useless attacks north of Lutsk, an area manifestly unsuited for large-scale cavalry actions. Thus when the road to Kovel' lay practically undefended, the Russians had no forces at hand to take the city. The defenders could hardly believe their good fortune. As General Ludendorff, the German deputy commander in the east, later testified: "The Russians had not followed up very smartly in a westerly direction, although a great victory was beckoning them."[137]

At this critical juncture in the offensive Brusilov seems to have been almost as bewildered by his success as the Austro-Germans, as he watched his supporting attack quickly become the greatest Russian success of the war. However, instead of driving into the gap with the forces on hand, he now ordered his units to consolidate along the Styr' River and to expand the penetration along either flank, while the cavalry was to continue its efforts to break through to Kovel'. Brusilov's hesitation at this point shows that he had little in common with the romanticized "fighting general" image that he and successive generations of Soviet and Western historians have constructed.

The Stavka intervened to further complicate an already difficult situation on June 9, when Alekseev ordered Brusilov to call off the advance on Kovel' and, instead, move southwest on Rava-Russkaya. The same message also informed the front commander that Evert's attack had been postponed to June 17.[138] In an odd swing of moods, Alekseev's initial doubts about the wisdom of Brusilov's attack had been transformed by its unexpected success into a desire to achieve a larger decision. By moving on Rava-Russkaya, Alekseev evidently sought to turn the Austro-Hungarian flank in the north and split the Hapsburg armies off from their German allies. This was a task for which the front's meager resources were entirely insufficient, all the more so because the other fronts remained inactive.

The Eighth Army, temporarily diverted from Kovel', continued its attack due west, pushing across the Styr' against feeble Austro-Hungarian resistance. By now Brusilov had come to realize the futility of his cavalry attack and began switching what remained of this force southward to exploit the success around Lutsk, although valuable time had been lost. By June 15 the army had penetrated as far as the Stokhod River, equidistant from Kovel' and Vladimir-Volynskii. To the south, Eleventh Army was able to take advantage of its neighbor's success to push its right flank nearly to Brody. Matters developed less well on Seventh Army's front, where the Russians continued to flail ineffectually at the enemy's second defensive zone. Ninth Army renewed its offensive on June 10 and was immediately successful when the enemy withdrawal got out of hand and became a rout. On June 18 Ninth Army forced the Prut River and captured Chernovtsy.

As word of the Austro-Hungarian collapse spread, the Germans acted with their usual dispatch to shore up their faltering ally. The Dual Monarchy was forced to shut down its Italian offensive and move forces back to Volhynya, while the Germans began to frantically strip units from the eastern and western fronts and rush them to the Kovel' area. The Germans were immensely aided in these efforts by their highly developed rail net and their interior lines of communications, which enabled them to rapidly switch forces from one front to another.

On June 16 a mixed Austro-German force began a series of counterattacks along the entire perimeter of the Lutsk salient. However, the attacks achieved little and only succeeded in pushing the Russian lines back a few kilometers, flattening the bulge's nose. The German commander, General von Linsingen, had not waited to assemble a sufficient striking force but had committed his units into the battle as they arrived, thus reducing the counterattack's effectiveness. By June 21 the attack's impetus was spent, and the initiative once more passed into Russian hands.

However, Brusilov continued to be hobbled by the Western Front's delays in launching its Vilna attack. Evert's reluctance to move was well known, and his grand offensive was further postponed until early July. Furthermore, Evert suddenly decided to switch the main effort south to the Baranovichi area, a move that set back the timetable even more. This useless maneuvering gave the Germans a free hand to shift their troops from Evert's and Kuropatkin's fronts to meet the crisis at Lutsk. Brusilov was beginning to receive reinforcements as well from the other two fronts, whose commanders were probably just as glad to be deprived of the means for conducting offensive operations. On June 24 Evert's left-flank Third Army came under Brusilov's command, although this infusion of strength did nothing but lengthen the latter's front and could do little to restore the opportunity forfeited by repeated postponements of the main attack.

Brusilov's orders for the offensive's second round were issued on June 25. Third Army was to move due west toward Gorodok and Manevichi, while Eighth Army was to launch its main drive on Kovel', with a secondary blow aimed at Vladimir-Volynskii. Eleventh Army was to continue attacking toward Brody, and the Seventh to move on Monasterzhiska. Ninth Army would reorient its advance northwest, toward Stanislavlov and Galich, with the date of attack set for July 4.

For once the Russian high command managed to achieve a modicum of strategic coordination. The Western Front's Baranovichi offensive opened on July 2, although this ostensible main effort actually preceded the "supporting" attack by two days. But the lack of preparation in switching forces to this new front told early on, and the attack was a complete and bloody failure. Evert called off the offensive after just nine days, with a loss to the Russian Fourth Army of some 80,000 men.[139]

The Southwestern Front's renewed offensive now enjoyed only mixed success, with the armies on either wing (Third, Eighth, and Ninth) advancing farthest, while the center armies (Eleventh and Seventh) were held to minor gains.

In the south, Ninth Army continued its successful drive between the Prut and Dnester Rivers and pushed the Austro-Hungarians back still farther. The fighting was most fierce to the north, in the area between Lutsk and the Pripyat River, where Russian casualties were averaging 15,000 men per day.[140] Here Eighth Army was able to push only a few kilometers across the Stokhod River before being halted by German reserves. Third Army's attack gained considerable ground between the Styr' and Stokhod, and at one point seemed poised to break through to Kovel' from the northeast. Ludendorff called this time "one of the greatest crises on the Eastern Front," when it seemed unlikely that the Dual Monarchy's hapless troops could hold out against the repeated Russian attacks.[141] But stiffened with German reserves, they just managed to hold on, and the Russian attacks gradually exhausted themselves. Brusilov halted the offensive on July 11 and immediately set about reorganizing his forces for another effort.

By now the Stavka had realized the importance of Brusilov's attack and had begun shifting forces to the Southwestern Front in earnest. By the latter half of July Russian forces south of the Pripyat Marshes numbered 711,000 men against 421,000 Austro-Germans, a significant increase over the slight superiority of early June.[142] This reinforcement led to the creation of the "Special" Army, made up of three newly arrived Guards corps and two corps already in place. The army, under Gen. V. M. Bezobrazov, was inserted into the line between the Third and Eighth Armies and given the task of advancing on Kovel'. However, this added advantage served no particular purpose except to tempt Brusilov into making more expensive attempts to take the town. The element of surprise that had served the Russians so well at the beginning of the offensive was now entirely gone, and the Central Powers could make better use of their inferior numbers by using their rail system to switch troops to the threatened sectors.

Nonetheless, Brusilov resumed his attacks all along the front on July 28, with Third Army striking toward Kovel' and Eighth Army moving westward on Vladimir-Volynskii. However, lack of success along the main axis did not stop him from repeatedly throwing his troops into bloodily unsuccessful attacks against the enemy's positions along the Stokhod. General von Falkenhayn, the German chief of staff, recalled that the Russian losses during this period "must have been nothing short of colossal."[143] This was hardly the imaginative and resourceful commander of June, who sought to do his best with the small numerical superiority available to him. The end result of this senseless attrition was a few kilometers of ground gained before the attack was once again halted.

In the south the Russians fared better against armies that were substantially Austro-Hungarian in composition. Here the Russians were able to take Brody and advance to within 50 kilometers of the vital rail center of Lemberg. The greatest success continued to take place on Ninth Army's front, where the Russians took Stanislavlov and, in August, Galich and Kolomyya, and threatened to push through the passes of the Carpathian Mountains onto the Hungarian plains. However, given the secondary nature of this sector and the poor state of Russian communications in the area, the offensive here soon died out from lack of sustenance, although the fighting here and along the rest of the front sputtered on fitfully well into autumn.

By mid-August the Southwestern Front's great offensive, for all practical purposes, had ended as a result of the exhaustion and enormous casualties on both sides. Brusilov later claimed to have inflicted 1.5 million casualties on the enemy, plus another 450,000 captured through mid-November, although these numbers are surely inflated.[144] Russian casualties are more difficult to arrive at, although Falkenhayn was by no means exaggerating. Between June 5 and 29 Brusilov's forces suffered 289,298 casualties, according to a later Soviet source.[145] Another source puts the total Russian casualties for the summer, of which the great majority may be attributed to the Southwestern Front's offensive, at 1.2 million killed and wounded, with another 212,000 taken prisoner.[146]

Although intended purely as a secondary effort, the Southwestern Front's summer offensive did achieve a number of important and unexpected strategic results. The substantial drain in resources forced the Austro-Hungarians to call off their Italian offensive, which had enjoyed a good deal of initial success. In the west, the Germans had to forgo their plans for a preemptive attack against the British offensive preparations along the Somme in France.[147] The offensive's early success prompted Romania to join the Allies, although this belated effort was later crushed in a lightning campaign that left the Central Powers even stronger in the Balkans than before. Finally, the front's offensive completed the destruction of the ramshackle Austro-Hungarian army as an effective fighting force, at least on the eastern front.

However, it is at the operational level that the "Brusilov offensive" holds the greatest interest, particularly during the initial breakthrough phase and the early attempts at exploitation. Brusilov eschewed the practice of launching a single major attack along a narrow front in favor of several separate army and even corps efforts at widely separated intervals. This method of tactical-operational concentration along the projected breakthrough zones, against a background of operational-strategic dispersion south of the Pripyat Marshes and aided by the indifferent quality of the enemy forces, ensured a rapid breakthrough in several places at once, with the greatest success along the main sector. During the offensive's first two weeks Eighth Army advanced to a depth of 75 kilometers, which was quite good for the time, even in the more mobile conditions of the eastern front. Such rates also compare favorably with several of the 1918 offensives on the western front, which demanded a far heavier investment in men and matériel.

But the attack's initial impetus quickly exhausted itself, and after mid-June the gains were few and horrendously expensive, except in the south, where Ninth Army ultimately penetrated up to 150 kilometers. The explanations for the Russian failure to achieve a decisive operational success must be sought in the shortcomings of the front command and in the meager matériel support allotted to the offensive, which in turn was the result of prior decisions at the strategic level.

Brusilov's chief problem lay in the contradiction between his original conception of his front's supporting role and the great vistas revealed by the operation's first spectacular successes. His original desire to engage and occupy the enemy in as many places as possible led him to approve the Eighth Army commander's plan to launch two separate attacks on Kovel', leading to an unnecessary dispersal of force along the axis of the main advance. Thus the main, or northern, wing attacked with all its corps arrayed in a single echelon along the front, without a second echelon to impart depth and sustainability. The few reserve divisions available were inadequate and were, in any event, quickly consumed during the breakthrough. Thus the Russian attack remained a "one-punch" affair without the means for following up any success. The harsh lesson of the Lutsk operation was that in order to break through a deeply fortified enemy front and exploit the penetration, the attack must be organized in depth as well.

In spite of these faulty initial dispositions, Kovel' might have fallen in June had either Kaledin or Brusilov demonstrated the requisite flexibility in adapting to their unexpected success. Brusilov later blamed Kaledin for this failure, citing the latter's stubborn insistence on advancing in the direction of Vladimir-Volynskii, when the way to Kovel' lay open. However, Brusilov does not seem to have been particularly insistent on this point.[148] Moreover, the front commander's own conduct was marked by indecision during this time, when a commitment to a rapid push to Kovel', even without reserves, might well have been successful. Equally reprehensible was the conduct of the Stavka under General Alekseev. The Russian high command failed utterly to carry out its responsibilities in coordinating the activities of its subordinate fronts by insisting that Evert and Kuropatkin assist Brusilov. Nor did the high command ever succeed in reinforcing Brusilov's attack in a timely manner. This was due chiefly to the shortcomings, military and otherwise, of Nicholas II and his chief of staff, Alekseev, whose timidity and indecisiveness prevented them from taking advantage of the possibilities revealed by the offensive.

If Brusilov proved himself no better than his contemporaries in exploiting his opportunities, his actions, once the offensive's original impetus had exhausted itself, place him among the worst of a bad lot. By taking Lutsk, the Southwestern Front had already done far more than was ever expected of it, and Brusilov can hardly be held responsible for the Stavka's failure to insist on an immediate attack by the other fronts. Brusilov, having failed to push on to Kovel' after the breakthrough, should have been content to rest on his laurels. Unfortunately for the Russians, once the Southwestern Front became the "main front" and began to receive the lion's share of reinforcements, Brusilov seems to have lost the capacity for original thinking forced upon him by his former scarcity of resources and reverted to the laborious and grinding attacks favored by too many of his contemporaries. Far from bringing any benefit to the Russian cause, this senseless prolongation of the attack bled the army white and went far toward undermining what remained of its offensive spirit. As the fighting along the Stokhod continued into the autumn, incidents of entire regiments refusing to leave their trenches were reported, a development that presaged the army's final collapse a few months later.[149]

In retrospect, it would have been wiser to have shut down the offensive no later than mid-July, as its original justification as a prelude to the Western Front's main blow had by then evaporated. Soviet operational theoreticians of the 1920s would later make much of the notion of not pushing an offensive beyond a point where the risks and losses incurred begin to outweigh the results achieved. In the Lutsk operation, they found a lesson and a warning.

The Lutsk operation was the old regime's last significant military effort, and the remainder of 1916 passed without incident. Internally, however, the imperial system was breaking down, and with it the country's armed forces.

The Provisional Government, which succeeded the Romanov dynasty in March 1917, inherited a profoundly demoralized army that was showing increasing signs of war-weariness. The Petrograd Soviet's infamous Order Number 1, which authorized the election of officers by "soldiers' committees," had an immediate and disastrous effect on the armed forces' discipline. Matters were equally chaotic at the higher levels of command, where senior officers were often appointed and replaced for reasons having more to do with politics than with the situation at the front. In the span of six months five different men held the title of supreme commander in chief: Nicholas II, Alekseev, Brusilov, L. G. Kornilov, and A. F. Kerenskii, the latter of whom was a lawyer by training and a revolutionary by vocation.

Nevertheless, the Russians elected to attack once again with the forces of the Southwestern Front. This was a serious mistake. The Russian army, racked by massive internal problems, should have been content to remain on the defensive throughout 1917, while attempting to restore its morale for a possible offensive the following year. This was particularly the case because the Germans had their hands full staving off a series of Allied offensives in France. Nevertheless, the attack began on July 1, following a two-day artillery bombardment. At first the offensive made respectable progress against the equally dispirited Austro-Hungarian forces south of Lemberg. However, the defeatist rot that had seized the army was too far gone, and the attack soon broke down. The ensuing German counterattack quickly threw the Russian troops back to their starting positions and beyond. The retreat became a rout, causing one British observer to note that "the Russian army had been irretrievably ruined as a fighting organisation."[150]

The failure of the "July offensive" was the final blow to what remained of the imperial army. It was also a severe setback to the Provisional Government, which had staked its dwindling prestige on the attack and the continuation of the war. From this point on the large and disaffected mass of soldiery was increasingly willing to heed the Bolsheviks' calls for an immediate peace. Little did they suspect, however, that in choosing revolution over fighting, they would soon have more war than anyone could ever imagine.

However, in passing from the scene, the old regime nevertheless managed to leave a rich legacy in the area of operational art, one upon which its successor could build. Chief among these were the notion of the operational level of war itself, the front system of command, as well as nascent research into the idea of conducting a series of consecutive operations. That the imperial regime could not bring these ideas to fruition was due more to the internal ills of the entire czarist system than to any weaknesses in the armed forces. Now the torch would be passed to a new order—one infinitely more cruel than its predecessor but nevertheless infused with a brutal energy—that was more than ready to move the country and its military along its own peculiar path.

2
Wars Within and Without, 1918–1920

The radical turn that the Russian Revolution took upon the Bolsheviks' seizure of power on November 7, 1917, was one of the most catastrophic events of the twentieth century, in terms of both the immediate suffering it wrought and its consequences, which entailed even more misery. The civil war that accompanied the revolution was to last three long and terrible years and in some areas would continue with varying degrees of intensity until the end of 1922.

Given the population's accumulated grievances, it is likely that a revolution of some sorts would have eventually broken out in Russia, even without a major war. However, this would probably have taken a relatively moderate form, much like the events of February 1917. Unfortunately, the dislocations caused by the Great War ensured that the revolution, when it did occur, would take on a horrific character wholly unforeseen by its prophets and opponents alike.

The Bolsheviks proclaimed the Russian Soviet Federated Socialist Republic (RSFSR), which openly espoused a revolutionary ideology dedicated to overthrowing the existing order throughout the world. At the top stood the Council of People's Commissars, headed by the Bolshevik leader V. I. Lenin, in a coalition with a faction of the Socialist Revolutionaries. The first Soviet government included such notables as L. D. Trotskii and J. V. Stalin.

One of the new government's first steps was to outlaw all other political parties other than itself and its erstwhile allies. This move was enforced by the newly created secret police, the All-Russian Extraordinary Commission (VChK), headed by F. E. Dzerzhinskii, which quickly moved against opposition parties. That the Bolsheviks were not going to tolerate any manifestation of "bourgeois" democracy was made apparent in January 1918, when they dispersed the Constituent Assembly, which had been elected by popular vote the previous autumn. In this fashion, the short-lived Russian experiment in democracy came to an ignominious end.

Another pressing task was to seek peace with the Central Powers, which had been one of the Bolsheviks' rallying cries the previous summer. However, given the parlous state of the old Russian army, the Soviet government could not hope to negotiate with its enemies on anything like equal terms. A feeble attempt to resist the enemy's demands brought about an immediate German offensive, which threatened to topple the Bolsheviks from power. As a result, on March 3, 1918, the Soviets were forced to sign the punitive Brest-Litovsk peace, which surrendered to Germany and its allies Poland and part of the Baltic States. The treaty also obliged the Soviets to withdraw their forces from Finland, the remainder of the Baltic, Ukraine, and parts of the Trans-Caucasus, most of which were subsequently occupied by the Central Powers.

This act engendered the undying enmity of the Western Allies, who already suspected the Bolsheviks of being German agents. The Allies felt that the new Soviet government had betrayed them by concluding a separate peace with the Central Powers, and they retaliated by landing troops along the Russian periphery and rendering material aid to the fledgling anti-Bolshevik forces. Part of the old officer class also turned against the new government for abandoning the war with the hated Germans. However, the peace did afford the Bolsheviks the breathing space they needed to consolidate and implement the other tenets of their political program.

The latter included the nationalization of land and industry, and even such utopian measures as the abolition of money. Far more serious, however, was the Bolshevik policy of forcible payments in kind from the peasantry, which was bled dry in order to feed the urban proletariat.

By the summer of 1918 these multiple discontents burst forth in an open rebellion by the Bolsheviks' Socialist Revolutionary allies, which was quickly and bloodily put down. The Bolsheviks used the opportunity to throw off the charade of pseudodemocracy to outlaw all other political parties. This and a subsequent attempt on Lenin's life led to the proclamation of the "Red Terror," which quickly became a fixture of Soviet life during the regime's early years. Meanwhile, on the former empire's periphery, the anticommunist forces, known collectively as the Whites, were gathering their armies. These events mark the true beginning of the civil war.

As a purely military phenomenon, the civil war may be viewed as a subset of the Great War in the east, which continued to influence events on the western front, and vice versa, until November 1918. The most obvious evidence of this linkage was the Brest-Litovsk peace, which allowed the Germans to transfer large numbers of forces to France, where they were nearly able to turn the tide against the Western Allies that spring and summer. Conversely, the German collapse in the fall of 1918 caused them to withdraw their forces from Ukraine and south Russia, which proved to be a boon for the struggling Bolsheviks. War erupted again in the summer of 1920, in the shape of the follow-on conflict with Poland, which threatened to upset the entire structure of post-Versailles Europe.

The civil war was also a conflict of almost unimaginable savagery, in which centuries-old hatreds and ideological fanaticism were given free rein. For example, prisoners taken by either side were routinely shot, while reprisals and other atrocities against civilians unlucky enough to be members of a particular "class" were all too common. An estimated 16 million died as the result of World War I, the civil war, and the subsequent famine.[1] Millions of others, chiefly from the upper and middle classes, emigrated.

The economic disruptions were just as violent. As a result, production in the major industrial categories declined to a fraction of its prewar volume by 1920, due to the ravages of war and the almost-complete cessation of imported materials. The situation in the agricultural sector was nearly as catastrophic, due to the effects of war, as well as the Bolsheviks' own ruinous expropriation policies. By 1920 basic grain yields were only 54 percent of what they had been in the 1909–13 period, while the number of farm animals declined by more than 50 million head from the 1916 figure.[2] Even the sympathetic H. G. Wells spoke of "a vast irreparable breakdown," and it would be several years before the country could recover.[3]

By the end of 1920 the Soviet Republic lay isolated and prostrate. Among the country's other woes was the loss of large territories (Finland, the Baltic States, Poland, and Bessarabia) along the former empire's western frontiers. However, out of the destruction of this conflict would emerge a new force in world affairs—the Soviet Union.

THE MILITARY SPECIALISTS

It is one of the many ironies of the Russian civil war that the most pressing military problem the Bolsheviks faced during their first months in power was one of their own making. The Bolsheviks had spent much of 1917 undermining the former imperial army in order to deprive the successor Provisional Government (March–November 1917) of armed support. The Soviet leaders had not foreseen the need to create a regular army, believing that their coup would be the signal for similar uprisings in the west. Instead, the regime was immediately confronted with the prospect not only of civil war but also of intervention by a still-vigorous imperial Germany and was forced to build a new army almost from scratch. This would prove to be no easy task in a country already exhausted by more than three years of war and whose huge but demoralized army was incapable of offering effective resistance to anyone. For example, by the beginning of 1918, mass desertions had left only about 30,000 to 50,000 troops to maintain the semblance of a front against the Germans.[4]

In January 1918 this untenable situation compelled the Soviet government to establish the Red Army, units of which were soon in action against German troops. These early formations usually consisted of Red Guards, the party's military arm, and other volunteers. However, this expedient failed to provide a sufficient number of recruits to meet the regime's growing military responsibilities. By May 1918 the Red Army still numbered only 306,000 men, which was far from adequate to suppress the growing White resistance in the south and east or to fend off German probing in the west.[5] Accordingly, that same month the Soviets adopted working-class conscription, which obligated the urban proletariat and peasants to serve in the army. This move raised the size of the army to 800,000 by the end of 1918, and to over 5 million by the end of the war.[6]

However necessary, the army's rapid expansion and the inflation of its ranks with masses of untrained and semiliterate workers and peasants made the shortage of qualified officer cadres all the more acutely felt. The Bolsheviks, for so many years an underground political movement, were almost devoid of members with military command or staff experience, which stood in sharp contrast to the White armies, which contained a high proportion of experienced officers.

As the civil war approached its first crisis in the summer of 1918, the Soviet authorities were forced by circumstances to conscript their own cadre of former officers, although this policy was accompanied by a great deal of controversy. The Bolsheviks' anxiety about employing large numbers of former czarist officers is understandable, given the party's ideological hostility to the officer class as a matter of principle and the army's prerevolutionary role as the mainstay of the autocracy. Even Lenin, who supported the policy, felt that the former officers were "permeated throughout with bourgeois psychology" and that nine-tenths of them were "capable of treason at any opportunity."[7] For many veteran Bolsheviks the very idea of former czarist officers commanding units in the proletarian army was an abomination, and they waged an active campaign against this policy.[8] Among the fiercest critics were some of the younger former officers, who may well have resented their senior brethren's rapid advancement under the new regime. One of these was a twenty-six-year-old former junior officer, M. N. Tukhachevskii, who claimed that the Red Army had inherited the least capable remains of the old officer corps. This group, he charged, lacked both the requisite military skills and the political understanding to conduct operations in the radically different conditions of the civil war.[9]

The chief proponent of recruiting the former officers was Lev Davidovich Trotskii (Bronshtein). Trotskii, who was born in southern Ukraine in 1879, was a professional revolutionary who had followed the usual path of arrest, exile, and party-literary work abroad in the years before 1917. Returning to Russia after the autocracy's collapse, he aligned himself with Lenin, with whom he had clashed in the past; he quickly rose to the top of the party hierarchy and was instrumental in organizing the Bolshevik coup against the Provisional Government. Trotskii, following a disastrous stint as people's commissar for foreign affairs, took over the war commissariat in March 1918. In this post he truly came into his own, despite his complete lack of military experience, and his ruthless, uncompromising leadership was decisive to the Reds' victory. Trotskii's reasons for employing the former officers were entirely practical, and he castigated the bigoted attitudes of Bolshevik "semipartisans," for whom military science and the rational conduct of war were "identified with treason and treachery."[10] This bitter dispute festered throughout the remainder of 1918, and the policy was not officially adopted until the following March at the eighth party congress. However, the ill feelings engendered by this controversy would linger long after the war itself was over.

For their part, many of the former officers, particularly the older ones, detested the new regime, which they blamed for the collapse of the old army and the hated Brest-Litovsk peace, as well as the loss of their former privileges and authority. The latter included such "democratic" innovations of 1917 as the abolition of ranks and saluting and the election of officers by so-called soldiers' committees. As one former officer recalled, the "overwhelming majority" of officers viewed the idea of serving in the Red Army as "almost shameful."[11]

The former officers' reasons for serving were varied and sometimes contradictory. Some served the Reds for patriotic motives, in spite of the Bolsheviks' "internationalist" pretensions. Such feelings were certainly uppermost in the minds of those who joined during the winter of 1917–18, when a renewed German advance threatened to take Petrograd, and in the spring of 1920, following the Polish invasion. One of the latter was Brusilov, who joined the Red Army in 1920 despite having earlier been arrested and condemned to death by the regime.[12] Others, albeit a distinct minority, seem to have sincerely supported the party's program or had come to believe that the Bolsheviks represented the choice of the people.[13] Others joined because they knew no other profession and could have served the Whites just as easily.

The majority, however, undoubtedly served under some duress. This pressure took several forms, the most lenient of which was Trotskii's proposal to ensconce unwilling officers in concentration camps, while Lenin threatened "saboteurs" with shooting.[14] Certainly the most barbaric measure was the war commissar's order to arrest the relatives of commanders who defected to the Whites, a practice that foreshadowed one of the more odious practices of the Stalin era.[15] In such an atmosphere no former officer was above suspicion, and even the Red Army's first commander in chief, Vatsetis, was briefly arrested in 1919 on charges of treason.[16] Even the slavishly loyal M. D. Bonch-Bruevich later wrote that "many czarist generals and officers became victims of the red terror," although he excused the repression as justified by the Whites' actions.[17]

Prominent victims included N. N. Dukhonin, who served briefly as supreme commander in chief and was killed by mutinous soldiers in 1917, after they learned that he had freed the anti-Bolshevik generals Kornilov and A. I. Denikin. These two became the organizers of the White resistance in south Russia. Another was Renenkampf, the villain of the East Prussian and Lodz operations of 1914. He was executed by Soviet authorities in early 1918 for his part in quelling antigovernment uprisings during the 1905 revolution. The Whites were no less vengeful. Two former generals, A. V. Stankevich and A. P. Nikolaev, were executed following their capture by counterrevolutionary forces in 1919.[18]

Under these circumstances, one of the party's chief tasks was to assert and maintain its authority over this potentially treasonous group. The Bolsheviks achieved this through the institution of political commissars, an expedient of radical regimes since the French Revolution. Political commissars had served in the Russian army since the February Revolution of 1917, and following their seizure of power the Bolsheviks immediately set about expanding this system and bringing it under their control. In April 1918 the All-Russian Bureau of Military Commissars was established, which became the Revolutionary Military Council of the Republic (RVSR) Political Directorate the following year. Such future party leaders as K. E. Voroshilov, S. M. Kirov, N. S. Khrushchev, V. V. Kuibyshev, and Stalin gained considerable experience as "the eyes and ears" of the party during this period.

Military councils *(voennye sovety)* were created at the front and army level to ensure party control, while individual commissars were assigned to units down to the battalion level. The military councils generally consisted of two political commissars and the commander, who at the higher levels was almost always a former officer. In theory, the commander was to enjoy operational freedom, while the commissars answered for the unit's political loyalty. In practice, however, the commanders' prerogatives were often encroached upon by overzealous commissars intent on ferreting out "treason" and interfering in purely military matters. The key to the commissar's power was the provision that no operational directive could be implemented without his countersignature. The ambiguity inherent in this arrangement became fertile ground for mischief making by any ambitious commissar, as happened on a number of occasions. The system of dual command and the insecurity it bred among the former officers were among the prime causes of much of the red tape and inefficiency in the Red Army's conduct of operations during the war.[19]

One of the most egregious examples of political interference in the former officers' command functions took place in the summer of 1918. This incident is important not only because it illustrates the problems the former officers encountered in their work but also because it reveals the attitudes of two men, Stalin and Voroshilov, whose policies would shape the Red Army for a generation.

Stalin arrived in Tsaritsyn (Stalingrad/Volgograd) in June 1918 to supervise the requisitioning of the area's grain supplies for Russia's urban areas. The city was threatened at the time by P. N. Krasnov's Cossack troops, who were attempting to cut the Soviets' Volga River lifeline and link up with the White forces to the north and east. Stalin, although he had not been delegated military powers, used his political position (at the time he was a member of the party's Politburo and Central Committee, as well as people's commissar for nationalities) to usurp the city's defense from the military authorities. One of his first acts was to arrest the commander of the North Caucasus Military District, the former officer

Gen. Lt. A. E. Snesarev, and several of his staff on charges of treason. According to some émigré sources, Stalin later ordered the staff officers placed aboard a barge, which was towed to the middle of the Volga and sunk.[20]

The extent of Stalin's enmity toward the former officers may be gathered from two letters written to Lenin during this period. In the first, Stalin denounced the officers as "cobblers" (a slang term meaning "idiots") and blamed them for the city's defense problems. In the other, Stalin complained that the former officers were actually allies of the Cossacks and Anglo-French "interventionists."[21] As the letters indicate, Stalin's penchant for seeing "spies" and "saboteurs" everywhere was already highly developed. The dictator's hostility toward the former officers was confirmed years later by his lieutenant and eventual successor, Khrushchev, who wrote, "Stalin used to enjoy telling us that he refused to have anything to do with the bourgeois officers whom Trotskii dispatched to Tsaritsyn and that they invariably turned out to be traitors." Stalin, according to this source, remained a "specialist eater all his life."[22]

Stalin ruled virtually unhindered at Tsaritsyn for two more months, until mid-September, when the Southern Front was established, embracing the area along the lower Don and Northern Caucasus. Its military council consisted of Stalin, the former general major P. P. Sytin, Voroshilov, and S. K. Minin. This was an impossible arrangement, given the personalities involved and the political members' ingrained mistrust of the former officers. Trotskii called Voroshilov "the man who most detested the military specialists . . . , not overly intellectual but shrewd and unscrupulous." Minin, he said, "suffered from a blinding phobia of all tsarist officers."[23] The military council was continually torn by disagreements over command, supplies, and even the location of front headquarters.[24] The situation eventually became so intolerable that Stalin was recalled to Moscow in October, while Voroshilov was transferred to Ukraine two months later.

Although Stalin and his allies had been temporarily dispersed, they would be reunited with even more disastrous consequences in the war with Poland. Their defeat was thus by no means final, and their enmity toward Trotskii and the former officers had only increased. This group (Voroshilov, S. M. Budennyi, and E. M. Shchadenko) would later become the nucleus of the Stalinist faction within the army, which was to have tragic consequences for the country's defense.[25]

For all the commissars' vigilance, however, there were a number of cases of real treason by former officers. The most spectacular was that of former lieutenant colonel M. A. Murav'ev, the first commander of the Eastern Front. Murav'ev, a Socialist Revolutionary, joined his party's disastrous uprising against the Bolsheviks in July 1918 but failed and was killed in a gun battle. A similar fate awaited all those who betrayed Soviet power or failed to carry out orders with sufficient vigor—a policy that was applied to specialist and commissar alike. However, Trotskii's policy of executing commissars for their units' failures and his supposed favoritism toward the former officers soon became part of the growing indictment against him by many of the army's political officers. One of these later reported that by the time of the eighth party congress the majority of military delegates, who presumably, for the most part, were political officers, were personally opposed to Trotskii.[26]

Trotskii's alleged coddling of the former officers, to the detriment of party control, is one of the enduring myths of post–civil war Soviet historical writing.[27] This assertion has no basis in fact. As always, Trotskii's guiding principle was that "one cannot build an army without repressions," which he applied with even-handed vigor to commanders and commissars alike.[28]

However, the former officers' influence within the army was counterbalanced by the so-called "red commanders" *(krasnye komandiry)*. The great majority of these came from the ranks of those who had served as noncommissioned officers (NCOs) or enlisted men during the Great War, and there also were some with no military experience. Most of these men lacked specialized officer training, while many had only the rudiments of a grade-school education. In spite of these drawbacks, a number of these commanders eventually became accomplished soldiers, at least under the conditions of 1918–20. Among this group were such future notables as Budennyi, S. K. Timoshenko, I. E. Yakir, and G. K. Zhukov. For these men the civil war presented an opportunity for professional advancement as no other event could have done. They, in turn, repaid the debt by becoming the regime's most loyal supporters within the armed forces.

The most famous of the red commanders was Mikhail Vasil'evich Frunze, who was born in Russian Central Asia in 1885. Frunze joined the Bolsheviks in 1904 and spent the next several years between revolutionary activity, prison, and Siberian exile. He was instrumental in the Bolshevik seizure of Moscow in November 1917 and later served as military commissar of the Yaroslavl' Military District. During the civil war he commanded a series of armies, as well as the Eastern, Turkestan, and Southern Fronts. Following the war, Frunze commanded the armed forces of Ukraine and the Crimea and headed a diplomatic delegation to Turkey. He returned to Moscow in early 1924 as Trotskii's deputy on the Revolutionary Military Council and succeeded the former a year later. Frunze's tenure in the country's top military position was short-lived, however, and he died in October 1925 under mysterious circumstances.

In spite of these difficulties, the policy of recruiting the former officers was a great quantitative success. Beginning with the first partial mobilization of June 1918 and continuing through the end of the war in November 1920, nearly 75,000 former officers passed through the Red Army's ranks, although the exact figure remains in dispute.[29] This total accounted for 56 percent of the 130,914 Red Army line commanders of all backgrounds and nearly 30 percent of the prerevolutionary officer corps (career and wartime officers), according to the most reliable source. Those former officers who served in the White armies accounted for some 40 percent (100,000) of the total, while the remaining 30 percent (75,000) managed to avoid service on either side by going into hiding or emigrating.[30]

The Red Army's haul of former officers, despite the small overall percentage, was nevertheless impressive in terms of quality and included a significant number of those formerly attached to the czarist General Staff apparatus—the army's administrative and intellectual elite. A White source has calculated the number of General Staff officers at the end of 1917 at about 1,500, of whom 319 (21 percent) eventually served in the Red Army, although this figure is disputed by a number of other sources.[31]

These officers also had an especially important role to play in resurrecting the country's system of higher military education, where their knowledge of the arcana of staff work and military administration was particularly valuable. Their efforts were centered in the new Academy of the General Staff, which opened its doors in December 1918. This institution was the successor to the defunct imperial staff academy, which had led a curious twilight existence amid the turmoil of war and revolution and had continued to graduate students as late as the spring of 1918. The new academy's first chief was the former general major A. K. Klimovich; he was succeeded the following year by Snesarev, who was fortunate to be alive following his run-in with Stalin.[32] Among the teaching staff were such former General Staff officers as N. A. Danilov, V. F. Novitskii, N. A. Suleiman, Neznamov, and Svechin. Neznamov read the course on strategy, as he had done in prewar days, and Svechin taught the history of military art. These officers, as the living repositories of what was best in the Russian military tradition, no doubt had a great impact on their eager but untutored pupils. Among the first of these were the future marshals and General Staff chiefs K. A. Meretskov and V. D. Sokolovskii and one of the outstanding operational theorists of the interwar period, V. K. Triandafillov.[33]

Because of the widespread opprobrium attached to the word "officer" at the time, the first officer volunteers were called variously "military experts," "military consultants," or "technical leaders." It was only from the spring of 1918 that the term "military specialist" *(voennyi spetsialist)* became standardized in the army.[34] One Soviet source defines "military specialist" as "a general, admiral, officer or bureaucrat of the old Russian army and fleet, recruited for service in the Soviet army and navy during the civil war and foreign intervention in Russia."[35] However, this definition lacks precision, and the term requires closer examination.

First of all, the so-called military bureaucrats should be eliminated from the equation as having nothing in common with those officers serving in line, staff, or pedagogical positions. One should also exclude from this group the large number of wartime officers (approximately 90 percent of this total) who were commissioned from the ranks or otherwise made officers during World War I.[36] And while their experience was certainly greater than that of the military bureaucrats, it would be a gross error to equate the wartime officers' level of practical, and particularly theoretical, training with that of career officers commissioned before

1914. Despite their educational shortcomings, however, many wartime officers went on to highly successful careers in the postwar Red Army. Among these were F. I. Tolbukhin, Triandafillov, I. E. Petrov, I. P. Uborevich, A. I. Antonov, and A. M. Vasilevskii.

Qualitative judgments concerning the small number of former career officers who served in the Red Army must also be made, for the differences in training and education within this group were as profound as those separating them from the wartime officers.[37] The higher officers' ranks (general–field marshal, general, general lieutenant, general major) would have been overwhelmingly represented by men who had graduated from the old General Staff Academy and who had commanded operational-level formations, or who had served in field staffs at a corresponding level.[38] Among this group the Soviets managed to recruit such operational practitioners and theorists as Brusilov, A. A. Samoilo, Svechin, A. I. Verkhovskii, P. P. Lebedev, and Mikhnevich.

A slightly larger group consisted of those midlevel officers (colonels and lieutenant colonels) who threw in their lot with the Bolsheviks.[39] A number of these officers had attended the General Staff Academy before World War I, particularly during the relatively innovative period between 1906 and 1912. While these officers lacked the generals' command and staff experience at the operational level, they were probably less conservative and more open to new ideas—necessary qualities in the radically different conditions of the civil war and a new political order. In this respect, they may reasonably be compared to those middle-ranking Reichswehr officers (Guderian, von Manstein, etc.) whose ideas profoundly influenced the German army after 1933. Among this group were such notable commanders and staff officers as Vatsetis, S. S. Kamenev, A. I. Yegorov, Shaposhnikov, A. I. Gotovtsev, and F. P. Shafalovich.

The large group of lower-ranking officers (captain, staff captain, lieutenant, second lieutenant) was a potentially rich source of future commanders, even though their overall level of theoretical preparation was little different from that of the wartime officers. These officers' experience had been entirely at the tactical level, and only a very few had attended the imperial General Staff Academy, mostly in accelerated courses during 1915–18. Nevertheless, this inexperienced group was to furnish many of those who would later occupy important command positions in the wartime and postwar Red Army, and who would make a significant contribution to operational theory as well. These officers included A. I. Kork, N. E. Varfolomeev, E. A. Shilovskii, and Tukhachevskii.[40]

At first glance the overall contribution of the military specialists (in the narrow sense of the term used here) seems quite small—no more than 6 percent of the whole—compared with the much larger proportion of wartime officers, former NCOs, and others who constituted the Red Army's command element during the civil war. However, in qualitative terms, the specialists' influence was far greater than their numbers would indicate and ultimately was decisive to the conduct and outcome of the war. This was due to the former career officers' virtual monopoly of the army's most important administrative, command, and staff positions, which could only be filled by those with the requisite skills. This was particularly true at the strategic-operational level, where the chief operations were conceived and conducted.

For example, both commanders in chief (Vatsetis and Kamenev) were former colonels and graduates of the imperial General Staff Academy. Both finished their training at the academy during its most innovative period between 1906 and 1912. The commander in chief's executive organ, the RVSR Field Staff, was headed successively by N. I. Rattel', F. V. Kostyaev, Bonch-Bruevich, and Lebedev, all former general majors.[41] These officers provided a much-needed leavening of professionalism at a critical command juncture.

The situation was little different at the front level, where the specialists held the great majority of command and staff positions. Of the 20 men who commanded the chief fronts between 1918 and the end of 1920, 16 (80 percent) were military specialists, while the remainder were professional revolutionaries, of whom Frunze demonstrated the greatest military capabilities. Ten (50 percent) of the front commanders were graduates of the old staff academy, and two (10 percent) had completed the academy course between 1906 and 1912. Of the 28 men who served as front chief of staff, 27 (96 percent) were documented regular officers. Of this group, 26 (93 percent) had graduated from the imperial General Staff Academy, which was proof of the Bolsheviks' high opinion of their professional training. Moreover, 12 (43 percent) of the staff officers graduated between 1906 and 1912.[42] Thus of the 46 men who occupied one or both of these positions, 41 (89 percent) can be shown to have been former career officers, while 34 (74 percent) were graduates of the old staff academy. Of this number, 14 (30 percent) completed the course between 1906 and 1912.

At the army command and staff level the dominance of the military specialists remained strong, if somewhat reduced. Of the 85 men who commanded major armies between 1918 and the end of 1920, 66 (78 percent) can be shown to have been former career officers, although the actual percentage is probably higher, due to incomplete information. Of these, 39 (46 percent) were graduates of the imperial General Staff Academy, with 11 (13 percent) graduating between 1906 and 1912. In all, 130 men occupied the post of chief of staff in these armies, of which 86 (68 percent) were documented military specialists, although once again complete information is lacking. Of this number, 77 (59 percent) were graduates of the czarist staff academy, although this figure is almost certainly too low. Of these, 22 (17 percent) came from the 1906–12 classes.[43] In all, 182 men held one or both posts, of which 89 (49 percent) were former career officers. Of these, 89 (49 percent) had graduated from the old General Staff Academy, with 25 (14 percent) having completed the academy course during 1906–12.

These figures constitute overwhelming proof of the military specialists' decisive contribution to the planning and conduct of the Red Army's operations during the civil war. This is hardly to be wondered at, as the influence of the former czarist officers could only have been profound, given the army's primitive state during these years. This circumstance made it relatively easy to graft the czarist army's theory and practice of conducting operations upon the tabula rasa of the Red Army, which did not suffer from the weight of the past. In fact, it was this very combination of messianic revolutionary enthusiasm, tempered by the positive aspects of the old Russian military tradition and the peculiar conditions of the civil war, that created the conditions for a specifically Soviet approach to operations.

As to the larger question of the specialists' contribution to the Reds' ultimate victory, such judgments often have as much to do with the observer's political loyalties as anything else. For example, two Soviet historians have gone so far as to claim that the military specialists "were never the leading force of our command cadres, and did not play a decisive role" in defeating the Whites.[44] The opposing view, not surprisingly, was held by the White general Denikin, who, while he considered the specialists traitors to their country and class, nevertheless believed that the "Red Army was built exclusively by the brains and experience of the 'old czarist generals.'"[45] However, even Lenin, who certainly cannot be accused of any favoritism toward these representatives of a hated class, nevertheless believed that the Red Army had been able to win only with the aid of the former officers.[46]

CIVIL WAR OPERATIONS, 1919–20

As a background to the study of operational art, the Russian civil war constitutes an extremely interesting, although highly contradictory, phase in the operation's development. The peculiarities of the conflict, at once grandiose in its immense spatial scope and anachronistically small in the numbers of men and equipment actually engaged, represent a highly eccentric break with the heretofore orderly quantitative development of a number of operational indices. For example, at its greatest length in early 1919 the "front" stretched some 8,000 kilometers, from the Gulf of Finland south along the border with the Baltic States, then southeast across Belorussia and southern Ukraine to the Northern Caucasus, before looping back to the Caspian Sea. The line then moved north through the Volga-Kama basin, before turning to the northwest until it reached the Finnish border north of Petrograd (Leningrad/St. Petersburg). From mid-1918 the fighting centered along two main fronts, which alternated periodically in strategic importance. These were the eastern, generally between the Volga and the Ural Mountains, and the southern, embracing most of Ukraine, the Don River basin, and the northern Caucasus Mountains. During the follow-on war with Poland the front came to include the western districts of Ukraine and Belorussia, to the ethnic border of Poland and beyond. Secondary fronts also existed at various times west of Petrograd, the area south of Archangel and Murmansk, the Trans-Caucasus region, Central Asia, and the Far East. The Soviet forces held the interior of this line, while their enemies, the Whites, operated from the periphery.

The troops available to man this front were hopelessly inadequate to the task, due not only to an objective shortage of manpower but also to the troops' irrational employment. At its peak strength in 1920 the Workers' and Peasants' Red Army (RKKA) numbered 5.5 million men, of which only 700,000 to 800,000 were regular troops and a mere 400,000 to 500,000 were combatants.[47] The White armies, for their part, never totaled more than 640,000 men at best, although they made up somewhat for their inferiority by the high proportion of trained officers in their ranks.[48] In material terms the situation was even worse, and by the end of the civil war the Red Army still possessed only 2,300 artillery pieces, or about as many as were in the German Fifth Army, which attacked along a 15-kilometer front at Verdun in 1916.[49] Rarely in the history of modern warfare have the forces of the warring parties been so minuscule in relation to the stakes involved.

These factors made the maintenance of a continuous defensive front impossible and shifted the advantage decisively in favor of the attacker, who could generally break through the defender's porous line or turn his position by means of a flanking movement. This helped to make the civil war a conflict of exceptionally wide-ranging maneuver, particularly in comparison with the limited movement of the Great War. The scarcity of reserves on both sides made even the slightest breakthrough or turning movement a potential disaster for the defense. Thus while offensives on the western front in 1914–18 could often be measured in hundreds or thousands of meters gained, civil war operations flowed back and forth over hundreds of kilometers and more. For example, during the Red Army's 1919–20 offensive on the eastern front the White forces were driven all the way from the middle Volga to Lake Baikal, a distance of several thousand kilometers.

In brief, the military problem for the Bolsheviks was to break out of their central Russian redoubt and extend their control over the outlying areas of the country. The problem for the anticommunist forces was just the opposite: to pierce the Soviet heartland from one or more of their strongholds and bring down the regime by a march on Moscow. However, both sides were hobbled by a number of serious economic, military, political, and other liabilities. For example, the Whites at one time controlled territory that before the war produced 85 percent of the country's iron ore, 90 percent of the coal, three-quarters of the steel, and almost all of the oil and that housed two-thirds of its military factories.[50] The White forces could also count on significant aid from Western governments, although what direct military intervention there was by the Allies proved to be insufficient. The Whites also possessed greater military expertise at first, although this became less of a factor as the war progressed.

The Bolsheviks, however, were not without their advantages, which ultimately proved decisive. The Reds, although they initially occupied only a fraction of the country's territory, did hold the most populous areas and hence the larger recruiting base. They also enjoyed the inestimable benefit of interior lines, which allowed them to switch forces from one threatened front to another as the situation demanded. During the war 70 percent of the Soviet divisions fought on two or more fronts, with some employed on as many as five.[51] This was in contrast to the Whites, who were never able to establish a continuous front under a single commander in chief and whose offensive operations were consequently uncoordinated. The same was true in the political sphere, where the White effort suffered continuously from factionalism and the inability to articulate a coherent and popular program. This was opposed to the Bolshevik leadership, which combined superior political insight and flexibility of method with utter ruthlessness of execution.

Both sides relied on a small, solid core of ideologically committed volunteers, while the bulk of their forces consisted of reluctant peasant conscripts who were essentially indifferent to the political quarrels involved. Loyalties were particularly weak, and large-scale desertions were common on both sides. Between January 1919 and December 1920 the Red Army tallied 2,846,000 cases of desertion or otherwise absent without leave.[52] The fidelity of most soldiers was ensured by harsh discipline and consistent military success rather than any sort of political allegiance. Indeed, so great was the reluctance to fight in Russia that the Red Army throughout relied heavily on the military skills of former German and Austro-Hungarian prisoners of war who had converted to communism. About 50,000 Hungarians, Czechs, Germans, and other nationalities fought on the Soviet side during these years and accounted for as much as 10 to 11 percent of the Red Army's strength in late 1918.[53] The Whites also had their foreign allies, including former Czech and Slovak prisoners of war, who proved to be some of their most effective soldiers.

Along with the Red Army's numerical growth came a corresponding development of its organs of strategic and operational control. The Bolsheviks' first military body was the Military Revolutionary Committee, created by the Petrograd Soviet of Workers' and Soldiers' Deputies for the purpose of overthrowing the Provisional Government. This organization was followed in rapid succession by the Committee for Military and Naval Affairs, the Council of People's Commissars for Military Affairs, and, finally, the People's Commissariat for Military Affairs in late 1917. General Dukhonin briefly carried out the functions of supreme commander in chief under the Bolsheviks until his removal and murder in November 1917. He was succeeded by the lawyer and professional revolutionary N. V. Krylenko, who held the post until its abolition in early 1918.

By the summer of 1918 the outlines of a more permanent military organization had begun to take shape. At the top stood the Communist Party's Central Committee, although this body played a secondary role to the more powerful Politburo. The party exercised direct control over the war effort through the Council of Workers' and Peasants' Defense, created in November 1918 and renamed the Council of Labor and Defense in April 1920. The Bolshevik leader Lenin headed this body, which served as the prototype of the 1941–45 State Defense Committee under Stalin. Direct control of military operations was exercised through the RVSR, created in September 1918. Trotskii, who was also the people's commissar for military affairs, headed this body. The highest strictly military post in the Red Army was that of commander in chief *(glavnokomanduyushchii,* or *glavkom),* who was at the same time a member of the RVSR and carried out its directives. The first commander in chief was Vatsetis, a Latvian and former czarist colonel, who had graduated from the General Staff Academy in 1909 and occupied the post from its creation in September 1918 until his removal in July 1919, as the result of a policy dispute. He was succeeded by Kamenev, also a former colonel and 1907 academy graduate, who served in the post throughout the remainder of the war. The working organ of the RVSR and the commander in chief was the RVSR Field Staff, created in September 1918 and charged with drawing up strategic plans and transmitting orders to the fronts and independent armies.

The preponderant role of the "military specialists" in the Red Army is the most obvious point of continuity between the czarist regime and its communist successor. Another, but no less significant, link between the two is the enduring front system of command. The front existed in theory as early as 1900 and was already fully developed by the October Revolution. The Bolsheviks, for all their revolutionary ardor in abolishing the old regime's symbols, adopted this organizational expedient without any difficulty, and for many of the same reasons—broad frontages and a multiplicity of enemies.

The Red Army organized its first front, the Eastern, in mid-1918, which was followed over the next several months by the creation of the Northern, Southern, and Ukrainian Fronts, among many others. Civil war fronts, compared with those of the late empire, were quite small and technologically primitive, numbering only about 46,000 to 147,000 men and 245 to 660 artillery pieces. The armies of the period were also pale reflections of their imperial predecessors and contained anywhere from 14,000 to 28,000 men and 72 to 216 guns.[54]

The Eastern Front had its origins in the events of the spring and summer of 1918. Here resistance to Soviet power was based primarily on the Czechoslovak Corps, which had been formed from Austro-Hungarian prisoners of war to fight on the Allied side. The Czechoslovaks responded to the Bolsheviks' clumsy attempts to disarm them by seizing the Trans-Siberian Railroad from Vladivostok to the Volga and becoming the backbone of White resistance in Siberia. The latter also included elements of the short-lived Constituent Assembly, which had been dispersed by the Bolsheviks in early 1918, and other groups. In response, the Soviets created the Eastern Front in June and appointed as its first commander Murav'ev, a former lieutenant colonel and member of the Socialist Revolutionary Party. Following Murav'ev's death in an abortive uprising a month later, Vatsetis was appointed to the post.

These events coincided with the Soviets' first major military crisis in the summer of 1918, when the White forces began a broad offensive in the area between the Urals and the Volga. By mid-August the Whites had crossed the river and taken Samara, Simbirsk (Ul'yanovsk), and Kazan', and they threatened to link up with anti-Bolshevik forces advancing from the Don River area. Even more threatening was the possibility of an advance through Nizhnii Novgorod to Moscow. The Soviets recovered, however, and in a six-month series of offensive operations (September 1918–February 1919) threw the Whites back nearly to the Urals and restored communications with Soviet authorities in Central Asia. The Red Army's position was now better than it had been for some time, although new trials were not long in coming.

By early 1919 the White forces in the east had recovered from their defeats of the previous autumn and were once again ready to resume the advance on Moscow. This time they were led by Admiral A. V. Kolchak, who had seized control of the anti-Bolshevik movement in Siberia from more democratic elements the previous November. By the beginning of the offensive in early March, Kolchak's forces numbered some 113,000 men and more than 200 guns against 111,000 Red troops and 379 guns.[55] The White forces were organized into the Siberian and Western Armies in the north and the "Southern Army Group," Orenburg and Ural'sk Armies in the south. Opposed to them were the Soviet troops of the Eastern Front under Kamenev, who had replaced Vatsetis in September 1918 when the latter was called to Moscow to take up the newly created post of commander in chief. The Soviet armies were divided from north to south into the Third, Second, Fifth, Turkestan, First, and Fourth Armies. These forces occupied an 1,800-kilometer front that stretched from the forests north of Perm' to the Caspian Sea.

The White advance began on March 4 (see map 5) along a broad front from Perm' to Orsk, with the main effort concentrated along a 450-kilometer front from Perm' to Ufa. The Whites apparently were seeking to link up with allied forces near Kotlas and in the Kuban' region, which, if correct, represented a dangerous dispersion of scarce manpower. Nevertheless, this assault was initially successful against the scattered Soviet forces in the area, which had been neglected in favor of the armies currently fighting in Ukraine. Ufa fell on March 14, while to the south Kolchak's forces severed the tenuous Soviet link with Central Asia and threatened to cut off the Red garrisons at Orenburg and Ural'sk. The danger was particularly great in the center, where Gen. M. V. Khanzhin's Western Army was pressing Tukhachevskii's Fifth Army back to the Volga south of the Kama River. By mid-April Kolchak's forces had succeeded in opening a large gap between Tukhachevskii and the neighboring Second Army and threatened to break through to the river in the direction of Simbirsk and Samara.

Once the scale of the White advance became apparent, the Soviets quickly set about preparing a counterattack. Glavkom Vatsetis first broached this idea in a message to Kamenev on April 2, suggesting that the front gather a "strike fist" against the White forces advancing from Ufa.[56] A meeting between Trotskii, Vatsetis, and Kamenev on April 10 adopted and developed this idea further and

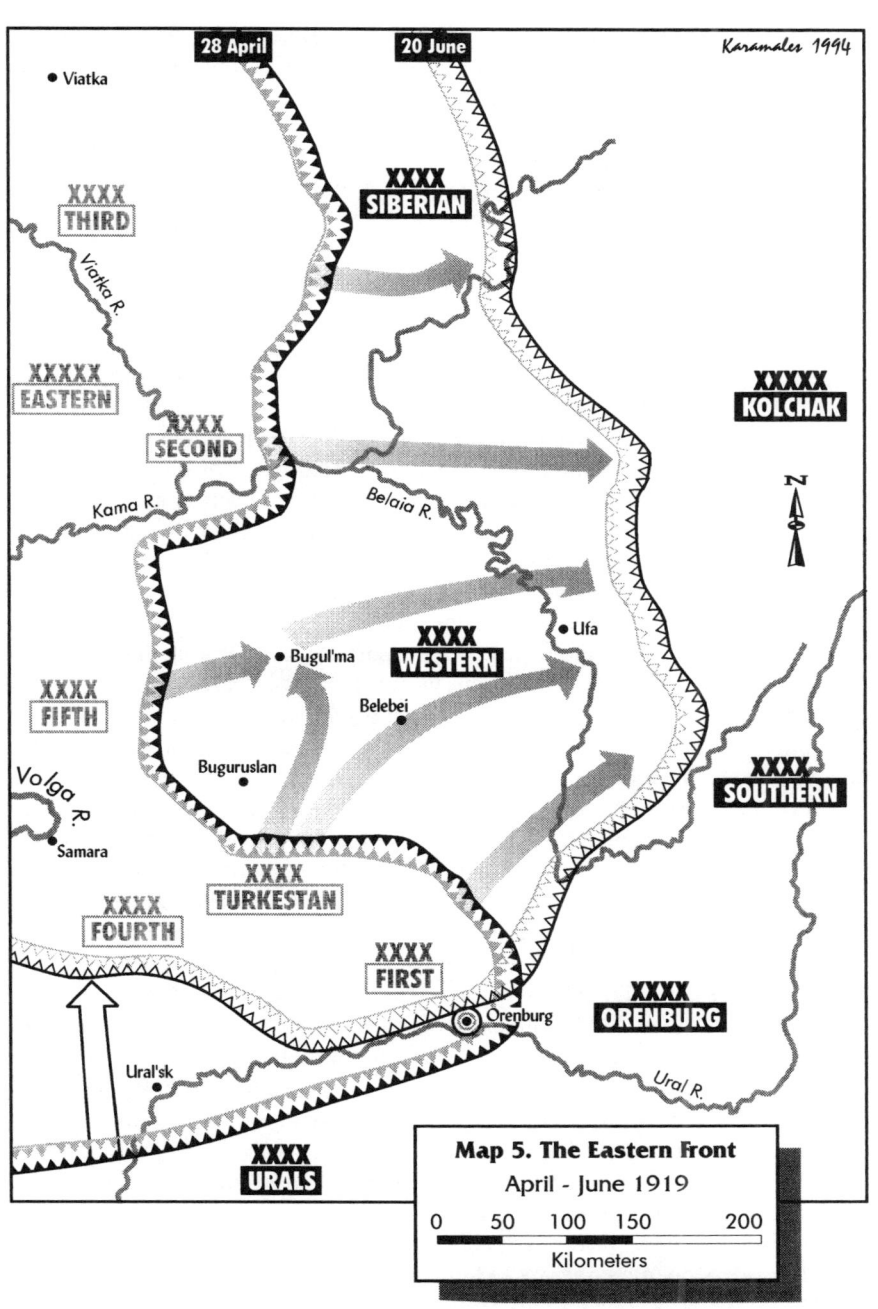

made a number of important organizational changes as well. The most visible response was to split the Eastern Front into two semi-independent groups for greater ease of control: the Southern (Fourth, First, Turkestan, and Fifth Armies), which incorporated Soviet forces south of the Kama, commanded by Frunze, and the Northern (Second and Third Armies), which included those forces north of the river, under the former czarist colonel V. I. Shorin. That same day Kamenev ordered Frunze to strengthen the Fifth Army and gather forces in the Buzuluk area, between Samara and Orenburg, for a counterattack.[57]

The energetic Frunze, together with his chief of staff, the former czarist major general and 1895 General Staff Academy graduate F. F. Novitskii, immediately set about drawing up plans for a counterstroke against the exposed southern flank of Khanzhin's widely scattered forces, which were nonetheless pressing inexorably toward the Volga. His initial plan foresaw the creation of a powerful infantry-cavalry strike force to attack the enemy's left flank and push him back to the north. However, numerous transport difficulties slowed the concentration of this force, and the necessity of shoring up Tukhachevskii's collapsing army soon forced Frunze to send part of his planned strike force north to reinforce the Fifth Army's left wing. Frunze, in a message to Kamenev before the start of the counteroffensive, outlined the operation's goals, which included launching a concentrated attack between the widely separated 3d and 6th Corps in the Buguruslan-Zaglyadino area, "for the purpose of separating these corps and routing them in detail."[58] To compensate for the loss of part of his strike force, Frunze directed Fifth Army to attack toward Buguruslan and Bugul'ma, while at the same time units of the First Army's left flank would pin down enemy forces and cover the advance from the right.

Frunze resorted to a good deal of internal regrouping to create his striking force. His final arrangements for the offensive are an excellent example of employing the maximum concentration of force at the point of decision, even given the watered-down version that he was forced to adopt. Of the approximately 70,000 troops under his command at the end of April, Frunze managed to concentrate for the attack 36,620 men and 152 guns along a 200- to 220-kilometer front against the two White corps' 7,400 men. The remainder of the Southern Group's front, stretching more than 700 kilometers, was manned by a mere 33,200 troops and 152 guns.[59] Thus by late April the Soviets, by ruthlessly scraping together men and matériel from the less active sectors, were able to achieve a hefty superiority over Khanzhin's army, which due to a combination of desertions and combat losses had shrunk to between 18,000 and 22,000 men.[60]

Frunze was so concerned by the Whites' continued progress against Tukhachevskii's left flank in the Sergievsk-Chistopol' area that he ordered his strike group to attack on April 28, before it had fully concentrated. Nevertheless, the offensive's opening phase was highly successful, as the Soviet units flowed easily into the 60-kilometer gap between the White corps, which was screened only by detachments. Resistance was therefore minimal at first, and by April 30 leading units of the Fifth Army had cut the Ufa-Samara railroad east of Buguruslan and were poised to continue the drive to the northwest in the direction of Belebei. Meanwhile, unmindful of the threat to his left, Khanzhin pressed on to Samara, which was practically undefended. The continuation of this advance would have soon put the Whites in the strike group's rear, even as the latter strove to cut them off from Ufa. Kamenev therefore ordered Frunze to shift the axis of the advance from the northeast to the north (Turkestan Army) and northwest (Fifth Army), in the general direction of Bugul'ma.[61] At a single stroke Frunze's deep flanking movement was reduced to an attempt at a shallow envelopment of the leading White units, while the attack's former spearhead, the Turkestan Army, became, in effect, the flank guard for Fifth Army's right wing.

Frunze's understandable irritation with his superiors' interference undoubtedly increased, due to personnel changes in the Eastern Front command caused by political intrigues in Moscow. On May 5 Kamenev was replaced by Samoilo, a czarist major general. Lebedev, also a former major general, became his chief of staff. Samoilo's first order of business upon arriving at front headquarters in Simbirsk was to remove the Fifth Army from Frunze's control and subordinate it directly to himself. This caused Tukhachevskii to later claim that Samoilo's interference "completely ruined the brilliant beginning of our counteroffensive and allowed the Whites to put their retreat in order."[62] Samoilo later stated that he had never wanted the job, which took him away from his command of the Sixth Army south of Archangel. He also accused S. I. Gusev, the leading member of the front's military council, Kamenev, and Tukhachevskii of conspiring against him.[63]

The second half of the Buguruslan operation saw considerable heavy fighting as the Soviets continued to press the Whites from the south, southwest, and west. Khanzhin correctly guessed the Soviets' intention to cut him off west of Bugul'ma and began to withdraw his troops through the town before the Reds could close the trap. To keep their lifeline open, the Whites made a number of spirited counterattacks north of Buguruslan in early May. The Soviets successfully fended these off but were delayed just long enough to enable the Whites to extricate their troops through Bugul'ma ahead of the Fifth Army. With the town's fall on May 13 the operation ended.

The ensuing Belebei operation (May 15–19) was the missing second half of Frunze's original plan for a drive to the northeast, which had been aborted by Kamenev's reorienting the strike group toward Buguruslan. The shallow and inconclusive movement that resulted made an advance on Belebei the logical next step in the unfolding Soviet counteroffensive toward Ufa. Indeed, the first clashes preceding the counteroffensive's next phase were already taking place north and west of the town even as the Buguruslan operation was drawing to a close.

However, Frunze's plan for reviving the advance to the northeast was very nearly upset by Samoilo's concern over the continuing White advance north of the Kama River. Here, the Czech Siberian Army, led by Gen. Lt. R. Gajda, was slowly pushing back the Soviet Second and Third Armies on Vyatka (Kirov) and

Kazan'. At this point the front commander began to entertain the vague notion of switching Tukhachevskii's army northward across the Kama against the enemy left flank. Orders to this effect were issued several times in mid-May, orienting the Fifth Army first one way, then another.[64] Frunze, who quickly saw that the diversion of the now-powerful Fifth Army away from the Belebei-Ufa axis would leave his remaining forces too weak for further offensive operations, took his case directly to Samoilo. In a heated exchange with the front commander on May 12, Frunze insisted on a deep turning movement by Fifth Army to cut off the enemy's retreat to the east. And although Frunze failed to reassert his control over Fifth Army, he did convince Samoilo to allot him two divisions to continue the attack.[65]

Frunze's plan aimed at the destruction of the White troops barring the way to Ufa. Due to the fighting for Buguruslan and Bugul'ma and the removal of Fifth Army from Frunze's control, most of what remained of the original striking force now lay along the Ik River on the Southern Group's extreme left. Frunze accordingly ordered the First and Turkestan Armies to move northeast along the Ufa-Samara railroad to pin down the enemy forces south of Belebei, while a mixed infantry-cavalry force was to attack north of the city "for a deep envelopment in order to cut the enemy off from his communications with Ufa."[66]

The Soviets moved out on May 15. They advanced slowly, however, although speed was essential if the railway was to be cut ahead of the retreating enemy. The White units slowly fell back on Belebei, and Soviet troops entered the town on the seventeenth. Farther north, Red units closed on the town from the west, although too slowly to block the Whites' retreat. Although Frunze had pushed the Whites back some distance during the short offensive, the Belebei operation must be regarded as a distinct disappointment for the Soviets. Once again, the Whites had slipped away and still barred the road to Ufa, although they were showing signs of tiring of the fight.

Undaunted, Frunze pressed his offensive and once again singled out the Turkestan Army to make the main assault. Cavalry and infantry would spearhead the latest effort, designed to push the Whites northeast across the Belaya River. Once across this formidable barrier south of Ufa, elements of Frunze's forces would move directly on Ufa from the south, while the movement's flanks would be covered by other units advancing on Birsk and Sterlitamak. For the operation, Frunze could count on only an equality of force of 49,000 men and 92 guns in his two attacking armies (Fifth and Turkestan) against Khanzhin's force of 46,000 to 47,000 men and 119 guns.[67] However, defeatism was spreading rapidly within the White ranks, and some units were already showing an alarming tendency to "turn their coats" when pressed.

Once the operation got under way on May 25, the Turkestan Army, subordinated for the duration directly to Frunze, had little trouble in achieving its preliminary objective of closing to the Belaya along the entire front, as the Whites elected to fall back and make a stand along the river. Farther to the north there was heavy fighting along Fifth Army's front, where the Whites suffered substantial losses in a vain attempt to halt the Soviet advance. This victory had important consequences for the Ufa operation by eliminating a potential threat to Frunze's left and allowing him to move up infantry reserves to assist the crossing south of Ufa. By the time the Turkestan Army closed to the river in early June, strong forces were available for crossings north and south of the city.

South of Ufa, heavy White artillery fire and the river's swift current foiled the southern wing's initial attempts to cross. The Soviets were more fortunate farther north, where as early as June 4 rifle units were able to secure a bridgehead below the city. By June 8 Frunze had ferried an entire division to the eastern bank in an improvised crossing, as further Red attempts to force the river south of Ufa were beaten back. The White command was alive to the danger that the northern crossing represented and launched repeated and bloody counterattacks against the Soviet bridgehead over the next two days. These attacks, however, led only to heavy casualties on both sides and an overall weakening of the White defense. The Soviets finally broke out of their bridgehead on June 9 and captured Ufa the same day. Meanwhile, Soviet cavalry and infantry units persisted in their efforts to cross the river south of the city, succeeding only on June 14. Red units continued to push to about 50 kilometers east of Ufa, where a shortage of troops and supply difficulties forced Frunze to call a brief halt in operations.

The fall of Ufa was the occasion for a good deal of high-level debate about the front's scope of future operations. Vatsetis, supported by Trotskii, wanted to halt the front's advance short of the Urals and throw the bulk of its forces south, in response to the worsening situation in Ukraine. Kamenev, who had been reappointed commander of the Eastern Front at the end of May, insisted on a continuation of the offensive. Both sides appealed to their political patrons for support. The party's Central Committee ultimately decided in favor of the front apparatus, and the advance continued. Trotskii offered to resign, but this move was rejected. His protégé, Vatsetis, did resign and was replaced as commander in chief by Kamenev in July.

Following the capture of Ufa, the Eastern Front's story is quickly told, as the Soviets resumed their advance in June against Kolchak's disintegrating armies. Operations in June and August cleared the important Urals industrial region of White forces and set the stage for the conquest of Siberia. The next series of operations (August 1919–January 1920) completed the destruction of the White armies and brought the Soviets as far east as Lake Baikal, where they were halted by the presence of foreign troops. Although more than two years of fighting remained before Soviet troops actually reached Vladivostok, the events of 1919 effectively ensured the triumph of Soviet power in Siberia and the Far East.

The civil war's other main front, the southern, had its beginnings on the morrow of the Bolshevik coup. Here the Reds scored their first military victories by defeating General Kaledin's Cossack forces and driving General Kornilov's newly created Volunteer Army back to the area of the Kuban' River. The Red Army, however, soon faced a new and more serious threat from Germany. The

Germans, following the Treaty of Brest-Litovsk, proceeded to occupy all of Ukraine and by May had advanced as far as Rostov. The Germans also began supporting General Krasnov's Don Army, which during 1918–19 made three unsuccessful attempts to take Tsaritsyn and advance up the Volga for a junction with the White Siberian armies.

The German collapse in November 1918 strengthened the Soviet position considerably, and the Red Army moved in to fill the vacuum left by the kaiser's retreating forces. By early 1919 the Soviets had reoccupied almost all of Ukraine, and the Don Army, deprived of German aid, quickly collapsed and was soon subordinated to the Volunteer Army, now commanded by General Denikin. In early 1919 Denikin reorganized his forces into the Armed Forces of South Russia, which included the Volunteer, Don, and, later, Gen. P. N. Wrangel's Caucasus Army. This force was based primarily on the Cossack populations of the lower Don and Northern Caucasus and those officers who had managed to make their way south following the Bolshevik coup. Also, thanks to Denikin's consistently pro-Allied orientation, the White armies here could count on Western aid, which began to arrive in increasing amounts through the reopened Turkish Straits.

The Soviets were indeed fortunate that the time of greatest danger in the east coincided with a period of relative calm in the south. Here Denikin's forces began to move in strength only in May 1919, after the tide had turned against Kolchak, although the Reds were still preoccupied by the situation along the Volga. The White advance was also greatly aided by large-scale Cossack uprisings in the Soviet rear along the middle Don. Denikin's forces successively defeated the qualitatively inferior Soviets north and east of Rostov and by early summer had taken Tsaritsyn and Khar'kov before turning west. The Whites soon captured Kiev and most of right-bank Ukraine before they turned north to resume the advance on Moscow. By early autumn the White armies were deployed along a huge arc, stretching east from Zhitomir through Chernigov, Orel, Voronezh, Tsaritsyn, and Astrakhan'. Elsewhere Polish troops menaced the Soviets in Belorussia, while farther north Gen. N. N. Yudenich advanced for the second time on Petrograd from his Estonian base.

However, much as Kolchak, Denikin's forces rested on an extremely weak political-military base, which collapsed almost immediately upon the first serious reverses. In the early autumn Denikin claimed to have had only 98,000 troops to man his 1,800-kilometer front against a Bolshevik force that he estimated at between 140,000 and 160,000 men.[68] Nor were Denikin's forces of a uniformly high quality. The summer's rapid advance had carried the Whites far from their anticommunist base and had entailed the drafting of large numbers of reluctant Russian and Ukrainian peasants. This diluted the army's strong officer base and led to an overall decline in the Whites' military efficiency, heretofore their strongest suit. Finally, Denikin's forces were greatly hampered by bands of semi-anarchist peasants in their rear under N. I. Makhno, who hated the Whites even more than the Reds, although he played both sides against the other. At the height of the October fighting, Makhno's forces numbered 28,000 infantry and cavalry, supported by 50 guns and 200 machine guns, and even briefly threatened Denikin's headquarters at Taganrog.[69] The necessity of dealing with this and other internal threats forced the White command to divert significant numbers of men from the front at critical moments and so helped pave the way for their ultimate defeat.

On September 13 the Soviet high command, in response to the rapid White advance, split off from the Southern Front the Ninth, Tenth, and Eleventh Armies to form the Southeastern Front, under Shorin, to man the line south of Voronezh. What remained of the Southern Front (Eighth, Thirteenth, and Fourteenth Armies, joined by the Twelfth Army from the Western Front in mid-October) continued under the command of former general lieutenant V. N. Yegor'ev. However, this reorganization was not actually effected until September 30, by which time the situation had changed considerably. Kursk had fallen to Denikin's forces on September 20, and it was now the White advance along the Orel-Tula axis (see map 6) that presented the greatest danger to the Soviet Republic. Here, what one participant described as the "threatening proportions of a strategic catastrophe" forced the Soviet command to shift its attention to the area immediately south of Moscow.[70]

The Soviets commendably resolved to halt Denikin's advance on Orel by launching an attack of their own. To this purpose, in late September Glavkom Kamenev ordered the concentration southeast of Bryansk of 10,000 infantry, 1,500 cavalry, and 80 guns, which was to form the core of the Soviet counterattack.[71] In an October 9 directive to his army commanders, deputy front commander Yegorov, a former czarist colonel, outlined the plan for the coming counteroffensive. The strike group, under the command of former general A. A. Martusevich, was to advance from the Kromy area and strike at Denikin's communications along the Orel-Kursk railroad in the general direction of Maloarkhangel'sk and Fatezh. The Thirteenth and Fourteenth Armies were to halt their withdrawal and support the strike group by pinning down what forces they could.[72]

The Soviet response to this latest crisis was as rapid and decisive as it had been on the eastern front. With the proclamation of the southern front as the main area of operations in early July, the Bolshevik military machine swung into action. The steady influx of men that this designation brought in its wake enabled the Soviets to bring the Southern Front up to a strength of 113,439 infantry, 27,328 cavalry, and 774 guns by the start of the operation, against a White force of 58,650 infantry, 48,200 cavalry, and 431 guns. In the center, however, the opposing forces were essentially equal. Here the Whites managed to concentrate 45,200 infantry and 13,900 cavalry, supported by 200 guns, against a Red force (Fourteenth, Thirteenth, and Eighth Armies) of 55,630 infantry, 1,820 cavalry, and 412 guns.[73]

Meanwhile, some 250 kilometers southeast of Orel, events were also reaching a crisis for the beleaguered Red forces. Here Gen. V. I. Sidorin's Don Army was pressing the Soviets back in the Voronezh area and had opened a 130-kilometer gap north of the city between the Thirteenth and Eighth Armies, which threat-

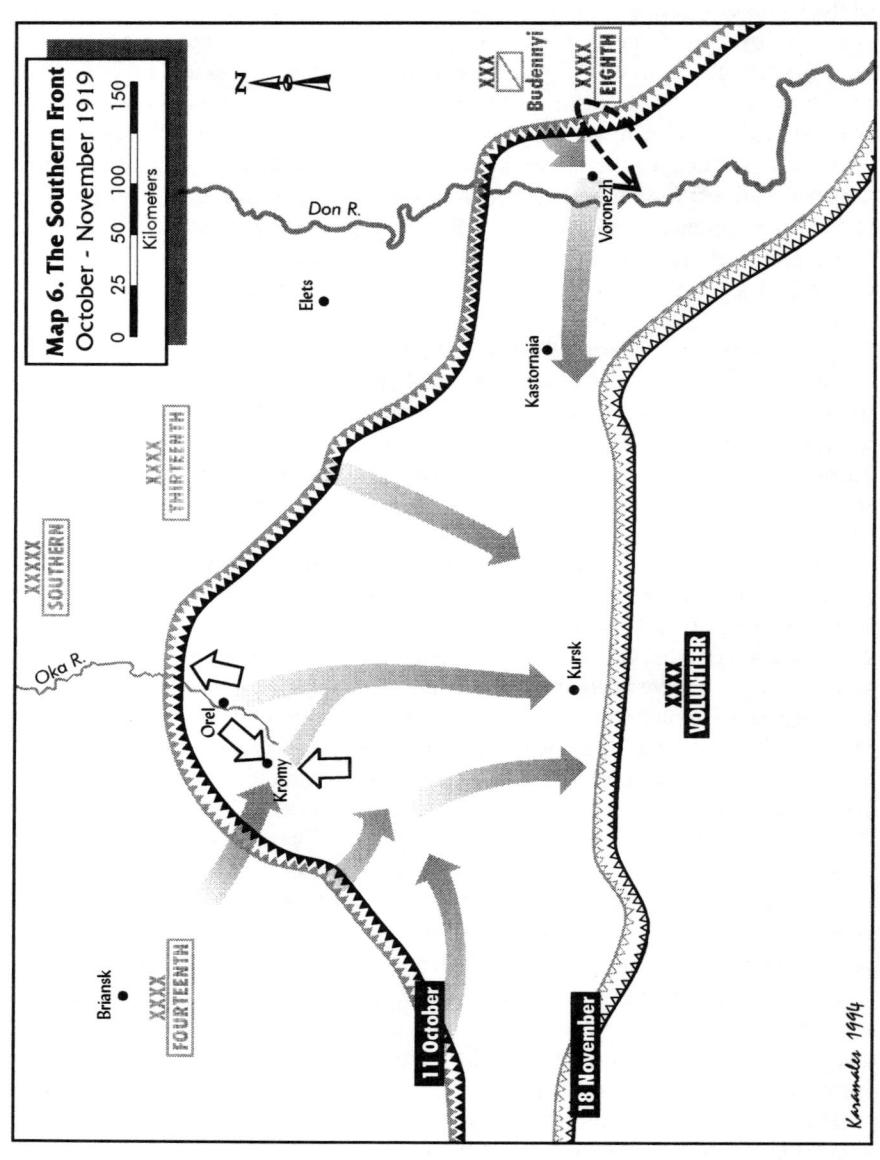

ened to split the Southern from the Southeastern Front and unhinge the entire Soviet position in the south. Kamenev, to forestall a disaster, ordered Budennyi's cavalry corps northward from the middle Don to shore up the front in the area of Voronezh, which had fallen on October 6. However, at this early stage in the operation's planning there was no attempt to link the Orel counteroffensive with events to the southeast, and from the very first the situation around Voronezh was of secondary importance in Soviet calculations.

The Soviet counteroffensive in the Orel area opened on October 11 in an extremely fluid situation that saw both sides advancing and withdrawing simultaneously. So lightly manned were the White lines west of Kromy that the initial assault hit only air and did not even encounter the enemy in strength until the next day. Nevertheless, the Soviets moved forward slowly and succeeded in taking Kromy only on the fourteenth. The group's plodding advance was due not only to stubborn White resistance but also to Martusevich's justified fear for his lengthening flanks, as he followed with growing concern the retreat of the Red infantry units on either side. These and other Soviet units were literally fighting for their lives as the White forces maintained the pressure, seemingly indifferent to the Soviet attack. The situation was even more critical to the northeast, where the Whites took Orel on the thirteenth, tearing a dangerous gap between the Thirteenth and Fourteenth Armies and opening the way to the military-industrial center of Tula.

For the strike group to have continued to advance in the original direction would have meant putting its head farther into the noose. Yegorov, recently appointed front commander, reacted to this new threat by changing the axis of the group's advance and orienting it due east toward Eropkino station to threaten the White communications and attack toward Orel from the southwest.[74] The primacy of Orel in the developing situation was reemphasized on October 17, when Yegorov ordered the newly arrived Estonian Rifle Division into the attack directly on the city.[75] Yegorov regretted having to make this change in plans but defended his decision by maintaining that to have continued to push the front's spearhead in the original direction "would have led to catastrophic results."[76]

Actually, very little now remained of the original plan for a deep strike against the White communications. Instead, the two exhausted armies continued to batter at each other in what had become an extended meeting operation along the entire front, and the strike group's efforts differed little from any of the other headlong collisions now taking place. The Whites continued to advance to the east of Orel and captured Novosil' on October 17. But the Soviet advantage in numbers was beginning to tell, and the Reds recaptured the town two days later. The Whites, by now beset on three sides, also abandoned Orel on October 20, although they continued to attack in the Kromy area.

While the fate of the Orel counteroffensive hung in the balance, Yegorov harried his left-wing units (Eighth Army and Budennyi's corps) to speed up their attack toward Voronezh. However, the Soviet units in this area seemed in no hurry to move and limited themselves to some heavy sparring with the White cavalry east and southeast of Voronezh. Yegorov's orders on October 18 were more detailed and for the first time implied a connection between the activities of his left wing and center. The front commander ordered Budennyi to defeat the enemy in the Voronezh area and to cover Eighth Army's advance across the Don. The cavalry was then to advance on Kastornaya and Kursk, which would put the Soviets in the rear of the Volunteer Army engaged around Orel and threaten it with the loss of its communications to the south.[77]

The skirmishing east of Voronezh climaxed on October 19, when the White cavalry struck Timoshenko's cavalry division, and the melee quickly expanded into a major encounter as units from both sides were fed into the fighting. The Whites were ultimately defeated in the brisk, close-quarters battle, and they withdrew into Voronezh. The Soviets failed in their attempts to take Voronezh on the march. They then brought up their forces for a coordinated assault and began their attack on the city on the twenty-third: the cavalry corps from the east and north, with the Soviet infantry attacking from the southeast. The Whites, to avoid encirclement, abandoned the city and took up defensive positions across the Don. Two days later the Eighth Army's left-flank units took Liski to the south.

Yegorov, with the initiative in the Orel area now in his hands, hurried his armies forward. His order of October 20 reoriented the axis of the spearhead's advance away from Orel and toward Fatezh and Kursk, while the remainder of Fourteenth Army was to continue its attack toward Dmitrovsk and Dmitriev, and Thirteenth Army moved south on Livny and Kastornaya.[78] Once again, however, the Soviet attacks became snarled in a series of costly frontal engagements all along the line. The lumbering Soviet style of attack did involve, however, an attrition that the Reds could afford far better than the Whites, whose meager resources were already stretched to the breaking point. Nevertheless, for the time being the Whites stubbornly answered each Soviet attack with an assault of their own during the seesaw fighting that characterized the next two weeks. Denikin's units, continually pressed by superior forces, gradually began to give ground.

As the fighting around Orel swayed first one way and then another, the Soviet command began to look more and more to Budennyi's corps to tip the scales. This was particularly true of the Novosil'-Elets area, where a White breakthrough toward Lipetsk and Tambov appeared imminent. Budennyi began crossing the Don on October 28 north of Voronezh and in the first days of November fought off numerous attacks in the Zemlyansk area. Here the Soviet cavalry was able to link up with the Thirteenth Army advancing south and close the gap in their line. By November 8 both units had closed to Kastornaya from north and east. The Whites could ill afford to lose this vital rail junction, which provided the most direct communications route between the Don and Volunteer Armies. Throughout the following week the Red and White cavalry traded blows in the surrounding villages, each side first advancing, then retreating.

The weight of numbers was decisive here as well, and Budennyi was able to maneuver southeast of the rail junction and drive a wedge between two White cavalry corps. Soviet cavalry finally took Kastornaya on November 15. With the town's fall the operation came to a close, with the Soviets well placed to continue the drive south. Although the Voronezh-Kastornaya operation had always occupied a secondary place in Soviet calculations, its importance had nevertheless increased as the counteroffensive around Orel faltered. No less an authority than Denikin credited the Soviet offensive out of Voronezh with forcing him to abandon Orel.[79]

Time was also running out for the White cause in the Orel area, where the Volunteer Army continued to fall back before spirited, if inept, Soviet attacks. The Whites tried to organize a defense in the Dmitrovsk-Eropkino area, but Soviet infantry broke through on the morning of November 3. Red cavalry surged into the breach and advanced to cut the Orel-Kursk railway at Ponyri the next day, while another unit raided as far south as Fatezh. The disorganization that these incursions caused in the White rear only served to speed up the defenders' collapse. Sevsk fell on the sixth, as the White front began to buckle. Dmitriev finally fell to the Reds on November 13, and another cavalry raid on Lgov captured that town on the seventeenth, cutting this vital east-west rail link. With the fall of Kursk the same day the operation came to an end.

In contrast to the rapid Soviet advance in the east, more than a month of heavy fighting during the Orel-Kursk (October 11–November 18) and Voronezh-Kastornaya (October 13–November 16) operations had thrown back the outnumbered Whites no more than 160 kilometers. Nevertheless, the two operations had brought about a complete reversal of military fortunes in favor of the Red Army. In the south the Soviets moved swiftly to realize their strategy of destroying Denikin by driving a wedge between the Volunteer and Don Armies and splitting the White forces in two against the Sea of Azov. An undertaking of this magnitude involved for the first time the cooperation of the Southern and Southeastern Fronts, making necessary their coordination by the commander in chief in what was a strategic operation by later Soviet standards. The Soviets cleared the eastern Ukraine and the middle Don of White forces in November and December and later that month captured the vital Donbass industrial region. The Soviet armies captured Rostov in January 1920, which irreparably split the White armies into eastern and western halves. A number of operations remained to be conducted before Soviet power was finally established in the south, notably in the Kuban' River area, the North Caucasus, and southwestern Ukraine, all in the face of military exhaustion and a typhus epidemic that ravaged both sides equally.[80] With the lone exception of the Whites' Crimean stronghold, by the spring of 1920 the war in the south was over.

Following the end of the Soviets' war with Poland, the last hope of the faltering White cause lay in the Crimea, where the shattered remnants of the Volunteer Army maintained a small bastion against the Red forces. Here Wrangel had succeeded Denikin in command of the remaining anticommunist forces in early 1920. Although Wrangel's rechristened "Russian Army" (First and Second Armies) was pitifully small, he was able to take advantage of the Red Army's preoccupation with the Poles to move successfully against the weak Thirteenth Army in June (see map 7). This offensive soon reached the line of the lower Dnepr but was halted. Likewise, an attempt to reestablish a front across the Kerch peninsula in the Kuban' region collapsed in early September, following a month's fighting. Still, by early September Wrangel was in a position to threaten Ekaterinoslav (Dnepropetrovsk) and the Donbass industrial area. However, spirited White attempts to take these areas were beaten back, and by early October Wrangel had been forced to retreat to a shorter line.

The Soviet high command responded to this latest challenge by reconstituting the Southern Front on September 21. This force initially included the Sixth and Thirteenth Armies, as well as the newly created Second Cavalry Army. This force was later augmented by the formation of a new Fourth Army and the arrival of Budennyi's First Cavalry Army from the Polish front in late October. Frunze, newly arrived from the Turkestan Front, was appointed commander. As long as the situation with Poland remained uncertain, Frunze remained on the defensive, content to repel White forays and build up his own forces. He fretted over the latter's slow arrival, fearing that Wrangel might foil his planned counteroffensive by withdrawing his forces into the security of the Crimean peninsula. By the end of October Frunze could count on a heavy numerical and technical superiority of 99,500 infantry, 33,685 cavalry, and 527 guns against a meager White force of only 23,070 infantry, 11,795 cavalry, and 213 guns.[81]

Frunze's October 26 directive described the goal of the operation as destroying the enemy's "main forces by a coordinated, concentric offensive" so as to cut off his retreat back into the peninsula. According to this plan, the Fourth and Thirteenth Armies would attack to the southwest, with the latter breaching the Melitopol' fortifications and pursuing the enemy with its cavalry. While this force occupied the defenders' attention, the main blow would come farther west, along the Dnepr. F. K. Mironov's Second Cavalry Army would attack due south out of its Nikopol' bridgehead toward Seragozy to "surround and destroy the enemy's main forces," which Wrangel had concentrated against the Soviets' Kakhovka bridgehead. Meanwhile, the Sixth Army would force its way out of the bridgehead and head south to cut off the Whites' retreat through the Perekop Isthmus. The army, at the same time, would open a path for the First Cavalry Army to drive to the east. The Soviet cavalry was to pour into the breach made by the infantry and, having advanced as far as Aksaniya-Nova, would then turn north with its main forces toward Seragozy to link up with the Second Cavalry Army to cut off the White forces in the area. Budennyi was also instructed to detach a small force to cut the railroad leading from Melitopol' into the peninsula through Sal'kovo.[82]

The evolution of Frunze's plan is noteworthy for what it reveals about the styles of individual commanders. Budennyi and his commissar, Voroshilov, had

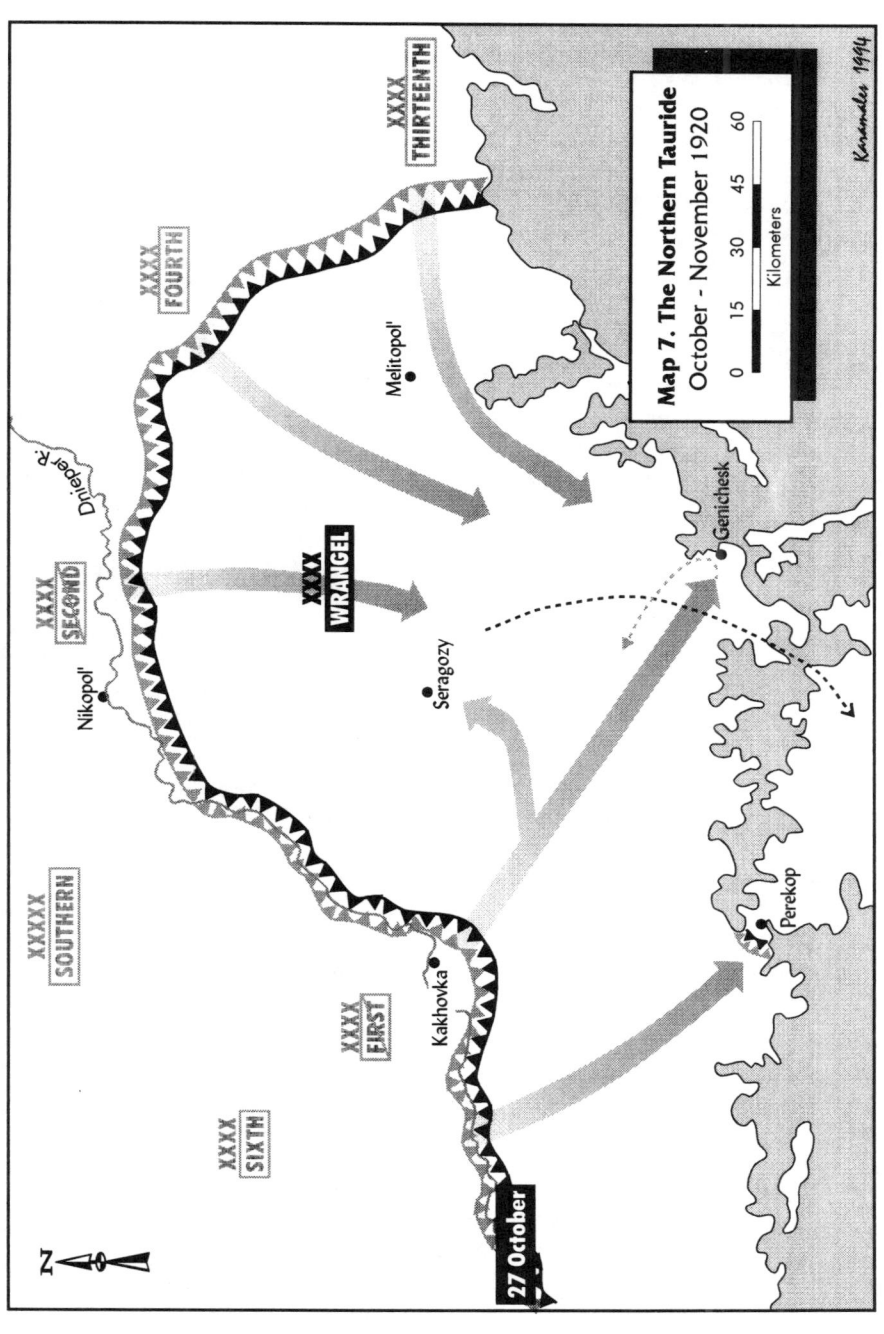

proposed that the First Cavalry Army deliver the main blow by driving due southeast to the Sal'kovo area to cut off the Whites' path of retreat into the Crimea. However, both Frunze and Kamenev rejected this proposal, probably on the grounds that it was too risky.[83] Frunze, for his part, suggested in mid-October moving the Second Cavalry Army south to the Kakhovka bridgehead to concentrate the bulk of the front's cavalry at a single point. Kamenev rejected this proposal as well, citing the problems of controlling such a large force.[84] The commander in chief's caution on both counts was probably due to a lingering respect for the Whites' abilities, even at this late stage. He was probably also reluctant to take any unnecessary chances while the peace negotiations with Poland were still in progress.

The most striking feature of the final Soviet plan was its multiplicity of objectives, even taking into account the Soviets' crushing superiority. Frunze, by leaving the Second Cavalry Army in the Nikopol' area, effectively divided the Soviets' most powerful strike arm into nonsupporting halves. Furthermore, the plan incorporated some elements of the First Cavalry Army's proposal for a dash across the base of the Northern Tauride, while denying it the necessary means to accomplish its goal. This meant that the Soviets would ultimately find themselves with insufficient forces at the battle's crisis.

Still, given the numbers involved and the unfavorable configuration of the Whites' 350-kilometer front, there could be little doubt about the final outcome when the Soviet offensive began on October 28. The fighting had actually begun two days before with the Second Cavalry Army's attack out of its Nikopol' bridgehead, although progress in this sector was limited at first. The Reds had greater success to the east, where the Whites methodically pulled back and the Fourth and Thirteenth Armies advanced as far as Balki and Bol'shoi Tokmak. Elsewhere, part of Sixth Army made good progress toward Perekop. Budennyi's army, arriving late and tired, was unable to advance much beyond Sixth Army's forward units in the Kakhovka area.

However, the first day's mixed success did nothing to dampen Frunze's enthusiasm. In fact, so impressed was the front commander by erroneous reports of Second Cavalry Army's progress south of Nikopol' that he radically altered his operational plan. On October 29 he ordered Budennyi to extend his attack to Sal'kovo and Genichesk (the latter on the Sea of Azov), which would cut off the Whites' escape route into the Crimean peninsula.[85] However, he failed to allocate additional forces for this new task, while the original goal of trapping the White forces around Seragozy remained in force. As a result, two cavalry divisions turned northeast toward Seragozy, while the other half of the army pushed southeast to the Azov coast. It was a division of effort that would cost the Reds dearly.

However, all seemed to go well at first, as Budennyi's cavalry moved almost effortlessly through the undefended White rear. By the evening of October 29 Soviet cavalry had advanced as far east as Novonikolaevka, barely 40 kilometers from the Sea of Azov. To the west, Sixth Army had reached the Black Sea coast and the White defenses athwart the Perekop Isthmus. Units of the First Cavalry Army reached the sea at Genichesk the next day, while to the northeast the Thirteenth Army finally captured Melitopol' in a disappointingly slow advance. For the moment, it appeared as though the Whites were trapped.

But Wrangel was not yet beaten. His forces facing the Thirteenth, Fourth, and Second Cavalry Armies had managed to break contact with their languid pursuers, which reduced the pressure from that quarter and gained the White commander valuable time to pull his forces south, where the fate of his army was being decided. Wrangel was quick to see the opportunity presented by Budennyi's overextended line in the Sal'kovo-Genichesk area, and he decided to attack in order to pin the Red cavalry against the Sivash, an arm of the Sea of Azov, just north of the peninsula. The White counterattack began on November 1, with particularly fierce fighting north of Sal'kovo. Here half of the First Cavalry Army was fighting virtually alone against an increasing number of White units being funneled through the remaining escape route to the peninsula. The Soviets were forced to abandon their blocking position and fall back to the west to rejoin the main forces. By November 3 the last White forces had passed through the bottleneck and taken up defensive positions covering the approaches to the peninsula. In spite of this incomplete success, the Reds had certainly weakened their opponents and were now poised to finish them off.

Final victory came in the course of the succeeding Perekop-Chongar operation (November 7–17, 1920), which drove the Whites from the Crimea and ended most organized resistance to Soviet rule. With the exception of minor fighting in the Caucasus, Central Asia, and the Far East, the civil war in Russia was over.

The end of hostilities provides a convenient backdrop against which to examine the Red Army's conduct of operations during the civil war. It should be emphasized once again that the civil war represents an extremely eccentric case of the operation's development, according to those operational indices already mentioned: length of front, the forces involved, the duration of operations, and other factors. Whereas on one hand the length of the various fronts increased geometrically, the size of the forces manning them shrunk to the level of the Napoleonic Wars and smaller. As these elements changed vis-à-vis each other, so did the Soviets' conduct of operations.

For example, the Eastern Front's April–May operations were conducted along an extremely broad front (1,800 kilometers) with only a minuscule number of troops (110,000) to man it. The Southern Front in the autumn of 1919 was more fortunate, holding a line approximately 1,000 kilometers in width with some 140,000 men. Continuing this trend, the reconstituted southern front in October 1920 attacked along a 350-kilometer front with a force of 133,000. Along with the increasing density of the front, there was a corresponding increase in the number of cavalry and artillery, which gradually brought the civil war's operational indices into something approximating modernity.

These changing factors had their greatest effect on the Red Army's employment of maneuver. The most signal characteristic in this regard throughout was the Soviets' frequent reliance on flank attacks. Frunze, in the Buguruslan and Ufa operations, would first pin down part of the enemy army with secondary attacks, then break through his front to launch turning movements against the Whites' flanks, aimed at cutting them off from their source of supply. The intermediate Belebei operation chiefly involved frontal attacks in what was essentially the postscript to an altered Buguruslan operation. That these flanking movements often fell short of expectations was primarily due to the Reds' overall insufficiency of force, their low mobility, and the disruptive changes in the Eastern Front's command and organization.

By the autumn of 1919 the situation had grown somewhat more difficult for the attacker, although opportunities for maneuver still existed. The Soviets' main effort during the Orel-Kursk operation was a flank attack aimed at Denikin's communications. Budennyi's flank attack toward Kastornaya was actually more successful, although it was planned as a strictly secondary effort.

However, the two operations also reveal a number of flaws in Soviet execution, particularly during the Orel fighting. While it must be acknowledged that in the Volunteer Army the Soviets faced an opponent of higher quality than Kolchak's ragtag legions, they often frittered away their advantage by ignoring the importance of maneuver. The Red Army displayed its usual skill in massing large numbers of men along the projected attack areas, although the widespread practice of launching frontal assaults all along the front did much to negate the advantage gained. This was particularly true of the front's shock group as it became increasingly drawn into the frontal battles for Orel. Yegorov had to constantly remind his subordinates to refrain from making frontal attacks and instead strike the enemy in the flank and rear with all available forces.[86] These clumsy efforts turned the operation into a grinding slugfest, which was won only through greater Soviet numbers. Later Soviet historians, in referring to the operation as an "attrition struggle," implicitly recognized their own shortcomings.[87]

During the October operation against Wrangel the Soviets again sought a decision based on turning the enemy's flanks, followed by a deep drive into his rear, for the purpose of surrounding his forces and cutting off their retreat. This was to be carried out in the form of a double envelopment by the two cavalry armies and testifies to growing Soviet skill, or at least ambitions. Unfortunately for the Soviets, this otherwise laudable approach was blunted by their failure to adequately reinforce their main strike arm. This was another instance of inadequate means in pursuit of decisive ends, which had led them into disaster in Poland just a few months before.

Essential to the Red Army's increased maneuverability was the growth of its cavalry arm, which flew in the face of much recent experience, in which the cavalry arm's role was sharply curtailed. This was most apparent during World War I and the formation of a continuous front. During that conflict the major belligerents continued to maintain large mounted establishments to exploit a breakthrough that never came. The conditions of the Russian civil war, with its almost nonexistent fronts, for a brief moment restored the cavalry to its former place of glory as the exploiter of success. However, this was not entirely a uniform development, given the laborious task of building the Red Army from scratch and the proletarian army's lack of familiarity with this historically aristocratic arm.

The growth of the Soviet cavalry arm may be followed through the operations in question. For example, on the Eastern Front the cavalry's role had been relatively minor due to its small numbers. By the autumn of 1919 this situation had changed considerably, and the cavalry was instrumental in the Soviet victory, particularly during the Voronezh-Kastornaya operation and the follow-up pursuit of the Whites during the winter of 1919–20. The Red Army was not slow to see the potential of even larger formations of this type. The creation of Budennyi's First Cavalry Army in November 1919 indicated the lines along which their thinking was to develop, and the creation of the Second Cavalry Army in July 1920 was the logical continuation of this process. As we have seen, the cavalry was absolutely essential to the Reds' victory in the Northern Tauride in 1920.

Hand in hand with the cavalry's quantitative growth was the Red Army's increased skill in employing these large cavalry formations. Of particular importance in this regard was the Soviet practice of creating strike groups with a heavy cavalry complement, which increased the range, shock power, and mobility of these units significantly. The Soviet cavalry's growth in numbers and skill during these years meant that these units could be used more effectively as a shock force to crack the enemy's thinly held positions and exploit the subsequent breakthrough in depth. This was hardly possible or necessary on the Eastern Front, given the small number of Soviet cavalry. By the autumn of 1919, however, the evolving conditions of the war had made the creation of such groups necessary, although the forces involved were still relatively small. By the time of the Soviet offensive in the Northern Tauride, their presence was absolutely essential, and the Soviets at last had the wherewithal to employ them to decisive effect.

The Soviets' use of their cavalry strike arm during the latter operation is especially noteworthy. It was not deemed expedient, given the heavy White fortifications ringing the Kakhovka bridgehead, to attempt a breakthrough with cavalry forces alone, as had been the case at Voronezh the previous autumn, when the mounted formations had breached the front without infantry support. The Kakhovka position was the one instance in the civil war in which conditions approached those of the Great War's trench system on the Western Front. At Kakhovka the Soviets were forced to break through the enemy's tactical defense with infantry before they could exploit the success in depth with their cavalry. This method of infantry-cavalry cooperation would serve as a point of departure for a technically updated Red Army's later theoretical work on the theory of the deep operation. The latter involved the traditional infantry-cavalry mix, plus tanks and mechanized units.

The Soviets' use of the cavalry arm during an operation's pursuit phase is also significant. Once again, the Eastern Front's experience is of marginal value because the pursuit of Kolchak's forces was carried out primarily by the infantry. The situation, however, changes dramatically when one examines the Southern Front's pursuit of Denikin's forces during the winter of 1919–20. In previous wars the cavalry arm was used to pursue the enemy from the tactical battlefield. Here for the first time is an instance of operational-strategic pursuit of a beaten enemy army. The Soviet pursuit of Wrangel's forces in October–November 1920 is less dramatic, if only because of the smaller distances involved, although the forces capable of such a task were certainly in place.

Finally, the fronts' various operations are significant for the *consecutiveness* of their conduct. As has been shown, pre–World War I Russian theorists such as Neznamov and Elchaninov predicted the appearance of a number of more or less consecutive operational efforts in the pursuit of a larger goal. This theory foresaw a series of offensive efforts, each punctuated by brief periods of rest and refurbishment, before the cycle would begin again. However, the Great War's positional stalemate negated this possibility, which was only revived under the more mobile conditions of the civil war. The latter conflict fairly teems with examples of this new phenomenon.

The Eastern Front's "Southern Group" carried out the Buguruslan, Belebei, and Ufa operations in April–June 1919, while at the same time the "Northern Group" conducted the Sarapul'-Votkinsk operation. This six-week period of almost nonstop fighting began with the Reds everywhere falling back and ended with the initiative firmly in their grasp. During the counteroffensive the Soviets advanced from 350 to 400 kilometers along a front several hundred kilometers in width. Following a brief pause, the front resumed its advance. The Perm', Zlatoust, Ekaterinburg, and Cheryabinsk operations, which carried the Reds over the Urals, some 300 kilometers from their starting point, were the next stage in this operational sequence. This lunge was followed by the Petropavlovsk, Omsk, Novonikolaevsk, and Krasnoyarsk operations, which brought the Eastern Front to Lake Baikal, a distance of nearly 3,000 kilometers.

In the same way, the Southern Front conducted the aforementioned Orel-Kursk and Voronezh–Kastornaya operations in October–November 1919, which succeeded in moving the front forward only about 160 kilometers, although it was decisive in breaking the back of the White resistance in Ukraine. Thereafter it conducted successively the Nezhin-Poltava, Khar'kov, Kiev, and Donbass operations in December, and the Rostov-Novocherkassk and Odessa operations in January–February 1920, the latter as the Southwestern Front. The Southeastern Front simultaneously conducted the Khoper-Don, Boguchar-Likhai, and Tsaritsyn operations in November–December and, together with the Southern Front, the Rostov-Novocherkassk operation in January. Renamed the Caucasus Front, these forces continued their drive with the Don-Manych, Tikhoretsk, and Kuban'-Novorossiisk operations in January–March 1920. Finally, Frunze's Southern Front conducted its October 23–November 3 counteroffensive, which was quickly followed by the Perkop-Chongar operation.

In some cases, one operation would succeed another, without a significant break. In others, there would ensue an operational pause, during which the armies would be reinforced for the next leap forward. The Red Army had encountered something new in military affairs, and the succeeding decade's theorists would make the theory of consecutive operations one of the cornerstones of their operational art.

OPERATIONS IN THE WAR AGAINST POLAND, 1920

The war with Poland was played out over the same corpse of empire as the Russian civil war. But whereas operations in the latter conflict were conducted by ragtag armies along widely separated fronts, the war with Poland involved relatively more sophisticated forces in an area confined to the former empire's western borders, under conditions similar to those of 1914–17 in the east. And whereas the civil war was primarily an internecine conflict, the Polish War involved the Soviets for the first time in a national struggle. This qualitatively new political-military situation would put the Red Army's military art to its harshest test yet while at the same time providing valuable lessons for the years to come.

As a result of the 1772, 1793, and 1795 partitions of Poland by Austria, Prussia, and Russia, the Polish state ceased to exist for more than a century. Poland was reborn, following the collapse of these same empires in 1917–18, and immediately set about reconstituting itself at the expense of its late masters. Chief among these was Russia, against which the Poles harbored territorial claims stretching far to the east of the country's ethnic boundaries. However, other than seizing large tracts of land in Belorussia and western Ukraine, Poland remained neutral in the conflict between Red and White, even when a determined offensive in conjunction with Denikin's advance in the summer of 1919 might well have meant the end of the Bolshevik regime. That the Poles ultimately refrained from intervening is hardly surprising, given that the White slogan "Russia, great and indivisible" was more hateful to them than even the pernicious social doctrines emanating from Moscow. By the spring of 1920 it had become clear with whom the Poles would have to deal, and they acted at last. The Poles, following a series of insincere negotiations on both sides, attacked in Ukraine on April 25, 1920, while the Soviet armies were still recovering from the previous winter's exertions. They chose not to move in Belorussia and were content to remain in the positions they had come to occupy the previous year. The invaders easily brushed aside the weak Soviet forces in the area and captured the Ukrainian capital of Kiev on May 6. This new threat, coupled with the increasing aggressiveness of the White forces holed up in the Crimea, meant that the Soviet Republic had reached another critical pass.

But the Polish invasion did not catch the Soviets completely off guard because the latter had been expecting war for some time and were already taking measures. The Soviet plan (see map 8) for first countering and then throwing back the Polish attack was conditioned by the Pripyat Marshes, a 270,000-square-kilometer expanse of forest and swamp between Gomel' and Brest. This feature made the large-scale lateral movement of troops difficult and effectively divided the western theater of war into northern and southern halves. These halves corresponded to the "theater of military activities," as defined by Leer, and were probably exactly the sort of geographic division he had in mind. At the beginning of the war the northern sector was held by Tukhachevskii's Western Front (Fifteenth and Sixteenth Armies, plus the "Mozyr' Group"). Yegorov's Southwestern Front (Twelfth and Fourteenth Armies) covered western Ukraine, with Thirteenth Army covering the exits out of the Crimea.

As early as March 18 Glavkom Kamenev informed Yegorov that the Western Front would constitute the counteroffensive's "main axis," while the Southwestern Front would conduct operations along the line Berdichev-Rovno-Kovel'-Brest in support of its neighbor. Kamenev also stated that his apparatus would be responsible for the strategic coordination of the two fronts' efforts.[88]

However, the Western Front's first attempt (May 14–June 8) to force the Polish front around Polotsk ended in failure, when a Polish counterattack from the Molodechno area threw the Soviets back nearly to their starting positions. The primary reason for the May offensive's failure was Tukhachevskii's haste in launching his attack before the arrival of sufficient reinforcements. The Western Front, according to the official Soviet history, had only a small superiority of 61,000 infantry and 5,000 cavalry against a Polish force of 50,800 infantry and 4,500 cavalry.[89] The Western Front's aborted offensive nonetheless drew off significant Polish forces north of the marshes, thus weakening their front around Kiev, where Yegorov was preparing his own attack.

The Polish advance in the south had carried Marshal Joseph Pilsudski's Southeastern Front (Third, Second, and Sixth Armies) as far as the Dnepr River south of Zhlobin, from whence the front followed the river to a point just south of Kiev before curving southwest back to the Romanian border along the Dnestr River. The Poles also held a small bridgehead on the Dnepr's left bank opposite Kiev. Here the Poles dug in, in effect, leaving the initiative to the Reds. The latter were not slow in taking advantage of the opportunity and immediately began reinforcing the area. Crucial to this effort was the arrival of the First Cavalry Army, following a fifty-three-day journey from the Northern Caucasus, where it had been engaged in mopping up the remnants of Denikin's shattered army. The army, in the course of its 1,000-kilometer trek to the west, also engaged in considerable fighting with anti-Soviet guerrillas in southern Ukraine. By late May the army finally reached its assembly point near Uman'.

Yegorov issued detailed instructions to his commanders on May 23. Budennyi's cavalry army would constitute the front's strike group, with the task

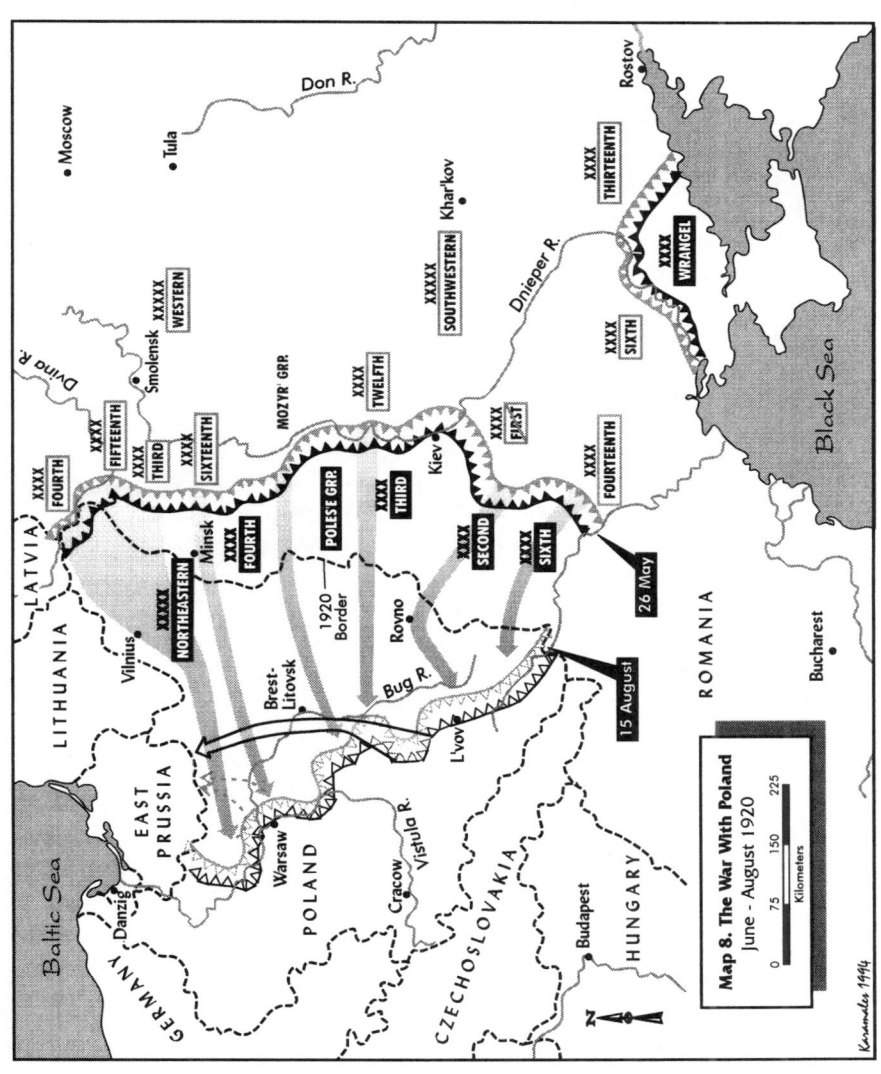

of splitting the Polish front in two. The First Cavalry Army, after taking Berdichev and Kazatin, was to "act in the enemy's rear," a vague order that was to cause a good deal of confusion later on. The Twelfth Army was to force the Dnepr north of Kiev and cut the railway to Korosten'. Yakir's "Fastov Group" and Uborevich's Fourteenth Army would assist the main effort by attacking and tying down enemy forces along their respective sectors.[90]

The most striking aspect of this order was its failure to call for the encirclement of the Polish Third Army, based on Kiev, in spite of the existence of advantageously placed Soviet forces on either flank. Yegorov's failure to employ the highly mobile cavalry army for anything more than extended raiding in the enemy rear, leaving the main task of cutting the enemy's communications through Korosten' to the slower Twelfth Army, is particularly incomprehensible. Added to the plan's flawed conception was the front's overall lack of means to achieve even these goals. The most evenhanded Soviet source gives the Poles a superiority of 60,000 to some 37,000 infantry and cavalry in the area south of the Pripyat Marshes.[91] However, Yegorov did follow standard Soviet procedure in providing for the maximum concentration of force along the decisive areas of his 400-kilometer front. This was in contrast to the Poles' practice of dispersing their forces more or less evenly along the front. This meant that the First Cavalry Army was able to field over 15,000 troops, most of them mounted, and fifty-three guns in its breakthrough sector, against a slightly smaller Polish force, only about half of which was cavalry, and seventy-seven guns.[92]

The Soviet attack jumped off on May 26 but met with varying success along the front. Twelfth Army, supported by units of the Dnepr flotilla, made a number of unsuccessful attempts to cross the river and only managed to secure a small bridgehead north of Kiev by June 1. The "Fastov Group" made good progress at first toward Belaya Tserkov', but a Polish counterattack on May 30 threw it back almost to its original position. The First Cavalry Army moved out on May 27 but had to spend several days dispersing mounted Cossack detachments, which had helped to screen the Polish front. The first days of June were spent probing the Polish lines in what was nonetheless heavy fighting, although Budennyi's languid approach is reminiscent of his conduct the previous autumn around Voronezh.

To crack the enemy front, Budennyi organized his army into two echelons for the breakthrough and exploitation along a narrow front. On June 5 the army broke through at the boundary of Third and Sixth Armies, and by the end of the day it had advanced some 30 kilometers into the enemy rear. The following day the cavalry army cut the Kazatin-Kiev railway. But the Poles reacted quickly to this threat and counterattacked, closing the break in their lines and effectively cutting off the First Cavalry Army. The Red commander's response to this dilemma was to continue his raid into the Polish rear, capturing Zhitomir and Berdichev on the seventh, before falling back toward Fastov to link up with Yakir, having covered some 140 kilometers.

However, wrangling within the Soviet camp ultimately nullified whatever success the cavalry could claim. Repeated altercations between Kamenev and Yegorov over what direction the operation should take led to the cavalry army being moved first to Fastov, back toward Zhitomir and Kazatin, then back on Kiev, over several days.[93] The constant changes in direction exhausted the troops and wasted precious time. The Soviets' problems were further exacerbated by Budennyi's loss of radio contact with front headquarters for several days, during which time his army roamed uselessly in the Polish rear. Twelfth Army's ineffectual attempts to cut the Poles' retreat through Korosten' also contributed to the Soviets' failure to encircle Third Army. The Southwestern Front did manage to retake Kiev on June 12, as the Polish armies began to fall back, but the Soviets' confusion enabled Pilsudski to extricate his forces in time. As a result, an operation that might have ended in the capture of considerable enemy forces merely succeeded in pushing them back.

For the time being, at least, this was sufficient, and the Kiev operation heralded the beginning of a lengthy Polish retreat, although the Poles managed to keep their forces together throughout. The Southwestern Front now pursued the Poles across Volhynya and Galicia. The pursuit, however impressive, failed to yield a decisive result, and the fighting here was eventually overshadowed by events to the north.

After the fall of Kiev, the Soviets shifted their attention back to the area north of the Pripyat Marshes. The Soviet high command, while fully recognizing the political and psychological importance of regaining the Ukrainian capital, never lost sight of the fact that the shortest and most decisive route to victory lay along the Minsk-Warsaw axis. Following the failure of the May operation, the Soviets took advantage of the Poles' preoccupation with western Ukraine to renew their attempts to break through to the Polish heartland. For this purpose, Tukhachevskii was reinforced with several fresh divisions, from which he formed two new armies, the Third and Fourth. This brought his total force at the beginning of July to 91,463 infantry and cavalry, against the Polish Northeastern Front (First and Fourth Armies, and the "Poles'e Group"), which numbered 72,600.[94]

Tukhachevskii's plan closely resembled his preparations for the May operation; it called for a concentrated blow by the front's powerful Fourth, Fifteenth, and Third Armies to the north of the Berezina River, which would then sweep around the Polish left toward Molodechno like the swinging of a giant gate. The southern wing (Sixteenth Army and the "Mozyr' Group") would tie down the Polish forces by attacking toward Minsk. Central to the main effort's success was G. D. Gai's 3d Cavalry Corps, which was positioned on the advance's right shoulder, with the task of operating in the enemy rear following the breakthrough. If the Soviets moved swiftly enough, so this proletarian version of the Schlieffen Plan proposed, the Polish units around Minsk and to the south would be pinned against the marshes and destroyed.

Tukhachevskii, in drawing up his plans for the new offensive, was aware that the conditions of the relatively static front along the Berezina more nearly approached those of the recent world war than had heretofore been the case in the civil war. Thus he would need to create a superiority of men and matériel along the axis of the main attack that would ensure the density of force necessary for the attack's success. Tukhachevskii, by the usual Soviet practice of ruthlessly skimming men from the more passive sectors of his front, thus managed to create a superiority of 60,000 to 33,000 along the strike group's 135-kilometer attack sector (Fourth, Fifteenth, and Third Armies), while the rest of the 450-kilometer front had to make do with the remainder.[95] Tukhachevskii was thus able to create what was, by civil war standards, a high concentration of men and matériel along his front. For example, along the Fifteenth Army's 35-kilometer front the density of troops reached 741 men per kilometer. Elsewhere, the Sixteenth Army, which had a supporting role in the attack, could muster only 125 men per kilometer of front.[96]

It is therefore hardly surprising, given this superiority, that the Soviet attack on July 4 enjoyed great success from the outset. The advance north of Minsk was steady, as the badly outnumbered Poles began to fall back to the southwest. Gai's advance was especially swift as he pushed his cavalry into the breach opened up by the Fourth Army. In less than a week the Soviet cavalry advanced some 120 kilometers to take Sventsyany (Svencionys) on the ninth. Progress was almost as swift to the south, where the Fifteenth Army took Molodechno on the eleventh, while Minsk fell to the Sixteenth Army the same day. The line of the old German trenches was quickly pierced, and on July 14 Gai's cavalry captured Vilna, followed quickly by Lida and Baranovichi to the south, as the Polish retreat gathered speed. In the latter half of July the Soviets crossed the Neman and Shara Rivers and took Grodno on the nineteenth, while to the south they occupied Pinsk on the twenty-seventh. By the end of the July operation the Soviet forces had advanced more than 300 kilometers in some places and were poised to cross over into ethnic Poland.

However, as spectacular as the operation had been in terms of territory regained, the overall military results for the Soviets were slim. While the Polish armies had been severely handled, they nonetheless managed to evade Tukhachevskii's trap and fall back relatively intact. This was due chiefly to the Red Army's low level of mobility, its primitive supply system, and the chaotic command and staff arrangements engendered by the Western Front's rapid growth in June. The marshy and wooded terrain of much of Belorussia and the proximity of the Latvian and Lithuanian borders also hindered the advance by constricting the area for maneuver and channeling the attack into predictable directions that could more easily be defended. But the absence of any decisive victory and the expected large haul of prisoners failed to temper the euphoria that seized the Soviet command beginning in late July. Indeed, there seemed little cause for concern at the time, as Yegorov's forces pressed on south of the marshes, capturing Rovno and Ternopol'.

In this buoyant atmosphere Kamenev became lax in his strategic coordination of the two fronts and allowed his subordinate commanders' immediate operational objectives to develop at variance with his own plans.

Before late July it had been understood by all parties that the axis of the Southwestern Front's advance would be to the northwest, in the general direction of Brest. However, emboldened by their success in Volhynya in June and July, Yegorov and his political commissar, Stalin, petitioned Kamenev on July 22 to reorient the axis of the front's advance on L'vov.[97] Kamenev agreed the next day, shortly after issuing instructions to Tukhachevskii for the final advance on Warsaw, the capture of which he scheduled for August 12.[98] That Kamenev was so quick to agree to this fundamental change in his plans is indicative of the unfounded optimism then reigning in Moscow. He may also have been unwilling to defy Stalin, a member of the party Politburo, whose intense dislike of the military specialists, of which Kamenev was one, was well known in the army. Whatever the reason, what was to have been a converging movement on Warsaw from the east and southeast had instead become a two-pronged assault along diverging axes. Kamenev, by agreeing to split the Soviet effort, had inadvertently set the stage for the Poles' "miracle on the Vistula."

At this juncture, however, there seemed little cause for alarm, as the Western Front continued to advance against spotty Polish resistance, which generally took the form of brief defensive battles organized along the river lines. The Red Army captured Belostok on July 29 and Brest three days later. The Soviets, pushing beyond the Bug and Narew Rivers, had by August 9 reached a point only about 35 kilometers from Warsaw. Tukhachevskii, in orders issued the next day, outlined his plan for piercing the line of the Vistula River. The front commander, who based his plan on the assumption that the main Polish forces were located north of Warsaw, ordered the Fourth, Fifteenth, and Third Armies, as well as most of the Sixteenth, to force the Vistula north of the city in order to cut the Poles' supply lines to their Western allies, which led through the Polish Corridor. The remainder of his forces were to close to the river south of the capital.[99]

Tukhachevskii's decision to weight the advance north of Warsaw put a serious strain on his weak left flank, which was already overextended by the deflection of Yegorov's front toward L'vov. The Western Front's left wing was now anchored on the weak "Mozyr' Group," which had been intended as the link between the two fronts as they traversed the marshes. With the fronts now going their separate ways, this minuscule force had become the linchpin of the Red Army's entire effort, and at the same time the most vulnerable sector of the entire Soviet front. The Western Front's situation was made worse by its staggering supply problems, the result of the previous month's rapid advance, which had carried some units as much as 600 kilometers. The miserable condition of the Soviet railroads meant that as many as 60,000 urgently needed reinforcements were stranded in the rear and unable to reach the front, just as the battle was approaching its climax.[100] Tukhachevskii's overconfidence and cavalier attitude toward his supply situation at this stage are inexplicable and can perhaps only be understood by the front commander's inexperience in commanding large forces (he was just twenty-seven at the time of the operation).

Tukhachevskii's manpower problems were further compounded by the Red Army's irrational allocation of forces among the various fronts. Although the army numbered some 3.5 million men by early August, 80 percent of these were stationed in internal military districts, while more than 200,000 others remained tied down in the Caucasus and the Northern Tauride against Wrangel. The Western and Southwestern Fronts, in comparison, together could field only slightly more than 87,000 active combatants against the Poles.[101] The problem of bringing sufficient forces to bear, despite a crushing overall superiority, was a constant drain on the Red Army's combat effectiveness. In percentages, these figures mirror almost exactly the condition of the old army at its nadir in late 1917, when it could put a mere 2 million men in the trenches, out of a total force of some 10 million.[102] It says much about the chaotic conditions in the army and the country as a whole that this situation was allowed to continue throughout the war.

Still Tukhachevskii pressed gamely on, although Polish resistance was beginning to stiffen noticeably all along the line, and it became apparent that the Poles were determined to give battle north and east of the Vistula. By mid-August the Western Front numbered only about 54,000 infantry and cavalry against 88,000 Poles. The two sides' forces were deployed as follows: north of the Bug River the Soviet Fourth, Fifteenth, and Third Armies (37,742 infantry and cavalry) were opposed by the Polish Fifth Army and the "Lower Vistula Group" (25,836 infantry and cavalry). South of the Bug the Sixteenth Army (10,328 infantry and cavalry) was approaching Warsaw and the middle Vistula, against the Polish First and Second Armies (33,000 infantry and cavalry), which disproved Tukhachevskii's contention that the chief enemy units were deployed north of the Polish capital. However, the real danger was on the Western Front's left, where the Polish Fourth and Third Armies (29,500 infantry and cavalry) were preparing a counteroffensive aimed at the sector held by the weak "Mozyr' Group" (6,600 infantry).[103] Tukhachevskii, true to his operational plan, had assembled most of his force north of the Bug and had even managed to create a small advantage in numbers here. But the Poles had been able to put together a crushing superiority of force in the Deblin area and were preparing to strike the Soviets' overstretched front and split it in two.

The Polish advantage need not have been decisive, however, had the Soviets carried out the planned regrouping of their forces in time. Kamenev, as early as August 3, had instructed both front commanders to prepare for the transfer of the Southwestern Front's Twelfth and First Cavalry Armies to the Western Front, followed three days later by an order transferring the Fourteenth Army as well, although this is difficult to square with the commander in chief's previous blessing of the L'vov operation.[104] And although Yegorov issued the necessary instructions to implement the order, he seems to have done everything in his power to hinder this movement by plunging his armies deeper into the L'vov fighting. Events finally reached a crisis on August 14, when Stalin, exercising his prerogative as a member of the front's military council, refused to countersign the necessary orders turning over the armies. They were finally signed by another member, after considerable delay. Had the Twelfth and First Cavalry Armies been dispatched to the Lublin-Deblin area in time, as Kamenev and Tukhachevskii had wished, the two armies' 26,000 troops (including 15,000 cavalry) would have eliminated the Polish advantage in the area and foiled their counteroffensive.[105] Stalin was recalled to Moscow following this incident, but the damage had already been done.

The Polish counteroffensive may be conveniently divided into two parts, embracing events north and south of Warsaw. The attack in the north began on August 14 with the Fifth Army's assault across the Wkra River, north of Modlin. The Soviet Fourth and Fifteenth Armies began to give way under the pressure, while to the south the Sixteenth Army took Radzymin and was approaching the outskirts of Warsaw. A surprise attack by Polish cavalry the next day broke through the Soviet lines and captured Fourth Army's headquarters at Ciechanow, which completely disrupted its communications with the front command in Minsk and with its own divisions. Gai, unmindful of the true state of affairs in his rear, continued to push his cavalry corps to the west, with the aim of cutting off the Polish corridor from the hinterland. Soviet cavalry even crossed the Vistula at Wloclawek on the sixteenth before being ordered back to participate in the counterattack being prepared against the Fifth Army. The fighting north of the Bug seesawed for several days, with the Poles gradually getting the upper hand as the Soviets, their communications in disarray, struggled to regroup. However, the Soviets were by no means beaten, and they still possessed a local superiority of force. To the south of Warsaw, units of the Sixteenth Army reached the Vistula opposite Gora Kalwaria, although they were halted by superior Polish forces short of the capital itself. However, these actions were quickly overshadowed by the decisive events taking place at the other end of the Vistula front.

Here Pilsudski launched his main attack on August 16 due north from the Deblin area against the Soviets' thin covering screen. The Poles easily brushed aside the defenders, pushing the "Mozyr' Group" to the east, and rushed into the yawning gap between the two fronts. By August 17 the Poles had reached Siedlce and were approaching Brest, well in the rear of the Soviet forces still tied down before Warsaw. Tukhachevskii, however, gamely continued to spur his armies onward. That same day the front commander ordered his three northern armies to continue their attacks, while Sixteenth Army was to pull back its left flank to cover the Soviet rear. He also ordered the Twelfth and First Cavalry Armies to assemble in the Chelm-Vladimir-Volynskii area, preparatory to taking the Polish forces in the rear.[106] But the Southwestern Front command continued to delay the dispatch of Budennyi's army, although it is doubtful if it would have made any difference at this late juncture.

By August 20 Tukhachevskii realized that he was beaten and ordered his armies to fall back from the Polish capital. He still seems to have considered the recent fighting only a temporary setback, from which he would soon resume the attack, for on the twenty-fourth he ordered the Twelfth and First Cavalry Armies to advance on Krasnystaw and Lublin, deep in the rear of the enemy's strike force.[107] This time the armies finally moved and managed to advance as far as the line Zamosc-Chelm before they were turned back at the end of August. Their arrival, in any event, occurred much too late to do anything other than discomfit the Poles, who had closed to the East Prussian border north of Ostrolenka, cutting off 3d Cavalry Corps, Fourth Army, and part of the Fifteenth Army. These units crossed into Germany, where they were interned for the duration of the war. The other Soviet armies managed to escape, although they were terribly worn down. Successive Polish attacks through the autumn gradually forced the exhausted and outnumbered Soviets back to approximately the line where they had begun the war in May. An armistice in October finally halted the fighting and allowed the Soviets to transfer troops south for the final confrontation with the Whites.

The Soviet conduct of operations during the war with Poland does not differ dramatically from that of the later civil war along the major fronts. Here we find the same features—maneuver against the enemy's flanks, the large-scale employment of cavalry, and the conduct of consecutive operations—that have already been noted in 1919–20.

For example, both the Western Front and the Southwestern Front used their cavalry arm as a maneuver spearhead, although in slightly different ways. This was due to the nature of the defenses they faced. In the Kiev operation, massed cavalry was employed to pierce the static Polish defense. After the defense was ruptured, the cavalry moved to develop the success in depth. The Soviet approach here represented a refinement of the methods used against Denikin's forces the previous autumn in the more open conditions of western Ukraine and testified to growing Soviet skill in handling large mobile formations.

In the north, the Polish defense was even stronger, while the Soviet cavalry was weaker in numbers. Here the front commander placed Gai's cavalry corps in echelon behind the Fourth Army, with the latter tasked with breaking through the enemy's front and opening the way for the cavalry's exploitation drive. This foreshadowed the methods used by the Southern Front command a few months later in organizing the First Cavalry Army's breakthrough out of the Kakhovka bridgehead. This method also had the advantage of maintaining the cavalry strike force's strength for its pursuit objective.

However, both cavalry drives ultimately failed. The Southwestern Front's counteroffensive accomplished nothing more than pushing the Poles out of Ukraine, due to the front commander's mistakes and those of his subordinates. Most egregious was Yegorov's failure to order the encirclement of the Polish forces around Kiev, despite the fact that the prerequisites for such a maneuver were in place. This oversight is reminiscent of Yegorov's failure the previous fall to see until the very end any connection between the Orel and Voronezh sectors of his front. The front command's mistakes were further compounded by the First Cavalry Army's pointless raiding in the enemy rear, instead of pursuing a more definite and decisive aim. Here Budennyi reverted to his true calling as a Cossack NCO who could not see the forest for the trees.

The ultimate failure of the Western Front's cavalry drive was due less to personalities than to the more difficult Belorussian terrain, compared with central and western Ukraine. And although Tukhachevskii's idea of turning the Polish flank and destroying the enemy against the Pripyat Marshes was a sound one, the insufficient maneuver forces allotted for the operation ensured its failure. Moreover, it is questionable whether the operation's aims could have been realized with a larger force. An operation of this dimension demanded the kind of mobility that the Soviets would not possess for another fifteen years—large mechanized and armored formations.

Both fronts conducted a number of consecutive operations. The Southwestern Front carried out the Kiev (May 26–June 27), Novograd-Volynskii (June 19–27), Rovno (June 28–July 11), and L'vov (July 23–August 20) operations, while the Western Front conducted the July (July 4–23) and Warsaw (July 24–August 25) operations. However, these operations do not represent a significant break with those conducted during the civil war.

What was distinct was the Red Army's command and control difficulties, particularly at the operational-strategic level. These problems had risen before, as, for example, on the Eastern Front a year earlier, when Kamenev was relieved as front commander as a result of intrigues in Moscow. However, this movement was not overly disruptive, and in any event Kamenev was soon back at his post. Moreover, the high command's strategic coordination of the Southern and Southeastern Fronts' pursuit of the White forces in the winter of 1919–20 was conducted with a minimum of friction.

However, it was during the Polish War that the evils inherent in the commissar system of dual command were fully realized in a way that doomed the entire Soviet effort. The Southwestern Front command acted with impunity throughout and consistently pursued secondary ends to the detriment of the common goal. Yegorov already seems to have been in Stalin's thrall. Kamenev, who may well have been reluctant to offend the powerful and vindictive commissar, allowed his headstrong subordinates' actions to dictate strategy. Kamenev's failure to assert his authority led to a situation whereby at the very moment when Soviet armies were facing disaster before Warsaw, Yegorov and Stalin felt free to continue their own private campaign against L'vov.

The Soviets' drive on Warsaw had been frustrated by a number of factors, most of them of their own making. To these and the Poles' unexpected powers of recovery must also be added the Soviets' tendency to push operations beyond the point where the army's rear organs could possibly sustain them. In retrospect, it would have been wiser to have halted the Western Front's advance along the Bug and Narew Rivers in order to rest and reinforce the troops before making a final effort that might well have been successful. As it was, the exhausted armies were driven beyond their endurance against an enemy who was able to fall back on his sources of human and matériel supply. And just as Tukhachevskii had hoped to defeat the Poles with his version of the Schlieffen Plan, so he was defeated on the Vistula as the Germans had been on the Marne in 1914, and for much the same reason.

The Warsaw operation seared itself into the Red Army's collective consciousness as did no other event of the 1918–20 period, and its lessons were not soon forgotten. Indeed, the notions of "operational exhaustion" and of not pushing operations to the point of diminishing returns were themes to which a number of the army's leading intellects, most of them former officers, would return often during the years to come.

3
The Birth of a Theory, 1921–1929

Marx's theory had predicated the outbreak of a proletarian revolution in a given country on the achievement of a sufficiently high level of industrial development and the presence of a working class that constituted the bulk of the population. In one of the great ironies of history, the Bolsheviks' coup had been carried out in a country that still lagged considerably behind the more developed capitalist economies of the West, and where the industrial working class was a very small minority in a society where the great mass of people were still peasants.

Moreover, the Bolsheviks' own harsh policy of "War Communism," combined with the widespread disruption of the civil war, had by the end of the conflict reduced the national economy nearly to the subsistence level. The decline in many areas of industry had been precipitous. For example, the production of coal fell from 29.1 million tons in 1913 to 9.5 million in 1921; oil from 9.2 to 3.8 million tons; iron from 4.2 million to 100,000 tons; and steel from 4.2 million to 200,000 tons.[1] The decline in production in many other areas was just as bad, or worse, and it was not until 1925–26 that the economy finally achieved the prewar level of production.

Given the country's weakened state, the USSR was fortunate not to have been involved in any major conflicts during the decade. The only clash of note occurred in late 1929 in Manchuria, where Soviet troops fought a brief war with the Chinese army. The dispute grew out of a local warlord's seizure of the Chinese Eastern Railroad, which belonged to the USSR and provided the shortest route between Vladivostok and the interior. The Soviets reacted by forming the Special Far Eastern Army, commanded by the civil war hero V. K. Blyukher. The Soviet offensive to regain the railroad began in October and lasted a little more than a month, ending in a complete victory over the technically inferior Chinese. An agreement between the two countries in December restored the prewar situation, after which Soviet troops returned home.

In a highly politicized society like the USSR, it would have been surprising had the armed forces managed to remain aloof from the fierce intraparty quarrels that characterized the period from the onset of Lenin's fatal illness to Stalin's consolidation of power at the end of the decade. In fact, the armed forces were torn by the same factional battles as the party, and as the only reasonably coherent institution apart from the party within the shattered society, their support was invaluable in the struggle for power. This fact and the presence of some of the major contenders in both political and military bodies ensured that the armed forces would be drawn into the political strife of the time, with significant repercussions for individuals and policies alike.

Lenin's great authority within the party had usually managed to curb the institutional and personal rivalries of its leading figures. However, his lingering illness from the end of 1922 allowed these pent-up tensions increasingly full play. Central to the struggle to succeed Lenin was Trotskii, who, as people's commissar for military and naval affairs, member of the Politburo, member of the Council of Labor and Defense, and chairman of the Military Revolutionary Council (RVS), wielded enormous power. He was opposed by the triumvirate of G. E. Zinov'ev, L. B. Kamenev (no relation to the commander in chief), and Stalin, the latter of whom had become the party's general secretary in 1922. The three began to savagely attack the war commissar even before Lenin's death, taking skillful advantage of the latter's unpopularity within some segments of the party. These efforts bore their first real fruit in early 1924 with the removal of Trotskii's ally, V. A. Antonov-Ovseenko, as chief of the armed forces Political Directorate and his replacement by A. S. Bubnov, who proceeded to subordinate the armed forces more closely to the party apparatus increasingly controlled by Stalin.

Trotskii's position had already been weakened by his wartime sponsorship of the military specialists and the wrangle over the formulation of a military doctrine for the Red Army. Matters came to a head shortly after Lenin's death in January 1924, when Trotskii's enemies ousted his deputy on the RVS and replaced him with Frunze, who certainly had no reason to support his new chief. And although Trotskii continued as RVS chairman, he was effectively excluded from most day-to-day activity, and it fell to Frunze to carry out the introduction of the cadre-territorial system and the concept of "unified command," which greatly increased the unit commanders' powers vis-à-vis the political officer. Under these circumstances, Trotskii's final humiliation was almost anticlimactic, when he was replaced by Frunze in January 1925 as both war commissar and chairman of the RVS.

However, Frunze's tenure at the top of the country's military establishment lasted a mere nine months. The war commissar, only forty years old, suffered from stomach ulcers and was ordered by the Politburo to undergo an operation, much against his will. An overdose of chloroform brought on a heart attack, and Frunze died on October 31, 1925.[2] He was succeeded by Voroshilov, the commander of the Moscow Military District and a follower of Stalin's from the early days of the civil war.

Voroshilov's appointment, while a political coup for the Stalin faction, ultimately proved disastrous for the armed forces and the country's defense as a whole. Under the war commissar's inept management the Soviet military establishment became the obedient tool of Stalin's personal dictatorship, although this did not save it from the tyrant's murderous purge of 1937–38, in which Voroshilov played a leading role. In other areas, Voroshilov's innate conservatism in military affairs repeatedly stymied the efforts of many of the Red Army's brightest minds to bring the armed forces up to the demands of modern war. His devotion to the civil war's outdated cavalry methods led him to promote to high posts such military nonentities associated with that arm as Budennyi and Shchadenko, whom one historian aptly called "the new type of political soldier, the ex-NCO associated with Stalin, possessing a rudimentary military education, . . . but a ruthless power of estimating situations in terms of narrow loyalties."[3] Voroshilov's incompetence was made manifest in the Red Army's poor showing during the 1939–40 war with Finland, and he was finally relieved soon after. However, fifteen years of mismanagement could not be overcome so easily, and Voroshilov must bear a large share of the responsibility for the disasters of 1941.

Frunze's death was extremely opportune for Stalin, whose marriage of convenience with his nominal allies was coming to an end. The breach in the trio's partnership came out into the open at the fourteenth party congress in December 1925, in which the "left opposition" of Zinov'ev and Kamenev was decisively defeated by Stalin and the party machine. The two, along with Trotskii, were in turn expelled from the Politburo the following year. This was followed by two years of relative peace, characterized by Stalin's adherence to Lenin's moderate New Economic Policy (NEP). However, this interlude was not fated to last, and Stalin next turned on his erstwhile supporters, N. I. Bukharin and A. I. Rykov, now styled the "right opposition." These two had become increasingly alienated by the general secretary's harsh ways and his radical program for transforming industry and agriculture. They were easily defeated, however, after a brief battle, and by the end of 1929 Stalin was the undisputed master of the party and the army.

DOCTRINAL AND STRATEGIC DEBATES

The armed forces were affected no less than the rest of society by the dislocations and shortages of these years. Upon the conclusion of the civil war in the European part of the country, it became apparent that the armed forces could no longer be maintained at their current size in light of the country's economic problems. During the first half of the 1920s the armed forces were drastically reduced from a high of 5.3 million at the end of 1920 to 1.6 million a year later, followed by further cuts that pared down the military establishment to a mere 562,000 by mid-1924. Of this number, nearly 530,000 served in the army, evidence of the military's primitive condition.[4] This figure was quite small for a country the size of the USSR, which still suffered from occasional domestic flare-ups, such as the Tambov uprising in 1921, and a protracted struggle against Central Asian nationalists throughout the decade.

The sharp decline in the army's numbers had an inevitable effect on the command element, which was successively reduced from a high of 130,932 at the end of 1920 to 49,319 at the beginning of 1924.[5] Much of this reduction came at the expense of the older generation of former officers, which had received its training in the imperial army. This is evident by the proportion of former military specialists (the term was abolished after the end of the civil war) serving in command positions, which fell from a high of 34 percent at the end of the civil war to 14.1 percent in 1925 and to a mere 10.6 percent in 1928.[6]

The army's greatly reduced size meant that only a small portion of the yearly draft contingent could be accommodated. The Soviets sought to resolve this problem by introducing a mixed cadre-territorial system, the latter units of which combined civilian labor with periods of military service over a period of several years. While the quality of the territorial units often left much to be desired, the Soviets had little choice but to press ahead with this system of recruitment, which soon came to occupy an important place in the armed forces.[7] By the end of 1923, territorial units accounted for 17.2 percent of all rifle divisions, a figure that had increased to 56 percent by 1928.[8]

Important changes were also taking place in the higher military organs during these years. Overall control of military affairs continued to be exercised through the Council of Labor and Defense and the RVSR, which in 1923 became the RVS USSR. During these years the RKKA completely dominated the structure of the People's Commissariat for Military and Naval Affairs, and the Workers' and Peasants' Red Navy (RKKF) played a distinctly secondary role. The air force was even more closely tied to the ground forces, existing merely, like the navy, as a directorate *(upravlenie)* within the defense commissariat. In 1921 the All-Russian Main Staff, a wartime administrative organ, was merged with the RVSR Field Staff to form the RKKA Staff, which continued to be run by Lebedev, an imperial General Staff Academy graduate. He was succeeded in this post by the impeccably proletarian Frunze in 1924, followed a year later by Kamenev, another academy graduate. Tukhachevskii, who in spite of his own "specialist" background was always one of the more virulent exponents of the party line, occupied the post from 1925 to 1928 and upon his resignation was succeeded by the 1910 academy graduate Shaposhnikov. The post of *glavkom* was abolished in 1924, and Kamenev was relegated to the military inspectorate, although he continued to hold a number of important positions until his death in 1936.

Despite its many weaknesses, the Red Army during the 1920s embarked upon an exciting period of theoretical discovery. And while a good deal of work remained highly speculative, many of the conclusions reached during these investigations had far-reaching consequences for the further development of operational art.

One of the chief tenets of Marxist-Leninist military thought holds that a state's military system is a product of the economic relationships between classes, whether the society in question is characterized by slave-owning, feudal, or capitalist productive relationships. It was in this vein that Friedrich Engels wrote in 1851 that "the emancipation of the proletariat . . . will have its own special expression in military affairs and will create its own special and new military method."[9] And just as the French Revolution had ushered in radical changes in the conduct of war, so the Soviets believed that their revolution would bring about similar changes. However, just as a number of prerevolutionary developments in France reached maturity only under Napoleon, the same was true of the Soviet Union after the civil war. Here the Red Army, for all its radical sloganeering, would continue to draw heavily from the czarist military legacy.

This link was particularly evident in the army's early attempts to elaborate a military doctrine tailored to the needs of the new proletarian state. This effort was in many respects a continuation of the doctrinal debate that took place in the czarist army in 1911–12. Among those who took an active part in this discussion were such future military specialists as A. M. Zaionchkovskii, Bonch-Bruevich, and Neznamov. However, this promising movement soon fell victim to the same reaction that had driven the "Young Turks" from the General Staff Academy, and the czar expressly forbade further debate on the subject.[10] The discussion was resumed briefly in 1920 on the pages of *Military Affairs,* the house organ of the Red Army's more intellectual military specialists before it was closed down that same year for views later described as "non-Marxist and under the influence of the old military thinking."[11] However, this episode was merely the prelude to the more intense and militarily significant controversy that followed.

The first shots in the renewed debate were fired at the tenth party congress in March 1921, during which Frunze and Gusev presented their proposals for the reorganization of the Red Army in peacetime. The most important point in their program was Frunze's call for transforming the army into a "unified organism," held together "by a unity of views as to the character of the military tasks facing the republic," which he called the "unified military doctrine" *(edinaya voennaya doktrina).*[12] At this time the imposition of an official system of military views was a key demand of the army's more earnestly proletarian military elements, of which Frunze himself was the most outstanding example. It was also a thinly veiled challenge to Trotskii, who had aroused a good deal of enmity among this group with his enthusiastic sponsorship of the military specialists during the civil war. There were more personal reasons as well. The pair's antipathy toward Trotskii dated from their service on the eastern front in 1919, when they successfully reversed the war commissar's removal of Kamenev as front commander during the spring 1919 counteroffensive. However, Trotskii's authority could not be overcome at this point, and the proposals were withdrawn.

But Frunze refused to be silenced for long. He renewed his attack later that year in a major article, "A Unified Military Doctrine and the Red Army," which developed his ideas on the subject more fully. Most important, Frunze defined his doctrine as

> that teaching adopted in the army of a given state, which establishes the character of the construction of the country's armed forces, the methods of the troops' combat training and their leadership on the basis of the state's prevailing views as to the character of the military tasks before it and ways of solving them, which spring from the class essence of the state and which are determined by the level of development of the country's productive forces.[13]

Frunze divided his doctrine into two parts—the technical and the political. The first is concerned with the more mundane aspects of military life and embraces such matters as troop training, organization, and military equipment. The second, and more important, is the product of the state's political system, which is determined by its dominant social class. Couched in these terms, Frunze's doctrine also constituted a clever appeal to the army's class-conscious coterie of red commanders, which had always resented Trotskii's employment of the politically suspect military specialists.

The peripatetic war commissar was not slow in rising to the challenge, and he summoned all his considerable polemical skill to rebut Frunze's proposal. In an article venomously entitled "Military Doctrine, or Pseudo-Military Doctrinairism," Trotskii proceeded to heap scorn on what he regarded as the juvenile ideas of Frunze and his allies. He charged that "only hopeless doctrinaires think that the answers to the problems of mobilization, organization, instruction, strategy and tactics can be derived from . . . the premises of sacred 'military doctrine.'"[14] On the contrary, he warned, "Military affairs are a very empirical, very practical matter," and any attempts to codify the art of war into a set of eternal laws run the risk of stultifying the development of thought in this area.[15]

It would be a mistake to conclude from this passage, however, that Trotskii was advocating anything like freedom of expression within the army, or that he was any less insistent than his opponents on the principle of party control of the armed forces. His political credentials on this score were every bit as good as Frunze's, and he had shown himself on several occasions to be utterly ruthless in carrying out the party's directives. His reasons for opposing Frunze's doctrine were more subtle than his words would indicate and had as much to do with the emerging political struggle within the party as with the issue at hand. The vehemence and length (thirty pages) of his reply suggest that Trotskii may well have suspected Frunze of being the cat's paw in an attempt to undermine his control of the armed forces.[16]

It was a considerably chastened Frunze who returned to the question in early 1922, with a lengthy article entitled "The Military-Political Education of the Red Army." Frunze had been deeply stung by Trotskii's criticisms and now went to some lengths to distance himself from his doctrine's more extreme tenets. A crucial concession involved the word "doctrine" itself, which, Frunze now admitted, indeed "smacks of something doctrinaire, opposed to that spirit of creativity, initiative and activity" that he believed should be the Red Army's hallmark.[17] This acknowledgment set the stage for a number of significant concessions on the points so beloved of the red commanders. Among the most important of these was the belief in the existence of a uniquely proletarian military art. Frunze was now ready to admit that the Red Army "had introduced nothing new into the fields of tactics and strategy" and, for the time being, at least, would have to make do with the equipment and methods of the old regime.[18] It was a bitter pill for Frunze and his allies to swallow, but they would have their revenge.

Neither Trotskii nor Frunze had much opportunity or wish to debate the issue further after 1922. More immediate problems, such as the army's ongoing demobilization and the crisis in the party caused by Lenin's illness, took precedence over such seemingly abstract concerns. Intellectually, Trotskii was the clear winner, and he had compelled Frunze to retreat from or modify some of his more extreme statements. The latter's capitulation on the main point of contention was made complete at a conference of military delegates to the eleventh party congress in March 1922, at which Trotskii was also able to engineer the removal of Frunze's ally, Gusev, as head of the armed forces' political directorate and replace him with his own man, Antonov-Ovseenko. Here Frunze conceded that "there can be no kind of revolution in the sense of creating an independent proletarian tactics and strategy," due to the inability of the country's economy to meet all but the army's most basic needs. However, he consoled himself with the belief that with the recovery of the country's industry, the development of a uniquely proletarian military art was inevitable.[19]

Ultimately, however, it was Frunze who replaced Trotskii as war commissar, just as it was his interpretation of military doctrine that was imposed, almost word for word, on the Red Army. This was because, despite his outward victory, the debate over military doctrine was deeply damaging to Trotskii's position in the army in a way that had little to do with the merits of the case and everything to do with the armed forces' ideological makeup and the ambitions of his enemies. At bottom, Frunze's proposal to create a proletarian military doctrine had an inherently greater appeal to the large number of politically minded red commanders who had come of age during the civil war and who constituted the largest and most ambitious of the army's various groups. This faction despised Trotskii for his intellectual arrogance and his sponsorship of the military specialists, who occupied positions of power and influence that its spokesmen felt belonged to them by right. One such red commander recalled that during this period "a sort of underground opposition to Trotskii . . . began to show its head both in the Party and in the Army. Its rallying points were Stalin and Voroshilov."[20] And whereas Trotskii seemed to relish insulting this group's theoretical pretensions, Frunze wisely appealed to its highly developed sense of mission as the herald of a new era in military affairs.

The doctrinal controversy, in turn, stimulated a wide-ranging debate among many of the army's leading theoreticians regarding the nature of a future war, the determination of which was one of the primary tasks of Frunze's doctrine. Prominent among those who took part were a number of former czarist officers and their red counterparts. However, this was no mere academic discussion but a matter of crucial importance to a military leadership that foresaw a renewed clash between the socialist and capitalist systems as inevitable. This apocalyptic mood was contained in a secret internal study, entitled *Future War,* prepared by Tukhachevskii's RKKA Staff apparatus in 1928. According to this study, in the event of a renewed capitalist assault on the USSR, the most likely belligerents would be Great Britain, France, Poland, Romania, Finland, the Baltic States, and Italy. Another group, which included Germany, Czechoslovakia, Hungary, Bulgaria, Yugoslavia, Greece, Belgium, Japan, and the United States, might be drawn into an anti-Soviet coalition at some point. A third group consisted of those countries that would likely remain neutral, including Sweden, Norway, Denmark, Switzerland, Austria, Albania, Iran, and Latin America. Finally, there were countries such as Turkey, Afghanistan, China, and European colonial holdings in the Middle East, Africa, and Asia that would remain friendly with the USSR.[21]

As the debate developed through the 1920s, the participants' attention increasingly focused on four major issues. The first of these concerned whether a future war would be a protracted struggle on the model of World War I or one resolved in a quick campaign. The second dealt with whether the Red Army should pursue an offensive or defensive strategy. Third, would a future war see a repeat of the Great War's positional stalemate, or would the art of maneuver reassert itself as it had during the civil war? Finally, would a future war be another clash of predominantly infantry armies, or would such armies be replaced by smaller, more mechanized forces? All of these problems lay squarely within the realm of military strategy and dealt with the nature and conduct of war at the highest level. Their resolution, for better or worse, would inevitably have a profound impact on the development of Soviet views on conducting operations.

The debate over the duration of a future war had its roots in the Red Army's defeat before Warsaw and the ebbing of the revolutionary tide elsewhere in Europe in the 1920s. This check forced the Soviets to face the fact of their own political isolation and caused them to make some adjustments to their revolutionary optimism. The capitalist world's unexpected recovery and the Soviets' own dire economic straits injected a further note of caution into the regime's military pronouncements, along with a growing realization that a future war, at least one involving one or more of the Great Powers, was likely to be an extended one. Thus even a man of Frunze's impeccably communist credentials could write in 1924 that a future war against the capitalist world would be a "protracted and cruel contest, putting to the test all the economic and political foundations of the belligerent sides."[22] He was seconded on this score by Tukhachevskii, who, in spite of his "specialist" background as a junior officer, or perhaps because of it, had emerged as one of the "redder" commanders in the debate. However, even the normally impetuous Tukhachevskii was forced to conclude that in a future war the Soviet Union would face an economically superior capitalist coalition, and that the ensuing struggle would be "protracted, stubborn and bitter."[23]

These conclusions, not surprisingly, found a good deal of support among an erudite group of former officers, whose professional training and lack of revolutionary zeal inclined them toward a more sober view. Among these was Svechin, an imperial academy graduate and a bitter enemy of the more radical commanders. Svechin's holistic view of war led him to conclude that a prolonged conflict was inevitable, due to the mobilization constraints inherent in modern economies and the extended time needed to accumulate the necessary resources. This, he argued, is because the nation's military economy always lags behind the overall growth in productive forces and the former's period of maximum exertion cannot usually be attained before the war's second year.[24] This would create a situation similar to that of the Western Allies during the greater part of 1915, when they were forced to forgo major offensive operations due to the exhaustion of prewar stockpiles. Svechin's colleague, Shaposhnikov, who had accommodated himself more successfully to the new regime, also stressed economic factors. Given the Soviet Union's reigning weaknesses in this regard, he urged the country's leadership to prepare for a *"protracted and intensive* exertion" in a war that would last at least as long as the 1914–18 struggle.[25]

The same held true of a war against the USSR's smaller western neighbors, particularly, if as expected, they were supported by the Great Powers. Incredible as it seems to a generation accustomed to viewing the former Soviet Union as a military superpower, Soviet military planners of the 1920s had to seriously consider the military strength of Poland and Romania. Thus the authors of *Future War* calculated that both Estonia and Latvia could be defeated in a single, quick campaign, due to their small territory and the insignificant size of their armies. Poland, however, could be expected to field as many as seventy divisions and could only be defeated in an arduous struggle lasting as long as three years, only *after* which could Romania be successfully engaged. The only hope the Soviets had of shortening such a war lay in achieving an overwhelming superiority in men and matériel and supplying the army with the necessary transportation resources. These, the study indicated, the Red Army neither possessed nor was likely to have in the near future.[26]

The surprising degree of unanimity regarding the notion of a prolonged war stood in sharp contrast to the bitter polemical debates that raged about some of the other questions. The resulting consensus was no accident, however, and was conditioned in large part by the experience of World War I and the Red Army's own protracted struggle in 1918–20. The Great War had convincingly demonstrated that modern wars could no longer be won in a single campaign and that victory demanded an intensive, sustained effort, in which a state's economic and political measures were as important as its military ones. The civil war only reaffirmed these lessons, even though both sides had relied on a far more primitive industrial base than had the main belligerents of 1914–18, and the Bolsheviks' victory was due as much to their enemies' political disarray as to their military superiority.

That the Red Army was able to accept the likelihood of a protracted war showed that its leaders could tolerate some limitations on their revolutionary optimism if they were faced with incontrovertible facts that did not clash excessively with their ambitions. This was certainly the case in the 1920s, when the Soviet Union, confronted with its own political, economic, and military inferiority, had no choice but to accept the premise of a prolonged conflict and to prepare for it accordingly.

However, this consensus was overshadowed by the bitter struggle over whether the Red Army should adopt an offensive or defensive strategy in a future war. In this area, more than any other, political considerations played a role in the final outcome. This was because the question of offense versus defense went to the very heart of the Red Army's conception of itself and what its leaders believed it should be. As in so much else, the controversy had its origins in the initial debate over military doctrine. Here, Frunze had admitted that the Red Army remained technologically inferior to the armies of the capitalist countries. However, he believed that this advantage could be negated by what he regarded as the Red Army's inherently offensive character, which was a product of its proletarian class composition. From this he concluded that the proletarian army "can and will attack," and that the Red Army should be trained in the spirit of "energetic, decisively and daringly conducted offensive operations."[27] This was the essence of what became the extreme "red" position, although Frunze's own ideas were to evolve significantly from this unsophisticated beginning.

The impetus for some of this change came from his enemy Trotskii, whose caustic attacks did much to quell Frunze's revolutionary ardor. The war commissar was particularly contemptuous of Frunze's attempts to extract an inherently offensive strategy on the basis of the Red Army's class composition and its experience during the civil war. Trotskii sought to undermine the notion of the army's offensive character by pointing out that the Red Army not only had not invented "offensiveness" *(nastupatel'nost')* but had actually learned from the Whites the art of "rapid breakthroughs, flanking movements and penetrations into the enemy rear."[28] Moreover, he added, strategic defense and retreat had also been major components of Soviet military strategy during the war, as the Red Army was forced more than once to abandon large areas on one front in order to build up forces for a counteroffensive on another. Trotskii concluded this broadside by denouncing the idea that an offensive strategy was peculiar to the Red Army and not the product of objective conditions prevailing in the civil war, which had affected both sides equally.[29]

However, Frunze was more hesitant to concede this point to Trotskii, and his modified position was hedged with reservations indicative of his reluctance to abandon a belief so dear to the militants in his own camp. The most he would do to temper his offensive-mindedness was to admit the expediency of a retreat under certain circumstances. However, he insisted that such a retreat be viewed merely as a "feature" of an overall offensive strategy and a forced measure prior to launching a "new and decisive offensive."[30] Frunze, as this example indicates, was maturing as a military thinker, although he was not entirely free of political prejudices, and his formula for adopting the defensive only under duress soon became standard policy in the Red Army.

The controversy soon shifted to the merits of the "strategy of destruction" *(strategiya sokrusheniya)* versus the "strategy of attrition" *(strategiya izmora)*. These terms came to define the debate over an offensive or defensive strategy, although in ways that could easily be misleading. The debate also came to be personified in the speeches and writings of the decade's two outstanding strategic theorists, Svechin and Tukhachevskii.

Aleksandr Andreevich Svechin was born into a military family in 1878 and graduated from an artillery school in 1897. He finished the General Staff Academy in 1903 and served briefly in Manchuria. Between wars Svechin occupied a number of command and staff positions and began a long, fruitful scholarly career as well. During World War I he served as a regimental and division commander and as chief of an army staff. Svechin joined the Red Army in 1918 and served briefly as chief of the All-Russian Main Staff, after which he devoted himself entirely to scholarly work in various military academies. During the 1920s he produced the multivolume *History of Military Art, The Evolution of Military Art,* and his famous *Strategy,* which remained the single most important work on the subject in the Soviet Union until the 1960s. As a theorist, Svechin was the most outstanding representative of the imperial military tradition in the Red Army, and his erudition and breadth of knowledge far exceeded that of any of the red commanders who so despised him, as well as many of the younger specialists who sided with them. However, a man of Svechin's forthright views could not survive what was coming in the army, and he was ultimately consumed by the vast killing machine in 1938.

Svechin was an unabashed defender of the strategy of attrition, which might just as easily be termed the strategy of the "indirect approach," in which such concerns as "geographic points, embodying political and economic interests, become paramount."[31] The strategy of destruction, on the other hand, is the strategy of immediacy, which seeks a decision in the shortest time possible by the application of the maximum force at the decisive point. The strategy of destruction is unilinear and sees the destruction of the main enemy force or coalition partner as the only correct solution. According to Svechin, in its violent, headlong pursuit of a rapid decision, the strategy of destruction disregards "all secondary interests and axes, all geographic goals."[32] And whereas the destructive approach recognizes no other factors in its search for an overwhelming victory, the strategy of attrition takes into account any number of intermediate military, political, and economic goals. And while this approach eschewed an immediate military decision as inexpedient, it was far from being a defensive strategy, as many of Svechin's critics charged. On the contrary, Svechin wrote, the strategy of attrition may pursue the "most decisive ultimate goals" and should never be confused with a war of limited aims.[33] Rather, the strategy of attrition would follow the path of least resistance, gradually accumulating political, economic, and military advantages, which would enable it eventually to deliver the final "knockout" blow. Svechin, by way of illustration, criticized the Western Allies' "destructive logic" in World War I of Paris-Berlin with the preferred and more gradual attrition strategy of Paris-Salonika-Vienna-Berlin.[34]

Nevertheless, it is hard to deny that a certain defensive bias is inherent in the strategy of attrition, particularly during the opening stages of the war. Trotskii had made this point in 1922 during the original doctrinal debates. This was the war commissar at his most "defensive," arguing that in the event of war with a technologically superior enemy possessing greater initial mobilization capabilities, Soviet strategy should be essentially defensive. He counseled that in such a case the Red Army should withdraw into the country's vast spaces in order to gain time and draw upon its greater recruiting base, which would ultimately allow it to launch a counteroffensive.[35] Svechin would later agree with the war commissar, arguing that the absence of "geographic values" along the Soviet Union's western frontier might justify a withdrawal at the beginning of a war.[36] Verkhovskii, Svechin's academy colleague, was more explicit in his recommendations and maintained that in such a situation it would be more expedient to withdraw and give up Minsk and Kiev than to take Belostok and Brest.[37] Unfortunately, such statements left their proponents open to charges of "defensivism" and lack of revolutionary spirit, which was by no means an idle charge. It is particularly ironic, then, that long after such ideas had been declared anathema, the Red Army was forced by circumstances to adopt an even more extreme variation of this strategy in 1941–42.

The man who led the attack against these views was Tukhachevskii, who had become the unofficial spokesman of the red commanders in spite of his own "specialist" background. Moreover, he had even been born into the provincial gentry in 1893. Upon graduation from a czarist military school in 1914, he served briefly in World War I until his capture the next year. Tukhachevskii succeeded in escaping two years later, and upon returning to Russia he aligned himself with the Bolsheviks. He held a number of high-ranking positions during the civil war, including the command of the Western Front during the latter's ill-fated invasion of Poland. The recriminations that followed that campaign made him several powerful enemies (Stalin and Voroshilov), who came to oppose many of his initiatives and ultimately precipitated his downfall. Tukhachevskii also served the Soviet cause in liquidating the Kronshtadt mutiny and ruthlessly putting down a peasant uprising in the Tambov area in 1921. Following a period of mixed command and academic activity, he headed the RKKA Staff from 1925 to 1928. Tukhachevskii, as the result of a policy dispute with Stalin and Voroshilov, resigned this post and was relegated to a sort of military exile as commander of the Leningrad Military

District, from whence he was summoned back to Moscow in 1931 to take charge of the armed forces' ambitious rearmament program. In 1935 he was made a marshal and the following year first deputy defense minister and chief of the RKKA directorate of military training. Tukhachevskii's fall, however, was even swifter. In May 1937 he was unceremoniously dismissed from his central administrative duties and relegated to the command of the Volga Military District. Shortly afterward he was arrested, quickly tried, and executed.

In his 1926 brochure "Problems of Modern Strategy," Tukhachevskii, in what could only have been a reply to Svechin and his followers, denounced as "military nihilism" the attitude that "rejects the possibility of changing the correlation of forces by military means" and reduces the entire conduct of war to economic competition alone.[38] This blast, however, indicated that its author had either completely misread Svechin or was deliberately distorting his opponent's views in order to score debating points. Svechin had never been an unquestioning advocate of a defensive strategy, although he clearly felt that the latter more closely suited the Soviet Union's existing capabilities. Svechin, in the same way he had opposed the imposition of a military doctrine before and after the revolution, was trying to educate the Red Army in a broader spirit of intellectual speculation and save it from doctrinaires of all stripes. Above all, his was a call for realism and moderation in military affairs. Ironically, his advocacy of the maximum flexibility in the pursuit of unchanging ends showed Svechin to be a better Leninist than many of his politically correct opponents.

Tukhachevskii doubted the USSR's capacity to wage the kind of incremental war preferred by Svechin, warning that the Soviet Union could not afford "to endlessly prolong its war," and that it must strive to achieve a military victory by the "swiftest and most economical means" possible, through an offensive strategy.[39] Tukhachevskii, given his lieutenant's knowledge of military history, no doubt saw parallels with Germany's strategic position in 1914, in which the only alternative to a slow but inevitable defeat lay in a quick offensive war to destroy the enemy coalition before it could mobilize fully. However, poor and all but isolated in the mid-1920s, the USSR was in no position to wage a lightning campaign against a superior capitalist coalition. Svechin, as always the more subtle thinker of the two, saw more deeply into the problem, realizing that for the Soviet Union to predominate in a major war, the war would have to be prolonged, so that its inherent advantages (its vast territory and large population) could come into play. In fact, this was the strategy the Soviets were ultimately forced to adopt in 1941–45, although under circumstances totally unforeseen by the Red Army's prewar strategists.

The response to these views in other quarters varied widely and often depended on political considerations as much as military ones. One of the most extreme positions was taken by the historian V. A. Melikov, who approvingly called the strategy of destruction "the soul of revolutionary class war."[40] He was supported in this instance by his literary associate N. E. Kakurin, a former czarist colonel and 1910 General Staff Academy graduate. Kakurin, writing in 1921, declared that "future class wars will always be *offensive*" and will be characterized by "extreme energy, decisiveness, and rapidity of execution."[41] A more moderate appraisal was offered by Kakurin's academy classmate Shaposhnikov, whose skill in negotiating the treacherous currents of Red Army politics ranks him as one of its great survivors. He artfully managed to keep a foot in both camps when he wrote that "*a future war will take on the character of an attrition struggle,*" although he did not altogether exclude the strategy of destruction.[42] Frunze, for his part, had also moderated his tone and sought to strike a balance between the two camps. By 1924 he had lost much of his former offensive spirit and was advocating a "transition from the strategy of lightning, decisive blows to a strategy of exhaustion" (*strategiya istoshcheniya*). This was a significant concession to Svechin's point of view. But for political reasons Frunze could not renounce entirely an offensive strategy and sought to salvage his position by stressing the shakiness of the enemy rear. A future war with the Soviet Union, according to this view, would so exacerbate class conflicts within the capitalist bloc that a determined offensive by the Red Army would be the signal for uprisings in the enemy rear, thus assuring a communist victory.[43] However, Frunze's clumsy compromise found few followers in either camp.

In fact, the increasingly tense atmosphere of the late 1920s allowed little scope for moderation of any kind in a party and army that were becoming more intolerant of deviations from the general line. Svechin was to come under even harsher criticism as the advocates of the destruction strategy gained the upper hand from the middle of the decade onward. Their victory was formally sealed in 1926 at the first all-union congress of the army's Military-Scientific Society, whose delegates overwhelmingly supported Tukhachevskii's formula. In retrospect, it is hardly surprising that the Red Army came to endorse such an approach, given the aggressive nature of Marxist-Leninist thought, and the primacy of the offensive was fundamental to Soviet military art from the beginning. Henceforth the Red Army would devote almost exclusive attention to the offensive and relegate defensive preparations to the backwaters of military thought.

Closely tied to this question was the controversy over whether a future war would see a reversion to positional fighting or whether maneuver would predominate. Trotskii, for his part, was particularly contemptuous of those revolutionary parvenus who sought to project into the future the limited experience of the civil war, particularly as it concerned the Red Army's supposedly "inherent" maneuver qualities. Such a notion was completely false, he maintained, and he pointed out that the Whites' strategy had been highly maneuverable from the start, due to their smaller numbers, and it had fallen to the Red Army to learn the art of maneuver from its enemies. Whatever maneuver qualities the army had demonstrated, he continued, were less the product of revolutionary virtue than of the objective conditions of the war itself, which had facilitated wide-ranging maneuver. Trotskii concluded that one therefore should not consider maneuverability *(manevrennost')* "a special expression of the Red Army's revolutionary character."[44]

The war commissar's attack had its usual sobering effect on Frunze, who had begun his peacetime career as an extreme proponent of maneuver. Frunze's retreat was a fence-straddling compromise in which he sought to reconcile his heart with his head. He now urged his followers to study the positional phase of the Great War, although he reaffirmed his belief that maneuver would predominate in a future conflict involving the Soviet Union.[45] However grudging, Frunze's acceptance of World War I's positional phase was significant. Now the trench deadlock on the western front could no longer be so easily dismissed as evidence of the failure of "bourgeois" military art. Rather, it was a legitimate, if regrettable, alternative brought about by objective conditions that someday might have application to the Red Army as well.

Frunze's shift also made it possible for a number of other commanders to make the transition to a more realistic point of view. One of these was Tukhachevskii, who, not surprisingly, had started as a maneuver advocate of the Frunze type. In 1923 he was adamantly opposed to any form of positional warfare and declared that a future war would feature "decisive and overwhelming" maneuver.[46] By 1928, however, he had retreated considerably from this position. The monumental *Future War,* edited by Tukhachevskii in his capacity as chief of the RKKA Staff, now dismissed as "simplified" those views which held that the Red Army was uniquely qualified to wage a war of maneuver. Moreover, the study directed the army to examine in particular the experience of the eastern front during 1914–17, while the civil war was to be studied chiefly for the influence of political factors.[47] This could not have been an easy step, since the notion of a war of maneuver was so tightly bound to the red commanders' strategy of destruction. Tukhachevskii's new formula was also significant for the way it so obviously denigrated the experience of the civil war in favor of the more technically advanced fighting of World War I as a guide for the Red Army's future development.

Svechin, not surprisingly, found the notion of a war of position more palatable, given his preference for the strategy of attrition. Svechin believed that the next war might well follow the pattern of the recent world war, in which an initial period of maneuver would give way to a "loss of offensive spirit" and the adoption of positional methods, as the weight of material factors began to assert itself. He predicted, however, that a positional war in the east would differ from one in the west, just as it had in the Great War, and for much the same reasons: the theater's greater spatial scope and the lower technical saturation of the front. This would result in "softer forms" of positional warfare, such as predominated on the eastern front in the winter of 1914–15, and which still offered some scope for maneuver.[48]

The idea that a future eastern front would differ from one in the west was readily accepted by Red Army theorists of various backgrounds. This is understandable because it allowed a measure of hope that the army could avoid the horrors of a trench stalemate. One of these theorists was the promising young staff officer Triandafillov. He believed that even though the favorable conditions of 1914 and 1920 would not be repeated, there still remained considerable scope for "broad maneuver activities," even though these would develop more slowly than in the west. This would involve, in particular, the widespread employment of large cavalry formations against the enemy's flanks and rear.[49] The former officer and imperial staff academy graduate N. Ya. Kapustin adopted a somewhat more optimistic view in 1927. Kapustin predicted that "spatial conditions alone" will impart to operations "a greater scope in both front and depth" than even the opening weeks of the 1914 campaign in the east.[50] Verkhovskii was even more sanguine and saw great prospects for maneuver in a future war in connection with the army's mechanization. He predicted that the opening battles of a future war would resemble those of 1918–20, and he called the Red Army's 1920 offensive against Poland the "prototype" of future battles.[51] This position, while wildly at odds with the army's existing capabilities, proved to be remarkably prophetic and was a fairly accurate forecast of several of the Soviets' major offensive operations during 1944–45.

The minor disagreements over the extent of maneuver in a future war only serve to emphasize the fair degree of unanimity that actually existed on this point toward the end of the 1920s. By 1928 the Red Army had arrived at a compromise of sorts in which a war of position was seen as a distinct possibility, although it was believed that the art of maneuver would ultimately reassert itself to a greater or lesser degree. Psychologically, it was probably asking too much of the generation of highly ideological commanders that had emerged from the civil war to consider the prospect of a positional stalemate with anything other than distaste. In much the same way, the belief in the prospects for maneuver was undoubtedly a source of consolation to an army painfully conscious of its own matériel inferiority.

The Soviet preference for a large citizen army had its political roots in the Bolsheviks' belief in the mass appeal of their program, which would, it was asserted, eventually lead the numerically superior working class to victory. Thus the idea of the "nation in arms," as much as any other, was inherent in Soviet military thought, as was the companion notion of total war, involving the complete mobilization of the state's human and other resources.

A corollary of this belief was the broad disdain felt in the Red Army for theories then current in the West, which advocated to varying degrees replacing the mass army with a smaller, highly mechanized force, staffed by a core of professional soldiers. Among those who objected to these ideas was Frunze, whose views were political rather than technical. He believed that by creating small professional armies, the capitalist states were attempting to substitute technology for mass, in order to secure the loyalty of the armed forces by creating a caste of professional mercenaries. According to this view, the exacerbation of the class struggle in the West meant that the ruling classes could no longer rely on the loyalties of a mass army based on universal military service. This conviction was fully in accord with the view that in a future war between the capitalist and communist camps, the latter would be able to count on significant working-class support in the enemy rear.[52]

The idea of a large national army found support in a more strictly military analysis as well. Writing in 1927, Triandafillov sought to substantiate the need for a large army by analyzing the mobilization capabilities of the Soviet Union's likely enemies. Triandafillov concluded that the improvements in production methods since 1918 had made it possible for the advanced capitalist nations to actually increase the percentage of the population drafted into the armed forces, compared with that of World War I, making it likely that future armies would be even larger than during 1914–18. On a grimmer note, he concluded that large armies would continue to be necessary because ongoing refinements in the means of destruction would lead to greater personnel losses, thus requiring larger drafts to maintain the army's strength.[53]

However, the preceding should not be taken to mean that the Red Army rejected the idea of mechanization. On the contrary, it impatiently awaited the time when the country's industrial base would have recovered sufficiently to supply the necessary numbers of tanks and aircraft to satisfy the dreams of the army's mechanization advocates. One of these was Frunze, who declared in 1925 that a future war, "to a significant degree, if not completely, will be a war of machines."[54] Another was Tukhachevskii, who had become an enthusiastic proponent of mechanization in all its forms and who was to conduct his own experiments in armored organization as commander of the Leningrad Military District. By 1928 the former zealot was writing that "revolutionary spirit, without the necessary equipment, cannot triumph in a future war."[55] It was a significant statement on Tukhachevskii's part, showing not only how his thinking had matured but also the direction in which he would lead the armed forces.

That direction was indicated most clearly on the pages of *Future War*, produced under Tukhachevskii's direction on the eve of the Red Army's massive mechanization effort. However, in 1928 the army was still a largely infantry and cavalry force, with the more technical arms composing only a small percentage of the total. A force as primitive as this lacked both the striking power and the mobility to penetrate modern defenses, or even the transportation means to maintain a successful advance to any appreciable depth, which raised the specter of a prolonged positional conflict. The study admitted the Red Army's shortcomings in this area and recommended that it be increasingly supplied with "*technical means, particularly the means of attack and suppression.*" Among the measures listed were those increasing the size, power, and mobility of the army's artillery park; introducing light, heavy, and "breakthrough" tanks; increasing the size of the air force; and strengthening the cavalry's firepower and armor.[56] By 1933 these recommendations would be well on their way to realization and would soon achieve a scope the authors had not dared dream was possible.

In fact, there had never really been a serious debate over the question of mass and mechanization, and the issue was resolved without the rancor that accompanied the era's other strategic controversies. Indeed, no one had seriously questioned the need for a large army, and the few proponents of a smaller, more mechanized force remained isolated and lacking in influence. Likewise, it had never been a question of whether the Red Army would adopt a large-scale mechanization program, but of when.

Thus by the end of the 1920s a theoretical compromise had been reached, which involved marrying Russia's traditional strength in numbers and the ideologically correct reliance on a large army with the military necessity of pushing ahead with mechanization in order to deal with future enemies on equal terms. There was really very little else the Soviets could do, since it would still be some time before the economy could hope to satisfy the army's technical needs. Likewise, the high command could hardly be expected to renounce its only asset—the country's enormous manpower reserves. With the benefit of hindsight one may conclude that the compromise reached, however dictated by circumstances, was the most intelligent solution for the time, and one adopted by all the major belligerents during World War II.

By the close of the 1920s, Soviet military thought had arrived at a more or less settled position as regards these four strategic questions. Their resolution was personified in Tukhachevskii, whose evolution as a thinker mirrored many of the army's shifting views on strategic policy. Tukhachevskii best summed up this view in his article "War as a Problem of Armed Struggle" (1928), in which he predicted that in a future war

> decisive actions may be punctuated by positional phases, dividing one period of war from the other. A prolonged struggle, with the exertion of all economic and social forces and accompanied by the exacerbation of class contradictions, characterizes modern mass wars, in which both sides strive to decisively defeat the enemy's armed forces, employing enormous forces and means.[57]

In broad outline, these were the conclusions reached. However, it is impossible to do justice to the intellectual complexity of these controversies in the small space allotted to them here. Also, the welter of political, bureaucratic, and personal loyalties highlighted here are also, to a certain extent, artificial. Thus even the most vigorous supporters of the mass proletarian army did not reject the prospect of mechanization, although for political reasons they were highly suspicious of similar efforts abroad. Likewise, the debate over the place of maneuver and positional warfare eventually found the participants separated by degrees of emphasis, in spite of the potential for disagreement because of ideological considerations. Also, the likelihood of a prolonged war was never seriously disputed, even by the proponents of a highly offensive strategy. As always, the main point of controversy concerned the question of the strategy of destruction versus the strategy of attrition, in which the myth of inherent proletarian offensiveness clashed repeatedly with certain theorists' more sober estimates of the Red Army's capabilities.

Nor should the reader view the strategic debate solely in terms of a "fathers and sons" confrontation between a young "red" cadre and an "old guard" of former military specialists, although some of the more zealous red commanders certainly tried to present their case in this light, for reasons that varied from sincere conviction to outright careerism.[58] Such an approach is too simplistic.

A more useful and accurate means of understanding the final result is to focus less on the debate's confrontational aspects and more on the final synthesis of the opposing sides' views. The terms of the debate were not always distinct, and there were numerous borrowings and changes of position along the way. Apart from the destruction versus attrition controversy, the results of these debates were never a clear-cut victory for one side or another but rather the melding of their parts to produce a recognizable body of Soviet strategic thought. The resulting alloy, for better or worse, represented a fusion of much of the prerevolutionary military legacy with the dynamism and aggressiveness of communist ideology. In turn, these strategic conclusions were to serve as the theoretical point of departure for the emerging Soviet theory of operational art.

THE SHAPING OF OPERATIONAL ART

The Soviet strategic debate of the 1920s ultimately led to a number of far-reaching conclusions regarding the nature of a future war. The most important of these from the operational point of view was the Red Army's adoption of the strategy of destruction, which posited the defeat of the enemy's forces by the overwhelming application of military power, in which all other considerations are secondary. Given the hierarchical nature of Soviet military art and operational art's subordination to strategy, the same political-military demands that shaped the strategic thought of the period had predictable consequences for the conduct of operations. Thus it was no accident that the desire for a decisive outcome by the most violent and direct means possible came to dominate the field of operations as well.

It should not be assumed, however, that the notion of destructive operations originated with the Soviets or that it was exclusively the product of the regime's ideological predilections. In fact, the quest for the enemy's destruction in battle has been a part of the modern Russian military tradition since the time of Peter the Great. Thus while many Western armies during the eighteenth century preferred to maneuver for an advantageous position rather than fight a battle, the Russian army showed a marked inclination to seek a battlefield decision, as at Poltava in 1709 and Kunersdorf in 1759. The same was true during the Napoleonic Wars in such battles as Eylau in 1807 and Borodino in 1812. And while neither of these encounters yielded a decisive result, they were among the bloodiest battles of the age and testify to a desire to destroy the enemy at almost any cost. This tradition remained strong among the army's healthier elements, in spite of the Russians' languid efforts in Manchuria and World War I, the conduct of which reflected a deep-set systemic decay as much as the incompetence of individual commanders.

The tradition was revived with a vengeance by the successor Red Army, whose more politically minded leaders favored the swift, decisive methods that had figured so prominently in the civil war. Among these was Frunze, then chief of the RKKA Staff, whose views were reflected in an operational manual issued under his aegis in 1924. In fact, the manual begins with the declaration that "the task of each operation and battle is the destruction of the enemy's armed force," which is to be achieved by "daring and decisive actions" employing wide-ranging maneuver.[59] These sentiments were echoed in another staff document, *Future War,* which was produced four years later. Here the authors stated that "operations must be waged with the greatest possible energy, to destroy the enemy," in order to exhaust him and create the conditions for a civil war in the enemy rear.[60]

These views found strong support among an influential group of young theorists who were just beginning their academic careers. Chief among these was Tukhachevskii, whose views on the strategy of destruction are already known, and whose approach to operations was no less aggressive. In his pamphlet "Problems of the High Command" (1924), Tukhachevskii unambiguously declared that "operations are conducted to destroy the enemy's armed force, which is necessary for achieving the war's aims."[61] Melikov reached the same conclusion in his history of recent military operations in France, Poland, and Turkey. The author fully endorsed the idea of the "destructive battle," which takes as its goal the "complete rout of the enemy army," according to the dictates of the strategy of destruction.[62] A. K. Kolenkovskii, a 1912 General Staff Academy graduate, wrote in 1929 that the "offensive operation must become dominant" in the Red Army's operational art.[63]

One of the few who opposed this view was Svechin, who courageously sought to resist the monolithic tide of offensivism in the operational sphere, just as he had in the strategic debate. As always, his reasons were subtle and reflected his reaction to the crude theories of the red commanders. He was particularly appalled at his opponents' single-minded search for a decision, which he felt limited the commander's freedom of choice in reacting to circumstances. Svechin roundly criticized the offensive operation conducted according to the strategy of destruction, which, he maintained, threatens to become an end in itself. He recommended instead waging operations with limited aims, which would ultimately bring about victory through the gradual accumulation of military and other advantages.[64] These views were later denounced by Triandafillov as "operational opportunism" and evidence of the author's "decadent attitudes."[65] Such charges were not only an unfair characterization of Svechin's views; they also amply illustrate the increasingly intolerant tone of the Soviet military debate toward the end of the decade.

However, Svechin was fighting a hopeless rearguard action; the issue had already been decided in favor of the offensive party, which is hardly surprising given the prevailing political climate. This took place at the same All-Union Congress of the Military-Scientific Society that had approved Tukhachevskii's destructive strategy. Here the assembled delegates wholeheartedly endorsed the views of Tukhachevskii, Triandafillov, and others and set the Red Army firmly on the path of offensive operations. Henceforth, the army's theorists would focus almost exclusively on the planning and conduct of the offensive, generally at the army level, while defensive operations remained little more than an afterthought in all but a very few works. The one-sided development of operational theory, as in the strategic sphere, while understandable, ultimately led to a serious neglect of defensive preparations that would cost the army dearly in 1941.

These and other important operational questions of the decade were thrashed out within the RKKA General Staff Academy—the lineal descendant of the imperial staff academy, which had gone out of existence in 1918. The institution was renamed the RKKA Military Academy in 1921 and became the Frunze Military Academy in 1925, in honor of the recently deceased war commissar. During these years the academy was headed by the former officers Snesarev (1919–21), Tukhachevskii (1921–22), A. I. Gekker (1922), Lebedev (1922–24), and R. P. Eideman (1925–32). Frunze, the only nonprofessional military man, headed the academy briefly in 1924–25. Of this group, Snesarev, Gekker, and Lebedev were graduates of the old General Staff Academy.

The czarist army's influence was just as strong among the faculty, which included such representatives of the old regime as Svechin, Verkhovskii, and V. F. Novitskii. Indeed, so heavily was the old professoriat represented that some complained that the academy was in danger of becoming merely a red imitation of its imperial predecessor.[66]

As the army's premier military educational establishment, the academy did not escape the bitter political struggles that racked the party and the armed forces throughout most of the decade. Here, as in other areas, the Stalinist faction gained the upper hand as successive groups of "Trotskyites" and "left" and "right deviationists" were defeated and expelled.[67] In spite of these interruptions, the academy was nevertheless able to make a significant contribution to the development of a Soviet theory of operations.

Easily the most important of these achievements was the creation of a separate theory of operational art. As we have seen, the development of operational thought during the late imperial period was hobbled by a chronic reluctance to make a clear distinction between the province of operations and the older disciplines of strategy and tactics. More often than not, operations were viewed as an adjunct of strategy and were not recognized as occupying a theoretically independent niche. This terminological confusion continued into the early post–civil war years, during which time the field of operations was variously referred to as the "operational direction of troops," the "tactics of mass armies," "operational affairs," the "tactics of the theater of military activities," and "strategic art in the operation," among others.[68] One Soviet historian has claimed that the term "operational art" did not appear in the military literature until 1922, although he unfortunately fails to cite the source for this claim.[69] Another participant in these events gives the despised Svechin credit for coining the term during the 1923–24 academic year.[70]

This remark may refer to a lecture Svechin gave in late 1924, entitled "The Integral Understanding of Military Art," which deserves to be quoted at some length. In this address Svechin declared that

> strategy and tactics are separated by an intermediate member—operational art; we think that retaining the old division of military art into strategy and tactics at the present time is absurd, because . . . the general engagement, which once served as the basis for this division, has disappeared. We believe that each of the disciplines, into which military art is divided, must embrace a field having a certain internal integrity. . . . For tactics, such a field is the modern reality of the battlefield. . . . Operational art organizes the separate tactical activities into the operation, proceeding from the criterion of the operation as a whole. Finally, the tasks of grouping operations for achieving the war's political aim fall on strategy.[71]

Svechin's formula was soon adopted within the Red Army, in spite of the deep-set hostility that many commanders felt toward his views.[72] One of Svechin's most erudite supporters on this score was an academic colleague, Varfolomeev, a former czarist captain and graduate of the final 1918 class of the old staff academy. In an important article entitled "Strategy in an Academic Setting" (1928), Varfolomeev stated that as a result of the appearance of large armies and the spatial growth of the former battlefield,

> the study of the operation has gone beyond the framework of tactics, the lot of which was the study of a single battle, but not of a group of them. The modern operation, in grouping battles, is a complex act; meaning the totality of maneuvers and battles in a given sector of the theater of military activities, directed at achieving the overall, final goal in a given period of a campaign. The conduct of operations is beyond the capacity of tactics. It has become the lot of *operational art.* Thus the former two-part formula of "tactics-strategy" is now becoming a three-part one—
>
> | *tactics* | *operational art* | *strategy* |
> |---|---|---|
> | combat | operation | war[73] |

By the end of the decade the need for a separate and independent sphere of operational art had been fully accepted within the army. Something approaching official recognition of this term appeared in a 1928 article in the *Great Soviet Encyclopedia*. The article, written by Svechin and edited by Voroshilov and Tukhachevskii, proclaimed operational art an independent component of military art.[74] The fact that the leading representatives of the Red Army's major factions—Voroshilov (the party), Tukhachevskii (the young commanders), and Svechin (the older generation)—were able to agree on this point is testimony to the degree to which it had become part of the army's intellectual baggage.

The army's changing view of operations was reflected in the academy's program of instruction. In the early years, studies were broken up into so-called cycles, of which the most important were strategy, tactics, and military history.[75] What later became known as operational art was initially taught as part of the strategic cycle, although the study of operations during this period tended to overshadow the cycle's actual designation and harked back to the prerevolutionary past, when even a corps was considered a unit of strategic significance.[76] This terminological dissonance led to a situation in which "higher strategy" (the study of war as a whole) remained tied to "lower strategy" (operations), which, in turn, became entangled with "higher tactics."[77] The resulting confusion can be directly traced to Leer's formula of more than thirty years earlier and indicated how much still needed to be done to establish operational art as a separate discipline.

The situation was clarified somewhat in 1924 with the division of the strategic cycle into two separate departments: the study of war and the conduct of operations *(vedenie operatsii)*, headed, respectively, by Tukhachevskii and Triandafillov. One participant in these events later noted that with the department's establishment, "*operational art* became a part of the academy's scientific-educational practice, both in the capacity of a definite scientific concept, and in the capacity of an educational discipline."[78] The study of operational art was further enhanced by the expansion of the academy's program in 1925 from two to three years. While the first two years were devoted chiefly to tactical problems, the third year was given over to the study of operational-strategic questions, in particular the conduct of operations at the army and front level.[79] However, the delineation of the various disciplines remained imprecise, particularly at the army-front nexus, and this problem was not satisfactorily resolved until the 1940s.

During these years the staff and graduates of the academy produced works that contributed greatly to the Red Army's understanding of operations. Among these were an important joint effort by Tukhachevskii, Varfolomeev, and Shilovskii entitled *The Army Operation: The Work of the Command and Field Directorate* (1926). Others included Svechin's *Strategy* (1923, 1927), Triandafillov's *The Character of Operations of Modern Armies* (1929), Kapustin's *Operational Art in a Positional War* (1927), N. N. Movchin's *Consecutive Operations According to the Experience of the Marne and the Vistula* (1928), and Kolenkovskii's *On the Offensive Operation of an Army as Part of a Front* (1929).

The academic developments of the 1920s represent the logical culmination of operational art's long struggle for theoretical independence. In retrospect, the most notable feature of this decades-long journey is not the length of time required but the fact that the final product so closely resembled what had gone before. From Leer's "tactics of the theater of military activities" to "operatics," and Neznamov's views on the place of operations in military art, it was but a short step to a formula that remained essentially unchanged for more than sixty years. The fact that the prime movers in this evolution's final steps were former czarist officers, by virtue of their superior training and expertise, should come as no surprise and illustrates once again the profound influence that the representatives of the imperial military tradition still wielded in certain areas of the Red Army.

One of the most interesting and productive areas of research during these years involved devising a method of conducting operations at the army level. As the "*smallest operational unit,*" an army was viewed as responsible for "grouping . . . a series of combats," while its own activities constituted one or more of the intermediate phases of a larger front operation.[80] In practical terms, the army organizes the numerous tactical actions of its subordinate divisions and corps, while at the same time it fulfills a similar function vis-à-vis the front, which pursues its own operational-strategic mission. Such statements also highlight the central position occupied by the army operation and, by extension, operational art, in the theoretical order of things. In 1928 this formula was aptly summed up by Varfolomeev, who wrote that "combat is the means of the operation, tactics—the material of operational art; the operation—the means of strategy, operational art the material of strategy."[81]

One author, Movchin, went to some lengths to explain the nature of the army operation, in particular as it differed from the front operation, which is at once both larger, in terms of the men and matériel involved, and more complicated as to the multiplicity of goals it can pursue. However, Movchin insisted that the army operation was not merely a subset of the front operation but a combat episode possessing independent elements, in spite of its subordinate status. He defined the army, or "simple," operation as one that, due to its limited resources, is capable of pursuing only one objective at a time; possesses sufficient resources for achieving this goal; has a command organization responsible for controlling the army's activities and establishing intermediate objectives; and encompasses all activities during the operation.[82]

Movchin's use of the term "simple" *(prostaya)* operation to describe the activities of an army pursuing a single objective is particularly interesting, given its historical antecedents. Mikhnevich was writing about the "simple operational line" as early as 1911, if not before, to describe an operation in which the army pursues "a *single* object of activities" along the front. He distinguished this from what he called the "complex operational line," whereby an army or group of armies pursues more than one objective simultaneously.[83] Mikhnevich's notion of "operational lines" was never adopted by the Soviets, but his division of operations into "simple" (army) and "complex" (front) types was employed by the Red Army to highlight the differences between these forms.

Soviet military theory during this period recognized three kinds of army operations, the approximate outline of which had been identified by Neznamov as early as 1911. The first and most intensively studied was the offensive against a defender awaiting attack. This form was considered the most likely to occur and reflected the experience of the Great War, in which positional forms had been dominant. Such a situation would require a breakthrough operation to restore maneuver, although the Soviets assumed that even a relatively stable front in the east would be more vulnerable to penetration than had been the case during the 1914–18 trench stalemate in France. The second form was the meeting operation, during which both sides launched attacks. This situation, it was believed, would most likely arise at the beginning of hostilities or in the presence of open flanks along an otherwise stable front. The third and final form was the much-ignored defensive operation, which was viewed as a forced measure, to be adopted only under duress.

The outstanding theorist of the army operation during the 1920s was Vladimir Kiryakovich Triandafillov, who for all his immense importance to the development of Soviet operational art is almost unknown in the West. Triandafillov was born in 1894 to a family of Greek descent near Kars, in what is now northeastern Turkey. He was drafted, like others of his generation, into the Russian army upon the outbreak of World War I and eventually rose to the rank of captain. Triandafillov, like many other specialists and wartime officers, joined the Red Army in 1918 and held various command and staff positions on the Eastern, Southern, and Southwestern Fronts in the civil war. He enrolled in the RKKA General Staff Academy in 1919, although combat postings and other assignments delayed his graduation until 1923. The following year Triandafillov was appointed chief of a section in the RKKA Staff's operational directorate; a year later he was head of the directorate, while also serving as head of the staff academy's operational department. In 1928 he became deputy chief of the RKKA Staff; he returned to that position in 1930, following a year's service as commander of a rifle corps.[84] Triandafillov died in an airplane crash near Moscow on July 12, 1931, an accident that also claimed the life of the Red Army's leading armored theoretician, K. B. Kalinovskii. As evidence of the great esteem in which he was held in the army, Triandafillov's ashes were interred in the Kremlin wall alongside those of other Soviet notables.

Triandafillov, as a young wartime officer, naturally gravitated to the camp of the "destructionists" and enthusiastically supported Tukhachevskii and other likeminded commanders in their bitter polemics with the older military specialists. However, Triandafillov was no single-minded bigot but a talented, innovative theorist and author of several articles on military history. His intellectual partnership with Tukhachevskii—what one observer called "a happy combination of two minds"—was particularly fruitful, and the two were able to implement a number of changes in the army, despite Stalin's objections.[85]

Triandafillov's writings reveal a convinced exponent of the offensive operation, conducted to destroy or capture the enemy force in the swiftest and most decisive manner possible.[86] However, Triandafillov's enthusiasm, unlike that of many of his contemporaries, was tempered by a sober calculation of those factors that had greatly increased the difficulty of realizing such an operation. Among these were the defense's vastly augmented powers of resistance, due to both qualitative and quantitative developments in weapons since the war. Triandafillov calculated that the density of machine guns per kilometer along a future eastern front would actually exceed the 1914 figure by some six to eight times, while similar improvements would also take place in the armies' artillery, air, and transportation arms.[87]

Another factor is the great spatial depth of modern defensive arrangements, which enables the defender to withstand serious offensive shocks without collapsing and to maneuver his reserves to meet any threat. Triandafillov calculated the depth of the enemy's tactical defense at between 8 and 10 kilometers, an area that embraced the front line to the limit of his corps reserves. He defined the operational defense as encompassing the defender's army reserves, which generally extend to a depth of 25 to 35 kilometers, although in certain cases this zone may reach back as far as 80 to 100 kilometers, given the presence of a sufficiently large truck park. He classified any deeper reserves as "strategic," which would be brought up to the front by rail.[88]

Triandafillov's chosen instrument for overcoming these formidable obstacles was the "shock army" *(udarnaya armiya)*, a combined-arms force designed not only to break through the enemy's tactical defense but also to continue the offensive through his operational depth and beyond. The shock army would ideally contain from twelve to eighteen rifle divisions, organized into four or five corps, yielding a structure similar in size to a number of prerevolutionary calculations for an army of 150,000 to 200,000 men.[89] However, the similarity here was in numbers only, for the shock army was vastly superior to its prewar counterpart in terms of both its striking power and its mobility. Triandafillov wanted to increase the former by reinforcing it with as many as sixteen to twenty artillery regiments for suppressing the enemy's machine guns and artillery fire during the critical breakthrough phase; greater mobility and depth to the blow would be imparted through the addition of eight to twelve tank battalions. He further proposed strengthening the army through the addition of two or three aviation brigades of light and heavy bombers, for strikes deep in the enemy rear, while four or five fighter squadrons would provide cover for the ground attack.[90]

Triandafillov modeled his shock army after the powerful German right-flank armies that invaded Belgium and France in 1914 and a similar grouping organized by the Tukhachevskii's Western Front in 1920. The shock army, as these examples indicate, was to assume the leading role in frontal operations along the most important strategic axes, although under conditions and in a technological form that differed radically from those of its predecessors.[91] With the prospect of some form of positional warfare seen as increasingly likely, the shock army had to be configured to the need for disrupting the enemy defense and maneuvering in depth.

This requirement, in turn, made it necessary to increase the proportion of specialized arms within the army. The idea of the shock army was quickly adopted by other Soviet theorists, and its composition was continuously debated throughout the 1930s. However, the shock army, as originally conceived, never lived up to its initial promise, although a number of such armies were eventually created during World War II.

Triandafillov rejected the idea of mounting an offensive along a narrow front, which had been the practice in both east and west during the greater part of World War I, the main exception being Brusilov's 1916 effort. He argued that an attack along a narrow front can destroy, at most, only an insignificant portion of the defender's frontline troops and reserves, leaving the remainder free to form a new defensive front or launch a counterattack. As proof, Triandafillov cited the Germans' great March 1918 offensive, which had unfolded along an 80-kilometer sector, or little more than 11 percent of the entire 730-kilometer western front. As a result, the German offensive initially affected only 29 Allied infantry divisions, leaving the remaining 146 divisions untouched and able to concentrate against the threat and thus halt the German advance.[92] On this basis Triandafillov concluded that "a breakthrough operation may count on success . . . only if it ties down a significant portion of the enemy's forces" occupying a given front, which he calculated at between one-third and one-half of the defender's total forces.[93] By this, the author evidently had in mind Tukhachevskii's opening offensive against the Poles in July 1920, which embraced the entire enemy army group north of the Pripyat Marshes, or approximately half of the total Polish forces at the front.

Triandafillov's views were supported by a broad spectrum of the Red Army's leading theorists of varying backgrounds. Among these was the young G. S. Isserson, who was just beginning his academic career and was destined to become one of the most influential authors on operational art during the 1930s. Isserson also chose as his point of reference the March 1918 offensive and, like Triandafillov, reproached the German high command for launching the offensive with less than a third of its forces along a strategically insufficient share of the front. He concluded that for the offensive to go beyond mere tactical success, "it is necessary to keep the enemy's reserves in place along the entire front," so as to prevent the defender from concentrating his unengaged forces against the breakthrough area.[94] Other supporters included Kamenev and Tukhachevskii, the latter of whom declared in 1924, "The wider the breakthrough front, the greater the destruction inflicted upon the enemy."[95] Triandafillov defined this necessary frontage at no less than 150 to 200 kilometers. He calculated that an attack of this scope would immediately engage anywhere from fifteen to twenty enemy divisions and would require as many more to seal the breach. He further concluded that such a large diversion of troops to the threatened sector would likely be beyond the capabilities of an army numbering only sixty to sixty-five divisions, by which he clearly meant Poland.[96]

That the Soviets came to prefer offensive operations along a broad front is hardly surprising, given the various political and military factors that entered into their calculations. Among these was the assumption that a future war might easily involve all the Soviet Union's western neighbors, creating a 3,000-kilometer front from the Barents Sea to the Black Sea. The absurdity of trying to achieve a decisive result along a narrow front, given the distances involved, was obvious, particularly given the high command's belief that an offensive along a 300-kilometer front might remove some of the smaller members (Estonia and Latvia) of the expected coalition at a single stroke.[97] Another was the proven effectiveness of the offensive launched on a broad front, particularly in the east, where the vast distances and the resulting lower troop densities made a war of maneuver more likely. This had been the case in 1916, when even the poorly supplied Southwestern Front defeated the Austro-Hungarians and came close to a stunning strategic result. The situation was somewhat different in the cramped conditions of France, but the Allies did ultimately adopt the strategy of launching multiple and continuous offensives along broad sectors of the front during their final summer and autumn drive in 1918.

The notion of the broad-front offensive quickly became official army policy, and its utility was never seriously questioned by any of the major theorists. During World War II these ideas were put into practice, and the conduct of offensive operations involving one or more fronts quickly became a standard feature of Soviet operational-strategic practice.

Triandafillov's solution for overcoming the enemy's tactical defense and carrying the offensive into his operational and strategic depth was twofold. The first step involved concentrating large numbers of men and matériel at the decisive point, in order to increase the initial weight of the attack and overwhelm the defense at the very outset. He calculated that even a reinforced shock army can mount an effective attack along a front of no more than 25 to 30 kilometers and recommended that the divisions carrying out this attack be assigned sectors of 2 to 3 kilometers in breadth, for a first-echelon strength of eight divisions along the projected breakthrough zone.[98] Artillery densities for the main attack would range from fifty guns per kilometer for purposes of infantry support to seventy-five guns per kilometer in those instances where the artillery has a counterbattery mission as well. In certain cases, the artillery may be partially replaced by tanks, which may be massed to a density of twenty to thirty machines per kilometer to support the infantry attack against a built-up defense. When extended operations are called for, this figure may rise to as many as sixty tanks per kilometer.[99]

The principle of the maximum concentration of force at a single point, in the context of an extended front and an overall scarcity of resources, was one with which the Red Army was familiar. The Soviets had amply demonstrated this ability on a number of occasions, as during the counteroffensive by Frunze's Southern Group and Yegorov's "shock group" near Orel in 1919, as well as Tukhachevskii's preparations for his summer 1920 offensive. This principle underwent fur-

THE BIRTH OF A THEORY, 1921–1929   147

ther theoretical elaboration following the civil war. Both Tukhachevskii and Kolenkovskii, for example, believed that army commanders should strive to achieve a five- or sixfold superiority over the defender to ensure success and should establish a threefold superiority as a minimal condition for a successful attack against an entrenched opponent.[100] Kapustin, in his work on army operations in a positional war, recommended an even greater concentration of force: twenty to twenty-five divisions attacking along a 15- to 20-kilometer breakthrough front, supported by approximately fifty guns per kilometer.[101] Kapustin, however, was writing two years before Triandafillov and was relying chiefly on the experience of the Great War, while the latter was already looking forward to a more technically advanced army that did not have to rely so heavily on large masses of infantry.

Triandafillov also recommended launching a number of secondary attacks to deceive the defender as to the place and direction of the main blow, and to pin down his frontline forces and reserves. These auxiliary attacks would involve two or three divisions, attacking along a 20- to 25-kilometer front. This would yield an offensive frontage of some 45 to 50 kilometers for the shock army as a whole, with a first-echelon strength of ten to eleven divisions. Due to the main attack's demands, however, those units making secondary efforts would have to rely on their organic means, although Triandafillov allowed that in exceptional cases they might be reinforced with units from corps artillery.[102] Kolenkovskii, in a similar fashion, divided his army into "shock," "holding," and "demonstration" groups. The shock group, according to this scheme, would make the main attack with no less than two-thirds of the army's forces. It would be supported by the other two groups along the attack front's secondary sectors according to their designation.[103]

The second ingredient of operational success, following the disruption of the enemy's tactical defense, is to sustain the force of the initial blow into the defender's operational depth and beyond. Triandafillov warned that this would be no easy task under modern conditions, and that the first-echelon divisions could expect to suffer 12 to 20 percent casualties in a period of five to six days.[104] He suggested that one way to compensate for the effects of these losses would be to arrange the army's main attack into second or third echelons, containing one-third to one-half of the first echelon's strength.[105] This backup force would enable the corps commanders to maintain the necessary attack densities along their lengthening fronts and sustain the offensive's momentum by continuously feeding the advance.

This arrangement was a radical departure from civil war practice, when even an army attacking along the main axis was lucky to have as much as a division in reserve, much less supporting echelons. Triandafillov's recommendations were further developed during the succeeding interwar years and took on a technical dimension with the advent of mechanized and armored forces. This development reached its apogee during the latter half of World War II when, in several of the larger front and multifront operations, entire armies came to constitute the follow-on echelons.

The theorists of the 1920s dealt briefly with the actual minutiae of the operation, so its unfolding can be only sketchily reconstructed through their writings. For Triandafillov, the key to success lay in quickly overcoming the enemy's tactical defense zone and defeating in succession his operational reserves as they arrived to seal the breakthrough. This method presupposed the enemy's suppression throughout his entire tactical-operational defense and is best illustrated by the activities of the shock army's air arm during the initial operation. Bomber aviation would begin the operation with strikes against the defender's frontline troops and immediate rear targets, such as troop concentrations and artillery positions, while fighter aviation would work to gain air superiority over the battlefield and secure the main attack's deployment and penetration of the tactical defense. As the offensive moved into the defender's operational zone, bomber aviation would gradually shift its efforts to disrupting the arrival of the enemy's reserves by concentrating on such rear-area targets as troop columns and rail junctions, while fighter aviation would protect those units advancing along the most important axes. The depth of air combat activity in such cases might reach 50 to 75 kilometers and more.[106]

Triandafillov calculated the daily rate of advance during the immediate breakthrough phase at 5 to 6 kilometers, which meant it would take two days to pierce the enemy's tactical defense, with another three to four days to clear the area of the defender's army reserves.[107] Kapustin recommended creating a special "breakthrough group" *(proryvayushchaya gruppa)* of first-echelon divisions to carry out the difficult task of overcoming the enemy's tactical defensive zone. He also anticipated Triandafillov in his insistence that this group be reinforced with extra artillery, tanks, and chemical weapons for the task. The shock army commander, once the defender's tactical position had been breached, would then, according to this plan, commit his "maneuver group" *(manevrennaya gruppa)* to develop the attack against the enemy's flanks and rear. The maneuver group would consist of infantry divisions and large numbers of cavalry, and its mission was quite distinct from that of the second and third echelons.[108] Whereas the latter were charged with reinforcing the advance, the maneuver group would spearhead the advance, raiding the defender's communications and disrupting the arrival of his reserves.

Triandafillov, for his part, did not assign this group a particular organizational status within the army, and he envisaged a formation composed primarily of so-called strategic cavalry, which was a more up-to-date version of Budennyi's First Cavalry Army. This group would be reinforced with mobile artillery, light tanks, and motorized machine gun units. This formation would operate on the shock army's flank to a depth of 75 to 100 kilometers, raiding and carrying out the tactical encirclement of the defender's forces.[109]

The idea of a special mobile force for exploiting infantry success is as old as the cavalry itself. However, the advent of trench warfare in 1914–18 seemed to herald the end of the mounted arm's usefulness, even on the eastern front. The situation changed dramatically during the civil war, where the cavalry was reborn under conditions that facilitated broad-ranging maneuver. As the Red Army became more skilled in their employment, large cavalry formations quickly became a decisive means for exploiting the infantry's success at the front level, most notably during the First Cavalry Army's breakout from the Kakhovka bridgehead in 1920. In this sense, the idea of a separate maneuver group in an army operation did not represent much of an advance over previous practice. However, the advent of large-scale mechanization during the 1930s created the technical basis for the development of a much more powerful maneuver group, composed of motorized infantry, cavalry, and tanks. These formations, whether known as the mobile group, maneuver group, or breakthrough development echelon, eventually became the cavalry-mechanized groups and tank armies of World War II, in which capacity they were often the decisive means for exploiting success during front offensive operations.

While tactics deals with zones, sectors, and densities, the proper sphere of operational art is the axis of advance, making the form and direction of the blow a matter of prime importance to the army commander. Soviet operational art during these years recognized three basic forms of offensive maneuver. These had been identified by Neznamov as early as 1911 and consisted of a movement to turn one of the enemy's flanks, a movement to turn both flanks, and a frontal attack resulting in a breakthrough.[110] The first two forms were more likely to be encountered in conditions of maneuver warfare, such as a meeting operation, in which the enemy's flanks would be open or lightly held, although frontal attacks were certainly not excluded. The latter case was much more likely to occur in a positional setting, in which case a successful breakthrough would almost always turn into a single or double turning movement.

Some theorists favored the so-called ram *(taran)* approach, which involves an offensive operation aimed at turning the enemy flank along a single axis; this could come about as the result of a meeting operation involving open flanks or following the breakthrough of the enemy's tactical defense under positional conditions. The maneuver had been tried most recently by the Germans during their 1914 advance to the Marne and by the Western Front during its ill-fated drive to the Vistula in 1920. Tukhachevskii continued to speak favorably of this maneuver, in spite of his own disastrous experience before Warsaw. However, he was not completely blind to its flaws, the most serious of which was that such a narrow approach quickly reveals its intentions to the enemy, thus giving him time to prepare a counterattack.[111] Kolenkovskii was even more guarded in his approach, although he allowed that a single turning movement might still be useful in certain cases. Among these were situations in which a single blow would enable the attacker to pin the outflanked enemy against a natural barrier or foreign border, resulting in his isolation and destruction.[112]

Triandafillov's rejection of the ram was more forceful, and he believed that such an expedient could rarely be effective because the defender would be able to ward off such an obvious maneuver by counterattacking or withdrawing to a new position. In purely logistical terms, a major offensive along a single axis would also be more difficult to supply over a limited road and rail net than a more dispersed effort, in which supplies and reinforcements could be brought up along more than one avenue of advance. Triandafillov, as had Kolenkovskii, saw the ram's usefulness limited to those exceptional cases where the presence of impassable natural obstacles or a neutral border would furnish the missing flank and allow a single blow to cut off the enemy.[113]

Triandafillov believed that the most decisive form of maneuver was a series of offensives "along intersecting axes," designed to "surround, capture, and destroy" the defender in a pincer movement. He recommended that the projected encirclement should cut off not only those elements of the enemy's tactical defense still holding out at the front but also his army reserves, and that the enveloping wings be heavily reinforced with mobile formations to carry the attack quickly to a depth of 35 to 50 kilometers. A movement of this scope implies the mounting of two major offensive operations along widely separated areas of the front; Triandafillov proposed an attack by two adjacent shock armies along an 80-kilometer front, in conjunction with an attack by another such army on a 40- to 50-kilometer sector along another part of the front.[114]

These recommendations had their roots in prerevolutionary theory, as well as the Red Army's own experience in the civil war. In the latter conflict, Soviet attempts at single or double turning movements usually failed due to a lack of troops and the army's low level of mobility, and there are no instances of a large haul of prisoners as a result. Despite these failures, the idea of cutting off and encircling the defender was never seriously questioned. Other theorists would develop this idea further in the next decade, and it would reach fruition in several of the Red Army's great encirclement battles of 1942–45.

Many of the recommendations put forward by the operational theorists of the 1920s applied equally to the army operation in a positional war, as well as to the more fluid conditions of the meeting operation. The latter, however, possessed a number of specific qualities that required further elaboration. The most important of these features was that the army would not be previously deployed, as in a positional situation, but would do so from the line of march, often with only a limited knowledge of the enemy's forces and deployment. Thus Triandafillov calculated that an army on the march would occupy a front 90 to 100 kilometers in breadth and 65 to 70 kilometers in depth within three to four days of the anticipated encounter, although he expected this frontage to contract to 50 kilometers by the eve of the battle.[115]

His recommendations concerning troop and artillery densities were similar to those he deemed necessary for success in a positional setting. According to this scenario, the army would launch its main attack along a 25-kilometer front, with eight divisions in the first echelon, while another two or three divisions would carry out supporting attacks along a 20- to 25-kilometer front. The army commander, with no field fortifications of substance to deal with, might vary the density of his artillery along the main attack front from as low as thirty guns to as high as sixty guns per kilometer. These calculations were supported in the main by Kolenkovskii, who recommended attacking along a 25- to 30-kilometer front, but with an artillery density of only twenty-four guns per kilometer along the main attack front.[116]

The attack was expected to conclude with a breakthrough of the enemy's front, followed by its subsequent exploitation in depth. Much the same applied to the turning movement directed against the enemy's open flank. Should either attack fail, it was likely that the front would stabilize in the immediate area, perhaps resulting in a positional stalemate, as had been the case after the first great clashes of 1914.

It is not surprising, given the marked Soviet penchant for offensive operations, that Triandafillov devoted so little time to their defensive counterpart, and even these remarks were imbued with an aggressiveness that viewed the defensive as a temporary, forced measure undertaken prior to launching a counteroffensive. Triandafillov's recourse to the defensive was the direct result of his offensive preparations, and he philosophically accepted the inevitability of defensive measures along sections of a lengthy front on which one cannot be strong everywhere, particularly if sufficient forces are to be gathered for a decisive offensive along another sector.

The army's defense rests primarily on its organic reserves. Once the enemy has penetrated the tactical defense zone, the defender's ability to restore the situation rests with the speed with which he can bring these reserves to the threatened area, a factor that also determines the ultimate depth of the defender's possible withdrawal. Triandafillov hoped to limit the retreat in most cases to 30 to 40 kilometers and finally bring the offensive to a halt by directing the reserve forces' counterattacks against the attacker's lengthening flanks. The defender, in the case of a particularly large breakthrough, may be forced to make use of his strategic reserves and carry out the lateral movement of other forces from the unaffected sectors of the front.[117]

The Character of Operations of Modern Armies was the single most important work on the subject of operations produced during the interwar period. The author's achievement is all the more remarkable in light of the Red Army's existing technical state at the end of the 1920s. At the time the army was still an overwhelmingly infantry force, which derived whatever mobility it did possess from its large but outdated cavalry arm. However, great changes were in the offing, and it is to the author's credit that he was able to see beyond the army's current backward state to a time when it would be technically capable of realizing his ambitious plans. Triandafillov was able to go beyond previous historically based studies and construct an "operational calculus" for determining the methods and resources for operational success in a future war. The result was a veritable primer for plotting the breakthrough of the enemy's front and conducting operations in depth. In fact, so prescient were many of his ideas that they were easily grafted onto the more mechanized Red Army of the 1930s. For this reason, Triandafillov was considered by a number of his contemporaries to be the father of what later became known as the "deep operation."[118] This theory, in turn, became the theoretical model for many of the Red Army's great wartime offensive operations.

THE THEORY OF CONSECUTIVE OPERATIONS

Soviet military theory in the 1920s had expressed itself forcefully in favor of the decisive offensive operation, aimed at the destruction or capture of the enemy army in the quickest and most violent manner possible. The chief drawback to this approach was the fact that "modern armies possess colossal survivability," as Frunze observed in 1924, and that a final military decision involving such armies "cannot be achieved by a single blow."[119] The then-deputy war commissar, in this statement, was merely acknowledging one of the salient characteristics of modern armies since the American Civil War, during which time their amazing resilience to destruction in a single great battle first became apparent. Even following such battles as Second Manassas, Chancellorsville, and Gettysburg, the defeated army escaped to fight another day, while as often as not, as at Shiloh and Stone's River, the two sides fought to the point of mutual exhaustion. The few exceptions to this trend occurred at Metz and Sedan in 1870, but these outcomes owed far more to the French command's shortcomings than to its armies' fighting capabilities.

The problem had been raised in Russia as early as 1911 by the future military specialist Neznamov, who declared that the decisive "general engagement," in which the outcome of a war is decided by a single battle, was a thing of the past. Oddly enough, Neznamov persisted in praising the single decisive battle as the "ideal of military art," although he admitted that such an event had occurred only once in recent history, at Jena in 1806, where Napoleon routed the main Prussian forces in a single day. He warned that in most cases any victory was likely to be incomplete, enabling the defeated army to withdraw intact, while its remnants would serve as the basis for a new line of resistance. In such cases, the victor might be as disorganized and exhausted as the loser, preventing him from quickly exploiting his success and causing the process to begin anew.[120] Neznamov may have had in mind the Battle of Borodino, in 1812, in which Kutuzov was defeated but managed to withdraw his army in the face of the equally exhausted French and recovered to drive the enemy out of Russia. He was also likely to have recalled his own experiences in Manchuria, where the Russians suffered a tactical defeat at Lyao-Yang and a near disaster at Mukden but were able to avoid final destruction. The Japanese, in each instance, were too bloodied to take advantage of their victories and finish off the Russians.

World War I and the Soviet-Polish War provided ample confirmation of this trend on an even larger scale, in spite of the vastly different material circumstances under which they were waged. By far the most notable example of a modern nation's inability to end a war in a single climactic battle was the failure of the Germans' 1914 advance to the Marne River, which was conducted under the auspices of the strategy of destruction. In this case the British and French were able to recover from their early reverses and throw the Germans back from Paris to the Aisne and nearly four years of trench deadlock. The Red Army attempted much the same feat in its headlong advance to the Vistula in 1920. However, the Soviets soon became the victims of their own success and arrived before Warsaw worn out and understrength; the devastating Polish counteroffensive that followed threw them back hundreds of kilometers, where the war soon ended in mutual exhaustion.

These and other events provided considerable grist for the Red Army's intellectual mills following the civil war. Among the many theorists who pondered the implications of this dilemma were a number of military specialists and nonprofessional commanders. Senior among these was Glavkom Kamenev, who may well have attended Neznamov's lectures at the imperial staff academy and who reached much the same conclusions ten years later. Kamenev wrote that in a modern war involving large armies, "general engagements . . . have lost their acute character" and are no longer capable of determining the outcome of a war at a single stroke.[121] Tukhachevskii's knowledge of modern armies' resilience had been learned the hard way against the supposedly defeated Poles in 1920. That sobering experience soon brought him around to his former commander in chief's views, and the difficulty or impossibility of deciding the outcome of a war in a single battle or operation was a theme to which he would return often during the decade.[122] Svechin, the bête noire of the red commanders, readily expressed his solidarity with this viewpoint, declaring that "only on very rare occasions" could a decision now be achieved in a single battle.[123]

The conclusions regarding the demise of the decisive general engagement were supported in a number of historical studies by other, less well known authors, who also shared the idea that the modern state had become impervious to a single "knockout" blow. Among these was Movchin, who wrote in 1928 that "in modern war it is impossible to destroy the enemy's entire army with a single blow."[124] In a similar vein, other theorists were struck by the enhanced ability of modern armies to sustain even serious defeats and recover relatively quickly by falling back on their sources of supply, as had been the case in both World War I and the Russian civil war.[125]

Probably the most comprehensive summation of the Red Army's views on the question was delivered by Triandafillov at the previously mentioned congress of the Military-Scientific Society. In a lengthy article based on his report to the congress, he declared that

> the experience of recent wars showed that it is impossible to achieve the enemy's major defeat by a single operation. A single operation engages only part . . . of the enemy's entire forces. A single operation, in conditions of

modern war, may result in the rout or capture of only a certain part of the foe's armed forces. "Cannaes"—as they were depicted in the prewar literature,—cannot be realized through a single operation.[126]

Thus during the 1920s the Red Army faced the critical problem of devising a successful offensive method under conditions in which many of the criteria that formerly constituted victory were no longer attainable. The impossibility of destroying the enemy's armies in a single battle or operation inevitably gave rise to the notion of achieving the same goal over an extended period, which would require several operations. Such a conclusion dovetailed with the growing realization in Soviet strategic circles that any future conflict was likely to be a prolonged affair and that even a war with the USSR's western neighbors "cannot be concluded within a few months," as the RKKA Staff's *Future War* cautioned in 1928.[127] The combination of these factors prompted many of the army's leading thinkers on a series of investigations that ultimately produced one of the Red Army's most interesting and least known contributions to military thought—the theory of consecutive operations.

Not surprisingly, this theory had its roots in the brief period of intellectual vigor that characterized parts of the Russian army from 1905 to 1914. Neznamov, as we have seen, was quite pessimistic about the efficacy of the general engagement in deciding the war's outcome and saw only the likelihood of renewed fighting against an enemy likely to grow stronger as he fell back on his sources of strategic supply and reinforcement. Neznamov sought a way out of this dilemma by maintaining the pace of the advance; he suggested that if the winner of the general engagement "could *uninterruptedly* continue his offensive," then "the war would soon become impossible" for the defeated party to prolong.[128] Elchaninov, his academic colleague, was more specific still, writing of a situation in which an "*unbroken series of local decisions*" would culminate in a decisive result, following a prolonged effort.[129] This, in rudimentary form, was a formula for conducting a series of consecutive operations in which each operation would succeed a previous one and would, in turn, create the conditions for launching the next one, according to a larger strategic plan. While admittedly sketchy, these ideas did establish the groundwork for further work in this area and are one more indication of the continuity of operational theory in Russian-Soviet military thought.

These views were realized, in part, during World War I, although the positional stalemate that characterized much of the fighting tended to obscure the conduct of consecutive operations. For example, one can detect elements of consecutiveness in the early weeks of the war in the west, which saw in quick succession the so-called Battle of the Frontiers, the German pursuit to the Marne River, and the Allied counterattack. In the east, the Germans and Austro-Hungarians eliminated the Russian salient in Poland in a series of operations during the summer of 1915, while a year later the Southwestern Front launched a number of consecutive offensives in the Lutsk area. The first systematic "dosing" of operations took place during the spring and summer of 1918 (the Somme, March 21–April 4; Flanders, April 9–29; the Aisne, May 27–June 4; Noyon-Montdidier, June 9–13; and Champagne-Marne, July 15–17), as Ludendorff's offensives unfolded consecutively in time but separately in space along the front. Equally impressive was the Allies' series of offensive operations (the Aisne-Marne counteroffensive, July 18–August 6; Amiens, August 8–September 4; St. Mihiel, September 12–26; and the various offensives against the German salient in northern France from late September to the Armistice) during the summer and fall, which ultimately achieved the desired strategic result.

And while the Red Army's offensive operations were distinguished by a spatial scope that far exceeded that of the Great War, the same pattern of consecutive operations held true in an even more pronounced fashion during the Russian civil war. In most cases, the final strategic objective was attained only after a series of consecutive operations. This was due not only to the great distances involved but also to the primitive supply situation that prevailed, especially in the Red Army. The first factor was more pronounced during the civil war, while the second asserted itself with a vengeance during the brief conflict with Poland, with disastrous results for the Soviets.

During 1918–20 the Red Army conducted a number of multiple-army and front consecutive operations. The most notable of these are listed, according to front, in Table 1.

In 1928 one of the most talented of the former military specialists wrote that "the theory of a series of consecutive operations is a direct reflection of the civil war's experience in the operational sphere."[130] The civil war and the war with Poland, more so than any other factor, were critical in shaping the Red Army's views on conducting consecutive operations. This is hardly surprising, since the great mass of commanders could hardly have been expected to be familiar with the small body of literature on the subject, and only a very few had the necessary command experience at the operational level during the Great War. For the greater part of the postwar command element during these years, the civil war had been the defining moment in their military careers, and they were eager to draw any number of theoretical conclusions from it. To a great extent, then, the theory of consecutive operations was to be the work of a small group of young former military specialists and wartime officers, with only a small assist from the older specialists.

The acceptance of this formula in the Red Army was reflected in the writings of a number of theorists of various backgrounds. One of these was Tukhachevskii, who on the basis of his experience against the Poles wrote in 1923 that the impossibility of destroying the enemy's forces in a single battle now compels the attacker to achieve this "through a series of consecutive operations," which served the same purpose as the discredited general engagement.[131] He was supported on this point by Kamenev, who stressed the "uninterruptedness" of the Red Army's civil war operations, as well as by Kolenkovskii.[132] Nor did Svechin have any

Table 1.
RED ARMY CONSECUTIVE OFFENSIVE OPERATIONS, 1918-1920
(Blacked-out portions of the graph indicate periods of offensive activity.)

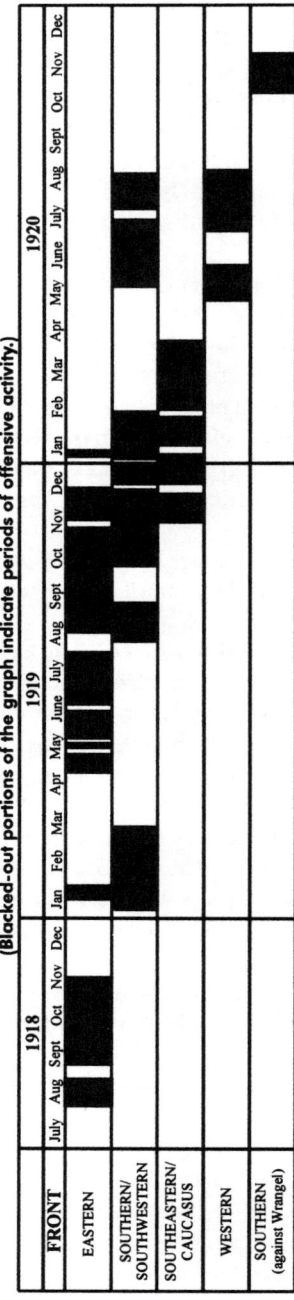

OPERATIONS

EASTERN FRONT: August (3-25 Aug., 1918); Kazan' (5-10 Sept.); Simbirsk (9-28 Sept.); Syzran'-Samara (14 Sept.-8 Oct.); Izhevsk-Votkinsk (15 Sept.-16 Nov.); Perm' (19-28 Jan., 1919); Buguruslan (28 Apr.-13 May); Belebei (15-19 May); Sarapul-Votkinsk (25 May-12 June); Ufa (25 May-19 June); Perm' (21 June-1 July); Zlatoust (24 June-13 July); Ekaterinburg (5-20 July); Chelyabinsk (17 July-4 Aug.); Petropavlovsk (20 Aug.-4 Nov.); Omsk (4-16 Nov.); Novonikolaevsk (20 Nov.-16 Dec.); Krasnoyarsk (4-7 Jan., 1920).

SOUTHERN/SOUTHWESTERN FRONT: Winter (4 Jan.-early March, 1919); Voronezh-Kastornaya (13 Oct.-16 Nov.); Nezhin-Poltava (12 Nov.-11 Dec.); Khar'kov (24 Nov.-12 Dec.); Kiev (1-16 Dec.); Donbass (18-31 Dec); Rostov-Novecherkassk (3-10 Jan., 1920); Odessa (11 Jan.-6 Feb.); Kiev (26 May-27 June); Novograd-Volynskii (19-27 June); Rovno (28 June-11 July); Lvov (23 July-20 Aug.).

SOUTHEASTERN/CAUCASUS FRONT: Khoper-Don (20 Nov.-8 Dec., 1919); Boguchar-Likhai (17 Dec., 1919-2 Jan., 1920); Tsaritsyn (26 Dec., 1919-3 Jan., 1920); Rostov-Novecherkassk (3-10 Jan., 1920); Don-Manych (17 Jan.-6 Feb.); Tikhoretsk (14 Feb.-2 March); Kuban-Novorossiisk (3 March-17 April).

WESTERN FRONT: May (14 May-8 June, 1920); July (4-22 July); Warsaw (23 July-25 Aug.).

SOUTHERN FRONT (against Wrangel): Counteroffensive (28 Oct.-3 Nov., 1920); Perekop-Chongar (7-17 Nov.).

trouble endorsing this position, and in language that was surprisingly similar to Tukhachevskii's. Svechin, in a typical historical analogy, noted that whereas the Battle of Marengo and the Battle of Jena had yielded Napoleon Italy and Germany at a single stroke, the French commander would now have to conduct a series of increasingly difficult consecutive operations to achieve the same ends.[133]

Another was Triandafillov, who devoted a good deal of thought to the subject in several of his works. For Triandafillov, a successful breakthrough of the enemy front and its subsequent development into the enemy's depth inevitably raised the prospect of conducting "a series of consecutive operations, following one after the other in time and space." He firmly believed in the efficacy of such operations as a means of achieving strategic goals; in fact, one of his primary demands of the shock army was that it be able "*to conduct a series of consecutive operations from beginning to end,*" based upon its own resources.[134]

The best summation of this theory was delivered in a 1928 article by Varfolomeev, one of the younger former military specialists. Victory is now achieved, he wrote, through

> an entire series of operations, consecutively developing one after the other, logically linked between themselves, united by the commonality of the final goal, and each achieving limited, intermediate goals ... the operation's goals—the destruction and complete rout of the enemy's armed force; the method—an uninterrupted offensive; the means—a prolonged operational pursuit, avoiding pauses and halts and realized by a series of consecutive operations, of which each is an intermediate link on the road to the final goal, achieved in the final, decisive operation.[135]

One of the most interesting and thorough analyses of the nature of consecutive operations was delivered by Nikolai Nikolaevich Movchin, an RKKA Staff worker and graduate of the Frunze Military Academy, whose *Consecutive Operations According to the Experience of the Marne and the Vistula* appeared in 1928. The book's title is indicative of the Red Army's continuing preoccupation with the Germans' 1914 advance on Paris and its own ill-fated war against Poland in 1920, the latter of which had left a deep and educational scar on the army's collective consciousness. The same theme was also taken up by the former specialist V. F. Novitskii's two-volume study of the 1914 campaign in Belgium and France, and by the red commander Melikov's history of the Marne and Vistula campaigns, as well as the Greek army's 1922 defeat by the Turks in Anatolia. This focus was not accidental, as all three episodes shared a number of operational-strategic traits: these were the dominant idea of "destruction"; the attacker's early victories, followed by a period of sustained and deep pursuit to the enemy's heartland; the attacker's growing weakness due to combat losses and supply problems; and the defender's ultimately successful counteroffensive, which the authors believed distinguish modern operations.

Movchin's work is particularly interesting for his remarks on the place of consecutive operations in the three-tiered Soviet formulation of military art. He believed that the theory of consecutive operations served as the "theoretical foundation" and "most important part" of operational art, while at the same time being an instrument of strategy, in accordance with the hierarchical subordination already established by such writers as Svechin and Varfolomeev.[136] However, by so closely identifying the theory with operational art, Movchin found himself disagreeing with some of his more famous colleagues, who tended to emphasize the theory's strategic applications. Indeed, Tukhachevskii had already identified the Red Army's willingness to conduct consecutive operations as "the foundation of our strategic success," while Triandafillov went even further, calling the theory "one of the chief questions of modern strategy."[137] The pair's wording is, at best, ambiguous, and it is difficult to determine whether they considered the theory of consecutive operations a branch of operational art or an integral part of the theory of strategy itself.

This lack of clarity was also apparent in determining the place of the front in the theory of consecutive operations, and in operational art altogether. This ambiguity was a function both of the czarist military legacy and of the varying missions that the Red Army's fronts were required to accomplish during the civil war. The czarist front/group of armies, occupying a theater of military activities, was a body designed for carrying out purely strategic tasks, as did the Northwestern and Southwestern Fronts, for example, in 1914. The Red Army copied this formula almost exactly with the creation of the Western and Southwestern Fronts in 1920, although these pursued more strictly operational objectives against a single opponent. At the other extreme were the Eastern Front's operations during 1919, which are a unique example of a front carrying out a strategic mission embracing an entire theater of war, despite the fact that the front was no larger than an average army. As a result, the inclusion of the front operation within operational art was gradual and not fully realized until the 1940s.

Triandafillov was primarily concerned with the operations of a single shock army and only briefly mentioned the front. His plan for a decisive offensive along a 200-kilometer front would require at least fifty divisions in the first echelon alone, a force that would necessarily entail the participation of several other armies as part of a larger front operation. These armies, inferior in strength to the shock army/armies, would mount supporting attacks simultaneously with the main effort because the main attack can succeed only if the defender can be prevented from shifting his reserves from the secondary sectors or withdrawing unhindered. Triandafillov recommended launching the front's secondary attacks with armies of three to four rifle corps in strength, each attacking along a 60- to 80-kilometer front. These attacks, because of the limited resources allotted to them, generally cannot count on significant success against a solidly entrenched defender, at least at the start of the operation. However, from the moment of the shock army's/armies' breakthrough along the main front it was expected that the secondary attacks would achieve "independent success."[138]

Movchin's focus, on the other hand, was primarily on the front, and in his more abstract analysis he tended to emphasize the distinctions between army and front operations more than had Triandafillov. The quantitative distinctions are obvious, as the army, which possesses fewer human and matériel resources than the front, is more restricted in its ability to conduct operations of the same duration or to the same depth as the latter. For example, Movchin calculated the average depth of a single army operation at 75 to 90 kilometers over a period of six to seven days, and that of a front at 120 to 150 kilometers over ten to fifteen days.[139]

However, although the front operation is composed of any number of separate army operations, the former is more than just the sum of its parts, and the qualitative distinctions between them according to goal are of a different order altogether. An army, given its limited resources, can safely pursue one operational objective at a time, while the front is capable of pursuing a number of such goals simultaneously. Movchin classified these operations as either "simple" (army) or "complex" (front), which recalls Mikhnevich's similar division of "operational lines" according to the number of objectives an army or front might have.[140] This distinction had important consequences for defining the front's role in conducting consecutive operations; only the front possessed the requisite strength to realize operations to the necessary depth and to simultaneously achieve the manifold objectives, such as a double envelopment, required to decisively disrupt the enemy front. Because only the front can carry out these tasks simultaneously, Movchin concluded that "the theory of a series of consecutive operations is the theory of a series of *complex* operations."[141]

Movchin argued that the demands of a modern war required the creation of the front level of control between the high command and the armies in the field. He singled out for criticism the younger von Moltke's 1914 attempt to coordinate his seven armies on the western front from general headquarters, when, in fact, these armies were conducting three separate front operations. Conversely, Movchin warned that the high command should not burden the front commander with the conduct of more than one series of complex operations and supported the creation of fronts containing as few as three to four armies.[142] In fact, the Soviets eventually came to practice a variation of this proposal in World War II, during which the Soviet-German front at one time contained as many as a dozen fronts. This was sharply at odds with the previous habit of creating only two or, at most, three fronts per theater of war.

Triandafillov favored the Stavka-front-army system of subordination for controlling the multiplicity of front and army operations, as had been the imperial practice in World War I. The Stavka, as the supreme arbiter of military activities, outlines the fronts' operational-strategic tasks and provides the forces and material for achieving them. In certain cases, such as an offensive launched at the juncture of two fronts, the commander in chief may take direct control of operations. The Soviets eventually came to adopt an enlarged version of this proposal during World War II, whereby high-ranking Stavka representatives would sometimes coordinate the operations of as many as three fronts.

In the same fashion, the front commander would assign purely operational objectives to his subordinate armies in accordance with his plans. These included the latters' immediate objectives to a depth of 30 to 50 kilometers, in which the army commanders enjoy a good deal of latitude, beyond which they are assigned subsequent objectives in the enemy's operational-strategic depth.[143]

Finally, Soviet writers also sought to distinguish a series of operations from the broader concept of a campaign. This was a simple task because the groundwork for such a distinction had already been laid by Mikhnevich, who wrote in 1911 that "each war consists of one or several *campaigns;* each campaign—of one or several *operations,* . . . from the initial strategic deployment to the final battle."[144] Tukhachevskii reached a similar conclusion in 1926 when he defined the campaign as that portion of a war that may coincide with a series of consecutive operations; Movchin saw the campaign as the "totality of actions in a defined theater of military activities over an extended period of time," which may include a number of consecutive operations, as well as nonconsecutive ones.[145] This definition was in accord with the Soviets' own recent experience, in which a number of fronts had conducted one or more series of consecutive operations as part of a larger campaign. This pattern would be repeated during World War II, most strikingly during the 1943–45 period, when the Red Army conducted a large number of consecutive offensive operations along the entire length of the Soviet-German front.

Equally interesting were Movchin's thoughts on the "operational anatomy" of the two campaigns. From this he concluded that consecutive operations by large, modern armies in conditions of mobile warfare have certain elements in common. Chief among these was their division into three identifiable stages: the initial operation, the pursuit operation, and the decisive operation (see map 9).

The most important of these is the initial operation *(iskhodnaya operatsiya),* which begins the cycle and whose result inevitably has a great influence on the conduct and outcome of succeeding operations. This operation—or operations, as several initial operations may unfold simultaneously along modern broad fronts—proceeds directly from the belligerents' strategic deployment plans and encompasses the first, large cross-border collisions. In those cases where both sides pursue offensive aims, the initial operation may develop as a meeting engagement of strategic proportions, as when the Allied and German armies collided in the "Battle of the Frontiers" in August 1914. At other times, the operation may unfold more one-sidedly, as when the Western Front attacked the Poles in Belorussia along a static front, where the latter had long since renounced any offensive intentions.

Movchin stated that in most cases a clear-cut victory in the initial operation would ensure success in the succeeding ones. Neznamov had earlier voiced the same hopes, although in 1911 he was still thinking in terms of one or two opening general engagements of a less than decisive variety.[146] However, the most salient feature of the 1914 and 1920 campaigns' initial operations had been their strategically indecisive result, even though one of the sides suffered a sharp reverse. In both cases the loser was able to avoid a decisive defeat by disengaging and withdrawing into his country's interior. The inconclusive result, in turn, laid the foundation for the conduct of future operations in depth. However, Movchin warned

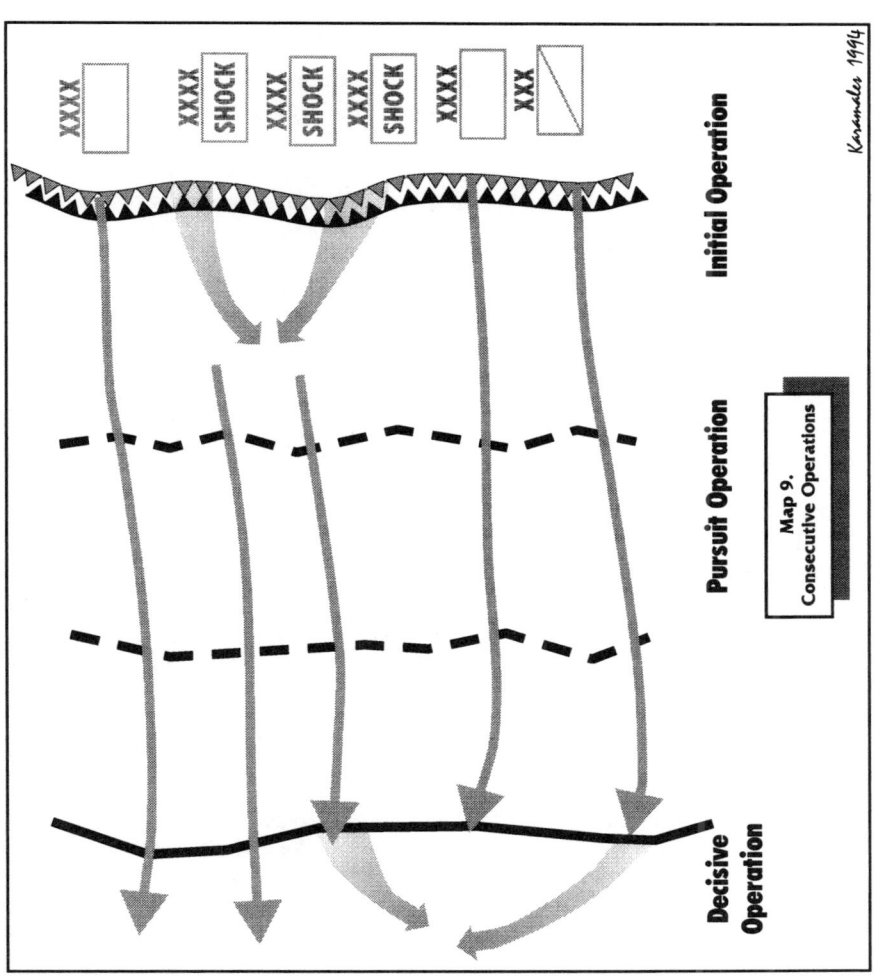

that in certain extreme cases the opening operation might yield such meager results that the entire continuity of operations is disrupted at the outset, and the attacker must undertake a new initial operation/operations, although this time from a point considerably closer to his opponent's vital areas.[147]

The pursuit operation *(operatsiya po presledovaniyu)* begins when the defender admits defeat in the initial operation and attempts to save himself by retreating in the face of superior forces. In modern conditions this phase differs greatly in scope from earlier notions of pursuit, in which the dispirited elements of the defeated army were ridden down within the tactical radius of the battlefield. In the twentieth century pursuit may be strategic in its scope and involve the greater part or all of the loser's armies along a broad front to a depth of several hundred kilometers. This was certainly the case in the two campaigns under study and encompasses the Allies' withdrawal from the Meuse and Sambre Rivers to the Marne, and the even deeper Polish retreat from central Belorussia to the area between the Bug and Vistula Rivers. Thus the pursuit phase had ceased being the finale of a single battle and had become an operationally distinct part of a larger entity.

Movchin divided the pursuit operation into two distinct phases, based on the defender's reaction to his initial defeat and the emerging strategic situation. The first phase comes about as the result of the defender's unwillingness to accept the magnitude of his defeat and sacrifice large territories by means of a strategic retreat. During this period he attempts to halt the attacker along a number of intermediate lines, such as at Le Cateau and Guise in 1914, and in some instances may mount local counterattacks. The second stage begins when the defender realizes the inadequacy of these measures against an attacker who is still considerably stronger and makes the decision to avoid a further, and possibly decisive, defeat by falling back on his heartland. This phase also witnesses the extensive regrouping of the defender's forces to the threatened sector. The attacker, meanwhile, is hobbled by a damaged rail net and is unable to shift his own forces laterally to meet this challenge. This caused Movchin to note that while the pursuit's first phase is the "logical conclusion of the initial operation," its second phase already contains a number of "elements of a new operational grouping for the forthcoming decisive operation."[148]

The "decisive operation" *(reshitel'naya operatsiya)* comes about as the result of the attacker's desire to seize the enemy's political and economic heartland and the defender's resolve not to relinquish it without a major battle. For the former, it is the capstone of the aforementioned operational cycle, while the defender finds himself in a classic "backs against the wall" situation, in which the loss of these areas means losing the war as well. The latter is a debatable point, as even an Allied defeat along the Marne and the subsequent loss of Paris in 1914 would by no means have meant a final German victory. On the other hand, barring sizable foreign intervention, a Polish defeat on the Vistula and the fall of Warsaw would certainly have meant the Sovietization of Poland. What is not in question is that in both cases the defenders were able to mount a devastating counteroffensive that changed the course of the war. How this came about and how to avoid a similar catastrophe in a future war was to prove one of the knottier problems the Red Army encountered in formulating a theory of consecutive operations.

For if the conditions of modern warfare had created a situation in which the consecutive conduct of operations was all but inevitable, these same conditions also rendered final victory increasingly difficult and drawn out. One of the chief reasons for modern armies' enhanced viability, even in defeat, is the enormous strain the fighting puts on the winner, who may emerge nearly as weakened and disorganized as the loser. The problem, which is as old as war itself, has become particularly acute in an age of mass armies, with their heightened demands on equipment and personnel. Clausewitz had defined the problem a century before in his apt phrase "friction in war" *(Friktion im Kriege),* a collective term for the innumerable factors that reduce an attacker's combat effectiveness over time. Among the operationally significant factors contributing to "friction" during the course of a lengthy advance are the loss of troop strength to occupation duties, fighting, and sickness; the attacker's growing distance from his sources of supply; and the necessity of conducting sieges. Clausewitz believed that should the attacker persist in his advance the gradual accumulation of these factors "will usually swallow up the superiority with which one began or which was gained by the victory."[149]

By far the most important of these factors is the problem of supply, for a continuous series of operations must be supported by the uninterrupted flow of men and equipment to the front. The great increase in the size of modern armies, the growing complexity of weapons, and their increased rate of fire put enormous supply strains on twentieth-century armies that had not been felt by the mass armies of the Napoleonic era, and which even the great improvements in transportation could only partially alleviate. Neznamov had noted this problem earlier and ranked supply difficulties and the necessity of "ensuring the *uninterrupted* influx" of forces from the rear as the prime component of operational success.[150] The validity of this statement was borne out several times during World War I, during which the inability of the armies' rear services to meet their offensive requirements often had as much to do with their failure as with enemy resistance, as had been the case during the Russians' 1916 summer offensive. Even the 1918–20 struggle in the former Russian Empire, although waged at a lower level of military technology, confirmed in the end the importance of continuous material supply to operations.

At first it seemed otherwise, however, due to the highly politicized nature of the civil war. The Eastern Front, for example, was able to conduct a lengthy offensive and pursuit over several thousand kilometers, with only minor interruptions, from April 1919 to January 1920. The same was true of the Southern Front's offensive against Denikin, during which the Red Army was able to maintain almost continuous offensive pressure on the White forces for over five months. In both cases the Soviets were able to maintain or even increase their strength by mobilizing the human and material resources of the politically friendly areas through which they passed, even as their organic supply means fell hopelessly behind. Tukhachevskii's Fifth Army, for example, actually grew in size from 24,000 to 37,000 men during August–October 1919, while the Southern Front, which began the autumn 1919 campaign with around 100,000 men, finished it with the same number, in spite of heavy losses due to fighting and disease.[151] The Whites, on the other hand, could rarely count on substantial local support outside certain regions, and their armies tended to melt away rapidly when the fighting moved beyond these areas and became prolonged or heavy. The Western Army, for example, began the Ufa operation with 46,000 men and ended it less than a month later with a mere 18,000, for a loss rate of 61 percent, mostly through desertion.[152] The difference in the two armies' conditions underlines the vital role that political loyalties played in the war.

However, once the struggle shifted to Poland and became a war not of classes but of nations, the Soviets were no longer able to rely on the support of a sympathetic local population to cover their supply and recruitment needs, and the farther the Red Army pressed into Poland, the more its ability to "live off the land" declined. Thus the Western Front, during its six-week offensive, lost up to 40 percent of its strength and was unable to make good its losses, and many of the divisions that had begun the campaign with 6,000 to 8,000 men arrived at the Vistula with no more than 2,500 to 3,000.[153] There were more than enough replacements available in the rear areas, but they could not be brought up in time because of damage to the rail network and the chaotic condition of the Soviet quartermaster system. As one historian later put it, the Red Army's attempt to "mechanically apply" the "methods and routines" of the civil war ended in disaster, as Tukhachevskii's exhausted armies collapsed in the face of a renewed Polish attack.[154]

The Polish campaign's sobering experience did much to impress the Soviets with the importance of the smooth functioning of the rear services. By 1924 Frunze was writing that operational success now depended more on the proper organization of the rear organs than on battlefield control.[155] Even writers normally as divergent in their views as Svechin and the red commander Melikov found that they could agree at least on the critical importance of uninterrupted matériel supply.[156] The best distillation of the new Soviet thinking on the subject was delivered by Varfolomeev in 1928. He declared that success in a series of consecutive operations carried to a great depth now depends on proper supply, which he termed "the successful struggle against the consequences of accompanying strategic exhaustion."[157]

In this regard, the most important factor affecting the attacker's ability to conduct a series of consecutive operations over an extended period was the likely heavy losses in men and equipment. Triandafillov calculated that the attacker's losses might reach 12 to 20 percent of the first echelon's divisions in the initial operation, and no less than 20 to 30 percent of all units during succeeding operations. He proposed to offset these losses by creating reserve regiments equal to 20 to 25 percent of the first echelon's corps to make good the losses suffered during the initial operation, while army reserve units, amounting to 20 to 25 percent of the army's total strength, would follow in the advance's second echelon to maintain the attack's momentum.[158] Movchin put the front's probable losses in the course of a month's fighting at 30 percent, which he believed could be made good by preparing immediate reserves totaling 10 percent of the front's strength, with the remainder arriving during the course of operations.[159] The common thread running through all these comments was that failure to take into account the critical factor of uninterrupted supply would be a repetition of the attackers' mistakes along the Marne and Vistula, when they arrived for the decisive battle exhausted, understrength, and in no condition to meet the enemy counteroffensive.

However, the attacker's ability to satisfy these requirements collides with the inherent contradictions of the pursuit phase itself, which tend to work against the pursuer. On the one hand, effective pursuit requires that the attacker's rate of advance equal or exceed the defender's rate of retreat, in order to cut off the latter's withdrawal and prevent the establishment of a new defensive front. Triandafillov calculated the defender's capacity to retreat along an undamaged rail network at up to 25 to 40 kilometers per day, while the pursuer is limited to no more than an 8- to 12-kilometer advance.[160] Triandafillov and Varfolomeev both sought technical solutions to close the gap. These consisted of creating highly mobile pursuit units of tanks and motorized infantry to carry out a parallel pursuit along the enemy's flanks, attacking his rear units and otherwise disrupting his withdrawal.[161] However, the means to accomplish this were not yet available to the Red Army and would remain so for some years.

Furthermore, any effort to increase these meager rates of advance with the primitive means at hand ran into the seemingly intractable problem of adequately supplying the troops by rail. This is because the rear organs' ability to keep the armies at strength during the course of such a lengthy offensive is directly dependent on the rail system's optimal functioning. However, given the railroads' vital importance, a retreating army is likely to carry out the systematic destruction of not only the tracks but also bridges and supporting structures. This, in turn, necessitates a great deal of repair work by the pursuer, with serious implications for the conduct of operations to any appreciable depth. Triandafillov predicted that future major operations would involve widespread rail destruction on the defender's part, with the attacker capable of repairing on the average only 5 to 6 kilometers per day, although this figure might rise to as high as 15 to 20 kilometers in especially favorable circumstances. Kolenkovskii was in agreement with the first figure, while Movchin was slightly more optimistic, calculating the average speed of railroad repair at 8 to 10 kilometers per day.[162] Moreover, even a restored rail line could not be brought up to full capacity immediately, causing further delays in the delivery of men and supplies. Based on these figures, Triandafillov calculated that a series of consecutive operations, conducted to a depth of 300 to 350 kilometers over a month, would outstrip the refurbished railroads by as much as 150 to 200 kilometers, while Movchin predicted that operations conducted to a depth of 300 to 400 kilometers over the same period would outrun their railroads by 120 to 150 kilometers.[163]

Nor was the situation improved appreciably by the inclusion of horse or automobile transport into this system, due chiefly to the primitive road network along the USSR's western frontier and the Red Army's own low level of mechanization. Triandafillov calculated that an army based exclusively on horse transport for the final stage of supply delivery may conduct consecutive operations only to a depth of 135 to 150 kilometers, which he declared insufficient for decisive success against an opponent occupying a broad front. Even the addition of thousands of supply trucks, which the Red Army did not possess, would extend the attacker's reach by no more than 140 kilometers. These bleak figures forced him to conclude that existing conditions of matériel supply limited the maximum depth of a series of consecutive operations to 250 kilometers, and then only if the attacker was well supplied with motorized transport.[164]

Thus the vagaries of the attacker's supply situation tended to put certain "natural limits" on the depth and duration of a series of consecutive operations. Movchin believed that these limits would come into play during the transition between the pursuit and decisive operations.[165] To ignore these limits and enter into the final battle with an exhausted, undersupplied army was to risk a decisive counteroffensive and defeat by a revived opponent.

Movchin's ideas on "operational exhaustion" had much in common with Clausewitz's earlier belief that even an advance begun under the most favorable circumstances cannot be sustained indefinitely, due to the inevitable "frictions" of war. Clausewitz had noted the offensive's tendency to wane over time and spoke of the "culminating point of the attack" *(Kulminatsionpunkt des Angriffs)* as that unseen line beyond which "the scale turns and the reaction follows with a force that is usually much stronger than that of the original attack."[166] Thus even a successful operation, because of its dependence on uninterrupted matériel supply and its tendency to outrun the latter, carries within itself the seeds of its own destruction, to paraphrase Marx. These notions had a particular resonance for an army still smarting from its defeat in 1920 and inspired a number of theorists to seek a way out of the dilemma.

One of the most thoughtful of these was Svechin, who was no doubt attracted to Clausewitz's ideas regarding offensive "overreach" by the points they shared with his own views concerning a more moderate approach to conducting operations. Svechin's work reveals a conscious effort to find a formula for conducting operations that would impose some constraints on the more offensive-minded commanders, whose enthusiasm for the uninterrupted offensive was pregnant with the very dangers that Clausewitz had pointed out. Svechin emphasized that the attacker's decision to continue the offensive, following the initial operation, places a growing strain on his communications and ability to maintain his strength; the farther he moves into enemy territory, the weaker he becomes vis-à-vis the defender, who is able to draw upon an undamaged resource base and a shorter supply line to alter the correlation of forces in his favor. The experience of recent campaigns caused Svechin to conclude that "the responsibility of strategy is to not allow offensive operations to drag out to the last gasp" and "to halt the offensive in time."[167]

This warning found a surprisingly sympathetic response among the more offensive-minded commanders, perhaps because they had seen for themselves what becomes of an offensive operation pushed beyond its limits. These included one writer who echoed Svechin nearly word for word, writing that a commander must "foresee the culmination point" of an operation and halt it in time.[168] The same point was also made by Melikov and Novitskii in their works on recent consecutive operations.[169] Triandafillov wrote in the same vein that "the art of the strategist and operator is to correctly feel that limit in human and matériel means" beyond which follow exhaustion and defeat.[170]

Movchin offered two practical recommendations for avoiding such an outcome. The first was to bring the initial operation closer to the enemy's vital areas by beginning the war with a number of limited operations along the frontier. Such a move, he argued, not only would place the enemy's heartland within range of any subsequent operational sequence but also would ease the attacker's later supply problems because of his more advanced state of mobilization. He also recommended a halt in the advance at the close of the pursuit operation. This would enable the pursuer to bring up his lagging supply organs and be reinforced so as to resume the offensive and enter the decisive operation with a good chance of success.[171]

Triandafillov also recommended shutting down operations at some stage to avoid overtaxing the pursuer's forces. Given the likely rate of railroad repair, he calculated this pause at a minimum of two to three weeks, in order to accumulate sufficient matériel supply before resuming operations along the same axis. Rather than grant the defender a respite during this period, he recommended mounting new operations elsewhere along the front.[172] The latter presupposes the attacker's having the overall strategic initiative, which allows him to strike at will along widely separated sectors of the front, and forecast in broad outline the strategy that the Soviets eventually pursued so skillfully in 1943–45.

The Soviets' obvious enthusiasm for this and other mechanistic formulas should not cause the reader to think that the Red Army was deficient in devising more concrete plans for conducting consecutive operations against its enemies during the 1920s. These plans were directed chiefly against the USSR's western neighbors and conditioned by the belief that the Soviet Union would have to wage a future war against a coalition of these and other powers. Added to this was the knowledge that the Red Army could not eliminate all of these countries in a single campaign but would require a series of sustained efforts to complete the task.[173] That the conduct of consecutive operations against these countries was a part of

Soviet strategy is clear from Tukhachevskii's 1926 exhortation that the Red Army must have a plan for eliminating the enemy coalition "in detail, consecutively and systematically."[174] As chief of staff, Tukhachevskii took a leading part in drawing up these plans.

Practically speaking, the swift conquest of Estonia and Latvia did not present a particular problem because their inconsequential depth and small armed forces offered little hope of prolonged resistance against a major attack. Tukhachevskii, in this case, favored a decision in the course of a "single decisive operation," which would secure these countries before the British fleet could intervene. The conquest of Romania promised to be more difficult than that of the Baltic States, due to its larger army and greater territorial depth. However, this was by no means an insuperable problem, and it was calculated that a series of consecutive operations would soon carry the Red Army to the political and economic center of Bucharest and quickly end the war.[175]

However, the Soviet Union's own military weakness dictated that Romania could not be effectively dealt with until after the defeat of Poland, the strongest military power in eastern Europe and, as such, the key to Soviet strategy in the region. Tukhachevskii's views on this question ran the gamut from wildly optimistic to deeply pessimistic. In 1926 he wrote that it was "theoretically possible" to defeat the Poles "by a series of consecutive, uninterruptedly conducted, operations," which would climax in a decisive battle along the middle Vistula, some 300 to 350 kilometers from the Soviet border.[176] However, only two years later his views and those of the RKKA Staff had sobered considerably; he had renounced the possibility of defeating Poland in a rapid series of such operations and was now predicting a much longer struggle, which might last as long as three years.[177]

By the end of the 1920s the theory of consecutive operations had become one of the prime components of Soviet operational theory. This theory, for all its schematic quality and reliance on the evidence of past wars, nevertheless performed the service of focusing the Red Army on the critical role played by the rear organs in offensive operations. In recognition of this fact, questions of matériel supply soon came to occupy a prominent place in the Frunze Academy's course of operational instruction.[178] Moreover, the theory of consecutive operations, like that of the army operation, proved quite adaptable to the technically more advanced army that was coming. It also served as the theoretical basis for many of the Red Army's great front and multifront offensive operations during the latter half of World War II and remained a fixture of Soviet operational thinking for many years beyond.

4
Maturation, 1930–1936

It was a basic tenet of the Soviet view of war that a country's military art is determined chiefly by its level of economic development. This maxim applies to capitalist and socialist states alike, and its disturbing consequences were becoming increasingly obvious to the Soviet leadership as the 1920s drew to a close. Although it was true that by 1928 the USSR had regained or surpassed the prewar (1913) level of production, the country still lagged dangerously behind the developed capitalist powers, which had used the years since 1918 to move even further ahead in the area of military technology. For the ever-suspicious Soviet leadership the situation was pregnant with disaster. Joseph Stalin stated the problem succinctly at a plenum of the party's Central Committee in late 1928. "It is impossible to defend our country's independence," he said, "lacking a sufficient industrial base for defense." Stalin, honing the point further, stressed the military necessity of economically overtaking the advanced capitalist nations. "Either we achieve this," he warned, "or they will wipe us out."[1]

The dictator and his henchmen were determined to transform backward, peasant Russia into a modern industrial and military power overnight, regardless of the cost. They were determined that the next war, when it came, would not find the country in the same situation as czarist Russia, which had been defeated by a smaller but industrially superior Germany. Nor were Stalin's concerns on this score completely unfounded, as had been the case with previous "war scares." The 1930s saw the overall worsening of the USSR's strategic position in both Europe and Asia, due to the revival of Japanese expansionism and Hitler's accession to power in Germany. Japan's conquest of Manchuria and Germany's ambitious rearmament program exacerbated these fears. The Soviet Union's diplomatic isolation and the prospect of a two-front war with what were regarded as the harbingers of a renewed capitalist assault caused Stalin to press his "revolution from above" with even greater ferocity.

The heart of the Stalinist program lay in the two Five-Year Plans (1928–37) for the social transformation of the country. The outlines of the first Five-Year Plan (1928–32) were drawn up at the fifteenth party congress in December 1927. However, the relatively modest growth rates then envisaged were progressively radicalized throughout 1928 and gave Stalin the issue he needed to break with his former allies, Bukharin and Rykov. The sixteenth party conference in April 1929 adopted in full the dictator's plan for the forced industrialization of the economy and the mass collectivization of private peasant holdings. During this period the remaining opponents of Stalin's policies were quickly defeated and removed from their positions, leaving the dictator and his followers free to pursue their course without hindrance.

The overall quantitative results of this policy were certainly impressive, and Stalin succeeded in transforming the Soviet Union into a modern industrial state of sorts within a few short years, even as the capitalist world was sliding into depression. In fact, so great was the growth in industrial production that by the end of 1937 the Soviet Union was in some areas the leading industrial power in Europe and lagged only behind the United States in the world. Table 2 gives an idea of the surge in industrial production during these years, according to a number of indices.[2]

But the cost in human suffering was enormous and far exceeded that of the harshest periods of development in the capitalist countries during the nineteenth century. Hardest hit were the country's peasants, whose centuries-old way of life was brutally turned upside down within a few years. By 1937 nearly all of the country's peasants had been herded into the new collective and state farms, in one of the worst and least known human disasters of the century. It has been estimated that as many as 14.5 million peasants died as the result of starvation and the various punitive measures that accompanied collectivization.[3] The situation was hardly better in the cities, as millions of industrial workers were crowded into the new towns and factories springing up all over the country and were forced to labor and live under the most primitive conditions. The standard of living plummeted drastically, as every fiber of the nation was strained to meet the goal of building "socialism in one country."

Equally grim was the growth in the network of labor camps and other mechanisms of the modern police state. The camps had existed in one form or another since the early days of the Soviet regime, but their numbers increased dramatically as the scale of repression rose sharply after 1929. Forced labor played a key role in the construction of such prestige projects as the Baltic–White Sea Canal and the Moscow-Volga Canal, which cost thousands of lives. By the beginning of 1937 as many as 5 million prisoners may have been held in these camps, and forced labor had become an essential component of the Soviet economy.[4]

Despite the suffering, these were happy times for the Red Army, which until 1937 remained the favored child of party and state and was spared, at least temporarily, many of the horrors being visited upon other parts of Soviet society.

Table 2. Soviet Industrial Production, 1928-37

Product		1928	1932	1937
Oil	(millions of tons)	11.6	21.4	28.5
Coal	" "	35.3	64.4	128.0
Cast iron	" "	3.3	6.2	14.5
Steel	" "	4.3	5.9	17.7
Iron ore	" "	6.1	12.1	27.8
Automobiles	(thousands)	.84	23.88	199.9

However, there were also disturbing signs, which the army's leadership would ignore at its peril. Among these was the growing imposition of Stalinist orthodoxy in all walks of life, including the military. This phenomenon coincided with the dictator's achievement of unchallenged authority and was tirelessly propagated throughout the armed forces by his creature, Voroshilov.[5]

Equally worrisome were the Shakhty trial (May–July 1929) and the trial of the so-called Industrial Party leadership (November–December 1930) on charges of "wrecking," which were indicative of a growing mania in society for rooting out "spies" and "saboteurs." The trials also represented the party's decision to break with the "bourgeois specialists" in favor of Soviet-era cadres, a move that had fateful consequences for the remaining former czarist officers in the army. Prominent among those who fell afoul of the new order were Svechin, Verkhovskii, and the civil war historian Kakurin, who were arrested in 1930. Svechin and Verkhovskii were released in 1932 and allowed to return to their teaching duties at the Frunze Military Academy, while Kakurin languished in prison until his death in 1936.

THE RED ARMY'S TECHNICAL RECONSTRUCTION

The sweeping changes taking place in the country's economy had an equally dramatic effect on the growth of the Red Army, which more than doubled in size from 617,000 men in 1928 to 1,433,000 by 1937.[6] The transition to a larger and more technically sophisticated army was the beginning of the end for the mixed territorial-cadre system, which was increasingly incapable of meeting the army's needs. In May 1935 the decision was made to gradually put the army on a single cadre system of recruitment, and by the end of the year 77 percent of all divisions were of the cadre type.[7]

Important changes were also taking place in the higher military organs. In June 1934 the People's Commissariat of Military and Naval Affairs became the People's Commissariat of Defense. Although Voroshilov continued to head the military establishment, it was widely recognized that the defense commissar lacked "any practical and theoretical basis in the field of military science and military art" and had to rely on Tukhachevskii, Triandafillov, and others.[8] At the same time, the civil war–era Revolutionary Military Council was abolished and its functions taken over by the existing Defense Commission, a permanent body attached to the Council of People's Commissars. Later that same year the Military Council was created as an advisory body to the defense commissariat. In September 1935 the RKKA Staff was renamed the RKKA General Staff. Yegorov, who had succeeded Shaposhnikov as chief of staff in 1931, continued at this post. Ya. B. Gamarnik, who had succeeded Bubnov as head of the RKKA Political Directorate in 1929, served as the armed forces' chief commissar throughout this period.

The armed forces' leadership had good reason to be pleased with the amount and variety of modern equipment it was receiving and remained firmly behind the regime even through the worst of the collectivization crisis. The army's loyalty was rewarded in September 1935 with the introduction of officers' ranks, although the term itself remained politically taboo. Two months later, Voroshilov, Budennyi, Yegorov, Tukhachevskii, and Blyukher were created marshals of the Soviet Union. Other commanders, such as Kamenev, Uborevich, Shaposhnikov, Yakir, Ya. Ya. Alksnis, Vatsetis, and Kork, among others, were created army commanders first and second class.

The armed forces were the chief beneficiary of the USSR's superhuman industrialization effort during the 1930s. While the great majority of the population endured unimaginable hardships, those sectors of the economy linked to defense production were comparatively well off. The military's total share of budgetary allocations, for example, rose from 11 percent during the first Five-Year Plan to 16.4 percent in the second.[9] If anything, the figures probably underestimate the military's share of the budget and include only those expenditures directly related to the maintenance of the armed forces, with other, related costs hidden within other commissariats. Whatever the actual state of affairs, there is no doubt that Soviet arms production did increase dramatically during this period, as illustrated in Table 3.[10]

An important milestone in the Red Army's technical makeover was the Central Committee's July 1929 decree "On the State of the USSR's Defense," which charted in broad outline the future growth of the nation's military and stressed the need for increasing the proportion of technical troops by greatly expanding the numbers of tanks, artillery, armored cars, and aircraft.[11] This general directive was continually refined, and a new plan for the 1934–38 period was adopted four years later. Separate plans for the technical renovation of the navy, air force, and artillery were also drawn up during 1933–35. In 1929 the post of chief of RKKA Armaments was established to oversee this ambitious program. The first chief was the former czarist ensign Uborevich, who was succeeded in 1931 by Tukhachevskii. In 1936 a separate People's Commissariat of the Defense Industry was established.

Table 3. Soviet Weapons Production, 1930-37

Weapons	Average Yearly Production		
	1930-31	1932-34	1935-37
Aircraft (total)	860	2,595	3,578
Bombers	100	252	568
Fighters	120	326	1,278
Tanks	740	3,371	3,139
Artillery (total)	1,191	3,778	5,020
Small-caliber	1,040	2,196	3,609
Medium-caliber	870	1,602	1,381

The rearmament program did not always proceed smoothly, however, and there inevitably arose a number of problems connected with an undertaking of this magnitude. The breakneck speed with which the program was adopted and the unthinking zeal for mechanization in any form led to an enormous waste of resources and several quantitative excesses in certain of the combat arms, particularly the armored branch. Moreover, a chronic shortage of factories, materials, skilled workers, and experienced weapons designers plagued the military industry throughout most of this period. In 1929, for example, only 20 percent of the planned output for tanks was achieved, and as late as 1937 rifle and artillery production was only 70 percent of projections.[12] The qualitative results were frequently disappointing as well, and many of the early tank and aircraft models were decidedly inferior to their Western counterparts. Nevertheless, in spite of enormous difficulties, the USSR's rearmament drive was, quantitatively speaking, a huge success, as revealed in Table 4.[13]

The steady influx of new weapons and equipment also gave rise to plans for reorganizing the Red Army along more modern lines. By far the most ambitious

Table 4. The Red Army's Weapons Park, 1928-35

Weapons and Equipment	1928	1932	1935
Rifles (thousands)	1,596	2,292	3,050
Machine guns (light)	8,811	22,553	83,922
Machine guns (heavy)	24,230	33,118	53,492
Artillery (76-mm and larger)	6,645	10,684	13,837
Tanks (mostly light)	92	1,053	7,633
Tankettes	0	348	2,547
Armored cars	7	213	464
Automobiles	1,050	5,669	35,303
Aircraft	1,394	3,285	6,672

of these was put forward by Tukhachevskii in early 1930, when the rearmament program was barely under way. He drew up the plan from his semi-exile as chief of the Leningrad Military District, to which he had been dispatched in 1928 following a policy dispute with Voroshilov. Tukhachevskii, in a report to his nemesis, emphasized that the emergence of a qualitatively new army made it necessary to expand its size and increase its mobility and offensive striking power by employing large numbers of tanks and aircraft. He proposed creating the foundations of an army that could mobilize to a strength of 200 divisions in twenty-eight days, with the vast majority arrayed against the USSR's western neighbors, particularly Poland. The remainder would be confined to internal military districts and the high command reserve. This force would be further supported by 50 high command artillery divisions, plus heavy gun and mortar units, 225 reserve machine gun battalions, 40,000 aircraft, and 50,000 tanks.[14]

Tukhachevskii's proposal is an example of the Soviet penchant for gigantism at its worst and would be beyond the country's productive capacity to fulfill, or the army's capacity to absorb, for many years to come. Stalin and Voroshilov brusquely rejected the plan as "red militarism" and likely to undermine the national economy if it were attempted.[15] Tukhachevskii's views, however, were partially vindicated in 1931, when he was recalled to Moscow to oversee the implementation of a more modest version of his plan.

The practical effects of the army's makeover were not long in making themselves felt in the army's organization and equipment mix, and that of its component parts. At the beginning of the 1930s the Red Army was divided into four services: the ground forces, air force, navy, and air-defense forces. Of these, the ground forces were by far the largest and most important. They also dominated the Defense Commissariat and upper echelons of the RKKA, where the three other services existed as mere directorates. However, this situation began to change with the arrival of more sophisticated equipment and the consequent strengthening of the more technical services at the expense of the ground forces, with its heavy infantry complement. Thus despite the more than twofold increase in the armed forces' size during these years, the ground forces' relative weight within the RKKA actually fell from 92.6 percent in 1928 to 79.3 percent in 1935. Conversely, the air force's share grew from a mere 2 percent in 1928 to 9.6 percent in 1935, and that of the navy increased from 5.4 to 8.9 percent. The air defense forces, which did not even exist as a separate directorate in 1928, accounted for 2.2 percent of the total by 1935.[16]

Within the ground forces (rifle troops, cavalry, armored and mechanized troops, artillery, airborne troops, and others), similar changes were taking place in favor of the more technical arms. This led to an overall decline in the proportion of rifle troops from 58 to 49 percent, despite a twofold growth in their absolute numbers between 1929 and 1938.[17] At the same time, the infantry arm benefited tremendously from the rearmament program in the direction of increased firepower and mobility. Whereas a rifle division in 1925 had an authorized strength of 12,800 men, 54 guns, 189 heavy machine guns, and 81 light machine guns, its 1935 counterpart contained slightly more men but had become much "heavier" in other respects. It now included 57 tanks, 96 guns, 180 heavy machine guns, 354 light machine guns, and 18 antiaircraft machine guns. A rifle corps, the largest tactical formation, contained three rifle divisions, plus two artillery regiments, an antiaircraft battalion, a sapper battalion, a communications battalion, and other units.[18] Nevertheless, the growth of the other combat arms failed to impinge upon the infantry's role as the centerpiece of the combined-arms battle. As Tukhachevskii, one of the Red Army's more zealous mechanization advocates, wrote in 1931: "Tanks only support the infantry in battle, but do not replace it."[19]

The Red Army's mounted arm also changed considerably during these years and, like the infantry, became "heavier" in terms of firepower. By 1936 a cavalry division contained four cavalry regiments, a mechanized regiment, an artillery regiment, and smaller specialized units. The infusion of modern technology had the effect of reducing the percentage of actual horse soldiers in cavalry units from 80 percent at the end of the 1920s to 60 percent in 1938. However, in contrast to the cavalry's precipitous decline in the armies of the other industrialized nations, the absolute numbers of cavalry actually increased within the Red Army in the 1930s. Thus the number of cavalry formations grew from fourteen divisions and seven brigades in 1929 to thirty-two divisions and two brigades by 1938, while the number of cavalry corps (two to three divisions) increased from four to seven.[20]

While the retention of a large cavalry arm may have been justified by the army's earlier low level of mobility, by the mid-1930s this reason no longer sufficed. That a large cavalry establishment lingered on so long within the Red Army was primarily due to the influence of two men, Voroshilov and Budennyi, who had been associated with the mounted arm since their service together in the First Cavalry Army in 1919–20. Voroshilov's military ignorance and resistance to change were well known, while Budennyi continued to propagate the virtues of cavalry from his post as RKKA cavalry inspector, where he denounced as "wrecking" those attempts to limit its employment.[21]

The Red Army's artillery arm benefited enormously from the flow of new weapons and was almost completely overhauled during the 1930s. Among the new weapons that entered service were the 45-mm antitank gun, 76-mm field gun, and 122-mm howitzer, all pulled by horse transport. Corps artillery received the 122-mm gun and 152-mm howitzer, while the heavy gun park included the 203-mm howitzer—all towed by mechanized transport, which would enable them to keep up with the tanks and motorized troops. There were problems, however, mostly in the number of guns produced. One observer recalled that at one point the enthusiasm for tanks in the Red Army was such that artillery production suffered and had to be made up for during succeeding Five-Year Plans.[22]

This massive influx of weapons naturally had an effect on the organization and distribution of the Red Army's artillery park. During the 1930s Soviet artillery was divided into troop and reserve artillery, with the former receiving the lion's share of the guns. Thus a rifle division was reinforced with an antiaircraft battalion, and its organic artillery regiment was increased from three to four battalions. Rifle corps were supplied with an extra artillery regiment and an antiaircraft battalion. The High Command Artillery Reserve (ARGK), on the other hand, would parcel out the forces at its disposal to strengthen the offensive power of those formations carrying out important tactical and operational missions. By 1939 this force had grown to a strength of twenty-four artillery regiments and a number of heavy-caliber battalions, from a mere four regiments in 1929.[23]

No single weapon was more important in transforming the Red Army into a modern force than the tank. Prior to 1927 the Soviet tank park consisted almost entirely of foreign models and captured holdovers from the civil war. Following the appearance of the T-18 light tank that year, new models succeeded each other in a bewildering array of types throughout the first two Five-Year Plans. Among these were the T-19, T-20, T-26, BT-2, BT-5, BT-7, BT-8, BT-IS, and T-46-5 light tanks; the T-17, T-23, and T-27 tankettes; the T-37 and T-38 amphibious models; the T-24, T-28, and T-29 medium tanks; and the heavy T-35. The Soviets quickly surpassed their Western counterparts in the sheer number and variety of armored vehicles, and by 1937 the Red Army's tank park was the largest in the world, numbering some 15,000 vehicles, of which nearly 12,000 were light T-26 and BT models.[24] However, the haste with which this force had been assembled was evident in the high proportion of light tanks and tankettes, many of the latter of which were little more than armored machine gun platforms. All these models lacked adequate armor protection and, with the exception of the T-28 and the T-35, were too lightly armed.[25] At this point the Soviets began to cut back the production of light tanks and concentrated instead on designing a new generation of medium and heavy tanks, which began to appear in significant numbers only in 1940.

The spectacular growth in the number of tanks engendered equally important changes in their organizational structure. This was the province of the Motorization and Mechanization Directorate, established in 1929, and its leading lights, I. A. Khalepskii and Kalinovskii. The directorate divided all armored and motorized troops during this period into three types: armored and mechanized battalions and mechanized regiments, as organic components of infantry and cavalry formations; and tank battalions, regiments, and brigades, as part of the High Command Tank Reserve (TRGK), which, like its artillery counterpart, was to reinforce offensive operations along the most important axes. Finally, there were the mechanized brigades and corps, which were to carry out operational missions in conjunction with the other combat arms.[26] The directorate also set up an experimental mechanized regiment in 1929, which was expanded into a brigade in 1930. In the autumn of 1932 two mechanized corps were formed, followed by two more in early 1934. Each corps, according to a 1935 organizational scheme, was to consist of two mechanized brigades, a rifle–machine gun brigade, a tank reconnaissance battalion, and a communications battalion—in all 8,965 men, 463 medium tanks and tankettes, 1,444 automobiles, plus supporting artillery.[27] In strictly organizational terms, this move put the Red Army well ahead of the German army, which did not establish its first three tank divisions until 1935.

After 1934, however, no new mechanized corps were created, due chiefly to the opposition of Voroshilov, who thought the whole idea of large armored formations was "far-fetched."[28] The Red Army did continue to form other, smaller units and by 1936 had, aside from the mechanized corps, six independent mechanized brigades, six independent tank regiments, fifteen mechanized regiments as organic parts of cavalry divisions, and eighty-three tank battalions and companies as organic components of rifle divisions.[29] However, the practice of distributing armored units within existing units for infantry support did not prevent some Soviet theorists from speculating on the creation of armored armies along the lines advocated by some in the west. Among these was Tukhachevskii, who allowed that future mechanized armies might someday be employed to carry out "independent operations."[30] But Tukhachevskii would not live to see this, and the Soviet tank park would undergo several major organizational changes prior to the formation of the first tank army in 1942.

The Red Army's airborne forces, even more so than the armored troops, were indebted to the country's industrialization program for their rapid development. The Soviets had carried out a number of small airborne landings in the struggle against Central Asian insurgents in the late 1920s, although the numbers involved were militarily insignificant. Experiments continued in peacetime, and in 1931 a small parachute unit was formed in the Leningrad Military District, a move that was successful enough to warrant the creation of similar units elsewhere. In 1933 the first "special designation brigade" was formed, consisting of a parachute battalion, an artillery battalion, and three squadrons of aircraft for transporting troops and equipment.[31] Two similar brigades were established in 1934–36, and airborne and parachute troops played a prominent role in several of the larger military maneuvers of 1935–36. In the 1935 Kiev Military District maneuvers 1,200 paratroopers were dropped, followed by a further 2,500 men, plus equipment, landed by plane.[32] Similar jumps made the following year in the Belorussian Military District maneuvers caused one Western observer to praise them as being "well ahead of their time."[33]

These years also saw the creation of an entirely new service—the air defense forces (PVO), which from 1927 had existed only as a section of the RKKA Staff. The PVO was raised to the status of an RKKA directorate, which became responsible for the air defense of the entire country and the coordination of related civil defense measures. In 1934 Kamenev, the former commander in chief, became head of the service; upon his death two years later, he was succeeded by A. I. Sedyakin. The PVO was outfitted with such new weapons as the 76.2-mm antiaircraft gun and smaller ground-based weapons. The Soviets also conducted their first experiments with radar during these years. By 1935 twenty-nine fighter squadrons were available for air defense purposes, although these remained under the operational control of the military district air force chiefs. In organizational terms, the PVO grew from a collection of antiaircraft battalions and regiments to include brigades and divisions. In 1937 the first PVO corps were created to defend such major cities as Moscow, Leningrad, and Baku and included antiaircraft divisions, searchlight, early-warning, barrage balloon, and machine gun regiments.[34]

The air force, under the stewardship of P. I. Baranov and Alksnis, was completely remade during the 1930s. New aircraft such as the I-5, I-15, I-16, and I-53 fighters and the TB-1, TB-3, DB-3, and SB-3 heavy and medium bombers entered service and transformed, at least quantitatively, the USSR into a major air power, with a force of 10,000 combat aircraft by the end of 1937.[35] Unlike the armored forces, however, the trend here was toward a heavier force. Whereas in 1929 reconnaissance aircraft had accounted for a staggering 82 percent of all combat aircraft, by 1935 bomber and assault aviation made up 51 percent of combat planes, and reconnaissance vehicles a mere 19 percent.[36] This growth was reflected in organizational changes as well. Assault, fighter, and light bomber aviation was organized into both mixed and homogeneous air divisions, and in 1933 all long-range (heavy) bombers were grouped into corps, each consisting of three brigades. In 1936 several heavy-bomber brigades were consolidated to form a "special designation army" (AON), which was subordinated directly to the high command for carrying out independent operational-strategic missions.

The appearance of the heavy bomber naturally gave rise to discussions about the air force's chief mission: ground support or strategic bombing operations against political and economic targets. Soviet ideas at this time were sharply at odds with the more extreme "airpower" theories then in vogue in the West, which saw the bomber playing a decisive role in a future war, through terror bombing and strikes against the enemy's war industry. Most representative in this regard were the views of A. N. Lapchinskii, the Red Army's chief air theorist during this period. Lapchinskii stressed the air force's role in ensuring the success of ground operations through its reconnaissance functions and strikes against ground and air targets in the enemy's tactical and operational zones. Lapchinskii, although he supported the idea of independent air operations against military targets deep in the enemy rear, dismissed the notion that airpower alone could win a war.[37]

Stalin himself put to rest any idea of an independent role for the air force when he declared in 1937 that "he who thinks that one can win a war by powerful aviation alone is deeply mistaken."[38] The early evidence of the Spanish civil war bore Stalin out, and, like the other great land powers, Germany and France, the Soviet Union would also relegate its air force to an almost exclusively ground support role.

The Soviet navy enjoyed a potentially more independent status than its air counterpart, but it also played a very secondary role to the ground forces during this period. Among the major problems the navy faced was a shortage of bases, particularly in the northwest, where the postrevolutionary independence of Finland and the Baltic States had deprived it of its forward positions and confined the Baltic Fleet to the eastern end of the Gulf of Finland, from which it could be easily blockaded. The Black Sea Fleet's situation was only marginally better, and in the Far East the coastline was open to a renewed Japanese attack. This gloomy picture was made worse by the pre-1933 prediction that Great Britain was the most likely future maritime enemy. This meant dealing with the world's strongest fleet, which was capable of striking with virtual impunity anywhere along the Soviet coast. The Soviets concluded that any attempt to build a large surface fleet and attempt to take on the British in their native element would be worse than useless, and that such a diversion of resources would only derail ongoing efforts to construct an effective interim defense. The Soviets thus rejected the idea of a large surface fleet built around capital ships in favor of a smaller and less expensive shore defense force.

This program was partially realized during these years, although visible improvements came about more slowly, due to the longer construction schedules involved. Submarine construction was particularly pushed as a quick means of building a relatively inexpensive defensive force capable of inflicting disproportionate damage on a stronger enemy. The Soviets managed to build only 6 modern submarines during the first Five-Year Plan but 137 during the second, of which 85 were of the large or medium type.[39] Shore-based aviation also grew at an impressive rate, and by 1937 the navy possessed 1,215 combat aircraft, divided almost equally between bombers, fighters, and reconnaissance aircraft.[40] This and similar growth in other areas enabled the Soviets to establish the Pacific Fleet in 1935 and to upgrade the status of the Northern Flotilla to that of a fleet two years later. By the end of this period the Soviet navy was on the verge of administrative independence from the ground forces, although the gathering purge, which hit the navy especially hard, would soon render such considerations academic.

The first half of the 1930s saw the Red Army transformed from an overwhelmingly infantry-cavalry force into a relatively modern army equal to those of the other major powers. The greater numbers of tanks, motorized troops, aircraft, and artillery, and their coalescence into operationally significant divisions and corps, inevitably influenced the development of the army's military theory. Tukhachevskii had foreseen this as early as 1930, when writing of the army's "new proportions" of modern weaponry, which, he asserted, "will call forth new forms of operational art."[41]

STRATEGY AND TACTICS

For all of the developments that were taking place in the Red Army's weapons and equipment park, the basic assumptions underlying Soviet military strategy changed relatively little during these years. Questions of strategy, being more closely tied to political and economic considerations, are generally less subject to the influence of new technology than the subordinate fields of operational art and tactics. What effect there was would continue to be secondary to such realities as the USSR's ongoing ideological confrontation with most of the rest of the world and its resulting political isolation. These and other factors combined to ensure that the basic premises of Soviet military strategy would continue to resemble closely the conclusions already reached during the previous decade.

As before, the Soviets viewed a future war as the inevitable clash of two irreconcilable systems, the capitalist and socialist, in which each side would strive to overthrow the other's social order and replace it with its own. A high-stakes conflict of this sort left no room for compromise and would be waged in the most decisive manner possible.[42] It was widely believed that this would be a war not of nations but of social classes. The USSR, which was admittedly far weaker than its likely opponents, would thus enjoy the advantage, it was said, of working-class support within the capitalist camp, which one author described as a "landing force" in the enemy's rear. In the same vein, the Soviets continued to count on the support of the inhabitants of the European colonial holdings and other dependencies.[43] These factors, it was believed, would force the capitalist nations to withdraw troops from the anti-Soviet front to put down internal uprisings, thus realizing the Bolshevik slogan of changing the "imperialist" war into a civil war. Finally, a future war would pit the USSR against a coalition of its immediate western neighbors, supported materially by such larger capitalist powers as Britain, France, and Japan.[44]

The conclusions reached by Soviet theoreticians during the strategic debates of the 1920s regarding the military conduct of a future war retained, for the most part, their validity well into the next decade and would serve as the basis for planning at the operational level. These debates had revolved chiefly around the question of a future war's duration; whether it would be a struggle of mass armies or of smaller, highly mechanized forces; whether the Red Army should pursue an offensive strategy of "destruction" or an essentially defensive one of "attrition"; and the relative place of maneuver and positional warfare. The preponderance of opinion came to view a future war as a lengthy and exhaustive struggle, waged by mass armies outfitted with the latest technological innovations. The Red Army would pursue an offensive strategy, geared to decisively defeating the chief members of the capitalist coalition as quickly as possible, although a defensive posture on secondary fronts was not ruled out. Finally, while the army leadership preferred a war of maneuver, it did not exclude positional methods, particularly along the less decisive axes.

These basic tenets were reaffirmed by a number of theorists during the 1930s. Among these was S. M. Belitskii, who declared that a future war would become an "extended and cruel contest," due to its coalition character. He also predicted that a future war would be a conflict of mass armies in which technology would aid, but not replace, the national army.[45] This view was supported by Tukhachevskii, who remained a zealous advocate of the mass army, coupled with a high level of mechanization, and was outspoken in his contempt for Western theories that called for the creation of small, highly mechanized professional armies.[46] He also took the lead in reiterating the Red Army's commitment to an offensive strategy, which had been the point of greatest contention during the 1920s. As before, his views were expressed in ad hominem attacks on the theories of his old rival, Svechin, who was derided for his alleged "pacifism" and willingness to accept capitalism's military superiority. In 1930 Tukhachevskii accused Svechin of renouncing the offensive, which another author praised as the *"single expedient form of struggle"* in an era of revolutionary wars.[47] Finally, while the Soviets continued to prefer a war of maneuver over positional forms, they had become increasingly resigned to the fact that the growing power of defensive weapons had made periods of positional warfare more likely in the future.[48]

The interplay of these and other factors in the Red Army's strategic calculations is most clearly illustrated in an exchange of internal documents between Svechin and Chief of Staff Shaposhnikov in early 1930. The dialogue between the two former czarist officers and imperial academy graduates regarding the possible contours of a future war and the army's proper strategy provides a fascinating insight into the thinking of the army's best minds.

Svechin opened the discussion with a detailed report to War Commissar Voroshilov in early March. Svechin outlined a future war against the USSR as a coalition affair, led by Britain and France, in which Poland and Romania would bear the brunt of the fighting as the coalition's cat's paw in the west. To the north, Latvia, Estonia, and Finland would maintain an "armed neutrality" in order to tie down Soviet forces along their borders. The Soviet Union would enter such a war much the weaker party against opponents who possessed significant technical advantages over the Red Army and who could mobilize their forces more quickly. Svechin sharply criticized Tukhachevskii and Triandafillov for overselling the technological benefits of the army's reconstruction program and predicted that the armed forces would not achieve a technical parity with its likely enemies for another fifteen years. Nor could the USSR count on significant support from working-class uprisings within the enemy camp, he said, because these could be easily suppressed.[49]

Svechin predicted that the capitalist coalition would make its main effort in the south, along the Black Sea coast, with the aim of creating a continuous front from the Caspian Sea to the Pripyat Marshes. The British, according to this scenario, would land in the Trans-Caucasus, with the object of seizing the oil centers of Baku and Groznyi. The French would land in the Crimea and seize the Donets Basin and the lower Dnepr River area, while Poland and Romania would join in the attack along their own frontiers. Svechin predicted that the achievement of these objectives would put the enemy in possession of the USSR's chief industrial and extractive areas and render a subsequent advance on Moscow relatively easy, or even unnecessary.[50]

Svechin proposed a political-military counterstrategy to take advantage of the coalition's lack of internal unity to prevent the union of the coalition armies and the formation of a continuous front along the USSR's southern periphery. To achieve this, the Red Army must remain on the defensive along most of the front, while directing its initial offensive efforts at Romania, which he correctly identified as the coalition's "weakest link." Svechin rather optimistically calculated that the Romanians could be defeated in a quick, two-week campaign, which would drive a wedge in the enemy front and isolate the Polish forces to the north from their allies along the Black Sea coast. He warned that at all costs the Red Army should refrain from making its first major offensive against Poland, either in Galicia or toward Warsaw. Svechin believed that such an attack would only involve the army in an extended and indecisive campaign, even as coalition forces linked up in the south, and might even bring Germany into the war on the Allied side. Likewise, he denounced any major effort in the Baltic as a "false step," which would only take away forces from the southern front.[51]

Shaposhnikov, in his reply, was quick to agree with Svechin about the coalition nature of a future war and its likely composition. Nor did he dispute the notion that the enemy would make its main effort along the country's Black Sea coast, although he disagreed about the scale of the fighting. Shaposhnikov believed that the British and French fleets would probably attack the USSR's southern and other ports, although he considered it unlikely that they would undertake any large-scale land operations in the interior.[52] Rather, the main point of contention between the two lay in Shaposhnikov's preference for the strategy of destruction, which he defined as "beginning the war with the defeat of the strongest and most dangerous enemy" and avoiding secondary distractions. He contrasted this to Svechin's strategy of attrition, which he characterized as the "strategy of limited goals, the strategy of circuitous routes to the objective."[53]

In practical terms this meant launching the initial attack against Poland, which Shaposhnikov identified as the coalition's strongest direct partner, and delaying the attack against Romania until the latter's defeat. Neither would Romania's defeat be the simple task that Svechin imagined, and Shaposhnikov calculated that the Red Army could reach Bucharest only on the fortieth day following its complete concentration along the Dnestr. Such a move, if undertaken first, would also be threatened along its right flank by a major Polish attack from Galicia. Launching the first attack against the Poles would also be a major undertaking and would require eighty-five to ninety-five divisions north of the Pripyat Marshes, as well as another forty divisions to the south, including those defending the Romanian frontier. An attack of this magnitude would also involve a secondary effort through the Baltic States to turn the Polish flank. Shaposhnikov calculated that an advance from the Polish border to the middle Vistula would take fifty days. This would not include the initial mobilization and deployment period, meaning that the decisive operations would take place sometime during the war's third month.[54]

While both men's analyses contained much that was intelligent and insightful, their judgment was often clouded by wishful thinking and ideological prejudice. The former was particularly true of Svechin's rosy predictions of a swift victory over Romania, while Shaposhnikov could not resist the temptation to fall back on political clichés to support his argument, knowing that Svechin was particularly vulnerable on that score.[55] Before too long, however, such interesting speculation would become superfluous, and the vague specter of an enemy coalition would be replaced by a new and very real enemy—Nazi Germany.

One of the most interesting aspects of the Soviet strategic debate during these years was the question of the so-called beginning period of the war *(nachal'nyi period voiny)* and the problems peculiar to it. One of the first to raise the question was Svechin, who in 1927 had written of the "premobilization" period and the measures needed to shield the armed forces' concentration and deployment upon the outbreak of war.[56] A number of articles on this subject followed at the end of the 1920s, although they were often too narrowly focused on the role of airpower or else ignored the influence of new military technology altogether.[57]

By the early 1930s, however, developments within the Red Army and abroad were leading many theorists to reexamine the problem in the light of recent advances in military technology. Whereas in the past, military operations had developed slowly along a relatively shallow front of strategic efforts, the appearance of such new weapons as long-range bomber aviation and mechanized forces meant that henceforth "from the very beginning combat activities will take on a deep and spatial character," as one Soviet author described it.[58] The vastly increased importance of the time factor, combined with the deep strike range of modern weapons, had obvious consequences for the mobilization and deployment of a nation's armed forces. Military planners could now no longer assume that their country's mobilization and concentration of its armies on the frontier would be allowed to proceed unhindered, as had been the case in 1914. The dangers and opportunities inherent in this new situation meant that the Red Army's efforts would be increasingly focused on what one theorist called "the right to deploy first," in which each side would actively seek to disrupt his opponent's military preparations at the beginning of a war in order to gain an advantage in the opening operations.[59]

However, despite the indisputable advantage of striking first, it was understood that no state can afford to maintain its armed forces in a full state of readiness in peacetime without provoking its neighbors. The problem for the Red Army and its foreign counterparts was to devise the most effective means of disrupting the enemy's mobilization and deployment at the beginning of a war, using a minimal initial amount of force. The Soviets' preferred instrument for carrying out this mission was the aptly named "invasion army" *(armiya vtorzheniya),* among other appellations. The invasion army, in order to strike quickly and deeply into enemy territory, would be maintained at nearly full strength and liberally reinforced with mechanized units, aircraft, and cavalry. The army constituted, in effect, the first echelon of the country's mobilization efforts, in which capacity it was charged not only with disrupting the enemy's deployment along the frontier but also with facilitating the eventual deployment of its own second and third strategic echelons inside enemy territory.[60] The latter, which greatly exceeded the first echelon in strength, would then quickly advance to support it upon the completion of their concentration.[61]

It was generally agreed that a future war would begin with air strikes in the enemy's strategic and operational rear, against his political and economic centers and his forces already in the field. These strikes, involving as many as 1,000 to 1,500 aircraft and carried out to a depth of 600 to 800 kilometers, would include among their military objectives rail junctions, large troop concentrations, and supply depots directly connected to the enemy's ongoing deployment efforts. Other targets included the enemy's war industry, mines, oil fields, and seaports. The attacker would also seek out the enemy's political and administrative centers for a terror bombing campaign, which would include among its weapons not only conventional ordnance but also incendiary and chemical weapons.[62]

The invasion army, simultaneous with the start of the air campaign, would begin its advance to the frontier. The army's composition and actions were outlined by S. A. Mezheninov, a former czarist captain and 1917 graduate of the imperial General Staff Academy, who served as deputy chief of the RKKA Staff/General Staff from 1933 to 1937. Mezheninov calculated the invasion army's strength at a mere one or two rifle divisions, backed by a cavalry corps, a mechanized corps, two or three antiaircraft battalions, plus a battalion each of motorized sappers and chemical troops and, in certain cases, bridging units. The army's advance would be covered by an air corps consisting of light bomber, assault, and fighter brigades. The preponderance of mobile arms and engineering troops clearly indicated that the army was intended to launch little more than deep "spoiling attacks" against the enemy's covering forces and his frontier obstacles. The army would advance into enemy territory in a series of incremental leaps, destroying the enemy's border troops and airfields, disorganizing his communications and control means, and, in general, disrupting the defender's efforts to hinder the Red Army's deployment. The mobile forces, having accomplished their mission, would then fall back on their own infantry and conduct a defensive battle until the arrival of the main forces, as represented by the second echelon's shock armies.[63]

The RKKA Staff had earlier calculated that an invasion of this size might penetrate up to 200 to 300 kilometers into enemy territory along a future western front. However, even a success of this magnitude could not be maintained for any length of time without sizable reinforcements. Elsewhere it was admitted that the invasion could, at best, only create a "series of crises" for the defender's force, and that decisive results would have to await the arrival of the attacker's main forces.[64]

As one of the Red Army's most gifted strategists, Tukhachevskii professed views on the nature and conduct of a future war's opening phase that are particularly important. These were revealed most clearly in his writings and conversations with fellow theorists. According to the latter, by the end of 1936

Tukhachevskii was firmly convinced of Nazi Germany's aggressive intentions and urged that it be considered the main opponent in future exercises. He was equally certain that the old formula of a country's unhindered mobilization and deployment was a thing of the past and that a future war would begin with surprise attacks by air, sea, and ground forces, as both sides would seek to disrupt the unfolding of the other's initial military preparations. This was particularly true of the air force, which, he believed, was capable of rendering a 250-kilometer border zone "off limits" to the enemy's mobilization efforts and force him to deploy deep in his own rear, while the attacker would be left free to deploy along the border. The air attacks would be accompanied by large-scale airborne landings to destroy rail lines, bridges, and isolated enemy garrisons within the 250-kilometer zone. Tukhachevskii, while his intentions were overwhelmingly offensive, did warn of similar enemy attempts to disrupt the Red Army's deployment by launching a preemptive strike of its own.[65]

Tukhachevskii advised that ground operations would probably unfold in a series of meeting engagements, particularly if both sides pursued an offensive strategy, and, in general, maneuver would predominate over positional forms. However, he did not exclude defensive operations and periods of positional warfare along the front's less-important sectors. The main ground force attack would be spearheaded by the "forward army" *(peredovaya armiya)*, generously equipped with mechanized units, cavalry, and motorized infantry. This army, deployed in peacetime near the border, would take advantage of the enemy's confusion in the frontier zone to invade the enemy's territory and hold it for the deployment of friendly forces advancing in succeeding echelons. However, Tukhachevskii warned that, as opposed to the past, future border operations might drag on for weeks. In such cases, the presence of "deep operational reserves" to maintain the attack would prove decisive.[66]

Unfortunately for the Red Army, Tukhachevskii had only a limited opportunity to test his theories at a war game conducted by the General Staff in early 1936. The strategic setting for the game envisioned a German-Polish invasion of the USSR, involving a force of eighty divisions, deployed between the Pripyat Marshes and the Dvina River. Uborevich, as commander of the Belorussian Military District, led the Soviet force, while Tukhachevskii commanded the enemy army. However, the latter's suggestion that the German-Polish forces preempt the Soviets' deployment efforts along the border with a surprise attack was brusquely rejected by Marshal Yegorov, who also dismissed Tukhachevskii's suggestion that the enemy armies enjoy an initial superiority of forces. In fact, according to the scenario laid down by Yegorov's General Staff apparatus, it was the Red Army that would complete its concentration and deployment first and enter the fighting with an equality of forces. Given these absurd restrictions, it is not surprising that the game ended in a series of frontal collisions along the frontier and failed to yield a decisive result. The upshot was that the Red Army was deprived of a valuable lesson for the future.[67]

Given the highly offensive nature of the Soviet approach to war, the fact that defensive considerations played such a small part in the formulation of strategy should come as no surprise. While it was true that the invasion army could also serve as a "cover army" *(armiya prikrytiya)* in the event of an enemy attack, the bias toward the offensive remained dominant.[68] Defensive arrangements, however, were more in evidence in the twelve "fortified areas" constructed along the USSR's western frontier (Karelia, Kingisepp, Pskov, Polotsk, Minsk, Mozyr', Korosten', Novograd-Volynskii, Letichev, Mogilev-Yampol'skii, Rybnitsa, Tiraspol') and in the interior (Kiev) between 1929 and 1938. These areas varied in length from 50 to 140 kilometers, with an approximate depth of 25 kilometers, while the flanks were usually anchored on some natural obstacle. However, in many cases these areas were too lightly armed, particularly in terms of antitank defense.[69]

Unfortunately for the Soviets, much of the creative work regarding the war's beginning ultimately came to naught, and the Red Army would shortly become the victim of the greatest surprise attack in military history. Zhukov, who at the beginning of the war served as chief of the General Staff, later admitted that the majority of the higher military leadership still expected a war to begin in the form of border engagements according to the pattern of 1914. No one, he claimed, believed that it was possible for a fully mobilized army to launch a full-scale attack of such magnitude.[70] That the Red Army high command continued to believe this in spite of the recent evidence of German methods in Poland and the west is indicative of a serious degradation in the quality of the army's strategic thinking following the 1937–38 military purges.

Equally important changes were also taking place from "below," in the realm of tactics. Here the Red Army faced the task of adapting its tactical doctrine, previously based on infantry and cavalry, to the increased fire and maneuver capabilities of the new weapons then entering service. In this respect, at least, Soviet theoreticians had much in common with their Western counterparts, who were also searching for ways to employ the new technology to avoid a repetition of the 1914–18 deadlock. The latter was certainly a possibility, for despite the impressive advances in offensive weaponry since 1918, the defense still retained a number of significant advantages vis-à-vis the attacker. This prospect was particularly distasteful to the Red Army, whose entire political-military ethos demanded decisive offensive actions.

The continued strength of modern defensive arrangements made it imperative that the problem of breaking through the enemy's tactical defense would first have to be solved. For without the disruption of the defender's tactical position there could be no question of the offensive's subsequent development into the enemy's operational and strategic depth. Or, as one author put it, the operation's outcome "is determined, in the final analysis, by tactical factors."[71] Soviet efforts to resolve this dilemma ultimately found expression in the theory of the "deep battle" *(glubokii boi),* which sought to employ the enhanced offensive qualities of the new technology to achieve a breakthrough of the enemy's tactical defense and set the stage for the operational exploitation of the success.

One of the earliest efforts in this area was a 1931 memorandum by Triandafillov, which laid the theoretical basis for the new approach in words that would be repeated many times in the years ahead. Triandafillov stated that the new military technology now made it possible to dispense with the method of "gnawing through" *(progryzanie)* the enemy's defensive position in favor of a *"simultaneous attack against the enemy throughout the entire depth of his tactical position."*[72] Equally intriguing, in light of the author's untimely demise, were Triandafillov's notes on the conduct of the deep battle, which were published in an appendix to a posthumous edition of his book *The Character of Operations of Modern Armies* in 1932. Triandafillov, at the time of his death, had been revising his magnum opus to take into account the army's ongoing technical transformation. From the outline it is evident that he was planning to devote special attention to the tactical problems of coordinating the different combat arms (infantry, armor, artillery, cavalry, aircraft, and airborne troops) during the attack.[73]

Triandafillov's pioneering work was taken up by others following his death in the summer of 1931. In early 1932 the Revolutionary Military Council commissioned Chief of Staff Yegorov to prepare a report on the army's tactical-operational views in light of its ongoing technical reconstruction. The result, "The RKKA's Tactics and Operational Art at a New Stage," was basically a distillation of Triandafillov's 1931 work, summing up the main theoretical conclusions reached up to that time while also establishing the general tone for succeeding discussions and works. The report's most important tactical conclusion was that the new military technology, due to its increased range, mobility, and destructive power, now

> *enables us to strike the enemy simultaneously throughout the entire depth of his position,* as opposed to current forms of battle and attack, which may be characterized as the consecutive suppression of successive parts of the battle order. The means are used so as to paralyze the fire of all defensive weapons, regardless of the depth of their deployment, to isolate one enemy unit from another, to disrupt cooperation between them, and to destroy them in detail.[74]

The report was circulated among the military district commanders and the heads of the various military academies, for their comments and criticisms. It subsequently became the basis for the "Provisional Instructions for Organizing the Deep Battle," which was issued in 1933 and became the Red Army's first manual on the subject.

The notions of simultaneity and depth in these and other writings are the cornerstone of the Soviet theory of the deep battle and distinguish its conduct from the tactical methods employed during the Great War.[75] For most of that conflict the method of attack had been consecutive and linear, with the slow-moving infantry having to bludgeon its way through the enemy's multilayered defensive zone in a series of grinding frontal collisions, which ultimately exhausted the attacker. The little simultaneity that could be achieved was limited to infantry-artillery interaction against the first defensive position, while the depth of the attack was restricted by the range and pace of the two arms' rate of advance. Moreover, the defense could usually bring up reinforcements to the battlefield without interference from the attacker. The appearance of large numbers of tanks, aircraft, and other weapons offered an escape from this positional "dead end" by enabling the attacker to group these arms' activities in such a way that both simultaneity of suppression and depth of attack would be achieved, and the battlefield isolated from the defender's reinforcements. This newfound capability, as one author noted, marked the transition from the old linear tactics to a new, multidimensional "deep tactics" *(glubokaya taktika)*.[76]

Of the new weapons, none was judged more important to the deep battle's success than the tank, and its means of employment was to be a source of intense debate for several years. One of the earliest references to the tank's emerging role in the deep battle appeared in the 1929 field manual, edited in large part by Triandafillov in his capacity as chief of the RKKA Staff's operational directorate. Perhaps most significantly, two of the manual's articles recommended the creation of special tank echelons to carry out the attack.[77] Triandafillov later advised forming three distinct tank echelons for operating to various depths of the defender's tactical defense zone and against specific targets. These echelons were first divided into "infantry accompaniment tanks," "machine gun destruction tanks," and "artillery destruction tanks," according to their mission. They were subsequently renamed "direct infantry support" *(neposredstvennaya podderzhka pekhoty)* tanks, or NPP; "long-range infantry support" *(dal'nyaya podderzhka pekhoty)* tanks, or DPP; and "long-range" *(dal'nee deistvie),* or DD, tanks, although their original mission remained the same.[78]

Another question concerned the relative importance of the tank in the deep battle vis-à-vis the other combat arms. Previous Soviet theory had stressed the tank's role as an infantry-support weapon, as when the 1929 field manual stated that the tanks' "chief task" was "to clear a path for the advancing infantry by suppressing the enemy's fire resistance and destroying his artificial obstacles."[79] As more and more tanks entered service, however, a number of theorists began to view the tank as the prime element in the combined-arms battle and to reduce the deep battle to the armored attack alone. This dalliance with the more extreme theories of tank warfare did not last long, however, as the weight of opinion in the army remained in favor of a more balanced approach. This was made official at a December 1934 meeting of the Military Council, during which Yegorov delivered a report reaffirming the supremacy of the infantry. He also condemned the existing three-stage (NPP, DPP, and DD) echelonment of tanks as cumbersome and unjustified, and recommended instead a two-echelon (NPP, DD) grouping. These recommendations were subsequently adopted and formed the basis for the army's new "Instructions for the Deep Battle," which was issued in March 1935.[80]

The new theory encountered other, more serious obstacles during these years, which threatened to channel its development in a more restrictive direction. One of the chief impediments was Voroshilov, whose reactionary views have been noted elsewhere. The war commissar maintained that the concept of the deep battle was applicable only to conditions of positional warfare, which required breaking through the enemy's static front. This view, however, ignored the theory's relevance to other, more mobile forms of warfare, such as the "meeting battle" *(vstrechnyi boi)*.[81] Tukhachevskii protested that Voroshilov's attitude was causing a good deal of confusion within the command element and had raised fears that the theory might be renounced altogether. Tukhachevskii's views ultimately prevailed, thanks to the support of such powerful allies as Kamenev, Uborevich, and Yakir, the commander of the Kiev Military District. Voroshilov's formal capitulation on this score came at the same December 1934 meeting of the Military Council at which he retracted his earlier statements and finally recognized the deep battle as a "new form" of military endeavor.[82]

The capstone of these years of effort was the Provisional Field Manual of 1936, which represented the final triumph of the Red Army's more progressive thinkers, many of whom had less than a year to live, and marks the high point of the deep battle's theoretical development in the prepurge period. The manual, as the army's guiding tactical document, codified several of the deep battle's basic tenets, among the most important of which was that it was above all a combined-arms effort, using the heightened strike and maneuver qualities of modern weaponry "*to achieve a simultaneous attack against the enemy's combat order throughout the entire depth of his position.*"[83] This applied to both defensive and offensive actions, although the latter was obviously preferred, culminating in the defender's encirclement and destruction. The manual also reaffirmed the infantry's primacy in the combined-arms battle, as all other combat arms were explicitly subordinated to the interests of the former.[84]

The manual divided the deep battle into three categories, according to designation: the meeting battle, the attack against an entrenched defender, and the defensive battle. These battles, despite their obvious differences, had several factors in common. Among them was the rifle corps, which as the largest tactical unit constituted the battle's organizational heart, usually as part of a larger operational effort. The corps, aside from its organic forces, might also be reinforced with tanks, artillery, and other weapons from the high command's reserve. The manual recommended dividing these forces into separate "shock" *(udarnaya)* and "holding" *(skovyvayushchaya)* groups in both offensive and defensive situations. Within the shock group are concentrated the greater part of the corps' organic weapons, as well as those allocated from above. The shock group's battle order is arranged to a depth of two to three echelons, which were to augment the first echelon's attack from the depth. Likewise, a breakthrough anywhere along the attack front was to be immediately exploited by units from the follow-on echelons and the reserve.[85]

The holding group would tie down the defender along secondary sectors and prevent him from concentrating his forces against the main effort. The holding group would generally not receive additional forces for its supporting mission and might be obliged to attack along a relatively broad front to facilitate the massing of men and weapons along the main sector. However, the holding group's attack cannot be limited to a mere demonstration, and it must carry out its mission to the best of its limited means. As soon as the enemy's defense along the main sector begins to give way, the holding group's attack must merge with the larger effort. Likewise, in a defensive battle, the holding group would try to weaken or halt the enemy attack before it reached the main defensive position. If this fails, the shock group would then launch a counterattack to restore the situation.[86]

Tank battalions, subordinated to the infantry division commanders, made up the bulk of the infantry support tanks. Tanks detailed from the high command reserve might be used to strengthen the infantry attack or would be formed into a separate long-range tank echelon under the control of the corps commander, or even of his division commanders. The corps commander would also allocate his organic and attached artillery park to special infantry support, cavalry support, and long-range tank support groups. In cases where the corps was attacking a fortified area, a special "destruction artillery" *(artilleriya razrusheniya)* group would be formed. Finally, assault aviation would disrupt the arrival of the enemy's reserves; support the ground attack; attack enemy rail lines and storage depots; disrupt his communications and control; and destroy his aircraft on the ground. Fighter aviation would destroy the enemy's planes, both in the air and on the ground; protect the ground assault; and, in certain cases, attack the defender's ground forces. Light-bomber aviation would direct its efforts against enemy troop concentrations, supply bases, communications and control, railways, and airfields.[87]

The meeting battle would unfold under conditions in which both sides were advancing toward each other in march formation. For this reason, the commander was advised to organize his forces along the line of march with an eye toward their rapid deployment at the start of the battle. To this end, the advancing column would generally consist of reconnaissance units, a vanguard, the main body, and a rear detachment. If possible, it was recommended that cavalry tank and motorized infantry, as well as attached artillery, advance in a separate column for ease of deployment.[88]

The meeting battle would usually begin with air strikes by both sides. These would be directed primarily at the enemy's troops, artillery park, and supply system through strafing and bombing attacks and the dropping of "poisonous substances." As the enemy approached, the vanguard would deploy against his forward units and engage them. Part of this force would attack the enemy in order to pin down his forward troops, while the vanguard's main body moved against the enemy's flanks in an effort to destroy the enemy's vanguard before it could fully deploy.[89]

Should both sides persist in their efforts until the arrival of their columns' main forces, further fighting would develop in the manner already described. In this case the attacker's vanguard would serve as the holding group for the formation's main effort by engaging the enemy in a frontal assault to divert his attention from the forthcoming attack. The column's main forces, liberally supplied with tanks, artillery, and airpower, would constitute the shock group, which would deploy behind the holding group's screen for an attack against the enemy's flanks and rear. If successful, the attack would hit the enemy's main forces before they had time to deploy, cutting off some units and destroying others. The battle would conclude with the relentless pursuit of the enemy forces until they were completely defeated.[90]

The "offensive battle" *(nastupatel'nyi boi)* was the name given to the attack against an entrenched defender, whether from the march or in circumstances in which the attacker occupies a fixed position. The manual also foresaw the necessity of attacking fortified positions and overcoming an enemy defense anchored on water barriers. The attack might also take place in a maneuver setting, in which the enemy's flanks are open and invite a turning movement, or along a continuous front, necessitating a breakthrough. In any event, the amount of space—at thirty-seven pages this was easily the manual's longest chapter—devoted to the subject indicates that the Soviets expected such situations to predominate in a future war, a contention supported by the editor's (Tukhachevskii's) public statements.[91]

Preparations for the attack were complicated, reflecting the difficulties in achieving the proper coordination of the dissimilar combat arms and the expected problems of assaulting prepared defenses. To carry this out, the commander was to concentrate two-thirds of his force at the point of decision. This meant that a reinforced rifle division would attack along a 3,000- to 3,500-meter front, with its regiments aligned in one or two echelons, while the regiments' battalions advanced in two to three echelons. The attacker's artillery, both organic and attached, would be grouped according to designation as previously described, as would the tanks. It was assumed that in most cases the DD tank attack would precede that of the infantry and its NPP tanks, although in terrain deemed difficult for tanks this order might be reversed. In such a case, the infantry and the NPP tanks would advance first, to seize the enemy's forward defensive zone and create gaps in his antitank defense. The long-range tanks would then be committed into these corridors for the subsequent drive into the enemy's defensive depth.[92]

Air strikes, conducted against the targets already described, signaled the beginning of the battle, while the attacker's "artillery preparation" augured the commencement of the ground assault. The artillery preparation might last as little as ten to fifteen minutes, or it might continue for several hours, depending on the number and type of guns available and the number of tanks slated to take part in the attack. The state of the enemy's defenses also had a bearing on the duration of this period, with permanent fortifications requiring a longer and more systematic bombardment. During this phase the artillery's chief targets were the defender's artillery, his antitank weapons, certain fortifications, and the defender's machine gun emplacements in those areas not slated for the tank assault. With the beginning of the long-range tank attack, the artillery would concentrate its fire on the defender's antitank weapons and artillery, while accompanying the tanks through the enemy defenses with either a rolling barrage or directed fire. The artillery, upon completing this phase, would switch its efforts to supporting the infantry-tank attack, during which it would concentrate its fire on the defender's remaining antitank weapons and machine guns.[93]

The long-range tanks would begin their attack immediately upon the cessation of the artillery preparation by moving into the gaps blasted in the enemy's antitank defense, while at the same time being covered by continuous artillery fire. The tanks were to avoid protracted fighting wherever possible and, by bypassing centers of resistance, would race into the enemy's rear to destroy his reserves, communications and control centers, and artillery and to cut off the retreat of those forces engaged at the front. Here the defender would already be contending with the infantry-tank attack, which was to begin immediately upon the DD tanks' passage into the rear, so as to take advantage of the disruption caused to the defender's fire system. The NPP tanks, supported by artillery fire, would then advance to clear a path for the infantry by suppressing the defender's machine gun system. As soon as the tanks passed through the forward defense line, the infantry would begin its attack, following the tanks at a distance of 200 meters and consolidating this success by exploiting gaps in the enemy defense and moving into his rear. Elsewhere, the attacker's forces would beat off enemy counterattacks, resulting in the defender's encirclement and destruction.[94]

With the rupture of the enemy's tactical defense along the main axis, the way was now open to exploit the success by a vigorous pursuit in depth. The corps commander would direct his mobile units to continue the attack along the enemy's flanks and in his rear. In the air, assault and light-bomber aviation would harry the defender's retreating columns, particularly at river crossings and other natural obstacles, while fighter aviation would cover the pursuing columns. The enemy forces still resisting along the attack's inner flanks would be cut off and surrounded by the attacker's mobile units in the rear, to be dealt with by the infantry units moving up from the rear. At this point the tactical phase would end, and the way now lay open to transforming the success into one of operational proportions.[95]

The manual viewed the tactical defense as an unpleasant but sometimes necessary measure to husband forces for an attack along another sector; to win time in order to gather forces for an attack; to occupy the enemy until the main attack has succeeded; to retain vital territory; and to foil the enemy's attack in order to launch a counterattack. The defensive battle might be waged along a broad front, based on noncontiguous but mutually supporting strongpoints, which would sacrifice territory in exchange for time, and along a continuous front, which was viewed as the most likely form.[96]

The defense, in most cases, would consist of a forward zone of engineering and chemical obstacles, up to 12 kilometers from the main position and manned by small infantry units and artillery. Behind this lay a somewhat stronger zone of defensive strongpoints, 1 to 3 kilometers from the main zone. The main defensive position contained the bulk of the defender's forces and weapons, including divisional shock groups. Behind this line, at a remove of 12 to 15 kilometers, lay the rear defensive zone. A rifle division in such an arrangement would occupy a front of 8 to 12 kilometers in breadth and 4 to 6 in depth, with its subordinate units occupying proportionately smaller frontages.[97]

The manual stressed that modern defense must be, above all, antitank in character, designed to isolate the enemy armor from its supporting infantry and destroy it in detail. This involved creating special antitank strongpoints within the main defensive zone, specially configured to create corridors for the passage and destruction of enemy tanks. Those enemy tanks that survived the defender's artillery barrage to reach the main defensive zone would be met by massed fire from antitank guns and the defender's own tanks. The greater part of the defender's artillery and all of his infantry weapons would be turned on the advancing infantry. Those enemy tanks that failed to penetrate to the main defense zone would, in turn, be attacked by the defender's antitank reserve and his tanks, as the prelude to a larger counterattack by the shock group. This attack, supported by artillery and aviation, would either restore the situation or exploit the success into the enemy's position.[98]

The usual gap between theory and practice would ultimately reveal a number of shortcomings in the Red Army's approach to the deep battle. The most serious of these was the order of attack by the long-range and infantry support tanks. Even the limited combat experience of 1939–40 would show how awkward this arrangement was in reality. Moreover, future combat in Mongolia and Finland would show that even a powerful artillery preparation could not be relied upon to destroy enough of the defender's antitank weapons to enable the long-range tanks to precede the ground attack without unacceptable losses. Instead, the infantry and its support tanks would have to clear a passage in the enemy's tactical defense for the long-range tanks in order to preserve the latter's strength for the attack in depth.

More laudable was the Red Army's balanced approach to the combined-arms battle, which avoided such extremes as the Germans' excessive reliance on the tank for achieving a breakthrough. This was offset, however, by the Soviets' continued emphasis on the employment of large cavalry formations, which was particularly anachronistic in light of the army's enthusiastic embrace of mechanization in all its forms.

THE DEEP OPERATION

Under modern conditions, however, it is not enough to simply break through the enemy's tactical defense, as crucial as that first step is, and the deep battle offers no solution to the problem of sustaining an advance beyond the immediate tactical defense zone. This is because modern defensive arrangements are distinguished above all by their great depth, and tactical success alone counts for little against an operational defensive zone extending dozens of kilometers behind the front line. This area, containing the defender's army and front reserves, presents a serious obstacle to any attack that seeks to develop a breakthrough beyond the initial tactical defense and to maintain the offensive's impetus against these forces. This had been shown to be the case repeatedly during the Great War, most notably during the Germans' March 1918 offensive in France, which for all its spectacular success failed to yield a decisive operational result.

Offensive gains during the war were confined to the defender's tactical zone because of the attacker's limited mobility and his inability to influence the fighting much beyond the immediate battlefield, due to the restricted range, speed, and reliability of existing weapons. Under these circumstances, the attacker was unable to exploit even the most favorable tactical success because he could not push his infantry into and beyond the breach rapidly enough, while the cavalry and armored forces at his disposal were too vulnerable or technically unreliable to be of much use. As a result, the defender's army reserves were usually free to move up relatively unhindered to the threatened area to seal the penetration and restore the situation because the attacker's nascent long-range weapons (tanks and aircraft) were as yet incapable of isolating the battlefield and preventing their arrival. Thus by the end of the war, despite a number of impressive tactical achievements, an operational solution to the trench deadlock seemed as remote as ever.

By the early 1930s, however, the new weapons had finally come into their own, and their potential could be fully realized. Ongoing improvements in their range, speed, and technical reliability had begun to shift the advantage increasingly in favor of the offensive, despite impressive parallel improvements in defensive means. At the same time, new tank and aircraft models were entering service in amounts sufficient to form motorized divisions, mechanized corps, and air armies. The convergence of these qualitative and quantitative trends prompted many of the Red Army's leading thinkers to take up the problem of adapting the conduct of offensive and defensive operations to the new technology.

The result was the theory of the "deep operation" *(glubokaya operatsiya)*, the development of which was substantially completed by 1936, although the basic idea was continually refined for many years afterward. The deep operation was geared toward operations at the army and/or front level and was larger, in terms of forces engaged, than the deep battle, which in organizational terms reached no higher than a corps. It was also considerably more ambitious in its goal of combining the efforts of ground, air, and airborne forces to launch a "simultaneous blow throughout the entire depth of the enemy's operational defense" in order to prevent or delay the arrival of his operational reserves by defeating these units in detail; to surround and destroy those units still at the front; and to continue the offensive into the defender's operational and strategic depth.[99]

Central to the deep operation's success was the composition of the shock army, acting either independently or with other armies as part of a larger front operation. However, during these years, as in the preceding decade, the single army operation remained the focus of attention. The term had been popularized by Triandafillov, who made the shock army the centerpiece of his *Character of Operations of Modern Armies,* and it retained its utility throughout the 1930s. The shock army, according to Triandafillov's original proposal, would consist of twelve to eighteen rifle divisions, grouped into four to five corps. These units would be supplemented with some sixteen to twenty artillery regiments and eight to twelve tank battalions, plus additional fighter and antiaircraft units to provide air cover, as well as two or three air brigades for offensive purposes, and miscellaneous chemical and other units.[100]

Although Triandafillov's original sketch was fairly modest by modern standards, it still vastly exceeded the Red Army's technical capabilities as of 1929. However, the quantitative achievements in military production resulting from the first Five-Year Plan soon caused Triandafillov to revise his projections. By 1931 he was proposing a number of variations on the theme of the shock army, comprising twelve to fifteen rifle divisions (four or five corps). The shock army, according to one proposal, would be reinforced for an offensive operation with six to nine artillery regiments, plus another two or three regiments of heavy guns. Another variant posited an additional twelve to eighteen tank and tankette battalions, supplemented by one or two additional battalions of heavy tanks. A third proposal foresaw a more balanced distribution of offensive weaponry of up to three or four artillery regiments, two to three heavy artillery regiments, and eight to twelve tank and tankette battalions. The shock army might be further reinforced by the inclusion of two or three aviation brigades of assault and light-bomber aircraft, plus six to eight fighter squadrons, for an overall strength, including organic air units, of 500 to 600 planes.[101] Triandafillov, to judge from the report, was not immune to the zeal for mechanization then sweeping the army, although even more equipment-heavy proposals were to appear.

Triandafillov died not long after submitting the report, but his work on the shock army's composition was continued by colleagues in the RKKA Staff apparatus. These ideas were elaborated in the report "The RKKA's Tactics and Operational Art at a New Stage," which was distributed in the summer of 1932 for study and comment by high-ranking officers. And although the document appeared over Chief of Staff Yegorov's signature, the ideas expressed are unmistakably Triandafillov's and represent a further distillation of his views.

One proposal, evidently tailored to an army attacking in an area unsuited for the mass employment of armor, posited a fifteen-division shock army, reinforced with 468 guns (108 of them of the heavy type) from the High Command Artillery Reserve. Combined with the rifle corps' organic complement of 1,515 small- and medium-caliber weapons, this yielded a total of 1,983 guns of all types, plus 250 tanks drawn from the corps' organic stocks. A second variant, intended for an army attacking in an area more favorable for tanks, proposed reinforcing the shock army with 348 guns, for a total of 1,863 artillery pieces, including 108 heavy guns. The reduction in firepower would be offset by the addition of twenty tank battalions (1,000 tanks) from the High Command Tank Reserve, or 1,500 tanks in all, including organic corps vehicles. The shock army might be further reinforced by the addition of between four and five assault and light-bomber brigades, two reconnaissance, and five to six fighter squadrons, which, including organic corps and other units, would raise the army's air strength to some 850 to 900 aircraft. In case of need, the shock army might also call upon the front's heavy-bomber units.[102]

Triandafillov's untimely death in the summer of 1931 left the small fraternity of operational theorists "orphaned" and lacking direction, according to one participant.[103] One of those who helped fill the gap was Nikolai Efimovich Varfolomeev, who was already known for his earlier writings on the theory of consecutive operations and the place of operational art in military art. Varfolomeev, who was born in 1890 and rose to the rank of captain in the czarist army during World War I, was a member of the old General Staff Academy's final graduating class in 1918. He joined the Red Army that same year and later served as chief of an army staff and deputy chief of staff of a front during the civil war. Varfolomeev's peacetime career included a stint as a military district chief of staff and service at the Frunze Military Academy, where he was awarded the distinguished title of professor. From this position he was ideally placed to pass on the old army's legacy to the new, which he did through a number of influential articles and books. Varfolomeev's last position was chief of staff of the Volga Military District, where he was arrested in 1938. He was shot a year later.

Varfolomeev's most important work was his book *The Shock Army* (1933), a detailed analysis of the cycle of German and Allied offensive operations conducted during the summer of 1918. The subject matter reflected the Red Army's ongoing preoccupation with the operational events of the war's climactic year and the lessons to be gleaned from them.[104] This was because it was assumed that many of the conditions that obtained in 1918 (continuous fronts, a deeply echeloned defense, etc.) would recur in a future war to greater or lesser degree. Moreover, the scope of the 1918 fighting was bound to excite the imagination of an army that more than anything else sought to avoid a repetition of the trench deadlock.

Varfolomeev's predominantly historical study was less concerned with the deep operation's quantitative indices than Triandafillov had been, and specific recommendations regarding the size and composition of the shock army are few;

however, the work's speculative sections certainly presuppose large numbers of aircraft, tanks, and mechanized troops. Rather, he focused on the mechanics of the shock army's mission, which he defined as "launching an uninterrupted, deep and shattering blow" along the main axis of advance. Such a task required that the shock army possess the requisite forces, firepower, and mobility to overcome the enemy's tactical defense and operational reserves and to complete the destruction of the main enemy force through a series of consecutive operations.[105]

Varfolomeev believed that the reality of deeply echeloned tactical and operational defensive zones called for comparable measures by the attacker. Or, as he stated in a previous article, "only a deep formation ensures the launching of a deep blow."[106] This suggestion was not new, and during 1918 the Germans had attacked using as many as three echelons. However, the attacks ultimately foundered because of the attacker's inability to strike deeply and quickly enough into and beyond the defender's army reserves, in order to prevent the establishment of a new defensive front. The resulting need to maintain the necessary tactical densities to carry out repeated breakthroughs robbed the succeeding echelons of the strength to sustain an advance into the operational depth. It was only the appearance of large numbers of new offensive weapons and their integration into the existing method of employment that enabled the attacker to simultaneously launch an assault throughout the entire depth of the enemy's army reserves and expand the initial breach of the defender's tactical zone into a breakthrough of operational proportions.

Varfolomeev accordingly divided his shock army into two echelons, distinguished by their differing objectives and the numbers and types of forces allotted to them. The first was the "tactical breakthrough echelon" *(eshelon takticheskogo proryva),* composed of several reinforced rifle corps. These would be backed up by a second line of divisions from the army's reserve to sustain the force of the initial breakthrough attempt. These forces would launch the initial assault against the defender's tactical zone to a depth of some 15 to 20 kilometers and contact with his army reserves.[107]

At this point the army commander would commit his second, or "operational breakthrough echelon" *(eshelon operativnogo proryva),* to expand the tactical breakthrough into one of operational scope by striking deep into the enemy rear. Whereas the first echelon emphasized raw striking power in order to pierce the layered enemy defense, the second relied on speed and mobility. This echelon, heavily reinforced with tanks, mechanized infantry, and cavalry units, would seek to turn the enemy's now-exposed flanks and encircle his forces still engaged along the front, possibly in conjunction with another shock army's attack. Other units, aided by deep air strikes, would press the attack into the operational and strategic depth, defeating the defender's reserves as they move up to the battlefield, and destroying his communications, command, and supply points. Varfolomeev stressed that to prevent the enemy's escape, those units pursuing from the front must advance at a rate of at least 20 to 25 kilometers per day, while those mobile units operating against his flanks and rear must cover as much as 40 to 45 kilometers per day.[108]

Several other proposals were offered during this period in an effort to "flesh out" the shock army's organizational structure. Among the most balanced of these was put forward by Varfolomeev's academic colleague P. I. Vakulich. The latter's projected shock army consisted of fifteen to sixteen rifle divisions; one motor-mechanized and one cavalry formation; twelve to fifteen tank battalions; nine to twelve additional artillery regiments; four to six light aviation brigades and a fighter unit; as well as other air and antiaircraft units and, if necessary, light and heavy bombers on loan from the front command.[109]

There were a number of excesses as well, which is hardly surprising, given the spirit of the times and the pace of the Red Army's mechanization drive. One of the more egregious examples was put forward in 1932 by Ya. M. Zhigur, an instructor at the Frunze Military Academy. Zhigur advocated creating a shock army of four to five rifle corps, motor-mechanized, and cavalry units, 2,000 tanks and as many aircraft, plus twelve to fifteen regiments of guns from the High Command Artillery Reserve.[110]

Even these figures are small compared with those contained in a report compiled by the staff of the Urals Military District in the autumn of 1936. A shock army, according to this proposal, would consist of twelve rifle divisions; a mechanized corps and an independent mechanized brigade; three cavalry divisions; a light-bomber brigade, two brigades of assault aircraft, and two squadrons each of fighter and reconnaissance planes; six RGK tank battalions; five RGK artillery regiments, plus two heavy artillery battalions; and two battalions of chemical troops. The shock army, at full strength, would number nearly 300,000 men, 100,000 horses, 1,668 small-caliber and 1,550 medium- and heavy-caliber guns, 722 aircraft, and 2,853 tanks.[111]

Such extreme proposals not only were far-fetched for the time but also, in numbers of armored vehicles, greatly exceeded even the large tank armies of World War II. Considerations of the Soviet penchant for gigantism aside, these and other, more moderate studies dealing with the shock army nevertheless represent one of the more intriguing and productive areas of military thought during the interwar period. By 1937 the Red Army possessed, at least in theory, a powerful instrument that would enable it to meet any operational eventuality.

The deep operation, like the deep battle, recognized three subordinate types: the meeting, breakthrough, and defensive operations. The latter is self-explanatory and will be dealt with later. Confusion most often arises when dealing with the other two types, which are variations of the generic offensive operation. Whereas the breakthrough operation against an enemy along a continuous front is by and large the defensive operation's opposite number, the meeting operation occurs when two or more armies, each attacking, collide. Such a situation most often arises at the beginning of a war, when both sides are pursuing an offensive strategy, and usually represents the first major operations along the belligerents' respective frontiers. The most noteworthy example of a series of meeting operations occurred along both fronts in August 1914, when the chief belligerents launched major offensives in the war's first weeks. A meeting operation might also take place along the still-open flanks of an otherwise-continuous front or, on rare occasions, following a particularly successful breakthrough operation, in which freedom of maneuver has been temporarily restored.

The meeting operation, because it is most likely to occur in the war's first weeks, is closely bound up with the armed forces' strategic deployment plans. These plans, dictating the army's placement and initial actions along the frontier, inevitably contain the germ of the war's opening operations, just as Neznamov had noted some twenty years earlier.[112] This was still the case, although the armed forces' technical composition had changed dramatically since 1911, with an emphasis on greater range, mechanization, and striking power. These developments, in turn, had a decisive effect at the strategic level, as reflected in various theories, discussed earlier, under the rubric of the "beginning period of the war."

The armed forces' mobilization and deployment efforts at the beginning of a war would consist of several strategic echelons, arriving consecutively from the interior. The first strategic echelon, according to one scenario, would actually consist of a number of smaller, operational echelons, divided among themselves according to their range, speed, and mobility. The first operational echelon would consist of aviation, both army organic and long-range front or strategic forces, capable of bombing targets in the enemy rear and clearing the way for the ground forces' advance. The latter would be spearheaded by the second echelon, or army "vanguard echelon" *(avangardnyi eshelon)*, or AE, made up of mechanized and motorized units, plus "mechanized cavalry." This would be followed by the third, or main, echelon, containing most of the army's men and matériel. Finally, the army's reserve echelon, consisting of late-arriving units and heavier weapons, would bring up the rear. In all, it was calculated that this invasion army would stretch some 250 to 300 kilometers to the rear as it advanced, while its front occupied a mere 75 to 100 kilometers in breadth.[113]

Such an extensive echelonment in depth creates several problems for the shock army commander. Chief among these is that the vanguard echelon would engage the enemy first, even as succeeding echelons were still far from the front. This raised the specter of the shock army being defeated by a superior enemy before the commander could bring his entire force to bear, making the uninterrupted replenishment of the forces at the front by succeeding echelons critical, lest the army be overwhelmed and defeated in detail. Such fears led one theorist, Isserson, to the somewhat schematic conclusion that in the meeting operation *"ultimate success will go to him whose operational formation is deeper."*[114]

Another difficulty was the importance that such a deep formation placed on the proper prebattle disposition of forces. That is, the speed at which the different echelons advance makes large-scale regroupings on the march exceedingly difficult. Therefore, it was vital that the future shock grouping or some other offensive intention already be present in the army's march order. A turning movement, under these circumstances, was deemed particularly promising, given the likelihood of open flanks at the onset of hostilities, and one theorist urged that front commanders organize their subordinate armies' marches so that even a frontal collision would lead to the turning of the enemy's flanks and the encirclement of his main forces.[115]

The meeting operation would actually begin in the air, preceding the collision of the ground forces. Prior to this, the army's "aviation group" would be primarily concerned with covering the forward units' march and deployment, and challenging the enemy for local air superiority. As the two forces approached, the aviation group's efforts would be increasingly directed against the enemy's troops, supply lines, and rail installations. In certain cases, bombing and other air activity may be conducted to a depth of 300 kilometers and be accompanied by gas attacks and airborne landings in the enemy rear.[116]

The ground battle would open with the vanguard echelon's attack against the approaching enemy's flanks. This echelon, as it closes with the enemy, may leap forward as much as 100 kilometers ahead of the main body, while remaining in supporting distance by the latter. Smaller forces will simultaneously launch a supporting attack to aid the main effort or, if defending, tie down enemy forces while the main attack progresses. The battle would continue with increasing intensity during the second and third days, as the vanguard echelon is steadily reinforced by infantry and other units arriving from the main body. The shock army, even while attacking, would still have to contend with the enemy's air and mechanized raids, as the battle ebbed and flowed along the front and in depth. In such a highly fluid situation the operation may develop on both sides to a depth of 150 to 200 kilometers.[117]

Should the army's main attack prove successful, its mechanized forces, having turned the enemy's flank, will break into his rear areas, followed by infantry units to consolidate the success. As the defender begins to withdraw, the shock army's motor-mechanized and cavalry units take up the pursuit by attacking his retreating columns to cut off and surround them. Meanwhile, the shock army's air arm would harry the retreat from above, attacking both troops and vital crossings. The pursuit would be pushed as far as possible until exhaustion sets in. At this point, it was predicted that the front would temporarily stabilize along positional lines, at which time preparations for a new operation would begin.[118] A variation of this scenario posited the failure of the vanguard echelon's initial assault during the first two days. In such an event, it was recommended that the mobile units be withdrawn from the battle to conserve their strength, with the main burden of the fighting then shifting to the infantry. Should the latter effort succeed, the vanguard echelon would then be recommitted into the battle to exploit the rifle corps' success in depth.[119]

Isserson paid special attention to the ambiguous nature of certain meeting operations, in which elements of the breakthrough operation are already clearly discernible. Such a situation might arise, he noted, when the vanguard echelon, having failed in its attack, is forced by enemy resistance to fall back upon the upcoming main echelon. In such a case, the vanguard echelon would be withdrawn and its place at the front taken by the main echelon. Isserson called this situation a "crisis" in the development of the meeting operation, in which the attacker has already lost the maneuver advantage afforded by the presence of open flanks and now faces the prospect of an impending solid front. However, he maintained that conditions still existed for successfully concluding the operation, due to the relative elasticity and undeveloped nature of the enemy's defenses, without resorting to a full-fledged breakthrough.[120]

This revived meeting operation would begin with an attack by the main echelon's infantry units, which would be supported by air strikes against the defender's frontline troops and his rear targets. The attack would develop slowly at first, achieving a depth of only 20 kilometers during the first two days. Isserson calculated, however, that by the third day the breach in the enemy front would be sufficiently wide and deep to commit the former vanguard echelon, now styled the "success development echelon" *(eshelon razvitiya uspekha),* or ERU, into the battle to carry it into the enemy's operational depth. By the end of the fourth day the main echelon might have advanced as far as 50 to 60 kilometers, while the ERU would resume its former place in the army's advance by penetrating up to 100 kilometers in pursuit of the enemy along the lines already described.[121]

However, the meeting operation, for all of the army's attention to the subject, never achieved the status of the breakthrough operation, chiefly because Soviet theorists, despite their declared preference for maneuver, fully expected that a future conflict would contain extended periods of positional warfare. This bias was further strengthened by the type of offensive operations the Red Army conducted during World War II, which chiefly involved breaking through fixed positions along a relatively static, although porous, front.

The breakthrough operation against an entrenched defender was the centerpiece of the Red Army's thinking about the deep operation during the 1930s. As such, the question attracted the army's best minds, who responded with a number of complex schemes, both open and classified, for breaking the positional deadlock and restoring maneuver to operations.

One of these was Tukhachevskii, who was now entering upon his most mature and productive period as a military theorist, in spite of the demands on his time as overseer of the armed forces' technical rearmament. A contemporary described Tukhachevskii as the army's "most outstanding military man, according to his strategic range of interests and operational capabilities."[122] These views found expression in his *New Problems of War,* the first part of a projected three-volume work, which the author dedicated to the recently deceased Triandafillov. Tukhachevskii, who began working on the manuscript in 1931, evidently saw the work as a technically more sophisticated update of his earlier *Future War*. Unfortunately, a revised draft was either lost or destroyed following Tukhachevskii's death in 1937, and only the earlier version remains.

Another, lesser-known, figure was Aleksandr Il'ich Yegorov, who during most of this period served as chief of the RKKA Staff, which in 1935 was renamed the RKKA General Staff. Yegorov, like most of those who occupied this position during the interwar period, was a former military specialist. Born in 1885, he rose to the rank of colonel during World War I before joining the Red Army in 1918, where he commanded the Southern and Southwestern Fronts and quickly fell under the influence of his political commissar, Joseph Stalin. Yegorov commanded a number of military districts after the war before becoming chief of staff in 1931. He has been unflatteringly described as a "figurehead" chief of staff who lacked the "drive or ability to initiate much on his own."[123] Yegorov, while he did not possess Tukhachevskii's brilliance, by virtue of his good relations with Stalin and Voroshilov could still push measures that his brash young counterpart could not. However, his long association with the Stalinist clique in the army did not save him in the end, and Yegorov fell victim to the purges in early 1939.

Yegorov's chief contribution to the theoretical debate was his sponsorship of the report "The RKKA's Tactics and Operational Art at a New Stage," which provides an interesting glimpse of the army's early official views on conducting the breakthrough operation. The report, modeled closely on Triandafillov's 1931 memorandum, echoed the latter's preoccupation with the strength of modern defense, which may extend up to 100 to 120 kilometers in depth and include both the defenders' tactical zone and his army reserves. The only hope of piercing this formidable barrier lay in the harmonious employment of the new combat arms, which the report identified as modern "strategic" cavalry, motorized and mechanized forces, aviation, airborne troops, and chemical weapons.[124] The resulting marriage of firepower and maneuver would enable the attacker to conduct an offensive throughout the entire depth of the enemy defense and to destroy the defender's frontline troops and deep reserves simultaneously.

Triandafillov's influence is evident in Tukhachevskii's insistence that the offensive be mounted along a sufficiently broad front to ensure a decisive outcome. He criticized the Germans' March 1918 decision to launch their attack toward Amiens along a narrow (80-kilometer) front, which, he contended, left the Allies free to shift reserves to the threatened area. Tukhachevskii's attitude is not surprising, as the vast spaces of eastern Europe made anything but a broad-front attack pointless. As we have seen, Brusilov reached the same conclusion in 1916 and enjoyed great initial success, although he lacked the technical means to exploit this victory to any great depth. This caused Tukhachevskii to conclude that in most cases "the wider the attack front, the greater . . . will be the operation's success."[125] The author also echoed Triandafillov's preference for an encirclement as the operation's culmination. This would be achieved either by twin blows along converging axes or through a single turning movement to pin the defender against a natural barrier or neutral frontier.[126]

Yegorov's shock army assault would begin with a predominantly infantry assault against the enemy's tactical defense zone along the lines already described. Upon penetrating to a depth of 6 to 10 kilometers, the army commander would commit his mobile forces to develop the attack in depth. Motor-mechanized units were expected to advance as deeply as 80 to 100 kilometers on the first day after commitment, with the more vulnerable cavalry covering the advance's flanks to a depth of 50 to 60 kilometers. These units would be supported by airborne landings in the enemy rear, to disrupt the arrival of the defender's reserves. Meanwhile, the army's mobile formations would continue their attack, successively defeating the defender's reserves and destroying his airfields. These units would press on until the "complete tactical encirclement" of the defender's forces still engaged at the front. Upon the defender's withdrawal, the pursuit phase would begin, with the infantry pressing him from the front, while motor-mechanized and cavalry forces would harry the retreat along the flanks, to cut off and encircle his retreating units.[127]

When Tukhachevskii began writing *New Problems of War*, the Red Army's mechanization program was just getting under way, and some of his early judgments betray an unreflective enthusiasm for the new combat arms and their potential. This was particularly evident in his comments concerning airborne forces, which he blithely assumed could act independently of the main forces for extended periods before returning to their base. Yegorov, on the other hand, suffered from a more lingering and archaic attachment to the cavalry arm, which doubtlessly sprang from his association with the Voroshilov-Budennyi clique, although his views elsewhere were progressive enough for the time. In this, as in other areas, the two men's differences were probably due as much to differences in temperament as to conviction.

Certainly one of the most talented and original, although least well known, operational theorists of this period was Georgii Samoilovich Isserson. Born in 1898, he was very much a product of the Soviet system, although like many others of his generation he undoubtedly owed much to the writings of his czarist predecessors. Isserson, following service in the civil war, graduated from the RKKA Military Academy in 1924 and held a variety of command and staff assignments over the next few years. In 1931 he was appointed to head the Frunze Academy's new "operational department," and in 1936 he became the first chief of the department of army operations in the new General Staff Academy, where he was subsequently awarded the title of professor. One officer who studied under him called Isserson "the most capable theoretician in the field of operational art" following Triandafillov's death, although he felt that Isserson overestimated his own importance.[128] Following service as an army chief of staff during the Finnish War, Isserson was arrested in July 1941 for criticizing the military leadership and spent the next fourteen years in labor camps and internal exile. He was rehabilitated and returned to Moscow only in 1955, although his health had been ruined for good. Isserson nonetheless continued his academic labors in retirement until his death in 1976.[129]

Isserson was one of the most prolific and erudite authors writing on tactics and operations during the 1930s.[130] Among his most important works on operational art were *The Evolution of Operational Art* (1932, 1937) and *Fundamentals of the Deep Operation* (1933), the latter of which remains classified to this day.

Isserson's idée fixe was the greatly enhanced role that the factor of depth had come to play in military affairs at all levels. According to this view, military strategy had developed from Napoleonic times and the "strategy of a single point," to the von Moltke era and the "epoch of linear strategy," as the increased importance of fire caused military activities to expand in terms of breadth. The latter form, with its distinctive flanking maneuver, was evident at Königgrätz (1866), Metz (1870), and Mukden (1905) and during the opening battles of World War I. However, Isserson argued that the disappearance of the open flank and the formation of a continuous front from the autumn of 1914 meant that this strategy was no longer viable. This meant, he wrote, resorting to Marxist terminology, that "the linear strategy had arrived at its antithesis," a theoretical dead end from which it could develop no further.[131] Military art now faced the task of breaking through a solid and deeply echeloned front, which brought to the fore the factor of depth. Its role in the Great War and the likelihood that similar conditions would obtain in a future conflict caused Isserson to conclude that *"we are at the dawn of a new epoch in military art, and must move from a linear strategy to a deep strategy."*[132]

This overall "deepening" of war affected all levels of warfare, as was shown in the section covering the war's beginning period and the deep battle. The effect on operational art was no less dramatic, and Isserson fully expected some form of positional warfare to recur following the clash of the sides' first strategic echelons in the war's opening meeting operations.[133]

This meant that the Red Army faced the prospect of having to break through a deeply echeloned front, whose depth Isserson calculated at between 100 and 120 kilometers. This area, he stated, consisted of three separate zones of varying depth. The first, or tactical, zone constituted the main line of resistance and was made up of two defensive positions. The first of these extended back some 5 to 6 kilometers from the front line, and a second 12 to 15 kilometers behind the forward edge of the first position. Behind this lay the operational zone, larger and less densely occupied than the first, embracing the railheads and supply stations to a depth of 50 to 60 kilometers. Here were concentrated the army's main reserves, airfields, and support troops. A third, or rear, zone completed the picture. This zone served as the link between the front and the country's strategic rear and included the area between the main rail distribution stations and the railheads. Also located in this zone were the front (strategic) reserves and heavy bomber airfields, as well as the army's, and perhaps the front's, headquarters.[134]

Such imposing depth raised the specter of a return to the conditions of 1914–18 and the dreary prospect of "gnawing through" the enemy's defenses. Isserson, to counter this, offered his own impressive shock army. This would comprise fifteen rifle divisions; two cavalry divisions; three mechanized brigades; a motorized division; twenty tank battalions; eight howitzer regiments; four ground-support air brigades; and two light-bomber brigades. This would yield, in raw figures, a force of 1,472 guns (575 of them heavy), 1,457 tanks (300 medium and the remainder light), and 1,045 aircraft (including 372 assault aircraft and 168 light bombers), for a total force of slightly over 350,000 men.[135] Experience would later show that Isserson's shock army was too large and cumbersome to be controlled by a single army commander. Indeed, such a formidable combination of men and matériel compared favorably in size to some of the wartime fronts a decade later.

Isserson, as had Varfolomeev, divided his army into two parts for conducting the breakthrough operation. By far the largest of these was the "attack echelon" *(eshelon ataki)*, or EA, which had the initial tactical mission of piercing the enemy's forward defensive zone. The EA would consist of five rifle corps, of which four would be reinforced with the twenty tank battalions and twelve artillery regiments to ensure a preponderance of force at the point of decision. Once the breach was made, the "breakthrough development echelon" *(eshelon razvitiya proryva)*, or ERP, would rush into the gap to exploit the success in depth. Configured for operating in highly fluid conditions, the ERP's strength lay in its mobility rather than its raw striking power, and accordingly consisted of a mechanized corps, a cavalry corps, a motorized division, and an airborne detachment.[136]

The breadth of the shock army's attack zone had always been another critical factor in Soviet calculations. Isserson believed that the army should attack along an overall frontage of 70 to 80 kilometers. According to this scenario, three or four reinforced rifle corps would make the main breakthrough attack along a front no less than 30 kilometers in width, which was considered the minimum necessary to allow for the ERP's passage through the gap without interference from the defender's artillery along the flanks of the penetration. The breakthrough zone, under especially favorable conditions, might be expanded to 48 to 50 kilometers, with the addition of another rifle corps. In this case, each reinforced rifle corps would attack along a 10- to 12-kilometer front, with each division in the corps' first echelon attacking along a 6-kilometer front, with a density of 18.5 guns, 13.1 aircraft, and 18.2 tanks per kilometer. The fifth rifle corps would launch a supporting attack along a 15- to 20-kilometer front.[137]

The breakthrough operation (see map 10) would begin in the air, one or two days before the start of the ground attack. This phase would immediately extend throughout the entire depth of the enemy's operational defense, with the main mass of the army's air strength (fighters and assault aircraft) directed against the defender's air strength and his frontline positions along the projected breakthrough zone. Bomber aviation would seek out targets deeper in the enemy rear, in order

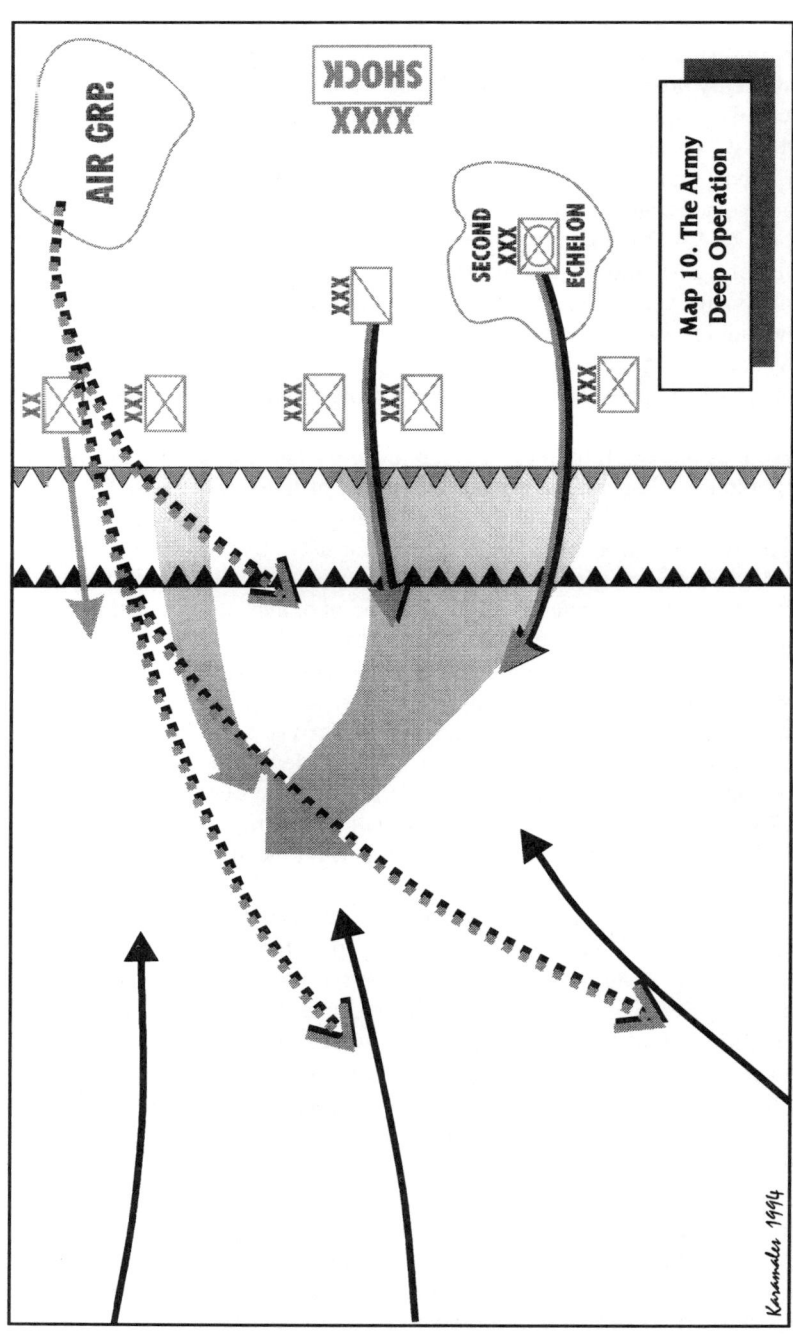

to isolate the battlefield and prevent the arrival of the defender's reserves to the threatened area. At the same time, the army's airborne detachment (ADO) would be dropped some 50 to 60 kilometers behind the front, with the task of disrupting the defender's command and control system.[138]

The ground attack would commence with the EA's assault against the defender's tactical zone in a combined ground-air attack along the lines of the deep battle. The defender's first position would receive the brunt of the assault, as the second position was rarely fully manned and served chiefly as a reserve position for the frontline troops. Isserson calculated that the fighting for the first position would continue for four or five hours, which he considered sufficient time to break through to a depth of 5 to 6 kilometers. At this point he recommended committing the ERP into the breach, a decision he called "one of the most complex and responsible" in the entire operation, requiring all the army commander's skill. To commit the ERP too early meant involving it in the battle for the first tactical position, from which it might emerge too weak to carry out its primary mission of striking in depth. To delay in committing the echelon would allow the first position's defenders time to fall back and occupy the second position and be reinforced by reserves from the defensive depth, which might well necessitate a repetition of the tactical breakthrough.[139]

The question of when to commit the ERP was studied intensively by Isserson's department of army operations during the winter of 1937. The study, entitled "The Army Offensive Operation in the Beginning Period of a War," examined in detail this and a number of other questions, many of which would remain a source of controversy for years.[140]

The study posited three possible scenarios for committing the ERP into battle. The first involved an attack against a weak defender lacking major reserves. In this case, the ERP would be committed at the beginning of the attack, or before the complete rupture of the tactical defense. The second alternative, however, was considered the most likely and involved an attack against a moderately strong defender. In this case, the ERP would be committed once the tactical defense had been pierced, preferably by the end of the first day. The third scenario was considered the most difficult and foresaw an attack against heavily fortified defensive positions. In such a situation the ERP would be committed along with the attack echelon to strengthen the weight of the blow against the tactical defense zone. This was considered the least preferable variant because it would involve heavy fighting through the tactical defense zone for several days, resulting in serious losses and a corresponding decline in the breakthrough development echelon's ability to subsequently exploit the success in depth.[141]

The department also examined the possible forms that the ERP's actions might assume after piercing the tactical defense. The first, or brief, variant pitted a relatively weak attacker and defender against each other. In this case, the ERP, having broken through the tactical zone's second position, would turn immediately inward to encircle the remaining defenders, leaving only a few mobile units to carry the advance to a depth of up to 50 kilometers. The second, or deep, variant involved an attack by a powerful breakthrough echelon to as deep as 100 kilometers. The ERP, in conjunction with air strikes and airborne landings in the rear, would engage and destroy the defender's operational reserves and block the retreat of those defenders still at the front. The third, or "combined," variant posited the actions of two separate armies' breakthrough development echelons as part of a larger front operation. In this case, the armies' two ERPs, operating along converging axes, would drive deep into the defender's rear to encircle large numbers of enemy forces.[142]

According to Isserson, the ERP's mechanized corps would be committed into the tactical breach on the first day, followed by the cavalry corps in the case of a single, large penetration. If more than one breakthrough zone developed, the two formations might be committed simultaneously along different sectors. This would be followed on the operation's second day by the introduction of the ERP's motorized division.[143]

The mechanized corps would quickly pass through the defender's unoccupied second tactical position and into the operational defense zone to a depth of 50 to 60 kilometers during the day following the breakthrough. The cavalry corps will advance along a slightly different axis to a depth of 30 to 40 kilometers. Together the two formations form the wedge of the shock army's projected turning movement, with the mechanized corps covering the longer, outer flank, and the cavalry the shorter, inner flank. By the end of the first day the ERP is to link up with the airborne forces in the enemy rear, while attacking and destroying the defender's operational reserves as they move up to the battlefield. These activities are supported by the greater part of the army's air group, which covers the ERP's advance and assists the attack by targeting the defender's reserves and communications. At the same time, strategic aviation would assist in isolating the battlefield by attacking mobilization, supply, and rail centers in the enemy's interior.[144]

By the end of the second day following the breakthrough, the ERP will in several places have penetrated throughout the rear zone to a depth of 100 to 120 kilometers. Here the echelon would continue its attacks against the defender's reserves, while at the same time seeking to complete the encirclement of those defenders now isolated along the original front, in conjunction with the infantry units. The EA's lead units, meanwhile, would clear the enemy's tactical zone by the end of the second day, where they would assist the army's mobile group in mopping up any lingering enemy resistance. Once this task was completed, the EA could then be brought up by auto transport over the next few days to the ERP's front.[145]

A success of this magnitude, as a result of the breakthrough operation, inevitably raised the question of the offensive's further development in depth. This, in turn, meant conducting a series of consecutive operations, the theoretical elaboration of which had been substantially completed by the end of the 1920s.

Isserson believed that the necessity for conducting such operations would quickly become evident, even as the initial breakthrough operation was reaching its zenith. This was because the defender, despite his defeat, would by the operation's fourth or fifth day have succeeded in bringing up sufficient forces from his deep reserves to construct the rudiments of a new front. Should these forces counterattack, a new operation would begin, unfolding along the lines of the meeting operation, as described earlier. In such a case, the ERP would automatically become the vanguard echelon, while the EA would assume the functions of the army's main echelon. Those units whose arrival is delayed by the need to finish off those defenders still at the front constitute the reserve echelon. Likewise, should the enemy's reserves succeed in halting the attacker and reestablishing a solid front, a new breakthrough operation would have to be organized.[146]

Isserson calculated that a series of consecutive operations launched from the USSR's western frontier against the Polish army would require a month to reach the line of the middle Vistula, a distance of some 400 kilometers. This meant an average daily rate of advance of 15 kilometers, not counting those relatively immobile days spent preparing new breakthrough operations.[147]

An uninterrupted advance to such a depth, while it held out the opportunity for great success, inevitably raised the specter of exhaustion. Success depends ultimately on the attacker's human and material superiority over the defender at every stage of a series of operations, and particularly at its culmination point. An operation without this superiority risks defeat even under the most favorable conditions, as had been the case in 1914 and 1920. If anything, the problem had grown more acute since then, as modern armies' matériel needs had increased substantially, even as the means of delivering the necessary supplies had changed very little. Varfolomeev, for example, calculated a shock army's daily supply needs at forty to forty-five trains during an offensive, which was moderate in comparison with other projections.[148] One author's gloomy reading of these statistics led him to conclude that supply problems would compel a future attacker to call a halt in the advance after only 150 to 200 kilometers to put his rear services in order.[149]

Isserson, however, was considerably more sanguine about the prospects of conducting operations to such a great depth, and his optimism was based primarily on his faith in the efficacy of modern technology to overcome most of the shock army's supply problems. He calculated that a series of operations carried to a depth of 400 kilometers would outstrip its rail lines by some 150 kilometers, given an average daily repair rate of 8 kilometers. The remaining distance could be filled by the army's organic transport system and divisional supply services to a depth of 125 kilometers, leaving a supply shortfall of 25 kilometers. Isserson maintained that this distance could easily be made up, either by increasing the rate of rail repair or by expanding the capabilities of the army's supply system.[150]

However, even Isserson was forced to admit that the carrying capacity of a newly restored rail line would probably be insufficient to meet all the shock army's supply needs during the course of a month's advance. Rather than halt the advance and allow the enemy to regroup and establish a new front, Isserson recommended detaching the most mobile elements (mechanized and cavalry corps and motorized units) from the main body to form a new vanguard echelon. This echelon, supported by the bulk of the army's air arm, would then continue the offensive, without pausing, ahead of the army's slower-moving rifle units until the operation's successful conclusion.[151]

From the preceding, it is evident that the basic theory of conducting consecutive operations had changed little since the 1920s, despite the advent of modern weapons. Here, as in so many other areas, Soviet practice continued to lag behind theory, and it was not until World War II and the arrival of large numbers of American and British wheeled and tracked vehicles that the Red Army finally attained the requisite transport capability to carry out sustained operations in depth.

However, an attack of this magnitude, even if carried out by a reinforced shock army, could not hope to achieve a decisive success, given the expected length of a future eastern European front. The fact that such an attack would have to be supported by other armies, acting in concert, inevitably raised the question of the front level of command and its place in the theory of operational art.

One of those who devoted a good deal of thought to the subject was Varfolomeev, whose views on the front and its relationship to its subordinate armies were solidly in accord with what was by now an established tradition in Russian-Soviet military thought. His thinking on the subject is particularly indicative of Mikhnevich's and Movchin's influence concerning the relationship of "complex" (front) and "simple" (army) operations. "In planning operations," Varfolomeev wrote,

> the front command establishes the final goal and breaks them [operations] up into a series of intermediate ones. The achievement of these latter goals is assigned to the armies (as part of a front) and is regulated by definite tasks. Within the framework of these tasks, forces, and means allotted by the front, the armies organize and conduct their operations. As opposed to the front, simultaneously pursuing several goals and acting along several operational axes, an army pursues one goal and acts along a single operational axis. The grouping of army operations in time and space issues from the overall idea of the front operation and is aimed at achieving intermediate front goals. The front's influence on the grouping of army operations is expressed in the distribution of forces and means between the armies and the regulation of activities in time (deadlines) and space (axes and lines).[152]

In certain cases, such as an operation involving the neighboring forces of two fronts, the high command may assume direct control over the armies' operations in order to more effectively coordinate their actions. In the majority of cases, however, the front commander will assign his subordinate armies initial objectives to a depth of 100 kilometers, or through the enemy's operational defense.

Upon achieving this initial task, the army commander will then receive additional orders from the front instance regarding the operation's subsequent development. Within the framework of the front commander's instructions, the several army commanders enjoy considerable freedom of action, in theory, in allotting forces and missions to subordinate units for both the breakthrough and the subsequent development phases.[153]

A number of Red Army theorists continued to subsume the front and the front operation under the rubric of strategy, rather than operational art, a terminological holdover from the late imperial era. One of the most influential of these was Isserson, who called the front a "formation of a strategic order" and considered the army the sole operational unit.[154] Varfolomeev did not address this question directly, although his writings provide some interesting insights into the place of front operations in the strategic sphere.

Varfolomeev believed, as had Triandafillov, that to achieve a decisive success, an operation must be launched along a sufficiently broad front. His solution was to group several shock armies (see map 11) into what he called a "shock front" *(udarnyi front),* calculating that an offensive of this magnitude not only would absorb a large number of enemy reserves but also would enable the front to launch deep attacks along intersecting axes to encircle the defender's forces still at the front.[155] The existence of a shock front presupposes the existence of other, passive, fronts or those playing an auxiliary role to the main offensive in a theater of military activities, much like secondary corps and armies in army and front operations. This form was employed successfully by the Red Army on a number of occasions during World War II, as during the Stalingrad counteroffensive of November 1942, when the Southwestern and Stalingrad Fronts struck the Axis defenders along both flanks, while the Don Front pinned the enemy down north of the city. Even more impressive is the example of the Belorussian strategic operation of 1944, which involved four fronts. Here the First Baltic, First, and Third Belorussian Fronts carried out shock missions, with the Second Belorussian Front consigned to a supporting role.

Other proposals for the organization and employment of the front were put forward during these years. Among the most interesting was that drawn up by the staff of the Urals Military District, which was commanded between 1935 and 1937 by I. I. Gar'kavyi, a former czarist lieutenant.

The staff's report clearly saw the front as a strategic factor, one capable of operating independently in a given theater of military activities. The proposed front might consist of several field armies; a "cavalry-mechanized army"; large airborne units; heavy and light aviation; tank, engineering, artillery, chemical, and transport units; as well as front reserves up to a rifle corps in strength. In certain cases, depending on geographic conditions, the front might even include such nontraditional units as river flotillas and even a fleet, if operating along a maritime axis. Such a concentration of force, the authors maintained, would enable the front to conduct a series of consecutive operations to a depth of 300 to 400 kilometers

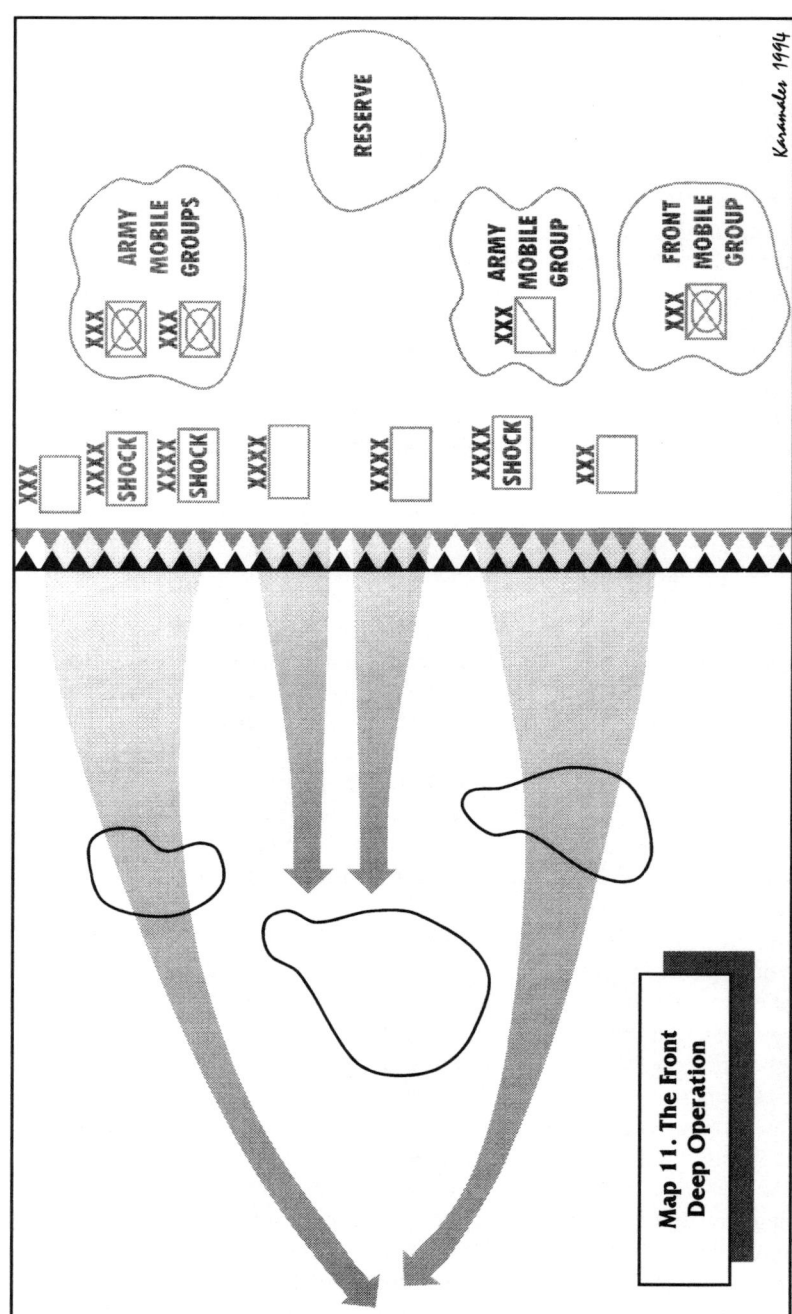

over a month or more, during which time its mobile formations might advance at times as much as 50 kilometers per day.[156]

It is clear from this description that the staff's notion of the front's role differed little in organization, aside from technological changes, from that of Leer and Neznamov. In fact, the authors' idea of the front's spatial responsibilities had more in common with earlier ideas of a single front occupying an entire theater of military activities than with the smaller, strictly operational force it would become during World War II. In other respects, particularly as regards the subordination of naval units to the ground forces commander, the staff's projected front recalls the breadth of Kuropatkin's responsibilities in 1904–5, as well as certain aspects of the Red Army's early creation of strategic "theater" commands in 1941–42 and 1945. Here, as in other areas, the Soviets clearly overestimated their capabilities, particularly as concerns the control of such a large force.

The authors did prove more prescient in forecasting the actions of certain of the front's subordinate units during an offensive, especially the aforementioned cavalry-mechanized army *(konno-mekhanizirovannaya armiya)*. According to the report, this army was a powerful force that might include as many as two mechanized corps; one or two cavalry corps; two motorized divisions; a brigade of medium tanks; two to three air brigades; plus additional artillery, chemical, and engineering troops. Clearly, it was designed for mobile operations in depth.[157] However, unlike the shock army, which it resembled in all but name, the cavalry-mechanized army was not intended to carry out a breakthrough on its own. Rather, it would be held in reserve as the front's mobile group, to be committed following a breakthrough by one of the regular armies. Once committed, the cavalry-mechanized army, in conjunction with the front's other armies, or a similar army from another front, would be able to carry out large-scale encirclements of the defender's frontline troops.

The idea of the cavalry-mechanized army had its genesis in the mounted arm's traditional exploitation role, although now on a much greater and technologically more advanced scale. A more recent source of inspiration was Budennyi's cavalry army and its dash from the Kakhovka bridgehead in 1920 as the Southern Front's mobile group. The cavalry-mechanized army did not appear as such during World War II but was transformed into the even more powerful tank armies, which served as the fronts' mobile group in a number of major operations. The Red Army did create several smaller formations, known as "cavalry-mechanized groups" *(konno-mekhanizirovannye gruppy)*, consisting of cavalry, tank, and mechanized corps, which were used extensively to exploit front breakthroughs during 1944–45.

Finally, the most forlorn branch of operational art during these years was, as always, the defensive operation. The subject received only passing attention from the army's leading theorists, who generally confined themselves to such generalities as stressing the heavily antitank nature of modern defense and the need to maintain adequate reserves to repel an attack.[158] For example, the army's leading theoretical journal, *War and Revolution,* published only a single article dealing with defense at the operational level during the period in question. In it, the author made the standard Soviet division of defense into two types, planned and forced, depending on the decisions of one's own high command and the enemy's actions. Either form could be employed actively or passively, although the author considered a passive defense more likely in those cases in which the army is forced to defend. The author, A. Anisov, considered the active variant superior because it gave the defender more time to organize and carry out the necessary measures, while the latter form suffered from its hurried and ad hoc character, generally as the result of a previous failure.[159]

Anisov divided the army's defense into three main zones. The first was the tactical zone, which consisted of two defensive belts. The first of these extended back some 6 kilometers from the front line, and the second was located another 10 to 12 kilometers back. The tactical zone, despite its designation, was the backbone of the army's defense, containing its main forces and most of its antitank weapons. Behind this lay the operational zone, which extended some 75 kilometers behind the front. This area contained the army's reserves, supply routes, and the greater part of its organic airpower. Behind this was a further rear zone, which contained supply depots, bomber airfields, deep army and front reserves, and, in some cases, a fortified rear army defensive line. This zone also contained the army and sometimes the front headquarters.[160]

The author put forward two proposals for conducting defensive operations. The first relied on a positional approach and was more or less static. It would be employed to hold particularly important areas whose retention was vital. One method was to heavily reinforce the tactical zone with reserves and attached units in order to prevent an enemy breakthrough from the very outset. A more active approach involved launching a preemptive attack against the enemy's penetrations, using tank and artillery units already concentrated in the tactical zone, as well as reserves from the army rear. Anisov believed that this would either thwart the enemy's offensive preparations altogether or at least force him to postpone his attack. However, should these measures fail and the enemy nonetheless penetrate the tactical zone, the army commander is to order a withdrawal to a new position, while continuing to counterattack, in order to slow the enemy's advance.[161]

The second proposal was less concerned with holding the tactical zone than with pinning down enemy forces and winning time for one's offensive endeavors on other portions of the front. In this case, as a rule, the front would be lightly held, with some sectors manned by covering forces only. Much more important is the army reserve, which contains the bulk of the army's mobile and attached units. This reserve would be echeloned in depth in the operational defense zone, from which it could be quickly concentrated and dispatched to the front to bolster the tactical defense by launching counterattacks to ease enemy pressure. Should the attacker nevertheless succeed in breaking through, the reserve units would cover the retreat to a new position by repeatedly counterattacking the pursuing forces.[162]

Significantly, none of the works from this period had anything to say about defensive operations at the front level, whether viewed through the prism of strategy or operational art. Indeed, strategic defense, much like its counterpart at the operational level, was woefully ignored during this period and beyond, a neglect that was to have near-fatal consequences for the Red Army in 1941–42. Entire Soviet armies were encircled and destroyed in the Wehrmacht's summer and fall offensive of 1941, although in many cases this was due to incompetence at the strategic level. Although the Red Army performed appreciably better in the defensive fighting of 1942, it nevertheless surrendered vast territories to the enemy and recovered only when the German advance faltered for logistical reasons. In fact, it was not until the Battle of Kursk, in the summer of 1943, that the Soviets finally succeeded in constructing an operational-strategic defensive system capable of halting the German army's attack from the outset.

The locus of the Red Army's work on the deep operation and other aspects of operational art during these years was the expanding network of military-educational establishments that were springing up around the country. Chief among these until 1936 was the Frunze Military Academy, which during this period was headed by Eideman (1925–32), formerly a junior officer in the czarist army; Shaposhnikov (1932–35), a former colonel and 1910 graduate of the imperial General Staff Academy; and Kork (1935–37), a former captain and 1914 graduate. Other important institutions included the RKKA Military Academy of Mechanization and Motorization and the RKKA Military-Chemical Academy, both of which were established in 1932.

The Frunze Academy, despite periodic campaigns against such unorthodox thinkers as Svechin and Verkhovskii, continued its efforts to turn out graduates versed in the ways of modern war. During the 1930s these increasingly took the form of investigating and disseminating the new theories of the deep battle and operation. The large numbers of tanks and other weapons then entering the army's arsenal lent an additional impetus to this search, so that as early as 1930 students were studying the fundamentals of the deep battle on the basis of the 1929 field manual and were conducting map and field exercises on the theme.[163]

However, the academy's increasingly tactical orientation was insufficient to further the development of operational thought, and in the summer of 1931 an operational department *(operativnyi fakul'tet)* was established as an adjunct to the academy. The department offered a one-year course of study to exceptional graduates to prepare them for staff work at the corps-army-front (military district) level, as well as within the RKKA Staff. The course consisted chiefly of lectures on the developing theory of the deep operation, as well as more practical exercises, such as war games. Isserson was appointed the first head of the department, which included among the faculty the imperial General Staff Academy graduate Kolenkovskii, as well as a number of former czarist officers such as S. N. Krasil'nikov and

Lapchinskii. The department, during its brief existence, was able to make a significant contribution to forming the next generation of high-ranking staff officers. Among its graduates were the future chiefs of staff Antonov and M. V. Zakharov.[164]

However, the department's limited facilities could not keep up with the army's growing demand for trained operational cadres. The high command sought to fill this need by establishing, on the basis of the operational department, a new General Staff Academy, in the autumn of 1936. D. A. Kuchinskii, a former czarist officer, was appointed to head the academy, which included among the faculty such graduates from its imperial predecessor as Svechin, Verkhovskii, Shilovskii, Gotovtsev, and Shafalovich.[165]

The academy initially consisted of five departments: army operations, renamed the department of operational art in 1937; the tactics of higher formations; organization and mobilization; military history; and foreign languages. The jewel in the academy's crown was the department of army operations, which embraced the army and front, the theory of military strategy, independent air operations, and land-sea operations. The department was headed by Isserson, whose students spent most of their time studying army and front operations through lectures and map exercises. Among the exercises conducted that first year were those on such themes as "Conducting a Front Offensive Operation in the Western Theater of Military Activities," "The Actions of the Breakthrough Development Echelon in a Front Offensive Operation," "Breaking Through a Prepared Defense," and "The Commitment of a Mechanized Corps into Battle."[166]

A serious drawback in the academy's curriculum was the lack of a concrete course in strategy, which might have served as the theoretical underpinning for further operational research. This was a particularly damaging omission because the front operation was still viewed by many at the time as an instrument of strategy. However, when Kuchinskii approached Yegorov about the possibility of instituting such a course at the academy, he was rudely cut off by the marshal and informed that strategic questions were the sole prerogative of the General Staff.[167]

Despite these and other shortcomings, overall the academy was successful in developing and spreading the tenets of the deep operation and raising the theory to a level consistent with, if not above, the degree of mechanization achieved in the army by 1936. The students of the first intake, in this respect, were particularly distinguished, and many of them went on to achieve fame during World War II and after. These included the wartime chiefs of staff Vasilevskii and Antonov; the front commanders I. Kh. Bagramyan, N. F. Vatutin, L. A. Govorov, and P. A. Kurochkin; as well as several front chiefs of staff, army commanders, and other high-ranking officers in the central military apparatus.[168]

The Soviets also tested their theoretical concepts in a number of large-scale maneuvers. One of the largest of these, held in September 1935 in the Kiev Military District, involved some 65,000 men and 3,000 vehicles, including 1,040 tanks, 600 aircraft, and 300 artillery pieces. The maneuvers began with an attack by the "blue" army toward Kiev, combined with an airborne landing east of the city. The attackers succeeded in breaking through the "red" army's defenses west of Kiev, whereupon they committed a cavalry-mechanized group into the breach to develop the success. This movement advanced rapidly until it was finally halted just short of Kiev. The defenders then launched a counterattack, spearheaded by a mechanized corps, which was able to turn the attacker's exposed flank and break into his rear area. The maneuvers were also noteworthy for the combined parachute-airborne landing of two rifle regiments and equipment.[169]

The deep operation was further tested a year later during maneuvers in the Belorussian Military District. A total of 85,000 troops, 1,136 tanks, 580 guns, and 638 aircraft took part in the exercise, which was designed to test the army's operational concepts for the outbreak of a war along the western frontier. Details of the exercise are sketchy, although two airborne brigades were dropped during the maneuvers, in which Isserson and such famous wartime commanders as Zhukov, I. S. Konev, and R. Ya. Malinovskii took part.[170]

By 1936 the basic precepts of the deep operation were firmly established in the Red Army, at least at the theoretical level. This was, overall, a triumph of Soviet military thinking and was indicative of how far intellectually the army had come in the two decades since the revolution. Moreover, it was a theory that was very much the product of Soviet circumstances, especially the country's momentous industrialization drive, which transformed the army and had no counterpart in the czarist era. Another was the changing composition of the theoretical cadres during this period and the clear dominance of such impeccably Soviet writers as Isserson, whose talents came to full fruition in the 1930s.

This is not to say that the former military specialists were by any means excluded from the theory's development. Such former officers and graduates of the old General Staff Academy as Varfolomeev and Shilovskii made important contributions to this work, while other former officers, such as Tukhachevskii, made important contributions as well.[171] On the whole, these tended to be younger men who had graduated from the academy or entered the czarist army not long before the revolution and who had adapted themselves to the new order without much difficulty. In this respect, they remained poles apart from Svechin and others like him, who essentially remained products of the old regime, and whose influence declined sharply during the decade.

5
The Road to War, 1937–1940

On December 1, 1934, Sergei Kirov, the Leningrad party boss and Politburo member, was assassinated. Stalin was quick to take advantage of this deed, which he may have engineered, to begin a wholesale purge of the party and government apparatus. The purge came to be known as the *Ezhovshchina,* after Stalin's notorious secret police chief, N. I. Ezhov, who himself became a victim. Among the others were almost all the dictator's defeated rivals, whom he proceeded to accuse of plotting with the exiled Trotskii to overthrow the state and restore capitalism. One by one, Zinov'ev, L. B. Kamenev, Bukharin, and other former notables were found guilty of various fantastic crimes in a series of "show trials" and subsequently executed. Thousands of lesser officials perished in the same fashion, while millions more were sentenced to almost certain death in the vast labor camp empire.

These years saw the final destruction of whatever opposition, real or imagined, remained in the party to Stalin's personal rule. This meant the extermination of practically all that remained of the Bolshevik old guard, as well as thousands of otherwise loyal Stalinists who had somehow run afoul of the tyrant. For example, of the 139 full and candidate members of the party's Central Committee elected at the seventeenth congress in 1934, 115 were gone by 1939, of whom 98 were shot. At the same time, 1,108 of the 1,966 delegates to the same congress had been arrested for "counterrevolutionary crimes."[1] The purge at the very top was just as complete, and such notables as G. K. Ordzhonikidze, P. P. Postyshev, S. V. Kosior, and others were eliminated by one means or another. They were replaced by such limited but loyal executors of the dictator's will as A. A. Zhdanov, G. M. Malenkov, and Khrushchev.

Against this background of horror, the national economy continued to make impressive strides as the country entered the third Five-Year Plan (1938–42). In 1940 the USSR produced 14.9 million tons of cast iron and 18.3 million tons of steel and extracted 166 million tons of coal and 31 million tons of oil.[2] New factories continued to be established in the Urals and Siberia, well beyond the range of enemy bombers. These and other measures were in part responsible for the Soviet Union's remarkable economic recovery during World War II. However, these achievements lay in the future, and the country's defense industry continued to have great difficulty in meeting the expanding armed forces' voracious demands for new equipment.

The Soviets adopted a typically Stalinist remedy to this problem by taking a number of steps that made the population's lot even more miserable. Among these were a number of decrees issued in 1940 that forbade workers to change their job without permission, measures to increase "job discipline," and a decree creating "labor reserves." These draconian measures furthered the growing militarization of Soviet life and in some areas put the economy on what amounted to a war footing months before the outbreak of hostilities.

The Soviet Union also fought two wars during this period, at either end of the far-flung country. The first, against the Japanese in Mongolia, ended in victory for the Soviets, even as World War II was beginning in the west. The second war, against Finland, although it, too, was ultimately successful, was a humiliating moral defeat for the USSR. More important, the war probably convinced Hitler that the Soviet Union could easily be conquered.

The immediate prewar years were also filled with complicated diplomatic maneuvering, as the European powers sought to contain an increasingly powerful and aggressive Germany. The Soviet Union at first played a leading part in these efforts, with its proposals for a united front against the Nazis. However, Stalin's party and army purge had so diminished the USSR in the eyes of Western diplomats that the Soviet Union was not even consulted during the Czechoslovak crisis in the fall of 1938. By the summer of 1939 the situation had changed dramatically in light of Germany's threats to Poland's independence. This caused Britain and France to actively court Stalin, so as to threaten Hitler with the prospect of a two-front war.

However, by now the Soviet Union was actively pursuing a rapprochement with Hitler, which culminated in the infamous Soviet-German nonaggression pact on August 23, 1939. This agreement, which enabled Hitler to begin his war of conquest, also divided much of eastern Europe into separate German and Soviet spheres of influence. The Soviet Union quickly moved to realize its ambitions by occupying the eastern half of Poland in September 1939, even as the latter was being subdued by Germany from the west.

However, Stalin's calculations that Germany would become bogged down in a long and debilitating war with the Western powers were upset by the Wehrmacht's unexpectedly rapid victory over the Anglo-French coalition in the spring of 1940. Stalin, alarmed at this sudden turn of events, acted with unseemly haste to occupy and incorporate into the USSR Lithuania, Latvia, and Estonia, as well as the Romanian provinces of Bessarabia and northern Bukovina in June–

July 1940. Hitler, for his part, was becoming increasingly obsessed with the idea of destroying the Soviet Union before the end of the war with Great Britain, and he began to make plans for this eventuality. Relations between the two powers deteriorated rapidly from the autumn of 1940, as the Germans began to transfer large forces to the east for the coming campaign. By the summer of 1941 the Soviet Union, now quite alone, was about to face the greatest test of its brief existence.

DISASTER AND RECOVERY

The armed forces at first seemed safe from the bloodletting that engulfed the country during these years. However, the logic of dictatorship decreed that this situation could not continue indefinitely, and by the winter of 1936–37 there were ominous signs that their privileged status was coming to an end. First Tukhachevskii was fleetingly implicated in one plot, while elsewhere a number of other officers were already under arrest by the secret police, the NKVD.

Nevertheless, in June 1937 the country was stunned to learn that a "treasonous, counterrevolutionary, military fascist organization" had been uncovered within the Red Army. The announcement went on to report that a group of high-ranking officers, led by Marshal Tukhachevskii, had confessed to charges of treason before a special military tribunal. "The loathsome traitors," the announcement continued, had been found guilty and executed.[3]

However, this was only the beginning, as the full power of the Stalinist terror machine was now turned against the armed forces. By the time the bloodletting subsided somewhat in the autumn of 1938, more than 40,000 people had been "purged" from the army.[4] And although to be purged was not necessarily synonymous with death, it can safely be assumed that most of the victims either were shot outright or died subsequently in the labor camps' harsh regime.[5]

The purge took an especially heavy toll among the senior and midlevel commanders, including two more marshals, Yegorov and Blyukher, the first of whom was shot, while the second died in prison. Among the other victims were all eleven deputy defense commissars and seventy-five of the Military Council's eighty members.[6] In all, three of five marshals died, leaving only the military nonentities Voroshilov and Budennyi. Both fleet admirals were "repressed" during this time, as were both admirals, all six vice-admirals, and nine of fifteen rear admirals. Of 4 army commanders first class, 2 were repressed, as were all 12 army commanders second class. Of 67 corps commanders, 60 fell in the purge, as did 136 of 199 division commanders and 221 of 397 brigade commanders.[7] During 1937–38 all but one of the military district commanders and all of their deputies and military district chiefs of staff were replaced, as were 79 percent of the regimental commanders, 88 percent of the regimental chiefs of staff, and 87 percent of all battalion commanders.[8]

Nor did the resumption of dual command in May 1937 spare the armed forces' political organs an equally severe bloodletting. Both army commissars first class fell victim to the purse, as did all 15 army commissars second class, and 25 of 28 corps commissars. Of 97 division commissars, 79 suffered, as did 34 of 36 brigade commissars.[9] P. A. Smirnov succeeded Gamarnik in May 1937 and was himself soon replaced by L. Z. Mekhlis as head of the newly created army political directorate (PU RKKA). Mekhlis, one of the more odious of Stalin's henchmen, ruthlessly set about bringing the army to heel and took an active and bloody part in gutting Marshal Blyukher's Far Eastern command in the summer of 1938. It was only when the armed forces had been sufficiently cowed that the system of unitary command was restored in 1940.

The purge indiscriminately cut down former military specialists and red commanders alike. Among the many victims were such former czarist officers as Gekker, V. M. Gittis, Shorin, N. N. Petin, and others who had joined the army during the civil war. Of this group, the most notable survivor was Shaposhnikov, who was reappointed chief of the General Staff in 1937 and promoted to the rank of marshal three years later.

Equally unfortunate were those commanders with impeccably proletarian credentials, such as I. P. Belov, P. E. Dybenko, Sedyakin, and Gai, who were shot. Others, such as K. K. Rokossovskii and A. V. Gorbatov, were luckier; they were imprisoned and, in some cases, tortured but managed to escape execution. They were released in 1940 and, despite their treatment, went on to enjoy distinguished careers during World War II. Zhukov, who later became a marshal and the Soviet Union's most decorated war hero, barely escaped arrest, but he survived to rise from division commander to chief of the General Staff in less than four years.[10]

Stalin's bloodlust even extended to the wives, children, and other relatives of the purged commanders, many of whom endured long prison sentences and worse. In a grisly but not uncommon example, the wives of Tukhachevskii, Uborevich, and Gamarnik were executed, as were other of the marshal's relatives.[11]

And although the purge's force slackened considerably after 1938, the machinery of repression continued to function, claiming several prominent victims in the years and months immediately preceding the outbreak of war. Among them was the veteran NKVD thug M. P. Frinovskii, who had been briefly placed in charge of the naval commissariat in 1938 and was shot the following year. Others included air force commanders A. D. Loktionov, Ya. V. Smushkevich, and P. V. Rychagov, all of whom were already under arrest at the start of the war and were executed in the dark days of October 1941. Another victim was G. M. Shtern, who briefly commanded the Red Army's Main PVO Directorate. He was arrested a week before the war began and shot with the others in October 1941, in the provincial city of Kuibyshev. Meretskov, who served a few months as chief of the General Staff in 1940–41, was arrested almost immediately upon the outbreak of war. He was fortunate enough to survive the ordeal and return to duty and a lackluster career as an army and front commander.

Aside from the purges themselves, the most significant personnel change to take place within the armed forces' command structure was Voroshilov's long-overdue removal as defense commissar in May 1940, as the result of the Red Army's poor showing in the 1939–40 war with Finland. Voroshilov was replaced by Timoshenko, who had most recently commanded Soviet forces in that war. Unfortunately, this meant that the army would continue to be dominated by hidebound veterans of the First Cavalry Army. This group had constituted Stalin's original base of support within the Red Army; it was known more for its political reliability than for any military acumen and in large part was responsible for the army's present troubles. However, if Timoshenko was by no means a military genius, he was certainly an improvement over Voroshilov, whose incompetence had become apparent even to Stalin. Under Timoshenko the Red Army embarked upon a series of measures designed to raise its combat capability. However, the mistakes of many years could not be rectified overnight, and the summer of 1941 found the Red Army ill prepared to meet the German onslaught.

The most important structural change to take place within the armed forces during these years was the navy's achievement of organizational independence from the defense commissariat, which was dominated by the ground forces. This came about with the creation of a separate People's Commissariat of the Navy on December 30, 1937, which was briefly headed by Smirnov before he, too, was removed and executed. Earlier that same year the Defense Commission had been renamed the Defense Council, with V. M. Molotov, chairman of the Council of People's Commissars, serving as chairman. In March 1938 separate main military councils were created within the army and navy commissariats to oversee technical and training matters.

The swift and unwarranted promotions of many officers to the top of the armed forces command structure date from this period. Among them was N. G. Kuznetsov, who rose from the position of naval attaché in Spain in 1936 to become head of the Soviet navy in 1939, at the age of thirty-seven. Even more spectacular were the rise and subsequent fall of Rychagov. He was appointed chief of the Red Army air force in 1940, at the age of twenty-nine, but was removed less than a year later, to be replaced by P. F. Zhigarev. Prior to 1937, Zhukov had had a fairly mediocre career and had managed to rise only as high as commander of a cavalry division, while his friend Rokossovskii was already commanding a cavalry corps. However, by the summer of 1938 Zhukov was a deputy commander of the Belorussian Special Military District, and a year later he was in charge of Soviet troops fighting the Japanese in Mongolia, even as Rokossovskii was undergoing torture in a Leningrad prison. By 1940 Zhukov, now a general, commanded the Kiev Special Military District, and in early 1941 he was moved to Moscow as chief of the General Staff.

This pattern was repeated in the army's most important field commands. For example, F. I. Kuznetsov was appointed commander of the Baltic Special Military District in 1941, having previously served as chief of the General Staff Academy. D. G. Pavlov had gained combat experience in Spain before being put in charge of the Red Army's Armor Directorate in late 1937. Following service in the Finnish War, Pavlov was promoted to general colonel in the summer of 1940 and appointed to command the Western (formerly Belorussian) Special Military District. M. P. Kirponos commanded a division in the Soviet-Finnish War; in 1940 he was promoted to command a rifle corps, then the Leningrad Military District. In early 1941 he was transferred to the command of the Kiev Special Military District, one of the country's most important. One of his subordinates recalled that "many generals had formed a bad impression" of Kirponos's abilities, and that the military district commander "was not up to handling this responsible position."[12]

This observation proved to be all too correct in the early days of the Great Patriotic War. Kirponos, then commanding the Southwestern Front, was killed and most of his forces surrounded in the great encirclement east of Kiev in September 1941. Pavlov, who commanded the Western Front at the outbreak of war, almost immediately lost control of his forces in the face of the German onslaught. He was recalled to Moscow a week after the war broke out and was executed along with most of his senior staff. Kuznetsov's fate was a kinder one, although he, too, proved to be unfitted for higher command. Relieved as commander of the Northwestern Front in 1941, he later served in a variety of field and academic positions but never regained his former status.

The General Staff, which was no less buffeted by the turbulence that swept the armed forces, saw four men occupy the post of chief of staff in as many years. Yegorov, soon to be purged himself, was relieved of his position in May 1937 and replaced by Shaposhnikov, who had preceded him at the post. Shaposhnikov was followed in August 1940 by Meretskov, who was in turn succeeded by Zhukov in early 1941. Of this group only the former czarist officer Shaposhnikov stood out, while Yegorov and Meretskov were mediocrities. Zhukov, the hero of the fighting in Mongolia, was neither trained nor temperamentally suited to fill this position, and a few weeks after the start of the war with Germany, Shaposhnikov was again made chief of staff.[13] Suffice it to say, the rapid turnover of chiefs could only negatively affect the General Staff's work as it sought to prepare the armed forces for war.

Nor did the purges spare the army's intellectual cadres. During this period the General Staff Academy went through five chiefs, of whom the first, Kuchinskii, was arrested in 1937 and died the following year. He was followed in quick succession by I. T. Shlemin, Kuznetsov, V. K. Mordvinov, and Shilovskii. Among other prominent victims was Vatsetis, the Red Army's first commander in chief, who was arrested between lectures at the Frunze Military Academy and shot in 1938.[14] Others, including many who had done so much to enrich Soviet military thinking, were also executed. These included Varfolomeev (1939), Verkhovskii (1938), A. M. Vol'pe (1937), Movchin (1938), and Svechin (1938), the latter of whom outlived his archrival Tukhachevskii by only a year. Melikov was shot in 1942. Belitskii (1938) and Kakurin (1936) died in prison. Others, such as A. V. Golubev and Isserson, were more fortunate and returned after long prison sentences.

The consequences for the development of military theory were devastating, particularly in the field of operations, where many of the victims had made their mark. And in a typical piece of Stalinist guilt by association, the execution of Tukhachevskii and other "enemies of the people" was sufficient to bring their theories under suspicion. Isserson, one of the lucky survivors, recalled that many of the most progressive theorists' writings were denounced and removed from circulation, while in the General Staff Academy the very fundamentals of the deep operation were viewed with suspicion.[15] Isserson himself continued to lecture on the subject, although he had to tread carefully. A student of Isserson's later recalled that "great bravery" was required by advocates of the deep operation, the teaching of which remained all but anathema until 1940.[16]

This assertion is somewhat exaggerated, as Isserson and a few other brave souls continued to employ the term, even during the darkest days of the purge. On the other hand, it cannot be denied that the execution of Tukhachevskii and his supporters dealt a severe blow to the development of operational theory. Instead of the lively theoretical debates of the recent past, Soviet military writings became increasingly dominated by bombastic declarations about the Red Army's "invincibility" and publications on the civil war, which were little more than hosannas to Stalin's "wise" leadership.[17] As a result, the quality of Soviet military thinking went into a steep decline from mid-1937 and was only just beginning to recover four years later.

Not surprisingly, the survivors often chose to avoid any sort of controversy as potentially fatal. Nowhere is this trend more evident than in the later writings of Shilovskii, a professor at and later chief of the General Staff Academy and previously one of the army's leading operational theorists. By the latter half of 1937 he had retreated into the relatively safe field of military history as a source of inspiration. The result was *The Operation,* which was a pale recapitulation of previous works, liberally sprinkled with quotes by Stalin and Voroshilov. In the book's meager theoretical section, the author's remarks on the nature of a future war, as well as such subjects as the meeting engagement, the breakthrough, and defensive and consecutive operations, contained nothing new.[18] Equally disappointing was his article "The Offensive Operation," which appeared several months later.[19] This piece, which was an examination of army and front operations, based on the Galician operation of 1914, contained nothing that had not been said as far back as the late 1920s.

Even Isserson, a man of considerable personal courage, was forced to proceed with caution, as was reflected in two articles that appeared in 1938. Both pieces prominently feature the author's idée fixe—the paramount importance of the role that depth had come to play in modern war—but otherwise broke no new ground.[20]

In no area was Soviet operational thinking during these years more remiss than in its evaluation of recent military conflicts, most notably in Spain and Finland. Soon after the uprising by General Franco's Nationalist forces in 1936, the Soviets moved quickly to shore up the beleaguered Republican army with matériel aid and advisers, among whom were such future marshals as Malinovskii, Meretskov, and N. N. Voronov. The Soviets, like the Germans, found in Spain a convenient testing ground for evaluating their military theory and equipment. However, contrary to expectations, the war rapidly took on positional characteristics reminiscent of World War I. The continuous front existed, with gradual changes, right up until the Republican collapse in early 1939. In none of the war's major operations (Guadalajara, Madrid, Aragon, etc.) were the army's views of the deep operation confirmed.

The Soviet military seems not to have taken into account several of the war's mitigating factors, such as rugged terrain over much of the country, which hindered maneuver, as well as the small armies fielded by both sides. One student attending the General Staff Academy at the time later wrote that the Soviet veterans of the Spanish war maintained that the next war would be a positional struggle. The veterans concluded that the "troops must be taught to conduct a positional defense and to try to break through strongly fortified zones by the 'gnawing through' method."[21]

This assessment, as events would soon show, was profoundly misguided. However, if the Spanish experience may be said to have had any positive effects, it is that the Red Army began to show an increased interest in questions of defense at the operational level. This was certainly a welcome move in an army where the very idea of an army defensive operation "was somehow considered indecent and almost in contradiction to our offensive doctrine."[22]

The pioneering work in this area was Isserson's *Fundamentals of the Defensive Operation,* which appeared at the end of 1938, as the pace of the executions began to slow down. In this work, Isserson not only performed the valuable service of raising the subject of the defensive operation but also put forth a number of quantitative indices, some old and some new, to guide commanders in this area.

Isserson believed that for the modern defense to be successful, it must be capable of opposing the attacker's deep-strike weapons with a comparable depth of its own. To this purpose, he divided the army's defensive area into a number of deep and mutually supporting zones.

The first, or forward zone, would be held by small mobile detachments, relying on a system of natural and artificial obstacles. This zone, which would stretch back some 20 to 25 kilometers, had as its primary task exhausting the attacker before he reached the defender's main position. This position, or the main zone, constituted the backbone of the army's tactical defense and was held by the greater part of its forces to a depth of 15 to 20 kilometers. This zone, in turn, consisted of two positions. The first of these was synonymous with the frontline divisions' defensive areas to a depth of 5 to 6 kilometers and represented the line along which the enemy's attack was to be halted. From 8 to 12 kilometers to the rear lay the second position, held by corps reserves and consisting of a broken series of obstacles and strongpoints. This would provide a refuge for those units falling back from the front.[23]

Behind the army's tactical defense lay the operational zone, extending to a depth of 20 to 25 kilometers. This area contained the army's reserves, which were based on an incomplete system of antitank and other defensive positions. These forces had the task of containing and destroying those enemy forces that had managed to penetrate the army's tactical defense. Finally, behind this zone lay the army rear zone, which might reach up to 50 kilometers in depth. This area, which contained the army headquarters and railheads, would not be held by large forces. Rather, it would consist primarily of occasional defensive positions and other obstacles, which could be occupied by the retreating defenders in the event of a major enemy breakthrough at the front.[24]

Isserson was also quite specific as regards the composition of an army in a defensive operation. Ideally, he wrote, the army would consist of ten to fifteen rifle divisions, which would be capable of holding a front approximately 100 kilometers in width. Of these, seven to ten divisions would be deployed in the first echelon, in the main zone's first defensive position. A further two to three divisions would occupy the second tactical position, with one to two divisions in the operational zone as a reserve. The army might be further reinforced with two to three RGK artillery regiments, as well as one to two tank brigades, four to five air regiments, chemical troops, and up to ten antiaircraft battalions. Isserson calculated that this would enable the defender to maintain a correlation of forces vis-à-vis the attacker of 1:3 along the main axis and 1:5 along secondary axes of the front. However, in the event of success and the decision to launch a counteroffensive, the army would have to rely on the front command for additional resources.[25]

However, as groundbreaking as Isserson's work was, it did not go nearly far enough. The author had severely limited his study to the army level, without even mentioning the possibility of a front defensive operation. This would inevitably have raised the question of conducting a strategic defense. That he refrained from doing so is hardly surprising, given the climate of fear in the army. But this reluctance, if understandable in 1938, made far less sense two years later, in the light of the German army's brilliant success in Poland and the west. However, despite this overwhelming evidence, the Soviet political-military leadership failed to consider or prepare for the possibility of conducting a strategic defense along the entire front.[26] This almost willful ignorance was to cost the Red Army dearly in 1941.

Isserson sought to make up for this omission in the relatively more tolerant atmosphere of 1940. The chief vehicle in this effort was his book *New Forms of Combat,* in which he skillfully mined the recent experience of the German-Polish War of 1939.

For Isserson, one of the more intriguing aspects of this new style of war was the manner of its beginning and the nature of its opening operations. He rightly noted that the German invasion of Poland represented a unique phenomenon in military history, which involved an all-out assault by a fully mobilized and deployed army, in which strategic air strikes and the start of hostilities on the ground had replaced the formal declaration of war. He contrasted this method favorably with the ponderous mobilizations that preceded the first clash of the belligerents' armies during World War I, while at the same time seeming to criticize the Red Army's own theory of the beginning period of the war and its chief component—the "invasion army."[27] This theory, he seemed to imply, had been overtaken by events.

Unfortunately, Isserson did not return to this theme, although its relevance to the Red Army was to become all too apparent before long.[28] His views stood in healthy contrast to the Red Army's outdated assumptions about how a war might actually begin. Zhukov later admitted that the reigning concept within the army high command saw a future war beginning as an updated version of World War I. This would involve an opening series of border clashes by the sides' covering armies, followed by the mobilization and commitment of the main forces.[29] Oddly enough, the thought of a fully mobilized enemy launching a surprise attack seems not to have occurred to anyone. How the Soviet high command could have continued to adhere to this outmoded scenario, in the light of the Germans' practice in Poland and the west, has never been satisfactorily explained.[30]

The German victory also had a bracing effect on the Red Army's operational theory, although its significance was not recognized immediately, chiefly for political reasons. At first, some theorists sought to dismiss the German triumph, ascribing the Polish defeat more to the political system's defects than to any military factors.[31] And while the interwar Polish state indeed suffered from any number of political defects, the Soviet effort to ascribe the country's defeat to purely political factors was no more than an exercise in self-delusion.

As usual, Isserson led the effort to put the Polish events in their proper operational perspective. He was openly dismissive of the Spanish experience and argued that the highly specific conditions of that conflict, which inevitably rendered it a war of position, held no lessons for the Red Army. He cautioned against drawing hasty conclusions about the operational utility of employing large mechanized forces based on this meager experience and went on to denounce as "exceptionally shortsighted" subsequent attempts to assign armored and motorized forces a purely auxiliary role in modern operations. For these and other reasons, Isserson concluded that the Spanish war was "still not a war of the *new forms of combat in action*" and warned that the fighting in Spain should not be taken as a "dress rehearsal" for a future war.[32]

Much more to the point, he argued, was the German invasion of Poland, where for the first time the new methods were applied with a vengeance. The Wehrmacht's smooth coordination of air, armor, and motorized infantry deeply impressed Isserson, who was anxious that the Red Army adopt the same measures. Without, of course, mentioning the disgraced Tukhachevskii, Isserson saw the massed employment of these weapons as fully justifying the late marshal's ideas and the lapsed theory of the deep operation. In Poland, he concluded, "The deep operation, as the simultaneous defeat of the entire depth of the enemy's operational base and the rapid spread of the blow to the deep rear, has effectively demonstrated its enormous practical significance."[33]

For Isserson, the German victory was a stunning confirmation of the ideas he and his circle had propagated so assiduously for the past several years. This was particularly heartening, following the period of terror within the army's ranks and the disappointing conclusions engendered by the predominantly positional character of the wars in Spain and Finland. The latter conflicts were particularly disturbing from the theoretical point of view, as they served to confirm the notion of the continuing efficacy of "linear" methods of warfare. According to Isserson, the German-Polish conflict had ushered in a *"new type of war,"* whose methods and conduct must be taken into account.[34]

However, if resistance to these new ideas remained, even the most ossified minds could not fail to ignore the lessons of the Germans' victory in the May-June 1940 campaign in the west. In less than two weeks German armored divisions had crossed the Meuse River at Sedan to reach the English Channel, cutting off the Allied forces in northern France and Belgium and effectively deciding the outcome of the campaign. Moreover, they had employed methods that fully vindicated the chief tenets of the deep operation.

Following the collapse of France, the theoretical reform movement went into high gear, as everywhere the "Spaniards," those who had brought home from Spain the lessons of that war, were discredited. One notable attempt in this movement was Gen. Maj. E. Tatarchenko's article "New Features of Modern Military Art," which appeared shortly after the French surrender. Tatarchenko found much to praise in the swift and decisive German conduct of the campaign and, obliquely, much to criticize in Soviet practice. While praising Guderian's armored dash to the Channel coast, he openly condemned the reigning Soviet practice of employing tanks "purely for the sake of interacting with the infantry," which he claimed shackled the tanks and motorized troops to the infantry's slower pace. This wasted the tank forces' great advantage in mobility and caused them to miss opportunities for the swift exploitation of a breakthrough. Tatarchenko closed his article with a call to arms that would be heard with increasing frequency during the remaining year of peace: "It is necessary to immediately employ the experience of the ongoing war in our theoretical and practical work."[35]

A corollary to the renewed Soviet fascination with modern operational methods was the derogation of the old ways, especially as they concerned the hoary traditions of the civil war. A particularly telling broadside was fired at the "old school" in the form of an article by V. Zakharov, aptly entitled "The Experience of the Civil War and Contemporaneity," which was remarkable for taking on one of the Red Army's most sacred cows—the cavalry forces. While praising the decisive role played by the First Cavalry Army in the events of 1919–20, the author made it clear that substantial changes had taken place since those halcyon days. These had drastically reduced the significance of the cavalry arm and, by inference, the validity of the civil war experience as a whole. "The Red Army must actively follow, carefully study and master the changes and shifts in the field of military affairs," he wrote. He went on to warn that in the light of changing circumstances, "it would be all the more harmful" to elevate the experience of the civil war "to a cult and ignore everything new that the practice of recent wars yields."[36]

The German victories also had other far-reaching effects on the Red Army. These took the form of a massive organizational and technical makeover, which primarily affected the tank and air forces, although nearly all the combat arms were affected to some degree. Many of these changes were comparable in their impact to those that had taken place during the frenzied mechanization drive of previous years. However, much still remained to be done, and time was rapidly running out. And, as in so many other fields, the German invasion in June 1941 caught the Red Army in an exposed state of technical makeover.

Chief among these changes was the armed forces' tremendous quantitative expansion. Their size increased from 1,513,400 men at the beginning of 1938 to 4,207,000 by January 1941. An emergency call-up of some 800,000 reservists in May and June of that year raised this figure to an eve-of-war high of 5,373,000 men, which included 4,553,000 in the ground forces and PVO, 476,000 in the air force, and 344,000 in the navy.[37]

One consequence of this rapid growth was the demise of the old territorial-cadre system, which could no longer meet the armed forces' manpower or training needs. On September 1, 1939, the armed forces became a fully cadre force.

On the eve of the German attack the Soviet armed forces were territorially organized on land into sixteen military districts and one front. Of the military districts, by far the most important were the five (Leningrad, Baltic Special, Western Special, Kiev Special, and Odessa) along the country's western frontier. These five districts contained fourteen army headquarters, of which three were still in the process of formation when the war broke out.[38] The western military districts contained 186 divisions, which was still far short of the mobilization plan figure of 240. These numbered 3.1 million men, more than 47,200 guns and mortars, and 12,800 tanks, of which 2,242 needed repairs. The air force in the area had about 7,500 combat aircraft, of which 6,400 were serviceable, while the Baltic and Black Sea Fleets had between them another 1,400 planes.[39]

The Far Eastern front, which had been re-formed in July 1940, contained four army headquarters and had the task of guarding against renewed Japanese probing along the Soviet Union's vulnerable eastern frontiers. Other armies were deployed or forming in the other eleven military districts (Archangel, North Caucasus, Trans-Caucasus, Moscow, Volga, Central Asian, Urals, Siberian, Trans-Baikal,

Khar'kov, and Orel). Four of these armies were already moving west in May and June 1941 and were only starting to arrive when the German invasion began.

At sea the armed forces included the Northern, Baltic, Black Sea, and Pacific Fleets, as well as the Danube, Pinsk, Caspian, Amur, and North Pacific Flotillas. Of these, the most powerful were the Baltic and Black Sea Fleets, which guarded the approaches to the USSR's northwestern and southwestern coasts.

The defense and naval commissars directly controlled this vast force through their respective executive organs, the RKKA General Staff and the Main Naval Staff. In theory, both commissars answered to the Main Military Council, the USSR Supreme Soviet, and the USSR Council of People's Commissars. In practice, all major decisions had to be approved by Stalin, as head of the ruling Communist Party. The latter's position was further strengthened in May 1941 by his assumption of the post of chairman of the Council of People's Commissars, a government post, as opposed to the strictly party positions he had occupied previously.

The ground forces were by far the largest service and accounted for 79.3 percent of the armed forces' total manpower at the beginning of the war.[40] These included 177 rifle, 19 mountain rifle, and 2 motorized rifle divisions, which were organized into sixty-two rifle corps. Also included were 13 cavalry, 31 motorized, and 61 tank divisions, as well as three independent rifle brigades and sixteen airborne brigades. These were grouped into four cavalry, twenty-nine mechanized, and five airborne corps. However, 81 of these divisions were still being formed when the war broke out.[41]

The mainstay of this force was the rifle division, which in 1941 contained three rifle and two artillery regiments, an antitank, antiaircraft, engineer, and communications battalions, as well as other, smaller support units. The rifle division underwent three reorganizations in less than two years, declining from a September 1939 high of 18,000 men to an April 1941 authorized wartime strength of 14,483 men, 78 field guns, 54 45-mm antitank guns, 4 76-mm and 8 37-mm antiaircraft guns, 66 82-mm and 120-mm mortars, and 16 light tanks.[42]

However, these figures considerably overstate the rifle divisions' true strength. A significant portion of these units were still being formed when the war began, and almost all were below authorized strength. For example, at the beginning of June 1941 the average strength of the rifle divisions in the five western military districts stood as follows: Leningrad, 11,985; Baltic Special, 8,712; Western Special, 9,327; Kiev Special, 8,792; and Odessa, 8,400.[43]

A cavalry division at this time contained four cavalry regiments, a tank regiment, an artillery and antiaircraft battalions, and supporting units. The Red Army's cavalry lost considerable ground to the other combat arms during this period. The number of cavalry divisions fell from 32 in 1938 to just 13 in 1941, of which 4 were mountain-cavalry divisions.[44] Many of the disbanded divisions' personnel were then used to staff the new mechanized corps. That these divisions survived at all was due mainly to the protection of such high-ranking First Cavalry Army veterans as Voroshilov, Timoshenko, and Budennyi, who occupied positions of great importance during this period and continued to trumpet the cavalry's "decisive" role in modern war.[45]

The Soviet artillery park continued to grow rapidly, although its development was hobbled by having the execrable G. I. Kulik as its head throughout this period. Fortunately, the able Voronov was able to mitigate some of his chief's incompetence. By the beginning of the war the Red Army had 91,493 guns and mortars. This figure included 30,166 45-mm and 76-mm guns, 158 50-mm mortars, and 1,382 37-mm antiaircraft guns, with the remainder consisting of higher-caliber guns, howitzers, mortars, and antiaircraft pieces.[46]

Organizationally, the Red Army's artillery remained divided into troop artillery and that of the High Command Reserve (RGK). The former included 92 percent of all weapons and constituted the rifle divisions' and other units' organic artillery. This consisted primarily of 45-mm and 76-mm guns, as well as 50-mm, 82-mm, and 120-mm mortars. Corps artillery included mixed 122-mm guns and 152-mm gun-howitzer regiments. The RGK numbered sixty howitzer and fourteen gun regiments.[47]

In April 1941 ten RGK antitank artillery brigades were established. These had an authorized strength of 48 76-mm antitank guns, 24 107-mm guns, 24 85-mm antiaircraft guns modified for an antitank role, and 16 37-mm antiaircraft guns.[48] However, there was not enough time left before the outbreak of war to organize these units properly.

In June 1941 an airborne forces directorate was established to oversee the formation of five new airborne corps, which had been created that same April. Each of these corps consisted of three airborne brigades, a tank battalion, and a communications platoon and had an authorized strength of 8,029 men.[49] Needless to say, none of these units were ready for combat at the start of the war.

During this period no other combat arm was more buffeted by organizational and technological changes than were the Red Army's armored forces. In 1938 the four existing mechanized corps were renamed tank corps and assigned a new organizational structure, which increased their authorized strength from 463 tanks and 8,965 men to 560 tanks and 12,710 men. Aside from this measure, no other major changes were introduced into a tank park that numbered 15,613 vehicles in 1938.[50]

However, doubts as to the expediency of maintaining large tank formations were growing, and in the summer of 1939 a high-level commission was set up to resolve the question. The commission ultimately voted to retain the tank corps, recommending only slight changes in their organizational structure. However, in November 1939 the Main Military Council overruled the commission and voted to disband the corps.[51] In their place it was resolved to create tank brigades. These were to include thirteen brigades, each outfitted with 258 BT-series light tanks and 2,562 men, plus three more BT tank brigades with 2,900 men, and twelve brigades with 258 light T-26 tanks and 2,470 men. Another four brigades were to be formed and detailed to the High Command Reserve. Three of these had an authorized strength of 156 tanks (117 T-28s and 39 BT-series tanks) and 2,500 men, while the other also contained 156 tanks (32 T-35s, 85 T-28s, and 39 BT-series tanks) and 2,640 men. Another 10 tank regiments were also to be established, which would be expanded into brigades (one BT-series and nine T-26) in wartime.[52]

The Main Military Council also moved to create 15 new motorized divisions as the army's largest armored formation. These were to have an authorized strength of 275 tanks (258 BT-series and 17 T-37s, T-38s, and T-40s), 12 152-mm and 16 122-mm howitzers, 20 76-mm guns, 30 45-mm antitank guns, 8 37-mm antiaircraft guns, 12 82-mm and 60 50-mm mortars, and 11,650 men. It was planned to deploy 8 of these in 1940 and another 7 in the first half of 1941. By May 1940 only 4 had been organized.[53]

However, this new organization was not fated to last long. Stalin had been deeply impressed by the performance of the German army's tank corps in Poland and the west in 1939–40. In May 1940 he ordered the General Staff to draw up plans for a new mechanized corps based on the German model of 2 tank divisions and a single motorized division. However, a Soviet mechanized corps was to be far stronger, at least on paper, with an authorized strength of 1,000 to 1,200 tanks.[54]

According to this new organization, the motorized division would remain unchanged from its 1939 authorized strength. The new tank divisions were to have an authorized strength of 413 tanks, of which 105 would be the new KV-series heavy tanks, 210 new T-34 medium tanks, 26 BT-7s, 18 T-26s, 54 T-26 flamethrower tanks, 11,343 men, and 91 guns and mortars, not counting 50-mm mortars.[55]

On the eve of the German invasion each mechanized corps had an authorized strength of 126 KV-series tanks, 420 T-34s, 316 BT-7s, 44 T-26s, 108 T-26 flamethrower tanks, and 17 T-38s and T-40s. The corps had 36,080 men and would be supported by 36 152-mm and 40 122-mm howitzers, 28 76-mm and 36 45-mm guns, 48 82-mm and 138 50-mm mortars, and 32 37-mm antiaircraft guns.[56] Nine corps were initially organized in 1940, and in February and March 1941 another twenty corps began the process of formation.

Thus by the beginning of the war the Red Army had a paper strength of 61 tank and 31 motorized divisions, which were organized into twenty-nine mechanized corps, with 3 tank and 2 independent motorized divisions. This was a fantastic figure by any standard and utterly dwarfed similar efforts by the Wehrmacht. However, this latest reorganization had done great violence to the Red Army's armored organization, which had only just begun to recover from the wrenching experience of 1939. One participant in these events later complained bitterly that

> the existing well-ordered and trained tank brigades were all simultaneously disbanded and dissolved in the new mechanized corps. The latter could become combat-ready only after several years. It is therefore not accidental that by the beginning of the war our mechanized corps reminded one more of training formations than combat units. The presence of outdated equipment in many mechanized corps aided only the teaching process.[57]

The latter statement highlights one of the most critical problems facing the Red Army during these years—the need to modernize its aging tank park, 50 percent of whose light vehicles had been built during 1931–35.[58] Soviet industry produced 2,986 tanks in 1939 and 2,666 in 1940. The latter figure included 1,549 T-26s (including the flamethrower model), 706 BT-7s, 41 T-40s, and 12 T-28s, as well as 115 T-34s, 141 KV-1s, and 102 KV-2s. The 1941 plan called for the production of 1,200 KV-series tanks, 2,500 T-34s, 550 T-50s, and 700 of the new light T-60s. However, the Soviet tank industry could not possibly keep up with these enormous demands and succeeded in producing only 393 KV-series and 1,110 T-34 tanks during the first six months of 1941.[59]

At the start of the war the Red Army's tank park numbered 13,088 battle-ready tanks, not including an unknown number of T-38s, T-40s, and flamethrower tanks. However, the newly created armored formations required 3,843 KV-series tanks, 12,810 T-34s, 9,584 BT-7s, 1,342 T-26s, 3,294 T-26 flamethrower tanks, and 527 T-38s and T-40s to bring these units up to their authorized strength, or 31,400 tanks. This meant that the Soviet tank park was some 18,000 vehicles under authorized strength as of June 1941, in what was still by far the world's largest armored force. Even had Soviet industry been able to meet its obligations for increasing tank production, the new mechanized corps would not have received their authorized allotment of KV-series and T-34 tanks before 1945.[60]

Similar sweeping changes were also taking place in the Red Army's air force. In this case the problems inevitably associated with such a large-scale organizational and technological makeover were exacerbated by a lack of continuity at the top; in four years the air force had five chiefs, four of whom were eventually shot.

At the start of 1938 the air force had 9,385 aircraft, including 1,386 planes subordinated to naval aviation. These were organized into seventy-seven brigades, including twenty-four heavy-bomber brigades, eighteen of medium bombers, one mine-torpedo, six light-bomber, ten light assault, fourteen fighter, and four mixed and reconnaissance brigades, plus another nine brigades assigned to naval aviation. The heavy-bomber brigades were further organized into three special designation armies (AON), whose commander reported directly to the defense commissar. Each army contained some 340 to 360 aircraft, with one based each in Moscow, Voronezh, and Rostov.[61]

The presence of these units and the disproportionately high number of bomber units in the Soviet air park indicate that the country's political-military leadership had seriously underestimated the importance of fighter aircraft in modern war, while conversely overestimating that of the bomber. This was a particularly egregious mistake for a land power, whose army would require a large degree of tactical air support.

In the summer of 1940 the brigade system was abandoned in favor of a division organization, as the air force embarked upon a massive expansion program. Each division was to consist of four to six regiments, with 60 to 63 aircraft in each.

By the beginning of the war the air force had 79 air divisions and five brigades. Of these, 13 bomber and 5 fighter divisions formed High Command (long-range) Aviation, which had replaced the special designation armies. The remaining 61 divisions were organized into front (military district), army, and troop (corps) aviation, of which there were 9 bomber, 34 mixed, and 18 fighter divisions. However, 25 of these divisions had not completed their organization when the war broke out.[62]

The war also caught the Soviet air force in a state of technological transition. During 1940–41 new aircraft such as the Yak-1, LaGG-3, and MiG-3 fighters, the Il-2 assault plane, and the Pe-2 bomber entered service. During the eighteen-month period from January 1940 through June 1941, the Soviet aircraft industry produced 2,030 new fighters, and in the first half of 1941, 458 Pe-2s and 249 Il-2s. Together, these new aircraft accounted for a mere 17.3 percent of the Red Army's air park at the start of the war.[63] This implies an overall strength of approximately 16,000 aircraft, of which the great majority were outdated models.[64]

The Soviet navy profited greatly from the USSR's westward expansion during 1939–40, particularly in the northwest, where the Baltic Fleet acquired valuable forward bases at Tallinn, Riga, and Liepaja. This advance coincided with the government's decision to move the Soviet Union into the front ranks of the world's naval powers. Molotov made this plain in a speech in early 1938. "The mighty Soviet power," he declared, "must have a sea and ocean fleet commensurate to its interests and worthy of our great cause."[65] This grandiose program of naval construction, more the product of Stalinist megalomania than of any realistic threat assessment, succeeded only in diverting scarce resources from existing programs more suited to the country's defense needs. To realize Stalin's vision, the country's third Five-Year Plan called for a far-reaching capital ship construction program centered around a new generation of battleships and heavy cruisers. However, the approach of war soon forced the Soviets to focus their energies on more immediate tasks, and in late 1940 the construction of capital ships was sharply curtailed.

Nonetheless, by the start of the war the Soviet navy could field a numerous, if light, force of three battleships, seven cruisers, 212 submarines, fifty-four destroyers of all types, and 287 torpedo boats. The navy's air arm consisted of 2,581 combat aircraft, of which most were older models, while the shore defense forces had more than 1,000 guns, ranging from 45-mm to 406-mm.[66]

In December 1940 the national air defense forces were elevated to the status of a main directorate within the defense commissariat. In early 1941 the service was reorganized and the country divided into air defense zones, each corresponding to the boundaries of a military district. All ground-based air defense forces within a zone were subordinated to the military district commander's deputy for air defense matters. The great majority of these forces were concentrated in the western military districts and the oil-producing area around Baku.

At the start of the war the national air defense troops had 3,329 medium-caliber and 330 small-caliber antiaircraft guns, as well as forty fighter regiments, numbering some 1,500 planes.[67] However, the latter remained under the operational control of the commanders of the military districts' air force. This practice effectively reduced the national PVO chief to the status of a quartermaster, responsible for the supply but not the employment of his forces.

The purges, along with the armed forces' expansion during these years, led to a severe shortage of officer cadres. As early as 1938 the armed forces were reporting a 34 percent shortfall in their authorized complement of officers, a problem that was particularly acute in the armored units.[68] The high command reacted to this problem by repeatedly promoting and shifting officers from one post to another, with predictable results for their units' efficiency. By the beginning of 1940 some 70 percent of division and regimental commanders had been at their posts for only a year.[69] In a particularly striking example of this practice, several of the new General Staff Academy's first-year students had their studies interrupted in the summer of 1937 and were posted to army and military district staff positions far above their previous station.[70]

One solution to this problem was the establishment of a massive officer training program during the years immediately preceding the outbreak of war. In 1940 alone, 42 military schools were set up, and by the summer of 1941 the country had nineteen military academies, seven higher naval schools, 203 military schools, sixty-eight supplementary training courses, and ten military departments within civilian higher education institutes, attended by more than 300,000 students.[71] Despite this mammoth effort, the overall level of officer training remained abysmally low. By the summer of 1941 only 7 percent of the armed forces' officers had a higher military education, while another 37 percent had not even completed a midlevel course of instruction.[72]

The purges and the accompanying charges of mass treason had also done much to undermine the officer corps' authority among the rank and file, and discipline had become a serious problem. The political and military leadership belatedly adopted a number of measures to make the officer's lot more attractive. The most important of these were the introduction of generals' ranks in May 1940 and the reinstitution of unitary command three months later. However, these measures could not alleviate the army's officer shortage overnight, and the problem remained acute during the remaining months of peace and beyond.

By June 1941 the Red Army was an outwardly impressive force, whose many defects would soon become all too clear. Many of its problems were certainly the result of the army's enormous prewar expansion, which did not entail a corresponding qualitative improvement. However, the army's quantitative growth is not by itself a sufficient explanation for the Red Army's disastrous performance in 1941–42. For example, the U.S. regular army and its subordinate air force had a strength of only 187,893 men as of July 1939. By June 1945 the army had ballooned to 8,291,336 men, a forty-four-fold increase, without experiencing such a decline in overall quality as did the Red Army, which grew by little more than a factor of three.[73]

Another explanation is the impact of Stalin's military purge, which hit the higher command echelon particularly hard. This sudden and brutal elimination of an entire generation of experienced commanders usually meant their replacement by officers who often lacked the necessary practical and theoretical training for their jobs. Those who remained were so cowed by the bloodletting that they often were afraid to exercise independent judgment. Another is the constant and ill-informed tinkering with the armed forces' organizational structure, particularly between 1939 and 1941, which saw units broken up and re-formed like so many pieces of clay. One observer called these measures "not only mistaken, but quite dangerous. The army was essentially rendered unfit for combat for a period of time."[74]

This view was echoed by the chief of the German General Staff, just six weeks before the start of the invasion of the Soviet Union. In his diary, Col. Gen. Franz Halder wrote: "Russian officer corps decidedly bad (depressing impression). Compared with 1933, picture is strikingly negative. It will take Russia twenty years to reach her old level."[75]

Ultimately, the explanation for the Red Army's manifold defects must be sought in the nature of the Stalinist system itself, which was responsible for these and other excesses. It was Stalin, for example, who had raised such nonentities as Voroshilov, Kulik, and other incompetents to their present station, just as he had destroyed many of their more talented fellow officers. By the same token, it was Stalin who, certain of his own infallibility, ignored the signs of the approaching Nazi invasion, against all evidence to the contrary. Thus the dictator himself bears the lion's share of responsibility for the disasters that befell the USSR during 1941–42. In a system of highly centralized one-man rule, there can be no other conclusion.

WARS EAST AND WEST, 1939–40

The Soviet Union took part in two serious conflicts during this period. These were the undeclared border war with Japan (May–September 1939) and the much larger and bloodier Soviet-Finnish War (November 1939–March 1940). The Red Army's actions in these two strikingly different theaters reveal Soviet prewar operational art at its best and worst.

Soviet-Japanese relations had been tense since the Russian civil war, during which Japanese forces took an active part in the anti-Bolshevik struggle and occupied large areas of the Soviet Far East. In fact, the last Japanese troops were withdrawn from Soviet northern Sakhalin Island only in 1925. Tensions rose sharply again with the Japanese conquest of China's strategic northeastern province of Manchuria in 1931–32, which brought the two countries into contact along a much lengthier frontier than had previously been the case. Relations deteriorated further after 1937, when open warfare broke out between Japan and Chiang

Kai-shek's Nationalist Chinese forces, which received political and military support from the Soviet government.

In response to this threat, the Soviets increased their forces in the Far East to 83,750 men, 946 guns, 890 tanks, and 766 aircraft by mid-1937, and they planned to dispatch more than 100,000 more men there in 1938.[76] The majority of these forces were organized into the Special Red Banner Far Eastern Army, under Marshal Blyukher.

These political frictions, combined with the Japanese Kwangtung Army's tendency to pursue an aggressive foreign policy independent of Tokyo, led to a number of border clashes with the Red Army. One of the most serious of these was the July–August 1938 fighting at Lake Khasan, along the border with Japanese-occupied Korea. In the end, both sides backed off after heavy fighting, with the chief casualty being Blyukher, commander of the newly created Red Banner Far Eastern Front. He was relieved of his command and summoned back to Moscow, where soon afterward he was arrested and died in prison.

The two sides collided again in the spring of 1939 along the disputed border between Mongolia and the Japanese puppet state of Manchukuo. Mongolia, previously a part of the Chinese empire, had later become a sideshow of the Red-White struggle late in the Russian civil war and was proclaimed a "people's republic" in 1924, thus becoming the Soviet Union's first satellite. The two countries were further bound in 1936 by a mutual assistance treaty, which allowed the Soviets to maintain troops on Mongolian territory. In May 1939 this force, the 57th Special Corps, was commanded by N. V. Feklenko.

The fighting flared up sporadically in the disputed area east of the Khalkhin-Gol (Halha) River during May (see map 12). The Japanese launched a sizable probing attack at the end of the month, but it was quickly wiped out by a combined Soviet-Mongolian force. However, this success failed to assuage the Soviet high command, which was becoming increasingly dissatisfied with Feklenko's handling of the situation. It was suggested that an experienced cavalry officer would be better suited to command a force composed primarily of cavalry and mechanized troops. Division Commander Zhukov, a cavalry corps commander from the Belorussian Special Military District, was dispatched to Mongolia in early June with a broad mandate to report on the situation.[77]

Upon arriving at corps headquarters, the energetic Zhukov quickly arranged to have himself appointed to replace Feklenko and began dunning Moscow for reinforcements. This included a request for no fewer than three rifle divisions, a tank brigade, and considerably more artillery.[78]

The buildup of Soviet forces was no easy task, however, and was made considerably more difficult by the great distances involved, as well as the extremes of climate and terrain. In a situation reminiscent of the imperial army's troubles during the Russo-Japanese War, men and supplies had to be transported thousands of kilometers along the Trans-Siberian railroad from European Russia. These could be delivered no farther than the spur line at Borzya, from whence they were shipped

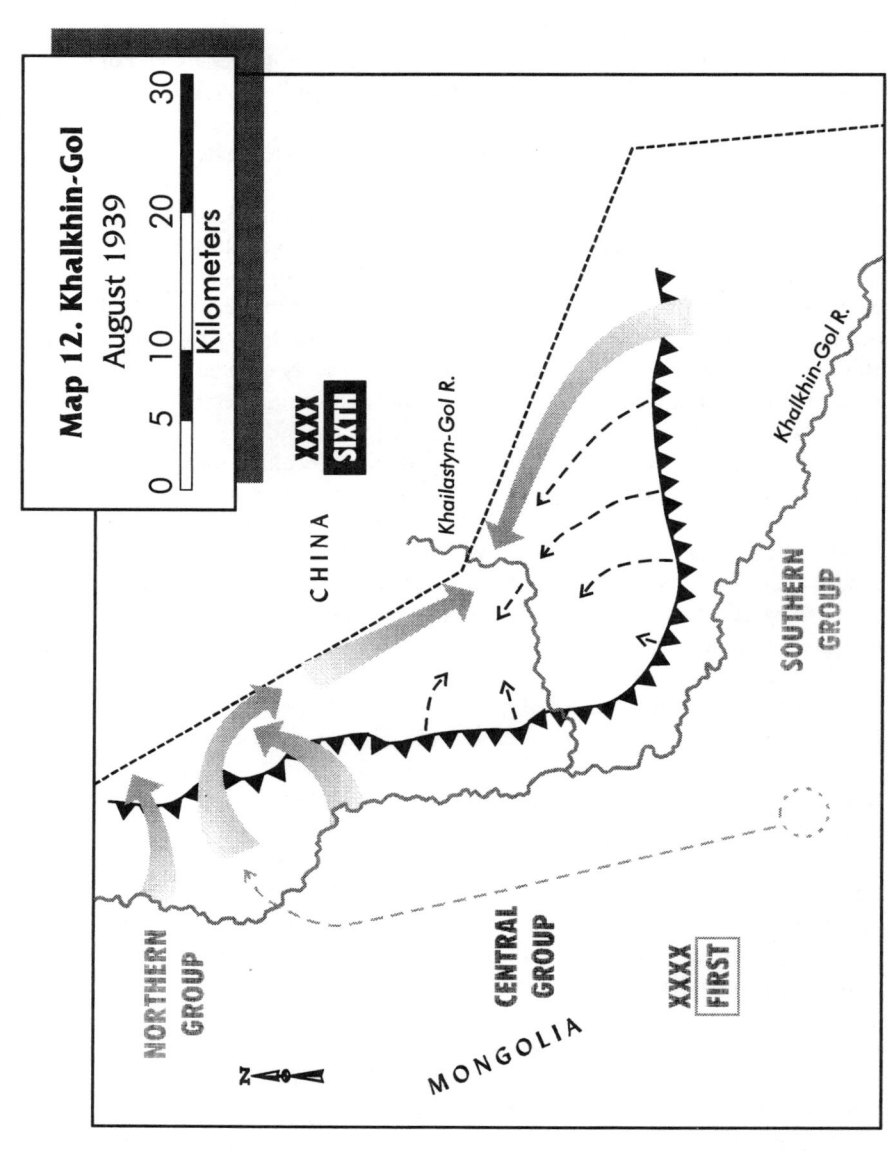

by truck nearly 700 kilometers to the battlefield, through a parched and treeless region, where even wood for cooking had to be brought in. In all, 4,000 vehicles took part in a supply effort that delivered thousands of tons of supplies and some 18,000 men to the area.[79]

Soviet efforts to organize a counteroffensive were further hobbled by a clumsy command arrangement. In mid-July the 57th Special Corps was redesignated the First Army Group, which was actually somewhere between a corps and an army in size. Zhukov, recently promoted to the rank of corps commander, remained in charge. The army group, in turn, was subordinated to a newly formed front directorate, which also included the First and Second Independent Red Banner Armies, although these took no part in the fighting. The directorate was commanded by Army Commander Second Class Shtern, who had replaced the unfortunate Blyukher the previous year. However, Shtern was charged only with supplying Zhukov's forces and lacked operational authority, as the latter answered directly to the defense commissar and could appeal any decision he disagreed with. This needlessly complicated system was to cause problems later on.[80]

Despite these difficulties, the Soviets were able to build up an impressive superiority of force, particularly in tanks, in the area of the projected counteroffensive. By mid-August the First Army Group numbered some 57,000 men, 498 tanks, 385 armored cars, 542 guns and mortars, and 515 combat aircraft. The Japanese, now organized into the Sixth Army under Lt. Gen. Ogisu Rippei, had approximately 38,000 men, 310 guns, 135 tanks, 10 armored cars, and 225 aircraft.[81]

Meanwhile, the fighting continued with varying intensity all along the front. The Japanese launched a particularly powerful assault across the Khalkhin-Gol on July 2 and a secondary attack against the Soviet-Mongolian positions north of the Khailastyn-Gol, a tributary. In the north the Japanese assault enjoyed initial success, scattering the Mongolian defenders and seizing Bain-Tsagan hill on the west bank. The Soviets counterattacked almost immediately, employing large numbers of tanks. Lacking support, the Japanese were soon forced to pull back across the river, pursued by the Soviets, who were able to secure several valuable bridgeheads along the eastern bank.

In the center the Japanese attack was less successful, and the Japanese were unable to dislodge the defenders from their positions. Nevertheless they continued to attack throughout most of July, although these engagements produced nothing but heavy casualties on both sides. In fact, the June–July fighting had yielded the Japanese little, except perhaps a newfound respect for their adversaries. The Soviets, on the other hand, had at least demonstrated their ability to withstand Japanese attacks and, if necessary, to attack themselves.

By mid-August a deceptive stalemate had set in along the front, punctuated only by heavy air battles and the Soviets' heavy and continuous employment of their artillery. The initiative, however, had clearly passed to the Soviets, who were gathering their forces to strike.

The Soviet offensive plan was simple.[82] Taking advantage of the favorable configuration of the arc-shaped Japanese front and the sizable bridgeheads on either flank, the Soviet-Mongolian forces planned to attack along converging axes to surround and destroy the Sixth Army. For this purpose, Zhukov divided his forces into three groups—Southern, Northern, and Central. The Southern Group (57th Rifle Division, 8th Mongolian Cavalry Division, the 6th Tank and 8th Armored Brigades, plus other smaller units) would make the main attack north-northwest toward the Nomon-Khan-Burd-Obo height. The Northern Group (6th Mongolian Cavalry Division, the 7th Armored and 11th Tank Brigades, plus supporting units) was to attack east-southeast toward the Southern Group to close the trap. The Central Group (82d Rifle Division, 36th Motorized Rifle Division, and the 5th Rifle–Machine Gun Brigade) would attack to hold the Japanese in place while the shock groups operated in their rear. Two brigades (212th Airborne and 9th Armored) and a tank battalion made up the reserve, to be committed along the flanks where needed.[83]

Zhukov's actions were also determined by a number of larger political questions rarely present in operations of this small size. Even as these plans were being drawn up, the Soviet Union was conducting negotiations with an Anglo-French delegation toward concluding an alliance to thwart Hitler's move against Poland. At the same time, Soviet-German contacts were increasing and would culminate in the infamous nonaggression pact of August 23, 1939. The last thing Stalin wanted was a full-scale war in the Far East while the situation in the west remained unsettled. He thus vetoed proposals that called for a deeper envelopment and restricted his commanders to defeating the Japanese within the bounds of the frontier claimed by Mongolia.[84]

Prior to the attack, the Soviets employed a variety of skillful ruses to deceive the Japanese. For example, all movements were carried out at night, masked by aircraft noise and special loudspeakers. False radio messages were sent in easily decipherable code, and field manuals, attesting to the command's defensive intentions, were liberally distributed among the Soviet troops, from which they quickly fell into Japanese hands. Planning for the offensive was restricted to a very small circle of officers, while the troops received their assignments only a few hours before the attack.[85]

The Soviet offensive opened at 5:45 A.M. on August 20, with an air strike by 153 bombers against the Japanese forward positions, artillery, and reserves.[86] At 6:15 A.M. there began an artillery bombardment that lasted nearly three hours. At precisely 9 A.M. the Soviet infantry moved out, supported by tanks, air, and artillery. The Japanese defenders seemed stunned by the ferocity of the attack and in the beginning managed only a weak show of resistance. By the end of the first day the attackers' progress was most pronounced on the southern wing, although movement here was hindered by the deep sands and the failure of the 6th Tank Brigade to cross the Khalkhin-Gol in time to take part in the assault. Success was less pronounced in the north, where Soviet units quickly butted up against strong Japanese defenders around the Fui Heights. Instead of bypassing this position with his mobile units, the Northern Group commander frittered away his numerical advantage in costly frontal assaults against the defenders' entrenchments. This delay forced Zhukov to dispatch his entire reserve to the heights, which finally fell on the twenty-third.

The Soviet advance continued on August 21–22, with the greatest progress still in the south. Here the attackers successfully passed through the Great Sands area and turned to the northeast. By the evening of the twenty-second these units were deep in the Japanese rear and were throwing out motorized and infantry flank guards as they pressed forward. In the center, however, events continued to develop slowly. Here the brunt of the Soviet attack was borne by the 82d Rifle Division, a territorial unit from the Urals Military District. This unit had broken under a Japanese artillery bombardment during the July fighting, and its level of training probably still left much to be desired.[87] In the north a special mobile group was created out of the newly arrived reserves. This group then proceeded to bypass and cut off the defenders along the Fui Heights and quickly get behind the Japanese positions north of the Khailastyn-Gol. Meanwhile, the Mongolian cavalry, which held the flanks of Zhukov's force, pushed to the border against light opposition, whereupon they halted.

On August 23 the Northern Group's 9th Armored Brigade reached the extreme rear of the Japanese position at Nomon-Khan-Burd-Obo. The next day the Southern Group's 8th Armored Brigade reached the Khailastyn-Gol to close the ring. The Soviets moved to tighten the encirclement throughout the following week, as the Japanese made desperate but uncoordinated efforts to break out to the east. One such attempt was made north of the Khailastyn-Gol on August 24. However, the weakened Japanese could make little progress against superior enemy forces, spearheaded by tanks, which proved to be far more effective than the outnumbered and outgunned Japanese models. This attack was halted well short of its goal, as were similar attempts elsewhere. The same fate befell a relief column dispatched from Hailar.

The Soviets, meanwhile, continued to press the Japanese on all sides. One by one the isolated units were either overcome or forced to surrender. By August 31 the last enemy units on the Mongolian side of the disputed border had been eliminated. This was very fortunate for the Soviets, and it preceded by only a day the beginning of the Nazi invasion of Poland.

There is a good deal of evidence that the Japanese, despite their defeat, were gathering forces and making plans for a renewed effort.[88] However, the high command in Tokyo did not relish the prospect of an autumn–winter campaign in the Mongolian wastes, all the more so because the Japanese had their hands full with the seemingly endless war against China. The Soviets, for their part, also had no desire to be drawn into a larger conflict, particularly in light of events in the west.

An armistice was accordingly concluded on September 15, which essentially left the opposing forces in place. Two days later Soviet units moved into Poland to claim their share of the spoils.

Thus Khalkhin-Gol proved to be an extremely timely victory for Stalin, although the battle was not without its cost. Soviet losses during May through September were 8,931 killed, died of wounds, or missing, with another 15,952 wounded and sick, or 24,883 total casualties.[89] The Japanese report 8,717 killed and missing and 10,997 sick and wounded, or 19,714 casualties.[90] However, the Japanese figures do not include the number of those captured, which presumably would have been fairly large. Mongolian casualties are unknown.

Khalkhin-Gol was a classic army operation of the "Cannae" type so beloved of Soviet military theorists. Here the basic tenets of the deep operation were confirmed, despite the usual problems of coordinating the various combat arms. Zhukov, despite his lack of an academic pedigree, seems to have absorbed much of the previous two decades' operational theory. This is particularly evident in his use of two shock groups, reinforced with armor and other mobile arms, on either flank. While his infantry-heavy center pinned down the enemy, the shock groups first broke through and then raced into the Japanese rear to encircle and destroy those units still at the front.

Khalkhin-Gol was also an impressive victory for the army's rear services, which demonstrated their ability to sustain a sizable force in the face of staggering transportation problems. Khalkhin-Gol also did much to restore the Red Army's faith in its abilities, which had been severely undermined by the purges. This confidence would soon be squandered in the ignominious war with Finland.

The operation was also a personal triumph for Zhukov, whose meteoric rise through the Red Army's ranks dates from this time. Within a year he had been promoted to the rank of general in command of the vital Kiev Special Military District, and within three years he was deputy supreme commander in chief, second only to Stalin in the military hierarchy. At Khalkhin-Gol the traces of the distinctive Zhukov style are clearly visible: the massing of overwhelming numbers of men and equipment at the point of decision and utter ruthlessness of execution, as the high proportion of Soviet dead and missing to wounded indicate.[91] For better or worse, this would become the Red Army's dominant method of conducting operations during World War II.

The next conflict, the 1939–40 war with Finland, had very little in common with the mainstream development of the Red Army's operational art. Played out in the highly specific terrain and climatic conditions of the Far North, the Finnish war should be viewed as a phenomenon of secondary importance, meriting only a brief description of the salient military and political events.

Ever since Finland won its independence from Soviet Russia in 1918, the Kremlin had eyed its small neighbor warily. The preternaturally suspicious Soviet leadership was especially concerned about its northwestern frontier, where the border with Finland ran a mere 32 kilometers from Leningrad, the USSR's second-largest city and a major industrial center. Moreover, with the Soviet Union practically shut off from the Baltic Sea by then-independent Estonia, Latvia, and Lithuania, the Baltic Fleet was dangerously bottled up in the eastern end of the Gulf of Finland. The Nazi-Soviet pact had assigned this region to the USSR's sphere of influence, and Stalin moved swiftly to consolidate his gains. In quick succession the Baltic States were forced to sign mutual assistance treaties with the Soviet Union, which allowed the latter to station troops on their territory and make use of their naval and air facilities. This was the prelude to their absorption into the USSR the following summer.

By the autumn of 1939 the Soviets had shifted their sights to Finland. The Finns were given a list of demands, which included the cession of part of the Karelian Isthmus, plus other territory in the Far North and along the Gulf of Finland. The USSR also offered to conclude a mutual assistance treaty similar to the ones imposed upon the Baltic States. As compensation, the Soviets offered Finland territory in central Karelia more than twice the size of that demanded, although the economic value of this land was practically nil.

To accept these conditions would have soon reduced Finland to the status of a vassal state, or worse. The Finns, all but cut off from the West by the world war and abandoned by their putative German allies, nevertheless rejected most of the Soviet conditions. Matters went quickly downhill from this point, although negotiations continued into November. On November 26 the Soviets denounced the 1932 nonaggression treaty with Finland, and a number of border "incidents" and the outbreak of hostilities followed on November 30.

All Soviet land, air, and naval forces in the area were subordinated to Meretskov, who also commanded the Leningrad Military District. This force initially numbered some 500,000 men.[92] These were organized, from north to south, into the Fourteenth, Ninth, Eighth, and Seventh Armies, numbering some twenty rifle divisions, three tank brigades, and seven RGK artillery regiments and smaller units.[93]

Finnish forces were commanded by Field Marshal C. G. E. Mannerheim, a former czarist officer who had been instrumental in winning the country's independence in 1918. The bulk of these were organized into nine divisions, of which six were concentrated along the Karelian Isthmus, the most direct route to the Finnish heartland, while one division remained in reserve along the coast. Two more divisions were deployed immediately north of Lake Ladoga, to ward off a flanking maneuver from that direction. The remainder of the 1,500-kilometer front was held by independent battalions and companies. The Soviets estimated Finnish strength at 260,000 men.[94]

Although the Finnish forces were pitifully small, the defenders nevertheless enjoyed a number of advantages. Chief among these were the forbidding terrain and harsh climatic conditions in a country, almost all of which is above sixty degrees north latitude. Dense forests cover the greater part of the country, and roads are few and primitive. The southeastern part of Finland is cut by countless lakes and swamps, which together make a formidable defensive barrier. Moreover, the Soviets would be attacking at the beginning of the long Finnish winter, during which temperatures regularly fall well below zero and daylight lasts only a few hours.

However, none of these considerations seemed to have unduly concerned the Soviet high command, whose approach to the forthcoming campaign bordered on the criminally irresponsible. Stalin, fearing the consequences of a protracted conflict, insisted that the war be concluded as rapidly as possible. The deadlines for completing the operation were eventually set at 8 to 10 days along the Karelian Isthmus, and 15 days north of Lake Ladoga.[95] The war was to eventually last 105 days and shake the Red Army to its foundations.

By mid-December the Seventh Army had pushed back the thin Finnish covering force along the frontier to a depth of 20 to 60 kilometers and had reached the "Mannerheim Line," which constituted the main Finnish defensive position. One source claims that the "Mannerheim Line" consisted of more than 1,000 earth and timber and concrete machine gun and artillery firing points. Mannerheim himself disputed this and maintained that this position contained no more than sixty-six machine gun nests, barbed wire entanglements, tank traps, and entrenchments, which were mostly out of date and lacking in depth.[96]

However, the first Soviet attempts to crack this zone proved to be costly failures. The Red Army lacked experience in breaking through fortified areas, and previous manuals on the subject had been destroyed when their authors fell victim to the purge.[97] Coordination among the combat arms was almost entirely lacking. An assault would typically begin with a poorly directed artillery barrage, which caused the defenders little or no harm. The heavy snow cover often forced the Soviet tanks to advance along the narrow forest roads, where they were easy targets for the Finnish artillery and infantry antitank weapons. The tanks would sometimes advance, fire, and then return to their starting positions before the infantry attack even began, leaving the latter to attack unsupported, across open ground, through the heavy drifts. Elsewhere along the front the story was much the same. Things were no better in the air, with the Soviet air force seemingly more intent on bombing cities and other rear area targets than on supporting the ground attack.

In late December the high command called off these useless attacks and set about reorganizing its forces for a new assault. During the next six weeks the Soviets worked feverishly to build new roads and railroads to the front. The troops began to receive better equipment, in particular warm clothing, the lack of which had caused so many problems at the start of the war. They were given special training in breaking through fortified areas, using methods that emphasized small-unit actions instead of mass assaults. Fresh units also continued to pour into the area, so that by the beginning of March Soviet forces numbered 760,578 men.[98]

Significant organizational changes took place as well. As early as December the Leningrad Military District's military council was removed from the direct control of operations. These were assumed by a new Stavka of the high command, consisting of Voroshilov as commander in chief, Kuznetsov, Shaposhnikov, and Stalin. Meretskov was demoted to the command of Seventh Army, while the commanders of Eighth and Ninth Armies were replaced as well. On January 7, 1940, the Northwestern Front was created, headed by Army Commander First Class Timoshenko, who had been dispatched to the area from Ukraine, where he had commanded the Kiev Special Military District. The front now included the Seventh Army and the newly created Thirteenth Army, with twenty-four divisions between them. Farther north, a new Fifteenth Army was formed. In this case, it was decided not to create a special Karelian Front directorate for those forces operating north of Lake Ladoga, and these armies (Eighth, Fifteenth, Ninth, and Fourteenth) remained subordinated directly to Moscow.[99]

By early February the Soviets were ready to renew their attack. Stalin was particularly insistent that the "Mannerheim Line" be breached before the onset of the spring thaw, which would render the ground impassable until summer. The Soviet dictator was terrified, lest the war drag on and bring about foreign intervention on the Finns' side.[100]

A massive artillery bombardment on the morning of February 11 heralded the start of the Soviet offensive. The main Soviet forces then moved out along a 40-kilometer front, along which they had concentrated 64 percent of their manpower and the greater part of their artillery.[101] Slowly the Finnish forces began to yield before the weight of the attack. The Soviets pressed their advantage by pouring infantry and tanks, including some new KV models, into the developing breach, although they moved too slowly to cut off any sizable Finnish units. By late February the Soviets had penetrated the main Finnish defensive position in most places and were approaching a second line in front of Viipuri.

The advance was renewed on February 28, with attacks along the entire front. The Finns managed to delay the advance by flooding the area near Viipuri. However, the Soviets were able to push across the frozen bay and establish a foothold on the opposite shore. The Soviets suffered heavily during this attack, but they continued to expand their bridgehead and were able to cut the main road to Helsinki and threaten the last rail line linking the Viipuri garrison to the interior.

Finland, with its small army bled white, could not hope to continue the war against these odds. And although the prospect of French and British aid must have been tantalizing, the Finns were at the end of their strength. On March 12 the Finnish government acceded to the Soviet demands and signed a peace treaty that ended the war the next day. The peace settlement was extremely harsh and went beyond even the original Soviet demands. The Finns were forced to cede 66,000 square kilometers of territory, mostly in the southeastern part of the country, and were saddled with a heavy indemnity.

The Finns also paid a heavy price in lives, losing 24,923 killed and missing and another 43,557 wounded.[102] The Red Army fared far worse, suffering 391,783 casualties, more than five times that of the Finns, and more than the entire Finnish army at the start of the war. Of this figure, 87,506 were killed or died of wounds and disease, with another 39,369 missing and presumed dead. The wounded accounted for 188,671 men, while another 76,237 were felled by disease or frostbite.[103]

The war with Finland showed the Red Army at its prewar nadir. It had taken the Soviets three and a half months to defeat a small nation in an operation that was supposed to last two weeks. The Finnish army had everywhere bested its opponent in the most basic elements of military skill, and the Red Army had only succeeded by grinding the Finns down under the sheer weight of manpower and metal. As one observer put it, Soviet methods were everywhere "clumsy, ruthless and extravagant."[104]

The lessons drawn from this conflict had serious consequences for the Red Army's operational art. Just as had been the case in Spain, the intellectually weakened Soviet high command drew a number of erroneous conclusions from the disastrous 1939–40 war. The campaign's salient feature had been the Red Army's ponderous and bloody reduction of the Finnish positions along the Karelian Isthmus. In this regard, their efforts had more in common with the senseless bludgeoning of Verdun and the Somme than with the slicing maneuver which the Soviets celebrated in their theoretical writings and which the Germans were beginning to realize in practice. On the other hand, it should be remembered that the heavily forested and marshy terrain of the Finnish theater had little in common with the war the army was ostensibly being trained to wage.

One young commander later complained that the "one-sided" experience of the Finnish campaign completely dominated the army's training during the final peacetime months. During this period, he wrote, the "fundamentals" of the deep battle were "consigned to oblivion," along with questions of maneuver warfare involving large mechanized formations. Instead, the army was trained in "overcoming the enemy's long-term defenses by gradually accumulating forces and patiently 'gnawing through' breaches in the enemy's fortifications, according to all the rules of engineering science."[105]

One contemporary charged that these views suited the deeply conservative outlook of the country's political leadership.[106] They certainly must have been pleasing to Voroshilov, whose thinking had not advanced much beyond the civil war and who had long resisted the various tenets of the deep operation. What comfort the Red Army could draw from this disastrous campaign came in the form of the incompetent Voroshilov's replacement as defense commissar by Timoshenko. The latter proceeded to subject the army to a furious and often brutal year of preparing to fight a modern war. Time, however, was running out.

ON THE EVE

At the end of 1940 a large group of general officers was summoned to Moscow to take part in a high-level discussion on the state of the army and its military theory. The participants included military district and front commanders, their political commissars and chiefs of staff, army commanders, high-ranking officers from the central administrative apparatus, and the heads of various military academies, as well as selected corps and division commanders. Several of the officers had less than a year to live and were to die either on the battlefield or at the hands of the NKVD. The conference sessions, which were held from December 23 to 31, were also attended by one or more leading representatives of the party and government, who reported their impressions back to Stalin. The conference was the last major military gathering before the war and thus is worthy of closer examination in order to determine the state of Soviet operational art during the final peacetime months.

The centerpiece of these proceedings consisted of the six reports that dealt with a number of tactical-operational problems, and the debates that accompanied them. These included General and Chief of the General Staff Meretskov's lengthy address, entitled "The Results and Tasks of the Ground Forces' and Air Force's Combat Training and the High Command's Operational Training"; General and Commander of the Kiev Special Military District Zhukov's "The Character of the Modern Offensive Operation"; General Lieutenant and Chief of the Main Air Force Directorate Rychagov's "The Air Force in an Offensive Operation and the Struggle for Air Superiority"; Gen. and Commander of the Moscow Military District I. V. Tyulenev's "The Character of the Modern Defensive Operation"; and General Colonel and Commander of the Western Special Military District Pavlov's "The Employment of Mechanized Formations in the Modern Offensive Operation and the Commitment of a Mechanized Corps into a Breakthrough." Gen. Lt. and General Inspector of Infantry A. K. Smirnov also delivered a report entitled "The Rifle Division's Battle in the Offensive and Defense," but because his speech dealt solely with tactical problems, it will not be discussed here. The conference concluded with a summary report by Marshal and Defense Commissar Timoshenko.

Meretskov's opening remarks contain little of interest, from the point of view of operational theory, because they were primarily devoted to the past year's training cycle and similar plans for 1941. However, his comments, and those of the other contributors, are important for the light they shed on the Red Army's precarious state just six months before the German invasion. The chief of staff highlighted in some detail shortcomings in the officer corps' training, both in the field and in the academies, as well as serious discipline problems among the rank and file. Other discussants complained of the poor quality of the army's recruits, which ranged from the draftees' small physical size to the inability of many to speak or understand Russian. Still others pointed to command problems caused by the continual shuffling of officer cadres and the disruption to training due to the troops' periodic assignment to civilian economic duties, such as helping with the harvest in the Far East.[107] The recitation of these problems, many of them systemic, completes the impression of an army in considerable disarray, even as it prepared to face its greatest test.[108]

The first and most important topic, an examination of the offensive operation, was entrusted to Zhukov, the Red Army's rising star. However, for all his success on the battlefield, Zhukov was no scholar and had only a rudimentary elementary and military education. For assistance he turned to Colonel Bagramyan, who had completed the course at the new General Staff Academy and taught there for two years, before being transferred to Kiev as chief of the district staff's operational section.[109] Bagramyan would later enjoy a successful career during the war, first in staff positions and then as an army and front commander.

Zhukov opened his remarks with a general review of the experience of recent wars. He quickly dismissed the relevance of Spain and China and made only the most perfunctory obeisance to the Soviet victory in Finland. Far more instructive, he claimed, were the Red Army's actions at Khalkhin-Gol and the Germans' equally rapid victories in Poland and the west. These three conflicts shared certain traits: the harmonious meshing of infantry, artillery, tanks, and airpower to destroy the enemy air force and gain air superiority; to break through the enemy's tactical defense, whether in field conditions or as part of a fortified position; and to commit a powerful mobile group, capable of destroying the defender's reserves and transforming the operational success into a strategic one.[110] This was essentially the old formula for the deep operation, although Zhukov himself did not use the term.

Of particular interest was Zhukov's use of the term "strategic success," which raised the stakes of an operational success by an order of magnitude. In this respect he was merely following in the footsteps of the majority of those theorists of the 1920s and 1930s who regarded the front as a strategic instrument, whereby final strategic success would come only at the conclusion of several purely operational efforts.

The Germans, however, in their recent campaigns, had shown the full possibilities of the new methods of waging war and may have influenced Zhukov's choice of a more ambitious phraseology. This was certainly the case during the brief war with Poland, which had begun as a single, uninterrupted operation and quickly brought about strategic results. The case of France and the Low Countries is somewhat more complicated. Here the German offensive unfolded in two stages: the armored breakthrough at Sedan and the drive to the sea; and the breakthrough of the Somme-Aisne line, followed by a subsequent strategic exploitation. And while this method validated previous Soviet theory regarding the consecutive conduct of operations, it could also be argued that the decisive strategic result of the latter campaign had been essentially achieved during the first phase.

Zhukov was on more traditional ground in his remarks about the role of the front level of command, which had long been recognized by imperial and Soviet theoreticians alike. The necessity for creating such a coordinating body followed naturally from Zhukov's calculations that an offensive operation conducted in the western theater of military activities must defeat from one-third to one-half of the enemy forces in order to achieve a strategic objective. This would involve an attack along a front of 400 to 450 kilometers in breadth, with the main effort made along a front of 100 to 150 kilometers. Anything less, he maintained, would enable the defender to bring up reinforcements and localize the attack. None of this was particularly new, however, and had already been raised by Triandafillov as far back as 1929.[111]

An attack of this magnitude would necessarily involve a large concentration of men and equipment, which Zhukov calculated at 85 to 100 rifle divisions, four to five mechanized corps, two to three cavalry corps, and thirty to thirty-five aviation divisions. These would be organized by the front into three to four shock and one or two auxiliary *(vspomogatel'nye)* armies. The front's long-range striking power would be concentrated in its mobile group, in the form of a cavalry-mechanized or motor-mechanized army, which was to be committed for the exploitation drive to a depth of 150 kilometers. The front mobile group would consist of two mechanized and one or two cavalry corps, plus appropriate air support. This force would also be supported by airborne units and 2 to 3 rifle divisions brought up from the rear. Finally, the front would also dispose of a reserve army, to meet enemy counterattacks, to secure the penetration's expanding flanks, and to strengthen the axis of the main advance.[112]

In the event of success, a front operation might reach a depth of 200 to 300 kilometers, or even more in certain cases. In an operation that might last anywhere from twelve to twenty days, this meant an average daily rate of advance of 10 to 15 kilometers.[113]

Zhukov devoted a fair amount of attention to the various forms of operational maneuver, which was another question that had been analyzed extensively during the previous decade. However, he did not add anything new to the debate and contented himself with a short recitation of each form's virtues and shortcomings.

Zhukov divided the forms of operational maneuver into two basic types: frontal and the turning movement. The first presupposes a more or less continuous front and may be encountered during a war's opening operations, although it is more likely later on, once a war of position has set in. Zhukov called this form the least "economical" because it requires a significant superiority of force on the part of the attacker and the deep echelonment of his combat formation to overcome the defending force. This may include an offensive by several armies along a single axis, with the subsequent development of the attack in depth and the encirclement of one or more of the isolated enemy groups. However, such an attack requires a well-developed rail net to supply such a large force, while it also enables the enemy to quickly concentrate his reserves against the breakthrough. Alternatively, piercing the enemy front at several widely spaced intervals held out the promise of disrupting the enemy's position along a broad front and then surrounding and destroying his isolated units in detail. Finally, there was the breakthrough of one or both wings of the enemy's front, with the latter particularly rich in possibilities for attacking along converging axes and surrounding the defender.[114]

Once the breakthrough of the enemy's front by one of these methods has been achieved, the attacker was to attempt to turn one or both of the defender's flanks, that is, undertake the second type of operational maneuver. Ideally, the turning force should drive to a depth of no less than 20 to 30 kilometers before turning inward against the defender's rear. Zhukov spoke highly of this maneuver and advised his listeners to employ it whenever possible, citing his own successful maneuver at Khalkhin-Gol as an example to be emulated.[115]

Zhukov's comments on the nature and conduct of the army operation reveal him to be well within the mainstream of operational thinking in this area as well. As opposed to the front operation, which unfolds simultaneously along several operational axes in the pursuit of its goal, the army operation is normally conducted along one axis and is more modest in its ambitions. Zhukov called the army operation a "derivative" of the front operation, bound by "narrower confines of time and space."[116]

The centerpiece of the army operation was, as before, the shock army, an already-large combined-arms army that had been further reinforced with attachments from the high command reserve. Zhukov's ideal shock army consisted of five rifle corps (fifteen to sixteen rifle divisions), three to five tank brigades, six or seven howitzer artillery regiments, two to three gun artillery regiments, six mortar battalions, seven or eight antiaircraft battalions, two to three fighter regiments, four to five bomber regiments, and two or three regiments of assault aircraft. This was a far more imposing force than the front's auxiliary armies, which contained no more than two or three corps.[117]

Zhukov assigned his shock army an attack frontage of 50 to 70 kilometers. This was small compared with that of an auxiliary army, which would launch supporting attacks along a projected 60- to 100-kilometer front. Moreover, the shock army would be making its main breakthrough effort along a 30-kilometer front. It was here that the shock army commander would concentrate three reinforced rifle corps and his reserve of two to three rifle divisions, while the two other corps occupied the remainder of the army's front. This worked out to a 10-kilometer attack front for each corps along the breakthrough zone, or 2.5 to 3 kilometers per rifle division. Concurrently with the main attack, one of the auxiliary corps was to launch a supporting drive along its 20- to 30-kilometer front.[118]

Zhukov calculated that this concentration of force would ensure a density of 60 guns per kilometer along the attack front, yielding a seven- to eightfold superiority over the enemy. The tank brigades were to be massed in the same fashion, one to one and a half per corps, for a density of forty tanks per kilometer. In all, it was planned to concentrate approximately 200,000 men, 1,500 to 2,000 guns, and a "mass of tanks" in a 30-by-30-kilometer area for the breakthrough, as well as a large number of transport vehicles and other equipment.[119]

Zhukov called the breakthrough of the enemy's front the "decisive act of the offensive operation." It would commence with a combined air and artillery assault, designed to gain local air superiority and to suppress the defender's antipersonnel and antitank weapons. The infantry-tank attack would follow upon the end of the artillery barrage, unfolding in successive waves to maintain the impetus of the assault. Zhukov felt that in certain favorable conditions the initial assault might be so successful as to occupy the defender's second tactical position by the end of the first day. If not, the position would have to be taken the next day in a renewed attack. Altogether, it was calculated that the breakthrough and defeat of the enemy in the immediate tactical defensive zone would take two to three days.[120]

The mobile group would be committed to exploit the success once the rifle corps had cleared the enemy's second position and reached the operational depth. This group would then move to defeat the defender's reserves as they moved up to the battlefield and to outflank and encircle those enemy forces still at the front, possibly in conjunction with a neighboring shock army's mobile group. The mobile group would be supported in its drive by organic army and front aviation, as well as through airborne landings in the enemy's rear. Zhukov calculated that this portion of the operation would last two to three days and conclude with the encirclement and destruction of a sizable enemy force.[121]

At this stage the operation would most likely end, having lasted seven to ten days and penetrated to a depth of some 100 to 150 kilometers. Zhukov's only advice at this point was that the army command prepare for a new operation, should this dovetail with the front commander's plans.[122] This left untouched the problem of conducting consecutive army operations as part of a larger front effort. However, nothing in Zhukov's subsequent wartime record as a front commander or Stavka representative implies that he was anything other than an adherent of this theory.

The comments attending Zhukov's speech reveal a fair degree of unanimity as far as the basic principles of the offensive operation were concerned, although the participants disagreed on a number of points. For example, Gen. Lt. P. L. Romanenko, a mechanized corps commander, criticized Zhukov's approach as outdated and reflecting the views and matériel situation of 1932–34.[123] There was more than a little truth to this accusation, as the further development of operational theory had all but ceased, beginning in mid-1937. This was due not only to the effects of the purges but also to the delayed transition to a new generation of tanks and aircraft, which meant that the army's operational theory continued to be based on outmoded equipment. Gen. Lt. F. I. Golikov, a deputy chief of staff and chief of the Red Army's Main Intelligence Directorate (GRU), called Romanenko's assertion "absurd." He went on to defend Zhukov, maintaining that the latter's calculations were based on the latest intelligence data from the recent campaign in the west.[124] However, the comments of Golikov, one of the prime culprits in the Soviet disaster of 1941 and a failed front commander, may be easily dismissed.

More to the point were remarks by General Colonel Shtern, commander of the Far Eastern Front, concerning the composition of the armies carrying out an offensive operation. Shtern's shock army was similar to Zhukov's and included four rifle corps and reserve divisions (twelve to fifteen rifle divisions), a mechanized corps as the army's success development echelon (ERU), consisting of two tank and one or two motorized rifle divisions, plus six to nine RGK artillery regiments. The RGK would also contribute another fifteen to twenty antiaircraft battalions and four or five tank brigades, which meant approximately 1,000 tanks for the immediate breakthrough stage. The army would be further reinforced with two or three airborne brigades and other units. Nor did Shtern's proposed auxiliary army differ markedly from Zhukov's; it included two to three rifle corps (six to eight rifle divisions), one or two tank brigades, and two or three RGK artillery regiments.[125]

However, even these figures seem small when compared with Romanenko's proposal to create shock armies of four or five mechanized corps, three to four air corps, one or two airborne divisions, and nine to twelve attached artillery regiments. Romanenko advocated deploying two such armies along the inner and outer flanks of two adjoining fronts. This would enable the attacker, he assured his audience, to deliver a blow so powerful as to ensure not only an operational but also a strategic success.[126]

Unfortunately, neither Zhukov nor Timoshenko addressed this issue in their closing remarks. One conference participant later cited this omission as evidence that the country's military leadership failed to fully understand the changing demands of modern war.[127] Whatever the truth of this statement, it still does not speak to the utility of creating such armies, nor to the difficulty in controlling them during an offensive. As it transpired, the 1943–45 authorized tank army strength of two tank and one mechanized corps was probably the solution best suited to Soviet circumstances.

Of more practical benefit were Shtern's thoughts on creating mechanized armies for carrying out independent offensive missions, or as a front mobile group. Such an army would consist of a tank group (one to two tank divisions), two or three light divisions, one to two airborne brigades, and three or four rifle divisions.[128]

Another area of contention concerned the amount of time to be allotted to preparations for the attack, for which Zhukov had set aside a mere two to three days.[129] This was disputed by several of the other speakers, who came out against forcing the pace of such activities. Romanenko, for example, ventured that this preparatory period might last anywhere from ten to fifteen days.[130]

A further point of debate dealt with the appropriate moment for committing the mobile group into the battle. Zhukov was in favor of a clear delineation of tasks, with the breakthrough of the enemy's second tactical position as the exclusive province of the shock army's first-echelon corps, followed by the commitment of the mobile group into a more or less unobstructed breach.[131] Shtern, while admitting the theoretical attractiveness of such an approach, maintained that more often than not the mobile group would have to be committed in order to complete the tactical breakthrough.[132] Shtern, in turn, was supported by Gen. Lt. and Commander of the Orel Military District F. N. Remezov, who favored committing the mobile group on the operation's second day. On this occasion, the mobile group's infantry units would assist the first echelon's rifle corps in completing the breakthrough.[133]

Finally, of particular interest for the near future were the remarks by Gen. Lt. P. S. Klenov, chief of staff of the Baltic Special Military District. Klenov criticized Zhukov for ignoring entirely the peculiar character of a war's opening operations. Here Klenov did not add anything new to the existing body of theory in this area, which dated from the 1930s, but he insisted that greater attention be paid to such questions. On the other hand, he also criticized Isserson's *New Forms of Combat* and rejected the author's assertion that wars now begin with an attack by one side's fully mobilized forces. Klenov labeled these assertions "hasty" and "premature" and too much based on the Wehrmacht's limited experience in the Polish campaign, with no particular relevance for the Red Army.[134] Klenov's remarks are more than ironic in light of the ferocity of the German attack, which developed precisely along the lines suggested by Isserson. Klenov was removed as chief of staff of the Northwestern Front in July 1941, was discharged from the army, and died soon after.

The next day's session was devoted to Rychagov's address on the uses of airpower. Unfortunately, Rychagov's report and the remarks of the speakers who followed him constitute the weakest of the conference. For the most part, the participants limited themselves to general declarations, while their remarks lacked the clarity and quantitative focus of the previous day. This may have been due to the very formulation of the problem, which served to divide the speakers' attention between questions of operational art and strategy.

Rychagov's address was devoted to the problem of air support for a front offensive operation, which he calculated might require as many as 3,500 to 4,000 aircraft. The air force's role in such an operation entailed the performance of a number of independent tasks, as well as those carried out in support of the ground forces. These included achieving and retaining air superiority, supporting the ground attack, providing air cover, attacking the defender's operational and strategic reserves, fulfilling reconnaissance duties, carrying out airborne landings, and airlifting supplies to units in the enemy rear.[135]

Rychagov divided air superiority into two types: strategic and operational. The first, he stated, is achieved by engaging the enemy's air force directly, and indirectly through air strikes aimed at his aviation industry and his equipment and fuel centers. This implies a strategic bombing campaign, although Rychagov did not elaborate. Operational superiority, on the other hand, is a narrower concept, embracing a particular geographic area for a limited time. This is achieved by repeatedly striking the defender's nearby airfields, repair shops, and fuel storage facilities; by destroying his airpower in combat directly over the battlefield; and by maintaining an overall numerical superiority in aircraft through constant reinforcement.[136]

The air force was also to support the ground forces during all phases of the operation. This would involve attacks against enemy ground forces immediately preceding and during the breakthrough stage. The air force would also delay the arrival of the defender's tactical and operational reserves to the breakthrough zone, attack his supply lines and headquarters, disrupt his defensive preparations in the rear, and harry his retreating units. Of particular importance was maintaining effective air support for the mobile group in the enemy rear. This task was entrusted primarily to front aviation.[137]

Finally, the air force was to attack the enemy's operational and strategic reserves, as well as other targets of military significance deep in his rear. The latter would take the form of long-range strikes, begun even before the start of the ground attack and aimed primarily at economic targets having a direct bearing on the forthcoming operation. Disrupting the arrival of the enemy's reserves would mainly involve attacks against his road and rail transport. This would force the enemy to move on foot and at night, thereby delaying his arrival on the battlefield and enabling the attacker to finish off those enemy forces slated for destruction.[138]

There were few outright objections to these principles expressed in the debates that followed Rychagov's report. However, a slightly discordant note was struck by Gen. Lt. E. S. Ptukhin, the air force commander of the Kiev Special Military District. Ptukhin, to judge from his remarks, was very much in favor of independent air operations aimed at achieving air superiority, with questions of ground support occupying a distant second place.[139] This approach was clearly disputed by Gen. Lt. K. M. Gusev, the Far Eastern Front's air force chief. Gusev proceeded to defend the army's traditional view in no uncertain terms, stating that the air force's tasks are "determined foremost by the front's missions."[140]

Another bone of contention was the problem of air subordination and the related question of the desired degree of air centralization. Gen. Lt. M. M. Popov, the commander of the First Red Banner Army, showed his infantry roots in arguing for a more decentralized system of air control. Popov, while claiming overall fealty to the principle of centralized control, nevertheless maintained that a certain portion of the attacker's air assets should be subordinated to the corps commanders during the operation's breakthrough phase. Other units should be "on call" to meet the mobile units' immediate tactical needs.[141] This view was challenged by General Lieutenant Kuznetsov, commander of the North Caucasus Military District, and Gen. Lt. G. P. Kravchenko, air force commander of the Baltic Special Military District. Both men, as well as Rychagov, insisted that in order to avoid a dangerous dispersal of force, the attacker's air assets should remain in the hands of the army and/or front commander.[142]

On December 27 General Tyulenev gave his address on the defensive operation, operational art's perennial stepchild. He began his remarks by admitting the army's deficiency in this area and the fact that it had nothing to which it could oppose the impressive body of work devoted to conducting the army offensive operation.[143] That the Red Army had come to such a sorry pass is hardly surprising and was the natural result of operational art's one-sided development during the previous twenty years. Given this background, Tyulenev did little more than cover the same theoretical ground that had already been explored in the 1930s, with only an occasional reference to more recent experience.

Thus Tyulenev was on familiar territory in relating to his audience why armies resort, or are forced to resort, to defensive operations. Such a move may be dictated by the war plan itself, particularly during a conflict's opening stages, or by the overall strategic situation as it develops during the course of the war. In either event, he said, a defensive operation will be undertaken in pursuit of three objectives: to economize force at one or more points in order to launch an offensive along the decisive axis; to win time so that this attack may be launched; and to protect important political and economic objectives, whose loss would be a severe blow to the country's war effort.[144]

What is striking in this formulation is the continuing degree to which offensive considerations, even if they concern activities on other areas of the front, animate the decision to adopt the defensive. The only exception is the third case, which is fixed due to more or less permanent circumstances. In fact, Tyulenev stated, the ideal defensive operation is one that, upon having achieved its primary objective of halting and exhausting the attacker, in turn creates the conditions for a counteroffensive.[145]

Nor did Tyulenev's detailed examination of the army's defensive preparations break any particularly new ground, although he did add several new quantitative elements. Ideally, the operation would be conducted by an army numbering four or five rifle corps (twelve to fifteen rifle divisions), one to two tank divisions, four or five RGK artillery regiments, twenty artillery battalions, two or three antiaircraft regiments, and a mixed air division, as well as smaller engineer and other units. This force would occupy a front approximately 100 kilometers in breadth. The army's first echelon would contain some ten rifle divisions, with the remainder, together with the tank divisions, relegated to the second echelon and reserves. In the first echelon, division frontages might be as narrow as 5 kilometers and as broad as 15, depending on the importance of the terrain. This worked out to an average artillery density of fourteen guns per kilometer of front, although Tyulenev favored massing as many as twenty to forty pieces along particularly important axes.[146]

Needless to say, these generous norms were rarely, if ever, met, particularly during 1941–42, when the Red Army was almost continuously on the defensive. It was only at Kursk in July 1943 that these figures were met or exceeded.

The army's defensive area would be somewhat greater in depth, thus matching the attacker's expected deep echelonment of his combat order. This defensive position, according to Tyulenev, would consist of four clearly defined zones. The first, or forward, zone extended back some 15 to 35 kilometers and consisted primarily of artificial and natural obstacles. The zone would be manned by small units whose task was to determine the axis of the enemy advance and to inflict as many casualties as possible in small holding actions. The heaviest fighting was to take place in the main defensive zone, which stretched back only 12 to 20 kilometers in depth. This zone included two positions, the first of which would be manned by the army's main forces and anchored on an interlocking system of antitank obstacles and firing points. The second position was less-developed but contained the army's second echelon, which was to be ready to launch a counterattack if the first position was unsuccessful in halting the attacker. The third, or operational maneuver, zone contained the army's reserve units and extended back some 25 to 30 kilometers. These reserves would cover particular axes in order to contain an enemy armored breakthrough. Finally, there was the rear zone, which might reach 50 kilometers in depth. This zone would be sparsely manned by antiaircraft units and mobile detachments for combating enemy airborne landings.[147]

Tyulenev calculated that to properly fortify the position the army would need some 300 tons of explosives, 2,500 tons of antitank mines, 1,000 tons of barbed wire, and up to 6,000 to 7,000 tons of other supplies. Large quantities of lumber and other construction materials would also be needed. This construction effort would require no less than ten to fifteen days to complete, plus the mobilization of 10,000 civilian workers.[148]

Tyulenev's remarks on the actual conduct of the defensive operation were not very specific and may be reduced to a few general statements. According to this scheme, the troops in the forward zone, reinforced with special "blocking detachments," were to delay the enemy advance and hinder his deployment before falling back on the main defensive zone. As the enemy approached the first position, he would be assailed by an intensive air and artillery bombardment, which might also be accompanied by limited tank sorties. As the fighting progressed into the main zone, the defender not only was to withstand the enemy assault but also was to counterattack when necessary. The chief goal at this stage was to conduct the battle in such a way as to separate the attacker's tanks from his slower-moving infantry, thus breaking up the assault into nonsupporting components. Once the enemy's attack had been halted or began to falter, the defender was to launch his own counteroffensive and restore the situation.[149]

Objections to Tyulenev's approach centered chiefly around his inflated expectations of the forces the army could be expected to dispose of for the operation. For example, Gen. Maj. V. E. Klimovskikh, the chief of staff of the Western Special Military District, claimed that Tyulenev's proposed army of fourteen to fifteen rifle divisions, plus a tank division, was more suited to attack than defend. He stated that nine to twelve rifle divisions, including reserves, would be adequate to man the front.[150] His contention was supported by his fellow chief of staff Klenov, who believed that the army commander should count on no more than ten divisions, plus a maximum of two to three RGK artillery regiments.[151]

Developing his remarks further, Klimovskikh claimed that even in its reduced state the army should be capable of defeating the enemy with the forces at hand. Should the enemy nevertheless break through, the front commander could move to seal off the breach by dispatching a mechanized formation to the threatened area. However, any major counteroffensive would require tank and mechanized formations, which the front would release as it saw fit.[152] These views also found favor in the remarks by General Lieutenant Kirponos, commander of the Leningrad Military District, and Gen. Maj. S. S. Biryuzov, a division commander and future chief of the General Staff.[153]

An interesting secondary discussion also developed in connection with the remarks by Gen. Lt. M. S. Khozin, the chief of the Frunze Military Academy. Khozin's researches had led him to the highly original conclusion to completely reverse the army's standard distribution of forces in the defense. Instead of two-thirds of these forces in the front line and one-third in the rear as a reserve, the rear was to contain two-thirds of the army's strength, leaving the front line to be held by little more than a covering force. He claimed that such a deployment would spare the forward units from being pummeled by the enemy's artillery and tank attack while the assault was at its height. A further advantage to such an arrangement, he said, was that such a disposition would ensure that any breakthrough would encounter increasing resistance as it advanced into the depth of the defender's position, just as the impetus of the original blow had begun to fade. In these remarks one hears echoes of the recent Finnish war and the subsequent Soviet tendency to overestimate the importance of artillery in a breakthrough operation.[154] This view was disputed by Tyulenev and his chief of staff, General Lieutenant Sokolovskii, who was also to rise to the position of chief of the General Staff. Both maintained, quite correctly, that such a deployment not only would do nothing to stop the attacker but also would leave the defender open to defeat in detail.[155]

On December 28 Pavlov presented his report on the employment of the mechanized corps. In many respects this represented a continuation of Zhukov's more wide-ranging remarks, with the emphasis in this case on the more narrowly defined circumstances of the corps' commitment into the offensive battle. This was a question that had intrigued Soviet theorists for the past several years. Zhukov himself admitted that prior to 1940 the Red Army's leadership lacked "a firm understanding of the significance of the methods and forms of employing large tank and mechanized formations, such as the corps and army, in modern war."[156] As the debate that followed Pavlov's remarks revealed, unanimity on this question was no closer six months before the start of the war.

At first glance, Pavlov appeared to be the officer best qualified to speak on the subject. He was one of the most experienced combat officers to have survived the purge and had commanded armored forces in Spain and Finland. Pavlov also possessed a solid academic background and was considered the army's leading expert on armored warfare. However, these qualifications proved to be of little value against the German onslaught in June 1941.

Pavlov devoted a good deal of attention to the new mechanized corps' strength and capabilities. This was premature, to say the least, as nearly all the corps were severely understrength in their authorized number of tanks and could not be expected to make up the shortfall for some time to come. However, this inconvenient fact did not stop Pavlov from making the then fantastic assertion that a Soviet mechanized corps was capable of defeating two German panzer divisions, or four to five infantry divisions.[157] Experience would soon show that these projections were wildly inflated.

Based on these supposed merits, the mechanized corps was capable of carrying out a number of tasks. Among these was the ability to disrupt the concentration and deployment of the enemy's main forces. This was likely to occur upon the outbreak of war and proceed along lines already examined under the rubric of "the beginning period of the war." However, the mechanized corps' prime task remained that of breaking through the defender's fortified position in the wake of the infantry-armored attack and then transforming the tactical success into an operational one. The corps was then to operate against the enemy's flanks and rear, cutting off and destroying those defenders still at the front, in conjunction with the infantry's advance. Pavlov did allow that in exceptional cases the mechanized corps might achieve a breakthrough on its own. This was most likely to occur when the enemy has established a hasty and unfortified defensive position. Rather than lose time in organizing a breakthrough in the traditional manner, the solution in this case was to organize an attack directly from the march. Ideally, this would involve an attack by two mechanized corps, supported by infantry and motorized infantry, attacking along converging axes. These forces would then smash through the defender's position to a depth of some 30 to 35 kilometers, whereupon the pincers would close around the remaining defenders and destroy them.[158]

However attractive this scenario may have been, Pavlov nevertheless expected the offensive operation to unfold along more traditional lines. This, he stated, would develop in three stages. The first embraced the complex preparatory measures and combat activities preceding the commitment of the mechanized corps into the battle and was calculated to last two or three days. During this period the entire weight of the attack would be carried by the rifle corps, which had the exclusive mission of piercing the enemy's tactical defense. The second stage involved the mechanized corps' commitment into the breach, which would take two or three hours. This stage might also see the commitment of even larger formations, such as a cavalry-mechanized group or a group of mechanized corps. This would be followed immediately by the exploitation phase, which was expected to last another two or three days and conclude with the defeat of the enemy's reserves and/or the encirclement and destruction of his forces still at the front.[159]

During the first phase the mechanized corps would be moved close to the front in preparation for the attack. Pavlov calculated that the corps would initially be concentrated some 60 to 70 kilometers behind the front line. This would lessen the chances of detection by the enemy's aerial reconnaissance. Under favorable terrain conditions, part of the corps might be moved up as close as 15 to 25 kilometers, which would also reduce wear and tear on the vehicles during the approach march, while at the same time remaining beyond the range of the enemy's artillery. During this period the corps commander's time would primarily be spent finalizing his plans and issuing orders for the approach march.[160]

Upon receiving the attack order from the army commander, the corps would move up to take its position for the assault. In march formation the corps would occupy a front 12 to 15 kilometers in width and 23 to 25 in depth, and would move at an average speed of 10 to 15 kilometers per hour. The most common approach order had the corps' two tank divisions advancing in a line, with the motorized division following behind in two echelons. This force would be spearheaded by a security detachment, followed by the divisions' heavy tanks, with lighter vehicles along the flanks. The divisions' motorized infantry would follow behind their tanks, with the motorized division bringing up the rear. In certain cases the situation might allow all three divisions to approach the front in a line.[161]

The mechanized corps' commitment into the breach was the most critical moment in the offensive operation, the success of which depended on the outcome of this maneuver. Thus the time and manner of the corps' commitment were of the utmost importance and caused Pavlov to dwell at length on its mechanics.

For Pavlov, speed was vital, lest the defender recover from the initial shock of the infantry attack and organize a new defensive position. Thus he spoke decisively in favor of committing the mechanized corps into the battle against the enemy's second defensive position, before it had been penetrated by the rifle corps' attack. To wait for the rifle corps to complete the task meant losing valuable time, which the defender would employ to bring up reserves and restore his front.[162]

During this phase the mechanized corps would be supported by one to two mixed air divisions, which would ensure air superiority over the breakthrough zone. The mechanized corps' heavy tanks would simultaneously move through the ranks of the rifle corps to attack the defender's field and antitank artillery. Following close behind, the medium tanks would finish off the remaining antitank guns and machine guns, thus clearing the way for the advance by the motorized infantry. Once the defender's tactical position had been penetrated to a depth of 20 to 25 kilometers, the corps' units would gather in a designated concentration area to receive their orders for the exploitation phase.[163]

The third stage was the least subject to planning, as its development depended to a great deal on the degree of success achieved during the preceding phases. As a general rule, at this point the mechanized corps moves to destroy those enemy reserves occupying the rear defensive position and block the retreat of those forces still at the front.[164]

The debates that followed these remarks revolved chiefly around two topics: the appropriate time to commit the mechanized corps, and who should give the order to commit it. The first question aroused the greatest degree of controversy and revealed a decided split in views between the commanders in the field and those in the central administrative apparatus. Among the latter was Gen. Maj. B. G. Vershinin, general-inspector of tank troops. Vershinin maintained that the rifle corps should complete the breakthrough of the defender's second tactical position unassisted, in order that the mechanized corps might enter the battle fresh and ready for action. To do otherwise, he warned, would weaken the mechanized corps and render it unfit for independent operations in the enemy rear.[165] His remarks were seconded by Gen. Lt. Ya. N. Fedorenko, Pavlov's successor as chief of the army's Main Armored Directorate. Fedorenko held that if the mechanized corps were used to complete the breakthrough of the enemy's tactical position, it would reach the defender's operational depth in a disorganized state. This would necessitate a significant halt in operations, he said, to put the corps in order before resuming the advance, causing a serious loss of time at a critical moment.[166]

These opinions were disputed by a number of mechanized corps commanders, who held a more practical view of the operation's development. Among these was Gen. Maj. M. G. Khatskilevich, who stated that if the defender's second tactical position was known to be occupied by strong forces, then the mechanized corps would be forced to attack and break through this position in tandem with the rifle corps. Above all, he warned, it would be a serious mistake to tie the actions of the mechanized corps to those of the rifle corps operating on their own.[167] This view received support from Gen. Lt. A. I. Eremenko, another mechanized corps commander. Eremenko opined that breaking through the defender's first position would require a regrouping, so that the second position could only be taken on the following day. This meant the commitment of the mechanized corps into the battle for the second position.[168]

Pavlov returned to the subject in his closing remarks. He repeated his contention that it was best to commit the mechanized corps into the battle for the enemy's second defensive position, lest time be lost in proceeding to the next, exploitation phase. He even went so far as to aver that in certain cases, such as a larger operation, it might be expedient for a single mechanized corps to draw the enemy's reserves upon itself to facilitate a breakthrough by other mechanized corps elsewhere along the front.[169]

With certain reservations, one must admit the validity of Pavlov's view regarding the primacy of completing the breakthrough of the defender's second position, using whatever forces are necessary. This approach, as opposed to the overly schematic views of the army operation held by others, recognized the importance of first piercing the enemy's tactical defense, without which any further talk of advancing into his operational depth is pointless.

Finally, there erupted a small flurry over the question of who should be responsible for committing the mechanized corps. Pavlov saw this as being solely the prerogative of the corps commander, a position that he repeated in his closing remarks.[170] However, he was opposed on this point by Gen. Col. I. R. Apanasenko, commander of the Central Asian Military District, and Gen. Lt. Ya. T. Cherevichenko, commander of the Odessa Military District. Both men argued that the decision to commit the mechanized corps should be made by the army commander, who by virtue of his position, possessed a broader operational perspective.[171] In this regard, they were undoubtedly correct in asserting that the army commander's operational needs must take precedence over the corps commander's purely tactical considerations.

On December 31 Timoshenko closed the conference with a major address, during which he summed up the proceedings and laid out his vision for the army's future development. For better or worse, the views he expressed became part of the Red Army's operational canon, to be consulted by commanders and staff officers in planning and conducting operations.

Timoshenko began his remarks with an examination of the army's tactical-operational defensive views. He rejected outright the notion that the military events of 1939–40 had revealed a defensive "crisis." He correctly pointed out that neither in Poland nor in France did the Wehrmacht encounter a defense worthy of the name. In Poland a fixed defense had not existed, whereas in France the Germans had simply outflanked the Maginot Line; nor was the hastily constructed Weygand Line much of a barrier. However, the defender could restore something of a balance by ensuring that his defensive arrangements were deeply echeloned and liberally reinforced with reserves and antitank and other units.[172]

Timoshenko discarded the previous distinction between "stubborn" and "mobile" defense, replacing them with the more precise terms "maneuver" and "positional." However, he devoted most of his remarks to the latter. This was a serious oversight, as events were to show, and the defense commissar's one-sided approach was no doubt influenced by his encounter with the "Mannerheim Line" in 1940. His erroneous fixation with the peculiar experience of the Finnish war was further highlighted by his remarks elsewhere that modern defense must be first of all antiartillery in orientation, and only then antitank. This view did much to negate the work of earlier theorists who had correctly identified the massed tank attack as the greatest threat.[173]

Timoshenko's examination of the army in a defensive operation broke no new ground and was mainly a recapitulation of those expressed earlier. The army defensive area, according to this scheme, would consist of the following: a forward operational obstacle zone, a tactical defense zone, and an operational defense zone. The first would be lightly held by the army's organic mobile units, or those specially allocated for this purpose by the front command.[174]

The tactical defense zone, according to Timoshenko, might be of two types. The first, or more traditional, variety included a security zone of 10 to 15 kilometers in depth. This zone would be manned by small units that, relying on a system of obstacles, would exhaust and slow down the attack and gain time for the defense. The bulk of the army's forces would be deployed along the tactical zone's main line of resistance, which extended back another 8 to 10 kilometers. These forces had the task of stopping the enemy attack. Behind this belt stood the tactical zone's second defensive line. This area housed the corps' reserves, which were to halt any breakthrough by the enemy's mechanized force and to spearhead any counterattacks.[175]

Another variation involved breaking the tactical defense zone into forward and main defensive positions, respectively. The first would extend 2 to 2.5 kilometers in depth and contain one-quarter to one-third of the army's forces. These were to halt the enemy attack or, failing that, fall back on the main defensive position, where the bulk of the army's forces were deployed. Behind this lay another two positions, which were occupied by the army's reserves.[176]

Timoshenko maintained that this variant "fully meets the demands of modern war" and has much in common with Khozin's proposals presented earlier in the week. And while the defense commissar's views on this score were motivated by the understandable desire to prevent the troops in the tactical zone's forward areas from being decimated by the attacker's artillery fire, once again the war with Finland led Timoshenko to draw the wrong conclusions.[177] Along the Karelian Isthmus it was the Red Army that had employed massed artillery to break the Finns' resistance. The Germans were planning to fight another kind of war entirely.

Behind either of the two tactical zones lay the operational defense zone. This area included the army's reserves, defending behind a network of artificial obstacles and antitank areas. These forces, which might be further strengthened with ARGK antitank units, were to halt any attack by large enemy mechanized forces that had managed to break through the tactical zone.[178]

Timoshenko's army in a defensive operation was to occupy a front of 80 to 100 kilometers in width and 50 to 60 kilometers in depth, not counting the forward obstacle zone. The army would dispose of ten to twelve divisions, enabling each to hold a frontage of 6 to 10 kilometers along the main sectors and 12 to 16 kilometers along secondary ones. The army might also be reinforced with ARGK artillery and mortar units, a brigade or two of tanks, an air division, and chemical troops.[179]

Timoshenko was on firmer and more congenial ground in his remarks on the conduct of the army offensive operation. However, he was forced to admit that the stock of a single army had fallen considerably over the years. Now, in an era of extended and continuous fronts, even the powerful shock army had lost much of its former independence and could achieve significant operational results only in conjunction with other armies as part of a larger front effort. The only exceptions, he stated, were to be found in such far-removed theaters as the Far East, Central Asia, and the Middle East, where the vast expanses involved and the absence of a continuous front would enable the army to reassert itself and gain a decision using its own resources.[180]

The defense commissar's ideal shock army differed little in strength and purpose from what previous speakers had proposed. The army would include fourteen to eighteen rifle divisions, ten to twelve ARGK artillery regiments, six to eight tank brigades, two to three air divisions, and a mobile group. The latter would presumably include at least one mechanized corps and perhaps a cavalry corps, as well as smaller motorized units. Such an accumulation of force, it was calculated, would enable the shock army to launch its main attack along a front of 20 to 30 kilometers and be capable of penetrating some 100 to 120 kilometers in depth. The army was expected to advance at an average rate of 10 to 15 kilometers per day, while the mobile group might achieve rates as high as 40 to 50 kilometers.[181]

But it was the breakthrough phase that determined the operation's success or failure and, as always, generated the most speculation. Timoshenko posited two variations of this attack, which were nothing more than simplified versions of the proposals put forward two days earlier by Pavlov and his colleagues.

The first involved an attack against a well-entrenched defender, or one whose position ran through an area difficult for tanks to traverse. According to this scenario, the army's rifle units, backed by a powerful echelon of infantry support tanks, would break through the enemy's tactical defense in the traditional manner. This would be followed by the mobile group's commitment for the exploitation drive. However, Timoshenko particularly favored the second variant, which posited an attack against an enemy occupying a poor defensive position. In this case, the army commander would forgo the standard echelonment of efforts in favor of the immediate commitment of his mechanized forces. These would pierce the defender's position on their own, followed immediately by the drive to the rear.[182]

The shock army's overall attack might also take one of several forms. Timoshenko believed that the most likely of these would involve a blow launched along the center of the army's front, or from one of its wings, followed by the commitment of the mobile group into the breach. Another foresaw a situation in which the army consisted entirely of shock corps. These would attack along a narrow front, with the subsequent breakthrough exploited by the mobile group. Another, exceptional, case would involve converging attacks launched along the army's wings. A single mobile group would then be committed into one of the breakthrough zones, followed by the encirclement of the defending force.[183]

Timoshenko had a much higher regard for the front operation, which he hailed as the pinnacle of modern operational art. At the same time, he moved to redefine the front operation's scope downward from its previous strategic designation to one he classified as "operational-strategic."[184] This was an important terminological step in the gradual evolution of the front from a strategic instance to one that pursued purely operational goals. That this was not an entirely straightforward process is shown by the creation of just three fronts (Northwestern, Western, and Southwestern) at the beginning of the war. Each of these fronts corresponded to a separate theater of military activities, having obvious strategic responsibilities. However, with the lengthening of the front and the corresponding growth in the number of front commands, the front at last arrived at its true operational designation.

Timoshenko did not assign the front any concrete strength norms, as these would vary greatly in accordance with its mission. Suffice it to say that the front was to be supplied with the necessary resources, in the form of one or more shock armies and units from the ARGK reserve, to enable it to undertake major offensive operations. The defense commissar stated that the front might be called upon to conduct an offensive along a front 80 to 300 kilometers in breadth, although the shock armies' actual breakthrough zones would be much narrower. The front must also be prepared to conduct an operation to a depth of 60 to 250 kilometers and, in the case of a series of consecutive operations, "significantly more."[185]

The type of maneuver employed in a front offensive operation would also vary greatly. The first involved a concentrated blow by several shock armies along a narrow sector of the front, followed by the commitment of the front's mobile group into the breach, which had much in common with the Germans' March 1918 offensive in France. This maneuver had the advantage of ensuring a devastating initial blow. Among its many disadvantages, however, were that such a narrowly focused effort could expect to tie down only a small portion of the enemy's forces, thus making it easy for him to transfer forces from the quiet sectors. At the same time, such a narrow concentration of force would make it more difficult to supply the attacker.[186]

The second approach involved a simultaneous attack along a broad front by several shock armies, followed by the commitment of the front's mobile group along one of the breakthrough zones. Such a maneuver held out the promise of engaging and defeating a large enemy force at a single blow, to the point where even the defender's strategic reserves would not be able to restore the situation. This form had been used with decisive success during the Germans' June 1940 offensive along the Somme-Aisne position. Timoshenko warned, however, that such an operation must be supported by a well-developed transportation network, lest it collapse because of its own supply difficulties.[187]

The third alternative foresaw the launching of several army operations along widely separated breakthrough zones, following the example of Brusilov's 1916 offensive. In each case, the breakthrough would be followed by the commitment of the respective shock armies' mobile groups. These would then race into the enemy's operational depth to encircle his units still at the front. This maneuver had much to recommend itself to Soviet planners, especially because it required the least-developed transportation system to support it.[188]

Timoshenko also raised the possibility of conducting two or more such operations simultaneously in order to inflict a strategic defeat on the defender.[189] The Soviet command would eventually come to heed this advice, and the employment of one or more of these methods became the hallmark of the Red Army's operational practice during World War II.

Most of the conference participants returned to their duties after hearing Timoshenko's closing remarks. A small group of senior officers remained behind, however, to take part in two operational-strategic war games in early January. These games, conducted with an eye toward testing the high command's response to an invasion from the west, offer a fascinating insight into the Red Army's ambitions and illusions during the final peacetime months.

Both games were based on the premise of a war against an enemy coalition, collectively referred to as the "western," or "blue," powers. These represented the

Soviet Union's most likely enemies in a future war—Germany, Finland, Hungary, and Romania. According to this scenario, these powers had launched an attack against the "reds," or "easterners," along the entire length of the latter's western frontier.

The primary assumption underlying both games was that the "blues" would make their main effort in the south, where they had concentrated 140 to 150 divisions. The enemy would also make a supporting attack with up to 60 divisions in the area north of Brest, while a smaller effort would be made against Leningrad.[190] Naval operations would also be conducted in the Baltic and Black Seas along the "reds'" maritime flanks.

This was a serious mistake and sharply at variance with the Axis forces' eventual deployment in June 1941. The driving force behind this assumption was Stalin's conviction that the Germans would deliver their main blow in the area south of the Pripyat Marshes, in order to seize Ukraine's rich industrial and agricultural areas.[191] As a Marxist and a military dilettante, Stalin was inclined to give priority to purely economic factors, often at the expense of military ones.

Other, more personal, considerations may also have influenced the decision to orient the main axis of the enemy advance to the south. One well-informed chronicler ascribed this to the influence of so many officers (Timoshenko, Zhukov, and General Lieutenant Vatutin, the deputy chief of the General Staff) from the Kiev Special Military District who occupied important posts in the army's central apparatus.[192]

Another mistake was the games' working assumption that a Soviet division was one and a half times as strong as its enemy counterpart. This was evidently supposed to make more palatable the enemy's initial superiority, which he had achieved by preempting the "easterners'" deployment and striking first.[193] However comforting this assumption may have been to the Soviet players, it was wildly at odds with reality. As the war would soon reveal, a German army was usually the equivalent of a Soviet front, a corps equal to an army, a division as strong as a corps, and so on.

The first and most instructive of these exercises was played out in the area to the north of the Pripyat Marshes. According to this scenario, the enemy's Northeastern Front (Eighth, Ninth, and Tenth Armies), commanded by Zhukov, had attacked on July 15, 1941. Zhukov's forces, which numbered fifty-nine infantry divisions, plus 3,516 tanks and 3,336 aircraft, had the mission of defeating the Soviet covering armies and advancing by mid-August to the line Riga–Dvinsk–Baranovichi.[194] Significantly enough, the game did not foresee an enemy attack from along the Brest-Baranovichi axis, which actually happened six months later.

He was opposed by Pavlov's Northwestern Front (First, Fourteenth, Ninth, Nineteenth, and Twenty-seventh Armies, plus a cavalry-mechanized group), which numbered fifty-one rifle divisions, 8,811 tanks, and 5,652 aircraft. To the south of the Pripyat Marshes, Shtern commanded the Southwestern Front.[195]

Not surprisingly, this scenario had the Soviets halting the enemy advance well short of its objectives, and Zhukov was forced to fall back on his frontier fortifications by August 1. Farther to the north, a Finnish attempt to take Leningrad was also repulsed. The Northwestern Front, having thus restored the situation, was then to eliminate the enemy's salient around Suwalki before launching a general offensive. This attack, spearheaded by the front's cavalry-mechanized group, was to reach the lower Vistula by early September, trapping sizable enemy forces in East Prussia. Zhukov, in turn, was to await reinforcements before resuming his attack. On August 10 he was to launch a counteroffensive in conjunction with the neighboring Eastern Front with the aim of achieving his original objectives by September 5.[196]

However, at the very moment when the opposing commanders were finally allowed to use their creative judgment in pursuing their objectives, the historical narrative becomes strangely reticent and, in places, downright contradictory. For example, M. V. Zakharov merely states that the "westerners" won the operation, adding elsewhere that the game "abounded in dramatic episodes for the eastern side," which were very similar to those that unfolded in June 1941.[197] Zhukov repeats this phrase nearly verbatim in his memoirs but fails to provide any details of the game's actual conduct.[198]

The second war game featured an attack by two western fronts against Soviet forces south of the Pripyat Marshes. Here the roles of attacker and defender were reversed, with Pavlov commanding the enemy's Southeastern Front (Eighteenth, Sixteenth, Fourteenth, and Third Armies), which contained thirty-seven infantry divisions, 739 tanks, and 2,170 aircraft. To his right was General Lieutenant Kuznetsov's Southern Front (Fifth, Sixth, Fourth, and Second Armies), with forty-eight infantry divisions, 2,475 tanks, and 2,286 planes. Facing this force were the troops of Zhukov's Southwestern Front (Third, Twenty-fifth, Seventh, Ninth, Eleventh, Thirteenth, and Fifteenth Armies, plus a cavalry-mechanized army), which numbered eighty-one rifle divisions, 8,841 tanks, and 5,791 airplanes.[199] Once again, Soviet strength, particularly in tanks, was overwhelming.

According to this scenario, the "western" forces had attacked on August 2, 1941, upon completing their concentration and deployment along the frontier. The Southern Front made its main effort from the Chernovtsy area toward Ternopol' and Proskurov, with a secondary attack due east across the Prut River. The Southeastern Front sought to link up with this force, which would trap sizable Soviet forces in the area around L'vov. By September 10 both fronts were to have reached the line Sarny-Shepetovka-Vinnitsa-Odessa. However, the Southern Front could do little more than take Chernovtsy and seize a few small bridgeheads across the Dnestr, and it made no progress at all toward Kishinev. Things went much more badly for the enemy in Volhynya, where Pavlov's forces suffered heavy losses in the frontier battles. By August 8 the "blue" forces had been thrown back to a line running southwest from Brest along the Vistula, to the Carpathian Mountains at Grybow.[200]

At this point, as in the previous game, the umpires intervened to assign the two sides their respective strategic tasks. According to these orders, the Southern

Front was to renew its offensive in the direction of Ternopol' and Proskurov. To its left the Southeastern Front's Third Army would launch a converging attack toward Stryi. The Southeastern Front's center would continue to defend along the Dunajec, while the left wing would prepare an attack from the Warsaw-Siedlce area.[201]

However, if these objectives merely represent attempts to put the "western" offensive back on track, the tasks assigned to the Soviet forces were truly breathtaking in their scope. Zhukov's right-wing armies were to follow up their success in southern Poland by driving on Crakow and Katowice. His center armies had the most far-reaching assignment of all. Here the front's cavalry-mechanized army was to spearhead an attack through the Carpathians and onto the Hungarian Plain, taking Budapest. This would also split the enemy coalition into nonsupporting halves. Finally, Zhukov's left-wing armies were to pinch off the enemy salient north of Botosani, before driving south to Bucharest and the Romanian oil fields at Ploesti. All of these objectives were to be reached by October 16, 1941.[202] How ironic, then, to recall that on this very date the German forces stood at the approaches to Moscow.

To the north of the marshes the "reds'" Western Front was to attack on August 11, with the goal of taking Warsaw and closing to the Vistula as far west as Plock by September 9.[203] Presumably, this would be in conjunction with a more successful offensive by the neighboring Northwestern Front than had been the case in the previous game.

Unfortunately, there is no way of knowing the outcome of this grandiose design because the literature pertaining to the second war game is almost nonexistent. However, given the scenario laid down by the game's umpires, as well as the limited capabilities of the two "western" commanders, it is unlikely that the Soviets were defeated.[204]

However, it is also highly unlikely that the Southwestern Front was able to achieve all the ambitious goals assigned to it. One reason was that the front, with approximately 100 rifle, tank, mechanized, and cavalry divisions, was probably too large for one man to control effectively. It is also likely that a successful breakthrough along three such widely separated axes would have hopelessly exacerbated existing problems of command and control. Another negative factor was the multiplicity of objectives, which were beyond the capabilities of a single front. It is clear from the objectives the game's umpires assigned Zhukov that they continued to regard the front as a strategic body. In fact, in this case the front was made responsible for the entire southwestern theater of military activities. In retrospect, it would have been wiser to have broken up this gigantic effort among three fronts, with each being responsible for a single task. Finally, even a successful attack launched to such depths would have quickly broken down in a mountainous region with a notoriously poor transportation system.

Whatever the outcome of the second game, there is no doubt that Stalin was highly dissatisfied with the results of the first, for which he harshly criticized

Pavlov, although the latter remained at his post.[205] Meretskov, however, was not so fortunate and was removed as chief of staff, following his unsuccessful analysis of the war games.[206] He was replaced by Zhukov, whose transfer to Moscow set off a major reshuffle among the Soviet high command. Kirponos was sent from Leningrad to take Zhukov's place as commander of the Kiev Special Military District, and Popov was recalled from the Far East to take over the Leningrad Military District. Other transfers were General Colonel Apanasenko to command the Far Eastern Front, General Lieutenant Konev to command the North Caucasus Military District, Gen. Lt. P. A. Kurochkin to command the Trans-Baikal Military District, and Gen. Maj. S. G. Trofimenko to command the Central Asian Military District. However, the effect of these transfers, particularly in Kiev and in the General Staff, was to further weaken the Red Army as it approached its moment of truth.

In retrospect, Stalin had every right to be dissatisfied with his army's performance, although, as supreme ruler, he must bear the lion's share of the blame for the disasters that followed. The German onslaught that began on June 22, 1941, caught the Soviets completely off guard and came close to destroying the Red Army. By the autumn of 1941 the Germans had conquered the Baltic States, Belorussia, and almost all of Ukraine and the Crimea, and they came tantalizingly close to capturing Moscow, before being defeated. A renewed assault the following year brought them to the lower Volga and the Caspian Sea, where they were once again beaten back, this time for good.

Thus having survived the initial shock, the Soviets were able to recover and wage the kind of war that suited them. This turn of events had as much to do with what operational art is as what it is not. Operational art should never be confused with the German practice of blitzkrieg, with which it is often mistakenly coupled. While both concepts have a number of battlefield elements in common, blitzkrieg is, at heart, a *strategy* for waging war, while operational art is subordinated to strategy. As practiced, blitzkrieg was a military-economic means for achieving German hegemony in western and central Europe. Blitzkrieg is, fundamentally, war on the cheap, a perfect tool for subduing such small and medium-sized countries as Poland, Belgium, Yugoslavia, and even France. As long as Germany's smaller continental opponents could be individually dispatched in a single lightning campaign, the system worked perfectly. However, once such continental or transcontinental powers as the Soviet Union and the United States entered the contest, Germany, with its smaller industrial and population base, was doomed. This was precisely the situation Hitler found himself in from the end of 1941 onward.

Operational art, on the other hand, was closely tied to a series of strategic assumptions arrived at by the Soviets in the 1920s, that the next war would be a protracted struggle demanding every last ounce of the nation's strength. If the Soviets were ultimately mistaken that a world capitalist coalition would be directed against them, they were certainly correct in predicting the war's fundamental nature and shaped their operational art accordingly. Thus the beginning of the war found them, for all their manifold defects, politically, militarily, and economically better prepared than the Germans for waging a prolonged war. The Soviets could thus afford to lose millions of men and hundreds of thousands of square kilometers of territory, while the Germans had to win every time, or not at all. Operational art, with its emphasis on a continuing series of partial and consecutive victories, leading to an ultimate strategic result, was thus well suited to meet the rigors of the coming war.

Conclusion

Operational art's thirty-seven-year journey from the Russo-Japanese War to the eve of the German invasion covers an exciting era of political, technological, and theoretical change. From an infant discipline that struggled long and hard to free itself from the tutelage of its senior partners, strategy and tactics, by the start of the Great Patriotic War operational art had succeeded in becoming a recognized component of the country's military art. During the next four years it was to prove itself worthy on more than one occasion during some of the Red Army's most desperate campaigns.

In evaluating the late-czarist army's views on operations, certain dominant themes emerge that, taken together, form a recognizable, if nascent, body of operational thought. One of the most important of these involves the semantic evolution of the operation and its place in the hierarchy of military art. Operations during these years were usually viewed as a subset and tool of strategy for achieving strategic objectives in a theater of military activities. Indeed, important areas of contemporary operational art, such as front operations, were seen as falling into the strategic realm, a trend that continued well into the 1930s. Nevertheless, important theoretical distinctions had been made, and these served as the point of departure when the debate resumed in the 1920s.

Not the least of that decade's accomplishments was the Red Army's liberation of operational art from the spheres of strategy and tactics and its recognition as a separate theoretical entity. The Soviets inherited the czarist army's terminological confusion about the place of operations in the hierarchy of military art, and this was reflected initially in the army's academic offerings. However, by the mid-1920s the situation had begun to change, and the current ranking of strategy, operational art, and tactics came into being. This was due primarily to the efforts of Svechin and such younger former officers as Varfolomeev, whose theoretical influence in the Red Army was considerable, despite their less than auspicious social origins.

Easily the most observable line of continuity between the imperial army and its successor is the persistent notion of the front (group of armies) level of command, in both theory and practice. The growth of modern armies and the vast distances anticipated in a war in eastern Europe compelled the Russians to adopt this form long before anyone else. Thus Leer's ruminations on a group of armies operating in a single theater of military activities found concrete expression in the Russian army's 1900 war plan, which envisaged the creation of two fronts in the western theater of war. Kuropatkin's armies in Manchuria constituted a front in everything but name, while such postwar theorists as Neznamov and Mikhnevich refined the concept and its commander's responsibilities in relation to its subordinate armies and the high command. Thus was born the Stavka-front-army system of subordination, which remained a fixture of Soviet operational organization for many years.

However, a key point of terminological ambiguity continued to dog the notion of the front for many years afterward. This confusion, which had its origins in the imperial army's designation of the front as a force capable of performing strategic missions, was reflected in the army's 1900 and succeeding war plans, in which each front was given the strategic task of defeating a member of the enemy coalition. This system was adopted virtually without change during the civil war, which saw the Red Army conduct a number of single-front operations along a theater of military activities, or two fronts operating in tandem in a single theater of war. The idea of the front as a strategic unit persisted well into the 1930s, which meant that for many years the army remained the sole operational formation. However, by the end of the decade the situation had changed, so that by the time the USSR entered World War II the front instance of command had become firmly entrenched as a key aspect of operational art.

Another, if more tenuous, area of continuity between the two armies lay in the area of conducting consecutive operations. This possibility had been raised as early as 1911 by Neznamov, who, unfortunately, devoted little space to the subject other than emphasizing the likely need for them. It fell, instead, to the Red Army, which had the benefit of the examples of 1914 and 1918–20 to guide it, to devise a method for conducting extended operations and to determine what, if any, were the inherent limits of such operations. The result of this work was the theory of consecutive operations, in which one operation flows from and succeeds another in pursuit of a larger strategic objective. In this area, as in so many others, such former officers as Svechin, Varfolomeev, Movchin, and Triandafillov played a crucial role.

Another of the imperial army's legacies had less to do with a particular tradition than with the vagaries of conducting operations along the extended fronts of eastern Europe. This concerned the efficacy of launching major offensive efforts along sufficiently broad frontages, in pursuit of a decisive result. Most of this experience was gained firsthand, notably during Brusilov's 1916 offensive, which owed part of its success to the front commander's novel expedient of launching several, smaller supporting attacks along widely separated sectors of the front in support of a more-concentrated main effort elsewhere. The method was adopted by the Red Army out of sheer necessity during the civil war, given the extended fronts of that conflict. Postwar theorists developed this idea further in a number of historical studies that supported the idea of launching broad-front offensives.

However, despite the evidence of a good deal of theoretical and practical continuity between the two armies, there are significant areas of divergence as well. Most of these have to do with the Red Army's ideological and technical composition.

The first quality set the Red Army decisively apart from its imperial predecessor, which was fairly apolitical. The ideological absolutes and political controls imposed on the army created an ethos not disposed to recognize limits, and which could hardly have failed to have an impact on the nature of its military operations. Consequently, the political-military belief that the communist ideology represented the most dynamic historical forces naturally inclined the army toward offensive operations.

Whatever one may think of the Bolsheviks' political goals, there is nonetheless a refreshing vitality in the Red Army's conduct of civil war operations. This stands in marked contrast to the Russian army's disgraceful performance in Manchuria and throughout much of World War I, and is evidence of the czarist regime's overall decline as much as of any specifically military shortcomings. However, the Red Army's laudable preference for offensive operations was purchased at what later proved to be a stiff price. It is hardly surprising, given these muscular attitudes, that the army's study of defensive operations was seriously neglected, which carried over into all aspects of its post–civil war strategy, operational art, and tactics.

The other dissonant note is the Red Army's technical makeover in the 1930s, which also set it apart from its predecessor. The army, in recasting itself as a modern force, thus broke decisively with the czarist tradition of technological inferiority vis-à-vis the West. By 1936–37 this process was substantially completed. The Red Army had become the equal of any of the major European powers, and its military might easily surpassed that of Nazi Germany, whose rearmament program was barely under way. This quantitative growth ushered in equally impressive changes in the armed forces' organization and saw the introduction of such operationally significant formations as mechanized brigades and corps, which had no counterpart in the czarist army.

The Red Army's transformation, from a force not markedly different in technical prowess from its czarist predecessor to a truly modern army, also had profound effects on the development of its operational theory. This was most evident in what later became known as the deep operation, which sought to exploit the striking power and mobility of modern weapons to resolve the problem of breaking through a solid defensive front.

The appearance of a new, mechanized Red Army also heralded the breakdown of the old imperial-Soviet synthesis, as personified by the older military specialists, and their replacement by younger, more self-consciously Soviet, cadres. For the most part, it fell to such younger specialists as Tukhachevskii, Varfolomeev, and Shilovskii, as well as such wholly Soviet products as Isserson, to rework the army's operational theory in accordance with its new capabilities. Likewise, while Soviet operational theory of the mid-1930s retained many features that linked it to the past, it was at the same time heavily obliged to exclusively Soviet circumstances for its birth and development.

The Soviets came dangerously close to throwing this heritage away during the military purge of 1937–38, which saw the destruction of practically all the old specialist cadres, as well as a good proportion of the nonspecialist ranks, and their replacement with officers who, with a few exceptions, were almost entirely unaware of the old army's theoretical heritage. In a typical piece of Stalinist guilt by association, operational art's more progressive tenets became suspects when their creators were "unmasked" as "enemies of the people." It was only through the efforts of a few brave individuals that such concepts as the deep operation survived at all. Prodded by the spectacular German successes of 1939–40, the Soviets spent the last year before the war desperately trying to relearn what they had so foolishly discarded.

Thus in spite of the ideological and technological dissimilarities dividing the czarist and Soviet systems, the military-theoretical continuity between the two is striking. This is not accidental, and it speaks to a greater imperative at work in the development of operational art than the transient interests of a particular regime. And while the imperial and Soviet military were influenced by foreign developments, their operational theory was much more than an unthinking copy of Western models, as is sometimes maintained. Rather, operational art should be viewed as a distinctly Russian response to the problems of conducting war in the twentieth century.

Notes

INTRODUCTION

1. W. D. Jacobs, "The Art of Operations," *Army* 12, no. 4 (1961): 64.

2. Department of the Army, *FM 100-5: Operations* (Washington, D.C., 1982); Department of the Army, *FM 100-5: Operations* (Washington, D.C., 1986); Department of the Army, *FM 100-5: Operations* (Washington, D.C., 1993). See also C. Dick, "Soviet Operational Art. Part 1: The Fruits of Experience," *International Defence Review* 21, no. 7 (1988): 755–61; and his "Soviet Operational Art. Part 2: The Keys to Victory," *International Defence Review* 21, no. 8 (1988): 901–8.

3. B. N. Morozov, ed., *Kratkii Slovar' Operativno-Takticheskikh i Obshchevoenykh Slov (Terminov)* (Moscow, 1958), 188.

1. TWILIGHT OF EMPIRE

1. V. T. Chuntulov, *Ekonomicheskaya Istoriya SSSR* (Moscow, 1969), 156, 230; V. T. Chuntulov, *Istoriya Narodnogo Khozyaistva SSSR. Dooktyabrskii Period* (Kiev, 1964), 175.

2. N. N. Golovin, *Voennye Usiliya Rossii v Mirovoi Voine* (Paris, 1939), 1:82, 150.

3. C. von Clausewitz, *On War*, ed. and trans. M. Howard and P. Paret (Princeton, N.J., 1984), 258.

4. A. A. Humphreys, *The Virginia Campaign of '64 and '65* (New York, 1885), 118. In this vein, one author has made an interesting argument for the appearance of the operation as far back as the American Civil War. See J. Schneider, "The Loose Marble—and the Origins of Operational Art," *Parameters* 19, no. 1 (1989): 85–99.

5. I. Marievskii, "Stanovlenie i Razvitie Teorii Operativnogo Iskusstva," *Voenno-Istoricheskii Zhurnal* (hereafter *V-IZh*), no. 3 (1962): 28.

6. Morozov, *Kratkii Slovar'*, 189.

7. N. A. Levitskii, *Russko-Yaponskaya Voina 1904–1905 gg.*, 3d ed. (Moscow, 1938), 65.

8. V. A. Apushkin, *Russko-Yaponskaya Voina, 1904–1905 g.* (Moscow, 1910), 133.
9. Levitskii, *Russko-Yaponskaya Voina,* 167, 169.
10. I. I. Rostunov, ed., *Istoriya Russko-Yaponskoi Voiny 1904–1905 gg.* (Moscow, 1977), 285.
11. Quoted in S. M. Belitskii, *Strategicheskie Rezervy* (Moscow and Leningrad, 1930), 44.
12. A. A. Kersnovskii, *Istoriya Russkoi Armii* (Belgrade, 1933–38), 3:575.
13. I. Hamilton, *A Staff Officer's Scrap Book During the Russo-Japanese War* (London, 1905–7), 2:185.
14. Levitskii, *Russko-Yaponskaya Voina,* 182.
15. V. A. Cheremisov, *Russko-Yaponskaya Voina 1904–1905 Goda,* 2d ed. (St. Petersburg, 1909), 163.
16. A. A. Svechin, *Evolyutsiya Voennogo Iskusstva* (Moscow and Leningrad, 1927–28), 2:508.
17. Levitskii, *Russko-Yaponskaya Voina,* 238–40.
18. M. Carver, *Twentieth-Century Warriors* (London, 1987), 333, 336–38.
19. Levitskii, *Russko-Yaponskaya Voina,* 252.
20. Cheremisov, *Russko-Yaponskaya Voina,* 242.
21. Levitskii, *Russko-Yaponskaya Voina,* 263.
22. Ibid., 292.
23. Rostunov, *Istoriya Russko-Yaponskoi,* 346.
24. Levitskii, *Russko-Yaponskaya Voina,* 286.
25. N. Stone, *The Eastern Front, 1914–1917* (New York, 1975), 17.
26. A. A. Neznamov, *Sovremennaya Voina: Deistviya Polevoi Armii* (St. Petersburg, 1911), v.
27. A. A. Samoilo, *Dve Zhizni* (Moscow, 1958), 58.
28. G. A. Leer, *Strategiya (Taktika Teatra Voennykh Deistvii),* 4th ed. (St. Petersburg, 1885–87), 1:1.
29. Ibid., 10.
30. Ibid., 6–10.
31. G. A. Leer, *Strategiya (Taktika Teatra Voennykh Deistvii),* 6th ed. (St. Petersburg, 1898), 1:4.
32. Leer, *Strategiya,* 4th ed., 2:13–14.
33. Ibid., 21.
34. Ibid.
35. P. I. Izmest'ev and E. E. Messner, comps., *Konspekt Strategii* (St. Petersburg, 1899), 12, 53–54.
36. Samoilo, *Dve Zhizni,* 63–64.
37. A. A. Kersnovskii, *Filosofiya Voiny* (Belgrade, 1939), 31–32.
38. Kersnovskii, *Istoriya,* 3:608.
39. Ibid.
40. Ibid., 609.
41. Samoilo, *Dve Zhizni,* 61; A. I. Denikin, *Put' Russkogo Ofitsera* (New York, 1953), 87–89.
42. B. M. Shaposhnikov, *Vospominaniya. Voenno-Nauchnye Trudy* (Moscow, 1974), 135.
43. I. I. Vatsetis, *O Voennoi Doktrine Budushchego* (Moscow, 1923), 100–101.

44. E. E. Messner, et al., *Rossiiskie Ofitsery* (Buenos Aires, 1959), 38.
45. Shaposhnikov, *Vospominaniya*, 143.
46. B. V. Gerua, *Vospominaniya o Moei Zhizni* (Paris, 1969), 1:252.
47. Vatsetis, *O Voennoi Doktrine*, 97.
48. For more about Neznamov, see A. Ageev, "Voenno-Teoreticheskoe Nasledie A. A. Neznamova," *V-IZh* no. 11 (1983): 84–89.
49. Neznamov, *Sovremennaya Voina*, 14.
50. Ibid., 15.
51. Ibid., 12–13; Leer, *Strategiya*, 4th ed., 1:23.
52. Neznamov, *Sovremennaya Voina*, 136.
53. Ibid., 137, 155.
54. Ibid., 21–22.
55. Neznamov was known at the academy as a devotee of the German school of operations. See Shaposhnikov, *Vospominaniya*, 144. Overall, the influence of German military thinking at the academy seems to have been considerable. See Vatsetis, *O Voennoi Doktrine*, 98.
56. Neznamov, *Sovremennaya Voina*, 21, 198–99.
57. Ibid., 178.
58. Ibid., 184.
59. Ibid., 24, 62.
60. Ibid., 194.
61. Ibid., 194.
62. Ibid., 196.
63. Ibid., 197.
64. Ibid., 10.
65. Ibid., 12.
66. Shaposhnikov, *Vospominaniya*, 145.
67. N. P. Mikhnevich, *Strategiya*, 3d ed. (St. Petersburg, 1911), 1:152.
68. N. P. Mikhnevich, *Osnovy Strategii* (St. Petersburg, 1913), 127.
69. Mikhnevich, *Strategiya*, 1:178, 180.
70. Mikhnevich, *Osnovy*, 73.
71. Ibid., 246.
72. A. G. Elchaninov, *Strategiya* (St. Petersburg, 1912), 201, 206–7, 387.
73. Ibid., 309.
74. General'nyi Shtab, *Polozhenie o Polevom Upravlenii Voisk v Voennoe Vremya* (St. Petersburg, 1914), 1, 3–4, 6.
75. Ibid., 1.
76. Ibid., 11.
77. Ibid., 54.
78. A. A. Brusilov, *Moi Vospominaniya* (Riga, 1929), 79.
79. Samoilo, *Dve Zhizni*, 140.
80. Yu. N. Danilov, *Rossiya v Mirovoi Voine 1914–1915 g.g.* (Berlin, 1924), 32.
81. N. B. Pavlovich, ed., *Flot v Pervoi Mirovoi Voine* (Moscow, 1964), 2:10.
82. Kersnovskii, *Istoriya*, 3:626–27.
83. A. M. Zaionchkovskii, *Podgotovka Rossii k Imperialisticheskoi Voine* (Moscow, 1926), 94.
84. Ibid., 101.

85. A. M. Zaionchkovskii, *Mirovaya Voina 1914–1918,* 2d ed. (Moscow, 1931), 30.
86. Kersonvskii, *Istoriya,* 3:610–11.
87. Zaionchkovskii, *Mirovaya,* 7, 21.
88. General'nyi Shtab RKKA, *Vostochno-Prusskaya Operatsiya.* This is part of the series *Sbornik Dokumentov Mirovoi Imperialisticheskoi Voiny na Russkom Fronte (1914–1917 gg.)* (Moscow, 1938–41), 61–62. This volume is hereafter referred to as *Vostochno-Prusskaya.*
89. Ibid., 64–65, 68.
90. Ibid., 63–64, 69.
91. Zaionchkovskii, *Podgotovka,* 213–22.
92. Ibid., 257–65.
93. V. A. Melikov, *Problema Strategicheskogo Razvertyvaniya po Opytu Mirovoi i Grazhdanskoi Voiny* (Moscow, 1935), 256.
94. Zaionchkovskii, *Podgotovka,* 124.
95. Ibid., 398–99.
96. Brusilov, *Moi Vospominaniya,* 64–66.
97. Yu. N. Danilov, *Velikii Knyaz' Nikolai Nikolaevich* (Paris, 1930), 123.
98. Morozov, *Kratkii Slovar',* 188.
99. A. I. Verkhovskii, *Na Trudnom Perevale* (Moscow, 1959), 26; B. Gourko, *Memoirs and Impressions of War and Revolution in Russia, 1914–1917* (London, 1918), 9–10.
100. *Vostochno-Prusskaya,* 12; I. I. Rostunov, ed., *Istoriya Pervoi Mirovoi Voiny, 1914–1918* (Moscow, 1975), 1:250, 252.
101. Zaionchkovskii, *Mirovaya,* 75–76.
102. *Vostochno-Prusskaya,* 146–47, 157.
103. Ibid., 263.
104. M. Hoffman, *War Diaries and Other Papers* (London, 1929), 2:35.
105. *Vostochno-Prusskaya,* 302.
106. Hoffman, *War Diaries,* 2:328.
107. *Vostochno-Prusskaya,* 332.
108. Ibid., 377–78.
109. N. N. Golovin, *Nachalo Voiny i Operatsii v Vostochnoi Prussii* (Prague, 1926; Paris, 1930, 1936–40), 408. This volume is part of the series *Iz Istorii Kampanii 1914 Goda na Russkom Fronte.*
110. Brusilov, *Moi Vospominaniya,* 67.
111. Ibid. Brusilov's views on Alekseev may well have been influenced by the diverging paths both men took during the Russian civil war. Alekseev was one of the early organizers of the White movement in south Russia before his death in 1918, while Brusilov was one of the most prominent czarist generals to offer his services to the Reds.
112. A. S. Beloi, *Galitsiiskaya Bitva* (Moscow and Leningrad, 1929), 54–56.
113. A. Kolenkovskii, *Manevrennyi Period Pervoi Mirovoi Imperialisticheskoi Voiny, 1914 g.* (Moscow, 1940), 81.
114. Beloi, *Galitsiiskaya Bitva,* 56.
115. Ibid., 54–55; Kolenkovskii, *Manevrennyi,* 81.
116. The army's wanderings are described in Stone, *Eastern Front,* 72–79.
117. Danilov, *Rossiya,* 158–59. The Russians' assumption was based on outdated intelligence of the Austro-Hungarians' mobilization plans. Once the leak was discovered, the Austro-Hungarian command changed its plans, although the Russians did not know this.

118. Zaionchkovskii, *Mirovaya,* 107.
119. Ibid., 126–27, 131.
120. Beloi, *Galitsiiskaya Bitva,* 353.
121. Kolenkovskii, *Manevrennyi,* 263–64; Zaionchkovskii, *Mirovaya,* 135.
122. Verkhovskii, *Na Trudnom,* 27–28.
123. Danilov, *Velikii,* 122–24.
124. Zaionchkovskii, *Mirovaya,* 182.
125. Golovin, *Voennye,* 2:139.
126. P. V. Cherkasov, ed., *Mirovaya Voina, 1914–1918. "Lutskii Proryv." Trudy i Materialy k Operatsii Yugo-Zapadnogo Fronta v Mae-Iyune 1916 Goda* (Moscow, 1924), 186.
127. A. Vol'pe, *Frontal'nyi Udar* (Moscow, 1931), 275–76.
128. Brusilov, *Moi Vospominaniya,* 106.
129. Ibid., 181–83.
130. Ibid., 186.
131. Vol'pe, *Frontal'nyi Udar,* 296.
132. Ibid.
133. Brusilov, *Moi Vospominaniya,* 196.
134. Zaionchkovskii, *Mirovaya,* 263.
135. E. von Falkenhayn, *General Headquarters 1914–1916 and Its Critical Decisions* (London, 1919), 246.
136. Brusilov, *Moi Vospominaniya,* 199.
137. E. Ludendorff, *My War Memoirs, 1914–1918* (London, 1919), 1:222.
138. Zaionchkovskii, *Mirovaya,* 267–68; Brusilov, *Moi Vospominaniya,* 199.
139. Zaionchkovskii, *Mirovaya,* 269.
140. Cherkasov, *Mirovaya,* 15.
141. Ludendorff, *My War Memoirs,* 1:226.
142. Cherkasov, *Mirovaya,* 8.
143. Falkenhayn, *General Headquarters,* 270.
144. Brusilov, *Moi Vospominaniya,* 210.
145. Vol'pe, *Frontal'nyi Udar,* 310.
146. Golovin, *Voennye,* 2:167.
147. Falkenhayn, *General Headquarters,* 250.
148. Brusilov, *Moi Vospominaniya,* 203. This is another instance in which Brusilov's postwar recollections may well have been colored by political considerations. Kaledin was another of the early organizers of the anti-Bolshevik movement in south Russia, before committing suicide in 1918.
149. Cherkasov, *Mirovaya,* 15.
150. A. Knox, *With the Russian Army, 1914–1917* (London, 1921) 2:648.

2. WARS WITHIN AND WITHOUT

1. D. H. Aldcroft, *The European Economy, 1914–1970* (London, 1978), 16.
2. Chuntulov, *Ekonomicheskaya,* 206, 214.
3. H. G. Wells, *Russia in the Shadows* (London, 1920), 11.
4. F. Nikonov, "Glavneishie Momenty Organizatsii Krasnoi Armii," in *Grazhdanskaya Voina v SSSR, 1918–1921,* ed. A. S. Bubnov, S. S. Kamenev, and R. P. Eideman (Moscow,

1928–30). Vol. 2, *Voennoe Iskusstvo Krasnoi Armii,* 50. M. N. Tukhachevskii was added as an editor to the third volume.

5. Ibid., 2:76.

6. Ibid., 87, 89.

7. V. I. Lenin, *Polnoe Sobranie Sochinenii,* 5th ed. (Moscow, 1958–65), 38:142; 43:242.

8. See E. Yaroslavskii, "Kak Vossozdat' Armiiu," *Izvestiya* (Moscow), June 15, 1918, 1–2; V. Sorin, "Komandiry i Komissary v Deistvuyushchei Armii," *Pravda* (Moscow), November 29, 1918, 2. For some pertinent remarks on the tensions between political rectitude and military professionalism in an earlier civil war, see B. Catton, *Mr. Lincoln's Army* (Garden City, N.Y., 1951), 204–13.

9. M. N. Tukhachevskii, *Izbrannye Proizvedeniya* (Moscow, 1964), 1:27–30.

10. L. D. Trotskii, *Kak Vooruzhalas' Revoliutsiya* (Moscow, 1923–25), 1:172–73.

11. M. D. Bonch-Bruevich, *Vsya Vlast' Sovetam* (Moscow, 1957), 284. The author, a former general-major, was one of the first high-ranking officers to serve in the Red Army. His brother was the veteran Bolshevik V. D. Bonch-Bruevich.

12. Brusilov, *Moi Vospominaniya,* 260.

13. One of these was Gen. Maj. A. I. Verkhovskii, a former war minister in the Provisional Government. He joined the Red Army in 1919 after spending several months in prison for plotting against the state. For an account of his "conversion," see *Na Trudnom,* 415–20.

14. Trotskii, *Kak Vooruzhalas',* 1:225; Lenin, *Polnoe,* 50:141.

15. The text of this decree is reprinted in Trotskii, *Kak Vooruzhalas',* 1:153. This was actually done in May 1919, during the Whites' first attempt to take Petrograd. See Bubnov, Kamenev, and Eideman, vol. 3, *Operativno-Strategicheskii Ocherk Boevykh Deistvii Krasnoi Armii,* 160.

16. L. D. Trotskii, *Stalin,* ed. and trans. C. Malamuth (New York, 1941), 315–16.

17. Bonch-Bruevich, *Vsya Vlast' Sovetam,* 283.

18. L. V. Nikulin, *Tukhachevskii* (Moscow, 1964), 43.

19. E. Shilovskii, "O Tekhnicheskoi Storone Upravleniya Armii v Grazhdanskuyu Voinu," *Voennaya Nauka i Revolyutsiya,* no. 2 (1922): 13–27.

20. V. Rapoport and Yu. Alexeev, *High Treason: Essays on the History of the Red Army, 1918–1938,* ed. V. Treml, trans. B. Adams (Durham, N.C., 1985), 128; A. Antonov-Ovseenko, *The Time of Stalin,* trans. G. Saunders (New York, 1981), 8. Although these authors cite no evidence for their claim, the incident was obliquely confirmed by Soviet sources during the dictator's lifetime. See E. Yaroslavskii, ed., *Vos'moi S"ezd RKP(b)* (Moscow, 1933), 148.

21. I. V. Stalin, *Sochineniya* (Moscow, 1946–52), 4:118, 124.

22. N. S. Khrushchev, *Khrushchev Remembers,* ed. and trans. S. Talbot (London, 1971), 18, 20.

23. Trotskii, *Stalin,* 289–90.

24. For a description of these events, see I. Kolesnichenko, "K Voprosu o Konflikte v Revvoensovete Yuzhnogo Fronta (Sentyabr'–Oktyabr' 1918 Goda)," *V-IZh,* no. 2 (1962): 39–47.

25. One Soviet historian has recently claimed that Voroshilov "maintained his prejudice and dislike of the old army's former officers and fully displayed these during the massive Stalinist repressions against the Red Army's command staff in 1937–38." See V. M. Ivanov, *Marshal M. N. Tukhachevskii* (Moscow, 1990), 32.

26. S. I. Gusev, *Grazhdanskaya Voina i Krasnaya Armiya* (Moscow and Leningrad, 1925), 214–15; S. I. Aralov, *Lenin vel Nas k Pobede* (Moscow, 1962), 99.

27. See S. M. Klyatskin, *Na Zashchite Oktyabrya* (Moscow, 1965), 353; Yu. I. Korablev, *V. I. Lenin i Zashchita Zavoevanii Velikogo Oktyabrya,* 2d ed. (Moscow, 1979), 280, 358, 426–27, 435, 444.

28. L. D. Trotskii, *Moya Zhizn'* (Berlin, 1930), 2:130, 141.

29. A. G. Kavtaradze, *Voennye Spetsialisty na Sluzhbe Respubliki Sovetov 1917–1920 gg.* (Moscow, 1988), 176. This source puts the exact figure at 73,311. This is indirectly supported by another source that calculates the Red Army's entire command element at the end of 1920 at 217,000, of which 34 percent (73,780) were former officers. The 217,000 figure obviously includes thousands of noncombat command positions, which were not counted in the 130,914 figure cited by Kavtaradze. See M. V. Zakharov, ed., *50 Let Vooruzhennykh Sil SSSR* (Moscow, 1968), 159. The most commonly cited figure is that of 48,409 former officers drafted between 12 June 1918 and 15 August 1920. See N. Efimov, "Komandnyi Sostav Krasnoi Armii," in Bubnov, Kamenev, and Eideman, *Grazhdanskaya,* 2:95. However, the author excludes from this figure the large number of officers who volunteered before June 1918 and the former White officers who voluntarily joined the Red Army, as well as those called up between August 15 and the end of the war. Kavtaradze (*Voennye Spetsialisty,* 175) calculates the number of officers in the first two categories alone at 20,000. In another article, Kavtaradze restates the 75,000 figure, and breaks it down further into those former officers who joined the Red Army voluntarily (8,000–10,000), those who were drafted (48,500), and those who either defected from the anti-Soviet forces or were captured (about 14,000). See P. S. Grachev, ed., *Voennaya Entsiklopediya* (Moscow, 1994–), 2:202. Two émigré sources do nothing more than repeat the standard figure of 48,409. See A. Zaitsov, *1918 God. Ocherki po Istorii Russkoi Grazhdanskoi Voiny* (Paris, 1934), 183; N. V. Pyatnitskii, *Voennaya Organizatsiya Gosudarstvennoi Oborony SSSR* (Paris, 1932), 116.

30. Kavtaradze, *Voennye Spetsialisty,* 176–77.

31. A. Baiov, "General'nyi Shtab vo Vremya Grazhdanskoi Voiny," *Chasovoi,* no. 84 (1932): 3–4. Soviet sources, not surprisingly, tend to place the figure somewhat higher. Kavtaradze (*Voennye Spetsialisty,* 196) maintains that of 1,932 General Staff officers, 639 (33 percent) served the Reds, while another author states that the number varied from 526 (36 percent) to 407 (28 percent) of a total prerevolutionary General Staff complement of 1,450. See L. M. Spirin, "V. I. Lenin i Sozdanie Sovetskikh Komandnykh Kadrov," *V-IZh,* no. 4 (1965): 12–13. However, both Soviet authors include postrevolutionary (1918) General Staff academy graduates, a method that inflates the percentages.

32. Even in the relatively peaceful setting of the academy, Snesarev and the other specialists were still subjected to persecution. One student later recalled that the former officers were often used as hostages and "were regularly put behind bars each time the internal situation took a turn for the worse." See A. Barmine, *Memoirs of a Soviet Diplomat,* trans. G. Hopkins (London, 1938), 108.

33. T. P. Bulgakova, ed., *Akademiya General'nogo Shtaba,* 2d ed. (Moscow, 1987), 12, 14, 17.

34. Kavtaradze, *Voennye Spetsialisty,* 13.

35. A. A. Grechko, ed., *Sovetskaya Voennaya Entsiklopediya* (Moscow, 1976–80), 2:274. The post-Soviet *Voennaya Entsiklopediya*'s definition does not differ dramatically

from this, although the amount of space devoted to the problem is much greater. See Grachev, *Voennaya,* 2:202.

36. Kavtaradze (*Voennye Spetsialisty,* 222) calculates the number of wartime officers at more than 65,000 of the nearly 75,000 former officers recruited by the Red Army. This view is partially supported by Voroshilov, who pointedly excluded from the category of specialist the lowest-ranking junior officers, the *praporshchiki,* an exclusively wartime rank. See K. E. Voroshilov, *Stat'i i Rechi* (Moscow, 1937), 227. However correct, Voroshilov's well-known antipathy toward the military specialists probably drove him to minimize their contribution.

37. The exact size of this group is difficult to determine, and estimates vary. Kavtaradze (*Voennye Spetsialisty,* 222) states that there were fewer than 10,000 former career officers in the Red Army. Another source puts the figure at 6 percent (13,020) of 217,000 Red Army commanders. See Zakharov, *50 Let,* 159.

38. Kavtaradze (*Voennye Spetsialisty,* 178) claims that 775 former generals served the Reds. Another Soviet source puts the figure at more than 1,000. See S. Fedyukin, "Ob Ispol'zovanii Voennykh Spetsialistov v Krasnoi Armii," *V-IZh,* no. 6 (1962): 39.

39. Kavtaradze (*Voennye Spetsialisty,* 178) claims that 980 former colonels and 746 lieutenant colonels served in the Red Army.

40. Tukhachevskii did not attend the General Staff Academy, having been commissioned a second lieutenant only in July 1914. However, a recent biographer states that Tukhachevskii was already familiar with the works of Leer and Mikhnevich. See Ivanov, *Tukhachevskii,* 24.

41. Kavtaradze, *Voennye Spetsialisty,* 109, 238, 243, 245–46, 251; S. S. Khromov, ed., *Grazhdanskaya Voina i Voennaya Interventsiya v SSSR. Entsiklopediya* (Moscow, 1983), 71, 87, 152, 251, 289, 319.

42. Kavtaradze, *Voennye Spetsialisty,* 109, 207–8, 236–37, 239–46, 248–54, 256, 259–62; Khromov, *Grazhdanskaya,* 39, 48, 51, 68, 87, 117, 149, 152, 205, 216, 245, 251, 263, 289, 316, 319, 362, 366, 394, 412, 424, 451, 483, 521, 527, 555, 575, 605–6, 612, 631, 666, 675–76, 678; N. N. Azovtsev et al., *Direktivy Komandovaniya Frontov Krasnoi Armii (1917–1922 gg.)* (Moscow, 1971–78), 4:529–33. Kavtaradze states that of the twenty main fronts, seventeen were commanded by military specialists, and that of twenty-eight front chiefs of staff, all were military specialists. See his article in Grachev, *Voennaya,* 2:203.

43. Kavtaradze, *Voennye Spetsialisty,* 16, 109, 145, 193, 199, 206, 208–9, 216–18, 236–39, 241–62; Khromov, *Grazhdanskaya,* 22, 29, 40, 48, 51, 65, 78, 86–87, 115, 118, 131–32, 138, 140–41, 149, 152, 154, 172–73, 186, 205, 219, 249, 260–62, 288, 311–12, 316, 318–19, 331, 343, 345, 352, 354, 366, 394, 411, 421, 443–45, 451, 486, 521, 530–31, 536, 544–555, 568, 594, 597, 601, 606–7, 631, 633, 636, 651, 653–56, 661, 663–65, 668–69, 679; Azovtsev et al., *Direktivy,* 4:533–44. Kavtaradze states that of 100 army commanders, 82 were military specialists, as were 83 percent of the army chiefs of staff. See his article in Grachev, *Voennaya,* 2:203.

44. D. A. Voropaev and A. M. Iovlev, *Bor'ba KPSS za Sozdanie Voennykh Kadrov,* 2d ed. (Moscow, 1960), 41.

45. A. I. Denikin, *Ocherki Russkoi Smuty* (Paris, 1921–22; Berlin, 1924–26), 3:144.

46. Lenin, *Polnoe,* 40:199.

47. N. Movchin, "Komplektovanie Krasnoi Armii v 1918–1921 gg," in Bubnov, Kamenev, and Eideman, *Grazhdanskaya,* 2:89.

48. S. S. Kamenev, *Zapiski o Grazhdanskoi Voine i Voennom Stroitel'stve. Izbrannye Stat'i* (Moscow, 1963), 58.
49. I. Kravchenko, "Kharakternye Cherty Operativnogo Iskusstva i Taktiki RKKA v Gody Grazhdanskoi Voiny," in *Iz Istorii Grazhdanskoi Voiny i Interventsii, 1917–1922 gg.*, ed. I. I. Mints (Moscow, 1974), 208.
50. Zakharov, *50 Let*, 46.
51. Kamenev, *Zapiski*, 77.
52. G. F. Krivosheev, ed., *Grif Sekretnosti Snyat. Poteri Vooruzhennykh Sil SSSR v Voinakh, Boevykh Deistviyakh i Voennykh Konfliktakh. Statisticheskoe Issledovanie* (Moscow, 1993), 39.
53. S. E. Rabinovich, *Istoriya Grazhdanskoi Voiny*, 2d ed. (Moscow, 1935), 63.
54. I. I. Kravchenko, "Kharakternye Cherty Nastupatel'nykh Operatsii Krasnoi Armii v Grazhdanskoi Voine," *V-IZh*, no. 3 (1976): 97–98.
55. Bubnov, Kamenev, and Eideman, *Grazhdanskaya*, 3:172–73. The strengths of both sides given here and elsewhere in this chapter indicate fighting strengths only and do not include rear, staff, and other noncombat services.
56. G. A. Belov et al., eds., *Direktivy Glavnogo Komandovaniya Krasnoi Armii (1917–1920)* (Moscow, 1969), 548.
57. Azovtsev et al., *Direktivy*, 2:648.
58. M. V. Frunze, *Izbrannye Proizvedeniya* (Moscow, 1957), 1:176.
59. Bubnov, Kamenev, and Eideman, *Grazhdanskaya*, 3:182–84.
60. Ibid., 190.
61. Azovtsev et al., *Direktivy*, 2:663.
62. Tukhachevskii, *Izbrannye*, 2:224.
63. Samoilo, *Dve Zhizni*, 248, 250–51.
64. Azovtsev et al., *Direktivy*, 2:667, 670, 676–77, 680.
65. Ibid., 673, 676.
66. Frunze, *Izbrannye*, 1:187.
67. Bubnov, Kamenev, and Eideman, *Grazhdanskaya*, 3:202.
68. Denikin, *Ocherki*, 5:230.
69. Bubnov, Kamenev, and Eideman, *Grazhdanskaya*, 3:282.
70. A. I. Yegorov, *Razgrom Denikina, 1919* (Moscow, 1931), 133.
71. Bubnov, Kamenev, and Eideman, *Grazhdanskaya*, 3:264; Belov et al., *Direktivy*, 472, 478.
72. Azovtsev et al., *Direktivy*, 2:349–50.
73. Bubnov, Kamenev, and Eideman, *Grazhdanskaya*, 3:262.
74. Azovtsev et al., *Direktivy*, 2:354.
75. Ibid., 356.
76. Yegorov, *Razgrom Denikina*, 164.
77. Azovtsev et al., *Direktivy*, 2:359–60.
78. Ibid., 360.
79. Denikin, *Ocherki*, 5:233.
80. It is significant that of the 5,024,088 casualties suffered by the Red Army in 1918–20, fewer than 700,000 were combat-related deaths. Around 4 million casualties were attributable to diseases, generally caused by lack of food and medicine, and the low level of hygiene. See Krivosheev, *Grif Sekretnosti Snyat*, 54.

81. I. S. Korotkov, *Razgrom Vrangelya*, 3d ed. (Moscow, 1955), 206.
82. Azovtsev et al., *Direktivy*, 3:484–85.
83. Bubnov, Kamenev, and Eideman, *Grazhdanskaya*, 3:514.
84. Azovtsev et al., *Direktivy*, 3:475–76.
85. Ibid., 488–89.
86. Ibid., 2:343–44, 346–47, 350, 357, 359, 365, 367.
87. Bubnov, Kamenev, and Eideman, *Grazhdanskaya*, 3:279.
88. Belov et al., *Direktivy*, 674–75.
89. Bubnov, Kamenev, and Eideman, *Grazhdanskaya*, 3:342.
90. Azovtsev et al., *Direktivy*, 3:158–59.
91. Bubnov, Kamenev, and Eideman, *Grazhdanskaya*, 3:352.
92. F. Zhemaitis, "Proryv Pol'skogo Fronta 1-i Konnoi Armiei," *V-IZh*, no. 6 (1940): 6.
93. Belov et al., *Direktivy*, 689–93, 695–99; Azovtsev et al., *Direktivy*, 3:168, 178, 184–85.
94. Bubnov, Kamenev, and Eideman, *Grazhdanskaya*, 3:366–67.
95. Ibid., 364.
96. Ibid., 366.
97. Azovtsev et al., *Direktivy*, 3:225–26.
98. Belov et al., *Direktivy*, 704–5, 643–44.
99. Azovtsev et al., *Direktivy*, 3:78–79.
100. Tukhachevskii, *Izbrannye*, 1:145.
101. Bubnov, Kamenev, and Eideman, *Grazhdanskaya*, 3:393.
102. Samoilo, *Dve Zhizni*, 176.
103. Bubnov, Kamenev, and Eideman, *Grazhdanskaya*, 3:436–37.
104. Belov et al., *Direktivy*, 646–47.
105. Bubnov, Kamenev, and Eideman, *Grazhdanskaya*, 3:437.
106. Azovtsev et al., *Direktivy*, 3:84–85.
107. Ibid., 89, 92.

3. THE BIRTH OF A THEORY

1. Chuntulov, *Ekonomicheskaya*, 230.
2. Frunze's death was extremely opportune for Stalin, and a number of historians have speculated on the dictator's complicity in the former's demise. See J. Erickson, *The Soviet High Command: A Military-Political History, 1918–1941* (London, 1962), 199–200; and R. Medvedev, "O Smerti M. V. Frunze i F. E. Dzerzhinskogo," *V-IZh*, no. 3 (1989): 54–61.
3. Erickson, *Soviet High Command*, 179.
4. I. B. Berkhin, *Voennaya Reforma v SSSR (1924–1925 gg.)* (Moscow, 1958), 40, 77.
5. Movchin, in Bubnov, Kamenev, and Eideman, *Grazhdanskaya*, 2:96, 102.
6. A. M. Iovlev, *Deyatel'nost' KPSS po Podgotovke Voennykh Kadrov* (Moscow, 1976), 77.
7. Marshal G. K. Zhukov later recalled, "Our territorial units were wretchedly trained," and "were in no way comparable to the cadre units." See K. Simonov, "Zametki k Biografii G. K. Zhukova," *V-IZh*, no. 6 (1987): 53.

8. Zakharov, *50 Let,* 174.
9. F. Engel's, *Izbrannye Voennye Proizvedeniya* (Moscow, 1957), 635.
10. P. A. Zhilin, ed., *Russkaya Voennaya Mysl'. Konets XIX–Nachalo XX v.* (Moscow, 1982), 143–46; and his "Diskussiya o Edinoi Voennoi Doktrine," *V-IZh,* no. 5 (1961): 61–74.
11. O. Yu. Shmidt, ed., *Bol'shaya Sovetskaya Entsiklopediya* (Moscow, 1926–47), 12:217.
12. Frunze, *Izbrannye,* 2:3.
13. Ibid., 8.
14. Trotskii, *Kak Vooruzhalas',* vol. 3, bk. 2, 238.
15. Ibid., 219.
16. Trotskii seems to have felt no great personal dislike for Frunze, although he considered him prone to abstractions and a poor judge of people. See Trotskii, *Moya Zhizn',* 2:254.
17. Frunze, *Izbrannye,* 2:35.
18. Ibid., 43.
19. Ibid., 97.
20. Barmine, *Memoirs,* 164.
21. *Budushehaya Voina,* Rossiisskii Gosudarstvennyi Voennyi Arkiv, fond 33988, opis' 2, delo 682, pp. 35–36. This archive is hereafter abbreviated as RGVA.
22. Frunze, *Izbrannye,* 2:133.
23. Tukhachevskii, *Izbrannye,* 1:255.
24. A. A. Svechin, *Strategiya,* 2d ed. (Moscow, 1927), 43.
25. B. M. Shaposhnikov, *Mozg Armii* (Moscow, 1927–29), 1:245; RGVA, fond 4, opis' 2, delo 515, p. 4.
26. RGVA, fond 33988, opis' 2, delo 688, pp. 22, 57, 60–61.
27. Frunze, *Izbrannye,* 2:17.
28. Trotskii, *Kak Vooruzhalas',* vol. 3, bk. 2, 232.
29. Ibid., 232–33.
30. Frunze, *Izbrannye,* 2:49.
31. Svechin, *Strategiya,* 181.
32. Ibid., 174.
33. Ibid., 41.
34. Ibid., 181.
35. Trotskii, *Kak Vooruzhalas',* vol. 3, bk. 2, 256.
36. Svechin, *Strategiya,* 165.
37. A. I. Verkhovskii, *Osnovy Nashei Taktiki. Ogon', Manevr, Maskirovka* (Moscow, 1928), 131.
38. Tukhachevskii, *Izbrannye,* 1:257.
39. Ibid.
40. V. A. Melikov, *Marna-1914 Goda. Visla-1920 Goda. Smirna-1922 Goda* (Moscow and Leningrad, 1928), 96.
41. N. E. Kakurin, *Strategiya Proletarskogo Gosudarstva* (Smolensk, 1921), 22, 28.
42. Shaposhnikov, *Mozg Armii,* 1:245.
43. Frunze, *Izbrannye,* 2:133–34.
44. Trotskii, *Kak Vooruzhalas',* vol. 3, bk. 2, 228–29.
45. Frunze, *Izbrannye,* 2:46–47.

46. Tukhachevskii, *Izbrannye*, 1:110.
47. RGVA, fond 33988, opis' 2, delo 688, pp. 53–54.
48. Svechin, *Strategiya*, 171, 189.
49. V. K. Triandafillov, "Vozmozhnaya Chislennost' Budushchikh Armii," *Voina i Revoliutsiya*, no. 3 (1927): 42–43. This journal is hereafter abbreviated as *V&R*.
50. N. Ya. Kapustin, *Operativnoe Iskusstvo v Pozitsionnoi Voine* (Moscow and Leningrad, 1927), 14.
51. Verkhovskii, *Osnovy*, 232.
52. Frunze, *Izbrannye*, 2:40.
53. Triandafillov, "Vozmozhnaya," 20, 34.
54. Frunze, *Izbrannye*, 2:343.
55. Tukhachevskii, *Izbrannye*, 2:27.
56. RGVA, fond 33988, opis' 2, delo 688, pp. 72–73, 93–94, 96.
57. Tukhachevskii, *Izbrannye*, 2:23.
58. Barmine, *Memoirs*, 163–64.
59. Shtab RKKA, *Vysshee Komandovanie. Ofitsial'noe Rukovodstvo dlya Komanduyushchikh i Polevykh Upravlenii Armii i Frontov* (Moscow, 1924), 5.
60. RGVA, fond 33988, opis' 2, delo 688, p. 98.
61. Tukhachevskii, *Izbrannye*, 1:185.
62. Melikov, *Marna*, 96.
63. A. K. Kolenkovskii, *O Nastupatel'noi Operatsii Armii, Vkhodyashchei v Sostav Fronta* (Moscow, 1929), 11.
64. Svechin, *Strategiya*, 177, 180–81.
65. V. K. Triandafillov, *Kharakter Operatsii Sovremennykh Armii* (Moscow and Leningrad, 1929), 161.
66. E. Shilovskii, "Evolyutsiya Akademicheskoi Podgotovki," *V&R*, no. 11 (1928): 24.
67. L. Papirmeister, "Partorganizatsiya Voennoi Akademii za 10 Let," *V&R*, no. 11 (1928): 35, 46–47; N. N. Voronov, *Na Sluzhbe Voennoi* (Moscow, 1963), 61; Barmine, *Memoirs*, 165–66.
68. F. Danilov and I. Kravchenko, "U Istokov Sovetskoi Teorii Operativnogo Iskusstva (1921–1930 gg.)," *V-IZh*, no. 11 (1973): 38.
69. V. A. Semenov, *Kratkii Ocherk Razvitiya Sovetskogo Operativnogo Iskusstva* (Moscow, 1960), 112.
70. N. E. Varfolomeev, "Strategiya v Akademicheskoi Postanovke," *V&R*, no. 11 (1928): 84.
71. A. A. Svechin, "Integral'noe Ponimanie Voennogo Iskusstva," *Krasnye Zori*, no. 11 (1924): 23.
72. Svechin's prickly relations with other faculty members and students are detailed in M. I. Kazakov, *Nad Kartoi Bylykh Srazhenii* (Moscow, 1971), 24, 38; L. M. Sandalov, *Perezhitoe* (Moscow, 1961), 8–9, 12–13.
73. Varfolomeev, "Strategiya," 83.
74. Shmidt, *Bol'shaya*, 12:218.
75. Shilovskii, "Evolyutsiya," 18.
76. Neznamov, *Sovremennaya Voina*, 194.
77. Varfolomeev, "Strategiya," 81–83.
78. Ibid., 84.

79. Shilovskii, "Evolyutsiya," 19; P. A. Kurochkin, ed., *Obshchevoiskovaya Armiya v Nastuplenii* (Moscow, 1966), 9.
80. Kapustin, *Operativnoe,* 20; Kolenkovskii, *O Nastupatel'noi,* 13, 15.
81. Varfolomeev, "Strategiya," 84.
82. N. N. Movchin, *Posledovatel'nye Operatsii po Opytu Marny i Visly* (Moscow and Leningrad, 1928), 19–20.
83. Mikhnevich, *Strategiya,* 1:178, 180.
84. A. Golubev, "Vydayushchiisya Sovetskii Voennyi Teoretik," *V-IZh,* no. 3 (1968): 107–14. One source states that Triandafillov also served briefly as chief of staff in 1931. See the article by M. V. Zakharov, in *Bol'shaya Sovetskaya Entsiklopediya,* 3d ed., ed. A. M. Prokhorov (Moscow, 1969–78), 6:224. Another claims that he was acting chief of staff in 1929. See A. B. Kadishev, ed., *Voprosy Strategii i Operativnogo Iskusstva v Sovetskikh Voennykh Trudakh (1917–1940 gg.)* (Moscow, 1965), 552. However, no other work on the General Staff or Triandafillov makes either of these claims. See the relevant articles in Grechko, *Sovetskaya,* 2:512, 8:107. Nor does Zakharov repeat the claim in his posthumous history of the General Staff. See M. V. Zakharov, *General'nyi Shtab v Predvoennye Gody* (Moscow, 1989), 311.
85. G. Isserson, "Zapiski Sovremennika o M. N. Tukhachevskom," *V-Izh,* no. 4 (1963): 69; N. I. Koritskii, S. M. Mel'nik-Tukhachevskaya, and B. N. Chistov, comps., *Marshal Tukhachevskii. Vospominaniya Druzei i Soratnikov* (Moscow, 1965), 133.
86. V. K. Triandafillov, *Razmakh Operatsii Sovremennykh Armii* (Moscow, 1926), 3.
87. Triandafillov, *Kharakter,* 75.
88. Ibid., 116.
89. Ibid., 97–98; Neznamov, *Sovremennaya Voina,* 194; Leer, *Strategiya,* 4th ed., 2:13.
90. Triandafillov, *Kharakter,* 98–99.
91. Ibid., 96.
92. Ibid., 120.
93. Ibid., 121.
94. G. S. Isserson, *Martovskoe Nastuplenie Germantsev v Pikardii v 1918 Godu* (Moscow, 1926), 47.
95. Kamenev, *Zapiski,* 71; Tukhachevskii, *Izbrannye,* 1:189.
96. Triandafillov, *Kharakter,* 122.
97. M. N. Tukhachevskii, N. E. Varfolomeev, and E. A. Shilovskii, *Armeiskaya Operatsiya. Rabota Komandovaniya i Polevogo Upravleniya* (Moscow and Leningrad, 1926), 24.
98. Triandafillov, *Kharakter,* 110, 121.
99. Ibid., 82–83.
100. Tukhachevskii, Varfolomeev, and Shilovskii, *Armeiskaya Operatsiya,* 53–56; Kolenkovskii, *O Nastupatel'noi,* 27.
101. Kapustin, *Operativnoe,* 79, 85.
102. Triandafillov, *Kharakter,* 110.
103. Kolenkovskii, *O Nastupatel'noi,* 28–29.
104. Triandafillov, *Kharakter,* 133.
105. Ibid., 97.
106. Ibid., 113; Kolenkovskii, *O Nastupatel'noi,* 61.
107. Triandafillov, *Kharakter,* 116.
108. Kapustin, *Operativnoe,* 18, 20, 213.
109. Triandafillov, *Kharakter,* 166.

110. Neznamov, *Sovremennaya Voina*, 21–22; Kolenkovskii, *O Nastupatel'noi*, 24.
111. Tukhachevskii, *Izbrannye*, 1:142.
112. Kolenkovskii, *O Nastupatel'noi*, 21.
113. Triandafillov, *Kharakter*, 163–65.
114. Ibid., 123–24, 165.
115. Ibid., 102, 104.
116. Ibid., 110–11; Kolenkovskii, *O Nastupatel'noi*, 64, 70.
117. Triandafillov, *Kharakter*, 130–31.
118. A. M. Vasilevskii, *Delo Vsei Zhizni* (Moscow, 1974), 78; Sandalov, 6.
119. Frunze, *Izbrannye*, 2:133.
120. Neznamov, *Sovremennaya Voina*, 10–11.
121. Kamenev, *Zapiski*, 64.
122. Tukhachevskii, Varfolomeev, and Shilovskii, *Armeiskaya Operatsiya*, 79; Tukhachevskii, *Izbrannye*, 1:107, 141–42, 261, 2:23.
123. Svechin, *Strategiya*, 14.
124. Movchin, *Posledovatel'nye*, 5.
125. V. F. Novitskii, *Mirovaya Voina, 1914–1918 gg. Kampaniya 1914 Goda v Bel'gii i Frantsii* (Moscow, 1926–28), 2:384–85; A. Vol'pe, "Presledovanie v Grazhdanskoi Voine," in Bubnov, Kamenev, and Eideman, *Grazhdanskaya*, 2:234.
126. Triandafillov, *Razmakh*, 3.
127. RGVA, fond 33988, opis' 2, delo 688, p. 62.
128. Neznamov, *Sovremennaya Voina*, 11.
129. Elchaninov, *Strategiya*, 309.
130. Shilovskii, "Evolyutsiya," 27.
131. Tukhachevskii, *Izbrannye*, 1:141–42.
132. Kamenev, *Zapiski*, 72–73, 75–76; Kolenkovskii, *O Nastupatel'noi*, 46–47.
133. Svechin, *Strategiya*, 177.
134. Triandafillov, *Razmakh*, 4; Triandafillov, *Kharakter*, 96.
135. Varfolomeev, "Strategiya," 88.
136. Movchin, *Posledovatel'nye*, 123.
137. Tukhachevskii, Varfolomeev, and Shilovskii, *Armeiskaya Operatsiya*, 86; Triandafillov, *Razmakh*, 4.
138. Triandafillov, *Kharakter*, 122, 125–26.
139. Movchin, *Posledovatel'nye*, 96, 101.
140. Ibid., 116; Mikhnevich, *Strategiya*, 1:178, 180.
141. Movchin, *Posledovatel'nye*, 120.
142. Ibid., 11, 120.
143. Triandafillov, *Kharakter*, 180–82.
144. Mikhnevich, *Strategiya*, 1:152.
145. Tukhachevskii, *Izbrannye*, 1:260; Movchin, *Posledovatel'nye*, 116.
146. Movchin, *Posledovatel'nye*, 23; Neznamov, *Sovremennaya Voina*, 11.
147. Movchin, *Posledovatel'nye*, 112.
148. Ibid., 28–29.
149. Clausewitz, *On War*, 527, 570.
150. Neznamov, *Sovremennaya Voina*, 33.
151. N. Varfolomeev, "Strategicheskoe Narastanie i Istoshchenie v Grazhdanskoi Voine," in Bubnov, Kamenev, and Eideman, *Grazhdanskaya*, 2:269, 273.

152. Ibid., 268.
153. Triandafillov, *Kharakter*, 132; Varfolomeev, "Strategicheskoe," 277.
154. V. Putna, *K Visle i Obratno* (Moscow, 1927), 240.
155. Frunze, *Izbrannye*, 2:177.
156. Svechin, *Strategiya*, 192; Melikov, *Marna*, 333.
157. Varfolomeev, "Strategiya," 88.
158. Triandafillov, *Kharakter*, 148, 160–61.
159. Movchin, *Posledovatel'nye*, 99.
160. Triandafillov, *Kharakter*, 164.
161. Ibid., 146; N. Varfolomeev, "Dvizhenie Presleduyushchei Armii k Polyu Reshitel'nogo Srazheniya," *Revoliutsiya i Voina*, no. 13 (1921): 80.
162. Triandafillov, *Kharakter*, 154; Kolenkovskii, *O Nastupatel'noi*, 53; Movchin, *Posledovatel'nye*, 104.
163. Triandafillov, *Kharakter*, 157; Movchin, *Posledovatel'nye*, 104.
164. Triandafillov, *Kharakter*, 157, 159–60.
165. Movchin, *Posledovatel'nye*, 113.
166. Clausewitz, *On War*, 528.
167. Svechin, *Strategiya*, 224–25.
168. Vol'pe, "Presledovanie," 234.
169. Melikov, *Marna*, 203; Novitskii, *Mirovaya Voina*, 1:506.
170. Triandafillov, *Kharakter*, 162.
171. Movchin, *Posledovatel'nye*, 110, 114.
172. Triandafillov, *Kharakter*, 170.
173. RGVA, fond 33988, opis' 2, delo 688, pp. 57, 91.
174. Tukhachevskii, *Izbrannye*, 1:256.
175. Tukhachevskii, Varfolomeev, and Shilovskii, *Armeiskaya Operatsiya*, 24, 29–30.
176. Ibid., 28–29.
177. RGVA, fond 33988, opis' 2, delo 688, pp. 56–57, 60–61.
178. Varfolomeev, "Strategiya," 91–92.

4. MATURATION

1. Stalin, *Sochineniya*, 11:248.
2. Tsentral'noe Statisticheskoe Upravlenie pri Sovete Ministrov SSSR, *Narodnoe Khozyaistvo SSSR 1922–1972 gg. Yubileinyi Statisticheskii Ezhegodnik* (Moscow, 1972), 136, 138.
3. R. Conquest, *The Harvest of Sorrow. Soviet Collectivization and the Terror-Famine* (London, 1986), 306.
4. R. Conquest, *The Great Terror. Stalin's Purge of the Thirties* (London, 1968), 532.
5. Two of the more egregious examples of the Stalin cult in the army are Voroshilov's article "Stalin i Krasnaya Armii," which appeared on the dictator's fiftieth birthday in 1929. See Voroshilov, *Stat'i i Rechi*, 346–64. See also R. Eideman, "K Izucheniyu Istorii Grazhdanskoi Voiny," *V&R*, no. 2 (1932): 90–99.
6. A. A. Grechko, ed., *Istoriya Vtoroi Mirovoi Voiny, 1939–1945* (Moscow, 1973–80), 1:270; P. N. Pospelov, ed., *Istoriya Velikoi Otechestvennoi Voiny Sovetskogo Soyuza, 1941–1945* (Moscow, 1960–65), 1:90.

7. Zakharov, *50 Let*, 198.
8. G. K. Zhukov, *Vospominaniya i Razmyshleniya*, 11th ed. (Moscow, 1992), 1: 186–87.
9. Grechko, *Istoriya*, 1:213.
10. Pospelov, *Istoriya*, 1:65.
11. N. I. Savinkin and K. M. Bogolyubov, comps., *KPSS o Vooruzhennykh Silakh Sovetskogo Soyuza. Dokumenty, 1917–1981* (Moscow, 1981), 259.
12. Grechko, *Istoriya*, 1:260, 2:90.
13. Ibid., 1:270.
14. *Dokladnaya Zapiska Komanduyushchego Voiskami Leningradskogo Voennogo Okruga Narodnomu Komissaru po Voennym i Morskim Delam K.E. Voroshilovu*, RGVA, fond 7, opis' 1, delo 170, pp. 12, 16–17.
15. S. Biryuzov, "Voenno-Teoreticheskoe Nasledstvo M. N. Tukhachevskogo," *V-IZh*, no. 2 (1964): 40.
16. Grechko, *Istoriya*, 1:270.
17. S. A. Tyushkevich, ed., *Sovetskie Vooruzhennye Sily. Istoriya Stroitel'stva* (Moscow, 1978), 203.
18. Zakharov, *50 Let*, 200.
19. Tukhachevskii, *Izbrannye*, 2:175.
20. Tyushkevich, *Sovetskie*, 199.
21. S. Budennyi, "Konnitsa v Sovremennoi Voine," *V&R*, no. 6 (1930): 23.
22. Zhukov, *Vospominaniya*, 1:224.
23. Tyushkevich, *Sovetskie*, 199.
24. Zakharov, *50 Let*, 202; P. A. Rotmistrov, *Vremya i Tanki* (Moscow, 1972), 46.
25. Both the T-28 and the T-35 mounted a 76.2-mm gun. The latter was also armed with two 45-mm guns and had a maximum armor protection of 30 mm. See V. D. Mostovenko, *Tanki*, 2d ed. (Moscow, 1958), 96–98.
26. N. G. Andronikov et al., *Bronetankovye i Mekhanizirovannye Voiska Sovetskoi Armii* (Moscow, 1958), 43–44.
27. A. Ryzhakov, "K Voprosu o Stroitel'stve Bronetankovykh Voisk Krasnoi Armii v 30-e Gody," *V-IZh*, no. 8 (1968): 108.
28. A. Iovlev, "Tekhnicheskoe Perevooruzhenie Krasnoi Armii v Gody Pervoi Pyatiletki," *V-IZh*, no. 12 (1964): 11.
29. Zakharov, *50 Let*, 202.
30. Tukhachevskii, *Izbrannye*, 2:210. See also S. N. Krasil'nikov, *Organizatsiya Krupnykh Obshchevoiskovykh Soedinenii* (Moscow, 1933), 311–12.
31. V. Kostylev, "Stanovlenie i Razvitie Vozdushno-Desantnykh Voisk," *V-IZh*, no. 9 (1975): 80–81.
32. I. I. Lisov, *Sovetskie Vozdushno-Desantnye Voiska* (Moscow, 1967), 19–20.
33. G. Martel, *The Russian Outlook* (London, 1947), 21.
34. P. F. Batitskii, ed., *Voiska Protivovozdushnoi Oborony Strany* (Moscow, 1968), 46.
35. P. Avdeenko, "Sovetskoe Samoletostroenie v Gody Predvoennykh Pyatiletok (1929–1940 gg.)," *V-IZh*, no. 7 (1974): 86.
36. Pospelov, *Istoriya*, 1:93; Grechko, *Istoriya*, 1:270.
37. A. N. Lapchinskii, *Bombardirovochnaya Aviatsiya* (Moscow, 1937), 42–43.
38. Quoted in I. S. Prochko, *Artilleriya—Bog Voiny* (Moscow, 1946), 4.

39. V. Dmitriev, "Stroitel'stvo Sovetskogo Podvodnogo Flota v Mezhvoennyi Period," *V-IZh*, no. 10 (1974): 85.
40. Tyushkevich, *Sovetskie*, 206.
41. RGVA, fond 7, opis' 1, delo 170, p. 12.
42. S. M. Belitskii, *Voina* (Leningrad, 1931), 11.
43. L. S. Amiragov, "O Kharaktere Budushchei Voiny," *V&R*, September–October (1934): 12–13.
44. Belitskii, *Voina*, 4, 12; R. Tsiffer, "Kharakteristika Predstoyashchei Voiny," *V&R*, no. 10–11 (1931): 5–6.
45. Belitskii, *Voina*, 11–12, 61.
46. Tukhachevskii, *Izbrannye*, 2:152–53.
47. Ibid., 134, 137–38; B. Burlak, "Nastuplenie kak Sil'naya Forma Revolyutsionnoi Voiny," *V&R*, September–October (1935): 40. See also Tukhachevskii's scurrilous attack on Svechin in K. Bocharov, I. Nizhechek, and P. Suslov, eds., *Protiv Reaktsionnykh Teorii na Voennonauchnom Fronte. Kritika Strategicheskikh i Voennoistoricheskikh Vzglyadov Prof. Svechina* (Moscow, 1931), 6–7.
48. Belitskii, *Voina*, 58; Tukhachevskii, *Izbrannye*, 2:247.
49. *Budushchaya Voina i Nashi Voennye Zadachi*, 1, 3–4. A number of considerations make it impossible at this time to cite this document in the usual manner. Instead, it will be referred to by title and page number only.
50. Ibid., 3, 6–7.
51. Ibid., 8–10, 12.
52. *Otvet na Zapisku A. Svechina "Budushchaya Voina i Nashi Voennye Zadachi,"* 3, 6, 8, 10. A number of considerations make it impossible at this time to cite this document in the usual manner. Instead, it will be referred to by title and page number only.
53. Ibid., 14, 29–30.
54. Ibid., 7, 14, 25, 28–29.
55. Ibid., 5, 33.
56. Svechin, *Strategiya*, 135, 138.
57. See G. Sokolov, "Sovremennaya Zavesa i Voprosy Strategicheskogo Prikrytiya," *V&R*, no. 4 (1928): 15–21; A. Lapchinskii, "Deistviya Aviatsii v Nachal'nom Periode Voiny," *V&R*, no. 6 (1929): 55–66; Ya. Alksnis, "Nachal'nyi Period Voiny," *V&R*, no. 9 (1929): 3–22; no. 10 (1929): 3–15.
58. E. Shilovskii, "Nachal'nyi Period Voiny," *V&R*, September–October (1933): 11.
59. R. Eideman, "K Voprosu o Kharaktere Nachal'nogo Perioda Voiny," *V&R*, no. 8 (1931): 12.
60. Melikov, *Problema*, 597, 599.
61. Belitskii, *Strategicheskie*, 255.
62. G. S. Isserson, *Osnovy Glubokoi Operatsii*, 54–56. A number of considerations make it impossible at this time to cite this document in the usual manner. Instead, it will be referred to by title and page number only. See also *Tezisy Doklada "Taktika i Operativnoe Iskusstvo RKKA na Novom Etape,"* RGVA, fond 31983, opis' 2, delo 18, pp. 145, 126–25; pagination in the original.
63. *Razrabotka o Nachal'nom Periode Voiny*, 4–5. A number of considerations make it impossible at this time to cite this document in the usual manner. Instead, it will be referred to by title and page number only.

64. RGVA, fond 31983, opis' 2, delo 18, p. 144.

65. Isserson, "Zapiski," 76; Tukhachevskii, *Izbrannye*, 2:213, 217–18, 221. The latter work, "The Character of Frontier Operations," was not published during Tukhachevskii's lifetime, although its contents were doubtlessly known to his associates.

66. Isserson, "Zapiski," 76–78; Tukhachevskii, *Izbrannye*, 2:218, 220.

67. Isserson, "Zapiski," 72–74; Zakharov, *General'nyi*, 105.

68. Melikov, *Problema*, 12.

69. S. Kh. Aganov, ed., *Inzhenernye Voiska Sovetskoi Armii, 1918–1945* (Moscow, 1985), 163–65; A. G. Khor'kov, "Ukreplennye Raiony na Zapadnykh Granitsakh SSSR," *V-IZh*, no. 12 (1987): 48.

70. Zhukov, *Vospominaniya*, 1:340, 354–55, 2:79. This view was supported by a postwar chief of staff. See S. S. Biryuzov, *Kogda Gremeli Pushki* (Moscow, 1961), 11.

71. G. Isserson, *Evolyutsiya Operativnogo Iskusstva*, 2d ed. (Moscow, 1937), 98.

72. *Osnovnye Voprosy Taktiki i Operativnogo Iskusstva v Svyazi s Rekonstruktsiei Armii*, 6–7. A number of considerations make it impossible at this time to cite this document in the usual manner. Instead, it will be referred to by title and page number only.

73. V. K. Triandafillov, *Kharakter Operatsii Sovremennykh Armii*, 2d ed. (Moscow, 1932), 177, 182–87.

74. RGVA, fond 31983, opis' 2, delo 18, p. 157.

75. See P. V. "Ispol'zovanie Sredstv Podavleniya v Operatsii Proryva," *V&R*, no. 10–11 (1931): 20–27; S. Ammosov, "Tanki v Operatsii Proryva," *V&R*, no. 5–6 (1932): 81–91.

76. Isserson, *Evolyutsiya*, 132.

77. Narodnyi Komissariat po Voennym i Morskim Delam, *Polevoi Ustav RKKA* (Moscow and Leningrad, 1929), 118, 127.

78. Triandafillov, *Kharakter*, 2d ed., 182, 184; *Osnovnye*, 7–8.

79. *Polevoi*, 127.

80. Zakharov, *General'nyi*, 90–91.

81. Ibid., 90.

82. Biryuzov, "Voenno-Teoreticheskoe," 44; G. Isserson, "Razvitie Teorii Sovetskogo Operativnogo Iskusstva v 30-e Gody," *V-IZh*, no. 1 (1965): 38; Zakharov, *General'nyi*, 91.

83. Narodnyi Komissariat Oborony, *Vremennyi Polevoi Ustav RKKA 1936* (Moscow, 1937), 10, 16.

84. Ibid., 9–11, 16.

85. Ibid., 59–61.

86. Ibid., 61–62.

87. Ibid., 63–68.

88. S. A. Smirnov, *Taktika* (Moscow, 1935), 176–79.

89. *Vremennyi*, 85, 91; Smirnov, *Taktika*, 192–93.

90. Smirnov, *Taktika*, 194–95.

91. Tukhachevskii, *Izbrannye*, 2:247.

92. Smirnov, *Taktika*, 155–56; *Vremennyi*, 102, 106.

93. *Vremennyi*, 111–12.

94. Ibid., 106, 115; Smirnov, *Taktika*, 165.

95. *Vremennyi*, 119–21.

96. Ibid., 132, 153–54.

97. Ibid., 134–35.
98. Ibid., 133, 136, 138–39, 149, 151.
99. N. Varfolomeev, "Operativnoe Iskusstvo na Sovremennom Etape," *Krasnaya Zvezda,* June 3, 1932, 2.
100. Triandafillov, *Kharakter,* 1st ed., 96–99.
101. *Osnovnye,* 4.
102. RGVA, fond 31983, opis' 2, delo 18, pp. 159–58; pagination in the original.
103. Isserson, "Razvitie," 39.
104. See also the articles by A. Myalkovskii, "Udarnaya Armiya," *V&R,* no. 2 (1931): 48–68; N. Varfolomeev, "Nastuplenie 18-i Germanskoi Armii Vesnoi 1918 g.," *V&R,* no. 7 (1931): 42–70; and Ia. Zhigur, "Proryv Oboronitel'noi Sistemy po Opytu Mirovoi Voiny," *V&R,* January–February (1935): 74–89.
105. N. E. Varfolomeev, *Udarnaya Armiya* (Moscow, 1933), 173.
106. N. Varfolomeev, "Glubokaya Operatsiya," *Krasnaya Zvezda,* November 5, 1932, 2.
107. Varfolomeev, *Udarnaya,* 174, 184.
108. Ibid., 173, 183.
109. P. I. Vakulich, "Sovremennaya Operatsiya," in *Voina i Voennoe Delo,* ed. V. N. Levichev (Moscow, 1933), 557.
110. Ya. Zhigur, "O 'Glubinnoi Taktike' i 'Prostranstvennoi Operatsii,'" *Krasnaya Zvezda,* August 15, 1932, 2.
111. *Proekt-Osnovy Vedeniya Operatsii,* 120–21. A number of considerations make it impossible at this time to cite this document in the usual manner. Instead, it will be referred to by title and page number only.
112. Neznamov, *Sovremennaya Voina,* 15.
113. Isserson, *Evolyutsiya,* 79–81; Isserson, *Osnovy,* 64; N. Varfolomeev, "Vstrechnaya Operatsiya," *V&R,* no. 7 (1930): 28.
114. Isserson, *Evolyutsiya,* 82.
115. E. Shilovskii, "Vstrechnaya Operatsiya," *Krasnaya Zvezda,* November 11, 1932, 2. Among others who felt that the army's march order should reflect its future battle order were Isserson, *Osnovy,* 66, and Varfolomeev, "Vstrechnaya," 29.
116. Isserson, *Osnovy,* 81.
117. Shilovskii, "Vstrechnaya," 2; Isserson, *Osnovy,* 76.
118. Shilovskii, "Vstrechnaya," 2.
119. Ibid.
120. Isserson, *Osnovy,* 83–84.
121. Ibid., 84–85, 87–88.
122. Isserson, "Zapiski," 65.
123. Martel, *The Russian Outlook,* 24.
124. RGVA, fond 31983, opis' 2, delo 18, pp. 141–39; pagination in the original.
125. *Novye Voprosy Voiny,* RGVA, fond 33987, opis' 3, delo 1257, pp. 194–96.
126. Ibid., 189–92.
127. RGVA, fond 31983, opis' 2, delo 18, p. 136.
128. I. Kh. Bagramyan, *Moi Vospominaniya* (Erevan, 1979), 158–59.
129. F. Sverdlov, "On Videl Budushchuyu Voinu," *Patriot* (Moscow), 1992, no. 19, p. 11.
130. Isserson's tactical works include "Kharakter Upravleniya Sovremennym Boem,"

V&R, no. 5 (1931): 56–62; "Istoricheskie Korni Novykh Form Boya," *Voennaya Mysl'*, no. 1 (1937): 3–27; and *Lektsii po Glubokoi Taktike* (Moscow, 1933).

131. Isserson, *Evolyutsiya*, 19–24, 40.
132. Ibid., 62.
133. Ibid., 58–59, 82; Isserson, *Osnovy*, 91.
134. Isserson, *Osnovy*, 95–99.
135. Ibid., 33.
136. Ibid., 30–31.
137. Ibid., 28–29, 32–34, 36, 109–10. Isserson's calculations were supported by several of his contemporaries. See Triandafillov, *Kharakter*, 1st ed., 121, 126; Varfolomeev, *Udarnaya*, 181–82; Vakulich, in Levichev, p. 555.
138. Isserson, *Osnovy*, 103, 113, 121.
139. Ibid., 105–6, 113–14.
140. Zakharov, *General'nyi*, 105; V. A. Anfilov, *Bessmertnyi Podvig* (Moscow, 1971), 143.
141. G. Isserson, "Razvitie Teorii Sovetskogo Operativnogo Iskusstva v 30-e Gody," *V-IZh*, no. 3 (1965): 53.
142. Ibid., 53–54.
143. Isserson, *Osnovy*, 114–17.
144. Ibid., 115–16, 118–20, 122.
145. Ibid., 117–18, 123; Varfolomeev, *Udarnaya*, 182; Vakulich, "Sovremennaya," 558; I. Savinov, "Operatsii Okruzheniia," *V&R*, July–August (1934): 23.
146. Isserson, *Osnovy*, 127–29.
147. Ibid., 130–31.
148. Varfolomeev, *Udarnaya*, 186. See also F. Trutko, "Material'noe Obespechenie Operatsii Udarnoi Armii," *V&R*, no. 12 (1932): 74.
149. Appen, "Problema Narastaniya i Istoshcheniya v Grazhdanskoi Voine, 1918–1920 gg.," *V&R*, no. 7 (1932): 64.
150. Isserson, *Osnovy*, 131.
151. Ibid., 132–33.
152. Varfolomeev, *Udarnaya*, 172.
153. Ibid., 188–89.
154. Isserson, *Osnovy*, 24.
155. Varfolomeev, *Udarnaya*, 173, 181.
156. *Proekt*, 89, 91–93.
157. Ibid., 100, 105.
158. *Osnovnye*, 45–47; Varfolomeev, "Operativnoe," 2.
159. A. Anisov, "Armeiskaya Oboronitel'naya Operatsiya," *V&R*, November–December (1934): 40–41.
160. Ibid., 44.
161. Ibid., 45.
162. Ibid., 47–48.
163. Kazakov, *Nad Kartoi*, 24; Isserson, "Razvitie," no. 1, p. 38.
164. Bulgakova, *Akademiya*, 26–27; Isserson, "Razvitie," no. 1, p. 44; V. G. Kulikov, ed., *Akademiya General'nogo Shtaba* (Moscow, 1976), 41.
165. Kulikov, *Akademiya*, 40; Bulgakova, *Akademiya*, 34.
166. Kulikov, *Akademiya*, 45–46; Bulgakova, *Akademiya*, 33; Kazakov, *Nad Kartoi*, 38; Vasilevskii, *Delo*, 92.

167. Isserson, "Razvitie," no. 3, pp. 49–50; Bagramyan, *Moi Vospominaniya,* 157.
168. Vasilevskii, *Delo,* 93.
169. A. M. Degtyarev, ed., *Kievskii Krasnoznamennyi* (Moscow, 1974), 102–3; A. I. Eremenko, *V Nachale Voiny* (Moscow, 1965), 8–11.
170. Zakharov, *General'nyi,* 101.
171. Isserson, "Razvitie," no. 1, p. 42.

5. THE ROAD TO WAR

1. Conquest, *Great Terror,* 471.
2. V. E. Motylev, *Narodnoe Khozyaistvo SSSR v Period Osushchestvleniya Tret'ego Pyatiletnogo Plana* (Moscow, 1959), 16–17.
3. K. E. Voroshilov, "Prikaz Narodnogo Komissara Oborony SSSR," *Krasnaya Zvezda,* June 14, 1937, 1. The other victims were I. P. Uborevich, commander of the Belorussian Military District; I. E. Yakir, commander of the Kiev Military District; A. I. Kork, head of the Frunze Military Academy; R. P. Eideman, chairman of the *Osoaviakhim* civil-military organization; B. M. Fel'dman, chief of the RKKA Main Administration; V. M. Primakov, deputy commander of the Leningrad Military District; and V. K. Putna, most recently military attaché in Great Britain. Ya. B. Gamarnik, head of the RKKA Political Directorate, was to have been part of this group, but he committed suicide before his arrest.
4. D. A. Volkogonov, *Triumf i Tragediya. Politicheskii Portret I. V. Stalina,* 2d ed. (Moscow, 1990), 1:513. The author cites as a source for this figure a Voroshilov speech at the end of November 1938. Another source supports this figure and claims that during 1937–38 more than 35,000 officers were "dismissed" from the ground forces, 3,000 from the navy, and more than 5,000 from the air force. See V. V. Karpov, *Marshal Zhukov. Ego Soratniki i Protivniki v Dni Voiny i Mira* (Moscow, 1992), 74. Another source mentions the figure of 35,000 victims in the officer corps. See W. G. Krivitsky, *In Stalin's Secret Service* (New York, 1939), 232. Erickson (*The Soviet High Command,* 506) puts the loss at 20,000 to 25,000.
5. One source states that 13,000 men were later reinstated in the RKKA, or about one-third of the total number purged. This also tends to confirm the overall figure of 40,000 purge victims. See V. L. Petrov, "Osobennosti Politicheskoi Sistemy Pered Voinoi," in *Velikaya Otechestvennaya Voina, 1941–1945,* ed. V. A. Zolotarev and G. N. Sevast'yanov (Moscow, 1998–99). Vol. I, *Surovye Ispytaniya,* 64.
6. Erickson, *The Soviet High Command,* 505.
7. Karpov, *Marshal Zhukov,* 73; O. F. Suvenirov, "Vsearmeiskaya Tragediya," *V-IZh,* no. 3 (1989): 41. Both sources cite the late A. I. Todorskii, whose breakdown of the victims by rank has become standard among Russian-Soviet historians.
8. Karpov, *Marshal Zhukov,* 75–76. One source states that of the RKKA's 767 senior officers (brigade commander and higher, and their naval equivalents), 412 were shot outright, 29 died in prison, 3 committed suicide, and only 59 were later released, or 503 victims of repression (65.5 percent). These figures are somewhat inflated, however, because they cover the period 1936–41 and therefore include those who were promoted to these ranks after 1936 and who were later repressed. See O. F. Suvenirov, *Tragediya RKKA, 1937–1938* (Moscow, 1998), 315.

9. Karpov, *Marshal Zhukov*, 75.

10. For an interesting account of his arrest, imprisonment, transportation, and ultimate release, see A. V. Gorbatov's *Gody i Voiny* (Moscow, 1965), 126–72. Unfortunately, Rokossovskii's memoirs, released during the Brezhnev years, do not mention these events. See K. K. Rokossovskii, *Soldatskii Dolg* (Moscow, 1968). The details of Zhukov's narrow escape became known only in the later, glasnost-era edition of his memoirs. See Zhukov, *Vospominaniya*, 1:241–44. For another version, see Simonov, "Zametki," no. 6, p. 54.

11. N. M. Yakupov, *Tragediya Polkovodtsev* (Moscow, 1992), 304; Nikulin, *Tukhachevskii*, 191; A. I. Todorskii, *Marshal Tukhachevskii* (Moscow, 1963), 8; Ivanov, *Marshal M. N. Tukhachevskii*, 311.

12. K. K. Rokossovskii, "Soldatskii Dolg," *V-IZh*, no. 4 (1989): 53. This passage is missing from the marshal's pre-glasnost-era memoirs of the same name and was replaced with a milder criticism. See Rokossovskii, *Soldatskii*, 8.

13. Simonov, "Zametki," no. 9, p. 50.

14. A. T. Stuchenko, *Zavidnaya Nasha Sud'ba* (Moscow, 1964), 63–64. This passage and other mentions of the purge were omitted from the 1968 edition.

15. Isserson, "Razvitie," no. 3, pp. 54–55; Eremenko, *V Nachale Voiny*, 14.

16. P. G. Grigorenko, *V Podpol'e Mozhno Vstretit' Tol'ko Krys* (New York, 1981), 212.

17. See V. A. Melikov, *Stalinskii Plan Razgroma Denikina* (Moscow, 1938); G. Fadeev, "Dvadtsat' Let Raboche-Krest'yanskoi Krasnoi Armii i Voenno-Morskogo Flota," *Voennaya Mysl'*, no. 2 (1938): 3–21; V. Solov'ev and A. Tsaritsyn, "Stalinskoe Uchenie o Voine i Armii," *V-IZh*, no. 5 (1939): 58–70.

18. E. A. Shilovskii, *Operatsiya* (Moscow, 1937), 54–55, 57–58, 64–66, 68–71.

19. E. Shilovskii, "Nastupatel'naya Operatsiya," *Voennaya Mysl'*, no. 6 (1938): 57–78.

20. G. Isserson, "Vstrechnoe Srazhenie Budushchego," *Voennaya Mysl'*, no. 7 (1938): 10–26; G. Isserson, "Operativnye Perspiktivy Budushchego," *Voennaya Mysl'*, no. 8 (1938): 14–26.

21. Grigorenko, *V Podpol'e*, 212. For a contemporary view of this conflict, see S. Lyubarskii, *Nekotorye Operativno-Takticheskie Vyvody iz Opyta Voiny v Ispanii* (Moscow, 1939); N. Korsun, "Nekotorye Operativnye Vyvody iz Poslednikh Voin," *V-IZh*, no. 1 (1939): 24–37; and A. Serebryakov, "Katalonskaya Operatsiya," *V-IZh*, no. 2 (1940): 74–93.

22. Isserson, "Razvitie," no. 3, p. 57. Shilovskii later described the defensive operation as having been until recently "in the shadows." See his "Vidy Operatsii," *Voennaya Mysl'*, no. 1 (1941): 22.

23. G. S. Isserson, *Osnovy Oboronitel'noi Operatsii* (Moscow, 1938), 21–24.

24. Ibid., 24–25.

25. Ibid., 27–31.

26. Zhukov, *Vospominaniya*, 1:306.

27. G. S. Isserson, *Novye Formy Bor'by* (Moscow, 1940), 22–25.

28. Isserson was soon to become a victim of his own outspoken views. In July 1941 he publicly stated in the General Staff Academy that if the army's leadership had adopted even some of the ideas put forth in his book, "We would have halted the enemy at Minsk."

As a result of this brave, if foolhardy, declaration, Isserson was immediately arrested and dispatched to the camps and internal exile, to return only in 1955. As a result of his arrest, his manuscript, dealing with the military events of 1940 in the west was confiscated and lost. See Sverdlov, "On Videl," 11.

29. Zhukov, *Vospominaniya,* 1:340, 354; V. Anfilov, ". . . Razgovor Zakonchilsya Ugrozoi Stalina," *V-IZh,* no. 3 (1995): 42.

30. Isserson later argued that the fault lay with a high command that lacked the experience and intellectual flexibility to respond to changing circumstances. Unfortunately, he concluded, those commanders who might have understood and adapted to the lessons of recent wars were no longer alive. See Isserson, "Razvitie," no. 3, p. 61.

31. See A. De-Lazari, "Voennoe Porazhenie Pol'skogo Gosudarstva," *V-IZh,* no. 1 (1940): 65–66.

32. Isserson, *Novye,* 22–25.

33. Ibid., 52.

34. Ibid., 65.

35. E. Tatarchenko, "Novye Cherty Sovremennogo Voennogo Iskusstva," *Krasnaya Zvezda,* July 10, 1940, 2. Other works on this subject include I. Ionov's "Ispol'zovanie VVS v Voine na Zapade," *Voennaya Mysl',* no. 10 (1940): 34–47, and I. Ratner's "Proryv na Maase," *V-IZh,* no. 5 (1941): 3–21.

36. V. Zakharov, "Opyt Grazhdanskoi Voiny v SSSR i Sovremennost'," *Krasnaya Zvezda,* February 8, 1941, 3.

37. Zakharov, *50 Let,* 198, 234; Grechko, *Istoriya,* 3:440, 4:18. A more recent source puts the armed forces' strength at some 5,700,000 men, although this figure includes NKVD troops as well. See Grachev, *Voennaya,* 2:35.

38. Tyushkevich, *Sovetskie,* 233, 237.

39. Grachev, *Voennaya,* 2:36. This version was chosen because, as the most recent, it presumably is less prone to the Soviet-era tendency to undercount Soviet troop strength in the area at the start of the war. Unfortunately, it does not offer a breakdown of divisions by type. Other sources exist, which offer different figures. One of these states that at the start of the war the Red Army had in its five frontier military districts 103 rifle, 7 cavalry, 40 tank, and 20 motorized divisions, plus 2 rifle brigades, or 171 divisions. These forces are said to have numbered 2,360,000 men, 11,000 tanks, 45,556 guns and mortars, and 8,030 aircraft. The lower personnel numbers may be due to not counting NKVD troops or those serving in the Baltic and Black Sea Fleets. See V. T. Iminov, ed., *Nachal'nyi Period Velikoi Otechestvennoi Voiny. Vyvody i Uroki* (Moscow, 1989), attachment 6. Two earlier works (Grechko, *Sovetskaya,* 2:55; Grechko, *Istoriya,* 4:25) repeat Iminov's figures for the number of divisions, while offering a lower figure of 37,500 guns and mortars. However, they are less than forthcoming regarding the actual number of tanks and aircraft at the start of the war. Both sources state that the Red Army had in the frontier military districts 1,475 new T-34 and KV-series tanks, as well as 1,540 modern aircraft. This begs the question of how many older-model tanks and aircraft there were, while serving the purpose of making the army's weapons park seem quite small in comparison with that of the Germans, who also had a significant number of obsolete tanks. These sources also offer a higher figure of 2,680,000 men in the five districts. The discrepancy also may be due to the latter sources counting border guards and internal troops as part of the total, and may also include personnel from the Baltic and Black Sea Fleets.

40. Grechko, *Istoriya*, 3:418.
41. M. V. Zakharov, *Nakanune Velikikh Ispytanii* (Moscow, 1968), 145; Zakharov, *50 Let*, 235.
42. Zakharov, *50 Let*, 235; Grechko, *Istoriya*, 3:418–19.
43. Grechko, *Istoriya*, 3:419.
44. Zakharov, *50 Let*, 236.
45. K. Voroshilov, "XX Let Raboche-Krest'yanskoi Krasnoi Armii i Voenno-Morskogo Flota," *Voennaya Mysl'*, no. 3 (1938): 13.
46. Zakharov, *50 Let*, 236; Grechko, *Istoriya*, 3:421; Zakharov, *Nakanune*, 176. Another source states that the Red Army had over 110,000 guns and mortars. See Grachev, *Voennaya*, 2:35.
47. Zakharov, *50 Let*, 236; Grechko, *Istoriya*, 3:421.
48. Grechko, *Istoriya*, 3:421.
49. Zakharov, *Nakanune*, 176.
50. Ryzhakov, "K Voprosu," 108–9; Zakharov, *Nakanune*, 21.
51. This decision and the debates accompanying it constitute one of the most controversial problems of the Red Army's interwar history. Marshal Zakharov maintains that the decision to disband the tank corps was a serious miscalculation that was based on incorrect conclusions drawn from the experience of employing armored forces during the Spanish civil war, which were not applicable to Soviet conditions. Zakharov also singles out D. G. Pavlov, a commission member and chief of the army's armored directorate, as the prime culprit in this decision. See Zakharov's introductory remarks in Kadishev, *Voprosy Strategii*, 22; and his own *Nakanune*, 48–50, 82. Ryzhakov ("K Voprosu," 109–10), however, defends the decision and claims that the September 1939 advance into Poland showed that the tank corps were difficult to control. Meretskov, another commission member, defends Pavlov and states that the latter's opposition to tank corps composed entirely of light tanks was well founded. See K. A. Meretskov, *Na Sluzhbe Narodu* (Moscow, 1968), 200–201.
52. Ryzhakov, "K Voprosu," 110; Zakharov, *Nakanune*, 51.
53. Ryzhakov, "K Voprosu," 110; I. Krupchenko, "Razvitie Tankovykh Voisk v Period Mezhdu Pervoi i Vtoroi Mirovymi Voinami," *V-IZh*, no. 5 (1968): 43; Zakharov, *Nakanune*, 212.
54. Zakharov, *Nakanune*, 82.
55. Ryzhakov, "K Voprosu," 110.
56. Zakharov, *Nakanune*, 211.
57. Ibid., 186.
58. Tyushkevich, *Sovetskie*, 230.
59. A. Nikitin, "Sostoyanie Vazhneishikh Otraslei Promyshlennosti SSSR Nakanune Velikoi Otechestvennoi Voiny," *V-IZh*, no. 3 (1960): 22–23; Zakharov, *Nakanune*, 147.
60. Zakharov, *Nakanune*, 147, 176; Zakharov, *50 Let*, 236. Another source states that the Red Army had at this time more than 23,000 tanks, of which 18,700 were combat-ready. The discrepancy, though large, may be accounted for by tanks in training and other units. See Grachev, *Voennaya*, 2:35.
61. Zakharov, *Nakanune*, 24; Grechko, *Sovetskaya*, 1:259.
62. Tyushkevich, *Sovetskie*, 243; Grechko, *Istoriya*, 3:424.
63. Nikitin, "Sostoyanie," 22.
64. Grachev (*Voennaya*, 2:35) states that the air force had about 13,000 serviceable combat aircraft at the start of the war.

65. "Rech' Predsedatelya Sovnarkoma SSSR, Deputata V. M. Molotova," *Pravda*, January 16, 1938, 4.

66. Grechko, *Istoriya*, 3:427. Another source states that the navy had 2,800 combat aircraft. See Grachev, *Voennaya*, 2:35.

67. Grechko, *Istoriya*, 3:425. Another source puts the PVO's prewar strength at 4,500 antiaircraft guns. See Grachev, *Voennaya*, 2:35.

68. Tyushkevich, *Sovetskie*, 247–48.

69. P. N. Pospelov, ed., *Velikaya Otechestvennaya Voina Sovetskogo Soiuza, 1941–1945. Kratkaya Istoriya* (Moscow, 1965), 40.

70. Zakharov, *General'nyi*, 52–53; Vasilevskii, *Delo*, 93–94; Sandalov, *Perezhitoe*, 22–23; Kazakov, *Nad Kartoi*, 40–41.

71. Grechko, *Istoriya*, 3:417.

72. Pospelov, *Istoriya*, 6:125.

73. M. A. Kreidberg and M. G. Merton, *History of Military Mobilization in the United States Army, 1775–1945* (Washington, D.C., 1955), 549, 623.

74. Zakharov, *Nakanune*, 186.

75. F. Halder, *The Halder Diaries* (Boulder, Colo., 1976), 2:904.

76. Grechko, *Istoriya*, 2:210.

77. Zakharov, *General'nyi*, 153–54; Zakharov, *Nakanune*, 44; Zhukov, *Vospominaniya*, 1:251. Zhukov later admitted his concern that the unexpected summons to Moscow meant that he was about to be arrested. See Simonov, "Zametki," no. 6, p. 52.

78. Zhukov, *Vospominaniya*, 1:254.

79. Ibid., 261–62; N. F. Kuz'min, *Na Strazhe Mirnogo Truda (1921–1940 gg.)* (Moscow, 1959), 212.

80. Simonov, "Zametki," no. 6, p. 53; Grigorenko, *V Podpol'e*, 234.

81. Grechko, *Istoriya*, 2:215, 217. Unfortunately, Soviet data concerning the size of the Japanese forces are shrouded in evasions and half-truths. The figure quoted is actually the number that the official history claims were moved up to the battlefield after May. The same history also states (p. 216) that the Sixth Army actually numbered 75,000 men, 500 guns, 182 tanks, and more than 300 planes. The former figure was chosen, however, because it coincides closely with figures given in other Soviet works. For example, Zakharov (*50 Let*, 227) states that the Soviets outnumbered the Japanese by a factor of 1.5 to 1 in infantry, nearly 2 to 1 in artillery, and 4 to 1 in tanks. Kuz'min (*Na Strazhe*, 212–13) cites nearly the same percentages, while adding that the Soviet superiority in aircraft was 515 to 303 planes.

82. There is some disagreement over who was the actual author of the plan, Zhukov or Shtern. See Simonov, "Zametki," no. 6, p. 47; Grigorenko, *V Podpol'e*, 234.

83. *Doklad Komandovaniya Gruppy ob Itogakh Operatsii v Raione r. Khalkhin-Gol*, RGVA, fond 32113, opis' 1, delo 207, p. 22.

84. Zakharov, *General'nyi*, 157.

85. Zhukov, *Vospominaniya*, 1:262–65.

86. Grechko, *Istoriya*, 2:218; Voronov (*Na Sluzhbe Voennoi*, 128–29) states that the Soviets attacked on Sunday because many Japanese officers would be on leave, while their men would be relaxing with prostitutes brought up from the rear.

87. Simonov, "Zametki," no. 6, pp. 53–54. Zhukov wrote at the time that 20 percent of this unit had never even so much as held a rifle and was completely unprepared for combat. He added, in a comment typical of the times, that the division also contained

"hostile elements" that carried out "counterrevolutionary work," which led to insubordination and murder. RGVA, fond 32113, opis' 1, delo 207, p. 38.

88. A. D. Coox, *Nomonhan: Japan Against Russia, 1939* (Stanford, Calif., 1994), 2:916.

89. Krivosheev, *Grif Sekretnosti Snyat,* 125.

90. Coox, *Nomonhan,* 2:916. Zhukov claims that the Japanese suffered 52,000 to 55,000 casualties from mid-July, including at least 23,000 to 25,000 killed. RGVA, fond 32113, opis' 1, delo 207, p. 27.

91. Grigorenko (*V Podpol'e,* 237) states that Zhukov ordered the handing out of death sentences during the battle to those who failed to carry out their mission, and that it required Shtern's intervention to have the sentences countermanded. Two years later, during the defense of Leningrad, Zhukov was still using these methods. See B. V. Bychevskii, *Gorod-Front* (Moscow, 1963), 99. Also instructive is General Eisenhower's description of Zhukov's view of casualties. See D. D. Eisenhower, *Crusade in Europe* (Garden City, N.Y., 1948), 467–68.

92. C. G. E. Mannerheim, *The Memoirs of Marshal Mannerheim,* trans. E. Lewenhaupt (London, 1953), 330. These figures are essentially confirmed in Erickson (*Soviet High Command,* 552). Krivosheev (*Grif Sekretnosti Snyat,* 96) states that on January 1, 1940, the Soviet forces deployed against Finland numbered 550,757 men, so the initial half-million figure may have been augmented by reinforcements.

93. Zakharov, *Nakanune,* 59–60.

94. Ibid., 55.

95. Meretskov, *Na Sluzhbe Narodu,* 178–79; Zakharov, *General'nyi,* 182; Zakharov, *Nakanune,* 58. For other examples of Soviet optimism on the eve of the war, see Khrushchev (*Khrushchev Remembers,* 152) and Voronov (*Na Sluzhbe Voennoi,* 136).

96. Kuz'min, *Na Strazhe,* 234; Mannerheim, *Memoirs,* 325, 371. The "Mannerheim Line," for obvious reasons, has acquired a near-mythic stature in Soviet-era histories. Meretskov (*Na Sluzhbe Narodu,* 176), for example, compares the position to the Siegfried and Maginot Lines.

97. Zakharov, *Nakanune,* 64.

98. Krivosheev, *Grif Sekretnosti Snyat,* 96. This figure probably includes only the ground forces. Soviet sources fail to cite the number of divisions involved. Both Mannerheim (*Memoirs,* 365) and Erickson (*Soviet High Command,* 552) cite a figure of forty-five divisions.

99. Zakharov, *General'nyi,* 183–84; Grechko, *Istoriya,* 3:363.

100. Meretskov, *Na Sluzhbe Narodu,* 187, 189.

101. Kuz'min, *Na Strazhe,* 241.

102. Mannerheim, *Memoirs,* 370.

103. Krivosheev, *Grif Sekretnosti Snyat,* 125.

104. Mannerheim, *Memoirs,* 367.

105. Biryuzov, *Kogda,* 31–32. A similar, if somewhat less harsh, verdict was also delivered by Marshal Zakharov. See his *Nakanune,* 113. For contemporary evidence of the Soviets' sudden interest in the subject of overcoming permanent fortifications, see the articles by M. Knyazev, "Ataka Ukreplennykh Raionov," *Voennaya Mysl',* no. 6 (1940): 10–38; K. Golubev, "Operatsiya po Proryvu UR," *Voennaya Mysl',* no. 2 (1941): 12–43; and V. Gorskii, "Material'noe Obespechenie Armii v Operatsii po Proryvu UR," *Voennaya Mysl',* no. 4 (1941): 29–52.

106. Grigorenko, *V Podpol'e,* 212.

107. V. A. Zolotarev, ed., *Russkii Arkhiv. Velikaya Otechestvennaya* (Moscow, 1993–), XII.1, 19, 25–27, 43, 57–58, 75, 77, 80, 85, 96, 118.

108. This statement is by no means an exaggeration, as was affirmed years later by the Soviet Union's greatest wartime general. In May 1941, Zhukov, then chief of the General Staff, and Timoshenko were becoming increasingly concerned with the concentration of German forces along the USSR's western frontier. Emboldened by a recent bellicose speech by Stalin, they drew up a plan for a preventive attack against Germany and presented it to the dictator for his approval. Stalin rejected the proposal out of hand, fearing that the preparations for such an attack would provoke the Germans into war. Zhukov, speaking nearly a quarter of a century later, expressed his relief that the plan had been turned down. The Red Army was in such a poor state, he said, that had the attack been mounted, it might have suffered a "disaster" much greater than its defeat at Khar'kov in May 1942. See Anfilov, "Razgovor," 41.

109. Zhukov, *Vospominaniya,* 1:303; I. Kh. Bagramyan, *Tak Nachinalas' Voina* (Moscow, 1971), 16.

110. Zolotarev, *Russkii Arkhiv,* XII.1, 130–33.

111. Ibid., 134–35; Triandafillov, *Kharakter,* 1st ed., 121–22. Zhukov singles out Triandafillov for praise in his memoirs (*Vospominaniya,* 1:169–70, 186), although he did not credit him in his December address.

112. Zolotarev, *Russkii Arkhiv,* XII.1, 135, 138–39.

113. Ibid., 135–36.

114. Ibid., 137.

115. Ibid., 137–38.

116. Ibid., 136.

117. Ibid., 138, 140–41.

118. Ibid., 138–39, 141.

119. Ibid., 140, 143.

120. Ibid., 142, 146–48.

121. Ibid., 142, 149–50.

122. Ibid., 139, 142, 150.

123. Ibid., 154.

124. Ibid., 165.

125. Ibid., 159–60.

126. Ibid., 155.

127. Eremenko, *V Nachale Voiny,* 38. This statement should be taken with a grain of salt, however. Eremenko was an ally of Khrushchev, who removed Zhukov from his post as defense minister in 1957 and was so obliged to denigrate the latter's reputation. After Khrushchev's own ouster in the autumn of 1964, a book review appeared attacking Eremenko's version of these and other events. See V. Ivanov and K. Cheremukhin, "O Knige 'V Nachale Voiny,'" *V-IZh,* no. 6 (1965): 72–80. There is much to the review's indictment, as even a cursory reading of the conference's stenographic record refutes Eremenko's tendentious remarks.

128. Zolotarev, *Ruskii Arkhiv,* XII.1, 159–60.

129. Ibid., 142.

130. Ibid., 155, 166–67.

131. Ibid., 149.

132. Ibid., 158.
133. Ibid., 171.
134. Ibid., 153.
135. Ibid., 174–76.
136. Ibid., 176–77.
137. Ibid., 177–78.
138. Ibid., 180.
139. Ibid., 189–91.
140. Ibid., 191.
141. Ibid., 188.
142. Ibid., 193–94, 201, 206.
143. Ibid., 209–10.
144. Ibid., 222.
145. Ibid., 210–11, 220.
146. Ibid., 216, 218.
147. Ibid., 214–15.
148. Ibid., 215.
149. Ibid., 219–20.
150. Ibid., 227.
151. Ibid., 248.
152. Ibid., 227.
153. Ibid., 228, 237.
154. Ibid., 238–39.
155. Ibid., 245–46, 249.
156. Zhukov, *Vospominaniya,* 1:304. This passage was deleted from earlier pre-glasnost editions.
157. Zolotarev, *Russkii Arkhiv,* XII.1, 257.
158. Ibid., 257–58.
159. Ibid., 259–60.
160. Ibid., 261.
161. Ibid., 263–64.
162. Ibid., 269.
163. Ibid., 269–70.
164. Ibid., 270.
165. Ibid., 289–90.
166. Ibid., 296.
167. Ibid., 275.
168. Ibid., 284.
169. Ibid., 299.
170. Ibid., 269, 299.
171. Ibid., 287, 294.
172. S. K. Timoshenko, *Zaklyuchitel'naya Rech' Narodnogo Komissara Oborony Soyuza SSR, Geroya i Marshala Sovetskogo Soyuza S. K. Timoshenko, na Voennom Soveshchanii, 31 Dekabrya 1940 g.* (Moscow, 1941), 10–11.
173. Ibid., 13, 15–16.
174. Ibid., 16, 18.
175. Ibid., 18.

176. Ibid., 20.
177. Ibid., 18, 20.
178. Ibid., 22.
179. Ibid., 22–23.
180. Ibid., 36, 44.
181. Ibid., 34, 38–39.
182. Ibid., 30–32.
183. Ibid., 39–40.
184. Ibid., 23–24.
185. Ibid., 25.
186. Ibid., 25–27.
187. Ibid., 27–28.
188. Ibid., 27, 29–30.
189. Ibid., 30.
190. Zakharov, *Nakanune*, 124. Elsewhere Zakharov puts the strength of the southern armies at 160 divisions. See his *General'nyi*, 240.
191. Vasilevskii, *Delo*, 110; Zhukov, *Vospominaniya*, 1:348–49; Zakharov, *General'nyi*, 220.
192. Zakharov, *General'nyi*, 221.
193. Zakharov, *Nakanune*, 124, 140.
194. Ibid., map 8.
195. Ibid.; Simonov, "Zametki," no. 9, p. 50. However, his own figures do not stop Zakharov (*Nakanune*, 140) from claiming that in both games the "westerners" had a superiority of forces. A possible explanation for this contradiction is examined more fully in note 198.
196. Zakharov, *Nakanune*, 125–26, map 8.
197. Ibid., 140; Zakharov, *General'nyi*, 240.
198. Zhukov, *Vospominaniya*, 1:307. A possible explanation for these events comes from a post-Soviet historical novel covering the immediate prewar years. The author states that the first war game was actually played out twice. The first time, he maintains, the game ended in the complete rout of Zhukov's forces between Warsaw and Konigsberg, very much according to the scenario outlined by Zakharov. This is understandable because the correlation of forces established for the game practically guaranteed a "western" defeat. The author goes on to state, however, that Zhukov, whose vanity had been stung by this defeat, appealed for a rematch to Chief of Staff Meretskov, who proceeded to heavily reinforce Zhukov's front to the level indicated by the latest intelligence data. Thus strengthened, Zhukov was able to launch a devastating opening blow and defeat the "red" forces. This implies that the game was replayed from the beginning, as it is unlikely that even a reinforced enemy front could have recovered from the kind of defeat inherent in the initial correlation of forces. This source further states that the Soviet rout was so complete that the "red" forces to the south of the Pripyat Marshes could not even carry out their planned counteroffensive. See I. L. Bunich, *Operatsiya "Groza"* (St. Petersburg, 1994), 2:324–27. Unfortunately, the author, who claims to base his narrative on the historical record, cites no documentary evidence to support his assertions. Indeed, Bunich's entire analysis is driven by his highly tendentious thesis that the Soviets were actually war-gaming a surprise attack ("Operation Storm") against Germany. Nevertheless, his interpretation of at least some of the first war game's particulars is obliquely confirmed by

two of the participants. One states that many officers were puzzled by the western armies' "insignificant superiority," by which the author is evidently referring to the initial lineup of forces. See Kazakov, *Nad Kartoi,* 57. As we have seen, however, it was the attacking "western" armies that were inferior to their opponents, particularly in the number of tanks. Elsewhere, Zhukov states that based on "real starting data," his forces were able to advance as far as Baranovichi in just eight days, despite being artificially slowed down by the game's umpires. The phrase "real starting data" also tends to confirm Bunich's version of events. However, Zhukov does not state whether this victory flowed from the original scenario or whether it was the result of a second "amended" game, although it is hard to imagine his achieving any successes, given the original correlation of forces. Furthermore, nowhere in this account does Zhukov mention a withdrawal or defeat by his forces. See Simonov, "Zametski," no. 9, p. 50. Another source supports Zhukov's version, stating that the "westerners" launched a number of converging attacks, which broke through the defender's frontier fortifications, followed by an advance as far east as Lida. See Anfilov, *Bessmertnyi,* 147. The author's phrasing indicates that these events occurred at the beginning of the war game. If there were indeed two war games played along this front, it is unclear from these remarks which one he is referring to. Once again, however, given the original correlation of forces, it is difficult to imagine Zhukov's forces advancing anywhere. As in so much else, the truth will emerge only when the Russian government fully opens its archives to all researchers.

199. Zakharov, *General'nyi,* 243–45; Zakharov, *Nakanune,* map 9. This scenario begs the question of why, if the Soviets believed that the Germans would make their main attack south of the Pripyat Marshes, the wargame planners made the enemy Southeastern Front so weak.

200. Zakharov, *Nakanune,* 127–28.

201. Ibid., 134.

202. Ibid., 134–35, 139.

203. Ibid., 135.

204. Zhukov considered Pavlov and Kuznetsov "poorly prepared" as commanders of major operational forces. See Anfilov, "Razgovor," 42.

205. Zhukov, *Vospominaniya,* 1:308–9.

206. Ibid., 308–11. Meretskov (*Na Sluzhbe Narodu,* 200) writes that Stalin was very dissatisfied with his (Meretskov's) intelligence data on the German forces. This version at least indirectly supports Bunich's two-game thesis.

Bibliography

This book's conclusions are primarily based on the original, open-source works of those theorists who participated in the development of operational art during the period in question. These include such outstanding studies as A. A. Neznamov's *Modern War: The Activities of a Field Army,* the first czarist-era work devoted entirely to military affairs at the operational level. Neznamov, who was already a senior officer in 1917, later enjoyed a career in the Red Army's system of military education. Also included in this group are N. N. Movchin's *Consecutive Operations According to the Experience of the Marne and Vistula,* V. K. Triandafillov's *The Character of Operations of Modern Armies,* and N. E. Varfolomeev's *The Shock Army.* The latter three authors all served as junior officers in the czarist army and saw their academic talents come to fruition under the Soviets.

Other valuable sources are the collected works of some of the major theorists and anthologies of other writings of the period in question. These include the *Selected Works* by both M. V. Frunze and M. N. Tukhachevskii, and S. S. Kamenev's *Notes on the Civil War and Military Construction: Selected Articles.* While Frunze was a professional revolutionary who found his true calling as a military leader during the civil war, both Kamenev and Tukhachevskii were former czarist officers who rose to high command positions in the Red Army. Another important work is *Problems of Strategy and Operational Art in Soviet Military Works (1917–1940),* edited by A. B. Kadishev. This collection of pre–World War II writings was at the time of its publication in 1965 one of the best insights into the Red Army's theoretical life, although it has since been superseded by greater access to the original publications.

The book also makes use of the extensive memoir literature covering the period. Chief among these is B. M. Shaposhnikov's *Memoirs: Military-Scientific Works,* which gives an invaluable insight into life at the imperial army's leading academic institution and the place operations occupied in the curriculum. Other works, such as A. M. Vasilevskii's *The Cause of a Lifetime,* L. M. Sandalov's *My Past,* and N. N. Voronov's *On Military Service,* are mined for their insights into people and problems. These works not only provide useful factual information and character portraits of leading military figures but also vividly portray the tenor of the times.

Also of great value are a number of official publications, particularly those of the Soviet period. Among these are such groundbreaking documents as the *RKKA Field Manual* of 1929 and the *1936 RKKA Provisional Field Manual.* While these are deeply tactical works, they nevertheless have significance for operational art, in that they lay out in great detail the forces and means necessary for carrying out the "deep battle," which is the tactical prerequisite for the conduct of the "deep operation" of the 1930s.

Finally, a number of journals contain a great deal of original literature on the subject, written by the major participants. These were generally showcased in *War and Revolution,* which was the Red Army's premier military-historical and theoretical journal in the 1920s and 1930s, until its replacement by *Military Thought* in 1937. Among these articles are Varfolomeev's excellent piece, "Strategy in an Academic Setting" (1928), which examines, among other questions, the place occupied by operational art in the leading Soviet military-educational institution at the end of the 1920s.

Of particular interest to the military specialist are a handful of archival documents, which were compiled during the late 1920s and 1930s. Some of these have appeared, in abbreviated form, in various Soviet publications, while others are presented here for the first time. Among these are *Future War,* a massive study edited by Tukhachevskii, which lays out on a grand scale the strategic tasks facing the USSR and the operational problems proceeding from these assumptions. Of equal interest is A. A. Svechin's report *A Future War and Our Military Tasks,* which persuasively presents an alternative strategy to that advocated by his archrival, Tukhachevskii. Triandafillov's *Fundamental Problems of Operational Art and Tactics, in Connection with the Army's Reconstruction,* drawn up shortly before the author's death, points the way for the Red Army's mechanization efforts, with inevitable consequences for operational art.

However, the jewel in the archival crown is undoubtedly G. S. Isserson's 1933 work, *Fundamentals of the Deep Operation,* which is to the 1930s what Triandafillov's *The Character of Operations of Modern Armies* was to the 1920s. Here the author lays out in enviable detail the means and methods for conducting a "deep operation." The lessons outlined in this manual retained their vitality well into World War II and may be profitably read even today. It is to be hoped that the Russian authorities will one day assent to this document's full declassification, as it does great honor to the intellectual vigor of the prewar Red Army.

Before proceeding to an examination of the Soviet secondary-source literature, a few words must be said regarding the veracity of the materials in question. The difficulty inherent in such research stems from the long-standing Russian-Soviet tradition of state interference in scholarly matters, with predictably deleterious consequences for the latter. This has often resulted in a situation in which history, in particular, has been employed as much to obfuscate as to illuminate. While this policy was by no means confined to the Soviet regime, the late system's far-reaching ideological pretensions exacerbated the situation immeasurably. The effects are particularly evident in much of the secondary-source literature since the end of the 1920s and have varied since then in accordance with the transient needs of the particular leadership group. Depending on the period in question, political considerations have led to the glorification of the military roles of some (Lenin, Stalin, Voroshilov) and the denigration or historical "disappearance" of others (Trotskii, Tukhachevskii, Svechin). Even the brief period of openness at the end of the 1950s and first part of the 1960s was motivated a great deal by N. S. Khrushchev's campaign to denigrate the late Joseph Stalin's role in Soviet history. The latest period of revelations, begun under M. S. Gorbachev, while highly uneven and sometimes given to sensationalism, has been far more objective and promises to have more long-lasting effects.

As one might expect, the volume of literature in Russian devoted to the problem of the country's military legacy and operational art is much greater than in the West. However, at least until recently, political constraints frequently hindered an objective examination of the country's military past.

Unfortunately, those Soviet works dealing with the former czarist officers' practical and theoretical contribution to the Red Army are almost exclusively concerned with the period encompassing the Russian civil war, 1918–22. This fixation, while somewhat understandable, necessarily fails to address the officers' role during the prerevolutionary and post–civil war years covered by this work and constitutes a serious oversight in Soviet historical research. Among these works are several official histories of the civil war, including *The History of the Civil War in the USSR,* which appeared in several volumes from 1935 to 1960. Other examples from this genre are the three-volume *From the History of the Civil War in the USSR* and the more recent two-volume *The Civil War in the USSR.* However, these works' worth is often diminished by a politically motivated tendency to dismiss or ignore the role of the former czarist officers in the Red Army and a predilection for empty sloganeering.

Among other useful publications dealing with the civil war are two collections of orders issued by the Soviet high command and the various front commands during these years: *Directives of the Red Army High Command (1917–1920)* and the four-volume *Directives of the Red Army Front Commands (1917–1922).* Both works are primarily documentary and refreshingly free of the usual political clichés. Together they convey an unintended but profound impression of the former czarist officers' degree of involvement in day-to-day military affairs at the operational-strategic level.

There are also many more general works that touch upon the role played by the former czarist officers during these years. These generally focus on the Communist Party's efforts to recruit the former officers into the Red Army and to establish effective control over them. Others fleetingly treat the problem of the former officers as part of the Soviet regime's larger effort to enlist the "bourgeois intelligentsia" to its cause. Several of these works contain valuable details regarding the employment of the former czarist officers and the controversy this policy engendered in both the party and the army. Among these are an article by S. A. Fedyukin: "On the Employment of Military Specialists in the Red Army," *Military-Historical Journal,* no. 6 (1962), and his broader work, *Great October and the Intelligentsia.*

Easily the most important work on the subject of the former officers is A. G. Kavtaradze's 1988 study of their role in the Red Army during the civil war: *Military Specialist on Service to the Soviet Republic, 1917–1920.* In this work the author uses a wealth of archival and secondary literature to construct a detailed picture of the officers' life in the army, including data on their social origins, methods of recruitment, their command and staff roles, and the problems and prejudices they encountered in their work. Kavtaradze also provides a useful listing of those former officers who served in the Red Army's general staff apparatus or commanded armies. The book is also refreshingly free of much of the ideological boilerplate that mars so many Soviet histories of the period. On the other hand, the work is necessarily limited, due to its narrow focus on the civil war and its failure to examine problems of military theory.

The large body of Soviet literature devoted to the development of the operation and operational art is equally impressive, although the quantity of the work often exceeds its quality. The Soviets were among the most prolific publishers of military-historical and military-theoretical books and articles, and operational art was no exception. This is hardly surprising, as Soviet historians always made much of the Red Army's contribution to the development of operational theory. Among these are such operationally significant studies as N. A. Levitskii's *The Russo-Japanese War, 1904–1905* and A. S. Beloi's *The Battle of Galicia*. Despite the fact that these works were published during the Stalinist years, they manage to remain professional military histories with a minimum of political commentary.

The Soviets have also produced a large body of work on the military operations of the civil war, such as K. V. Agureev's *The Rout of Denikin's White Guard Troops* and a joint work by N. E. Kakurin and V. A. Melikov, *The War with the White Poles*. Unfortunately, while a number of works are highly detailed and offer a great number of interesting facts, the value of many others has been reduced by an overtly propagandistic tone, and some, such as S. M. Budennyi's *The Road Traveled,* read more like didactic novels than history. This is also the period most affected by the Stalin cult, when the civil war's history was distorted almost beyond recognition. One of the most egregious offenders in this regard is Melikov's *The Heroic Defense of Tsaritsyn (1918),* among many others.

A much more valuable source for understanding the problem, and the civil war in general, is the three-volume history of the conflict published at the end of the 1920s, *The Civil War in the USSR, 1918–1921*. This is a deeply military history of the war, in spite of a fair amount of political boilerplate, and many of the articles were in fact written by former officers. Despite the creeping Stalin cult, this history remains by far the best and most objective account from the Soviet side, and it contains numerous facts and interpretations that were omitted from later official histories.

More impressive is the amount and quality of work published after Stalin's death in 1953, which covers the theoretical and technical developments of the interwar (1921–41) period. Among these is V. A. Semenov's *A Short Essay on the Development of Soviet Operational Art,* although this work is focused primarily on World War II and is badly dated. Far more impressive is R. A. Savushkin's short but excellent *The Development of the Soviet Armed Forces and Military Art in the Interwar Period (1921–1941)*. Savushkin's work is valuable not only in terms of archival access but also for his insights into this extremely rich period.

Two other recent works are also worthy of note: I. A. Korotkov's *A History of Soviet Military Thought* and P. A. Zhilin's *The Birth and Development of Soviet Military Historiography, 1917–1941*. The two works are notable for their efforts to more or less objectively discuss the role of the former czarist officers in elaborating a specifically Soviet theory of war and operational art, although the treatment of the latter subject is not as complete as one would like. Nor are the authors wholly free of a number of standard formulations and a somewhat condescending attitude toward the military specialists. On the other hand, Korotkov's discussion of the officers' contribution to the doctrinal and strategic debates of the 1920s is informative and generally fair, while Zhilin's section on their prerevolutionary writings is particularly good. It is unfortunate that the limited size of the two works and their broad scope of inquiry do not allow the authors to examine these questions in greater depth.

Use will also be made of a small number of Russian-language émigré sources, which deal primarily with the prerevolutionary and civil war periods. Among these are A. A. Kersnovskii's *A History of the Russian Army,* which offers an excellent insight into military developments up to 1917. Also of interest is N. N. Golovin's *Russia's Military Efforts in the World War,* which covers World War I. Finally, mention must also be made of A. I. Denikin's multivolume *Essays on the Russian Troubles,* which offers invaluable insights into the Russian conduct of operations in World War I and the civil war, the latter from the White perspective. Unfortunately, the value of these sources is limited exclusively to the prerevolutionary and civil war years, and they have no relevance to the post-1920 period. Also, while helpful, the worth of these sources, like that of their communist counterparts, is often impaired by their stridently polemical tone and a desire to settle old scores with adversaries.

However, if Soviet-era research was often hobbled by political considerations, a good deal of the pertinent Western scholarship tends to be superficial, in part due to the archival inaccessibility of much of the material, as well as our long-standing ignorance of what constitutes operational art. The great majority of these works overlook the operational level of war entirely and mention the role of the former czarist officers in the Red Army only in passing. At their worst, these works rarely rise above the level of popular history. Many rely heavily on unsupported anecdotes and lack a solid documentary base, while most tend to stress the Red Army's technological development and give short shrift to the theoretical side of affairs. Among the many offenders in this regard are E. Wollenberg's *The Red Army,* M. Garder's *A History of the Soviet Army,* and B. H. Liddell Hart's *The Soviet Army.* The latter is particularly disappointing in light of the author's earlier work.

Other works by British and American authors are considerably higher in quality. However, even such superior studies as M. Mackintosh's *Juggernaut: A History of the Soviet Armed Forces* and H. F. Scott and W. F. Scott's *The Armed Forces of the USSR* tend to focus on the Red Army's technological-administrative development at the expense of theory. Moreover, the authors' strictly Soviet approach leaves untouched the entire question of the imperial army's role in the army's evolution.

The best single work on the development of the Red Army is still John Erickson's *The Soviet High Command: A Military-Political History, 1918-1941,* which retains its value and freshness nearly four decades after its publication. Erickson's treatment of his subject is both sweeping in its scope and meticulous in its research. His comments on the recruitment of the former czarist officers into the fledgling Red Army are especially good, and their influence is felt throughout, although this was surely not the author's intent. However, many of Erickson's comments on the former officers' role are made only in passing, without any reference to their prerevolutionary activities or their significance to the army's later development. Moreover, the author rarely touches on the subject of operational art per se, although his treatment of the Red Army's theoretical growth in other areas is informative.

Another outstanding general work is D. Fedotoff White's *The Growth of the Red Army,* which is all the more impressive because the author, working in 1944, relied on a much smaller documentary base. Nonetheless, Fedotoff White produced an eminently readable and superior work. Unfortunately, while the problem of integrating the former imperial officers into the Red Army is touched upon fleetingly, the development of the army's military theory is almost entirely ignored. Still, one cannot but marvel at the author's solid grasp of the material.

A particularly bright spot in the English-language body of work dealing with the Russian imperial army is Bruce Menning's *Bayonets Before Bullets,* which covers the 1861–1914 period. Solidly researched and written in an easily accessible style, the book is indispensable for understanding developments within the army as it sought to come to grips with the new military technology in the years before World War I. The author's tactical-operational description of the Russo-Japanese War is far superior to anything available in English to date, although his conclusions about the war's operational significance are not as complete as one would like.

Menning is at his best when describing theoretical developments. His examination of the army's theoretical growth during the 1905–14 period is excellent, as are his intellectual and personal portraits of such theorists as Leer, Mikhnevich, and Neznamov. Here the author performs a great service in demonstrating, albeit unintentionally, that what was later to become the Soviet theory of operational art had its roots in the late imperial period.

In much the same way, Norman Stone's *The Eastern Front, 1914–1917,* is probably the best English-language treatment of this little-known aspect of World War I. The book provides a cogent description and analysis of the old army's collapse, both on the battlefield and in the rear. On the other hand, the narrative is often so sweeping that there is little analysis of the army's failures at the operational level. On a more positive note, the chapter dealing with the prewar intrigues and cliques within the army is informative and provides a complement to Menning's analysis.

Among those works dealing with the Russian civil war are W. H. Chamberlain's *The Russian Revolution, 1917–1921* and John F. Bradley's *Civil War in Russia, 1917–1920.* While all three are decent treatments of the war, the purely military aspects of the conflict do not receive the attention they deserve. Unfortunately, the definitive English-language military history of the civil war is yet to be written.

A different matter entirely is *White Eagle, Red Star,* by Norman Davies, which is an excellent military history of the Soviet-Polish war of 1920. The narrative, while chiefly from the Polish point of view, is nonetheless good at portraying the situation in the Soviet camp.

Also superior is Francesco Benvenuti's *The Bolsheviks and the Red Army, 1918–1922,* which tracks the army's growth during its early years. Of particular interest are chapters 5 and 8, which deal with the controversy surrounding the employment of former czarist officers and the political-military maneuverings after the civil war. The author's examination of the political motivations inherent in these disputes is particularly good.

A worthy complement to this volume is Mark von Hagen's *Soldiers in the Proletarian Dictatorship: The Red Army and the Soviet Socialist State, 1917–1930,* which traces the army's growth from its inception to the onset of mechanization. This work also contains a number of interesting passages on the role of the former czarist officers. However, it is deficient in its lack of attention to the army's theoretical growth, although, again, this was evidently not the author's intent.

The twenty-year period between the end of the civil war and Hitler's invasion of the Soviet Union is less amenable to delineation than preceding eras, which were conveniently broken up by wars. This often causes scholars to divide the period into segments corresponding to the political and technological currents that buffeted the Red Army during these years. The one work that comes closest to embracing the era with the necessary thoroughness is still Erickson's previously cited *The Soviet High Command.* However, as mentioned earlier, this work tends to slight theoretical developments in favor of a political-technological-administrative analysis of events.

Another Erickson work, *The Road to Stalingrad,* contains a good deal of valuable introductory material on theoretical developments from 1936 to 1941, and the author's treatment of the 1940–41 period is particularly good. However, the book's focus on World War II leaves no time to examine the operationally significant events of 1921–35.

In the same vein, David Glantz's two recent works, *When Titans Clashed* (coauthored with Jonathan M. House) and *Stumbling Colossus,* focus on the details of the 1941–45 struggle, or on the period immediately preceding the German invasion. The author's discussion of such prewar theoretical concepts as the "deep battle" is informative, if brief.

Another interesting work is *High Treason: Essays on the History of the Red Army, 1918–1938,* by émigré scholars Vitaly Rapoport and Yuri Alexeev. This book combines an eccentric and highly impressionistic view of events, which distinguishes it from any other work on the subject. The authors' examination of the theoretical debates of the 1920s is particularly good, although their tendency to see issues in terms of personalities can sometimes be misleading.

Of particular interest are two compilations of articles on strategy, published some forty years apart. The first is Edward Earle's "Lenin, Trotsky, Stalin: Soviet Concepts of War," which appeared in the 1943 version of *Makers of Modern Strategy,* which he also edited. The article, while chiefly concerned with military doctrine, nonetheless has, by extension, significance for operations. Unfortunately, the article is elsewhere marred by the spirit of wartime boosterism and outright gaffes (i.e., Voroshilov and Gusev as "brilliant, self-made commanders"), but it may still be read with profit.

Much better is Condoleezza Rice's "The Making of Soviet Strategy," which appears in Peter Paret's revised edition of *Makers of Modern Strategy.* The article's title aside, Rice makes a number of insightful forays into the Red Army's operational theory in the 1920s and 1930s. A better synopsis of Soviet interwar theoretical developments would be hard to find.

The upsurge in Soviet military studies, which began in the West in the late 1970s, has spawned a number of attempts to understand operational art as a distinct sphere of military endeavor. A few of the more representative works, for better or worse, are examined here.

One such effort is Edward Luttwak's "The Operational Level of War," *International Security,* vol. 5, no. 3 (1980–81), in which the author delivers an interesting critique of America's "Anglo-Saxon" failure to understand operational art. The author maintains that our logistics-driven tradition of waging war leads inevitably to an attrition struggle at the expense of such vital operational elements as maneuver. He errs, however, in ignoring the Soviet experience and in identifying the German blitzkrieg, a strategic concept, with operational art.

Less successful is James Schneider's "Theoretical Implications of Operational Art," *Military Review,* vol. 70, no. 9 (1990). The author, while rightly criticizing the American military's ignorance of operational art, does little to advance our understanding and engages in a hodgepodge of unrelated verbiage that even includes the national debt. Moreover, while Schneider makes brief reference to Soviet sources, he ultimately falls prey to the American military's long-standing vice of worshiping at the shrine of German military art.

Even more disappointing is an article by Jay Luvaas, entitled "Thinking at the Operational Level," *Parameters,* vol. 16, no. 1 (1986). Unfortunately, this piece contains very little in the way of thinking or operational art.

By far the best study of operational art in English is Glantz's *Soviet Military Operational Art. In Search of Deep Battle* (1991). In this book the author traces the phenomenon of operational art from its infant beginnings in an infantry-cavalry world to an era dominated by armor, airpower, and nuclear weapons. Glantz also performs the service of placing the theory within a hierarchical ordering of military doctrine, military science, military art, operational art, and tactics.

The author's treatment of the 1917–41 period is also superior, although his purely Soviet focus necessarily means skipping over the theory's imperial roots. His description of the doctrinal struggles of the 1920s is good, although more attention might have been paid to the theory of "consecutive operations"—one of the main results of the decade. The author's discussion of the theory of the "deep operation" of the 1930s is also good. The book is liberally supported by tables and maps, which graphically bring to life the theory.

Aside from the explicitly bad books and articles cited here, none of the previous commentary is meant to be a criticism of this or that work. Rather, I have sought in this brief section to highlight those areas where the scope of previous works corresponds with mine and, even more important, where it does not. All of these works have one or more points of contact with this book, whether the 1904–17 period, the civil war, or the interwar years. However, none of the works cited embraces the 1904–41 period, being generally divided into prerevolutionary and post-1917 studies.

This is even more the case when reviewing those books dealing with operational art as a separate theory. Those few works that mention it at all are almost exclusively concerned with the post-1917 years, while only Menning's book does any justice to the pre-1917 period, without, however, taking the narrative beyond 1914. In short, none of the works cited unite the two periods in Russian military history and attempt to determine the degree of theoretical continuity between them.

UNPUBLISHED WORKS

Budushchaya Voina. Moscow, 1928. RGVA, fond 33988, opis' 2, dela 682–88.

Budushchaya Voina i Nashi Voennye Zadachi. Moscow, March 8, 1930. A number of considerations make it impossible at this time to cite this document in the usual manner.

Doklad Komandovaniya Gruppy ob Itogakh Operatsii v Raione r. Khalkhin-Gol. 1939. RGVA, fond 32113, opis' 1, delo 207.

Doklad Nachal'nika Shtaba Predsedatelyu Revolyutsionnogo Voennogo Soveta Soyuza S.S.R. Moscow, March 9, 1929. RGVA, fond 4, opis' 2, delo 515.

Dokladnaya Zapiska Komanduyushchego Voiskami Leningradskogo Voennogo Okruga Narodnomu Komissaru po Voennym i Morskim Delam K.E. Voroshilovu. Leningrad, January 11, 1930. RGVA, fond 7, opis' 1, delo 170.

Novye Voprosy Voiny. Moscow, 1932. RGVA, fond 33987, opis' 3, delo 1257.

Osnovnye Voprosy Taktiki i Operativnogo Iskusstva v Svyazi s Rekonstruktsiei Armii. Moscow, 1931. A number of considerations make it impossible at this time to cite this document in the usual manner.

Isserson, G. S. *Osnovy Glubokoi Operatsii.* Moscow, 1933. A number of considerations make it impossible at this time to cite this document in the usual manner.

Otvet na Zapisku A. Svechina "Budushchaya Voina i Nashi Voennye Zadachi." Moscow, March 28, 1930. A number of considerations make it impossible at this time to cite this document in the usual manner.
Politburo TsK VKP(b) Tovarishchu Stalinu, Predsedatelyu SNK SSSR Tovarishchu Molotovu. Moscow, May 27, 1940. RGVA, fond 40442, opis' 2, delo 169.
Postanovlenie Glavnogo Voennogo Soveta Krasnoi Armii. Moscow, November 21, 1939. RGVA, fond 40442, opis' 2, delo 128.
Proekt-Osnovy Vedeniya Operatsii. Sverdlovsk, October 10, 1936. A number of considerations make it impossible at this time to cite this document in the usual manner.
Razrabotka o Nachal'nom Periode Voiny. Moscow, July 8, 1934. A number of considerations make it impossible at this time to cite this document in the usual manner.
Sovremennaya Operatsiya. Moscow, July 25, 1937. RGVA, fond 37977, opis' 4, delo 258.
Tezisy Doklada "Taktika i Operativnoe Iskusstvo RKKA na Novom Etape." Moscow, 1932. RGVA, fond 31983, opis' 2, delo 18.

OFFICIAL PUBLICATIONS

Department of the Army. *FM 100-5. Operations.* Washington, D.C.: U.S. Government Printing Office, 1982.
———. *FM 100-5. Operations.* Washington, D.C.: U.S. Government Printing Office, 1986.
———. *FM 100-5. Operations.* Washington, D.C.: U.S. Government Printing Office, 1993.
General'nyi Shtab. *Polozhenie o Polevom Upravlenii Voisk v Voennoe Vremya.* St. Petersburg: Voennaya Tipografiya Imperatritsy Ekateriny Velikoi, 1914.
General'nyi Shtab RKKA. *Vostochno-Prusskaya Operatsiya.* This volume is part of the series *Sbornik Dokumentov Mirovoi Imperialisticheskoi Voiny na Russkom Fronte (1914–1917 gg.)* 4 vols. Moscow: Gosudarstvennoe Voennoe Izdatel'stvo, 1938–41.
Narodnyi Komissariat Oborony. *Vremennyi Polevoi Ustav 1936.* Moscow: Gosudarstvennoe Voennoe Izdatel'stvo, 1937.
Narodnyi Komissariat po Voennym i Morskim Delam. *Polevoi Ustav RKKA.* Moscow and Leningrad: Gosudarstvennoe Izdatel'stvo, 1929.
Shtab RKKA. *Vysshee Komandovanie. Ofitsial'noe Rukovodstvo dlya Komanduyushchikh i Polevykh Upravlenii Armii i Frontov.* Moscow: Vysshii Voennyi Redaktsionnyi Sovet, 1924.
Tsentral'noe Statisticheskoe Upravlenie pri Sovete Ministrov SSSR. *Promyshlennost' SSSR. Statisticheskii Sbornik.* Moscow: Gosudarstvennoe Statisticheskoe Izdatel'stvo, 1957.
———. *Strana Sovetov za 50 Let. Sbornik Statisticheskikh Materialov.* Moscow: Izdatel'stvo "Statistika," 1967.
———. *Narodnoe Khozyaistvo SSSR 1922–1972 gg. Yubileinyi Statisticheskii Ezhegodnik.* Moscow: Izdatel'stvo "Statistika," 1972.

NEWSPAPERS

Ivanov, N. "O Vstrechnoi Operatsii." *Krasnaya Zvezda* (Moscow), August 24, 1932, 2.
———. "Kastrirovannaya 'Glubinnaya Taktika.'" *Krasnaya Zvezda* (Moscow), August 27, 1932, 2.

Krasil'nikov, S. "Nachal'nyi Period Budushchei Voiny." *Pravda* (Moscow), May 20, 1936, 2.

"Rech' Predsedatelya Sovnarkoma SSSR, Deputata V. M. Molotova." *Pravda* (Moscow), January 16, 1938, 4.

Shilovskii, E. "Prostranstvennaya Operatsiya." *Krasnaya Zvezda* (Moscow), July 2, 1932, 2.

———. "Vstrechnaya Operatsiya." *Krasnaya Zvezda* (Moscow), November 11, 1932, 2.

Sorin, V. "Komandiry i Komissary v Deistvuyushchei Armii." *Pravda* (Moscow), November 29, 1918, 2.

Sverdlov, F. "On Videl Budushchuyu Voinu." *Patriot* (Moscow), no. 19, 1992, 11.

Tatarchenko, E. "Novye Cherty Sovremennogo Voennogo Iskusstva." *Krasnaya Zvezda* (Moscow), July 10, 1940, 2.

Varfolomeev, N. "Evolyutsiya Tekhniki i Sovremennaya Operatsiya." *Krasnaya Zvezda* (Moscow), June 2, 1932, 2.

———. "Operativnoe Iskusstvo na Sovremennom Etape." *Krasnaya Zvezda* (Moscow), June 3, 1932, 2.

———. "Glubokaya Operatsiya." *Krasnaya Zvezda* (Moscow), November 5, 1932, 2.

Voroshilov, K. E. "Prikaz Narodnogo Komissara Oborony SSSR." *Krasnaya Zvezda* (Moscow), June 14, 1937, 1.

Yaroslavskii, E. "Kak Vossozdat' Armiyu." *Izvestiya* (Moscow), June 15, 1918, 1–2.

Zakharov, V. "Opyt Grazhdanskoi Voiny v SSSR i Sovremennost'." *Krasnaya Zvezda* (Moscow), February 8, 1941, 3.

Zhigur, Ya. "O 'Glubinnoi Taktike' i 'Prostranstvennoi Operatsii.'" *Krasnaya Zvezda* (Moscow), August 15, 1932, 2.

BOOKS

Aganov, S. Kh., ed. *Inzhenernye Voiska Sovetskoi Armii, 1918–1945*. Moscow: Voennoe Izdatel'stvo, 1985.

Agureev, K. V. *Razgrom Belogvardeiskikh Voisk Denikina*. Moscow: Voennoe Izdatel'stvo, 1961.

Aldcroft, D. H. *The European Economy, 1914–1970*. London: Croom Helm, 1978.

Anan'ev, I. M. *Tankovye Armii v Nastuplenii: Po Opytu Velikoi Otechestvennoi Voiny 1941–1945 gg*. Moscow: Voennoe Izdatel'stvo, 1988.

Andronikov, N. G., A. S. Begishev, I. G. Kalachev, I. I. Krasnov, and P. V. Terekhov. *Bronetankovye i Mekhanizirovannye Voiska Sovetskoi Armii*. Moscow: Voennoe Izdatel'stvo, 1958.

Anfilov, V. A. *Bessmertnyi Podvig*. Moscow: Izdatel'stvo "Nauka," 1971.

———. *Doroga K Tragedii Sorok Pervogo Goda*. Moscow: Izdatel' stvo Akopov, 1997.

Antonov-Ovseenko, A. *The Time of Stalin*. Translated by G. Saunders. New York: Harper and Row, 1981.

Apushkin, V. A. *Russko-Yaponskaya Voina, 1904–1905 g*. Moscow: Russkoe Tovarishchestvo, 1910.

Aralov, S. I. *Lenin vel Nas k Pobede*. Moscow: Gosudarstvennoe Izdatel'stvo Politicheskoi Literatury, 1962.

Azovtsev, N. N., ed. *Grazhdanskaya Voina v SSSR*. 2 vols. Moscow: Voennoe Izdatel'stvo, 1980–86.
Azovtsev, N. N., P. N. Dmitriev, V. V. Dushen'kin, S. F. Naida, and S. N. Shishkin, eds. *Direktivy Komandovaniya Frontov Krasnoi Armii (1917–1922 gg.)*. 4 vols. Moscow: Voennoe Izdatel'stvo, 1971–78.
Bagramyan, I. Kh. *Tak Nachinalas' Voina*. Moscow: Voennoe Izdatel'stvo, 1971.
———. *Moi Vospominaniya*. Erevan: Izdatel'stvo "Aiastan," 1979.
———, ed. *Istoriya Voin i Voennogo Iskusstva*. Moscow: Voennoe Izdatel'stvo, 1970.
Barmine, A. *Memoirs of a Soviet Diplomat*. Translated by G. Hopkins. London: Lovat Dickson, 1938.
Batitskii, P. F., ed. *Voiska Protivovozdushnoi Oborony Strany*. Moscow: Voennoe Izdatel'stvo, 1968.
Belitskii, S. M. *Strategicheskie Rezervy*. Moscow and Leningrad: Gosudarstvennoe Izdatel'stvo, 1930.
———. *Voina*. Leningrad: Izdatel'stvo "Molodaya Gvardiya," 1931.
Beloi, A. S. *Galitsiiskaya Bitva*. Moscow and Leningrad: Gosudarstvennoe Izdatel'stvo, 1929.
Belov, G. A., A. F. Butenko, B. A. Gavrilov, P. A. Golub, A. F. Gorlenko, N. F. Kuz'min, V. P. Moskovskii, S. F. Naida, G. D. Obichkin, A. A. Struchkov, N. I. Shatagin, and L. I. Yakovlev, eds. *Iz Istorii Grazhdanskoi Voiny*. 3 vols. Moscow: Izdatel'stvo "Sovetskaya Rossiya," 1960–61.
Belov, G. A., A. V. Golubev, P. A. Zhilin, D. I. Kurtov, S. F. Naida, and S. N. Shishkin, eds. *Direktivy Glavnogo Komandovaniya Krasnoi Armii (1917–1920)*. Moscow: Voennoe Izdatel'stvo, 1969.
Benvenuti, F. *The Bolsheviks and the Red Army*. Translated by C. Woodall. Cambridge: Cambridge University Press, 1988.
Berkhin, I. B. *Voennaya Reforma v SSSR (1924–1925 gg.)*. Moscow: Voennoe Izdatel'stvo, 1958.
Biryuzov, S. S. *Kogda Gremeli Pushki*. Moscow: Voennoe Izdatel'stvo, 1961.
Bocharov, K., I. Nizhechek, and P. Suslov, eds. *Protiv Reaktsionnykh Teorii na Voennonauchnom Fronte. Kritika Strategicheskikh i Voennoistoricheskikh Vzglyadov Prof. Svechina*. Moscow: Gosudarstvennoe Voennoe Izdatel'stvo, 1931.
Bogdanovich, P. N. *Vtorzhenie v Vostochnuyu Prussiyu v Avguste 1914 Goda*. Buenos Aires: Imprenta "Dorrego," 1964.
Bonch-Bruevich, M. D. *Vsya Vlast' Sovetam*. Moscow: Voennoe Izdatel'stvo, 1957.
Bradley, J. F. N. *Civil War in Russia, 1917–1920*. London: B. T. Batsford, 1975.
Brusilov, A. A. *Moi Vospominaniya*. Riga: Knigoizdatel'stvo "Mir," 1929.
Bubnov, A. S., S. S. Kamenev, and R. P. Eideman, eds. *Grazhdanskaya Voina 1918–1921*. 3 vols. Moscow: Izdatel'stvo "Voennyi Vestnik," 1928–30.
Budennyi, S. M. *Proidennyi Put'*. 3 vols. Moscow: Voennoe Izdatel'stvo, 1958–73.
Bulgakova, T. P., ed. *Akademiya General'nogo Shtaba*. 2d ed. Moscow: Voennoe Izdatel'stvo, 1987.
Bunich, I. L. *Operatsiya "Groza."* St. Petersburg: "Oblik," 1994.
Bychevskii, B. V. *Gorod-Front*. Moscow: Voennoe Izdatel'stvo, 1963.
Carver, M. *Twentieth-Century Warriors*. London: Weidenfeld and Nicolson, 1987.
Catton, B. *Mr. Lincoln's Army*. Garden City, N.Y.: Doubleday, 1951.

Chamberlain, W. H. *The Russian Revolution, 1917–1921.* New York: Macmillan, 1935.
Cheremisov, V. A. *Russko-Yaponskaya Voina 1904–1905 Goda.* 2d ed. St. Petersburg: Izdatel'stvo V. Berezovskogo, 1909.
Cherkasov, P. V., ed. *Mirovaya Voina, 1914–1918.* "Lutskii Proryv." *Trudy i Materialy k Operatsii Yugo-Zapadnogo Fronta v Mae-Iyune 1916 Goda.* Moscow: Vysshii Voennyi Redaktsionnyi Sovet, 1924.
Chuntulov, V. T. *Istoriya Narodnogo Khozyaistva SSSR. Dooktyabrskii Period.* Kiev: Izdatel'stvo Kievskogo Universiteta, 1964.
———. *Ekonomicheskaya Istoriya SSSR.* Moscow: Izdatel'stvo "Vysshaya Shkola," 1969.
Clausewitz, C. von. *On War.* Edited and translated by M. Howard and P. Paret. Princeton, N.J.: Princeton University Press, 1984.
Conquest, R. *The Great Terror: Stalin's Purge of the Thirties.* London: Macmillan, 1968.
———. *The Harvest of Sorrow: Soviet Collectivization and the Terror-Famine.* London: Hutchinson, 1986.
Coox, A. D. *Nomonhan: Japan Against Russia, 1939.* Stanford, Calif.: Stanford University Press, 1994.
Danilov, Yu. N. *Rossiya v Mirovoi Voine 1914–1915 g.g.* Berlin: Knigoizdatel'stvo "Slovo," 1924.
———. *Velikii Knyaz' Nikolai Nikolaevich.* Paris: Imprimerie de Navare, 1930.
Davies, N. *White Eagle, Red Star: The Soviet-Polish War, 1919–20.* New York: St. Martin's Press, 1972.
Degtyarev, A. M., ed. *Kievskii Krasnoznamennyi.* Moscow: Voennoe Izdatel'stvo, 1974.
Denikin, A. I. *Ocherki Russkoi Smuty.* 5 vols. Paris: J. Povolozky, 1921–22; Berlin: "Slovo," 1924–25; Berlin: "Mednyi Vsadnik," 1926.
———. *Put' Russkogo Ofitsera.* New York: Izdatel'stvo imeni Chekhova, 1953.
Earle, E. M. *Makers of Modern Strategy: Military Thought from Machiavelli to Hitler.* Princeton, N.J.: Princeton University Press, 1943.
Eisenhower, D. D. *Crusade in Europe.* Garden City, N.Y.: Doubleday, 1948.
Elchaninov, A. G. *Vedenie Sovremennykh Voiny i Boya.* St. Petersburg: Tipografiya Gr. Skachkova s S-mi, 1909.
———. *Strategiya.* St. Petersburg: Tipografiya I. Trofimova, 1912.
Engel's, F. *Izbrannye Voennye Proizvedeniya.* Moscow: Voennoe Izdatel'stvo, 1957.
Eremenko, A. I. *V Nachale Voiny.* Moscow: Izdatel'stvo "Nauka," 1965.
Erickson, J. *The Soviet High Command: A Military-Political History, 1918–1941.* London: St. Martin's Press, 1962.
———. *The Road to Stalingrad.* Boulder, Colo.: Westview Press, 1983.
Falkenhayn, E. von. *General Headquarters 1914–1916 and Its Critical Decisions.* London: Hutchinson, 1919.
Fedotoff White, D. *The Growth of the Red Army.* Princeton, N.J.: Princeton University Press, 1944.
Fedyukin, S. A. *Velikii Oktyabr' i Intelligentsiya.* Moscow: Izdatel'stvo "Nauka," 1972.
Frunze, M. V. *Izbrannye Proizvedeniya.* Moscow: Voennoe Izdatel'stvo, 1957.
Fugate, B. I. *Operation Barbarossa: Strategy and Tactics on the Eastern Front, 1941.* Novato, Calif.: Presidio Press, 1984.
Galaktionov, M. *Tempy Operatsii. Parizh-1914.* Moscow: Gosudarstvennoe Voennoe Izdatel'stvo, 1936.

Garder, M. *A History of the Soviet Army*. London: Pall Mall Press, 1966.
Gareev, M. A. *M. V. Frunze: Voennyi Teoretik*. Moscow: Voennoe Izdatel'stvo, 1985.
———. *Obshchevoiskovye Ucheniya*. 2d ed. Moscow: Voennoe Izdatel'stvo, 1990.
Gershel'man, F. *Mysli o Yaponskoi Voine*. St. Petersburg: Sklad V. A. Berezovskogo, 1908.
Gerua, B. V. *Vospominaniya o Moei Zhizni*. Paris: "Tanais," 1969.
Glantz, D. M. *Soviet Military Operational Art: In Pursuit of Deep Battle*. London: Frank Cass, 1991.
———. *Stumbling Colossus: The Red Army on the Eve of World War*. Lawrence: University Press of Kansas, 1998.
Glantz, D. M., and J. M. House. *When Titans Clashed: How the Red Army Stopped Hitler*. Lawrence: University Press of Kansas, 1995.
Golovin, N. N. *Vvedenie v Kurs Taktiki*. 2d ed. St. Petersburg: Ekonomicheskaya Tipolitografiya, 1912.
———. *Nachalo Voiny i Operatsii v Vostochnoi Prussii*. This volume is part of the series *Iz Istorii Kampanii 1914 Goda na Russkom Fronte*. 3 vols. Prague: Izdatel'stvo "Plamya," 1926; Paris: "Rodnik," 1930; Paris: Glavnoe Pravlenie Zarubezhnogo Soyuza Russkikh Voennykh Invalidov, 1936–40.
———. *Voennye Usiliya Rossii v Mirovoi Voine*. Paris: Tovarishchestvo Ob"edinennykh Izdatelei, 1939.
Gorbatov, A. V. *Gody i Voiny*. Moscow: Voennoe Izdatel'stvo, 1965.
Gor'kii, A. M., V. M. Molotov, K. E. Voroshilov, A. A. Zhdanov, A. S. Bubnov, Ya. B. Gamarnik, and I. V. Stalin, eds. *Istoriya Grazhdanskoi Voiny v SSSR*. 5 vols. Moscow: Gosudarstvennoe Izdatel'stvo "Istoriya Grazhdanskoi Voiny," 1935–60.
Gor'kov, Yu. A. *Kreml', Stavka, Genshtab*. Tver': "RIF LTD," 1995.
Gourko, B. *Memoirs and Impressions of War and Revolution in Russia, 1914–1917*. London: John Murray, 1918.
Grachev, P. S., ed. *Voennaya Entsiklopediya*. 8 vols. Moscow: Voennoe Izdatel'stvo, 1994–.
Grechko, A. A. *Vooruzhennye Sily Sovetskogo Gosudarstva*. 2d ed. Moscow: Voennoe Izdatel'stvo, 1975.
———, ed. *Istoriya Vtoroi Mirovoi Voiny, 1939–1945*. 12 vols. Moscow: Voennoe Izdatel'stvo, 1973–80.
———, ed. *Sovetskaya Voennaya Entsiklopediya*. 8 vols. Moscow: Voennoe Izdatel'stvo, 1976–80.
Grigorenko, P. G. *V Podpol'e Mozhno Vstretit' Tol'ko Krys*. New York: Izdatel'stvo "Detinets," 1981.
Gusev, S. I. *Grazhdanskaya Voina i Krasnaya Armiya*. Moscow and Leningrad: Gosudarstvennoe Izdatel'stvo, 1925.
Hagen, M. von. *Soldiers in the Proletarian Dictatorship: The Red Army and the Soviet Socialist State, 1917–1930*. Ithaca, N.Y.: Cornell University Press, 1990.
Halder, F. *The Halder Diaries*. Edited by A. Lissance. Boulder, Colo.: Westview Press, 1976.
Hamilton, I. *A Staff Officer's Scrap Book During the Russo-Japanese War*. 2 vols. London: E. Arnold, 1905–7.
Hoffmann, M. *War Diaries and Other Papers*. Translated by E. Sutton. London: Martin Secker, 1929.

Humphreys, A. A. *The Virginia Campaign of '64 and '65.* New York: Scribner's, 1885.
Iminov, V. T., ed., *Nachal'nyi Period Velikoi Otechestvennoi Voiny. Vyvody i Uroki.* Moscow: Akademiya General'nogo Shtaba, 1989.
Iovlev, A. M. *Deyatel'nost' KPSS po Podgotovke Voennykh Kadrov.* Moscow: Voennoe Izdatel'stvo, 1976.
Isserson, G. S. *Martovskoe Nastuplenie Germantsev v Pikardii v 1918 Godu.* Moscow: Gosudarstvennoe Voennoe Izdatel'stvo, 1926.
———. *Kanny Mirovoi Voiny (Gibel' Armii Samsonova).* Moscow: Gosudarstvennoe Voennoe Izdatel'stvo, 1932.
———. *Lektsii po Glubokoi Taktike.* Moscow: Voennaya Akademiya imeni M. V. Frunze, 1933.
———. *Evolyutsiya Operativnogo Iskusstva.* 2d ed. Moscow: Gosudarstvennoe Voennoe Izdatel'stvo, 1937.
———. *Osnovy Oboronitel'noi Operatsii.* Moscow: Akademiya General'nogo Shtaba, 1938.
———. *Novye Formy Bor'by.* Moscow: Voennoe Izdatel'stvo, 1940.
Ivanov, S. P., ed. *Nachal'nyi Period Voiny. Po Opytu Pervykh Kampanii i Operatsii Vtoroi Mirovoi Voiny.* Moscow: Voennoe Izdatel'stvo, 1974.
Ivanov, V. M. *Marshal M. N. Tukhachevskii.* Moscow: Voennoe Izdatel'stvo, 1990.
Izmest'ev, P. I., and E. E. Messner, comps. *Konspekt Strategii.* St. Petersburg: Tipografiya A. E. Landau, 1899.
Kadishev, A. B., ed. *Voprosy Strategii i Operativnogo Iskusstva v Sovetskikh Voennykh Trudakh (1917–1940 gg.).* Moscow: Voennoe Izdatel'stvo, 1965.
———, ed. *Voprosy Taktiki v Sovetskikh Voennykh Trudakh (1917–1940).* Moscow: Voennoe Izdatel'stvo, 1970.
Kakurin, N. E. *Strategiya Proletarskogo Gosudarstva.* Smolensk: Redaktsionno-Izdatel'skii Otdel pri RVS Zapadnogo Fronta, 1921.
———. *Kak Srazhalas' Revolyutsiya.* Moscow and Leningrad: Gosudarstvennoe Izdatel'stvo, 1925–26.
Kakurin, N. E., and V. A. Melikov. *Voina s Belopolyakami 1920 g.* Moscow: Gosudarstvennoe Voennoe Izdatel'stvo, 1925.
Kamenev, S. S. *Zapiski o Grazhdanskoi Voine i Voennom Stroitel'stve. Izbrannye Stat'i.* Moscow: Voennoe Izdatel'stvo, 1963.
Kapustin, N. Ya. *Operativnoe Iskusstvo v Pozitsionnoi Voine.* Moscow and Leningrad: Gosudarstvennoe Izdatel'stvo, 1927.
Karpov, V. V. *Marshal Zhukov. Ego Soratniki i Protivniki v Dni Voiny i Mira.* Moscow: Voennoe Izdatel'stvo, 1992.
Kavtaradze, A. G. *Voennye Spetsialisty na Sluzhbe Respubliki Sovetov 1917–1920 gg.* Moscow: Izdatel'stvo "Nauka," 1988.
Kazakov, M. I. *Nad Kartoi Bylykh Srazhenii.* Moscow: Voennoe Izdatel'stvo, 1971.
Kenez, P. *Civil War in South Russia, 1918.* Berkeley: University of California Press, 1971.
———. *Civil War in South Russia, 1919–1920.* Berkeley: University of California Press, 1977.
Kersnovskii, A. A. *Istoriya Russkoi Armii.* 4 vols. Belgrade: "Tsarskii Vestnik," 1933–38.
———. *Filosofiya Voiny.* Belgrade: "Tsarskii Vestnik," 1939.
Khromov, S. S., ed. *Grazhdanskaya Voina i Voennaya Interventsiya v SSSR. Entsiklopediya.* Moscow: Izdatel'stvo "Sovetskaya Entsiklopediya," 1983.

Khrushchev, N. S. *Khrushchev Remembers*. Edited and translated by S. Talbot. London: Andre Deutsch, 1971.
Kir'yan, M. M., ed. *Voenno-Tekhnicheskii Progress i Vooruzhennye Sily SSSR*. Moscow: Voennoe Izdatel'stvo, 1982.
———. *Fronty Nastupali. Po Opytu Velikoi Otechestvennoi Voiny*. Moscow: Izdatel'stvo "Nauka," 1987.
Klyatskin, S. M. *Na Zashchite Oktyabrya*. Moscow: Izdatel'stvo "Nauka," 1965.
Knox, A. *With the Russian Army, 1914–1917*. 2 vols. London: Hutchinson, 1921.
Kolenkovskii, A. *O Nastupatel'noi Operatsii Armii, Vkhodyashchei v Sostav Fronta*. Moscow: Voennaya Akademiya RKKA im. Frunze, 1929.
———. *Manevrennyi Period Pervoi Mirovoi Imperialisticheskoi Voiny, 1914 g*. Moscow: Gosudarstvennoe Voennoe Izdatel'stvo, 1940.
Korablev, Yu. I. *V. I. Lenin i Zashchita Zavoevanii Velikogo Oktyabrya*. 2d ed. Moscow: Izdatel'stvo "Nauka," 1979.
Koritskii, N. I., S. M. Mel'nik-Tukhachevskaya, and B. N. Chistov, comps. *Marshal Tukhachevskii. Vospominaniya Druzei i Soratnikov*. Moscow Voennoe Izdatel'stvo, 1965.
Korotkov, I. A. *Istoriya Sovetskoi Voennoi Mysli*. Moscow: Izdatel'stvo "Nauka," 1980.
Korotkov, I. S. *Razgrom Vrangelya*. 3d ed. Moscow: Voennoe Izdatel'stvo, 1955.
Kozlov, S. N., ed. *Spravochnik Ofitsera*. Moscow: Voennoe Izdatel'stvo, 1971.
Krasil'nikov, S. N. *Organizatsiya Krupnykh Obshchevoiskovykh Soedinenii*. Moscow: Gosudarstvennoe Voennoe Izdatel'stvo, 1933.
Kreidberg, M. A., and M. G. Merton. *History of Military Mobilization in the United States Army, 1775–1945*. Washington, D.C.: Department of the Army, 1955.
Krivitsky, W. G. *In Stalin's Secret Service*. New York: Harper, 1939.
Krivosheev, G. F., ed. *Grif Sekretnosti Snyat. Poteri Vooruzhennykh Sil SSSR v Voinakh, Boevykh Deistviyakh i Voennykh Konfliktakh. Statisticheskoe Issledovanie*. Moscow: Voennoe Izdatel'stvo, 1993.
Kulikov, V. G., ed. *Akademiya General'nogo Shtaba*. Moscow: Voennoe Izdatel'stvo, 1976.
Kurochkin, P. A., ed. *Obshchevoiskovaya Armiya v Nastuplenii*. Moscow: Voennoe Izdatel'stvo, 1966.
Kuz'min, N. F. *Na Strazhe Mirnogo Truda (1921–1940 gg.)*. Moscow: Voennoe Izdatel'stvo, 1959.
Lapchinskii, A. N. *Bombardirovochnaya Aviatsiya*. Moscow: Gosudarstvennoe Voennoe Izdatel'stvo, 1937.
Leer, G. A. *Strategiya (Taktika Teatra Voennykh Deistvii)*. 4th ed. 2 vols. St. Petersburg: Tipografiya V. Bezobrazova, 1885–87.
———. *Strategiya (Taktika Teatra Voennykh Deistvii)*. 6th ed. St. Petersburg: Izdatel'stvo V. A. Berezovskogo, 1898.
Lenin, V. I. *Polnoe Sobranie Sochinenii*. 5th ed. 55 vols. Moscow: Gosudarstvennoe Izdatel'stvo Politicheskoi Literatury, 1958–65.
Levichev, V. N., ed. *Voina i Voennoe Delo*. Moscow: Gosudarstvennoe Voennoe Izdatel'stvo, 1933.
Levitskii, N. A. *Russko-Yaponskaya Voina 1904–1905 gg*. 3d ed. Moscow: Gosudarstvennoe Voennoe Izdatel'stvo, 1938.
Liddell Hart, B. H., ed. *The Soviet Army*. London: Weidenfeld and Nicolson, 1956.

Lincoln, W. B. *Red Victory: A History of the Russian Civil War.* New York: Simon and Schuster, 1989.
Lisov, I. I. *Sovetskie Vozdushno-Desantnye Voiska.* Moscow: Izdatel'stvo DOSAAF, 1967.
Lizichev, A. D. *Put' Peremen, Vremya Deistvii.* Moscow: Voennoe Izdatel'stvo, 1989.
Luckett, R. *The White Generals: An Account of the White Movement and the Russian Civil War.* New York: Viking Press, 1971.
Ludendorff, E. *My War Memoirs, 1914–1918.* 2 vols. London: Hutchinson, 1919.
Lyubarskii, S. *Nekotorye Operativno-Takticheskie Vyvody iz Opyta Voiny v Ispanii.* Moscow: Gosudarstvennoe Voennoe Izdatel'stvo, 1939.
Mackintosh, M. *Juggernaut: A History of the Soviet Armed Forces.* New York: Macmillan, 1967.
Mannerheim, C. G. E. *The Memoirs of Marshal Mannerheim.* Translated by E. Lewenhaupt. London: Cassell, 1953.
Martel, G. *The Russian Outlook.* London: Michael Joseph, 1947.
Marushevskii, V. V. *Upravlenie Voiskami na Teatre Voiny i na Pole Srazheniya.* St. Petersburg: Tipografiya A. S. Suvorina, 1912.
Mawdsley, E. *The Russian Civil War.* Boston: Allen and Unwin, 1987.
Medvedev, R. A. *Let History Judge: The Origins and Consequences of Stalinism.* Edited by D. Joravsky and G. Haupt. Translated by C. Taylor. New York: Knopf, 1971.
Melikov, V. A. *Marna-1914 Goda. Visla-1920 Goda. Smirna-1922 Goda.* Moscow and Leningrad: Gosudarstvennoe Izdatel'stvo, 1928.
———. *Problema Strategicheskogo Razvertyvaniya po Opytu Mirovoi i Grazhdanskoi Voiny.* Moscow: Voennaya Akademiya imeni M. V. Frunze, 1935.
———. *Geroicheskaya Oborona Tsarytsina (1918 g.).* Moscow: Gosudarstvennoe Voennoe Izdatel'stvo, 1938.
———. *Stalinskii Plan Razgroma Denikina.* Moscow: Gosudarstvennoe Voennoe Izdatel'stvo, 1938.
Menning, B. *Bayonets Before Bullets: The Imperial Russian Army, 1861–1914.* Bloomington: Indiana University Press, 1992.
Meretskov, K. A. *Na Sluzhbe Narodu.* Moscow: Voennoe Izdatel'stvo, 1968.
Messner, E. E., S. Vakar, F. Verbitskii, V. Granitov, S. Kashirin, A. Petrashevich, M. Rozhchenko, V. Tseshko, V. Shaiditskii, and I. Eikhenbaum. *Rossiiskie Ofitsery.* Buenos Aires: Yuzhno-Amerikanskii Otdel Instituta po Issledovaniyu Problem Voiny i Mira imeni Generala Prof. N. N. Golovina, 1959.
Mikhnevich, N..P. *Vliyanie Noveishikh Tekhnicheskikh Izobretenii na Taktiku Voisk.* St. Petersburg: Tipografiya S. N. Khudekova, 1893.
———. *Strategiya.* 3d ed. 2 vols. St. Petersburg: Izdanie V. A. Berezovskogo, 1911.
———. *Osnovy Strategii.* St. Petersburg: Tipografiya Trenke i Fyusno, 1913.
Mints, I. I., ed. *Iz Istorii Grazhdanskoi Voiny i Interventsii, 1917–1922 gg.* Moscow: Izdatel'stvo, "Nauka," 1974.
Morozov, B. N., ed. *Kratkii Slovar' Operativno-Takticheskikh i Obshchevoennykh Slov (Terminov).* Moscow: Voennoe Izdatel'stvo, 1958.
———. *Slovar' Osnovnykh Voennykh Terminov.* Moscow: Voennoe Izdatel'stvo, 1965.
Mostovenko, V. D. *Tanki.* 2d ed. Moscow: Voennoe Izdatel'stvo, 1958.
Motylev, V. E. *Narodnoe Khozyaistvo SSSR v Period Osushchestvleniya Tret'ego Pyatiletnego Plana.* Moscow: Ministerstvo Vysshego Obrazovaniya SSSR, 1959.

Movchin, N. N. *Posledovatel'nye Operatsii po Opytu Marny i Visly.* Moscow and Leningrad: Gosudarstvennoe Izdatel'stvo, 1928.
Neznamov, A. A. *Sovremennaya Voina. Deistviya Polevoi Armii.* St. Petersburg: Tipografiya Gr. Skachkova s S-mi, 1911.
Nikulin, L. V. *Tukhachevskii.* Moscow: Voennoe Izdatel'stvo, 1964.
Novitskii, V. F. *Mirovaya Voina 1914–1918 g.g. Kampaniya 1914 Goda v Bel'gii i Frantsii.* 2 vols. Moscow: Gosudarstvennoe Voennoe Izdatel'stvo, 1926–28.
O'Ballance, E. *The Red Army.* London: Faber and Faber, 1964.
Ogarkov, N. V. *Istoriya Uchit Bditel'nosti.* Moscow: Voennoe Izdatel'stvo, 1985.
Orlov, A. *Tainaya Istoriya Stalinskikh Prestuplenii.* St. Petersburg: Knigoizdatel'stvo "Vsemirnoe Slovo," 1991.
Paret, P., ed. *Makers of Modern Strategy, from Machiavelli to the Nuclear Age.* Princeton, N.J.: Princeton University Press, 1986.
Pavlovich, N. B., ed. *Flot v Pervoi Mirovoi Voine.* Moscow: Voennoe Izdatel'stvo, 1964.
Pipes, R. *The Russian Revolution.* New York: Knopf, 1990.
Plekhov, A. M., comp. *Slovar' Voennykh Terminov.* Moscow: Voennoe Izdatel'stvo, 1988.
Polyakov, Yu. A. *Sovetskaya Strana Posle Okonchaniya Grazhdanskoi Voiny. Territoriya i Naselenie.* Moscow: Izdatel'stvo "Nauka," 1986.
Pospelov, P. N., ed. *Istoriya Velikoi Otechestvennoi Voiny Sovetskogo Soyuza, 1941–1945.* 6 vols. Moscow: Voennoe Izdatel'stvo, 1960–65.
———. *Velikaya Otechestvennaya Voina Sovetskogo Soyuza, 1941–1945. Kratkaya Istoriya.* Moscow: Voennoe Izdatel'stvo, 1965.
Prochko, I. S. *Artilleriya—Bog Voiny.* Moscow: Gosudarstvennoe Izdatel'stvo Politicheskoi Literatury, 1946.
Prokhorov, A. M., ed. *Bol'shaya Sovetskaya Entsiklopediya.* 3d ed. 30 vols. Moscow: Izdatel'stvo "Sovetskaya Entsiklopediya," 1969–78.
Prokop'ev, N. P. *O Voine i Armii.* Moscow: Voennoe Izdatel'stvo, 1965.
Putna, V. K. *K Visle i Obratno.* Moscow: Izdatel'stvo "Voennyi Vestnik," 1927.
Pyatnitskii, N. V. *Voennaya Organizatsiya Gosudarstvennoi Oborony SSSR.* Paris: Ofitserskaya Shkola Usovershenstvovaniya Voennykh Znanii pri I Otdele Russkogo Obshchevoinskogo Soyuza v Parizhe, 1932.
Rabinovich, S. E. *Istoriya Grazhdanskoi Voiny.* 2d ed. Moscow: Gosudarstvennoe Sotsial'no-Ekonomicheskoe Izdatel'stvo, 1935.
Radzievskii, A. I., ed. *Akademiya imeni M. V. Frunze.* Moscow: Voennoe Izdatel'stvo, 1973.
Rapoport, V., and Yu. Alexeev. *High Treason: Essays on the History of the Red Army, 1918–1938.* Edited by V. Treml. Translated by B. Adams. Durham, N.C.: Duke University Press, 1985.
Riasanovsky, N. V. *A History of Russia.* 3d ed. New York: Oxford University Press, 1977.
Rokossovskii, K. K. *Soldatskii Dolg.* Moscow: Voennoe Izdatel'stvo, 1968.
Rostunov, I. I. *Russkii Front Pervoi Mirovoi Voiny.* Moscow: Izdatel'stvo "Nauka," 1976.
———, ed. *Istoriya Pervoi Mirovoi Voiny, 1914–1918.* Moscow: Izdatel'stvo "Nauka," 1975.
———. *Istoriya Russko-Yaponskoi 1904–1905 gg.* Moscow: Izdatel'stvo "Nauka," 1977.
Rotmistrov, P. A. *Vremya i Tanki.* Moscow: Voennoe Izdatel'stvo, 1972.
———, ed. *Istoriya Voennogo Iskusstva.* 2 vols. Moscow: Voennoe Izdatel'stvo, 1963.

Rybkin, E. I. *Voina i Politika*. Moscow: Voennoe Izdatel'stvo, 1959.
Samoilo, A. A. *Dve Zhizni*. Moscow: Voennoe Izdatel'stvo, 1958.
Sandalov, L. M. *Perezhitoe*. Moscow: Voennoe Izdatel'stvo, 1961.
Savinkin, N. I., and K. M. Bogolyubov, comps. *KPSS o Vooruzhennykh Silakh Sovetskogo Soyuza. Dokumenty, 1917–1981*. Moscow: Voennoe Izdatel'stvo, 1981.
Savkin, V. E. *Osnovnye Printsipy Operativnogo Iskusstva i Taktiki*. Moscow: Voennoe Izdatel'stvo, 1972.
Savushkin, R. A. *Razvitie Sovetskikh Vooruzhennykh Sil i Voennogo Iskusstva v Mezhvoennyi Period (1921–1941 gg.)*. Moscow: Tipografiya VPA imeni V. I. Lenina, 1989.
Schlieffen, A. von. *Kanny*. 2d ed. Moscow: Gosudarstvennoe Voennoe Izdatel'stvo, 1938.
Scott, H. F., and W. F. Scott. *The Armed Forces of the USSR*. Boulder, Colo.: Westview Press, 1979.
———. *The Soviet Art of War: Doctrine, Strategy, and Tactics*. Boulder, Colo.: Westview Press, 1982.
———. *Soviet Military Doctrine. Continuity, Formulation, and Dissemination*. Boulder, Colo.: Westview Press, 1988.
Semenov, V. A. *Kratkii Ocherk Razvitiya Sovetskogo Operativnogo Iskusstva*. Moscow: Voennoe Izdatel'stvo, 1960.
Shaposhnikov, B. M. *Mozg Armii*. 3 vols. Moscow: Izdatel'stvo "Voennyi Vestnik," 1927–29.
———. *Vospominaniya. Voenno-Nauchnye Trudy*. Moscow: Voennoe Izdatel'stvo, 1974.
Shilovskii, E. A. *Operatsiya*. Moscow: Akademiya General'nogo Shtaba, 1937.
Shmidt, O. Yu., ed. *Bol'shaya Sovetskaya Entsiklopediya*. 65 vols. Moscow: Aktsionernoe Obshchestvo "Sovetskaya Entsiklopediya," 1926–47.
Shtemenko, S. M. *General'nyi Shtab v Gody Voiny*. 2 vols. Moscow: Voennoe Izdatel'stvo, 1968–73.
Smirnov, S. A. *Taktika*. Moscow: Gosudarstvennoe Voennoe Izdatel'stvo, 1935.
Sokolovskii, V. D., ed. *Voennaya Strategiya*. Moscow: Voennoe Izdatel'stvo, 1962.
Spirin, L. M. *Razgrom Armii Kolchaka*. Moscow: Izdatel'stvo Politicheskoi Literatury, 1957.
Stalin, I. V. *Sochineniya*. 13 vols. Moscow: Gosudarstvennoe Izdatel'stvo Politicheskoi Literatury, 1946–52.
Stone, N. *The Eastern Front, 1914–1917*. New York: Scribner, 1975.
Strokov, A. A. *Vooruzhennye Sily i Voennoe Iskusstvo v Pervoi Mirovoi Voine*. Moscow: Voennoe Izdatel'stvo, 1974.
Stuchenko, A. T. *Zavidnaya Nasha Sud'ba*. Moscow: Voennoe Izdatel'stvo, 1964.
Sukhomlinov, V. A. *Vospominaniya Sukhomlinova*. Moscow-Leningrad: Gosudarstvennoe Izdatel'stvo, 1926.
Suverinov, O. F. *Tragediya RKKA, 1937–1938*. Moscow: Izdatel'stvo "Terra," 1998.
Svechin, A. A. *Strategiya*. 2d ed. Moscow: Izdatel'stvo "Voennyi Vestnik," 1927.
———. *Evolyutsiya Voennogo Iskusstva*. 2 vols. Moscow and Leningrad: Gosudarstvennoe Voennoe Izdatel'stvo, 1927–28.
Timoshenko, S. K. *Zaklyuchitel'naya Rech' Narodnogo Komissara Oborony Soyuza SSR, Geroya i Marshala Sovetskogo Soyuza S. K. Timoshenko, na Voennom Soveshchanii, 31 Dekabrya 1940 g*. Moscow: Voennoe Izdatel'stvo, 1941.
Todorskii, A. I. *Marshal Tukhachevskii*. Moscow: Izdatel'stvo Politicheskoi Literatury, 1963.

Triandafillov, V. K. *Razmakh Operatsii Sovremennykh Armii.* Biblioteka Vsesoyuznogo S"ezda VNO, no. 5. Moscow: Izdatel'stvo "Voennyi Vestnik," 1926.
———. *Kharakter Operatsii Sovremennykh Armii.* Moscow and Leningrad: Gosudarstvennoe Izdatel'stvo, 1929.
———. *Kharakter Operatsii Sovremennykh Armii.* 2d ed. Moscow: Gosudarstvennoe Voennoe Izdatel'stvo, 1932.
Trotskii, L. D. *Kak Vooruzhalas' Revolyutsiya.* 3 vols. Moscow: Vysshii Voennyi Redaktsionnyi Sovet, 1923–25.
———. *Moya Zhizn'.* Berlin: Izdatel'stvo "Granit," 1930.
———. *Stalin.* Edited and translated by C. Malamuth. New York: Harper, 1941.
Tukhachevskii, M. N., *Izbrannye Proizvedeniya.* Moscow: Voennoe Izdatel'stvo, 1964.
Tukhachevskii, M. N., N. E. Varfolomeev, and E. A. Shilovskii. *Armeiskaya Operatsiya. Rabota Komandovaniya i Polevogo Upravleniya.* Moscow and Leningrad: Gosudarstvennoe Voennoe Izdatel'stvo, 1926.
Tyulenev, I. V. *Sovetskaya Kavaleriya v Boyakh za Rodinu.* Moscow: Voennoe Izdatel'stvo, 1957.
Tyushkevich, S. A., ed. *Sovetskie Vooruzhennye Sily. Istoriya Stroitel'stva.* Moscow: Voennoe Izdatel'stvo, 1978.
Varfolomeev, N. E. *Udarnaya Armiya.* Moscow: Gosudarstvennoe Voennoe Izdatel'stvo, 1933.
———. *Nastupatel'naya Operatsiya.* Moscow: Gosudarstvennoe Voennoe Izdatel'stvo, 1937.
Vasilevskii, A. M. *Delo Vsei Zhizni.* Moscow: Izdatel'stvo Politicheskoi Literatury, 1974.
Vatsetis, I. I. *O Voennoi Doktrine Budushchego.* Moscow: Gosudarstvennoe Izdatel'stvo, 1923.
Verkhovskii, A. I. *Osnovy Nashei Taktiki. Ogon', Manevr, Maskirovka.* Moscow: Izdatel'stvo "Voennyi Vestnik," 1928.
———. *Na Trudnom Perevale.* Moscow: Voennoe Izdatel'stvo, 1959.
Voinov, A. A., ed. *Istoriya Voennogo Iskusstva.* Moscow: Voennoe Izdatel'stvo, 1984.
Volkogonov, D. A. *Triumf i Tragediya. Politicheskii Portret I. V. Stalina.* 2d ed. Moscow: Izdatel'stvo "Novosti," 1990.
———. *Trotskii. Politicheskii Portret.* Moscow: Izdatel'stvo "Novosti," 1992.
Vol'pe, A. *Frontal'nyi Udar.* Moscow: Gosudarstvennoe Voennoe Izdatel'stvo, 1931.
Voronov, N. N. *Na Sluzhbe Voennoi.* Moscow: Voennoe Izdatel'stvo, 1963.
Voropaev, D. A., and A. M. Iovlev. *Bor'ba KPSS za Sozdanie Voennykh Kadrov.* 2d ed. Moscow: Voennoe Izdatel'stvo, 1960.
Voroshilov, K. E. *Stat'i i Rechi.* Moscow: Partizdat TsK VKP(b), 1937.
Wells, H. G. *Russia in the Shadows.* London: Hodder and Stoughton, 1920.
Wildman, A. K. *The End of the Russian Imperial Army.* 2 vols. Princeton, N.J.: Princeton University Press, 1980–87.
Wollenberg, E. *The Red Army.* Translated by C. W. Sykes. London: Secker and Warburg, 1938.
Yakupov, N. M. *Tragediya Polkovodtsev.* Moscow: Izdatel'stvo "Mysl," 1992.
Yaroslavskii, E., ed. *Vos'moi S"ezd RKP(b).* Moscow: Partiinoe Izdatel'stvo, 1933.
Yegorov, A. I. *L'vov-Varshava. 1920 God. Vzaimodeistvie Frontov.* Moscow and Leningrad: Gosudarstvennoe Voennoe Izdatel'stvo, 1929.
———. *Razgrom Denikina, 1919.* Moscow: Gosudarstvennoe Voennoe Izdatel'stvo, 1931.

Zaionchkovskii, A. M. *Lektsii po Strategii, Chitannye na Voenno-Akademicheskikh Kursakh Vysshego Komsostava i v Voennoi Akademii RKKA 1922–23 gg. Chast' I.* Moscow: Voennaya Akademiya RKKA, 1923.

———. *Podgotovka Rossii k Imperialisticheskoi Voine.* Moscow: Gosudarstvennoe Voennoe Izdatel'stvo, 1926.

———. *Mirovaya Voina 1914–1918.* 2d ed. Moscow: Gosudarstvennoe Voennoe Izdatel'stvo, 1931.

Zaitsov, A. *1918 God. Ocherki po Istorii Russkoi Grazhdanskoi Voiny.* Paris: Privately printed, 1934.

Zakharov, M. V. *Nakanune Velikikh Ispytanii.* Moscow: Voennoe Izdatel'stvo, 1968.

———. *General'nyi Shtab v Predvoennye Gody.* Moscow: Voennoe Izdatel'stvo, 1989.

———, ed. *50 Let Vooruzhennykh Sil SSSR.* Moscow: Voennoe Izdatel'stvo, 1968.

Zhilin, P. A., ed. *Russkaya Voennaya Mysl'. Konets XIX–Nachalo XX v.* Moscow: Izdatel'stvo "Nauka," 1982.

———. *Zarozhdenie i Razvitie Sovetskoi Voennoi Istoriografii 1917–1941.* Moscow: Izdatel'stvo, "Nauka," 1985.

Zhukov, G. K. *Vospominaniya i Razmyshleniya.* 11th ed. Moscow: Izdatel'stvo "Novosti," 1992.

Zolotarev, V. A., ed. *Russkii Arkhiv. Velikaya Otechestvennaya.* 32 vols. Moscow: Izdatel'stvo "Terra," 1993–.

Zolotarev, V. A., and G. N. Sevast'yanov, eds. *Velikaya Otechestvennaya Voina, 1941–1945.* 4 vols. Moscow: Izdatel'stvo "Nauka," 1998–99.

ARTICLES

Ageev, A. "Voenno-Teoreticheskie Vzglyady N. P. Mikhnevicha." *V-IZh*, no. 1 (1975): 90–95.

———. "Pervaya Frontovaya Operatsiya Krasnoi Armii." *V-IZh*, no. 8 (1979): 62–67.

———. "Kontrnastuplenie Krasnoi Armii na Vostochnom Fronte Osen'yu 1918 Goda." *V-IZh*, no. 3 (1982): 66–73.

———. "Voenno-Teoreticheskoe Nasledie A. A. Neznamova." *V-IZh*, no. 11 (1983): 84–89.

———. "Oborona Voisk Krasnoi Armii na Vostochnom Fronte Vesnoi 1919 Goda." *V-IZh*, no. 10 (1984): 75–81.

Ageev, A., and G. Solonitsyn. "Razgrom Vrangelya." *V-IZh*, no. 11 (1980): 9–16.

Algazin, A. "Samostoyatel'nye Vozdushnye Sily." *Voennaya Mysl'*, no. 1 (1937): 68–95.

———. "Primenenie i Organizatsiya Vozdushnoi Armii." *Voennaya Mysl'*, no. 2 (1937): 116–40.

Alksnis, Ya. "O Kharaktere Budushchei Mobilizatsii Burzhuaznykh Armii." *V&R*, no. 7 (1927): 3–15.

———. "Nachal'nyi Period Voiny." *V&R*, no. 9 (1929): 3–22; no. 10 (1929): 3–15.

Amiragov, L. S. "O Kharaktere Budushchei Voiny." *V&R*, September–October (1934): 3–17.

Ammosov, S. "Reidy Motomekhsoedineniya." *V&R*, no. 6 (1931): 42–58.

———. "Tanki v Operatsii Proryva." *V&R*, no. 5–6 (1932): 81–91.

Anfilov, V. "... Razgovor Zakonchilsya Ugrozoi Stalina." *V-IZh*, no. 3 (1995): 39–46.
Anisov, A. "Armeiskaya Oboronitel'naya Operatsiya." *V&R*, November–December (1934): 40–50.
Anuchin, V., and O. Zdorov. "Zarozhdenie i Razvitie Teorii Boevogo Primeneniya VVS (1917–1938 gg.)." *V-IZh*, no. 8 (1988): 19–26.
Apanasenko, I. "Pervaya Konnaya." *V-IZh*, no. 4 (1939): 35–42.
Appen. "Problema Narastaniya i Istoshcheniya v Grazhdanskoi Voine, 1918–1920 gg." *V&R*, no. 7 (1932): 44–64.
Avdeenko, P. "Sovetskoe Samoletostroenie v Gody Predvoennykh Pyatiletok (1929–1940 gg.)." *V-IZh*, no. 7 (1974): 84–89.
Avdeev, V. "Voenno-Istoricheskie Issledovaniya v Akademii General'nogo Shtaba Russkoi Armii." *V-IZh*, no. 12 (1987): 77–80.
———. "Posle Mukdena i Tsusimy." *V-IZh*, no. 8 (1992): 2–9.
Azovtsev, N., and A. Selyanichev. "Rukovodyashchaya Rol' Kommunisticheskoi Partii v Organizatsii Pobedy Sovetskogo Naroda v Gody Grazhdanskoi Voiny." *V-IZh*, no. 12 (1970): 3–12.
B., E. "Voprosy PVO Nastupatel'noi Operatsii Udarnoi Armii." *V&R*, March–April (1935): 31–47.
Bagramyan, I. "Dushevnyi Chelovek i Talantlivyi Voenachal'nik." *V-IZh*, no. 12 (1962): 58–68.
Baiov, A. "General'nyi Shtab vo Vremya Grazhdanskoi Voiny." *Chasovoi*, no. 84 (1932): 3–5.
Barantsev, G. Review of *Evolyutsiya Voennogo Iskusstva*. *V&R*, no. 8 (1928): 148–56.
Batashev, M. Review of *Udarnaya Armiya*. *V&R*, March–April (1935): 114–24.
Bazarevskii, A. "Vstrechnaya Operatsiya." *Voennaya Mysl'*, no. 3 (1937): 97–118.
Belitskii, S. "K Voprosu o Strategicheskikh Rezervakh." *V&R*, no. 2 (1925): 14–20.
———. "M. V. Frunze-Komanduyushchii Yuzhnoi Gruppoi Vostochnogo Fronta v 1919 g." *V&R*, no. 7–8 (1925): 17–31.
———. "Eshelonnaya Voina." *V&R*, no. 10–11 (1927): 197–207.
———. Review of *Mirovaya Voina 1914–1918 gg. Kampaniya 1914 Goda v Bel'gii i Frantsii*. *V&R*, no. 7 (1928): 150–56.
———. "Podvizhnost' Sovremennykh Armii." *V&R*, no. 11 (1930): 3–9.
Belyanovskii, B. "Deistviya Tankovykh i Makhanizirovannykh Voisk v Pol'she, Bel'gii i Frantsii." *Voennaya Mysl'*, no. 8 (1940): 39–58.
Belyavtsev, I. "Vosstanovlenie Voenno-Morskogo Flota SSSR v 1921–1928 Godakh." *V-IZh*, no. 3 (1963): 106–11.
Berends. "Taran." *V&R*, no. 4 (1927): 93–96.
Berkhin, I. "O Territorial'no-Militsionnom Stroitel'stve v Sovetskoi Armii." *V-IZh*, no. 12 (1960): 3–20.
Biryuzov, S. "Voenno-Teoreticheskoe Nasledstvo M. N. Tukhachevskogo." *V-IZh*, no. 2 (1964): 37–49.
Bobylev, P. "K Istorii Sozdaniya Zapadnogo Fronta (Mart 1918 g.–Fevral' 1919 g.)." *V-IZh*, no. 3 (1972): 32–40.
———. "Opredelenie Glavnogo Fronta Vesnoi 1919 Goda." *V-IZh*, no. 7 (1974): 69–75.
———. "O Roli Zapadnogo Fronta v Period Razgroma Denikina." *V-IZh*, no. 6 (1979): 62–67.

Bogolyubov, A. "Razgrom Kolchaka." *V-IZh*, no. 1 (1939): 9–23.
Bonch-Bruevich, M. "Nekotorye Osnovy Operativnogo Rukovodstva v Sovremennoi Voine." *V&R*, no. 12 (1927): 46–63.
———. "Nekotorye Problemy Budushchei Voiny". *V&R*, no. 5 (1929): 60–64.
Botner, S. "Voennaya Podgotovka Imperialistov i Problema Oborony SSSR v Svete Osushchestvleniya Pyatiletki." *V&R*, no. 2 (1930): 33–47.
Brusilov, A. "Proryv Avstro-Germanskogo Fronta v 1916 Godu." *V&R*, no. 4 (1927): 67–83; no. 5 (1927): 129–48.
Budennyi, S. "Konnitsa v Sovremennoi Voine." *V&R*, no. 6 (1930): 3–23.
———. "Moguchaya Konnitsa Proletarskoi Revolyutsii." *V-IZh*, no. 4 (1939): 17–26.
———. "Geroi Proryva Vrazheskogo Fronta." *V-IZh*, no. 4 (1963): 55–63.
Burlak, B. "Nastuplenie kak Sil'naya Forma Revolyutsionnoi Voiny." *V&R*, September–October (1935): 39–49.
Bushmanov, N. "Razgrom Vrangelya v Severnoi Tavrii." *V-IZh*, no. 4 (1939): 74–105.
Chikalin, S. "Organizatsiya i Ispol'zovanie Takticheskikh Tankovykh Soedinenii." *V&R*, no. 3 (1930): 12–28.
———. "Ob Osnovakh Primeneniya i Organizatsii Operativnykh Tankovykh Soedinenii." *V&R*, no. 4 (1930): 25–35.
Daines, V. "Razvitie Taktiki Obshchevoiskovogo Boya v 1929–1941 gg." *V-IZh*, no. 10 (1978): 96–101.
———. "Kontrnastuplenie Yuzhnogo Fronta v Oktyabre-Noyabre 1919 Goda." *V-IZh*, no. 10 (1986): 64–68.
———. "Podavlenie Kronshtadtskogo Antisovetskogo Myatezha." *V-IZh*, no. 3 (1988): 86–90.
———. "Konets Beloi Gvardii." *V-IZh*, no. 10 (1989): 27–35.
Danilevskii, A. "Bor'ba V.I. Lenina s 'Voennoi Oppozitsiei' na VIII S"ezde RKP(b)." *V-IZh*, no. 4 (1961): 3–11.
Danilevskii, A. F. "Tverdaya Liniya." *V-IZh*, no. 4 (1989): 14–21.
Danilov, F., and I. Kravchenko. "U Istokov Sovetskoi Teorii Operativnogo Iskusstva (1921–1930 gg.)." *V-IZh*, no. 11 (1973): 38–45.
Danilov, V. "Stroitel'stvo Tsentral'nogo Voennogo Apparata v 1921–1923 gg." *V-IZh*, no. 1 (1971): 9–16.
———. "Sozdanie Shtaba RKKA (Fevral' 1921–Mart 1924 g.)." *V-IZh*, no. 9 (1977): 85–89.
———. "General'nyi Shtab RKKA v Predvoennye Gody (1936–Iyun' 1941 g.)." *V-IZh*, no. 3 (1980): 68–73.
———. "Sovershenstvovanie Sistemy Tsentral'nykh Organov Voennogo Rukovodstva v 1929–1939 gg." *V-IZh*, no. 6 (1982): 74–79.
———. "Organizatsiya Strategicheskogo Rukovodstva Sovetskimi Vooruzhennymi Silami (1917–1920 gg.)." *V-IZh*, no. 3 (1988): 17–25.
———. Review of *Voennye Spetsialisty na Sluzhbe Respubliki Sovetov 1917–1920 gg. V-IZh*, no. 5 (1989): 84–85.
De-Lazari, A. "Voennoe Porazhenie Pol'skogo Gosudarstva." *V-IZh*, no. 1 (1940): 63–74.
Dick, C. "Soviet Operational Art. Part 1: The Fruits of Experience." *International Defence Review* 21, no. 7 (1988): 755–61.

―――. "Soviet Operational Art. Part 2: The Keys to Victory." *International Defence Review* 21, no. 8 (1988): 901–8.
Dmitriev, P. "Sozdanie Strategicheskikh Rezervov Krasnoi Armii v Gody Grazhdanskoi Voiny." *V-IZh*, no. 6 (1974): 64–73.
―――. "Ispol'zovanie Strategicheskikh Rezervov Krasnoi Armii (Fevral' 1918 g.–Fevral' 1919 g.)." *V-IZh*, no. 11 (1975): 64–69.
―――. "Strategicheskie Rezervy Krasnoi Armii v Letnei Kampanii 1919 Goda." *V-IZh*, no. 7 (1977): 85–92.
―――. "Ispol'zovanie Strategicheskikh Rezervov Krasnoi Armii v Osenne-Zimnei Kampanii 1919–1920 gg." *V-IZh*, no. 10 (1979): 45–49.
Dmitriev, V. "Stroitel'stvo Sovetskogo Podvodnogo Flota v Mezhvoennyi Period." *V-IZh*, no. 10 (1974): 81–86.
Domnikov, V. "Velikii Oktyabr' i Sozdanie Sovetskikh Voennykh Kadrov." *V-IZh*, no. 11 (1967): 14–25.
Dudorova, O. "Neizvestnye Stranitsy 'Zimnei Voiny'." *V-IZh*, no. 9 (1991): 12–23.
Dzhambaev, N. "Aktivnoe Prikrytie v Nachal'nyi Period Voiny." *Voennaya Mysl'*, no. 1 (1937): 46–67.
―――. "Ispol'zovanie Aviatsii v Nastupatel'noi Operatsii." *Voennaya Mysl'*, no. 3 (1941): 36–58.
Efimov, N. "Evolyutsiya Sistemy Vooruzheniya." *V&R*, no. 10 (1928): 24–44.
Eideman, R. Review of *Osnovy Nashei Taktiki. Ogon', Manevr, Maskirovka. V&R*, no. 7 (1928): 148–50.
―――. "Desyat' Let." *V&R*, no. 11 (1928): 5–14.
―――. "K Voprosu o Kharaktere Nachal'nogo Perioda Voiny." *V&R*, no. 8 (1931): 11–17.
―――. "K Izucheniyu Istorii Grazhdanskoi Voiny." *V&R*, no. 2 (1932): 90–99.
Ernest, N. "Izpol'zovanie Tankov v Nastupatel'noi Operatsii." *Voennaya Mysl'*, no. 1 (1941): 46–54.
Evseev, A. "Voenno-Teoreticheskie Vzglyady M. V. Frunze." *V-IZh*, no. 1 (1985): 53–63.
Fadeev, G. "Dvadtsat' Let Raboche-Krest'yanskoi Krasnoi Armii i Voenno-Morskogo Flota." *Voennaya Mysl'*, no. 2 (1938): 3–21.
Favitskii, V. "Bol'shaya Malaya Voina." *V&R*, no. 2 (1925): 52–64.
―――. "Podvizhnaya Oborona." *V&R*, no. 3 (1932): 28–42.
―――. "Rol' Mekhvoisk v Sovremennoi Operatsii." *Mekhanizatsiya i Motorizatsiya RKKA*, no. 2 (1933): 60–71.
Fedorenko, L. "K Voprosu o Konnykh Massakh." *V&R*, no. 6 (1930): 24–43.
―――. "Konnitsa v Razvitii Proryva." *Voennaya Mysl'*, no. 8–9 (1937): 42–58.
Fedorov, A. "Osnovnye Etapy Stroitel'stva Krasnoi Armii." *V-IZh*, no. 2 (1940): 3–17.
Fedotov, A. "Ispol'zovanie Sredstv Podavleniya v Proryve." *V&R*, no. 8–9 (1932): 44–63.
Fedyukin, S. "Ob Ispol'zovanii Voennykh Spetsialistov v Krasnoi Armii." *V-IZh*, no. 6 (1962): 32–44.
Frolov, B. "Russko-Yaponskaia Voina 1904–1905 gg." *V-IZh*, no. 2 (1974): 83–90.
G. Review of *Protiv Reaktsionnykh Teorii na Voenno-Nauchnom Fronte. V&R*, no. 12 (1931): 77–81.

G-g. "Voina, Avtotransport i Problema Motorizatsii Armii." *V&R*, no. 8 (1928): 93–105.
Galaktionov, M. "Bronya i Motor." *V&R*, no. 4 (1932): 79–91.
———. "Artillerya i Tanki." *V&R*, no. 12 (1932): 38–64.
———. Review of *Udarnaya Armiya. V&R,* November–December (1933): 106–12.
———. "Moto-Mekhsily i Aviatsiya v Operatsii 'Kanny'." *V&R*, July–August (1934): 26–41.
Galistan, A. "Vydayushchiisya Sovetskii Gosudarstvennyi i Voennyi Deyatel'." *V-IZh*, no. 2 (1971): 47–50.
Gapich, N. "Deistviya 4-1 i 13-1 Armii v Severnoi Tavrii v Oktyabre-Noyabre 1920 g." *V&R*, no. 10 (1930): 64–85.
———. "Operativnyi Proryv." *Voennaya Mysl'*, no. 12 (1938): 146–48.
Geronimus, A. "Sushchnost' Krasnoi Armii kak Armii Diktatury Proletariata." *V&R*, no. 2 (1931): 9–28.
Girl', K. "Rezervy v Razlichnye Epokhy." *V&R*, no. 4 (1929): 28–40; no. 6 (1929): 17–35.
Glagolev. "Evolyutsiya Vzglyadov v Oblasti Taktiki Tankov za Poslednie Tri Goda." *V&R*, no. 3 (1928): 60–70.
Golubev, A. "Kak Zarozhdalsya Krymskii Front." *V&R*, no. 10 (1930): 45–63.
———. "Operatsii na Okhvat i Okruzhenie v Grazhdanskoi Voine 1918–1921 gg." *V&R*, January–February (1933): 4–17.
———. "Novyi Etap Voiny v Evrope." *Bol'shevik*, no. 10 (1940): 64–81.
———. "Obrashchena li Byla v Proshloe Nasha Voennaya Teoriya v 20-e Gody?" *V-IZh*, no. 10 (1965): 35–47.
———. "Vydayushchiisya Sovetskii Voennyi Teoretik." *V-IZh*, no. 3 (1968): 107–14.
Golubev, K. "Operatsiya po Proryvu UR." *Voennaya Mysl'*, no. 2 (1941): 12–43.
Gorelik, Ia. "O Voennoi i Nauchnoi Deyatel'nosti B. M. Shaposhnikova v Sovetskoi Armii." *V-IZh*, no. 10 (1960): 53–60.
———. "O Polkovodcheskoi i Voenno-Nauchnoi Deyatel'nosti Marshala Sovetskogo Soyuza M. N. Tukhachevskogo." *V-IZh*, no. 7 (1961): 45–55.
———. "O Voenno-Teoreticheskom Nasledii M. N. Tukhachevskogo." *V-IZh*, no. 2 (1963): 107–14.
———. "Predvideniya M. N. Tukhachevskogo." *V-IZh*, no. 9 (1988): 18–22.
Gorev, B. "Voennaya Istoriya i Marksizm." *V&R*, no. 4 (1927): 43–48.
———. "Marksizm i Leninism v Voennoi Akademii." *V&R*, no. 11 (1928): 29–34.
Gorodovikov, O. "2-ya Konnaya Armiya v Severnoi Tavrii." *V-IZh*, no. 10 (1940): 109–28.
Gorskii, V. "Material'noe Obespechenie Armii v Operatsii po Proryvu UR." *Voennaya Mysl'*, no. 4 (1941): 29–52.
Grebel'skii, Z. "X S"ezd Partii o Dal'neishem Stroitel'stve Krasnoi Armii." *V-IZh*, no. 3 (1971): 3–10.
———. "XI S"ezd Partii i Dal'neishee Ukreplenie Krasnoi Armii." *V-IZh*, no. 3 (1972): 3–10.
Grendal', V. "Artilleriiskii Rezerv Glavnogo Komandovaniya—'ARGK.'" *V&R*, no. 4 (1925): 30–38.
Gromakov, A. "Politika Kommunisticheskoi Partii v Oblasti Voennogo Stroitel'stva (1920–1923 gg.)." *V-IZh*, no. 6 (1970): 3–11.
———. "Deyatel'nost' Kommunisticheskoi Partii po Razvitiyu Oboronnoi Promyshlennosti (1921–1925 gg.)." *V-IZh*, no. 10 (1975): 84–89.

Gulevich, A. "Imperatorskaya Nikolaevskaya Voennaya Akademiya." *Chasovoi*, no. 93 (1932): 4–13.
Hartgrove, J. D. "Chronicling Soviet Military History: The Major Works of John Erickson." *Russian History/Histoire Russe* 12, no. 1 (1985): 95–100.
Holder, L. D. "Training for the Operational Level." *Parameters* 16, no. 1 (1986): 7–13.
Ionov, I. "Gospodstvo v Vozdukhe." *Voennaya Mysl'*, no. 5–6 (1937): 74–87.
———. "Ispol'zovanie VVS v Voine na Zapade." *Voennaya Mysl'*, no. 10 (1940): 34–47.
Iovlev, A. "Podgotovka Komandnykh i Politicheskikh Kadrov Sovetskoi Armii v 1929–1933 Godakh." *V-IZh*, no. 5 (1960): 63–75.
———. "Tekhnicheskoe Perevooruzhenie Krasnoi Armii v Gody Pervoi Pyatiletki." *V-IZh*, no. 12 (1964): 3–13.
———. "Stanovlenie i Razvitie Voenno-Uchebnykh Zavedenii Krasnoi Armii (1918–1920 gg.)." *V-IZh*, no. 9 (1974): 86–90.
Iovlev, A., and A. Cheremnykh. "Razvitie Voenno-Uchebnykh Zavedenii v 1929–1937 gg." *V-IZh*, no. 7 (1980): 72–76.
Isserson, G. "Kharakter Upravleniya Sovremennym Boem." *V&R*, no. 5 (1931): 56–62.
———. "Istoricheskie Korni Novykh Form Boya." *Voennaya Mysl'*, no. 1 (1937): 3–27.
———. "Vstrechnoe Srazhenie Budushchego." *Voennaya Mysl'*, no. 7 (1938): 10–26.
———. "Operativnye Perspektivy Budushchego." *Voennaya Mysl'*, no. 8 (1938): 14–26.
———. "Nachalo Boevogo Puti." *V-IZh*, no. 2 (1963): 71–75.
———. "Zapiski Sovremennika o M. N. Tukhachevskom." *V-IZh*, no. 4 (1963): 64–78.
———. "Razvitie Teorii Sovetskogo Operativnogo Iskusstva v 30-e Gody." *V-IZh*, no. 1 (1965): 36–46; no. 3: 48–61.
Ivanov, N. "Udary po Skhodyashchimsya Napravleniyam." *V&R*, March–April (1935): 14–30.
———. "Bor'ba s Obkhodom Flangom i Proryvom." *V&R*, May–June (1935): 56–69.
Ivanov, V., and K. Cheremukhin. "O Knige 'V Nachale Voiny.'" *V-IZh*, no. 6 (1965): 72–80.
Jacobs, W. D. "The Art of Operations." *Army* 12, no. 4 (1961): 60–64.
K., V. Review of *Protiv Men'shevistvuyushchego Idealizma v Voprosakh Voiny i Voennogo Dela*. *V&R*, no. 3 (1932): 82–86.
Kakurin, N. "Vnutrennie Operatsionnye Linii v Grazhdanskoi Voine." *V&R*, no. 4 (1928): 65–85.
———. Review of *L'vov-Varshava*. *V&R*, no. 5 (1929): 144–55.
Kalinovskii, K. "Tanki v Oborone." *V&R*, no. 8 (1927): 117–24.
———. "Bystrokhodnye Tanki vo Vstrechnom Boyu." *V&R*, no. 1 (1929): 61–68.
Kamenev, S. "K Desyatoi Godovshchine." *V&R*, no. 2 (1928): 3–11.
Kapustin, N. "Oborona v Pozitsionnoi Voine." *V&R*, no. 7–8 (1925): 156–76.
Kartavtsev, I. "Prepodavanie Istorii Voennogo Iskusstva v Voennoi Akademii imeni M. V. Frunze v 1918–1978 gg." *V-IZh*, no. 12 (1979): 57–61.
Kavtaradze, A. "Iyun'skoe Nastuplenie Russkoi Armii v 1917 Godu." *V-IZh*, no. 5 (1967): 111–17.
———. "Iz Istorii Russkogo General'nogo Shtaba." *V-IZh*, no. 7 (1972): 87–92.
———. "Iz Istorii Russkogo General'nogo Shtaba (1909–Iyul' 1914 gg.)." *V-IZh*, no. 12 (1974): 80–86.
———. "Iz Istorii Russkogo General'nogo Shtaba (Avgust 1914 Goda–Mai 1918 Goda)." *V-IZh*, no. 3 (1976): 103–9.

Kazakov, M. "O Lyudskikh Rezervakh Krasnoi Armii v Gody Grazhdanskoi Voiny." *V-IZh*, no. 9 (1973): 54–60.

Kellerman, G. "Nastuplenie Tankov." *V&R*, no. 8–9 (1932): 64–75.

Khor'kov, A. G. "Nekotorye Voprosy Strategicheskogo Razvertyvaniya Sovetskikh Vooruzhennykh Sil v Nachale Velikoi Otechestvennoi Voiny." *V-IZh*, no. 1 (1986): 9–15.

———. "Tekhnicheskoe Perevooruzhenie Sovetskoi Armii Nakanune Velikoi Otechestvennoi Voiny." *V-IZh*, no. 6 (1987): 15–24.

———. "Ukreplennye Raiony na Zapadnykh Granitsakh SSSR." *V-IZh*, no. 12 (1987): 47–54.

Khvesin, T. "Deistviya Mozyrskoi Gruppy v 1920 Godu." *V&R*, no. 2 (1928): 113–31.

Kiselev, I. "Motorizovanno-Mekhanizirovannye Soedineniya." *V&R*, no. 5 (1930): 41–64.

———. "Ryad Kraine Nevernykh Polozhenii." *V&R*, no. 8–9 (1930): 75–84.

———. "K Voprosu ob Ispol'zovanii Russkoi Armii dlya Nuzhd Oborony Sovetskoi Respubliki." *V-IZh*, no. 12 (1961): 24–35.

Klimovskikh, V. "Vstrechnoe Srazhenie." *Voennaya Mysl'*, no. 8 (1938): 27–51.

Klyatskin, S. "Problemy Voennogo Stroitel'stva na Zavershayushchem Etape Grazhdanskoi Voiny." *V-IZh*, no. 3 (1964): 3–16.

Knyazev, M. "Ataka Ukreplennykh Raionov." *Voennaya Mysl'*, no. 6 (1940): 10–38.

Kokordinov, P. "Kharakter Sovremennogo Boya." *Voennaya Mysl'*, no. 2 (1941): 72–86.

Kolenkovskii, A. "Nastupatel'naya Operatsiya Protiv Ostanovivshevogosya Protivnika." *V&R*, no. 7 (1931): 33–41.

Kolesnichenko, I. "K Voprosu o Konflikte v Revvoensovete Yuzhnogo Fronta (Sentyabr'–Oktyabr' 1918 Goda)." *V-IZh*, no. 2 (1962): 39–47.

Kononenko, A. "Boi vo Flandrii." *V-IZh*, no. 3 (1941): 3–25.

Korneev, G. Review of *O Nastupatel'noi Operatsii Armii, Vkhodyashchei v Sostav Fronta*. *V&R*, no. 5 (1930): 139–42.

Korotkov, I. "V Reshayushchikh Boyakh Protiv Vrangelya." *V-IZh*, no. 10 (1940): 87–108.

———. "Voenno-Nauchnye Zhurnaly kak Istoricheskii Istochnik." *V-IZh*, no. 1 (1970): 83–91.

———. "Obobshchenie Opyta Voin v Mezhvoennyi Period." *V-IZh*, no. 6 (1976): 95–100.

———. "Voprosy Obshchei Taktiki v Sovetskoi Voennoi Istoriografii (1918–1941 gg.)." *V-IZh*, no. 12 (1977): 86–91.

Korsun, N. "Nekotorye Operativnye Vyvody iz Poslednikh Voin." *V-IZh*, no. 1 (1939): 24–37.

Kosogov, I. "Konnaya Armiya na Vrangelevskom Fronte." *V&R*, September–October (1935): 13–20.

Kostylev, V. "Stanovlenie i Razvitie Vozdushno-Desantnykh Voisk." *V-IZh*, no. 9 (1975): 80–85.

Kovalev, I. "Zadachi Bombardirovochnoi Aviatsii." *V&R*, no. 5 (1928): 39–47.

———. "Aviatsionnye Rezervy." *Voennaya Mysl'*, no. 3–4 (1937): 128–42.

———. "Aviatsionnaia Podgotovka Nastupleniya." *Voennaya Mysl'*, no. 6 (1940): 56–77.

Kozlov, S. "K Voprosu o Razvitii Russkoi Voennoi Teorii v Khode Pervoi Mirovoi Voiny." *V-IZh*, no. 9 (1970): 28–36.
Krasil'nikov, V. "Nekotorye Voprosy Voennonauchnoi Raboty." *V&R*, no. 12 (1931): 45–49.
———. Review of *K Kharakteristike Novykh Tendentsii v Voennom Dele*. *V&R*, no. 1 (1932): 96–104.
Kravchenko, I. "Kharakternye Cherty Nastupatel'nykh Operatsii Krasnoi Armii v Grazhdanskoi Voine." *V-IZh*, no. 3 (1976): 96–102.
———. "Vedenie Oborony Krasnoi Armiei v Khode Grazhdanskoi Voiny." *V-IZh*, no. 12 (1977): 74–78.
Kremkov, S. "Operativnye Nabroski." *V&R*, no. 8–9 (1930): 38–58.
Krupchenko, I. "Razvitie Tankovykh Voisk v Period Mezhdu Pervoi i Vtoroi Mirovymi Voinami." *V-IZh*, no. 5 (1968): 31–45.
Kr-v, N. "Vpolzanie v Voinu." *V&R*, March–April (1934): 34–37.
Kryzhanovskii, V. "Legkie Motomekhanizirovannye Soedineniya v Armeiskoi Operatsii." *V&R*, no. 10–11 (1931): 45–75.
———. "Samostoyatel'noe Motomekhanizirovannoe Soedinenie na Otkrytom Flange Armii v Nastupatel'noi Operatsii." *V&R*, no. 1 (1932): 13–33.
———. "Nastuplenie Shturmovoi Pekhoty Motorizovannogo Tipa na Oboronyayushchegosya Protivnika v Manevrennoi Voine." *V&R*, no. 8 (1932): 64–75.
Kuchinskii, D. "Neotdel'naya Armiya." *V&R*, no. 4 (1927): 84–92.
Kudryavtsev, A. "Operativnyi Otskok kak Odna iz Form Uskol'zaniya iz-pod Udara Protivnika." *V&R*, no. 4 (1929): 3–27.
Kuksha. "Vzaimodeistvie Tankov DPP i DD s Aviatsiei i Artilleriei pri Proryve Oboronitel'noi Polosy Protivnika v Manevrennoi Voine." *V&R*, no. 1 (1932): 1–12.
Kutyakov, I. "Operativno-Takticheskie Uroki Kievskoi Operatsii 1920 g." *V&R*, March–April (1935): 48–64.
Kuz'min, N. "Voennyi Vopros na VIII S"ezde Partii." *Voprosy Istorii KPSS*, no. 6 (1958): 174–88.
———. "Ob Odnoi Nevypolnennoi Direktive Glavkoma." *V-IZh*, no. 9 (1962): 49–66.
Ladukhin, V. "Nachal'nik Polevogo Shtaba Revvoensoveta Respubliki." *V-IZh*, no. 4 (1972): 59–64.
Lapchinskii, A. "Aviatsiya nad Polem Srazheniya." *V&R*, no. 11 (1928): 141–52.
———. "Deistviya Aviatsii v Nachal'nom Periode Voiny." *V&R*, no. 6 (1929): 55–66.
———. "Vozdushnye Desanty." *V&R*, no. 6 (1930): 87–100.
———. "Vozdushnaya Voina Budushchego." *V&R*, no. 3 (1931): 3–15.
———. "Osnovnye Voprosy Sovremennoi Aviatsii." *Voennaya Mysl'*, no. 3–4 (1937): 85–95.
Leer, G. "Vyyasnenie Nekotorykh Dannykh, Otnosyashchikhsya do Slozhnykh Operatsii Massovykh Armii, na Osnovanii Opyta Osennego Pokhoda 1813 Goda." *Voennyi Sbornik*, no. 3 (1888): 45–98.
Leonov, K. "Protivovozdushnaya Oborona Vnutrennei Territorii Strany." *Voennaya Mysl'*, no. 3–4 (1937): 96–116.
Levichev, V. "'Genshtab' i Voennaya Akademiya." *V&R*, no. 7 (1928): 74–77.
Lobov, V. "Aktual'nye Voprosy Razvitiya Sovetskoi Teorii Voennoi Strategii 20-kh—Serediny 30-kh Godov." *V-IZh*, no. 2 (1989): 41–50.

Lomov, N. Review of *Voprosy Strategii i Operativnogo Iskusstva v Sovetskikh Voennykh Trudakh (1917–1940 gg.)*. *V-IZh*, no. 1 (1968): 101–7.
———. "General Armii A. I. Antonov." *V-IZh*, no. 9 (1976): 115–21.
———. "Marshal Sovetskogo Soyuza B. M. Shaposhnikov." *V-IZh*, no. 9 (1982): 54–57.
Lozovoi-Shevchenko, V. "VVS v Armeiskoi Nastupatel'noi Operatsii." *Voennaya Mysl'*, no. 2 (1941): 44–60.
Ludri, I. "Morskie Operatsii." *Voennaya Mysl'*, no. 2 (1937): 75–86.
Luttwak, E. "The Operational Level of War." *International Security* 5, no. 3 (1980–81): 61–69.
Lyubarskii, S. "Nekotorye Vyvody iz Opyta Voiny v Ispanii. Nastuplenie." *Voennaya Mysl'*, no. 10 (1938): 12–31.
———. "Nekotorye Vyvody iz Opyta Voiny v Ispanii. Oborona." *Voennaya Mysl'*, no. 11 (1938): 95–109.
Malevskii, A. "Osnovy Upravleniya Moto-Mekhanizirovannymi Soedineniyami." *Voennaya Mysl'*, no. 2 (1937): 87–101.
———. "Mekhanizatsiya Sovremennykh Armii." *Voennaya Mysl'*, no. 3–4 (1937): 117–27.
Marievskii, I. "Operativnyi Plan Razgroma Belopolyakov na Ukraine v 1920 Godu." *V-IZh*, no. 5 (1939): 124–40.
———. "K Dvadtsatiletiyu Pobedy nad Panskoi Pol'shei." *V-IZh*, no. 5 (1940): 3–24.
———. "Stanovlenie i Razvitie Teorii Operativnogo Iskusstva." *V-IZh*, no. 3 (1962): 26–40.
Marinov, A. "U Istokov Voenno-Istoricheskoi Literatury o Grazhdanskoi Voine." *V-IZh*, no. 6 (1980): 76–79.
Matsulenko, V. "Razvitie Taktiki Nastupatel'nogo Boya." *V-IZh*, no. 2 (1968): 28–46.
Medvedev, R. "O Smerti M. V. Frunze i F. E. Dzerzhinskogo." *V-IZh*, no. 3 (1989): 54–61.
Melikov, V. Review of *Mozg Armii*. *V&R*, no. 7 (1929): 137–46.
———. "Srazhenie na Visle v Svete Opyta Maisko-Avgustovskoi Kampanii 1920 g." *V&R*, no. 10 (1930): 9–44.
———. "Vtoraya Marna." *V&R*, no. 5 (1931): 3–33.
———. "Tvorcheskii Voenno-Nauchnyi Put' V. Triandafillova i K. Kalinovskogo." *V&R*, no. 8 (1931): 3–10.
———. "Konnye Massy v Grazhdanskoi Voine." *V&R*, July–August (1933): 3–16.
———. "Geroicheskaya Oborona Tsaritsyna." *Voennaya Mysl'*, no. 2 (1937): 3–33.
———. "Lenin i Stalin-Organizatory Pobed Grazhdanskoi Voiny." *V-IZh*, no. 5 (1939): 6–47.
Meretskov, K. "Komandarm 1 Ranga I. P. Uborevich." *V-IZh*, no. 9 (1962): 74–90.
Mezheninov, S. "Boevaya Aviatsiya." *V&R*, no. 1 (1929): 14–31.
Mikhailov, S. "Rol' Artillerii v Sovremennoi Voine." *Voennaya Mysl'*, no. 2 (1937): 34–59.
Mikulin, V. Review of *L'vov-Varshava*. *V&R*, no. 10 (1929): 141–50.
Murakhver, N. "Podgotovka Komandnykh Kadrov Krasnoi Armii v Gody Grazhdanskoi Voiny v SSSR (1917–1920 gg.)." *V-IZh*, no. 6 (1940): 72–87.
Myalkovskii, A. "Udarnaya Armiya." *V&R*, no. 2 (1931): 48–68.
Nastusevich, Ya. Review of *The Reformation of War*. *V&R*, no. 4 (1932): 100–106.
Naumov, N. "Teoriya Proryva Oborony Protivnika v Predvoennye Gody." *V-IZh*, no. 1 (1975): 57–63.

Nenarokov, A. "Istorik Grazhdanskoi Voiny." *V-IZh*, no. 11 (1965): 42–49.
Nikitin, A. "Sostoyanie Vazhneishikh Otraslei Promyshlennosti SSSR Nakanune Velikoi Otechestvennoi Voiny." *V-IZh*, no. 3 (1960): 14–26.
Nikitin, E. "KPSS i Stroitel'stvo Sovetskikh Vooruzhennykh Sil v Mezhvoennyi Period." *V-IZh*, no. 10 (1977): 95–101.
Nikolin, I. "Pyatiletka i Oborona." *V&R*, no. 5 (1929): 3–16.
Nikol'skoi, M. "VVS v Voine na Zapade." *Voennaya Mysl'*, no. 11–12 (1940): 50–59.
Nizhichek, I. "Politika i Voina." *V&R*, January–February (1933): 30–48.
Novikov, G. Review of *Marna, Visla, Smirna*. *V&R*, no. 5 (1928): 154–60.
Novitskii, F. "Kontrudar po Kolchaku." *V-IZh*, no. 10 (1940): 29–55.
Novitskii, V. Review of *Strategiya*. *V&R*, no. 1 (1928): 152–58.
———. "Desyat' Let Prepodavaniya Voennoi Istorii v Voennoi Akademii RKKA." *V&R*, no. 11 (1928): 66–77.
———. "Bor'ba za Kharakter Budushchei Voiny." *V&R*, no. 3 (1929): 3–13.
———. "Deistviya Aviatsii v Nachal'nom Periode Voiny." *V&R*, no. 9 (1929): 23–31.
———. "Voennomorskie Sily v Nachal'nyi Period Voiny." *V&R*, May–June (1935): 46–55.
Nozdrunov. "Pochemu ne Udalos' Okruzhit' Pol'skuyu Armiyu 4–7 Iyulya 1920 Goda na Zapadnom Fronte." *V&R*, no. 7 (1930): 78–100.
Ogorodnikov, F. "Krizisy Bol'shikh Srazhenii." *V&R*, no. 7 (1928): 16–28.
Papirmeister, L. "Partorganizatsiya Voennoi Akademii za 10 Let." *V&R*, no. 11 (1928): 35–49.
Pauka, I. "Eshche o Kontrudare Yugo-Zapadnogo Fronta v Mae–Iyune 1920 g." *V&R*, May–June (1935): 15–35.
Pavlenko, N. "Iz Istorii Razvitiya Teorii Strategii." *V-IZh*, no. 10 (1964): 104–16.
———. "Nekotorye Voprosy Razvitiya Teorii Strategii v 20-kh Godakh." *V-IZh*, no. 5 (1966): 10–26.
Petrov, Yu. "Deyatel'nost' Kommunisticheskoi Partii po Provedeniyu Edinonachaliya v Vooruzhennykh Silakh (1925–1931 Gody)." *V-IZh*, no. 5 (1963): 12–23.
Pfaff, I. "Praga i Delo o Voennom Zagavore." *V-IZh*, no. 11 (1988): 47–56; no. 12 (1988): 61–69.
Plyachenko, P. "Trudy po Teorii Boevogo Primeneniya Sovetskikh VVS (1918–1940 gg.)." *V-IZh*, no. 8 (1970): 82–88.
Pugachev, S. Review of *Osnovy Nashei Taktiki. Ogon', Manevr, Maskirovka*. *V&R*, no. 7 (1928): 145–48.
Ramanichev, N. "Razvitie Teorii i Praktiki Boevogo Primenenie Vozdushno-Desantnykh Voisk v Mezhvoennyi Period." *V-IZh*, no. 10 (1982): 72–77.
Ratner, I. "Proryv na Maase." *V-IZh*, no. 5 (1941): 3–21.
Rokossovskii, K. "Soldatskii Dolg." *V-IZh*, no. 4 (1989): 52–57.
Rostunov, I. "U Istokov Sovetskoi Voennoi Istoriografii." *V-IZh*, no. 8 (1967): 84–96.
———. "Sovetskaya Voennaya Istoriografiya v Mezhvoennyi Period." *V-IZh*, no. 11 (1967): 86–93.
———. "Memuary Brusilova kak Istoricheskii Istochnik." *V-IZh*, no. 8 (1972): 97–104.
———. "Uroki Russko-Yaponskoi Voiny 1904–1905 gg." *V-IZh*, no. 2 (1984): 73–79.
Rotermel', A. Review of *Kharakter Operatsii Sovremennykh Armii*. *V&R*, no. 3 (1930): 140–47.
Rymshan, M. "Revvoensovet Respubliki za Desyat' Let." *V&R*, no. 2 (1928): 42–52.

Ryzhakov, A. "K Voprosu o Stroitel'stve Bronetankovykh Voisk Krasnoi Armii v 30-e Gody." *V-IZh*, no. 8 (1968): 105–11.
S. "Artilleriya pri Proryve." *V&R*, no. 9 (1931): 14–34.
———. "Obshchevoiskovoi Boi." *V&R*, no. 8–9 (1932): 1–14.
Salitan, I. "Operativnaya Deyatel'nost' Armeiskoi Konnitsy po Opytu Voiny s Pol'shei 1920 g." *V&R*, no. 12 (1928): 67–86.
Samoilov, A. "Deyatel'nost' Kommunisticheskoi Partii po Osushchestvleniyu Voennoi Reformy 1924–1925 gg." *V-IZh*, no. 11 (1985): 60–64.
Savinov, I. "Operatsii Okruzheniya." *V&R*, July–August (1934): 15–25.
Savinskii, M. "Zhurnal 'Voennaya Mysl' i Revolyutsiya' kak Istochnik po Istorii Sovetskikh Vooruzhennykh Sil." *V-IZh*, no. 2 (1974): 100–105.
Savushkin, R. "K Voprosu o Vozniknovenii i Razvitii Operatsii." *V-IZh*, no. 5 (1979): 78–82.
———. "K Voprosu o Zarozhdenii Teorii Posledovatel'nykh Nastupatel'nykh Operatsii (1921–1929 gg.)." *V-IZh*, no. 5 (1983): 77–83.
———. "Evolyutsiya Vzglyadov na Oboronu v Mezhvoennye Gody." *V-IZh*, no. 1 (1987): 37–42.
———. "Zarozhdenie i Razvitie Sovetskoi Voennoi Doktriny." *V-IZh*, no. 2 (1988): 19–26.
Savushkin, R., and N. Ramanichev. "Razvitie Taktiki Obshchevoiskovogo Boya v Period Mezhdu Grazhdanskoi i Velikoi Otechestvennoi Voinami." *V-IZh*, no. 11 (1985): 21–28.
Schneider, J. "The Loose Marble—and the Origins of Operational Art." *Parameters* 19, no. 1 (1989): 85–99.
———. "Theoretical Implications of Operational Art." *Military Review* 70, no. 9 (1990): 17–27.
Sedyakin, A. Review of *Evolyutsiya Operativnogo Iskusstva*. *V&R*, January–February (1933): 113–18.
———. "Tanki i Protivotankovaya Oborona." *V&R*, November–December (1933): 29–36.
Serebryakov, A. "Katalonskaya Operatsiya." *V-IZh*, no. 2 (1940): 74–93.
Shatsillo, K. "Podgotovka Tsarizmom Vooruzhennykh Sil k Pervoi Mirovoi Voine." *V-IZh*, no. 9 (1974): 91–96.
Sheideman, E. "Deistviya Konnogo Korpusa v Proryve Nepriyatel'skogo Fronta." *V&R*, no. 3 (1930): 40–64.
———. "Vzaimodeistvie Konnitsy s Motomekhanizirovannymi Soedineniyami." *V&R*, no. 6 (1930): 44–59.
Shelakhov, G. "Problema Vstrechnogo Boya." *V&R*, July–August (1935): 60–70.
Shelakhov, G., and Yu. Geller. "O Polkovodcheskoi i Voenno-Organizatorskoi Deyatel'nosti I. E. Yakira." *V-IZh*, no. 5 (1962): 25–43.
Sherstyuk, A. "Razvitie Teorii Boevogo Primeneniya Sredstv Protivovozdushnoi Oborony (1917–1941 gg.)." *V-IZh*, no. 4 (1988): 74–77.
Shilovskii, E. "O Tekhnicheskoi Storone Upravleniya Armii v Grazhdanskuyu Voinu." *Voennaya Nauka i Revolyutsiya*, no. 2 (1922): 13–27.
———. "K 10-mu Uchebnomu Godu." *V&R*, no. 7 (1927): 88–96.
———. "Evolyutsiya Akademicheskoi Podgotovki." *V&R*, no. 11 (1928): 15–28.
———. "Nachal'nyi Period Voiny." *V&R*, September–October (1933): 3–11.

———. "Nastupatel'naya Operatsiya." *Voennaya Mysl'*, no. 6 (1938): 57–78.
———. "Podgotovka i Vedenie Operativnogo Proryva." *Voennaya Mysl'*, no. 8 (1939): 15–29.
———. "Vidy Operatsii." *Voennaya Mysl'*, no. 1 (1941): 20–31.
Shishkin, S. "O Planakh Bor'by s Armiei Denikina." *V-IZh*, no. 2 (1963): 21–36.
———. "Kommunisticheskaya Partiya-Organizator Pobed Sovetskoi Respubliki nad Interventami i Belogvardeitsami v 1920 Godu." *V-IZh*, no. 11 (1970): 26–32.
Shpektorov, N. "Vysshee Upravlenie v Imperialisticheskoi Koalitsionnoi Voine." *V&R*, no. 6 (1927): 14–30.
Shtromberg, A. "Tankovye Voiska v Nastuplenii." *Voennaya Mysl'*, no. 6–7 (1941): 15–28.
Shukevich, I. "Taktika i Oruzhie Budushchego." *V&R*, no. 10 (1929): 38–62.
Shvarts, M. "K Postanovke Voprosa Issledovaniya Grazhdanskoi Voiny 1917–21 gg." *V&R*, no. 1 (1928): 48–60.
———. "Nekotorye Uroki Varshavskoi Operatsii 1920 g." *V&R*, no. 4 (1931): 34–60.
Simonov, K. "Zametki k Biografii G. K. Zhukova." *V-IZh*, no. 6 (1987): 46–54; no. 7 (1987): 45–56; no. 9 (1987): 48–56; no. 10 (1987): 56–63; no. 12 (1987): 40–46.
Smirnov, A. "K Voprosu ob Operativnom Iskusstve v Grazhdanskuyu Voinu 1918–1920 gg." *V&R*, January–February (1933): 18–29.
Smirnov, P. "Pervye Pyatiletki i Voenno-Tekhnicheskaya Politika Partii." *V-IZh*, no. 4 (1979): 66–69.
Sokolov, G. "Sovremennaya Zavesa i Voprosy Strategicheskogo Prikrytiya." *V&R*, no. 4 (1928): 15–21.
———. "Problema Reorganizatsii Konnitsy." *V&R*, no. 8–9 (1930): 59–74.
Sokolov-Strakhov, K. "K. E. Voroshilov o Kharaktere Sovremennoi Voiny." *V&R*, no. 2 (1931): 3–8.
———. "Neobkhodima Korennaya Reorganizatsiya Voenno-Issledovatel'skogo Dela." *V&R*, no. 9 (1931): 62–65.
Solov'ev, V., and A. Tsaritsyn. "Stalinskoe Uchenie o Voine i Armii." *V-IZh*, no. 5 (1939): 58–70.
Spirin, L. "V. I. Lenin i Sozdanie Sovetskikh Komandnykh Kadrov." *V-IZh*, no. 4 (1965): 3–16.
Starunin, A. "Operativnaya Vnezapnost'." *Voennaya Mysl'*, no. 3 (1941): 27–35.
Stebakova, L. "Glavkom Respubliki S. S. Kamenev." *V-IZh*, no. 4 (1971): 56–58.
Stepnoi, K. "Tanki i Operativnoe Iskusstvo." *Voennaya Mysl'*, no. 1 (1937): 28–45.
Stukov, N. Review of *L'vov-Varshava*. *V&R*, no. 10 (1929): 129–41.
Sudakov, F. "Voennoe Iskusstvo na Poroge Novogo Etapa Razvitiya." *V-IZh*, no. 1 (1940): 20–36.
Suvenirov, O. F. "Esli b ne ta Vakkhanaliya." *V-IZh*, no. 2 (1989): 51–59.
———. "Vsearmeiskaya Tragediya." *V-IZh*, no. 3 (1989): 39–47.
Svechin, A. A. "Integral'noe Ponimanie Voennogo Iskusstva." *Krasnye Zori*, no. 11 (1924): 15–23.
———. "Izuchenie Voennoi Istorii." *V&R*, no. 4 (1927): 49–66.
———. "Gosudarstvennyi i Frontovoi Tyl." *V&R*, no. 11 (1928): 94–108.
Svetlishin, N. "Marshal Sovetskogo Soyuza S. K. Timoshenko." *V-IZh*, no. 2 (1975): 43–48.
———. "Problemy Protivovozdushnoi Oborony v Trudakh Sovetskikh Avtorov (1920–1941 gg.)." *V-IZh*, no. 4 (1979): 76–79.

Tatarchenko, E. "Vozdushnyi Flot v Budushchei Voine." *V&R*, no. 9 (1929): 32–51.
———. "Operativno-Strategicheskaya Podvizhnost' Vozdushnykh Sil." *V&R*, no. 7 (1932): 30–35.
Tikhonov, M. "Nachal'nyi Period Sovremennoi Voiny." *V&R*, March–April (1933): 31–33.
Timoshkov, S. "Razgrom Yuzhnoi Armii Kolchaka." *V-IZh*, no. 3 (1940): 33–56.
Tolchenov, M. "Vtoraya Imperialisticheskaya Voina na Zapade." *Voennaya Mysl'*, no. 8 (1940): 16–38.
Tomashevskii, Ia. "K Voprosu o Vosstanovlenii Zheleznykh Dorog." *V&R*, May–June (1933): 24–29.
Triandafillov, V. K. "Vzaimodeistvie Mezhdu Zap. i Yugo-Zap. Frontami vo Vremya Letnego Nastupleniya Krasnoi Armii na Vislu v 1920 g." *V&R*, no. 2 (1925): 21–51.
———. "K Pyatiletnei Godovshchine Likvidatsii Vrangelya." *V&R*, no. 7–8 (1925): 32–49.
———. "Vozmozhnaya Chislennost' Budushchikh Armii." *V&R*, no. 3 (1927): 14–43.
Trifonov, I., and O. Suvenirov. "Razgrom Kronshtadtskogo Kontrrevolyutsionnogo Myatezha 1921 Goda." *V-IZh*, no. 3 (1971): 88–94.
Trutko, F. "Material'noe Obespechenie Operatsii Udarnoi Armii." *V&R*, no. 12 (1932): 65–84.
Tsiffer, R. "Kharakteristika Predstoyashchei Voiny." *V&R*, no. 10–11 (1931): 3–19.
Tukhachevskii, M. "Novye Voprosy Voiny." *V-IZh*, no. 2 (1962): 62–77.
Ul'yanov, V. "Razvitie Teorii Glubokogo Nastupatel'nogo Boya v Predvoennye Gody." *V-IZh*, no. 3 (1988): 26–33.
Unsigned. "Zadachi Bol'shevistkoi Kritiki na Voennonauchnom Fronte." *V&R*, no. 1 (1932): 93–96.
Unsigned. "Voennye Voprosy na VIII S"ezde Partii." *V-IZh*, no. 3 (1984): 19–26.
V., P. "Usilennyi Strelkovyi Korpus pri Proryve." *V&R*, no. 6 (1931): 3–13.
———. "Usilennyi Strelkovyi Korpus vo Vstrechnom Srazhenii." *V&R*, no. 9 (1931): 3–13.
———. "Ispol'zovanie Sredstv Podavleniya v Operatsii Proryva." *V&R*, no. 10–11 (1931): 20–27.
Varfolomeev, N. E. "Dvizhenie Presleduyushchei Armii k Polyu Reshitel'nogo Srazheniya." *Revolyutsiya i Voina*, no. 13 (1921): 69–96.
———. "Manevry na Zapfronte." *Revolyutsiya i Voina*, no. 19 (1923): 5–26; no. 21 (1923): 77–105.
———. "Operativnaya Vnezapnost' i Maskirovka." *V&R*, no. 3 (1927): 96–111.
———. "Strategiya v Akademicheskoi Postanovke." *V&R*, no. 11 (1928): 78–93.
———. "Vstrechnaya Operatsiya." *V&R*, no. 7 (1930): 11–42.
———. "Nastuplenie 18-i Germanskoi Armii Vesnoi 1918 g." *V&R*, no. 7 (1931): 42–70.
———. "Podgotovka Operatsii Udarnykh Armii." *V&R*, no. 3 (1932): 1–13.
Vashchenko, P., and V. Runov. "Voennaya Reforma v SSSR." *V-IZh*, no. 12 (1989): 33–40.
Vasilevskii, A. "Marshal B. M. Shaposhnikov." *V-IZh*, no. 9 (1972): 32–37.
———. "Soldat, Polkovodets." *V-IZh*, no. 10 (1973): 39–43.
Verkhovskii, A. "Novaya i Staraya Shkola." *V&R*, no. 4 (1928): 99–112.
———. "Evolyutsiya Prepodavaniya Taktiki v Voennoi Akademii v 1918–1928 gg." *V&R*, no. 11 (1928): 50–65.

Vetoshnikov, L. "Brusilovskii Proryv (Kratkii Operativno-Strategicheskii Ocherk)." *Voennaya Mysl'*, no. 7 (1939): 70–91.
Viktorov, B. "'I Postavili Svoyu Podpis' . . ." *V-IZh*, no. 4 (1989): 45–51.
Vishnev, S. Review of *The Reformation of War*. *V&R*, no. 1 (1925): 283–87.
———. "Ekonomicheskaya Podgotovka k Voine za Rubezhom." *V&R*, no. 7 (1928): 3–15.
Voinov, V. "Planirovanie Armeiskoi Nastupatel'noi Operatsii." *Voennaya Mysl'*, no. 6–7 (1941): 7–14.
Vol'pe, A. Review of *Strategiya*, 2d ed. *V&R*, no. 5 (1927): 182–86.
———. "Nekotorye Mysli o Dialektike Voiny." *V&R*, no. 5 (1929): 36–54.
———. "Korni Operativnogo Plana Voiny (Vliyanie Politicheskikh Faktorov na Strategicheskoe Razvertyvanie Germanii, Frantsii i Rossii v 1914 g." *V&R*, no. 1 (1930): 13–54.
———. "Vnezapnost'." *Voennaya Mysl'*, no. 3 (1937): 3–34.
Voronkov, V. "Kontrudar M. V. Frunze na Vostochnom Fronte." *V&R*, July–August (1933): 17–38.
———. "Razgrom Kolchaka." *V&R*, March–April (1934): 58–64.
Voroshilov, K. "XX Let Raboche-Krest'yanskoi Krasnoi Armii i Voenno-Morskogo Flota." *Voennaya Mysl'*, no. 3 (1938): 3–22.
Voskanov, G. "O Kontrudare Yugo-Zapadnogo Fronta v Mae-Iyune 1920 g." *V&R*, May–June (1934): 50–66.
Yegorov, A. "Goryachii Bol'shevistskii Privet Voennoi Akademii RKKA Imeni M. V. Frunze." *V&R*, January–February (1934): 3–7.
———. "Taktika i Operativnoe Iskusstvo RKKA na Novom Etape." *V-IZh*, no. 10 (1963): 30–39.
Zakharov, M. "O Teorii Glubokoi Operatsii." *V-IZh*, no. 10 (1970): 10–20.
———. "Kommunisticheskaya Partiya i Tekhnicheskoe Perevooruzhenie Armii i Flota v Gody Predvoennykh Pyatiletok." *V-IZh*, no. 2 (1971): 3–12.
Zakutnyi, D. Review of *Taktika*. *V&R*, September–October (1934): 122–24.
Zavalishin, N. "Vstrechi s Marshalom A. I. Yegorovym." *V-IZh*, no. 11 (1963): 72–75.
Zhemaitis, F. "Proryv Pol'skogo Fronta 1-i Konnoi Armiei." *V-IZh*, no. 6 (1940): 3–23.
Zhigur, Ya. "Perspektivy Sozdaniya Antisovetskogo Bloka." *V&R*, no. 2 (1925): 137–48.
———. "Angliya i SSSR." *V&R*, no. 4 (1925): 7–14.
———. "Vliyanie Sovremennoi Voennoi Tekhniki na Kharakter Budushchikh Voin." *V&R*, no. 8 (1927): 14–26.
———. "Zadachi Usileniya Tekhniki Krasnoi Armii." *V&R*, no. 10 (1928): 45–66; no. 12 (1928): 21–33.
———. "Operativnyi Plan Voiny Shliffena i Sovremennaya Deistvitel'nost'." *V&R*, no. 6 (1929): 3–16; no. 7 (1929): 3–14.
———. "Proryv Oboronitel'noi Systemy po Opytu Mirovoi Voiny." *V&R*, January–February (1935): 74–89.
———. "Proryv i ego Razvitie." *Voennaya Mysl'*, no. 5–6 (1937): 17–53.
Zhilin, P. "Diskussiya o Edinoi Voennoi Doktrine." *V-IZh*, no. 5 (1961): 61–74.
———. "Kharakternye Cherty Sovetskoi Voennoi Strategii v Gody Grazhdanskoi Voiny." *V-IZh*, no. 2 (1973): 21–33.
———. "Bol'shaya Programma po Usileniyu Russkoi Armii." *V-IZh*, no. 7 (1974): 90–97.

———. "Nastuplenie Russkoi Armii Letom 1917 Goda v Voenno-Politicheskikh Planakh Antanty." *V-IZh,* no. 3 (1982): 59–66.
Zhuravlev, N. "Operativnoe Sosredotochinie." *V&R,* November–December (1935): 41–47.
Zimin, Ya. "V. I. Lenin i Sozdanie Vysshikh Organov Voennogo Rukovodstva Sovetskogo Gosudarstva (1917–1920 gg.)." *V-IZh,* no. 6 (1968): 3–16.
Zotov, S. "Proryv Pol'skogo Fronta." *V&R,* May–June (1935): 36–45.

Index

Afghanistan, 126
Aircraft
  DB-3, 178
  I-5, 178
  I-15, 178
  I-16, 178
  I-53, 178
  Il-2, 234
  LaGG-3, 234
  MiG-3, 234
  Pe-2, 234
  SB-3, 178
  TB-1, 178
  TB-3, 178
  Yak-1, 234
Aisne River, 153, 155, 248, 264
Albania, 126
Aleksandr III, 6
Alekseev, M. V., 52, 62, 66, 70–71
Alksnis, Ya. Ya., 172, 178
Allies (World War I), 69, 85, 146, 162
All-Russian Bureau of Military Commissars.
  See Red Army Political Directorate
All-Russian Main Staff, 35, 122, 129
Amiens, 155
Amur Flotilla, 230

Anatolia, 157
Anisov, A., 214
Antonov, A. I., 82, 216
Antonov-Ovseenko, V. A., 120, 125
Apanasenko, I. R., 260, 268
Archangel, 84, 91
Archangel Military District, 229
Armed Forces of Southern Russia
  (Whites), 94
Armies, Russo-Japanese War (1904–1905)
  1st Army, 17, 19–22
  2d Army, 17, 20, 22
  3d Army, 17, 20–22
  First Army (Japanese), 13, 21
  Second Army (Japanese), 15, 19–21
  Third Army (Japanese), 19
  Fourth Army (Japanese), 15, 19–21
  Fifth Army (Japanese), 19, 21
Armies, World War I (1914–1918)
  1st Army, 43, 45–46, 48–51, 56, 61
  2d Army, 43, 45–46, 48–50, 56, 60–61
  3d Army, 43, 52–57, 60, 67–68
  4th Army, 43, 52–57, 60–61
  5th Army, 43, 52–57, 60–61
  6th Army, 43
  7th Army, 43, 63, 65–67

(Note: Numbered armies are Russian-Soviet, as is the Turkestan Army. All others are White Civil War–era or foreign armies.)

Armies, World War I (1914–1918) (*continued*)
   8th Army, 52–54, 56–57, 60, 63, 65–70
   9th Army, 53, 55–57, 60–61, 63, 65–69
   10th Army, 51
   11th Army, 63, 65–67
   Fifth Army (German), 85
   Eighth Army (German), 45, 47, 51
   Ninth Army (German), 60–61
   Southern Army (German), 63
   First Army (Austro-Hungarian), 42, 52–53, 56–58, 60–61, 63
   Second Army (Austro-Hungarian), 42, 53, 55–56, 58, 63
   Third Army (Austro-Hungarian), 42, 52–53, 55–56, 58
   Fourth Army (Austro-Hungarian), 42, 52–58, 63, 65
   Seventh Army (Austro-Hungarian), 63
Armies, Civil War (1918–1920)
   1st Army, 88, 90, 92
   1st Cavalry Army, 100, 102–3, 105, 108, 110, 114–17, 148–49, 175, 222, 229–30
   2d Army, 88, 90
   2d Cavalry Army, 100, 102–3, 105
   3d Army, 90, 111–14
   4th Army, 88, 90, 100, 102–3, 111–16
   5th Army, 88, 90–92, 164
   6th Army, 91, 100, 102
   8th Army, 95, 97–98
   9th Army, 95
   10th Army, 95
   11th Army, 95
   12th Army, 95, 108, 110–11, 114–16
   13th Army, 95, 97–98, 100, 102–3, 108
   14th Army, 95, 97, 108, 110, 114
   15th Army, 108, 111–16
   16th Army, 108, 111–15
   Caucasus Army (Whites), 94
   Don Army (Whites), 94–95, 98–99
   First Army (Polish), 111, 114
   Second Army (Polish), 108, 110
   Third Army (Polish), 108, 110–11, 114
   Fourth Army (Polish), 111, 114
   Fifth Army (Polish), 114–15
   Sixth Army (Polish), 108, 110
   First Army (Whites), 100
   Second Army (Whites), 100
   Orenburg Army (Whites), 88
   Siberian Army (Whites), 88, 91
   Southern Army Group (Whites), 88
   Volunteer Army (Whites), 93–94, 98–99, 104
   Western Army (Whites), 88, 164
   Turkestan Army, 88, 90–93
Armies, Soviet-Finnish War (1939–1940)
   7th Army, 243–45
   8th Army, 243, 245
   9th Army, 243, 245
   13th Army, 245
   14th Army, 243, 245
   15th Army, 245
Armies, others
   1st (Independent) Red Banner Army, 239, 254
   2d (Independent) Red Banner Army, 239
   Sixth Army (Japanese), 239–40
Artillery
   37-mm AA gun, 230–32
   45-mm anti-tank gun, 175, 230–31
   50-mm mortar, 231–32
   76-mm gun, 175, 230–32
   76.2-mm AA gun, 177
   82-mm mortar, 230–32
   85-mm AA gun, 230–32
   107-mm gun, 231
   120-mm mortar, 230–31
   122-mm gun, 175, 231
   122-mm howitzer, 40, 175, 232
   152-mm howitzer, 231–32
   155-mm howitzer, 40
   203-mm howitzer, 175
Artillery Academy, 35
Asiago, 63
Astrakhan', 94
Attack echelon (EA), 205, 207–9
Austerlitz, 10
Austria, 126
Austria-Hungary, 6, 9, 11, 26, 33, 37, 39–44, 52, 58, 63, 66–68, 107

Bagramyan, I. Kh., 216, 248
Baiov, A. K., 27

Baku, 178, 181, 234
Baltic Fleet, 5, 179, 229–30, 234, 243
Baltic Sea, 243, 265
Baltic Special Military District, 222, 229–30, 253–54
Baltic States, 74–75, 84, 126, 168, 178, 182, 243, 268
Baltic-White Sea Canal, 170
Baranov, P. I., 178
Baranovichi, 62, 67, 112, 265
Barents Sea, 146
Battle of the Frontiers, 154, 160
Beginning Period of War, 183–86
Belaya River, 92
Belebei, 91–92, 104, 106
Belgium, 6, 126, 144, 157, 228, 268
Belitskii, S. M., 180, 223
Belorussia, 84, 94, 107, 112, 160, 162, 268
Belorussian Military District, 177, 185, 217, 222–23, 229, 230, 237, 247, 256
Belorussian Special Military District. *See* Belorussian Military District
Belostok, 42, 49, 113, 130
Belov, I. P., 221
Berdichev, 108, 110
Berezina River, 111–12
Berlin, 26, 42, 44, 130
Bessarabia, 75, 219
Bezobrazov, V. M., 68
Bil'derling, A. A. 13, 17
Biryuzov, S. S., 257
Black Sea, 102, 146, 181–82, 265
Black Sea Fleet, 179, 229–30
Blitzkrieg, 268
Blyukher, V. K. 119, 172, 220–21, 237, 239
Bohm-Ermolli, Gen., 55, 63
Bonch-Bruevich, M. D., 77, 83, 123
Borodino, Battle of, 11, 137, 152
Bothmer, Gen., 63
Boxer Rebellion, 12
Breakthrough development echelon (ERP), 205, 207–9
Brest (Brest-Litovsk), 42, 53, 108, 113, 115, 130, 265–66

Brest-Litovsk, Treaty of, 74, 77, 94
Brody, 66–68
Brudermann, Gen., 53
Brusilov, A. A., 52, 54–55, 62–63, 65–71, 77, 82, 145, 202, 264, 271
Bryansk, 95
Bubnov, A. S., 120, 172
Bucharest, 168, 182, 267
Budapest, 26, 44, 267
Budennyi, S. M., 79–80, 97–100, 102–5, 108, 111, 115, 121, 148, 172, 175, 203, 213, 220, 230
Bug River, 43, 53–54, 113–15, 118, 162
Buguruslan, 90–92, 104, 106
Bukharin, N. I., 121, 170, 218
Bukovina, 63, 219
Bulgaria, 6, 126

Carpathian Mountains, 42, 44, 52, 57, 61, 68, 266–67
Caspian Flotilla, 230
Caspian Sea, 84, 88, 181, 268
Caucasus Front (World War I), 44
Caucasus Front (Civil War), 106
Caucasus Mountains, 84, 103, 114
Cavalry-Mechanized Army, 211, 213, 266–67
Cavalry-Mechanized Group, 149, 213, 217, 265–66
Central Asia, 45, 80, 84, 88, 103
Central Asian Military District, 229, 260, 268
Central Committee, Communist Party, 78, 86, 93, 169, 172, 218
Central Group (Khalkhin-Gol), 240
Central Powers, 6, 62, 68–69, 74
Champagne, 155
Chancellorsville, Battle of, 152
Chelm, 53–56, 115–16
Chelyabinsk, 106
Cherevichenko, Ya. T., 260
Chernigov, 94
Chernovtsy, 52, 66, 266
Chiang-Kai-Shek, 236–37
China, 41, 126, 236, 241, 248
Chinese Eastern Railroad, 119
Civil War, American (1861–1865), 7, 9, 152

Civil War, Russian (1918–1920), 34, 74–75, 84, 103, 105, 107, 123, 128, 130, 133–34, 153, 155, 158, 203, 237, 271
Civil War, Spanish (1936–1939), 178, 196, 222–23, 225, 227–28, 246, 248, 257
Clausewitz, C. von, 10, 163, 166
Cold Harbor, 8
Committee for Military and Naval Affairs, 86
Complex Operation, 36, 142, 159, 210
Conrad von Hotzendorf, F., 52–53, 56–58
Consecutive Operations, 29, 34, 37, 71, 106, 152, 154–55, 157–68, 208–9, 228–29
Constituent Assembly, 73, 87
Cossacks, 79, 93–94, 110
Council of Labor and Defense, 86, 120, 122
Council of People's Commissars for Military Affairs, 86
Council of People's Commissars, 73, 172, 222, 230
Council of Workers' and Peasants' Defense, 86
Cover Army, 186
Cracow, 60, 267
Crimea, 80, 99–100, 102–3, 107–8, 181, 268
Crimean War (1853–1856), 4
Czechoslovak Corps, 87
Czechoslovakia, 126

Danilov, N. A., 81
Danilvo, Yu. N., 60
Dankl, Gen., 53
Danube Flotilla, 230
Daugavpils (Dvinsk), 62, 265
DD tanks, 188, 191–92
Deblin, 114–15
Deep Battle, 186–94, 246
Deep Operation, 152, 194–217, 228, 248
Defense Commission, 172, 222
Defense Council, 222
Defensive Operation, 32, 151, 213–15, 225–26, 254–57

Denikin, A. I., 77, 84, 94–95, 98, 100, 104, 107–8, 116, 163
Denmark, 126
Desert Storm, Operation, 1
Dnepr River, 100, 108, 181
Dnestr Detachment, 52
Dnestr River, 52, 57, 63, 68, 108, 182, 266
Donets Basin, 99–100, 106, 181
Don Front (World War II), 211
Don River, 79, 84, 88, 97–99, 106
DPP tanks, 188
Dubno, 55
Dukhonin, N. N., 77, 86
Duma, 5
Dunajec River, 57, 267
Dvina River, 185
Dybenko, P. E., 221
Dzerzhinskii, F. E., 73

Eastern Detachment (Russo-Japanese War), 13, 15
Eastern Front (Civil War), 79–80, 87–88, 90–91, 93, 103, 105–6, 117, 143, 158, 163
East Prussia, 31, 42–45, 47, 50–51, 53, 56, 58–59, 62, 266
Eideman, R. P., 139, 215
Ekaterinburg, 106
Ekaterinoslav (Dnepropetrovsk), 100
Elchaninov, A. G., 35–38, 106, 154
Engagement, 30–31
Engels, F., 123
English Channel, 228
Eremenko, A. I., 260
Estonia, 127, 146, 168, 181, 219, 243
Evert, A. E., 54, 62, 66–67, 70
Eylau, 137
Ezhov, N. I., 218

Falkenhayn, E. von, 68–69
Far Eastern Front, 229, 237, 251, 254, 268
Fastov Group (Southwestern Front), 110
February Revolution, 78
Fedorenko, Ya. N., 260
Feklenko, N. V. 237
Ferdinand, Archduke, 52, 63

Finland, 74–75, 121, 126, 178, 181, 193, 219, 222, 225, 228, 242–43, 245–46, 248, 257, 262, 265
First Army Group (Khalkhin-Gol), 239
First Baltic Front (World War II), 211
First Belorussian Front (World War II), 211
Five-Year Plans (1928–1941), 170, 172, 175, 179, 195, 218, 234
Flanders, 155
Forward Army, 185
France, 6, 9, 41–43, 53, 69, 71, 74, 123, 126, 138, 143–44, 146, 155, 157, 178, 180–81, 219, 228, 248, 261, 264, 268
Franco, F., 225
Franco-Prussian War (1870–1871), 8, 10, 32
French Revolution, 9, 78, 123
"Friction in war," 163, 166
Frinovskii, M. P., 211
Front, 2–3, 8, 11, 13, 17, 25–26, 29, 33, 36–38, 158–59, 210–11
Frunze, M. V., 80, 90–93, 100, 102, 104, 106, 120–26, 128–29, 132–35, 138, 146, 152, 164
Frunze Military Academy, 139, 143, 157, 168, 171, 196, 198, 203, 215, 223, 257

Gai, G. D., 111–12, 115–16, 221
Gajda, R., 91
Galich, 52–53, 55, 63, 67–68
Galicia, 42–44, 50, 53, 58–60, 62, 111, 182
Galicia, Battle of, 31, 53, 58–59, 224
Gamarnik, Ya. B., 172, 221
Gar'kavyi, I. I., 211
Gekker, A. I., 139, 221
General engagement, 30–31, 35, 59, 140, 152, 154
General Staff (imperial), 40–41, 81
General Staff Academy (imperial), 24, 26–27, 29, 35, 44, 81–83, 87, 123, 129, 132, 138–39, 196, 215, 217
General Staff Academy (Soviet), 203, 216, 222–25, 235, 248
German-Polish War, 226, 228

Germany, 4, 6, 7, 11, 26, 33, 37, 40–44, 74–75, 93, 116, 126, 131, 157, 169, 178, 182–83, 185, 219, 223, 265, 271
Gerua, A. V., 26
Gettysburg, 152
Gittis, V. M., 221
Gnilaya Lipa River, 55, 58
Golikov, F. I., 251
Golovin, N. N., 27
Golubev, A. V., 224
Gomel', 108
Gorbatov, A. V., 221
Gorlice, 61
Gorodok, 56–57, 67
Gotovtsev, A. I., 82, 216
Govorov, L. A., 216
Grand Tactics, 28
Great Britain, 3, 6, 40, 126, 179–81, 219–20
Great Program, 40
Greece, 126
Grodno, 112
Group of Armies. *See* Front
Grozny, 181
Guderian, H., 82, 228
Gulf of Finland, 84, 179, 243
Gusev, K. M., 254
Gusev, S. I., 91, 123, 125

Hailar, 241
Halder, F., 236
Helsinki, 245
High Command Artillery Reserve (ARGK), 176, 196, 198, 226, 231, 243, 252, 255–56, 262–63
High Command Aviation, 234
High Command Tank Reserve (TRGK), 176, 196, 198, 231
Higher Tactics, 24, 28, 141
Hindenburg, P. von, 47, 51
Hitler, A., 169, 219–20, 268
Hungary, 52, 126, 265
Hun-ho River, 19–22

Industrial Party, 171
Industrial Revolution, 4, 7–9
Invasion Army, 183–84

Iran, 126
Isserson, G. S., 145, 199–200, 203–5, 207, 209–11, 216–17, 224–28, 253, 273
Italy, 6, 126, 157
Ivanov, N. I., 52, 54–56, 59

Japan, 11, 19, 23, 41, 126, 169, 180
Jena, Battle of, 152, 157

Kakhovka, 100, 102, 105, 116, 149, 213
Kakurin, N. E., 131–32, 171, 224
Kaledin, A. M., 63, 70, 93
Kalinovskii, K. B., 143, 176
Kama River, 84, 88, 90–92
Kamenets-Podol'skii, 52
Kamenev, L. B., 120–21, 218
Kamenev, S. S., 82–83, 87–88, 90–91, 93, 95, 102, 108, 111, 113–15, 117, 122–23, 145, 153, 155, 172, 177
Kapustin, N. Ya., 134, 141, 147–48
Karelia, 186, 243
Karelian Isthmus, 243–44, 246, 262
Kastornaya, 98–99, 104–5
Katowice, 61, 267
Kaulbars, A. V., 17
Kawamura, Gen., 19–20
Kazan', 88, 92
Kazan' Military District, 52
Kerch Peninsula, 100
Kerenskii, A. F., 71
Khalepskii, I. A., 176
Khalkhin-Gol River, 237, 239–40, 242, 248, 250
Khanzhin, M. V., 88, 90–92
Khar'kov, 94, 106
Khar'kov Military District, 229
Khatskilevich, M. G., 260
Khozin, M. S., 257, 262
Khrushchev, N. S., 78–79, 218
Kiev, 94, 107–8, 110–11, 116–17, 130, 186, 217, 223, 248, 268
Kiev Military District, 52, 177, 189, 216, 222–23, 229–30, 242, 245, 247, 254, 265, 268
Kiev Special Military District. *See* Kiev Military District
Kirov, S. M., 78, 218

Kirponos, M. P., 223, 257, 268
Kishinev, 266
Klenov, P. S., 253, 256
Klimovich, A. K., 81
Klimovskikh, V. E., 256
Kolchak, A. V., 88, 93–94, 104, 106
Kolenkovskii, A. K., 138, 141, 147, 149–50, 155, 165, 215
Konev, I. S., 217, 268
Königsberg, 46, 48
Königgrätz, 204
Korea, 237
Kork, A. I., 82, 172, 215
Kornilov, L. G., 71, 77, 93
Kosior, S. V., 218
Kostyaev, F. V., 83
Kovel', 63, 66–68, 70, 108
Kovess Group, 52–53
Kovno (Kaunas), 45
Krasil'nikov, S. N., 215
Krasnov, P. N., 78, 94
Krasnoyarsk, 106
Kravchenko, G. P., 254
Kronshtadt, 130
Krylenko, N. V., 86
Kuban', 88, 100, 106
Kuban' River, 93, 99
Kuchinskii, D. A., 216, 223
Kuibyshev, V. V., 78
Kulik, G. I., 231, 236
Kummer Group, 52
Kunersdorf, 137
Kurochkin, P. A., 216, 268
Kuroki, Gen., 13, 15, 19, 22
Kuropatkin, A. N., 12–13, 15–17, 19–23, 33, 38, 59, 62, 67, 70, 213, 271
Kursk, 95, 98–99, 104, 215, 255
Kutuzov, M. I., 152
Kuznetsov, F. I., 222–23, 254, 266
Kuznetsov, N. G., 222, 245
Kwangtung Army, 237

Lake Baikal, 85, 93
Lake Khasan, 237
Lake Ladoga, 243–45
Lake Naroch, 62
Lapchinskii, A. N., 178, 216

Latvia, 127, 146, 168, 181, 219, 243
Lebedev, P. P., 82–83, 91, 139
Lechitskii, P. A., 55, 63
Leer, G. A., 24–26, 28–30, 36–39, 108, 141, 213, 271
Leipzig, 16
Lenin, V. I., 73, 76–77, 79, 84, 86, 120–21, 125
Leningrad, 13, 43, 71, 76, 84, 178, 218, 222, 242, 265–66, 268
Leningrad Military District, 130–31, 135, 174, 177, 223, 229–30, 243, 257, 268
Linevich, N. P., 17, 19, 21–22
Linsengen, Gen. von, 67
Lipetsk, 98
Lithuania, 62, 219, 243
Lodz, 61
Loktionov, A. D., 221
Lower Vistula Group (Polish), 114
Lublin, 52–54, 56, 115–16
Ludendorff, E., 47, 51, 66, 68
Lutsk, 62–63, 65–68, 70–71, 154
L'vov (Lemberg), 52–53, 55–57, 59, 63, 68, 71, 113–15, 117, 266
Lyao-Yang, 12–13, 17, 34, 152

Maginot Line, 261
Main Air Force Directorate, 247
Main Armor Directorate, 223, 260
Main Intelligence Directorate (GRU), 251
Main Military Council, 172, 188–89, 220, 230–31
Main Naval Staff, 230
Main Operation, 36
Main PVO Directorate, 221
Makhno, N. I., 94–95
Malenkov, G. M., 218
Malinovskii, R. Ya., 217, 225
Manchukuo, 237
Manchuria, 5, 11–12, 23, 31, 34, 38, 119, 129, 138, 152, 169, 236, 270
Manchurian Army, 12, 23
Maneuver Group, 148–49
Mannerheim, C. G. E., 243
Mannerheim Line, 244–45, 261
Manstein, E. von, 82
Marengo, Battle of, 10, 157

Marne, Battle of, 31, 149, 153–55, 157, 162, 165
Martusevich, A. A., 95, 97
Marx, K., 119, 166
Mechanization Directorate, 176
Mechanized Corps, 176–77, 230–32, 271
Meeting Operation, 32, 143, 198–201
Mekhlis, L. Z., 221
Melikov, V. A., 131, 138, 157, 164, 167, 223
Melitopol', 100, 103
Messner, E. E., 26
Metetskov, K. A., 81, 221, 223, 225, 243, 245, 247, 268
Metz, 8, 10, 31, 152, 204
Meuse River, 162, 228
Mezheninov, S. A., 184
Mikhnevich, N. P., 35–36, 82, 142, 159–60, 210, 270
Military-Engineering Academy, 29
Military Revolutionary Committee, 86
Military-Scientific Society, 132, 139, 153
Military specialists, 81–83, 87, 120, 152, 155
Minin, S. K., 79
Minsk, 111–12, 115, 130, 186
Mironov, F. K., 100
Mobile Group, 249, 251, 264
Molotov, V. M., 222, 234
Moltke, H. von (the elder), 8, 25, 31, 33, 204
Moltke, H. von (the younger), 159
Mongolia, 193, 219, 222–23, 237, 240
Mons, Battle of, 31, 118
Mordvinov, V. K., 223
Moscow, 4, 79–80, 85, 88, 107, 113, 115, 117, 131, 143, 178, 181, 204, 223, 233, 237, 245–46, 268
Moscow Military District, 52, 120, 229, 247
Moscow-Volga Canal, 170
Movchin, N. N., 141–42, 153, 157–60, 162, 165–67, 210, 223, 271
Mozyr', 186
Mozyr' Group, 108, 111, 113–15
Mukden, 12, 19–23, 33–34, 59, 152, 204
Murav'ev, M. A., 79, 81

Murmansk, 84
Myshlaevskii, A. Z., 27

Napoleon, 9–10, 30, 123, 152, 157
Narew River, 46, 50, 53, 113, 118
National Air Defense (PVO), 177–78, 229, 234–35
Neman River, 46, 51, 112
New Economic Policy (NEP), 121
Neznamov, A. A., 28–36, 38, 58, 81, 106, 123, 142–43, 149, 152–54, 160, 163, 213, 270
Nicholas II, 5, 60, 62, 70–71
Nikolaev, A. P., 78
Nikolai Nikolaevich, Grand Duke, 44, 62
Nizhnii Novgorod, 88
NKVD (People's Commissariat for Internal Affairs), 220–21, 247
Nodzu, Gen., 15
Nogi, Gen., 19–21
Non-Aggression Pact, Soviet-German, 219, 240
North Caucasus Military District, 78, 229, 254, 268
Northeastern Front (Polish), 111
Northern Fleet, 179, 230
Northern Flotilla, 179
Northern Front (Civil War), 87
Northern Front (World War I), 44–45, 51, 62
Northern Group (Eastern Front), 90, 106
Northern Group (Khalkhin-Gol), 240–41
North Pacific Flotilla, 230
Northwestern Front (Soviet-Finnish War), 245
Northwestern Front (World War I), 44, 59–60, 158
Northwestern Front (World War II), 223, 253, 263
Norway, 126
Novitskii, F. F., 90
Novitskii, V. F., 81, 139, 157, 167
Novorossiisk, 106
NPP tanks, 188, 191–92

October Manifesto, 5
October Revolution, 87

Odessa, 106, 266
Odessa Military District, 229–30, 260
Ogisu, R., 239
Oku, Gen., 15–16, 21
Omsk, 106
Operatics, 26, 142
Operational breakthrough echelon, 197
Ordzhonikidze, K., 218
Orel, 94–95, 97–99, 104, 117, 146
Orel Military District, 229, 253
Orenburg, 90
Oyama, I., 12, 15, 19, 21

Pacific Fleet, 179, 230
Paris, 130, 153, 162
Pavlov, D. G., 223, 247, 257–60, 263, 265–66, 268
People's Commissariat for Military and Naval Affairs, 86, 122, 171
People's Commissariat of Defense, 171, 173
People's Commissariat of the Defense Industry, 172
People's Commissariat of the Navy, 222
Perekop Isthmus, 100, 102–3, 106–7
Perm', 88, 106
Peter I (the Great), 4, 137
Petin, N. N., 221
Petrograd. See Leningrad
Petrograd Soviet of Workers' and Soldiers' Deputies, 86
Petropavlovsk, 106
Petrov, I. E., 82
Pfanzer-Baltin, Gen., 63
Pilsudski, J., 108, 111, 115
Pinsk, 62, 112
Pinsk Flotilla, 230
Plan A, 43–44
Plan G, 43
Pleve, V. K., 52, 54
Ploesti, 267
Poland, 42–43, 50, 52, 62, 74–75, 79, 84, 99–100, 102, 104, 107, 112, 116, 126–27, 130, 134, 138, 145, 154–55, 162, 164, 168, 174, 181–82, 186, 219, 226–28, 232, 241–42, 248, 261, 267–68

Poles'e Group, 111
Polish Corridor, 113
Politburo, 78, 86, 113, 120–21, 218
Polotsk, 108, 186
Poltava, 106, 137
Popov, M. M., 254, 268
Port Arthur, 5, 11–13, 19, 39
Posen (Poznan), 42, 61
Postyshev, P. P., 218
Pripyat Marshes, 62, 68–69, 108, 110–11, 117, 145, 181–82, 185, 265–66
Pripyat River, 68
Prittwitz, M. von, 47
Proskurov, 52, 55, 266–67
Provisional Government, 7, 71, 75–76, 86
Prussia, 4, 9, 107
Prut River, 66, 68, 266
Przemysl, 52, 54, 57, 60–61
Pskov, 186
Ptukhin, E. S., 254
Puhallo, Gen., 63
PU RKKA. *See* Red Army Political Directorate

Rattel', N. I., 83
Rava-Russkaya, 54–55, 57, 66
Red Army (RKKA—Workers' and Peasants' Red Army)
 civil war operations, 87–107
 commissar system, 78–80, 120, 172, 221
 conflicts in the Far East, 119, 237–42
 creation of, 75–76, 86–88
 former officers in, 27–29, 35, 77–78, 80–84, 120, 129–31, 134, 138–42, 217
 manpower, 4, 85, 171, 229
 operations against Poland, 107–18
 organization, 86–87, 120–22, 171–72, 229–35, 268
 purge of, 220–24, 235–36
 rearmament, 135, 170, 172–79, 231, 233–34
 theoretical development, 120, 123–37, 143–68, 180–217, 224–29, 247–64
 theoretical heritage, 2–3, 24, 26, 34, 37–38
 war with Finland, 242–46

Red Army Political Directorate, 78, 120, 172, 221
Red Banner Far Eastern Front. *See* Far Eastern Front
Red Guards, 75
Red Terror, 74
Reichswehr, 82
Remezov, F. N., 253
Rennenkampf, P. K. von, 45, 47–51, 59, 61, 77
Revolutionary Military Council of the Republic (RVSR), 78, 80, 87, 120, 122, 172, 187
Riga, 62, 234, 265
RKKA General Staff. *See* RKKA Staff
RKKA General Staff Academy. *See* Frunze Military Academy
RKKA Military Academy. *See* Frunze Military Academy
RKKA Military Academy of Mechanization and Motorization, 215
RKKA Military-Chemical Academy, 215
RKKA Staff, 122, 126, 130, 133, 138, 154, 168, 172, 177, 184–86, 188, 195, 202, 215–16, 221–23, 230, 232, 247, 265, 268
Rokossovskii, K. K., 221–22
Romanenko, P. L., 251–52
Romania, 41, 69, 126–27, 168, 181–83, 265
Romanian Front (World War I), 44
Romanov (dynasty), 7
Rostov, 94, 99, 106, 233
Rovno, 42, 62–63, 108, 112, 117
RSFSR, 73
Russian Army (Whites), 100
Russo-Japanese War (1904–1905), 4–5, 27, 31–32, 34, 38–39, 45, 52, 58, 237, 270
Russo-Turkish War (1877–1878), 35
Ruzskii, N. V., 52, 55, 59
RVSR Field Staff, 83, 87, 122
RVSR Political Directorate. *See* Red Army Political Directorate
RVS USSR. *See* Revolutionary Military Council of the Republic

Rychagov, P. V., 221–22, 247, 253–54
Rykov, A. I., 121, 170

Sakhalin Island, 5, 236
Sakharov, V. V., 63
Salonika, 130
Samara (Kuibyshev), 88, 90–92, 221
Sambre River, 162
Samoilo, A. A., 82, 91–92
San River, 52–54, 56–57, 60
Schlieffen Plan, 8, 41, 111, 118
Sea of Azov, 102–3
Second Belorussian Front (World War II), 211
Second Manassas, Battle of, 152
Sedan, 8, 10, 19, 31, 52, 152, 228, 248
Sedyakin, A. I., 177, 221
Serbia, 6, 41, 58
Shafalovich, F. P., 82, 216
Sha-ho River, 12–13, 15–17, 19, 34
Shakhty Trial, 171
Shchadenko, E. M., 79, 121
Shcherbachev, D. G., 27, 63
Sheideman, S. M., 50
Shiloh, Battle of, 152
Shilovskii, E. A., 82, 141, 216–17, 223–24, 273
Shlemin, I. T., 223
Shock Army, 144–48, 150, 157–58, 195–200, 203, 205, 208, 213, 251–52, 263
Shock Front, 211
Shorin, V. I., 90, 95, 221
Shtakel'berg, G. K., 13, 15
Shtern, G. M., 221, 239, 251–52, 265
Siberia, 87–88, 93, 219
Siberian Military District, 229
Sidorin, V. I., 95
Silesia, 60–61
Simbirsk (Ul'yanovsk), 88, 91
Sivash, 103
Smirnov, A. K., 247
Smirnov, P. A., 221–22
Smushkevich, Ya. V., 221
Snesarev, A. E., 79, 81, 139
Socialist Revolutionaries, 73–74, 79, 87
Sokolovskii, V. D., 81, 257

Somme River, 246, 264
Southeastern Front (Civil War), 95, 97, 99, 106
Southeastern Front (Polish), 108, 117
Southern Front (Civil War), 79–80, 87, 95, 97, 99–100, 103, 106, 116–17, 143, 163–64, 202, 213
Southern Group (Eastern Front), 90, 92, 106, 146
Southern Group (Khalkhin-Gol), 240–41
Southwestern Front (Civil War), 106, 108, 111, 113–17, 143, 146, 154, 158, 202
Southwestern Front (World War I), 44, 52, 55, 60, 62–63, 65, 67–71, 158
Southwestern Front (World War II), 211, 223, 263
Soviet-Finnish War (1939–1940), 203, 223, 236, 242, 261
Soviet Republic. *See* USSR
Soviet Union. *See* USSR
Special Army (imperial), 68
Special Corps (57th), 237
Special Designation Army (AON), 178, 233–34
Special Far Eastern Army, 119
Special Red Banner Far Eastern Army, 237
Stalin, J. V., 73, 78–79, 81, 87, 113, 115, 117, 120–21, 125, 130, 143, 169–70, 174, 178, 202, 218, 222, 224, 230, 232, 234, 236, 240, 242, 244–45, 247, 265, 267–68
Stalingrad Front (World War II), 211
Stankevich, A. V., 78
State Defense Committee, 87
Stavka, 3, 44, 55, 60–62, 66, 68, 70, 159, 244, 270
St. Mihiel, 155
Stokhod River, 66, 68, 70
Stolypin, P. A., 6
Stone's River, Battle of, 152
St. Petersburg. *See* Leningrad
Strategic Operation, 26
Styr' River, 66, 68
Success development echelon (ERU), 201, 252

Sukhomlinov, V. A., 27–28, 44
Suleiman, N. A., 81
Supreme Soviet (USSR), 230
Svechin, A. A., 27, 81–82, 127, 129–33, 138–41, 155, 157–58, 164, 166–67, 171, 180–83, 215–17, 223, 270–71
Switzerland, 126
Sytin, P. P., 79

Tactical breakthrough echelon, 197
"Tactics of the battlefield," 24
Taganrog, 95
Tallinn, 234
Tambov, 98, 122, 130
Tank Corps, 231
Tanks
  BT-2, 176, 231–32
  BT-5, 176, 231–32
  BT-7, 176, 231–33
  BT-8, 176, 231–32
  BT-IS, 176, 231–32
  KV-1, 232–33
  KV-2, 232–33
  T-17, 176
  T-18, 176
  T-19, 176
  T-20, 176
  T-23, 176
  T-24, 176
  T-26, 176, 231–33
  T-27, 176
  T-28, 176, 232–33
  T-29, 176
  T-34, 232–33
  T-35, 176, 232
  T-37, 176, 232
  T-38, 176, 232–33
  T-40, 232–33
  T-46-5, 176
  T-50, 233
  T-60, 233
  Tannenberg, 44, 56
Tatarchenko, E., 228
Tatars, 4
Ternopol', 62, 112, 266–67
Theater of Military Activities, 24–26, 28, 33, 108, 141, 158, 160, 270

Theater of War, 25, 44, 158
Third Belorussian Front (World War II), 211
Three Emperors' League, 6
Timoshenko, S. K., 80, 98, 222, 230, 245–48, 261–65
Tiraspol', 186
Togo, Admiral, 11
Tolbukhin, F. I., 82
Trans-Baikal Military District, 229, 268
Trans-Caucasus Military District, 229
Trans-Siberian Railroad, 87, 237
Treaty of Portsmouth, 22
Triandafillov, V. K., 81–82, 134–35, 139, 141, 143–45, 147–53, 157–58, 164–67, 172, 181, 187–89, 195–96, 201–3, 211, 271
Triple Alliance, 6
Triple Entente, 6
Trotskii, L. D., 73, 76–77, 79–80, 87–88, 93, 120–21, 123–25, 128, 130, 132
Tsaritsyn (Stalingrad/Volgograd), 78–79, 94, 106, 211
Tsushima Strait, 5, 22, 39
Tukhachevskii, M. N., 76, 82, 88, 90–92, 108, 111–18, 122, 126, 129–33, 135–36, 138–39, 141, 143–47, 149, 153, 155, 157–58, 160, 164–66, 168, 172, 174, 177, 179–81, 184–85, 189, 191, 201–3, 217, 220–21, 223–24, 273
Tula, 95, 97
Turkestan Front (Civil War), 80, 100
Turkestan Military District, 45
Turkey, 6, 41, 80, 126, 138, 143
Turkish Straits, 94
Tyulenev, I. V., 247, 254–57

Uborevich, I. P., 82, 110, 172, 189, 221
Ufa, 88, 91–93, 104, 106, 164
Ukraine, 74, 76, 79–80, 84, 88, 93–94, 99, 107–8, 111, 116–17, 245, 265, 268
Ukrainian Front (Civil War), 87
United States, 3, 6, 9, 126, 170, 268
Ural Mountains, 84, 88, 93, 106, 219
Ural'sk Army (Whites), 88

Urals Military District, 198, 211, 229, 241
USSR, 4, 75, 95, 107, 119–20, 123, 126–29, 131–33, 135, 146, 153, 166–67, 169–70, 172–74, 178, 180–82, 185–86, 209, 218–20, 229, 234, 237, 242–43, 265, 268, 271

Vakulich, P. I., 198
Vanguard echelon (AE), 199, 210
Varfolomeev, N. E., 82, 140–42, 157–58, 164–65, 196–98, 205, 209–11, 217, 223–24, 270, 271, 273
Vasilevskii, A. M., 82, 216
Vatsetis, I. I., 28, 77, 82–83, 87–88, 93, 172, 223
Vatutin, N. F., 216, 265
VChK (All-Russian Extraordinary Commission), 73
Verdun, Battle of, 39, 84, 246
Verkhovskii, A. I., 82, 130, 134, 139, 171, 215–16, 223
Vershinin, B. G., 259
Vienna, 26, 44, 130
Vil'nius (Vilna), 45, 62, 67, 112
Vinnitsa, 266
Vistula River, 42, 47–48, 52–54, 58, 60, 113–15, 118, 149, 153, 157, 162, 164–65, 168, 182, 209, 266–67
Vladivostok, 87, 93, 119
Volga Military District, 131, 196, 229
Volga River, 78–79, 84–85, 87–88, 90, 94, 268
Volhynya, 67, 111, 113, 266
Vol'pe, A. M., 223
Voronezh, 94–95, 97–99, 105, 110, 117, 233
Voronov, N. N., 225, 231
Voroshilov, K. E., 78–79, 100, 120–21, 125, 130, 141, 171–72, 174–75, 177, 181, 189, 202–3, 220, 222, 230, 236, 245–46
Vyatka (Kirov), 91

"Waiting operation," 32
War Communism, 119

War Game (1941), 264–68
Warsaw, 42, 45, 50, 53, 56, 60, 111, 113–15, 117–18, 126, 149, 153, 162, 182, 267
Warsaw Military District, 45
Wehrmacht, 215, 219, 227, 232, 253, 261
Wells, H. G., 75
Western Detachment (Russo-Japanese War), 13, 15–16
Western Front (Civil War), 95, 108, 112–14, 116–18, 130, 144, 149, 158, 160, 164
Western Front (World War I), 62, 67, 71
Western Front (World War II), 223, 263
Western Special Military District. *See* Belorussian Military District
Weygand Line, 261
Workers' and Peasants' Red Navy (RKKF), 122
World War I, 4, 34, 39, 75, 80, 104, 126–27, 129–30, 133, 135, 138, 143, 145, 152–54, 159, 163, 196, 202, 204, 225, 227, 271
World War II, 27, 37, 136, 145–47, 159–60, 168, 198, 201, 210–11, 213, 216, 219, 242, 264, 271
Woyrsch Detachment, 52
Wrangel, P. N., 94, 99–100, 103–4, 106, 114

Yakir, I. E., 80, 110, 172, 189
Yalu River, 12
Yanushkevich, N. N., 44
Yaroslavl' Military District, 80
Yegor'ev, V. N., 95
Yegorov, A. I., 82, 95, 97, 104, 108, 110–14, 116–17, 146, 172, 185, 187–88, 195, 202–3, 216, 220, 223
Yudenich, N. N., 94
Yugoslavia, 126, 268

Zaionchkovskii, A. M., 123
Zakharov, M. V., 216, 266
Zakharov, V. 228
Zal'ts, A. E., 52–54

Zarubaev, N. P., 13
Zhdanov, A. A., 218
Zhigarev, P. F., 222
Zhigur, Ya. M., 198
Zhilinskii, Ya. G., 27, 44–51, 59
Zhitomir, 94, 110–11

Zhukov, G. K., 80, 186, 217, 222–23, 227, 237, 239–41, 247–53, 257, 265–68
Zinov'ev, G. E., 120–21, 218
Zlatoust, 106
Zolotaya Lipa River, 55, 58